W0254562

THE TRADER'S HANDBOOK

THE TRADER'S HANDBOOK

Winning Habits and Routines of Successful Traders

Richard Moglen, Nick Schmidt,
Ross Haber, Ameet Rai

HARRIMAN HOUSE LTD
3 Viceroy Court
Bedford Road
Petersfield
Hampshire
GU32 3LJ
GREAT BRITAIN
Tel: +44 (0)1730 233870

Email: enquiries@harriman-house.com
Website: harriman.house

First published in 2025 by Harriman House, an imprint of Pan Macmillan
EU Representative: Macmillan Publishers Ireland Limited, 1st Floor, The Liffey Centre, 117-126 Sherriff Street Upper, Dublin 1, DO1 YC45
Associated companies throughout the world
www.panmacmillan.com

Hardback ISBN: 978-1-80409-018-3
eBook ISBN: 978180409-019-0

British Library Cataloguing in Publication Data
A CIP catalogue record for this book can be obtained from the British Library.

Printed and bound in India by Thomson Press India Ltd.

For sale in the Indian subcontinent only

CONTENTS

FOREWORD BY DR. ERIC WISH

I wish I had been able to read this book when I started trading around 1964.

Richard Moglen took my undergraduate Honors course, Introduction to the Stock Market and Technical Analysis, at the University of Maryland in 2019. That course introduced young students to what I had learned about trading by studying the great traders, including Nicolas Darvas, William O'Neil, Stan Weinstein and Mark Minervini.

I first began teaching the course in 2006, after placing 5th in the 2005 Barron's Stock Challenge for business professors (which I was not), where I returned 30.8% during the 2.5-month contest. I convinced the University of Maryland Honors program to allow me, a Research Psychologist and Director of the Center for Substance Abuse Research, to offer a trading course, where my aim was to teach young students what I wish someone had taught me at their ages.

What links my two passions? Well, I reasoned that drugs and the stock market are both addictions!

Since then, I have offered the course each year and have published a free blog www.WishingWealthblog.com in which I tell people what I am doing in the market. I successfully avoided the steep market declines in 2000, 2008 and 2021-22 and in addition to protecting my university retirement accounts from huge declines, I have been able to increase my IRA trading account about 20x since the 1990s.

I tell my students to study the works of people who have "walked the talk" and have made fortunes in the stock market. Richard found his passion for trading in my class and upon graduating, went on to produce YouTube interviews with Weinstein, Minervini and a host of other market wizards. His growing reputation in the trading field led to his joining TraderLion and partnering with Ross Haber, a protégé of William O'Neil and prior Portfolio Manager at William O'Neil + Co.

Richard and his co-authors have pooled their 60+ years of extraordinary market experience to produce this book, and it shows. The book is filled with specific details about how to apply the actions they describe. And as an instruction manual, each chapter ends with a Trader's Handbook Challenge, really homework, that induces the reader to apply the concepts described in the chapter. The chapter on risk management is, perhaps, the most valuable, as it provides an excruciatingly detailed description of how to define and manage risk. Examples are given to show how to calculate each measure of risk. Many authors talk philosophically about managing risk. These authors show how they do it.

The TraderLion team has launched a new trading software, called Deepvue. It was Richard's goal to create an all-in-one tool that merges technical analysis with fundamental analysis and that would be priced much lower than competitors' programs. The book is infused with examples of how he uses Deepvue to create practical stock charts and scan for stocks worthy of purchase. This book is to Deepvue what William O'Neil's first book was to the *Investors Business Daily* newspaper and the CANSLIM strategy.

I hesitate to talk about any one chapter because all of them are essential. Discussions of the analysis of market trends, setups, setting stops, creating watchlists, preparing to trade, and post-trade evaluation of results are all invaluable. The book ends with examples of model stocks the authors have identified, but does not stop there. Readers are urged to compile their own collection of model stocks because of the knowledge gained by doing so.

The explicit details provided about the steps and challenges involved in trading reflect the fact that these authors are seasoned traders. I especially enjoyed Ross's descriptions of his experiences working with Bill O'Neil. My only advice for gaining the most from this book is that the reader first prepare by familiarizing himself with Nicolas Darvas' classic book, "How I made $2,000,000," and Stan Weinstein's concept of Stage Analysis, which guides my trades to this day.

If I had been able to read a book like this when I started trading, I believe I would have been able to trade profitably long before I did. Study this book and enjoy the journey!

Eric D. Wish, Ph.D.
WishingWealthblog.com and on X, @wishingwealth

PREFACE

WHAT THIS BOOK IS ABOUT

THIS BOOK IS about the key steps of developing a trading system and how you can practically go about executing an effective strategy.

This is not a book about the glam or glory of trading, but the hard work and processes necessary to perform it over the long term.

The principles we will cover are derived from the market itself and what has worked in the past and will continue to work in the future. We combine ideas from legendary traders such as William O'Neil, Nicolas Darvas, Jesse Livermore, and Stan Weinstein with current top traders such as Oliver Kell and Mark Minervini.

WHO THIS BOOK IS FOR

This book is for traders of all skill levels who want to keep improving and learning. While we build up the concepts from the ground up, there is no shortage of advanced techniques for more experienced readers.

We are primarily long-focused growth stock traders, and the specific examples and methods we share reflect that. This is not to say that the larger principles are not useful for traders who like to short, but that is not a focus of this book.

HOW THIS BOOK IS STRUCTURED

Each chapter of this book covers a key aspect of a trading system, from technical analysis to entries to exits, from risk management to post analysis, it is all discussed here. Not only do we present critical components of a trading system but we show how you apply them using real-world rules and techniques from our own combined 60+ years of trading.

With each chapter we have included challenges that help you apply the material. To get the most out of this book we highly encourage you to complete them and ideally exchange ideas with other traders.

We've designed this book to serve as a reference guide with each chapter covering a key aspect of trading.

Chapter 1 sets the stage and introduces five overarching principles to keep in mind as you read the book and refine your trading system.

Chapter 2 introduces the trader's journey and helps you identify your current stage.

Chapter 3 presents the key technical and fundamental foundations that form the basis of this book.

Chapter 4 dives into edges and setups in the market. We share our thought processes and the specific ones we use.

Chapter 5 discusses the entry tactics we use to enter positions, and briefly looks at how we manage risk along the way.

Chapter 6 dives deeper into risk management from both a portfolio and individual trade level. It also lays out a clear process for how to set position sizes.

Chapter 7 focuses on how to manage a trade once you have entered. This includes sell rules for swing and position traders.

Chapter 8 covers how to analyze the market to determine its trends and cycles. This is your guiding light that will inform you on how aggressive you should be with your trading.

Chapter 9 is where we share our screening process for finding new ideas and the repeatable routines we use to consistently perform.

Chapter 10 covers post analysis, journaling, and continuous improvement. We walk through how we analyze our own trading in order to improve with time.

Chapter 11 is for traders looking to find new edges, setups, and entry tactics. We discuss how to build model books of winners and how to perform a trading study on a trading concept or pattern.

Chapter 12 is a bonus chapter that shares many charts of top performers from the past few years to help speed up your learning curve.

We hope you enjoy this book, find it useful, and consider it a valuable reference as you progress as a trader.

Happy trading

—Richard, Rai, Nick, and Ross

CHAPTER 1

A LOOK IN THE MIRROR

IT WAS THE second week of April 1999, right during the peak of the internet bubble. I remember the feeling of delight as I hopped up and down cheering while CNBC covered Charles Schwab's standout stock performance. At that moment, SCHW, the ticker Charles Schwab traded under, was one of the largest positions in my portfolio at William O'Neil + Company.

The late 90s was a superb trading environment, and it felt like you could do no wrong buying breakouts in technology companies. The internet revolution was under way, and it was an amazing time to be a growth stock trader. A company could change their name, adding .com to the end, and double in value in a few days for no other reason.

I had started building a position in SCHW after it broke out from a 12-week cup and handle pattern in October of 1998. From the breakout it had acted perfectly, and proceeded to advance from $30 a share pre-split to well over 100% in just a matter of weeks.

In terms of fundamentals, Schwab seemed perfectly poised, taking market share and growing earnings at an accelerated rate each quarter.

Schwab had doubled down on the internet and was riding the wave of more and more clients looking to move their brokerage services online.

During this incredible run Charles Schwab never broke the 10-week moving average, which is a quality shared by many of the most impressive stocks in history. This sustained trend was likely due to accumulation by large institutions wanting to grab their pieces of the pie.

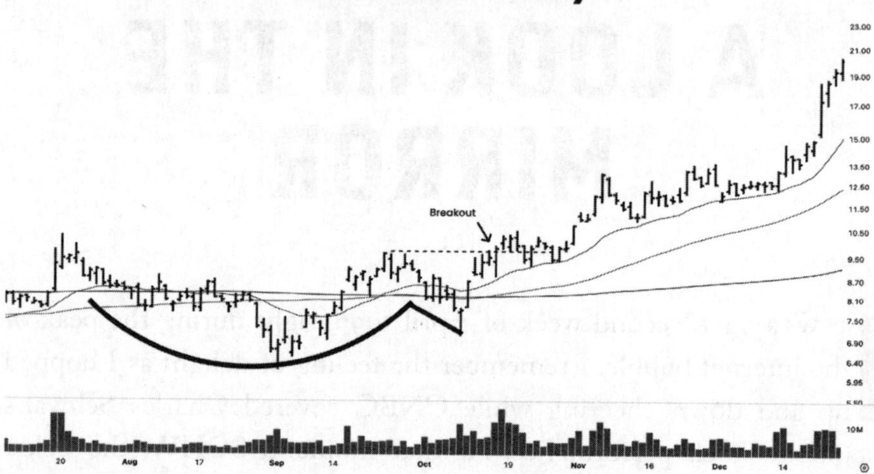

Standing in front of the TV on that day in April as CNBC highlighted Charles Schwab and what a tremendous stock it had been, I paused for a moment and some self-awareness pushed through the giddiness. Bringing up a chart, I took one glance, and it confirmed my suspicions. SCHW was forming a climax top after a 400% increase in just 24 weeks. I sobered up quickly, objectivity taking hold.

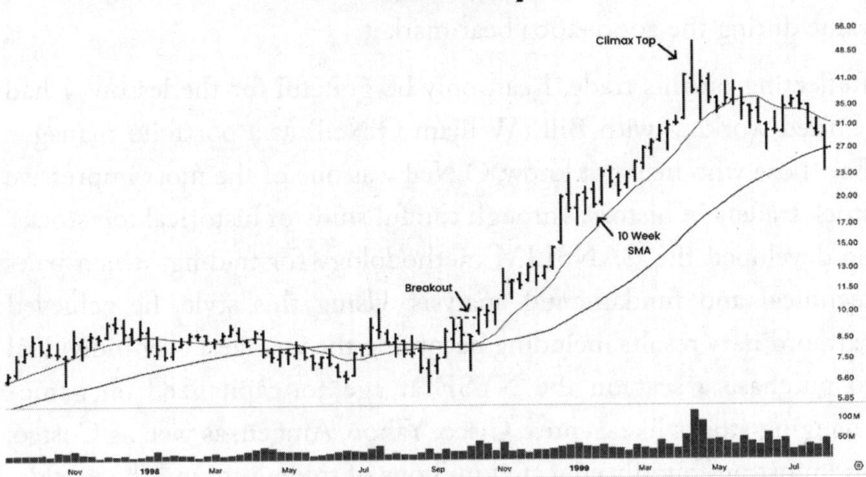

SCHW Daily

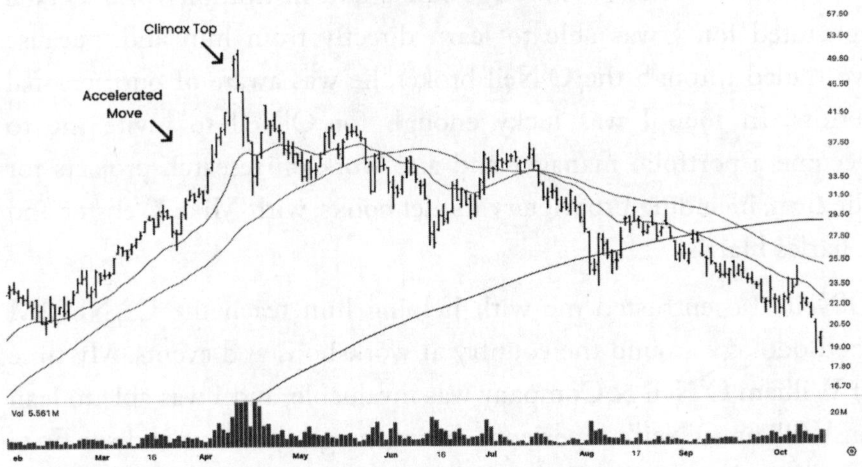

Climax tops occur after a stock has already made a major move and accelerates upward in a euphoric last push. This move, driven by greed, often marks the end of the rise of a model stock.

Realizing this, I immediately called my trader on the William O'Neil trading desk and told him to sell my entire position. By the time I sold, Schwab had fallen well off its highs for the day and had actually gone red. Looking back, this ended up being the top day in SCHW, which would fall over 65% in the next six months and lose 87% of its value during the 2000–2003 bear market.

Reflecting on this trade, I can only be grateful for the lessons I had learned working with Bill (William O'Neil) as a portfolio manager. For those who may not know, O'Neil was one of the most impressive stock traders in history. Through careful study of historical top stocks, he developed the CANSLIM methodology for trading, which pairs technical and fundamental analysis. Using this style, he achieved extraordinary results including becoming the youngest ever individual to purchase a seat on the NYSE at age 30, capitalized on game-changing stocks like Syntex, Cisco, Yahoo, Amgen, as well as Costco, and most profoundly educated millions of traders around the world.

I first joined O'Neil and company in 1998 in the institutional sales department, working with large funds and institutions who O'Neil consulted for. I was able to learn directly from him and, because we traded through the O'Neil broker, he was aware of our personal results. In 1999 I was lucky enough for O'Neil to invite me to become a portfolio manager and also work on research projects for the firm, including proprietary model books, with Mike Webster and Charles Harris.

O'Neil also entrusted me with helping him teach the CANSLIM methodology around the country at workshops and events. My time at William O'Neil & Company was invaluable, and I was able to lean on William O'Neil's experience during tough decisions and see first-hand how he traded and approached the markets.

During portfolio manager meetings, he reminded us consistently that although we buy based on both technicals and fundamentals, we must look to the charts to determine exactly when we should sell.

Despite Charles Schwab's great story and seemingly glowing future, the technicals revealed the raw truth. The large institutional investors were now net selling their shares to the general crowd, leading to the inevitable end of the stock's move.

My trade of SCHW remains one of my best executed, but it also serves as an important reminder to never let emotions get in the way of making the correct decisions while trading. When a stock is going up it feels amazing; it seems like we are able to print money at will. However, nothing is more important than managing risk and protecting the profits we gain during bull market runs.

Many new traders have felt the incredible potential of stock trading first-hand, but unless they also learn to respect risk and learn when to sell those stocks that had previously made them money when they change character and start downtrends, they will be hard pressed to keep what they have earned.

At TraderLion we've seen this many times with each bull market. Traders try to hold on to previously great stocks, unable to understand that, now, the prevailing trend is down.

We've learned to never fall in love with a stock, no matter how innovative the company seems or how charismatic the CEO may be. We've seen too many previously great stocks that rose tenfold, then lose momentum, and tumble 75% or more during downtrends. Often the fundamentals only seemed to deteriorate well after the stock had fallen from highs.

These hard-won lessons often take multiple market cycles of bear and bull markets to fully understand, and most people who start trading will become frustrated and quit long before they make the necessary breakthroughs.

This is one of our main motivations for writing this book—to pass on our learnings from our collective decades of market experience so that you can learn from both our triumphs and, ideally even more so, from the many mistakes we've made.

We hope we can help you learn the right approach and mentality that will enable you to create a successful trading system for yourself, so that you can protect your profits and compound your capital over a long career as a trader.

The barriers to entry for stock trading have never been lower. With commission-free trading, mobile apps, and online resources at your fingertips, anyone can open and fund an account in minutes and place their first trade.

You hear stories out there about million-dollar trades, new traders doubling and tripling their accounts in a matter of months, and otherwise fantastic feats which rightly show the incredible opportunity that exists in the markets. With the ease of access, more and more individuals are stepping into the arena with the professionals, with the hopes of obtaining *easy and fast money*.

Many of these new traders begin their journeys in the strongest bull markets when everyone seems to be making fortunes. The 90s were a perfect example, and more recently we saw many people start getting involved during the 2020 bull market. (You in fact may have picked up this book for the first time during the next great trading period.)

However, the reality of trading is that it is anything but easy. After the strong bull markets come bear markets and choppy periods which wipe out any progress from inexperienced traders, leaving them discouraged and likely to give up. To successfully navigate changing environments over decades it takes years of commitment, hard work, discipline, and the development of a time-tested process.

Newcomers to the markets hear about the headline trades, which are only the tip of the iceberg when it comes to real trading. In truth, every trader must go through a journey and evolution where they gradually learn the key lessons necessary to develop a personal, sustainable process.

Often, these lessons are learned at the cost of bumps and bruises, which, in the trading world, translates into losing trades and making significant mistakes. However, the most famous traders you have heard of—Stan Druckenmiller, George Soros, Paul Tudor Jones, and Mark Minervini—all had one thing in common: They persevered through early struggles until they found their style and gradually achieved super-performance.

Thinking you can jump into trading and be successful immediately is as misguided as believing you can pick up a baseball bat and produce the crucial game-winning hit in the bottom of the ninth in the World Series against an All-Star closer. Sure, it may look simple on TV to slap a fastball past the pitcher and into centerfield, but what is often forgotten by fans is all the hard work and preparation behind every single at bat.

This is the truth for any discipline, whether it's becoming a doctor, engineer, or musician. Each profession requires years of experience and hundreds of mistakes to turn a novice into a pro. It is the same story with stock trading, except from day one you are competing in the same market as hedge fund managers with decades of experience. What we hope to pass on in this book is a road map, a guide, and a resource that will allow you to progress as quickly as possible.

In this book we will present multiple edges and frameworks that are precisely relevant to the current markets. These edges come from our collective studies of setups and our analysis of the best-performing stocks over the past few decades. Even better, in Chapter 11, we will walk you through our process of performing a study to show you how you can find your own edges in the future.

You may ask yourself why, if we use these edges and setups, are we willing to share them?

The answer is that these edges are the result of market structure and human psychology, factors that have gone unchanged since the 1920s.

The methods we will share are the result of trend orders of magnitude bigger than us individuals and instead they are created by the actions of the largest funds and institutions on Wall Street.

These institutions manage billions upon billions of dollars and create the sustained trends we see in the market. Even collectively, individual retail investors cannot change the direction of a liquid stock for more than a few moments. And it is actually our relatively small size that allows us to capitalize on many of the setups and edges we will share.

Our general tactics may change over time, but the core strategy, riding the waves created by institutions, will remain the same. This is what O'Neil found when he first developed his system decades ago, and it will be true for the next market wizards years in the future.

Keep this in mind: Whenever you come across a saying taken as truth or a common trading method, test it out for yourself. By putting in the work and challenging the norms, you just might find a new edge that you can consistently use to take income from the market. We will show you how to do your own studies on the market and trading techniques, following the exact process that we have used to build our systems from the ground up.

In this handbook we will share what has worked and continues to work for us and the many thousands of traders we have worked with. Take what you find helpful, iterate to make it your own, and ignore the rest.

FIVE KEY PRINCIPLES OF TRADING

As you read this book, we want you to keep in mind the following five key principles that we have found successful traders fully embrace:

1. Keep it simple.
2. Stay focused.
3. Plan for failure.
4. Manage risk tightly.
5. Think in cycles.

1. KEEP IT SIMPLE

The best trading systems, routines, rules, etc., are remarkably simple. With simplicity comes robustness, as there are fewer cogs in the chain to jam, as well as polish and improve.

With your charts, focus on price action above all else, and potentially supplement with only a few key indicators. Make sure any indicator you use helps you analyze and manage a trade and does not add noise.

With your rules, be specific and clear about exactly what you mean. With your routines, make them easy to complete so that you will actually follow them consistently.

Complexity adds in randomness and confusion. Keep your trading as simple and clear as possible.

2. STAY FOCUSED

In trading, becoming a specialist is the path to success. This means one style—day trading, swing trading, position trading, investing. Pick one and master it.

Within your strategy, you also want to focus your attention on just a handful of stocks and a handful of chosen setups. We will show you how to build strict criteria for your stock selection so that you are focused on the top 1% of stocks for your strategy.

This focus and specialization allows you to build confidence in yourself, and become great at key processes that allow you to perform.

3. PLAN FOR FAILURE

As you create your system, you want to make sure that you are setting realistic expectations as well as building in failure. Planning for failure ensures that you can protect your capital even when you are trading at your worst.

There will be market environments where your setups are ineffective, or even simply just periods where you are not on your A game. Even just bad luck can lead to many losing trades in a row, gap downs, stop loss hits, etc. Your system and psyche must be resilient enough to handle these periods as well as drawdowns.

With this expectation in mind, building in failure is truly the key to success. If you can hold your own even when things are not going well and the wind is in your face, think of what you can achieve in periods when the wind is with you.

4. MANAGE RISK TIGHTLY

This follows closely with building in failure. Everyone says, "You have to manage risk." But what does that mean? We've dedicated the entirety of Chapter 6 to answering that question and it is likely the most important concept of this book. This is especially important for very new traders who are boom and busters.

Very simply, you will take losses, sometimes many in a row, while trading. You want to make sure that your losses are papercuts, and just one trade that performs well can pay for many of them. To do this you need to select and design setups and entry tactics that allow you to know quickly when a trade is not performing and allow you to exit with a minimal drawdown to your account.

If you can master this skill—the ability to always enter with both a tight and logical stop loss in a high potential stock and setup—you will succeed in the market.

5. THINK IN CYCLES

Both the market and individual stocks rise and fall in overall cycles created by supply and demand, fear, and greed.

You want to ensure that you are trading in the right direction relative to the current market trend and becoming aggressive at the right points. We will teach you in Chapter 8 how to identify market cycles and build a system for yourself that tells you how exposed you should be at any given point.

In addition, as a trader, you will go through cycles of learning and then testing. It's a process of continuous improvement. You will always be refining your system and slowly raising the bar. Chapters 10 and 11 are dedicated to frameworks that will help you study yourself and the markets.

There will be frustrating periods and drawdowns where it feels like you can't do anything right. Dig in and remember that just like with the market during a correction, a new uptrend is just around the corner.

When you feel yourself struggling, take a step away and review your system.

A LOOK IN THE MIRROR

Before we progress any further, we want to emphasize that the single most important factor that will determine how successful you will be at trading is your commitment to learning.

Passion and determination will sustain you through the early stages of your journey and help you persevere through any obstacle you experience.

To achieve outsized returns and consistently beat the market, you must be willing to put in the work that most traders shy away from.

Each of the following chapters will focus on a key element of a trading system. We will share our processes and lay out a specific blueprint for you to follow.

However, reading is one thing; applying the material is another. You need to study and work hard to become a successful trader; no one is going to give it to you.

So right now take a minute and get out a piece of paper and a pen. Once you have that ready, list all the reasons you have for learning to trade.

Finally, write a personal commitment to yourself (example below) declaring that you will put in the work to learn and improve your trading. You should also tweet this out or otherwise proclaim it to the world. You may find it a bit ridiculous, but written down goals have an interesting way of becoming true.

Remember, your choices and habits will over time form your reality. If you want to become a fantastic trader, it is fully within your power to do so. Read this book, perform studies, do your homework, and you will be well on your way to progressing along your trading journey.

It all starts with a look in the mirror and a commitment to yourself:

> I will do my utmost to make incremental improvements and put in the work that will allow me to learn and improve as a trader. I will establish routines, read books, conduct studies, and otherwise look for ways to extend my knowledge base and perform at my best.
>
> My reasons for learning to trade are:
>
> Sign here:

With that commitment made, let's get started.

CHAPTER 2
THE TRADER'S JOURNEY

> "The secret to being successful from a trading perspective is to have an indefatigable and an undying and unquenchable thirst for information and knowledge."
>
> —***Paul Tudor Jones, Market Wizard***

EVERY TRADER GOES through the trader's journey: A meandering path full of setbacks, breakthroughs, side quests, triumphs, pitfalls, and continuous learning. It often starts with early success that gets you hooked, that feeling that this is so easy, of limitless opportunity.

You may have even plotted performance on a spreadsheet and calculated how much your portfolio will grow in five years, ten years, 30 years from now.

Unfortunately, all traders soon learn that you must pay your dues to the market, learn to respect it, and that the only way forward is through hard work.

The journey is non-negotiable. Some traders may progress faster than others, other traders may have to double back and travel parts of the journey multiple times, but every trader must go its length before they can develop a consistent and successful trading system.

Even after this, top traders know all too well that there are always ways to improve and further paths to walk. The challenge of trading is unique in life. It always seems to come up with new obstacles and problems for you to tackle.

This book is focused on the *how* and *what* of trading, and the four stages that every trader must pass through to reach consistent profitability. We will strive to give you a blueprint, a guide, to help you along your path and hopefully help you avoid the many hazards that new traders face.

We will share what actually has worked, and continues to work, for us, and the hard lessons won over the years, not theoretical or academic hindsight observations.

You will find that it's much less about finding the perfect indicator or memorizing candlestick patterns and that true trading is much more about mindset, probabilities, execution, routines, and discipline. Doing the boring but effective and necessary work consistently.

Anyone can become a successful stock trader, but they must first make a commitment to themselves; a promise that they will approach trading like a business, instead of a hobby. To progress as a trader, whatever your current starting point, your *why* must be powerful enough to drive you to work hard, continue to learn, and apply yourself to this endeavor.

Real money is on the line and fortunes can be made, but until you respect the process and learn to manage risk, you will likely lose money over time instead of compounding.

Now let's dive into the four stages of trading, to help you identify where you are on your path and the steps you need to take to reach the next stage.

This chapter lays the groundwork for the rest of the book. If you are more experienced feel free to breeze through. However, if you are in your first few years of trading, or new to trend-following and momentum strategies, we urge you to read closely and study this chapter before moving on to the rest of the book.

THE STAGES OF TRADING

Along your trading journey you will go through four distinct stages. We've developed these categories through our work teaching thousands of traders over the past few years.

The stages are as follows:

- Stage 1: Unprofitable Stage
- Stage 2: Boom and Bust Stage
- Stage 3: Consistency Stage
- Stage 4: Performance Stage

Our goal with this book is to lay out the knowledge you need to move forward from whichever stage you are currently in. We will carefully describe commonalities between the stages as well as steps to take to continue your development.

As you are reading this section, be brutally honest with yourself about which stage you are currently in. Armed with this knowledge, focus on our recommendations for how you can progress to the next stage.

One key aspect of determining your stage is to plot your performance or portfolio value on a time series chart (many brokers show this natively). Scan out to a wide view, at least one year long.

This plot is called your Equity Curve. It represents the truth about your trading. Each of the four stages has a very particular look to the trader's equity curve. Have this plot ready for comparison as you continue to read.

Take a look at this graphic of the four stages.

The Evolution of a Profitable Trader TraderLion

Stage 1
Unprofitable Trader

Characteristics
- Small wins, larger losses
- Negatively trending equity

Reasons:
- Poor trade identification
- Poor risk management
- Poor profit-taking strategy

Stage 2
Boom-and-Bust Trader

Characteristics
- Roughly equal wins to losses
- Non-trending equity

Reasons:
- Better trade identification
- Poor risk management
- Profit-taking too early
- Over-trading

Stage 3
Profitable Trader

Characteristics
- Larger wins, smaller losses
- Positively trending equity

Reasons:
- Good trade identification
- Good risk management
- Lets profitable trades run
- Cuts losing trades quickly
- Knows when to be in cash

Stage 4
Performance Phase

Characteristics
- Achieved mastery of a system
- Looking for ways to improve edges
- Daily routines
- Confidence

We will now cover the stages in turn.

STAGE 1: UNPROFITABLE STAGE

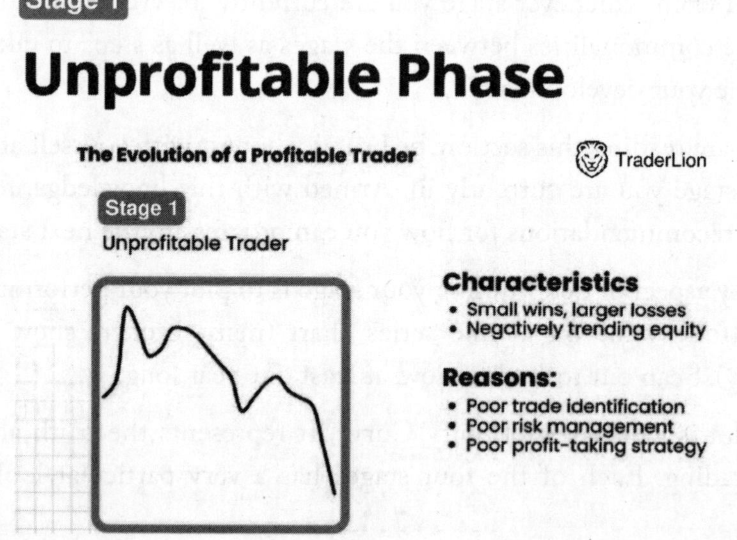

Every trader, no matter how experienced they are now, initially started in Stage 1. This stage is characterized by a volatile, downtrending equity curve. Traders in Stage 1 act randomly without a system and act on tips and impulses.

There is very little rhyme or reason when it comes to buys and sells, and often traders in this stage have not received any trading education outside of social media posts. Traders in this stage often begin trading during strong bull markets and achieve a few wins before the tides change and random entries are no longer as effective.

Traders in Stage 1 often use a wide variety of trading styles. They may swing trade, day trade, buy deep value, short, use options, trade futures… flitting from one thing to the next to try to chase the easy money.

They will often have no risk management process and likely do not use stop losses. They size their positions extremely large to try to capitalize on the next great opportunity. They are chasing the quick double, triple, or quadruple of their account.

Traders in this stage appear in every bull market. When the market changes, however, they will likely give back any gains they made and then some.

However, a fraction of these traders will have caught the trading bug and will become committed to improving. If this stage resonated with you, know that you only have to make the decision to treat trading seriously in order to progress.

The key elements of Stage 1 traders are:

- Lack of a system for buys/sells.
- Random entries and exits, and stock selection—all based on emotion and tips.
- Trying a variety of styles and trading instruments all at once.
- Lack of risk management such as using stop losses or a position sizing system.
- Interest is completely driven by the search for quick money.

HOW STAGE 1 TRADERS CAN PROGRESS TO STAGE 2

Stage 1 traders can very quickly progress to Stage 2 by seeking out resources and beginning to create their first trading system.

Their goals should be to:

- Commit to learning.
- Write their first set of trading rules (covered in Chapter 10).
- Build a consistent system for stock selection and entry setups (Chapters 4, 5, 9).
- Implement risk management systems through stop losses (Chapter 6).
- Adopt sell rules (Chapter 7).

In this stage there is so much to learn and improve on. Motivation is high and the traders who succeed dive into the work headfirst. What's great is that improvements come quickly and can keep you going.

STAGE 2: BOOM AND BUST STAGE

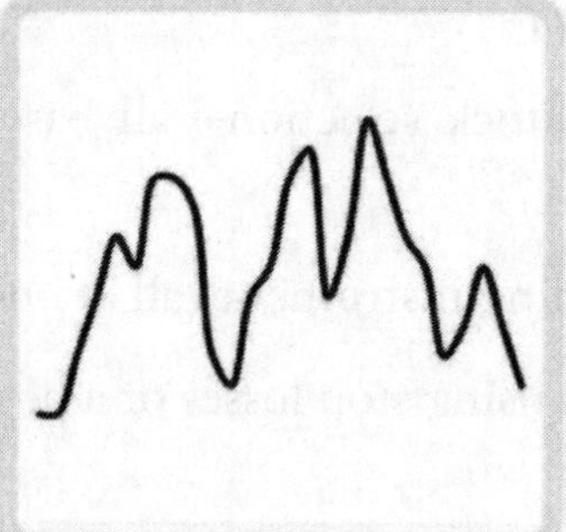

In this stage traders have often gotten more serious about trading and have done some research and even read a few books on strategies and setups.

However, they may struggle with consistently implementing a system and often lack proper risk management. Traders in Stage 2 have a volatile equity curve with upswings when the market is good and then they often give all their profits back when the market turns.

The key elements of Stage 2 traders are:

- Equity curve trends with the market.
- Risk management skills are still developing.
- Obsession with trying every indicator and strategy, albeit with more capability than Stage 1 traders.
- Lack of awareness of market cycles—long term and shorter term.

HOW STAGE 2 TRADERS CAN PROGRESS TO STAGE 3

Stage 2 traders' largest problem is that they are trying to focus on too much all at once. They are aware of all the resources and choices they can make and try to master all of them.

Their goals should be to:

- Focus on one time frame and one overall strategy.
- Study winning stocks and study traders who use their chosen strategy.
- Refine their rules and have rigid systems for entries, setting stop losses, position sizing, and selling.
- Gain more trading experience and knowledge.

This stage can be a turning point. The trader is now aware of the work ahead of them and it may feel very daunting and frustrating. Even with more knowledge and a starter system, Stage 2 traders may feel like they are not improving at all.

However, they should realize, and you should realize if you feel you are a Stage 2 trader, that Stage 3 is just around the corner after a few tweaks and refinements. Keep at it!

STAGE 3: THE PROFITABLE AND CONSISTENT STAGE

Stage 3

Consistency Phase

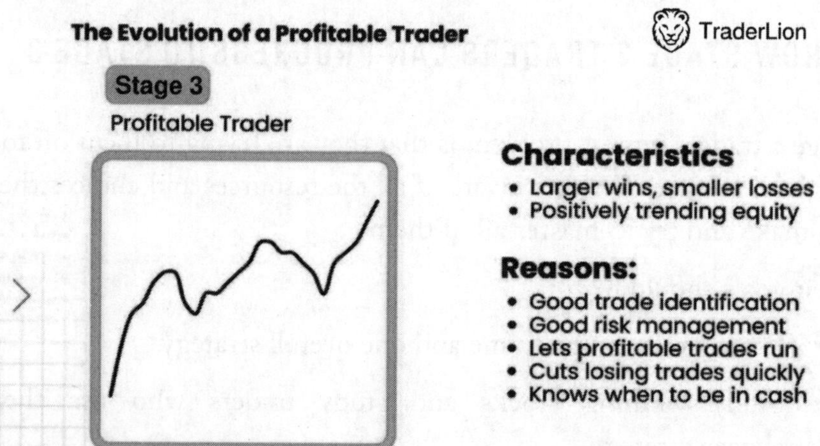

In this stage, traders have fully committed to learning and have often read multiple trading books and found a sound strategy that makes sense for them and their situation.

They may have also received mentorship from a more experienced trader using a similar style. At this point, they follow their system nearly all the time, they have improved risk management skills, and they also have awareness of the trends of the market and react accordingly.

The transition from Stage 2 to Stage 3 generally occurs when traders limit noise and focus on mastering one strategy and even just one setup. Proper risk management through position sizing and repeatable sell rules is also crucial to progressing to this stage.

In Stage 3, a trader's equity curve will generally be upward trending from left to right and will be forming higher lows as they protect their profits from one market cycle to the next. At this point they have started to build confidence, but still require many improvements and tweaks to start truly performing.

The key elements of Stage 3 traders are:

- Higher highs and higher lows in their equity curves.
- A strong focus on one strategy, a handful of setups, and position management rules.
- A basic understanding of market cycles.

HOW STAGE 3 TRADERS CAN PROGRESS TO STAGE 4

At Stage 3, traders are profitable, although they still may not be performing as well as they would like. However, the transition to Stage 4 is more nuanced.

Their goals should be to:

- Master and do deep dives into a small handful of edges, setups, and entry tactics.
- Trade in sync with medium-term market cycles.
- Continue to refine their rules to suit their own developing style.
- Double down on focusing on setups/tactics that produce tight and logical entries.

- With tighter entries, they can begin to position size higher, while keeping risk in check.
- Focus on the highest potential stocks of each cycle.

In Stage 3, traders are starting to see their work pay off and that will feel rewarding and motivate them to keep working. Performance is the end goal and at this point it's about refinements, working hard, and individual breakthroughs.

For Stage 3 traders working to progress, Chapters 10 and 11 should be a focus, as you work to develop your own system.

STAGE 4: THE PERFORMANCE STAGE

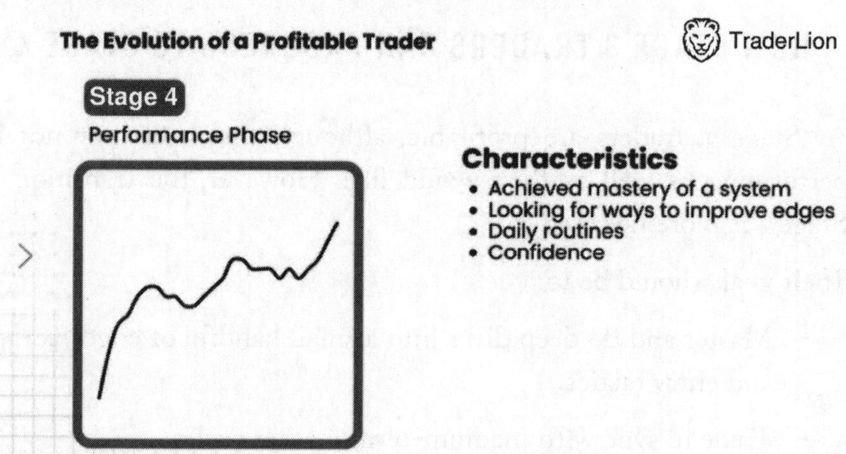

Stage 4 may be the last stage, but it by no means signifies that the learning or hard work is done. Traders in this stage have achieved mastery of their trading system, but they are continuously looking for ways to improve edges and their performance.

Performance stage traders have nailed down routines that keep them focused on the highest potential stocks for their system and aware of the current market conditions. They know when to press on the gas as well as when to take a step back and limit their involvement in the markets.

This does not mean that they do not go through drawdowns or experience setbacks. However, they have confidence in their process and method, and know that when the environment is right they can perform vastly better than the indexes.

This confidence allows them to be patient and selective when their style is not well suited for the market environment. They wait, stalk, and pounce when the time is right.

In Stage 4, your equity curve will have a sharp upward trend with higher lows. What differentiates it from Stage 3 is the steepness during uptrends and the shallowness of any drawdown.

The key elements of Stage 4 traders are:

- Higher highs and higher lows in their equity curves.
- Strong performance during opportunity periods and limited drawdowns.
- Strong confidence in themselves as traders, even with occasional setbacks and mistakes.

HOW STAGE 4 TRADERS CAN PROGRESS

Stage 4 is a continuation of Stage 3. The trader's goals should be to:

- Fully master a small handful of entry setups, defining their nuances.

- Anticipate and trade in sync with shorter-term market cycles.
- Size into the highest quality opportunities of their system at the correct moments.
- Limit drawdowns as cycles end.

Once a trader has reached Stage 4 they have a clear and consistent process that is unique to them. They have mastered particular setups and know intimately their nuances and what environments they work best in.

At this stage their goal is capital, time, and performance efficiency—to be concentrated on only the best opportunities coming out of the right setups in the right market environment.

DETERMINE YOUR STAGE

Think about your current trading ability and take a close look at your equity curve over the past year. It may be helpful to plot it against an index so you can have a visual representation of how the market was performing during different periods of time.

Look at how you have performed compared to the index. Is your curve trending upward or are you more of a boom and buster?

It may be hard to see the truth of your performance, but remember that no matter where you are now, with just a few tweaks and added experience, you will quickly progress to the next stage.

Likely if you are reading this book you are in the Stage 1+ to Stage 3+. This is an exciting time for a trader as you are committing to master this very difficult art and skill. Kudos to you for putting in the work.

THE MINDSET OF A WINNING TRADER

Once you have determined your stage, it is up to you to identify your strengths and weaknesses, and work hard to progress. The best part of trading is that your potential is unlimited.

Once you have developed your process and acquired the knowledge, no one can take that from you. It may take you years to progress from Stage 1 to Stage 3, but thereafter you will be able to benefit from every future market cycle and opportunity. Don't feel like there is a rush to perform; you need to build your foundation through studying price action, studying leaders, and studying yourself.

Then, from this strong foundation, you can build your system and success.

Most top traders take around two full bull-to-bear cycles to progress to Stage 3. It takes real experience trading, making mistakes, and learning from them to fully work out the kinks and to develop your own psyche. Approach trading like a student. Every loss is a learning opportunity that can help you improve.

The progression from Stage 3 to Stage 4 is about incremental improvements and mastery of yourself outside of trading.

It will take time to achieve, but once again if you refuse to quit then there is no doubt you can reach the performance stage and consistently see a rapid trend of higher lows within your equity curve.

KEY TAKEAWAYS

In this chapter we have discussed the stages of trading from unprofitable to boom and buster, to consistency, to performance.

We described each of the stages and how you can identify your current stage using your equity curve, and also how you can continue to progress.

BONUS RESOURCE

We recorded a webinar about common trading problems and the stages of trading. We discuss at length how you can work towards progressing along your journey.

You can watch it today at traderlion.com/handbook.

CHAPTER 3
FOUNDATIONS

BEFORE WE DIVE into building a system and more complex concepts such as setups, we wanted to emphasize some key technical and fundamental foundations that form the basis of this book. In this chapter we will focus on the most important aspects of reading price action, winning characteristics of high potential stocks, and what drives market trends.

More experienced traders can skim this, or skip to later chapters, but if you are in your first few years of trading, we highly encourage you to read this attentively. We will be sharing key observations about top-performing stocks that we have gathered from over 60 years of combined trading experience.

READING PRICE ACTION

Let's start from the very basics and quickly accelerate to the key price and volume characteristics that we look for.

First we encourage you to keep your charts as clean and simple as possible. Stick to a few key indicators, such as moving averages, to help you identify trends.

You can also choose to master a few indicators that help you identify edges, setups, or entry tactics that you use. However, we want to emphasize that the simpler you make your charts, the easier you will be able to focus on what truly matters: price and volume.

Here is the primary chart template that Richard Moglen uses in Deepvue.

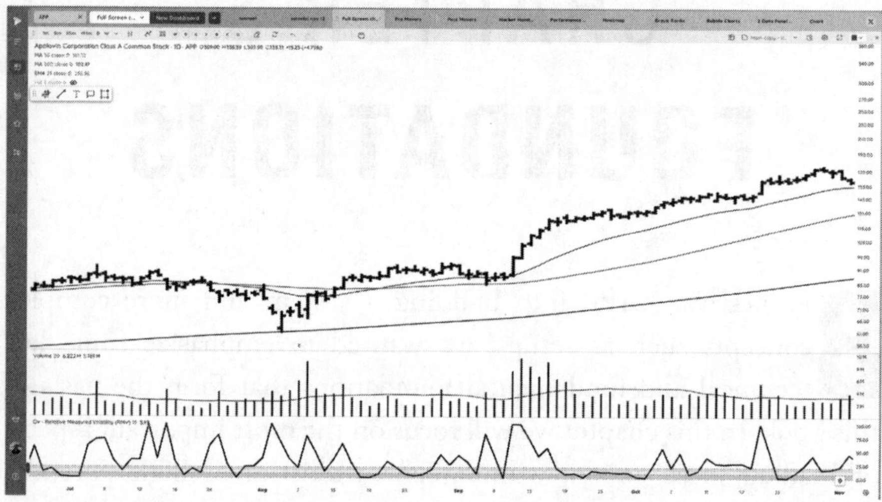

He is using three moving averages to judge trends over different periods, volume with a moving average to judge supply, and relative measured volatility to help identify tight price contraction areas.

Quick Tip! You can differentiate between the moving averages by how quickly they react to price movements – the 21ema is the most sensitive and the 200sma the least reactive.

Key moving averages and volume are a must, and you can decide for yourself if you'd like additional indicators that may help you analyze a stock, such as a Relative Strength line or other indicator.

The key point here is that there is no magic indicator combination—there is only what is most helpful to you and helps you quickly analyze charts. A common mistake of newer traders is to add many different indicators in a search for *the perfect signal.*

Less is more. You want to avoid analysis paralysis.

READING A SINGLE PRICE BAR

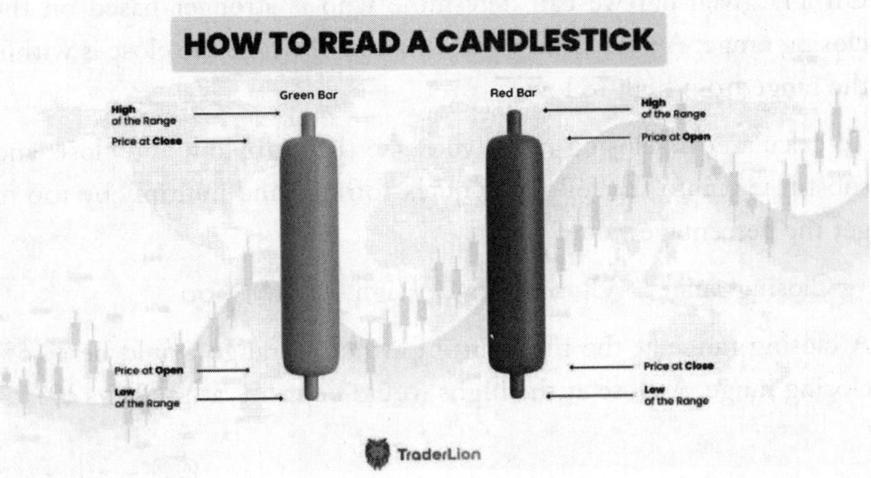

Charts are built from single bars or candlesticks. They can represent a minute's, a day's, or a week's worth of price action depending on the time frame.

How they are shaped and how they close relative to the price bars around them provides valuable clues about the forces of supply and demand. Larger patterns and higher time frames provide the context, the overall story, while individual bars write the new plot twists in words and sentences.

Instead of trying to memorize individual patterns and dozens of names, you should think of a price bar as a tug of war between buyers and sellers.

Buyers are trying to push the stock higher, closer to the top of the bar's range, while sellers are trying to pull the stock down toward the lows.

On any given bar we can determine who is stronger based on the closing range: A percentile representation of where the close is within the range from high to low.

To calculate the closing range you take the high, low, and close, and substitute it into the following quick formula and multiply by 100 to get the percentage value:

Closing range = (Close – Low / High – Low) * 100

A closing range at the midpoint of a trading range would be a 50% closing range. A close at the highs would be 100%, at the lows 0%.

$$\text{CLOSING RANGE} = \frac{\text{CLOSE - LOW}}{\text{HIGH - LOW}}$$

If a daily bar has a high of 100, a low of 90, and a current price of 98, then the daily closing range (DCR) is 80%.

A closing range of greater than 50% suggests that for that bar, buying pressure was stronger. The closer to the highs, the stronger the buyers; the closer to the lows, the stronger the sellers. A closing range of 50% suggests indecision and a balance.

By looking at the closing range of a single bar, you will start to be able to build an expectation of what can happen next and be able to differentiate between a constructive and non-constructive bar.

Here's a handy guide that combines the closing range with volume, which adds weight to what price is doing.

Constructive vs Non-Constructive Price Action

Type	Up Day / Down Day	Closing Range	Volume
Constructive	Up Day	>50%	Below Average/Average/Above Average
Constructive	Down Day	Any	Below Average
Non-Constructive	Up Day	<50%	Average/Above Average
Non-Constructive	Down Day	<50%	Above Average

It's important to remember that a single bar's price action should always be taken in the context of the larger pattern and price formation around it. Additionally, remember that higher time frames supersede lower ones.

Just because the stock is closing poorly on a five-minute bar near the end of the day on Friday, does not mean that the stock is doomed. Especially if the stock on a weekly time frame has a closing range of 95%, just broke out of a large base, and is making new highs.

VOLUME ANALYSIS

While reading price action at the end of the day is the most important aspect of analyzing a chart, volume provides helpful clues you can use to judge the conviction of buyers and sellers.

With volume, the first thing you want to be able to do is determine if a particular bar's volume was abnormally high or low. You would then pair that data point with analysis of the price action of the bar.

To judge if volume is high or low, you can use a moving average on the volume. For swing traders a 20-day period simple moving average is helpful, for position traders you can use a 50-day simple moving average. They will provide similar reference points in most cases.

Once the moving average is plotted, keep an eye out for bars where volume is around 25% more than average or 25% less. These are above or below average volume days.

You can also simply compare a bar's volume with the previous five-to-ten bars to see if in general it is high or low. We typically use a combination of the two methods.

High volume or low volume is most significant when it occurs in areas of similar action and when the stock is experiencing significant price expansions or contractions.

During contractions, low volume areas indicate a dry up in supply coming to market, which can make the eventual expansion more explosive.

High volume during expansions such as base breakouts indicates high demand, likely leading to a more powerful trend.

During a base you will often see a gradual decline in volume as an equilibrium is reached and there is less supply coming to the marketplace.

Because high volume is often helpful to recognize in real time, we recommend using a data point like volume run rate in Deepvue, which compares the current volume to the average at that time of day.

This data point will let you know if volume is above or below the average even after just a few minutes of trading.

PRICE TIGHTNESS AND VOLATILITY CONTRACTION

The overall range relative to recent price action is also important to note. If the stock normally trades with an average daily range of 5% from high to low and forms an inside day with only a range of 2%, then it is compressing in volatility. From these types of bars we can see expansion to the upside or downside. A tight open and close where they are similar in value is also a sign of contraction.

Looking at a series of bars we can also see ranges being built, then expansions upwards or downwards.

On the chart below, we've highlighted periods where bars were forming a range and tightening.

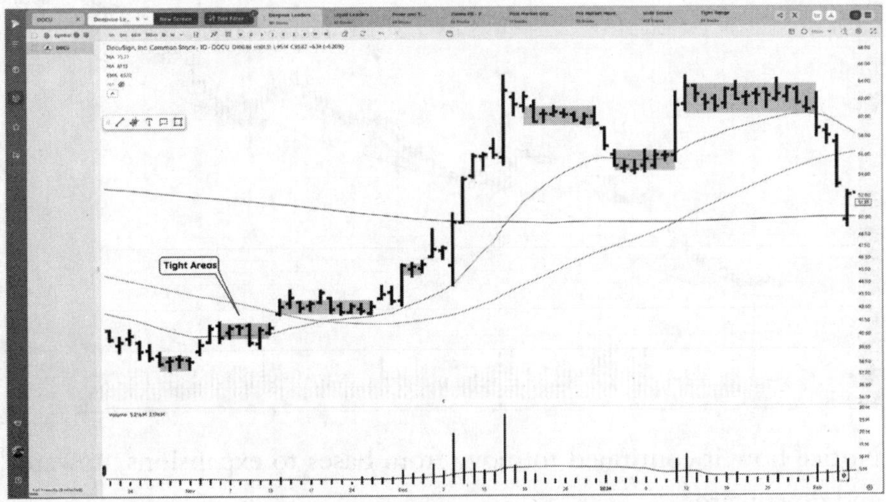

You can see how from these areas DOCU expanded and trended to the upside or downside.

In the markets, stocks on all time frames alternate between consolidation periods and trends upwards and downwards. From bases, consolidations, contractions, ranges—whatever you want to call them—come momentum moves and trends that we can take advantage of as traders.

This is a characteristic of markets where supply and demand control the prices as market participants buy and sell depending on their views of a stock's value on different time frames.

You can think of price tightness as the coiling of a spring. The tighter a stock gets relative to recent price action, the more explosive a momentum move is likely to be, once the stock emerges from the pattern.

This occurs intraday, on the daily time frame, and on even higher time frames setting up multi-month moves.

For instance, here is NVDA going back to 2015 on a monthly chart.

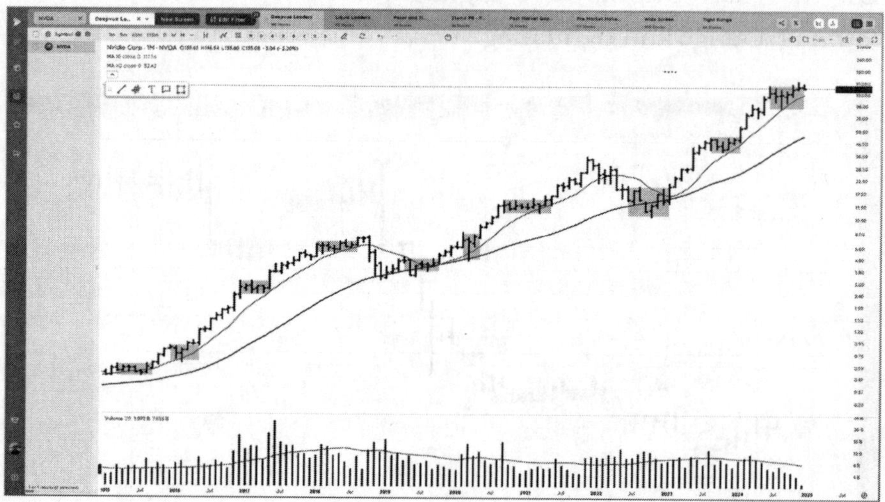

Notice how it continued to move from bases to expansions, upwards and downwards.

DEFINING TRENDS

Between consolidation periods, stocks move in trends. These sustained price increases or decreases are opportunities for traders to hold positions and profit.

It's important to recognize that even if a stock is in a sustained trend, there will be basing and counter trends along the way. Not every stock gives you an easy ride.

There are two simple but powerful ways that we want to teach you to define trends. The first is using market structure, and the second is by using moving averages.

USING MARKET STRUCTURE TO DEFINE TRENDS

The first way that you can define a trend is through simple market structure. You want to define local swing highs and swing lows. These turning points are when the stock changes direction meaningfully.

A simple way to do this is to define a turning point when a high or low is not overtaken for at least three bars.

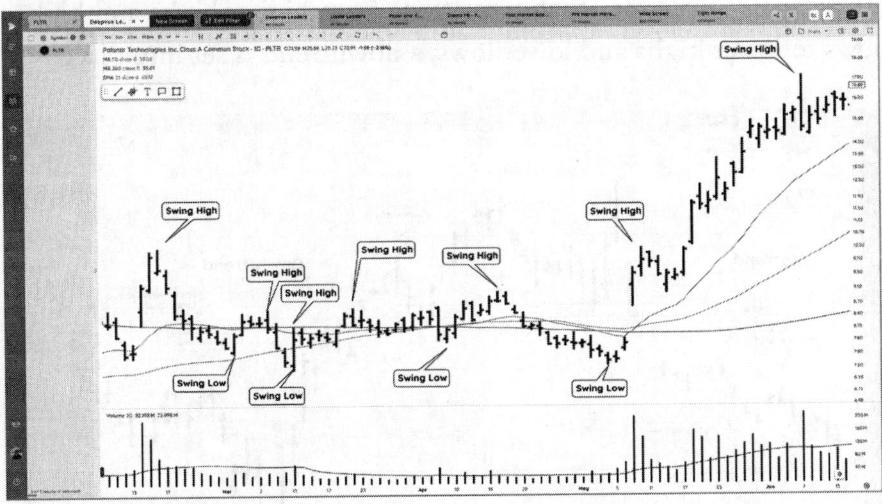

With these swing highs and lows set, an uptrend is defined as a period where the stock continues to make higher swing highs and higher swing lows.

During an uptrend there may be periods of basing in the short term where the stock may put in a lower high or lower low, but for the most part until the stock truly changes character and breaks structure, the uptrend is intact.

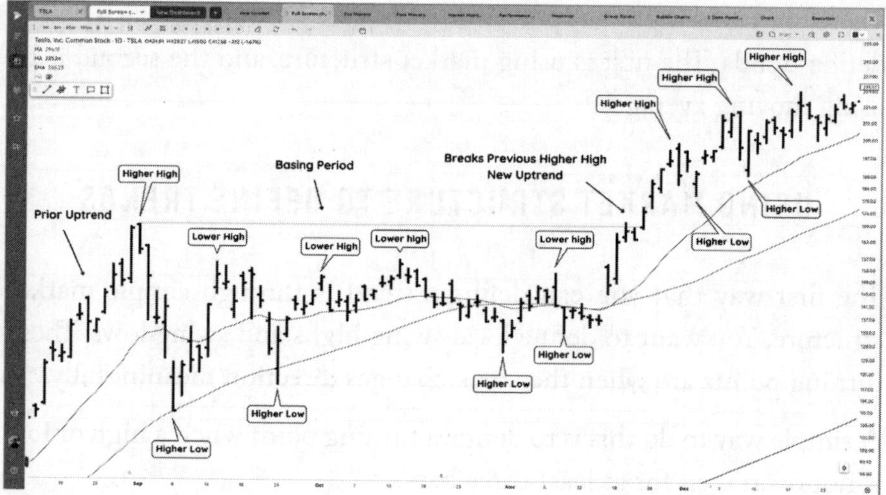

Then finally, once the stock transitions from higher highs and higher lows to lower highs and lower lows, a downtrend is set into place.

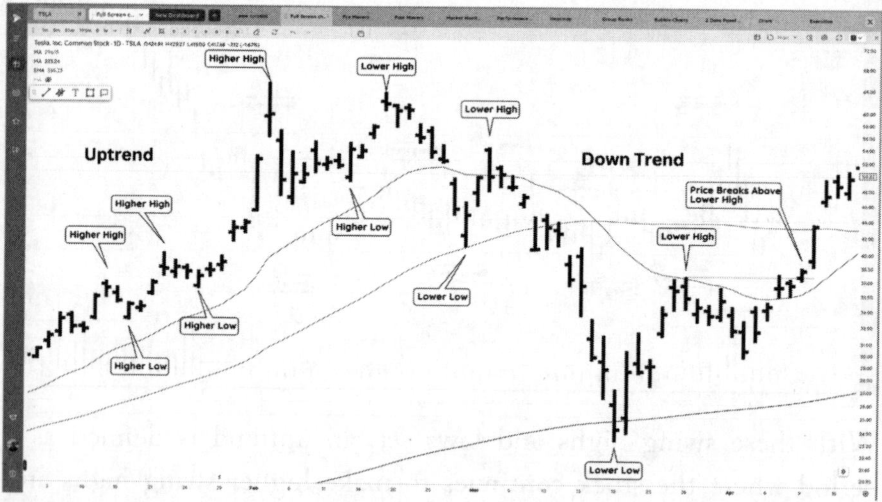

This continues until buying pressure once again overcomes supply and another break of structure occurs, resulting in a new uptrend.

This is a simple way to define uptrends and downtrends using price action.

USING MOVING AVERAGES TO DEFINE TRENDS

Another way to define trends is through using a moving average.

If the stock is moving higher above a rising moving average, by definition it is in an uptrend for that period.

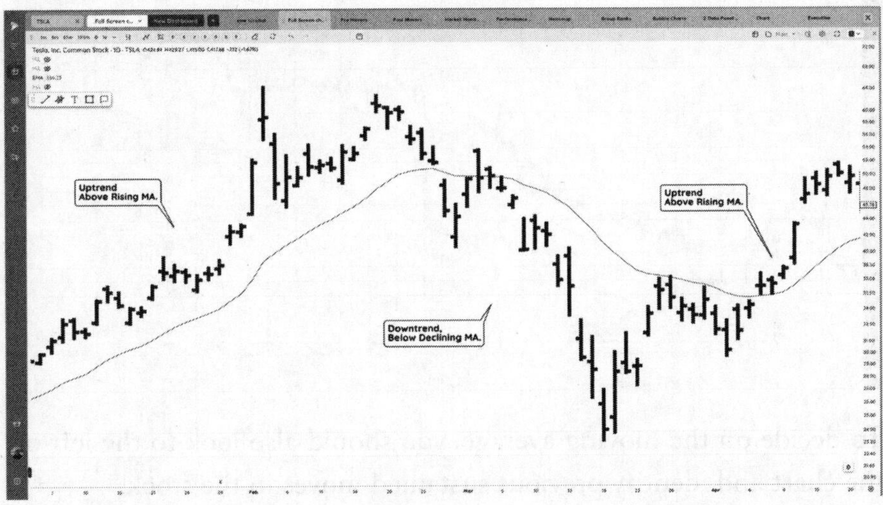

If it then undercuts the moving average and begins declining below the same moving average, it has transitioned into a downtrend.

KEY QUESTION: WHICH MOVING AVERAGE SHOULD YOU USE?

You should pick the moving average that makes sense for your trading time frame. If you are a day trader you will likely want to focus on shorter term moving averages such as the 5-day simple moving average (SMA) and ensure you are focusing on stocks in an uptrend for that period. Then you may even want to use intraday moving averages to define uptrends and downtrends.

Swing traders may prefer a 10-day SMA or 21-day EMA (exponential moving average), to focus on trends that last multiple weeks.

Position Traders and investors can focus on the 50-day SMA or even 200-day SMA to help identify the longer-term market cycle of the stock.

To decide on the moving average, you should also look to the left on the chart and identify previous sustained moves in the stock.

Which moving averages did the stock respect previously? Stocks have characters and you should use the moving averages that will keep you in the trade for your relevant time frame.

In the chart below, you can see that during both uptrends and downtrends NVDA tends to respect the 21-day EMA area.

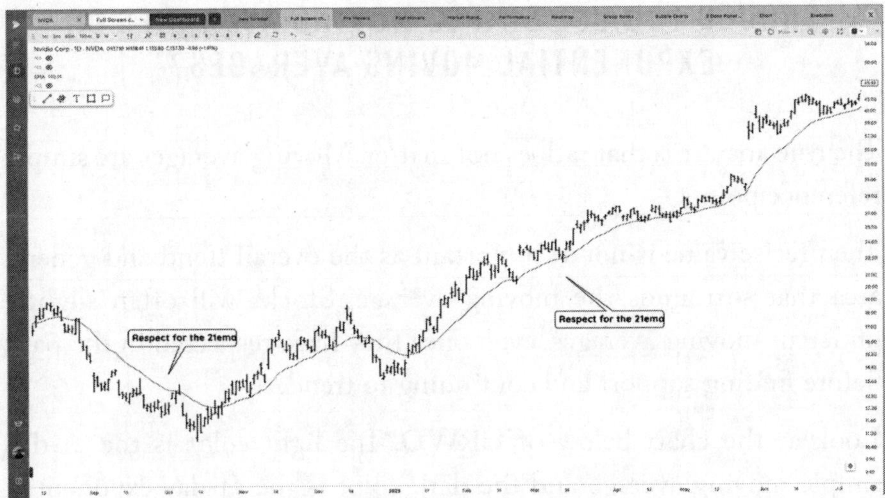

The 50-day SMA/10-week SMA, 200-day SMA/40-week SMA are often areas where institutions look to accumulate or add to positions. It's worth keeping an eye on those general levels since many market participants are watching them.

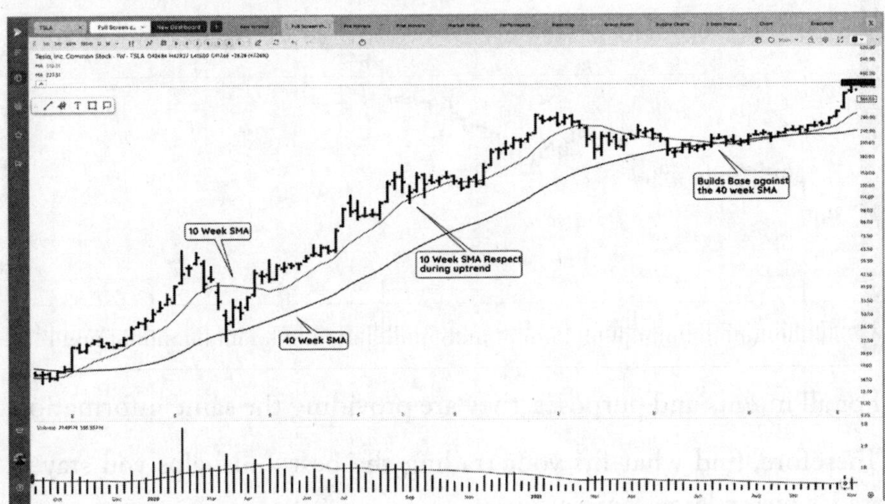

SHOULD YOU USE SIMPLE MOVING AVERAGES OR EXPONENTIAL MOVING AVERAGES?

The true answer is that it does not matter. Moving averages are simply reference points.

The precise value is not as important as the overall trend and general area that surrounds the moving average. Stocks will often slightly undercut moving averages, even ones they have respected in the past, before finding support and continuing to trend.

Look at the chart below of CRWD. The light color is the 21-day simple moving average and the dark color is the 21-day exponential moving average.

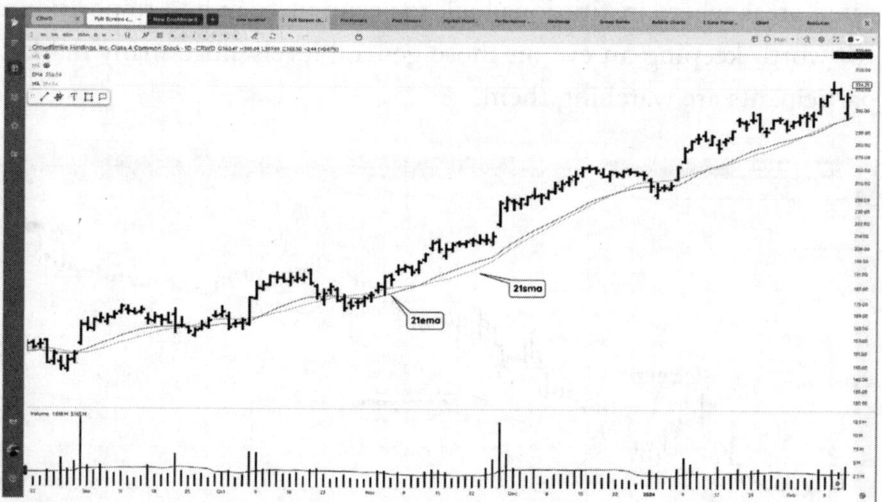

For all intents and purposes, they are providing the same information.

Therefore, find what fits your trading the best and helps you stay in trades over a large sample size.

USING MULTIPLE TIME FRAME ANALYSIS

The market is fractal, which means that trends and patterns occur on all time frames. The benefit of this is that by learning how to analyze price and volume action on one time frame, you can artfully determine supply and demand dynamics on any chart and time frame with the same process.

In addition, trends and levels become more powerful when they are aligned on multiple time frames.

If a stock on a daily chart is breaking out through yesterday's high and that high lines up with a key level on a weekly or monthly chart, then the breakout will involve participants of both the weekly and daily time frames. This adds fuel to the fire and increases the likelihood of the expansion holding and beginning a trend.

For instance, with CRSP we see a breakout through a daily high that coincides with a key level that had been resistant multiple times in the past few weeks. This led to a powerful expansion.

Another key thing to remember is that important levels from higher time frames are areas where trend changes can occur on lower time frames.

A prior swing low from a monthly chart is a spot where on a daily chart a trend of lower highs and lower lows may find support, start forming higher lows, and ultimately break structure and start a new daily uptrend.

Another example can be seen below with DOCU. First on the monthly chart you can see how the reversal in 2020 occurred right at the higher time frame IPO high that it set in 2018.

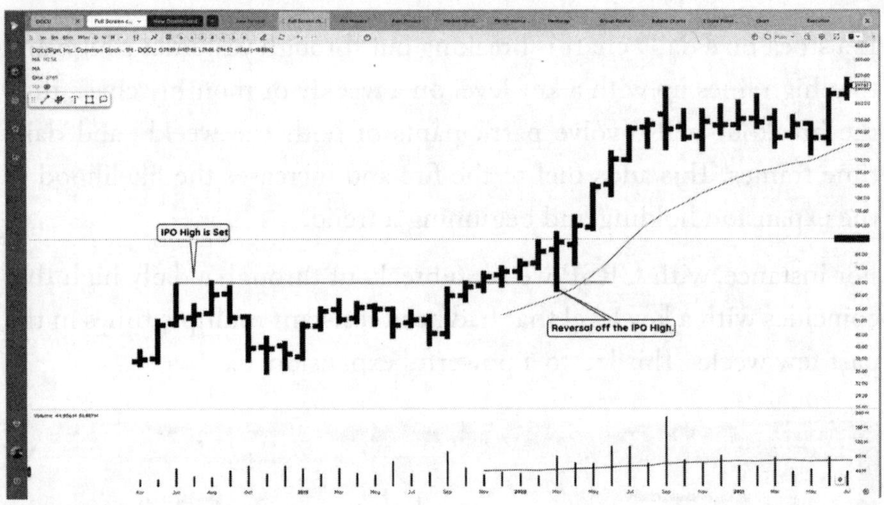

Zooming into a daily chart of the 2020 reversal we can see how DOCU was accumulated and supported right at that level.

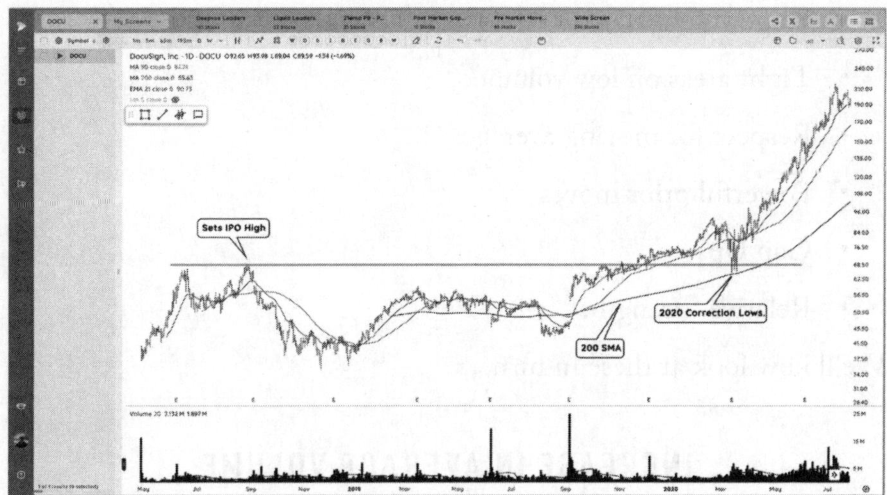

Even better, we have the confluence of the 200-day simple moving average in that same area.

When multiple key levels line up together, there is a stronger likelihood of an actionable pattern developing. Always keep an eye out for confluence.

Like with moving averages, price may undershoot or overshoot a level slightly. Think of them more as areas to be aware of—areas of interest.

WINNING CHARACTERISTICS

Now that we have covered the basics of reading price action, we wanted to share some key price and volume characteristics that the highest potential stocks share. These winning characteristics are based on observations and studies of the top-performing stocks from the mid-1990s onwards. They are shared by almost all stocks that double and triple.

The characteristics are:

- Increase in average volume

- Huge volume spikes
- Tight areas on low volume
- Respect for moving averages
- Powerful prior moves
- Gap Ups
- Relative Strength.

We'll now look at these in turn.

INCREASE IN AVERAGE VOLUME

As a stock is being accumulated, it will become more liquid as more institutions become involved. You will see a distinct step up in average volume. The start of this increase often occurs at the beginning of a new uptrend or after an earnings report.

HUGE VOLUME SPIKES

Oliver Kell, the US Investing Championship record holder, has a saying: Volume = Price, Cause = Effect.

Big volume is a signal of big accumulation. Along with the average increase in volume, you will often see large spikes of volume as trends get underway and at key moments such as on base breakouts and earnings reports.

Large volume is a sign of institutions stepping in and accumulating shares. On a daily chart look for the highest volume in a year or more and on a weekly look for large blue weeks during trends.

Here is an example of PLTR in 2023 which showed huge weeks of volume as it quickly doubled following an earnings report.

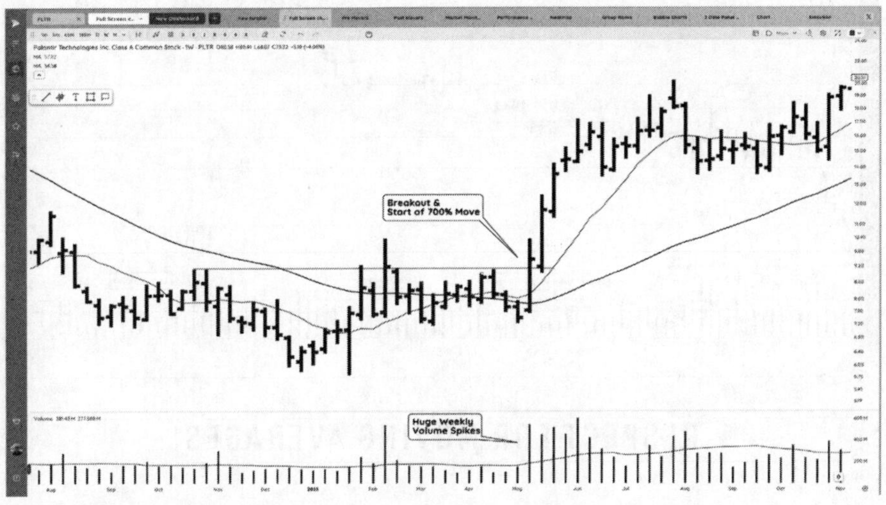

TIGHT AREAS ON LOW VOLUME

During both trends and consolidation periods, there will be moments where the stock pauses and forms tight areas, both in terms of overall ranges as well as closes.

Volume should decrease noticeably as, for a moment, there is an equilibrium reached in supply and demand. The key here is that these tight areas signify a lack of sellers and subtle accumulation by institutions as they support the stock and keep it within the range.

During a trend, these tight areas and pauses will often occur after a sharp increase in price. The stock should stair step higher in a very orderly and consistent manner above the moving averages.

It should expand up, go tight, expand up, go tight, and repeat as it trends. This is a clear sign that demand is continuing to support the stock even as it moves higher.

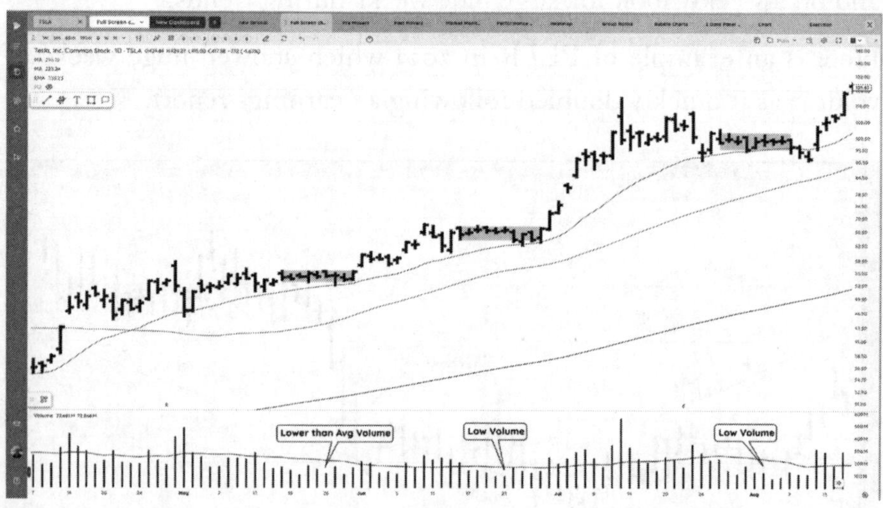

RESPECT FOR MOVING AVERAGES

Strong leaders during their moves will hold specific key moving averages for extended periods. This is a signal that the stock is still being accumulated during the trend.

During its 2020 250% move, ROKU showed clear respect for the 10-week simple moving average,

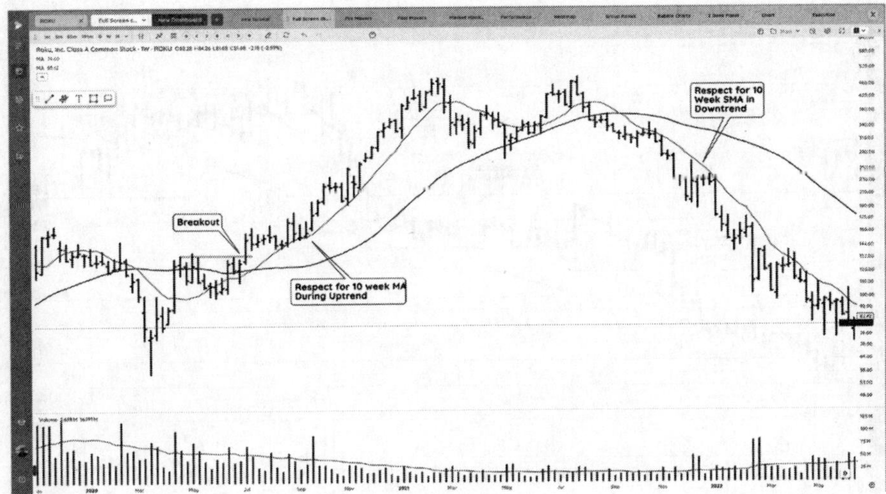

During its decline in 2021 it respected the 10-week to the downside as well.

The moving averages stocks respect become part of their character. Take note of when a stock finally seems to lose that respect because that could be a sign that the move is near the end or that the stock needs to build a longer base.

POWERFUL PRIOR MOVES

Winning stocks often continue to win. Stocks that have shown the ability to trend strongly in the recent past can perform once again after a base or longer corrective period.

SMCI in 2024 is shown in the graphic below.

On the flip side, if you look to the left in the chart and a stock trades weakly, does not progress well from proper bases, and trades choppy, then do not expect a nice clean trend unless you see a full change in character.

GAP UPS

Gap ups, often coinciding with earnings reports, are a key signature of market leaders. Stocks that make moves of 200%, 300%, 500%+ will often have multiple gap ups during their moves.

This price signature is a pattern that we will take advantage of later with our high volume edge and gapper setup.

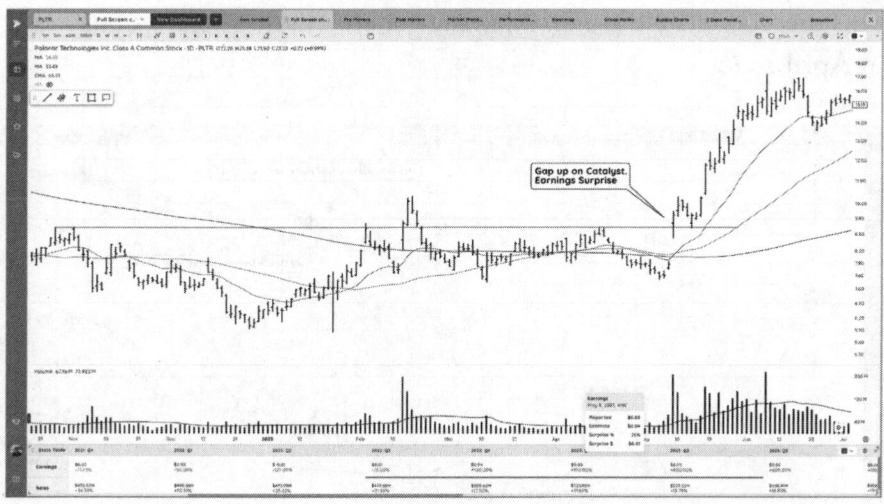

As we will mention later, the early gaps in a move have a higher probability of maturing into a trend as institutions are still accumulating shares aggressively due to changes in fundamentals, key news events, or other catalysts.

RELATIVE STRENGTH

The key leaders will always have periods where they stand out due to their Relative Strength. During a market correction they may be going sideways or advancing, even as the market is still pulling in.

This Relative Strength can be shown clearly in a Relative Strength line or screened for using the Relative Strength rating or absolute strength rating.

For instance, if a market correction is around three months long, you could use the 3-Month Absolute Strength Rating in Deepvue to find the top-performing stocks during that period.

A classic example of Relative Strength is Zoom (ZM) in 2020. Even as the market was correcting, institutions were accumulating this stock and it actually increased in value during the 2020 correction.

This preceded its 350% gain once the general market began an uptrend in April 2020.

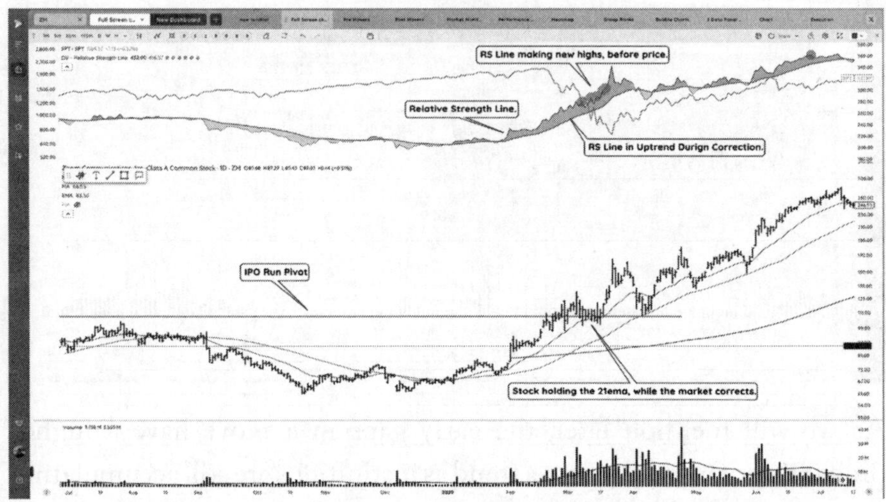

When the market weakens or consolidates, look for stocks that are standing out and diverging, fighting any drawdowns. These are potential leaders when the general market pressure is relieved.

LEARNING THE CHARACTER OF A STOCK

Along with recognizing winning characteristics, another key concept is learning the character of a stock. This will help you recognize how you should enter, manage, and exit a trade.

As you analyze thousands of charts, you will start to realize how each stock has its own patterns of movement.

Some are steady trenders, others are jumpy and volatile. Some stocks gap from base to base, others will go on strong momentum moves consistently. Some stocks respect the 21-day EMA, some the 50-day SMA.

These behaviors are a function of the particular supply and demand dynamics of that stock and the major participants who trade it.

There are a few key components that play a part:

- Liquidity, dollar volume, and institutional involvement
- Float
- Life cycle of the stock

As a general rule of thumb, the more liquid a stock is, the cleaner its trends will be and the more it will respect key levels and moving averages.

This is because when a stock has high dollar volume, which is defined by the average shares traded over a period multiplied by the current price, larger institutions can safely take positions. With larger players involved, bid and ask spreads tighten and a stock becomes less jumpy and trades smoother.

Does this mean the stock can't make extraordinary moves? Not at all!

In fact, many of the biggest moves in history occur as a young stock is becoming more liquid and larger institutions can take up stakes. This leads to the increase in average volume signature that we covered earlier.

Institutions also help dampen drawdowns by accumulating shares on weakness during a long-term uptrend. They tend to buy on pullbacks to key levels such as the 10-week or 40-week moving averages, creating bases.

Along with liquidity, the float of the stock can also impact how volatile a stock trades. Typically stocks with a lower float are more volatile, while stocks with more shares available to trade usually have gentler moves.

This goes hand in hand with where the stock is in its life cycle. Recent IPOs are often more volatile pre lock up because part of their float is restricted from trading. Post lock up, and after secondary offerings, stocks mature and become more liquid, leading to less volatility over time.

One of the most useful ways to express the volatility of a stock, and a parameter that we use frequently in screens, is average daily range (ADR). This can be expressed either as a dollar range or a % range. We prefer using the % version so it can be used to compare stocks of different share prices.

ADR is a measure of how much a stock typically moves during a trading day. There is a trade-off to be made since we want a stock that has strong movements but also trades tight enough that we can manage risk.

A good rule of thumb for growth and momentum trading is to focus on stocks with an ADR % of at least around 3–5%. At this level stocks can make powerful moves in just a few weeks.

CLEAN TRENDERS VERSUS CHOPPY TRADERS

One thing you will notice in charts is that some stocks trade cleanly, transitioning from uptrends to downtrends in an orderly fashion, respecting trend lines and moving averages, and also with few gap downs.

On the other side of the spectrum are what we call choppy traders. These are stocks that gap up and down frequently, lack tight areas on charts, and have little respect for key moving averages.

A good example of these stocks are oil and gas companies or other stocks that are influenced by an underlying commodity.

For instance, we have OXY. Even during an uptrend, it has the habit of gapping up and down with many false breakouts.

Both clean trenders and choppy traders can go on fantastic moves and double and triple, but we as a whole prefer the clean trenders. They are easier to manage, easier to position in, and respect key reference points along the way like the 50 SMA. A great trend only makes you money if you are able to stay in it.

CAN A STOCK'S CHARACTER CHANGE?

A stock's character can certainly change. This can occur when there is a catalyst that fundamentally changes a company or entire industry.

When this occurs, institutions have to recalibrate their models and allocate capital accordingly. This changes the supply and demand dynamic and can turn a once stagnant stock into a momentum mover.

Character changes show up in the charts often with a large increase in volume and powerful price moves. After this occurs stocks may have newfound respect for moving averages, trade more cleanly, and otherwise change their behavior.

WHAT DRIVES STOCK MARKET MOVES?

This is an important question that can help you determine which stocks have high potential and could produce meaningful trends.

To answer the *what*, we must first address the *who*. In the markets, the vast majority of trading volume—about 90%—is attributed to institutional investors, from hedge funds to pension funds to banks.

Only about 10% of trading volume can be attributed to retail and independent investors, according to research from Morgan Stanley.

So what are institutional investors looking for?

In short, they are looking to invest in companies which have increasing expectations for future earnings. They are looking for companies that will grow their value, develop new products, increase revenue, and improve margins.

How do we find companies like this? We've adapted the CANSLIM criteria, which was developed by William O'Neil, to suit the current markets.

CANSLIM is a trading and investing framework that consolidates the seven key criteria that defined the greatest performing stocks of all time. For an in-depth walkthrough of the system, we highly recommend you read *How To Make Money in Stocks* by William O'Neil.

Here is a brief overview of the seven CANSLIM criteria.

1. CURRENT QUARTERLY EARNINGS

Look for stocks with increases in quarterly earnings of at least 25% for the last two quarters. Ideally you will see strong earnings, sales, and profit margins growth in recent quarters. The faster the growth, the better.

2. ANNUAL EARNINGS GROWTH

On top of quarterly earnings, you want to be sure stocks are showing strong long-term growth.

This can be done by looking for stocks that have increased their earnings at least 25% for the past three to five years. In the case of unprofitability, you want to see a trend toward profitability. Also, take special note of significant annual earnings estimates over 25%, although the higher the better, for the current and successive year.

3. NEW PRODUCT/SERVICE/CEO/PRICE HIGH

All the studies of the greatest stock market winners have a new product or service in common. Look for the companies with the most innovative products/services. Ideally, these are companies that are changing the way we work, live, and play.

CEO changes can also lead to incredible turnaround stories, with Dr. Lisa Su of AMD being an excellent example. Since Dr. Su took the helm of AMD, the stock has risen from under $5 a share to well over $100 in under six years—greater than a 5,000% increase. Finally, many leadership stocks will be making new 52-week price highs over and over again during strong market trends.

4. SUPPLY AND DEMAND

This metric is where charts and technical analysis come into play. A stock's price goes up because more investors demand a limited supply of stock. You want to look for accumulation signs by institutions to gauge demand. We will teach you how to analyze a chart and be able to identify specific entry points where supply is limited and demand is exceptional.

5. LEADER OR LAGGARD

We want to focus on the best of the best stocks—these are the leaders. Leaders generally have a stronger chart and have superior earnings and sales growth versus similar companies. True market leaders will most likely be in top-performing industry groups and sectors as they are often innovative companies riding a disruptive theme.

6. INSTITUTIONAL SPONSORSHIP

We want to be focusing on young companies with rapidly growing fund ownership as well as high-quality funds establishing new positions in the stock. This institutional sponsorship will lead to clean trends and buy points during bull markets as funds accumulate shares.

7. MARKET DIRECTION

Finally, the most important factor in CANSLIM is the market direction, since three out of four stocks follow the trend of the general market. We always want to be aware of the overall trend and be trading when the deck is hot and the probabilities are with us. We want to be involved in uptrends, and conversely we want to be lightly exposed when conditions change and the market corrects.

We will never catch the low and never sell the high, but the goal when the market begins correcting is to step aside as a downtrend starts. Then we let institutions create the bases and join in ourselves after a new uptrend has been established.

HOW WE'VE ADAPTED CANSLIM

In current markets, CANSLIM still continues to point to many of the strongest institutional quality stocks in the market.

However, we have a few tweaks that we have made. First, we focus more on technicals than fundamentals. Fundamentals are important and are the driving factor in multi-year moves of a stock. But, for swing trades and even position trades, momentum and Relative Strength in technical screens will lead you to the strongest names.

In addition, although earnings growth is important, in recent times with more companies focusing on growth at all cost, revenue growth is often just as or more important for judging the potential of a stock.

The other key difference is that many stocks trade on catalysts even before growth shows up in earnings or sales data. These stocks can be found by looking for large gap ups and volume surges. We will discuss this in more depth in subsequent chapters.

In short, the key tenets of CANSLIM still hold true, although we personally focus more on price and volume signatures on the chart than on longer-term fundamental drivers. We also focus on the current strong themes in the market.

OPPORTUNITY ZONES

The final concept that we want to cover in the foundations chapter is that of the three opportunity zones. These are larger areas within a stock's trading history where we often see trends where stocks double and triple.

The three zones are:

- IPO Boom Zone

- Growth Transition Zone
- New Momentum Zone

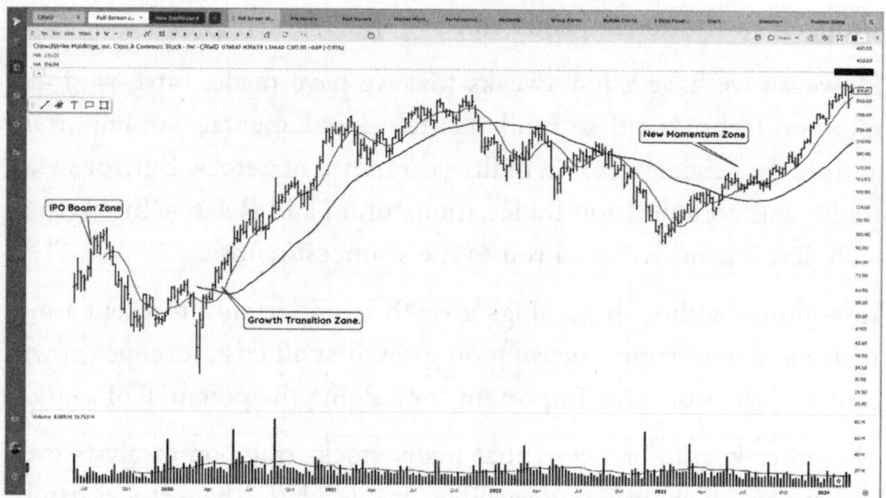

When a promising stock has entered one of these zones, you can zero in for further analysis, looking for price and volume signatures, entry setups, and finally entry tactics if a stock meets your criteria.

These zones build off the work of Mike Webster, Stan Weinstein, as well as the Lifecycle Trade team: Eve Boboch, Kurt Daill, Kathy Donnelly, and Eric Krull.

IPO BOOM ZONE

This is the first opportunity zone of a stock's life cycle. It occurs right after a stock IPO and often begins with an IPO base, a short consolidation of a few days to a few weeks. A recent IPO can make high momentum moves, especially if the stock is part of a current leadership group and theme.

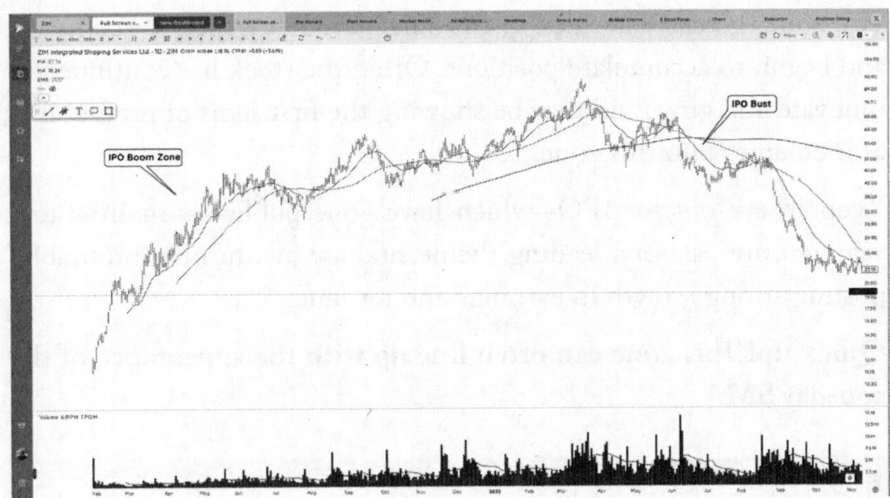

The main drawback of this zone is that it is short-lived and volatile. Still, traders can look for early entry points.

The supply and demand dynamics at play here are that because of a lock-up period, many of the stock's holders are unable to sell, leading to high potential for a trend if there is strong demand that comes in.

However, once the lock-up period ends, insiders are able to sell and there are often secondary offerings, leading to increased supply and the typical drawdown and basing period that the Lifecycle Trade authors coined the institutional due diligence phase.

GROWTH TRANSITION ZONE

This is the next opportunity that a stock will exhibit. This occurs as a stock establishes a trading range after the initial drawdown from its IPO and begins a new longer-term uptrend up the right side of the institutional due diligence stage.

Within this zone you can look for base breakouts off the bottom or along the trend closer to its previous IPO highs.

This zone is created because institutions have researched the company and begun to accumulate positions. Often the stock has continued to innovate and grow, and may be showing the first signs of profitability as it emerges into this zone.

Keep an eye out for IPOs which have gone public six months to a year ago, are part of a leading theme, and are just turning profitable/posting strong growth in earnings and revenue.

Quick tip! This zone can often line up with the appearance of the 200-day SMA.

NEW MOMENTUM ZONE

The final zone can occur multiple times during a stock's lifetime. The new momentum zone occurs anytime the stock has been declining or basing for some time, and then forms a base and begins a new strong Stage 2 uptrend.

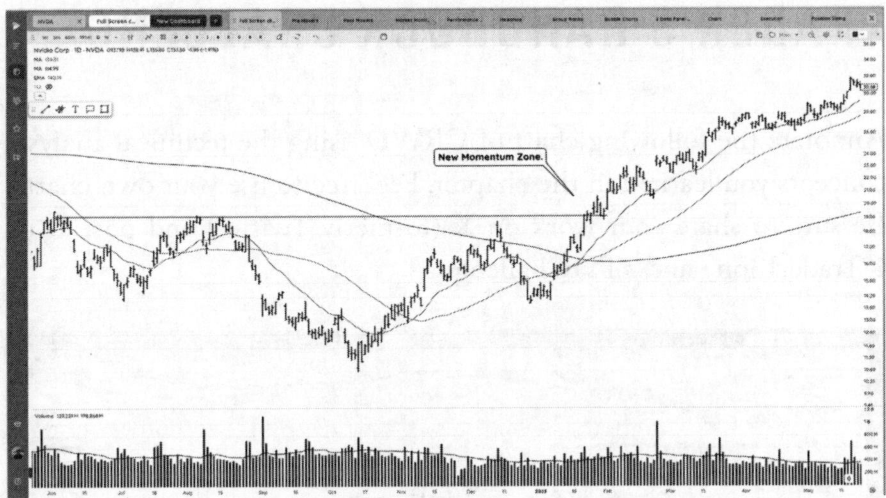

These zones often occur after the market has experienced a longer-term basing or correctional period.

The best stocks emerging into these zones will have a catalyst and leading theme associated with them, creating strong growth potential.

KEY FOUNDATIONAL TOPICS

There, we've done it! We've now covered the key building blocks that the rest of this book will be based upon.

Now let's quickly review before we move on to an exciting chapter on entry tactics.

We pivoted toward important technical analysis concepts that will form the basis for the edges, setups, entry tactics, and position management frameworks that we will discuss in the next few chapters.

Finally, we discussed winning characteristics, learning the character of a stock, and what drives market moves.

TRADER'S HANDBOOK CHALLENGE 1

Annotate the following chart of CRWD using the technical analysis concepts you learned in the chapter. Feel free to use your own charts. Be sure to share your work on X (formerly Twitter) and post at us @TraderLion_ and #THChallenge

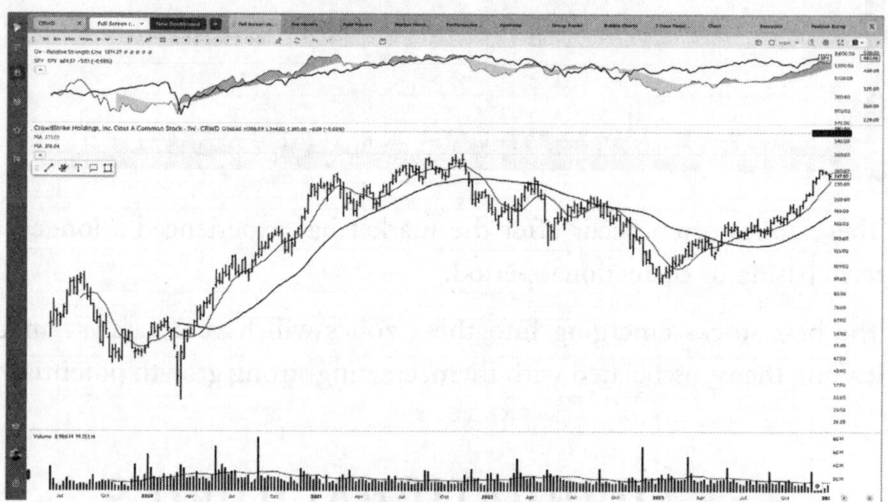

KEY TAKEAWAYS

Here are five key takeaways from this chapter:

1. Price action gives clues to the potential and trend of a stock. We can learn to recognize winning characteristics and build a template of what high potential stocks look like before and during their big moves.
2. Each stock has a particular character. This is due to its catalysts, institutional involvement, float, life cycle, and Average Daily Range (ADR). By learning these characteristics we can

recognize when a stock is under accumulation and learn to manage a position relative to this character.

3. Institutions drive stock market moves. They are responsible for the vast majority of trading volume, and they look to accumulate positions in stocks with strong growth and earnings potential. This accumulation creates trends that we can ride as retail traders.
4. There are certain opportunity zones that appear in stocks. The first is the IPO Boom Zone, the first potential momentum move in a stock's lifetime that starts shortly after a stock comes to market. The second is the Growth Transition Zone, which occurs after institutions have done their research and have started accumulating positions in force. The last zone is more cyclical, occurring after major bases or general market corrections. The new momentum zone occurs when a new Stage 2 uptrend begins, driven by a catalyst and often when the stock is part of an emerging theme.

BONUS RESOURCE

We recorded a webinar about reading price action and the foundations of technical analysis.

You can watch it today at traderlion.com/handbook.

CHAPTER 4
EDGES AND SETUPS

"Wall Street never changes, the pockets change, the suckers change, the stocks change, but Wall Street never changes, because human nature never changes."

—Jesse Livermore

EDGES AND SETUPS tactics are some of the most talked about aspects of trading. Newer traders strive to learn the secret patterns that lead to near 100% win rates and have the magical predictive ability to always lead to 1,000% moves in short order.

The reality of trading, however, is that the market is uncertain. We can focus on setups with higher probabilities of producing a strong return, but there is always a chance of a loss.

Therefore a proper setup is not necessarily special because of its ability to always produce strong returns consistently, but rather because it allows traders to manage risk tightly and logically.

The goal with edges and setups is to define frameworks for identifying and entering high potential stocks at a point where if you are right, you will quickly be at a profit, and where if you are wrong, you will quickly be stopped out for a negligible loss.

How does this work?

The setup in question must have a clearly defined entry level and a corresponding level where if the stock reverses, it would signal a current failure of the setup. The closer the failure level is to your entry point, the tighter your stop can be on the trade.

However, the stop level must also be logical—meaning that it reflects an important technical level that the stock should not violate given its current momentum if the trade is to be successful. This means that with normal trading of the stock, the level should not be breached. We will go much further into setting tight and logical stops in the risk management chapter.

How you define your setup will depend on your time frame and style of trading. Some traders reading this may be day traders, shorting artists, mean-reversion buyers... strategies that are very different from our approach. This is perfectly normal and each trader should study their own trades and develop their own unique styles that fit their method. However, the principles we will be discussing can apply to setups for all different styles.

A key point that we will emphasize again and again is that you do not need ten different strategies. Some of the best traders in history focused on only one setup that they mastered, then they waited and waited until the conditions were perfect. Specialization pays in trading.

If you can define just one to three repeatable setups that allow you to manage risk and show up during every market cycle in high-quality opportunities, you will excel as a trader.

So, as we go through the next two chapters, think about what your own unique edges, setups, and entry tactics are. Describe each of them in detail and include examples that you can refer back to.

Here's what we will cover in this chapter:

1. The S.N.I.P.E. framework
2. The high volume edges

3. The Relative Strength edge
4. The N-factor edge
5. The launch-pad setup
6. The gapper setup
7. The base breakout setup.

WHERE DO EDGES, SETUPS, AND TACTICS FIT INTO A TRADING SYSTEM?

Although entries are important, they are only one part of an overall trading system. Position management, among other concepts, is just as important, if not more so, and each of the chapters of this book plays a critical role.

We say this because often many beginning traders get obsessed with finding 'perfect' entries. In the reality of trading there is no such thing; there are only entries that fit a template for a high potential return to risk.

So how and where do entries fit into your trading system?

You can break down a trading system into five key processes. It may help you to remember them using the S.N.I.P.E. acronym, which in and of itself is a great reminder to focus, trade with discipline, and to specialize.

S.N.I.P.E. stands for:

1. **Search and scan**—Look for current opportunities.
2. **Narrow**—Focus your attention only on the stocks that fit your system and have strong potential.

3. **Identify**—Finalize your watchlists and analyze each opportunity looking for edges and setups.
4. **Plan**—For actionable names plan the setup and entry tactic that you will use to enter.
5. **Execute**—Enter your trade while managing risk and then manage the position.

SEARCH AND SCAN

This is your process for getting stocks that meet your most general criteria across your desk for further examination. This is the largest part of your funnel. We will explore this more in Chapter 5. This step could be requiring certain liquidity and dollar volume levels, or basic fundamental growth numbers.

NARROW

Focus your attention only on the stocks that are exhibiting edges and fit tighter criteria for a trade. This could be looking for necessary fundamentals, theme, story, momentum, trend, or price and volume signatures.

IDENTIFY

In this step you further restrict the flow of ideas and focus only on stocks that show edges and a specific setup that you have studied, and thrives in the current environment.

PLAN

For the names you are focused on, you will plan out the entry tactic you will use, how you will manage risk using stop losses and position sizing, and any other relevant criteria when making the trade.

EXECUTE

The final step of the process is to execute your plan, enter the position, and then manage the position using your position management rules. This includes both rules to sell into strength and rules to sell into weakness.

Now that we have the full context in mind, let's zoom in and explore trading edges and how they can help you identify high potential stocks.

WHAT IS AN EDGE?

In trading, the phrase "you need an edge" gets thrown around quite a bit, but what does that exactly mean?

Well, having an edge simply means that your process and its components allow you to have a winning expectation over time. The last two words "over time" are important because the markets are probabilistic. An edge or setup might be very successful over the long haul but may fail spectacularly the next time you use it. This is why risk management is a key part of successful trading as it allows you to protect yourself from large losses.

Edges come in all shapes and sizes. It can be Warren Buffett's ability to analyze a company's financials to find deals, Jim Simons' algorithms, or a news-based trader's ability to analyze information the fastest. In addition, the effectiveness of certain edges may fade over time due to changing market dynamics. This is why it's important to be fluid and bend with the market—to listen to what is working.

POSITION SIZING BASED ON EDGES

Position sizing is an extremely important part of trading. It is what ultimately contributes to performance by increasing the impact of a trending and well-performing position on your equity curve. However, you do have to balance this positive with the downside risk associated with any position if it goes against you.

As we've already discussed, edges are winning characteristics that indicate that a stock has high potential. It follows that the more edges a stock exhibits, the more evidence there is that it could be a top performer.

With this in mind, it stands to reason that when a stock shows more edges, we should increase our focus on that stock in order to execute and capitalize on a strong potential reward/risk opportunity. In this same vein, we should also commit more capital to that position, managing risk along the way.

Using a hypothetical portfolio of 100k, here is a breakdown of an example position sizing system based on the number of edges. The starter position here is 10k, or 10% of the total portfolio.

Base position	1 edge present	2 edges present	3 edges present	4 edges present
10% or 10k	12.5% or 12.5k	15% or 15k	17.5% or 17.5k	20% or 20k

This simplified system can serve as the base position sizing methodology that you should then tailor to your own trading while taking into account your own experience, skill level, and risk tolerance.

Maybe you are more comfortable setting your base sizing at 5%. That is perfectly fine.

What's important is that when your system has identified that a stock has many edges present and better fits your ideal template, you accordingly allocate more focus and capital to that opportunity.

You should also focus more on edges that are working in that current market cycle. It does not make sense to increase capital allocation based on an edge that is not working currently. Instead focus on recent edges that have proven themselves and focus on stocks in your universe that are exhibiting those criteria.

WHAT IS A SETUP?

If edges are repeatable winning characteristics that signify that an opportunity is developing, a setup is a repeatable larger pattern that signifies that there is a strong reward-to-risk ratio. It combines both the edges in play as well as the entry tactic that completes the larger pattern.

WHAT IS AN ENTRY TACTIC?

The last piece of this puzzle is entry tactics. Entry tactics are shorter-term patterns and methods that traders and investors use to establish positions within overall setups. Entry tactics allow you to manage risk tightly and logically while putting on enough size.

Entry tactics and trade execution will be the focus of the next chapter.

OUR PLAYBOOK

With the definitions set for edges, setups, and entry tactics, let's now dive into the specific ones that we use to position in the market leaders of each market cycle.

Reminder: These are the methods that we use. You may have your own setups. Organizing your own "playbook" with the characteristics you look for is an excellent exercise and may even be the challenge for this chapter (hint hint).

EDGES

THE HIGH VOLUME EDGES: HVE HVIPO HV1

The High Volume (HV) edges are a key part of our process. These volume signatures indicate that the stock is undergoing a potential significant character change.

A gap up on extremely large volume can lead to a strong momentum move and/or a long-term new trend in the stock.

HVE = Highest volume ever

HVIPO = Highest volume since the IPO week

HV1 = Highest volume in 1 year

The most promising HV edges occur when they are associated with a game-changing catalyst. This could be an earnings report where they announce profitability for the first time, a development and launch of a new product, or an industry-level change created by new legislation.

The larger the volume the better, and we want to see the stock change character and start a new uptrend; refer to the TSLA chart.

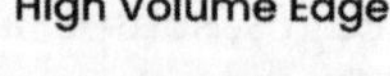

High Volume Edge

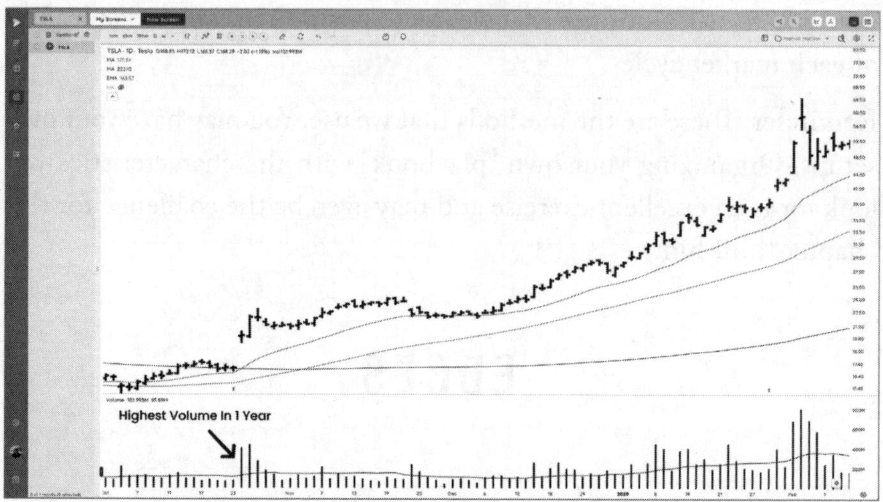

A great example of an HV1 is 24 April 2019 in TSLA. The company had reported earnings the previous day and announced a surprise profit, new over the air autopilot updates, and that a new factory was ahead of schedule.

This showed a dramatic change in the near-term future prospects of the company and changed how institutions viewed Tesla. The stock gapped up on the highest volume in a year and then rose the next day on *even higher volume*.

In this case the HV edge identified the character change that led to a 200% move in a few months.

You can easily create a screen for this edge using the logic that volume today is greater than the maximum volume of the past 250 days. We also have the logic built in as a data point in Deepvue.

We also like to specify that the closing range for the day was over 40%, the stock was up on the day, and the stock has at a bare minimum 3 million in dollar volume, but the key is the HV edge; refer to screen criteria.

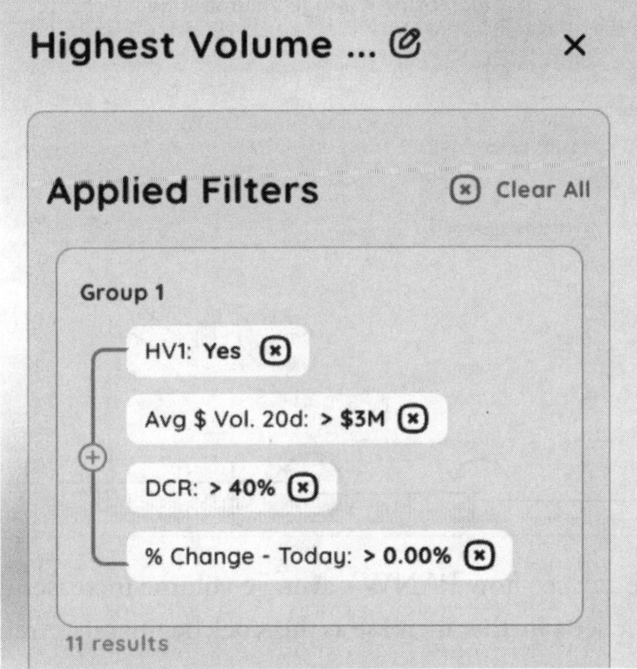

You will often see Biotech stocks on this screen. Although they can work, they often gap up on drug trial news which typically goes nowhere. We prefer stocks in other industries that again have a game-changing catalyst.

THE HIGH VOLUME EDGE

When looking at market leaders of the past you may notice that the average volume of a stock often significantly increases just as the move is getting underway.

This often indicates that the stock is becoming more liquid and is being traded more by more institutions. This change in supply/demand dynamics often contributes positively to the performance of the stock as larger institutions can get involved; refer to chart.

Increasing Average Volume Edge

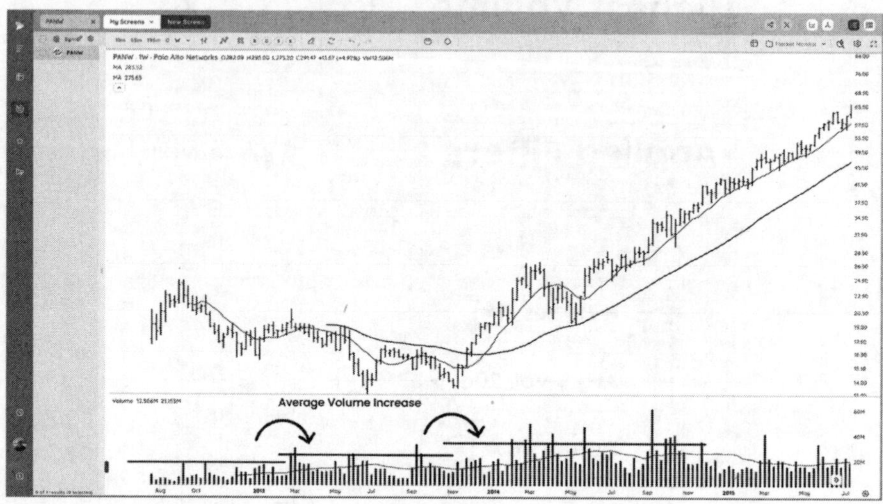

In 2013 we can see how PANW's average volume increases during the base and we see a further increase as the stock begins an uptrend in 2014.

Liquidity is key for institutions. They need to be able to build deca-million-dollar positions. As more institutions become involved in a stock, you'll see the daily average volume increase and often large weekly volume spikes.

THE RELATIVE STRENGTH EDGE

If you want to find a strong stock with the potential to make a powerful move, you often want to focus on stocks which have already shown outperformance.

Outperformance means that a stock was holding up better or rising faster than its peers over a certain time frame. It is often most apparent when the general market is undergoing a correction or pulling back. Institutions use these periods to add capital to their highest conviction ideas.

This demand supports the stock, so even though they may pull back with the rest of the market, they can stand out in various ways such as:

1. The Relative Strength Line in an uptrend and ideally making new highs.
2. On over 60% of days during a correction, the stock outperforms the market (a Relative Strength [RS] day).
3. The stock holds above key moving averages as the market undercuts them.
4. During a later part of a correction, the stock ignores market pullbacks and may form higher lows as the market forms lower lows.
5. As the market moves up the right side after consolidating, the stock "jumps up" and recovers faster, as if pressure on a spring has been released.

Once a new uptrend begins, it is often the stocks that showed Relative Strength, especially during the last third of the correction, that become leaders. Leaders will also often lead the market higher, meaning they will reclaim moving averages and make new highs ahead of the indexes; refer to the chart.

ZM during 2020 is an excellent example of RS. We've highlighted in the chart with vertical bars the period where the market was correcting. During this period ZM outperformed on 61% of the days as its RS line increased. It also held the 21 EMA as the market undercut and the RS line stayed in an uptrend and showed multiple new highs throughout the correction.

Relative Strength and High Momentum Edge

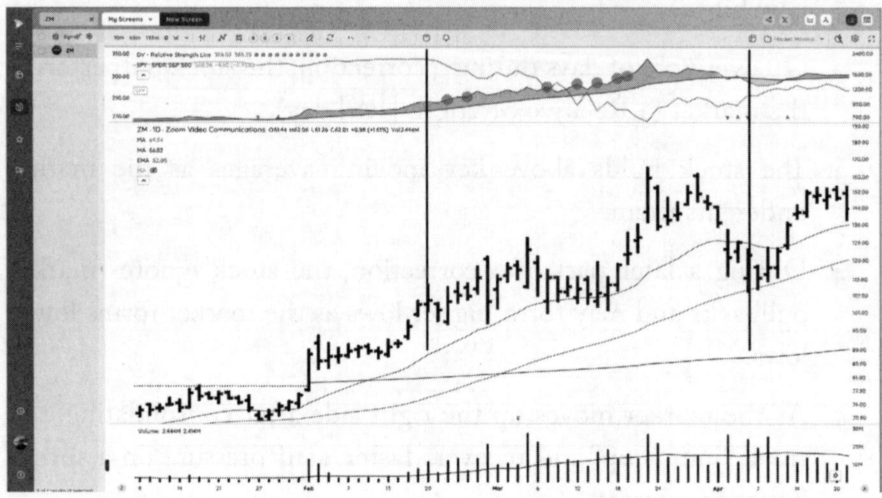

After the market correction ended, ZM led the work from home theme and increased a further 350%.

The RS line is an indicator that plots the ratio of the stock's price divided by an index ETF, typically the SPY. It is very different from the commonly used RSI or Relative Strength Index. An uptrend indicates outperformance versus the index; a downtrend indicates underperformance. The value itself is not meaningful—the trend is what matters.

During a normal uptrend you can use three-month absolute strength rankings to find the strongest stocks. You can also scan for stocks that are gapping up, or moving higher on volume. Essentially, you are watching for standout price action.

THE N-FACTOR EDGE

The next edge we will be discussing is more fundamental in nature. We are looking for a game-changing catalyst that can provide the story which leads to a significant advance in a stock. A common example is an EPS or revenue surprise where a company dramatically beats expectations and raises their guidance for upcoming quarters.

Surprises force large funds and institutions to accumulate or add to positions over time based on changing factors in their analysis and spreadsheets. This may result in a large gap up and potential trend which we as retail traders can take advantage of.

A game-changing catalyst can also appear at the industry level where perhaps regulation changes allow for significant development and growth. These changes can impact all stocks in that industry, but we like to focus on the strongest in the group.

Advances in technology can also lead to new industries being formed. For instance, the recent theme of AI has emerged after advances in computer hardware and software made it much more accessible and powerful.

Finally a company could introduce a revolutionary product/service and reinvent themselves. This "N-factor" can lead to new growth, and a great example is Netflix.

NFLX has undergone multiple reinventions starting first with mail-order DVDs and later introducing and becoming the market leader in both streaming and original content. These new areas of its business disrupted the industry and led to fantastic earnings and sales growth.

Each of these catalysts led to multi-month uptrends in the stock; refer to chart.

The N Factor Edge - A Game Changing Catalyst

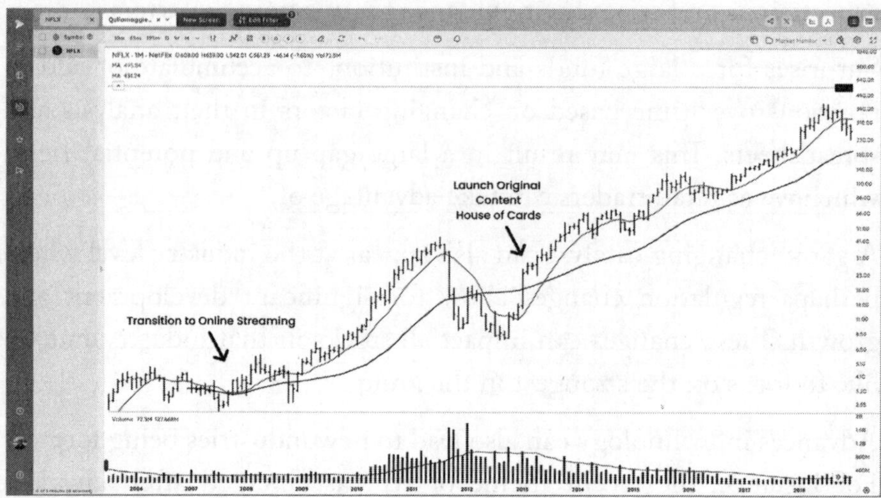

The N-factor is most effective when it is directly leading to growth in earnings and sales. We are always looking for companies with strong quarterly growth of over 25% at least and ideally triple digits and/or accelerating.

To use TSLA as a negative example, there has been talk for many years of how autopilot and robotaxis will be a dramatic growth driver. So far it has not yet materialized and TSLA has stagnated since late 2021. It may yet become another N-factor, but so far institutions are not buying it as of this writing in mid-2024.

Once they do it will be apparent in the price and volume action, and TSLA will again start an uptrend. Maybe by the time you are reading this book this next N-factor will be in play.

GROUP/THEME/MARKET STRENGTH

Stocks move in groups, with often a few groups making up the current leadership of the market cycle. These potential leadership groups (PLGs) are the result of outside factors such as game-changing catalysts for an industry as a whole.

When a stock is part of a PLG, the strength of the group contributes to its performance. This can have a significant impact and even average stocks in strong groups can outperform the strongest stocks in mediocre ones.

Market conditions add another level to this. Even strong stocks in strong groups may make little progress if the overall market is negative. This is why for the most part we want to always trade with the trend of the general market, group, and the stock. By aligning these forces, we have the strongest chance of success.

We will discuss more about the importance of group moves and themes in Chapter 9.

EDGES EXERCISE

Now that we have discussed the edges that we look for, it is time to apply what you have learned.

List out and describe the edges that you look for when analyzing and screening for ideas. For each edge, include an historical example.

Once you are done, remember to snap a picture and tweet us your work. We'd love to provide any feedback we can!

SETUPS

Edges help get promising stocks on our radar, but now it's about waiting for an applicable setup. Remember that the goal for a setup is to give us an opportunity to enter a high potential stock at a point where we are expecting a strong trend to begin.

Another key is that for each setup we want to be able to quickly know if we were wrong and be able to exit with a small loss.

An important reminder is that you can be stopped out of a trade once, even multiple times, and the overall setup can still be intact. This is where our entry tactics come into play, as we will discuss in the next chapter. So as long as the overall setup is still valid, keep watching stocks that stop you out.

Setups are larger chart patterns that take weeks to form but yield trends that can last months.

THE LAUNCH-PAD SETUP

The Launch Pad is one of our bread and butter setups of the TraderLion methodology, taught to Ross by Andre Neidich, his very first hedge fund client, when he worked in institutional sales at William O'Neil + Co. It is formed when all of our key moving averages converge and the stock begins to shape up within a consolidation.

With this type of setup, the focus is on stocks where the group as a whole is shaping up together and has the potential to lead. We typically use the 10-day SMA, 21-day EMA, 50-day SMA, 65-day EMA, and 200-day SMA.

This pattern often emerges after significant market corrections and bear markets as stocks form bottoms.

For instance, NVDA in 2023 formed a launch pad on January before advancing 400%; refer to chart.

The Launch Pad Setup

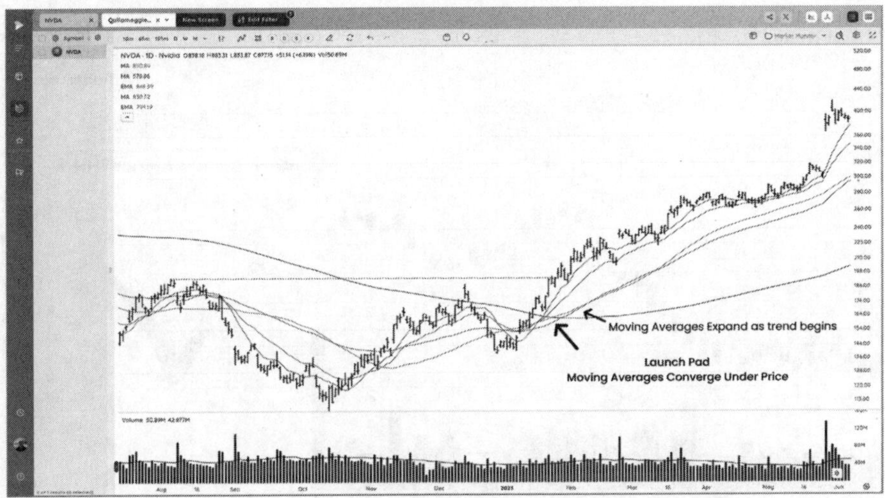

This pattern is particularly significant when a whole group sets up launch pads together. This is an indication that a group move is beginning to start.

Once a launch pad forms, we look to find clear consolidation pivots and other entry tactics that we can use to enter and manage risk.

THE GAPPER SETUP

The gapper setup relates closely to the HV edges. We want to see gap ups on large volume with a catalyst. Then we can look for entry areas using the tactics we will discuss shortly; refer to chart.

The Gapper Setup

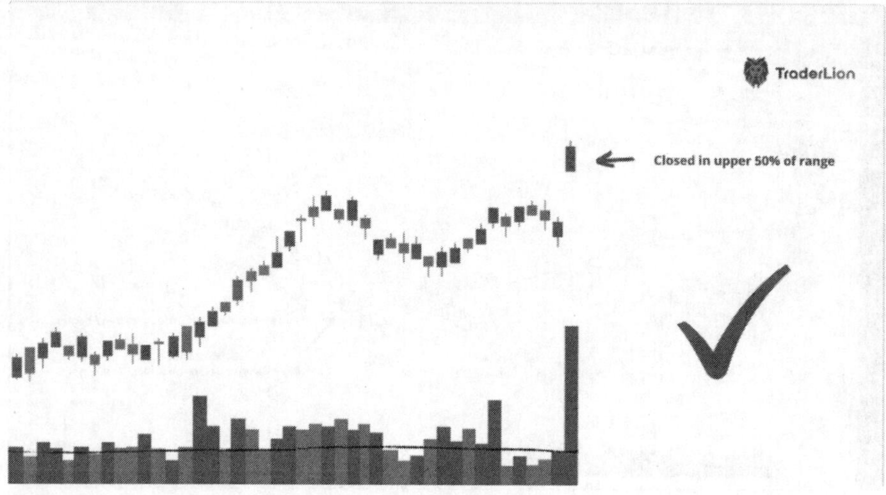

A stock may form multiple gappers during a strong uptrend. We want to focus on the first one or two to ensure that the stock still has a significant runway.

The later in the trend the more likely the momentum will deteriorate and gaps may be sold into as institutions take profit; refer to chart.

ELF 2022 - Gapper Setup

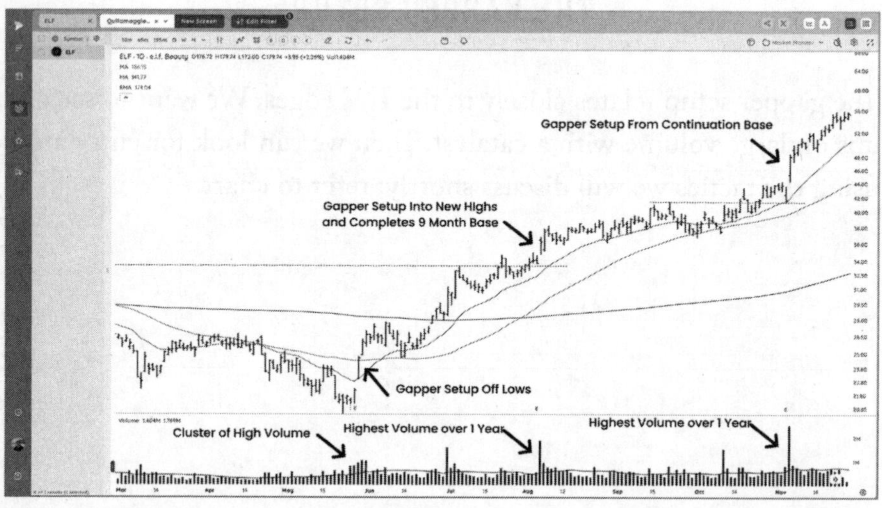

In 2022, ELF started its model book move with a gapper off the lows on earnings. It then formed another gapper setup on earnings as it emerged from the nine-month base to new highs and then another one on earnings in November. In this case the third gapper is actionable given the size of the base ELF had just emerged from and because the first gap was so low in the base.

These three gappers occurred as ELF accelerated EPS growth from −18% to +44% to +71%, and showed EPS surprises of +106%, +65%, and +126%, respectively.

From the closing price of the third gap shown, ELF has since advanced another 350% in 2023 to April 2024.

BASE BREAKOUT SETUP

This is a classic William O'Neil setup. We are looking for a multi-week consolidation within the context of a longer-term uptrend. The minimum we are typically looking for is five weeks.

While the launch-pad setup forms a bottom and starts a trend, these base breakouts are continuation setups as the longer-term trend resumes.

The healthiest bases tighten in price and volume from left to right, although shakeouts can form double bottoms which are certainly actionable.

On the breakout we are looking for a clean move through the line of resistance and a pick up in volume. These are the elephant tracks of the big institutions; refer to chart.

Base Breakout Setup

Like with the gapper setup, we want to focus on the first few bases in a stock's longer-term move. This is to ensure that the stock still has room to run.

One thing we have noticed in recent markets is that there are more breakout failures than there used to be in the 90s. This is why we usually look to enter earlier as a stock is moving up toward the breakout rather than waiting for it to be breached and potentially reverse. Another alternate entry point we use is when a stock stalls after a breakout and falls back to a key moving average like the 21 EMA, and resets.

We'll discuss how to do this using various entry tactics in the next chapter.

SPECIALIZATION

In this chapter we've covered many different examples of both edges and setups.

To start with, you should pick one that fits your style and study it carefully, looking up as many historical examples as possible. This will allow you to build intuition about when the setup will work and what should happen shortly after.

Then, only after applying that setup and entry tactic successfully can you look to build your repertoire of skills and master the next one. A common mistake that newer traders make is to try to master everything all at once. This leads to confusion, frustration, and often inferior execution.

Take the gapper setup or breakout setup and make it yours. Or pick a different setup such as a pullback to a key support level or moving average. The point is to master one blueprint and become an expert on when it works well, when it works alright, and when it does not work at all.

TRADER'S HANDBOOK CHALLENGE 2

With this in mind, pick one setup that we have covered and find five strong examples from the past five years.

Annotate them and label your buy point as well as any key price and volume characteristics that you notice.

Remember to tag us in your work by sharing it on X (formerly Twitter). Have fun with this! You are building your personal playbook that will help you catch future model book stocks. #THChallenge

KEY TAKEAWAYS

Here are four key takeaways from this chapter:

1. The S.N.I.P.E. framework can help you find and manage trading ideas:
   - Search and scan—Look for current opportunities.
   - Narrow—Focus your attention only on the stocks that fit your system and have strong potential.
   - Identify—Finalize your watchlists and analyze each opportunity looking for edges and setups.
   - Plan—For actionable names plan the setup and entry tactics that you will use to enter.
   - Execute—Enter your trade while managing risk and then manage the position.
2. Edges are repeatable winning characteristics that signify that an opportunity is developing.
3. A setup is a repeatable larger pattern that signifies that there is a strong reward-to-risk ratio.
4. Focusing on just a handful of edges and setups allows you to master them.

BONUS RESOURCE

We recorded a webinar about the top edges and setups we use in our trading and how we find them.

You can watch it today at traderlion.com/handbook.

CHAPTER 5
ENTRY TACTICS AND TRADE EXECUTION

"Strategy without tactics is the slowest route to victory. Tactics without strategy is the noise before defeat."

—***Sun Tzu***

IN THE PREVIOUS chapter we covered the key steps of trading and how we identify promising stocks. These edges and setups define the larger context of a trade, the *why*.

Now it's time to define the *how*, meaning the process by which we will enter a position while managing risk tightly and logically—namely, entry tactics. We spend more time on risk in Chapter 6.

Entry tactics are short-term processes and patterns that we use to build a position as a larger setup is being completed.

The benefit of entry tactics is that they allow us to size a position enough to make a difference if the trade moves in our favor, while also managing risk tightly enough if the trade fails.

Always thinking about the downside, we want to preserve the vast majority of our capital on any losing trade. This gives us both the confidence and flexibility to try a set up multiple times.

In this chapter we will cover the entry tactics we use as they correspond to each setup and also the key steps in the process of trade execution.

KEY COMPONENTS OF AN ENTRY TACTIC

An entry tactic has two main components. First is a well-defined level that becomes the pivot point, or the price that triggers the entry. The second component is the risk management level, where you are managing your risk against, exiting if the entry tactic fails.

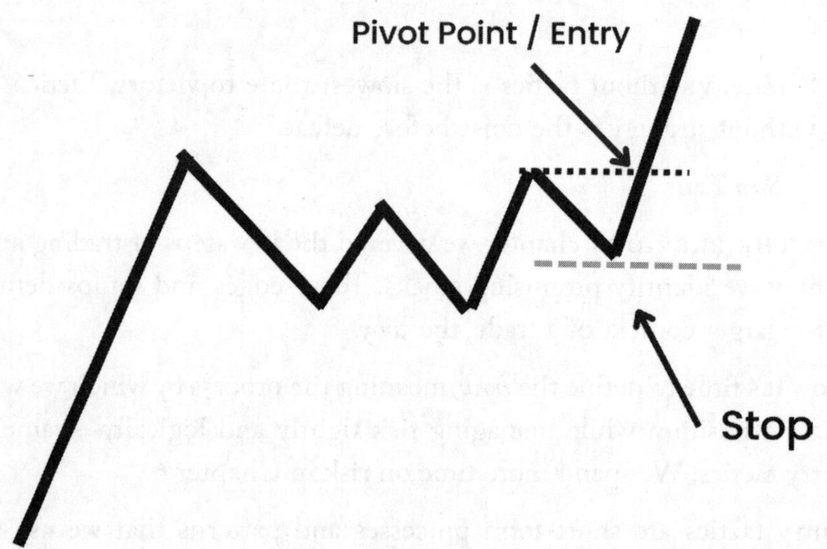

Remember that your risk management should be both tight and logical, allowing the stock to oscillate normally while keeping a loss small if the trade definitely resolves to the downside.

PAIRING ENTRY TACTICS WITH YOUR TRADE SETUPS

For the setups that you specialize in, you should have specific entry tactics that you use to execute that setup.

Not every setup will resolve in the same way, but your entry tactics should allow you to creatively enter the stock on the setup while managing risk.

Here are the entry tactics that we use in conjunction with each of our setups. For a particular trade we might use a subset of each of these entry tactics to establish our position.

Launch-pad setup and base breakout:

- Key Support Level Reclaim
- Consolidation Pivot Breakout
- Key Moving Average Pullback
- Oops Reversal
- Key Support Level Pullback.

Gapper Setup:

- Opening Range Breakout
- The Intraday Base Entry Tactic
- High-Volume Close Pivot.

We will now walk through each of these tactics and show them in action.

ENTRY TACTICS

KEY SUPPORT LEVEL RECLAIM

A key support level reclaim occurs when a stock has undercut a prior level of support such as a base low or 50-day moving average, and then surges back up through that level.

This entry tactic occurs in stocks that have already been basing and consolidating for a few weeks.

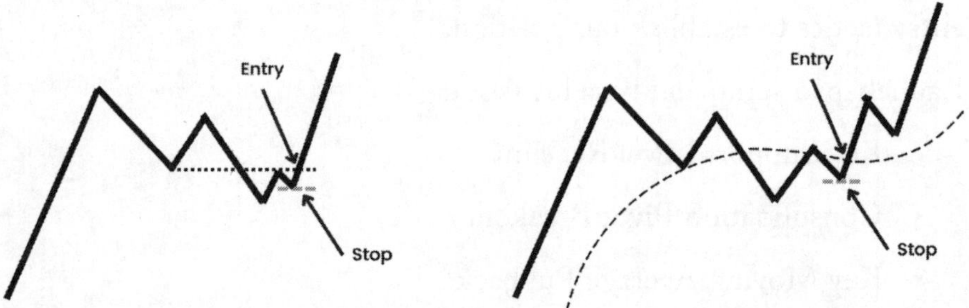

For this entry tactic the pivot point is the key level, and you want to use a relevant higher low or other key technical area as your stop loss point. Typically, we look to keep our stop losses for this tactic at less than 5% and ideally less than 3% on the position.

Once a stock has reclaimed the key level, this entry tactic fails if it loses that level. A key level reclaim can occur on different time frames. A stock may undercut that level for a few days or as little as a few minutes. The more powerful a stock is on the reclaim, the more likely the stock will continue its momentum and rise further in the base, toward the consolidation highs.

This entry tactic is often one of the first tradable spots in a stock's base.

CONSOLIDATION PIVOT BREAKOUT

The consolidation pivot was developed by Ross Haber when he started his hedge fund. With the higher amount of capital, he was unable to buy base breakouts in the traditional way and he had to find other methods to build positions.

He identified early entries where the stock would tighten and form pivots before the traditional breakout from a base.

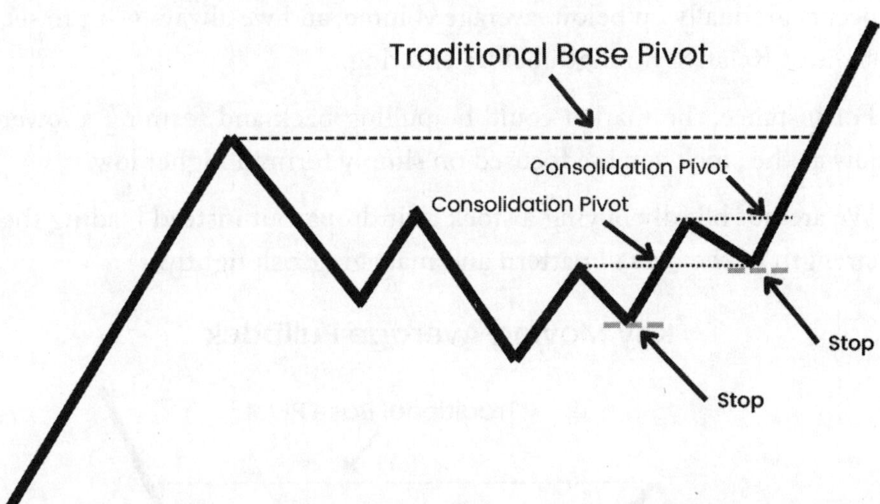

These consolidation pivot breakouts often present strong risk/reward opportunities and allow you to build a position up the right-hand side of a consolidation. To identify these consolidation pivots, you want to look for defined shorter-term resistance areas and swing highs. These become your pivot points.

To manage risk, we look for the nearest relevant technical area. Most commonly, we use the nearest higher low or key moving average. If you are using a moving average, you want to ensure that the stock has previously respected that moving average while in an uptrend.

Like with the key level reclaim, we are looking to keep our stop losses for this tactic at less than 5% and ideally less than 3% on the position. The idea here is to build a full position and have a profit cushion before a stock breaches the traditional base pivot.

KEY MOVING AVERAGE PULLBACK

Just as the consolidation pivot breakout is a buy on strength, you can also use a pullback to a key moving average or prior consolidation pivot within a consolidation as an entry point. Ideally the pullback occurs gradually on below-average volume, and we always want to see signs of Relative Strength before entering.

For instance, the market could be pulling back and forming a lower low as the stock you are focused on simply forms a higher low.

We are not blindly buying a stock as it drops, but instead reading the strength of the overall pattern and managing risk tightly.

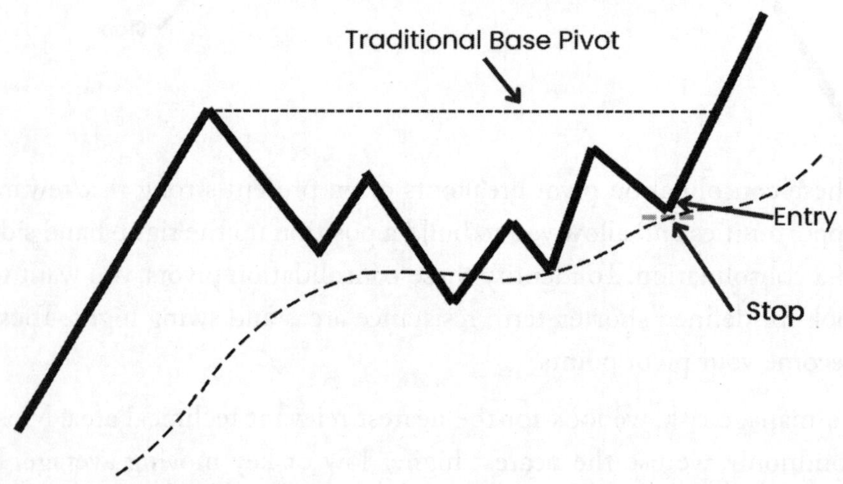

With a key moving average pullback the pivot is the moving average that the stock has respected previously. The stock may undercut the moving average slightly or even for a day or two, but we want to see demand come in and push the stock back higher.

Similarly, during the base-building process, there may be a sudden gap down to the moving average. If the stock responds to the level and closes strong off the moving average, that is often an excellent entry point.

The risk management level with this entry tactic is just below the moving average. If the stock pushes up from the moving average but then turns around and undercuts that level, the entry tactic has failed.

With this entry tactic we want to build the position as close to the moving average as possible. Our risk on the position can be very small, even below 1–2% if you are ready and able to give the stock multiple shots at working.

OOPS REVERSAL

The oops reversal is a very short-term pattern that can be within the other entry tactics we have mentioned.

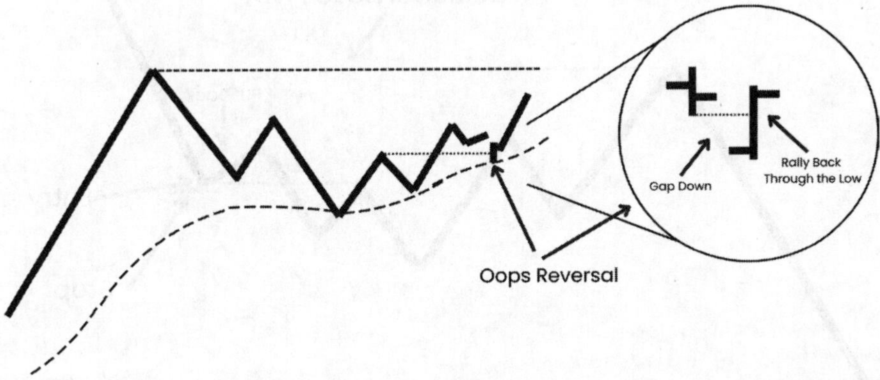

It was developed by Larry Williams and occurs when a stock gaps down below the prior day's low and then pushes back up through that low.

The *oops* is when all the market participants who sold out on the gap down have to buy their shares back, driving it higher.

The best oops reversals tend to occur up the right side of the base and when the gap down is right into a potential area of support, such as a moving average or consolidation pivot.

The strongest oops reversals immediately rebound and often finish with high daily closing ranges and ideally with an outside day.

The pivot for the oops reversal is the low of the prior day, and the risk management level is often the low of the day or a key support level if that is nearby.

KEY SUPPORT LEVEL PULLBACK

This is the same idea as the moving average pullback entry tactic, except the key level and pivot are the prior consolidation pivot or a base pivot. We are looking to enter as the stock rebounds from and shows respect for that level.

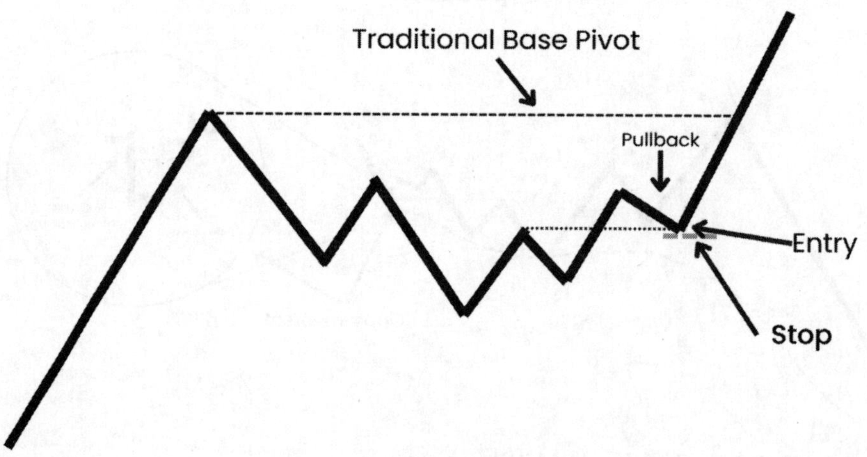

Ideally the pullback to the pivot is gradual and on lower than average volume. The risk management level is just below the pivot and higher low that is forming.

AFTER THE BREAKOUT

The entry tactics we've covered so far ideally will have you positioned in a stock before the traditional base breakout.

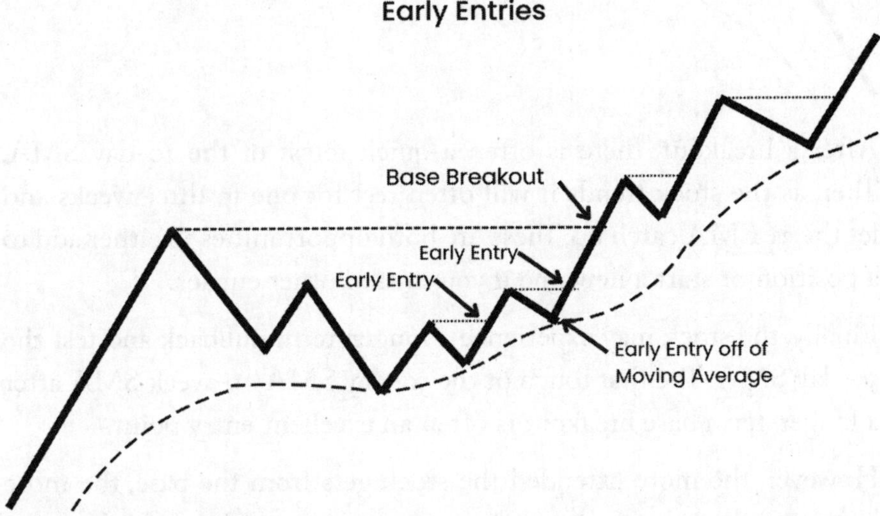

After a stock has broken out, especially if the base is one of the first in the longer-term uptrend, you can look to add to your position, or start swing trades, or add on entries.

The main two we use are moving average pullbacks or shorter-term consolidation pivots.

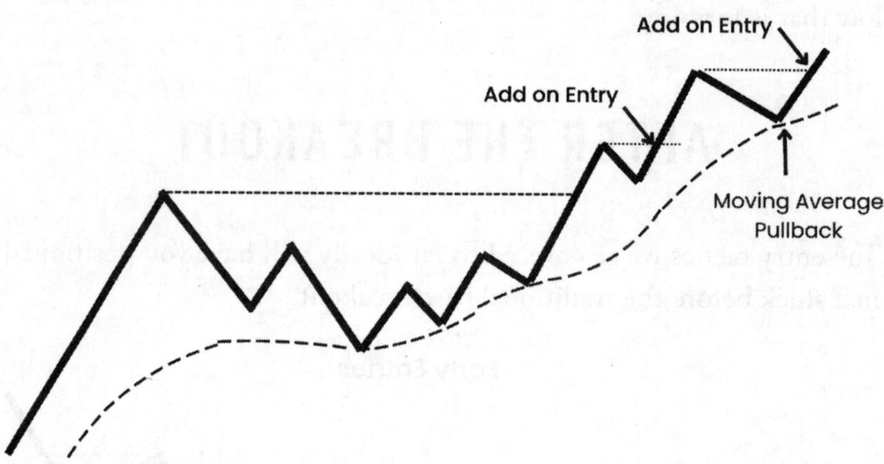

After a breakout, there is often a quick retest of the 10-day SMA. Then as the stock trends it will often rest for one to three weeks and let the 21 EMA catch up. These are both opportunities to either add to a position or start a new one if you missed other entries.

Finally, the stock may experience a longer-term pullback and test the 50-day SMA. The first touch of the 50-day SMA/10-week SMA after a longer-term base breakout is often an excellent entry point.

However, the more extended the stock gets from the base, the more likely it will need to form another one, so the second and third tests of the moving averages often are lower-quality opportunities.

ENTRY TACTICS FOR THE GAPPER SETUP

With the gapper setup, there are a few options for when you want to get involved:

Day 1 is the day of the gap up. There is often an opportunity on this day for intraday setups, although you would have to have been focused on the stock before the open, either by running screens for gaps or keeping an eye out for strong earnings reports/news events.

Day 2 is the following day. Waiting for this day gives you the ability to judge the power of the stock and there are clear levels to trade off, as we will discuss below.

After day 2 you can wait for a short consolidation to form or a moving average pullback. This is more like a normal trade entry, so we will focus on the day 1 and day 2 entry tactics here.

OPENING RANGE BREAKOUT

This Entry Tactic occurs on the intraday time frame on day 1. In the opening prints, a stock will often form a short range. This range can be viewed as an intraday base and the entry tactic is completed when the stock breaks out of the range.

You can trade a 15-minute opening range breakout, but for many gappers, a faster five-minute opening range breakout or a three-minute one is required. The best gappers on day 1 open and take off, trending above the daily volume weighted average price all day.

Key reminder: The shorter term the entry tactic, the likelier there is to be more noise and failures. Manage risk and expectations accordingly.

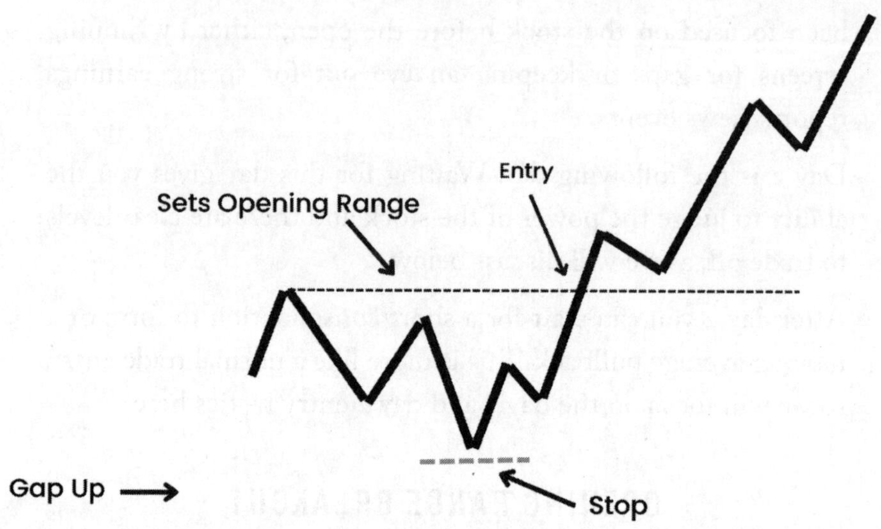

THE INTRADAY BASE ENTRY TACTIC

On day 1 of a strong gap up, the stock will often form intraday bases and pull back before continuing higher. These are opportunities to build your position. These will often coincide with a pullback to or compression beneath the intraday anchored volume weighted average price.

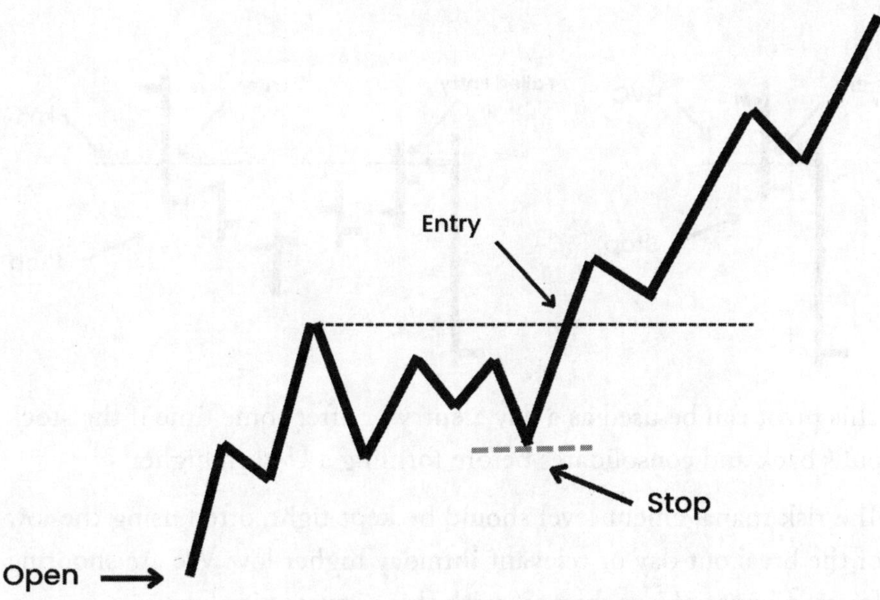

The entry point is a breakout from the intraday base. The risk management level is the recent higher low.

HIGH VOLUME CLOSE (HVC) PIVOT

The HVC entry tactic is a day 2 pattern where we are looking for a continuation move through the close of the gap up day. By waiting for the second day you get the benefit of being able to judge the quality of the gapper setup by looking at the amount of volume and the closing range.

High Volume Close Entry tactic

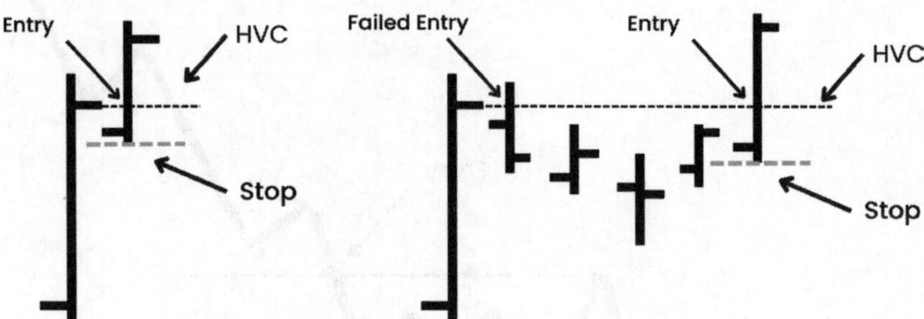

This pivot can be used as a day 2 entry or after some time if the stock pulls back and consolidates before forming a U-turn higher.

The risk management level should be kept tight, often using the low of the breakout day or relevant intraday higher low. We are shooting for stop losses of less than 3% with this entry tactic.

The HVC can also be used as the last addition as you build a position. You can use a combination of opening ranges, intraday bases, and the HVC to size up as the stock continues the momentum from the gap day.

Key reminder: Context matters.

Remember not to miss the forest for the trees. These entry tactics are best used in a strong stock showing institutional accumulation and as many edges as possible that we covered in Chapter 4. The stock must also be exhibiting a larger pattern and setup.

There will also be different market periods where certain setups and entry tactics work best. Keep an eye out during your routines for what types of patterns are acting well and following through.

Just like there can be a fundamental theme driving a group of stocks higher, there can also be a technical theme that is working at any moment in time.

TRADER'S HANDBOOK CHALLENGE 3

To apply what you have learned in this section, annotate in detail one base breakout setup and one gapper setup. Label the entry tactics you would use to build a position and where you would enter and set your stop loss. Be sure to share your work on twitter and tweet at us @ TraderLion_ and #THChallenge

KEY TAKEAWAYS

Here are five key takeaways from this chapter:

1. Entry tactics are short-term processes and patterns that we use to build a position as a larger setup is being completed.
2. The benefit of entry tactics is that they allow us to size a position enough to make a difference if the trade moves in our favor while also managing risk tightly enough if the trade fails.
3. For each setup you have, you should have associated entry tactics that allow you to execute within that larger pattern.
4. Each entry tactic has a pivot point and a risk management level.
5. Context matters: Setups and entry tactics have periods where they work well and periods where their performance declines.

BONUS RESOURCE

We recorded a webinar on our favorite entry tactics that we use to enter stocks while managing risk.

You can watch it today at traderlion.com/handbook.

CHAPTER 6

RISK MANAGEMENT

> "At the end of the day, the most important thing is how good are you at risk control. Ninety per cent of any great trader is going to be the risk control."
>
> ***—Paul Tudor Jones***

THIS CHAPTER IS likely the most important one in this book. Risk management is the skill that will allow you to protect both your principal as well as your profits. It will enable you to trade for decades, allowing you to fully take advantage of compounding.

But what does "managing risk" actually mean?

It's a phrase that is thrown around a lot but often with little substance. In contrast, in this chapter, we will fully define what it means to manage risk on both a position and portfolio level.

This includes a process for setting and managing stops, determining how to size positions, as well as when to lower your overall exposure.

WHAT IS RISK MANAGEMENT?

At its core, your risk is the amount of capital you have exposed in the markets at any given time. It's controlled by the number of positions you have on, the sizes of each of those positions, and where your stops are for each of those positions (where you will exit).

This resulting dollar value is the total amount you are currently risking and can lose if the market turns against you and stops you completely out of your positions.

However, as a trader, you need to put on risk to potentially profit from winning trades. The key is to develop a risk management system that keeps your losses small relative to your profits over time.

CALCULATING TOTAL OPEN RISK

In the previous chapter, we discussed different entry tactics and where we expect to cut our losses on a trade level. But it is also important to be able to track your risk at a portfolio level.

This data point is called total open risk or simply total risk for short.

As an example, if we are in a strong bull market, trading well, we may reach our highest total exposure, be completely invested and on 100% margin. With a 100k account in five hypothetical positions, our portfolio might look something like this:

- 40k in DEEP with our stop 5% below the current price.
- 40k in VUE with our stop 15% below the current price.
- 40k in TLDV with our stop 3% below the current price.
- 40k in WON with our stop 8% below the current price.
- 40k in TH with our stop 10% below the current price.

You'll notice that a few of these positions have tight stops. These represent stocks that potentially were just put on. With the others the stop is a bit wider, representing stocks that are trending with open profits. For these, we have trailing stops at a moving average further from the current price.

Let's now calculate the total risk. To do this, for each position multiply the position size in dollars by the distance to the stop loss in percentages. For each position this gives you the dollars at risk. Then to calculate the total risk you would sum all of these together.

The formula is:

Total risk (dollars) = Position size 1 * Stop 1 + Position size 2 * Stop 2 + ... Position size n * Stop n

Total risk (% of portfolio) = [Total risk (dollars)/Total portfolio value (dollars)] * 100

For the example above each position size is the same, so the calculation for total risk in dollars at the given moment is $40,000*(.05+.15+.03+.08+.10) = $16,400.

With an account of 100k the total risk in % is 16,400/100,000 or 16.4%.

So 16.4% of our principal is quite a high total risk amount. This may be suitable if the market is trending well and we have large profit cushions. However, if all our positions stopped out at once, it would be quite a drawdown from our peak equity.

For another example, here is another 100k portfolio that could be during a correction or very choppy environment where recent trades have not made any traction, volatility is high, and trends are short-lived. In this case all the trades are on a tight leash:

- 10k in AR with our stop 4% below the current price.
- 8k in NS with our stop 5% below the current price.
- 15k in RH with our stop 2% below the current price.

The total risk here is (10,000*.04) + (8000*.05) + (15,000*.02) = $1,100 or 1.1% total risk.

This is an example of perhaps three pilot trades with smaller position sizes which allow you to test the waters but would only draw your account down 1.1% if they all got stopped out.

You may notice that in this example, we have a 15% position size on one position, as well as a 10% size position, which may be considered very risky to investors who are used to diversification. However, despite relatively concentrated positions, the small stop size keeps the total risk in check.

In summary, the three factors that we use to calculate total open risk are: the number of positions we have open, the amount invested in each position, and the location of the stop loss on each position. All of these factors are completely within our control.

"Managing this risk" means adjusting at least one of the three factors described above to ensure that your total risk is acceptable given your risk tolerance, style, conditions of the market, extensions from moving averages, volatility, profits on the year… and any other factors.

Depending on your style you can focus on using one or more of the factors to manage risk. For instance, day traders may trade large positions but only one or two at a time with very tight stop losses.

Investors on the other hand often try to manage risk by increasing diversification (number of positions) and lowering positions sizes.

However, they often do not sell out of positions based on the market conditions or raise stop losses, and so risk is not necessarily managed. Additionally, they may find that stocks are not nearly as diversified as they thought.

In short, your total open risk allowance should fluctuate depending on the market conditions. Factors to consider are: the trend of the major indexes, health and breadth of market leadership, and the results from your past ten trades.

EXERCISE: CALCULATE TOTAL OPEN RISK

Using the figures below, calculate the total open risk in the portfolio. Assume a portfolio of 100k:

- 15k in Stock A with the stop 5% below the current price.
- 23k in Stock B with the stop 15% below the current price.
- 10k in Stock C with the stop 3% below the current price.
- 45k in Stock D with the stop 21% below the current price.
- 5k in Stock E with the stop 10% below the current price.
- 8k in Stock F with the stop 2% below the current price.

If the market were in an uptrend, would you be comfortable with this amount of risk? Why?

If the market were choppy, would you be comfortable with this amount of risk? Why?

How could you lower the total open risk?

LOWERING RISK

Say the market is starting to weaken or simply you haven't been trading well and have lost money on five out of the past six trades.

You have a few options to lower your risk in response to the trade feedback and changing market conditions.

LOWERING THE NUMBER OF POSITIONS

Sort your existing positions by your profit or performance over the past month. Grade the positions from A to D taking this into account and your view on the potential of each stock going forward.

As you look to lower the number of positions, eliminate the Ds first and look to keep the As if possible.

DECREASING POSITION SIZES

You can also consider selling portions of your positions to bring position sizes back down to what feels comfortable for the moment.

Again, look to preserve your strongest stocks first, but if the market seems to be turning and a winner is extended from a base and is showing weakening signs, you can always sell half and look to re-enter when conditions firm up.

If you are looking to lower risk, starting position sizes can also be adjusted down. For example, with a 100k portfolio you could use 5k positions in weak markets, 10k positions in normal markets, and 15k positions for strong markets.

ADJUSTING STOP LOSSES

A strong market is forgiving; a weak market is the opposite. When conditions worsen consider tightening up initial stop losses and being quicker to raise them to your breakeven level.

Each stock you buy has to prove itself to you that it is worth the risk.

INCREASING RISK

Coming out of a correction it's important that you test the waters and increase risk in response to positive feedback, such as new positions working well and other stocks on your watchlist moving higher.

As conditions improve, you build up a cushion and things are working, you can increase your total risk. As conditions worsen, size down, take fewer trades, and raise your stops to decrease your potential overall drawdown.

Trading is not an on-or-off business. Think of risk as a dial that you can turn in response to how things are going. As Mark Minervini says: "*You want to be trading your largest when you are trading your best and your smallest when conditions/your trading is at its worst.*" He coined the term progressive exposure, which describes this process of raising and lowering sizing in response to market feedback.

Managing risk in this way ensures your survival, allowing you to profit from uptrends and protecting yourself during corrections and bear markets.

Now that we have addressed the concept of risk management from a portfolio level, let's zoom into how you can manage it on individual positions using stop losses.

SETTING AND MANAGING STOP LOSSES

Stop losses are key to managing risk. Without a sound loss-cutting system, it is impossible to make consistent progress in the market over time.

Without a process for cutting losing positions, at best you will have some booms before you go bust.

Never forget, stop losses are what keeps you in the game to fight another day. Stop losses serve to protect and preserve your financial capital, as well as your mental/emotional capital.

It doesn't matter how good you are at picking stocks. At some point you are guaranteed to pick the wrong one and without a stop loss to protect you, it won't be long before your hard-earned money disappears, and your negative emotions come boiling to the surface.

Having a detailed plan to manage risk for the times when you are wrong is the only path to consistent success, as well as objective decision making when you are under pressure.

So let's dive into creating a detailed plan. We will cover setting an initial stop loss, common stop loss questions, adjusting your stop loss to breakeven, and trailing your stop loss when you are in a profit.

THE INITIAL STOP LOSS

When we first enter a trade anything is possible. There is excitement, potential, uncertainty, this trade you just put on could double and make your year.

However, we need to remember to take a step back and think about the overall system and the long-term view. What do we need to do with this trade to ensure that we preserve our capital and continue to make progress?

The best growth stock traders are right in strong markets about 50% of the time. The rest of the time they are cutting their losses short to ensure that they preserve the majority of their capital and try again.

Some of the top traders from the past year who have competed in the US Investing Championship and achieved well over triple digit returns are only right 30–40% of the time.

This means that the six out of ten times they lose they must have strict risk control so that when they are right, it more than pays for all the losses.

And it all starts with the initial stop loss.

You should place this stop loss immediately after placing the buy order. And in fact, you should know your stop level before you even enter the stock as it should be one of your determining factors of whether you will place the trade at all.

Before placing an order, ask yourself, can I manage risk in this stock if I enter here? Is there both a logical place on the chart to place my stop under, and is it also tight enough to my potential entry price to be a small loss if triggered?

Tight means that your loss on the position if your stop is triggered should be limited to just a few per cent. For swing/position trading we consider 1–4% to be a tight stop for your average growth stock and up to 6% for a more volatile name.

However, using a tight stop alone is not enough. It must also be logical.

A tight stop loss set to 2% does no good if your entry was at a place where a normal price fluctuation can easily stop you out.

If you are unable to place a tight and logical stop loss, then you are likely not using a sound entry tactic and pivot point. Until this is the case, wait for your spot to set up.

A logical stop loss means that a violation of your stop level invalidates your thesis and suggests that your entry tactic has failed for the time being. The stock may reset and set up again, but for now your rules state that you should be out of the stock.

This logical stop is likely defined by a significant technical level. This could be a moving average that the stock has shown respect for, a low of the range, or the low of the day.

This concept of requiring a tight and logical stop is one of the most important lessons we wish to share with you. It does not matter if you are a day trader trading one-minute charts or a long-term position trader trading weeklies, placing tight and logical stops is crucial to your long-term performance.

For your time frame, and style, a general rule of thumb for the % stop to be considered "tight" is to look at your average gain over a period of six months and divide by three.

Day traders may average 3% returns and be shooting for less than 1% stops. Investors may average 30% returns and shoot for less than 10% stops. Swing traders may average 10% returns and look for sub 3% stops.

This rule of three is a guideline and the tighter the better.

COMMON STOP LOSS QUESTIONS

SHOULD I SET MY STOPS RIGHT AT KEY LEVELS?

We typically set our stops a few cents below the key level. The "obvious" stop loss points sometimes get shaken out. That's trading. We are always ready to re-enter.

SHOULD I WAIT UNTIL THE END OF THE DAY TO HONOR MY STOPS?

In a strong bull market you should look to give your stocks the benefit of the doubt. You can also have an "intraday stop" that is your worst case but gives the stock a bit more room to maneuver.

For example, your stop could be 4% but intraday could be 7%. This stop should be decided in advance, not when the stock is already falling.

In a choppy market we don't wait to ask questions, we act in the moment and maybe cut a stock early if it does not act well.

We would rather be out of a stock wishing we were in than in a stock wishing we were out. This both protects your capital as well as your psyche.

SHOULD I SET HARD STOP LOSSES WITH MY BROKER?

It depends on your situation and your discipline. If you can watch the market and follow your rules you can use alerts. If not or if you work full time, hard stops may be the answer.

SHOULD I AVOID THE STOCK AFTER I HAVE BEEN STOPPED OUT?

Definitely not if the setup and story are still valid!

Sometimes the best trades take a few times to work. A shakeout that takes out the more obvious stop loss levels may even improve the setup!

However, if the bar that takes out your stop suggests significant distribution, you should be patient for the chart to heal itself.

WHAT IF I WANT TO ENTER A STOCK BUT THERE IS NO PLACE TO PUT MY STOP LOSS?

Then you can't place a tight and logical stop and are likely looking to enter in the middle of nowhere—have the discipline to wait.

WHAT IF I AM CONSTANTLY GETTING STOPPED OUT RIGHT BEFORE THE STOCK MOVES HIGHER WITHOUT ME?

If this is the case, analyze your entries. If normal fluctuations are stopping you out you may want to expand your typical stop loss slightly and lower your position size to balance the risk.

However, it may also be that your entries are not sound, so be sure to look at your entry tactics and setups as well to see if that is the issue.

WHAT IF A STOCK GAPS DOWN BELOW MY STOP LOSS?

This actually happens a lot less than traders expect. For the most part, beginner traders would do best honoring their original stops until they are further into Stage 2 and then Stage 3.

Once you have more experience you can judge the severity of the gap and catalyst, and make an informed decision of whether to give your stock a chance to recover.

Remember, however, that the goal is to preserve capital at all costs. If a stock has a large gap down on, then something isn't right and you are likely better off out of the stock and re-evaluating the situation.

ADJUSTING STOP LOSSES TO BREAKEVEN

Once a trade is on and makes progress for you, the next step in trade management is to raise your stop to protect your breakeven point, and then eventually backstop profits.

The faster your trading style—swing and day traders—the more quickly you want to move up your stops. This helps keep your losses as small as possible.

Investors and position traders can take a bit more time with this, although they still should have defined rules.

A good rule of thumb in a strong market is to move up your stop loss to your cost basis once you have a profit in the stock of two to three multiples of your initial stop loss.

This gives you some cushion to let the stock fluctuate while also capping your downside.

In a weak market you may want to move a lot quicker than this, maybe when you have even just a few % profit.

TRAILING YOUR STOP LOSS

Once your stop loss is at breakeven, the next step is to trail your stop loss behind the stock, leaving room for normal price action.

The higher your time frame the more room you should give your stock.

One of our favorite methods for trailing a stop loss is to use a moving average once it rises above our cost basis. For swing traders this could be the 21 EMA and for position traders this could be the 50 SMA.

Then we are waiting for two closes below the moving average to signal that our stop has been active. This works great in trending markets as stocks can make up to triple digit moves without breaking their key moving averages.

Another method would be to raise your stop loss once it has formed a new swing low and then continues higher. In this case you would back stop it just below the new swing low. Either way works—you just have to find the one that makes sense for you.

Stage 2 and 3 traders can look to adjust their trailing stops when they notice changes in character in a stock. For instance, if it starts an accelerated move upward after already being extended, you can switch to a shorter moving average or trailing at the low of two days ago. Or on the flipside, if a stock looks to be breaking down with obvious downside reversals and failed breakouts, there is no need to wait by law for a drop to the 50 SMA if that is not your style. You could adjust your stop to the low of the week or the 21 EMA.

The more experienced you are, the more you can let your judgment of price action dictate things. Early stage traders should try to use clear and objective rules.

The key is to have a general system for stop losses and sell rules that allow you to capture the majority of the trend for your style and time frame. We won't buy the low or sell the high, but if we can consistently catch the meat of the move, we will outperform.

POSITION SIZING

Along with stop losses, position sizing is a key determining factor to how much you can lose on a position if the trade goes against you:

A 3% loss on a 10% position is a 0.3% loss in your total portfolio.

A 3% loss on a 20% position is a 0.6% loss in your total portfolio.

A 3% loss on a 40% position is a 1.2% loss in your total portfolio.

One of the biggest mistakes traders make is trading too large, too soon. They see experienced traders using margin and taking 50% positions, and think that is the pathway to success.

It's very similar to going to the gym for the first time and putting 250 pounds on the bench press because you saw another lifter rep it out easily. That's a recipe for injuries. Instead, you have to start at what you are comfortable with and slowly scale up as you learn the proper techniques and get stronger.

You have to earn the right to lift heavier weights.

It's the same thing with trading—you have to earn the right to trade larger size. Larger positions can lead to bigger performance, but only if you can manage the risk correctly.

Many of the top traders don't buy a large position all at once. They string together entry tactics and put on 20% of their portfolio then 10%, then the last 20% as the stock is working for them and triggers new pivots. They have techniques to put on size while keeping their overall risk very small.

For Stage 1 and 2 traders, we would say that a base position of 10% is a nice sweet spot. Stage 1 traders should stay consistent with that as they work on their process, while Stage 2 traders can adjust their size up depending on the market and number of edges present to a maximum of 20%.

This would lead to a portfolio of around eight to ten stocks if completely invested.

Stage 3 traders can adjust these parameters as they see fit, but only after they have proven that they can manage risk over multiple market cycles.

Even the most experienced traders can get themselves into trouble by sizing too large or taking on too much risk at the wrong time.

Many of the very best traders also significantly pull back on their sizing if they don't feel in sync with the market or are trading badly.

The key is to take away your ego and adjust your sizing to the current situation and your skill level.

DETERMINING THE POSITION SIZE FOR INDIVIDUAL TRADES

For each trade you are considering, you should ask yourself these questions when determining the number of shares you will buy:

1. What is my current total risk and how much am I willing to add to that?
2. What is my expected stop loss level? What would be the % loss on the position?
3. What is my conviction in this stock and setup, and how many edges are present?
4. How is the health of the current market—are we in a weak, normal, or strong trending market?
5. How have my recent trades performed? Am I getting positive feedback?

In answering the first two questions, you will answer for yourself the maximum amount you could purchase in the stock.

In answering the last three questions, you can determine the final size you will put on relative to your normal starter position sizing.

Let's do an example.

If we are in a normal market and have currently 7% total risk and are comfortable taking that up to 10%, this means we could potentially add 3%. This does not mean we have to, but it means that we could add up to 3% and still be within our risk parameters.

The setup we are looking at is a consolidation pivot with a higher low 3.5% below. This also lines up with the 21 EMA which is 4% below the pivot. A tight and logical stop loss would be just below the moving average at 4.1%.

This means that the maximum size we could take is the 3% equity divided by 0.041 = 73% position size.

However, your maximum position size as a Stage 2 trader is 20%. So although you won't be taking a 73% position, you've confirmed that you have space in your portfolio for this new trade.

Next up is analyzing the current context and setup. It's a decent market so normal sizing is alright, but this stock is showing a few edges and is a potential leader in a strong theme. You decide that this stock is a B+ and worthy of slightly higher position sizing.

Recent trading has resulted in a normal win percentage and average gain.

Taking this all into account, you decide to take your base position sizing of 10% and raise it by 5% for this trade to a 15% position size.

This fits within your total risk parameters and for the individual trade, so you can go ahead and enter.

TRADER'S HANDBOOK CHALLENGE 4

List out the steps you take to set initial stops and adjust them. Annotate and label them on a previous trend of a market leader of your choice from one of your bread and butter setups. Be sure to share your work on twitter and tweet at us @TraderLion_ and #THChallenge

KEY TAKEAWAYS

Here are four key takeaways from this chapter:

1. Risk management is the key to longevity in trading.

2. The three factors that control open risk are the number of positions, the size of the positions, and the stop loss levels.
3. Stop losses should be tight and logical.
4. You need to earn the right to size up positions.

BONUS RESOURCE

We recorded a webinar on risk management, setting stop losses, and position sizing.

You can watch it today at traderlion.com/handbook.

A SMALL ASK THAT CAN HELP TRADERS JUST LIKE YOU

So far in this book we've covered key concepts that have hopefully helped guide you along your journey as a trader.

We strongly believe that the risk management chapter in and of itself can make a huge difference in helping you protect your hard-earned profits and capital.

It's part of our mission to educate as many traders and teach them the key principles that can keep them in the game for decades.

To help us achieve this goal, we need your help.

If this book has been helpful, can you take 30 seconds right now and leave us a quick review?

Because you picked up this book and have read this far, we know you are determined to improve your trading and care deeply about finding quality resources to expand your knowledge.

You may have read a review on Amazon or Goodreads that made you give *The Trader's Handbook* a chance.

Leave us a review to help other fellow traders out and let them know that it will be worth it.

On our website and in podcast comments, our favorite messages to receive are from past students or viewers a few years later where they mention how they had watched an interview, took a masterclass, or read an article, and it ended up being an inflection point in their trading.

This book could similarly impact a trader just like you. Someone who has dreams of turning profitable, managing their own accounts, or even having their first 50% year.

Your review means an immense amount to us *and* could make the difference in this book reaching fellow traders. The review is completely free and only takes 30 seconds.

You can visit the book's page on Amazon or whichever platform you purchased it on to leave a review. We read every one! And thank you in advance for sharing your thoughts with other traders.

Also, feel free to tell other traders about it in person or on X.

Cheers!

Richard, Rai, Nick, and Ross

Now back to the next chapters of the handbook.

CHAPTER 7

SELL RULES AND POSITION MANAGEMENT

"Buying a stock without knowing when or why you should sell it is like buying a car with no brakes, or being in a boat with no life preservers, or taking flying lessons that teach you how to take off but not how to land."

—William O'Neil, Market Wizard

So far we have covered the important topics of edges, setups, and entry tactics. We've discussed how to manage risk in order to keep losses and drawdowns small. However, this is only half of the trading equation.

We must also address sell rules and position management, which allows you to capture the trend for your time frame and yields strong winners. Although many traders focus on getting their entries perfect, position management is actually more crucial for achieving success over time.

In this chapter we will cover how we manage our positions and the clear steps of trade execution. After reading the next few pages, you should have a clear understanding of the last three letters in the S.N.I.P.E. framework: Identify, Plan, Execute.

KNOWING YOUR GOALS AND TIME FRAME

Before we discuss specific rules, you must define your personal style and time frame. There is a balance you must meet between holding a position for a larger move and the potential drawdown risk if that position moves against you over time.

Selling into strength allows you to sell at your equity peaks after a short duration. However, you will potentially lose out on profits if the stock continues higher.

Selling into weakness allows you to stay with a trend until it fully breaks down for your style. However, you will experience larger drawdowns in your equity curve, and may experience opportunity cost since your capital is locked into one idea.

Depending on your style and psychological make-up, one of these options, or a certain split between options, will give you the most peace of mind.

Swing traders will look to sell more into strength and then look for the next setup, focusing more on fast-moving stocks and quick trends.

Position traders will likely sell more into weakness as they look to play longer-term trends, even holding stocks throughout intermediate-term bases.

You will discover this balance through trial and error, many trades, and market cycles. Your preference may also shift over time as your account grows or your time constraints change.

GUIDELINES FOR DIFFERENT STAGE TRADERS

As we discussed in Chapter 2, depending on which stage you are in, your goals in the market should be different.

If you are a Stage 1 and early Stage 2 trader, your goal is to build consistency and look to gain experience in the market.

With this in mind, the sell rules for Stage 1 and 2 traders should be much more rigid, while Stage 3 traders can adapt to particular situations and use their experience and intuition to guide them more.

At late Stage 2 and once in Stage 3, you can then build off that foundation and tweak your rules to focus on performance.

Regardless of experience level, however, the goal of every trader when building sell and position management rules is the same: To ride a stock during the portion of the trend that is significant for their time frame.

SELL RULES FOR STAGE 1 AND 2 TRADERS

Let's begin by focusing on early stage traders. The goal here is to build a consistent system that nails down profits while playing a portion of your position for an intermediate-term trend.

Once your stock reaches a profit of 5%, immediately sell half your position and raise the stop on the balance of your position to breakeven.

From this point, if your stock ever breaches your maximum stop loss, the position should immediately be sold at the market, no ifs, ands, or buts.

If your stock continues to make progress without hitting your sell stops from this point, your goal is to then begin to use its relevant key moving averages to trail your position along the way. In the event that there are two closes below a relevant key moving average, your position must be closed immediately.

For swing traders we recommend using the 21 EMA moving average. The 21 EMA or similar timeframe EMA/SMA does a great job of tracking trends from base to base. For beginner position traders, we recommend starting with the 50 SMA. The 50 SMA can help position trades still with the longer term intermediate trend and hold through constructive bases.

Sell Rules with Moving Averages

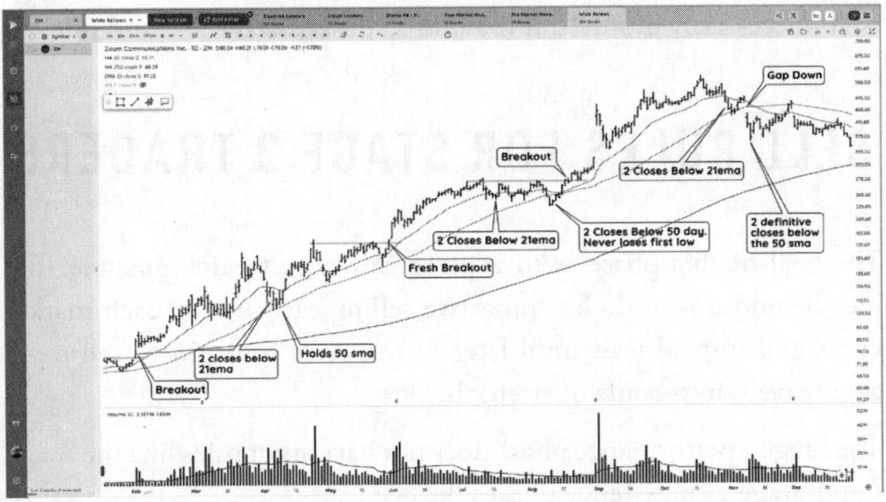

As you become comfortable with these sell rules, below are some progressions you can make. However, don't rush this process—make sure you are consistent in your process before adjusting:

1. Instead of selling half of your position at 5%, sell a third. Sell the next third at your average gain of the last 20 trades, and sell the last third on weakness using the moving averages.

2. Sell a third at 5%, a third into strength above your average gain when the stock gets visually extended from the moving average, and sell the last third on weakness using the moving averages.
3. Use the rule above but allow yourself to add back a third if the stock forms another low-risk entry tactic.
4. Sell a third at your average gain, a third into strength, and a third into weakness using the moving averages. Allow yourself to add back up to the two-thirds you sold previously if the stock forms another low-risk buy point.

Again, be very honest with yourself about where you are in your journey. Only move on to the next progressions if you feel like you are solidly in Stage 2 and getting closer to Stage 3. The goal of this stage is not necessarily profits, but to build a consistent process and rule set.

SELL RULES FOR STAGE 3 TRADERS

The goal of this phase is to capture the largest gains possible. The idea behind it is to do less proactive selling early within each market cycle, and instead wait until later in the cycle to begin to sell more aggressively, into bouts of strength.

The Stage 3 performance phase does not have strict rules like the Stage 1 and Stage 2 consistency phases do.

In essence, once you have reached the performance phase, you should possess the skill, confidence, and experience necessary to do the tactical selling needed to really enhance your performance when it matters.

In some cases, you will ultimately get forced out of a profitable position when your stock weakens and breaks below its key moving averages. In the case where you have enough of a profit cushion, it often makes sense to divide your sale between two different key moving averages, in an attempt to hold on to at least part of your position for a larger move.

Alternatively, as we've discussed above, you can use sell rule of 2 closes below a moving average. For Stage 3 traders, they can also consider how the stock is acting with those 2 closes. Are they sharp and definitive, or is the stock merely drifting below the moving average area. Also, sometimes the stock may have 2 closes below a moving average, but the second close is higher than the first one.

In short, Stage 3 traders can make more of a judgment call if they want to sell or give the stock a bit more of a benefit of the doubt.

There are also the times when you will find yourself proactively selling into strength. This is typically toward the end of a cycle or in choppier markets. For example, as one of your stocks becomes clearly extended above its 10 SMA, like it's done so many times before in the past, it may be prudent to sell a portion before it pulls back in hard.

A key part of Stage 3 position management is understanding your environment, as well as whether or not the stock you are trading is a true market leader worth trying to hold on to, or just a performance enhancer.

As a Stage 3 trader, if you get positioned with size early in a market cycle in a stock that you feel fits the template of a market leader in a leading theme, then your goal should be to let that position work for you, and to play for the larger move.

However, if a stock is more of a secondary name/performance enhancer, you can be quicker to sell into strength and use that cushion to feed your other positions or improve your confidence.

As a Stage 3 trader, pay attention to how your average winner over the past 20 to 30 trades has performed. If you find that your average winner is increasing, look to increase your holding periods. If it is declining, shorten things up and lean more into swing trading.

SELLING INTO STRENGTH

Between the two options, selling into strength is more nuanced. Psychologically, it can be difficult selling when a stock is moving up, fearing that it will continue on without you.

The most important thing, however, is that you do what is right for your equity curve. Selling into strength allows you to lock in profits and builds your confidence. And if you are selling a third or a half into strength, you still have the remainder of your position to ride the trend. You are also able to move the freed-up capital into another fresh idea that may not be as extended.

WHEN SHOULD YOU SELL INTO STRENGTH?

You can look to sell into strength at fixed intervals based on your entry or the stock's price structure, or on more fluid points such as when the stock becomes extended from a moving average or puts in a key reversal.

SELLING INTO STRENGTH AT YOUR AVERAGE GAIN AND R MULTIPLES

The first logical spots to sell some of your position into strength are at your rolling average gain and at R multiples from your entry point. (An r multiple means a multiple of your initial stop loss. For example a profit of 9% when your original stop was 3% means you have a gain of 3 r multiples.)

By locking some in at your average gain you are ensuring a profitable trade with the potential for the remainder of your position to increase that average.

R multiples are also useful as they allow you to focus on your risk and reward, and ensure that your winners are paying for any stop loss hits along the way.

SELLING INTO STRENGTH AT BASE EXTENSIONS

When stocks break out from a base, they typically progress strongly for a period before settling into a groove and trending. Often, there is a pause around 20–25% from the top of the base where the stock may pause, consolidate, and then continue higher.

As a stock approaches this level, it may increase in volatility, as different market participants take profits. For swing traders, you can also look to take some or all of your position off, having ridden a strong momentum move from the breakout.

SELLING INTO STRENGTH USING MOVING AVERAGES

When a stock is trending, it will naturally pullback, gather strength, and then continue higher. You will start to notice that it will form a habit of how far stretched it can be from the moving averages before pulling back in.

You can note the % it typically becomes extended from the moving average, or measure it in average true range (ATR), or simply eyeball it. Regardless of your method, the stock will be likely to continue with this character.

In Deepvue we've also developed an indicator that is trained on prior stock extensions versus a moving average and identifies where the current extension rates versus historical ones. When the Relative Measured Extension indicator approaches 100, it means that based on historical values, it is becoming stretched from the moving average.

Relative Measured Extension Indicator In Deepvue

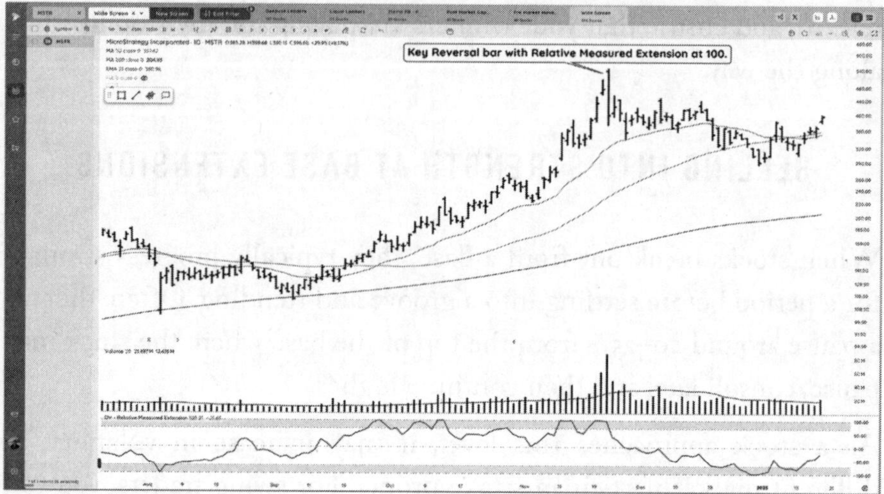

If it is already becoming stretched from the prior base, you may consider locking in a portion of your position when the stock approaches its extension level. This allows you to potentially get ahead of any key reversals or significant pullbacks to moving averages.

SELLING INTO STRENGTH ON KEY REVERSALS

This technique is slightly a hybrid of selling into strength and weakness. There are moments in a stock's move where it becomes slightly extended and closes significantly down on the day.

Key Reversal Bar

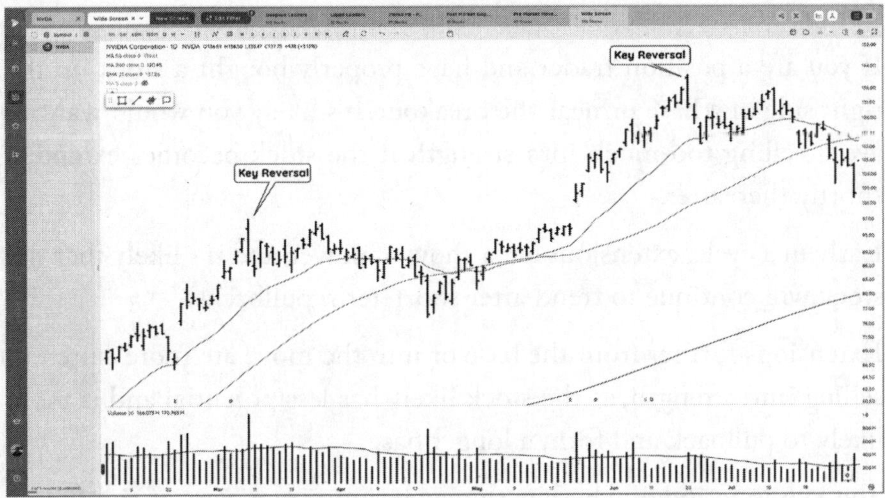

Ideally, you are already watching to sell into strength because of an extension from a moving average and you notice some of the characteristics in real time.

Here are some criteria to look for when identifying key reversals:

- At the high the stock was visually extended from the moving averages.
- The stock gaps up but quickly fills the gap and reverses downwards.
- The stock breaches a trend line of highs.
- The volume is abnormally high or the highest since the breakout.
- The stock forms the widest range bar since the breakout.
- The stock reverses below the prior day's low and closes low in the range.

These reversals can mark a change in momentum and potentially the start of a new base. It may be prudent to use these reversals to lock in some profits so you can move the capital toward a fresh opportunity as the original stock consolidates.

KEY REMINDER ON SELLING INTO STRENGTH

If you are a position trader and have properly bought a stock up the right side of a base or near the breakout, it's likely you would want to avoid selling too much into strength if the stock becomes extended shortly thereafter.

Early in a cycle, extensions are a show of power, and it's likely that the stock will continue to trend after short-term pullbacks.

Extensions further from the base or into the move are more suited to selling into strength, as the stock likely has less potential and is more likely to pullback and form a longer base.

The key is to judge whether the extensions are a sign of significant accumulation or are more indicative of exhaustion.

TRADE EXECUTION

Now that we have covered the key aspects of setups, entry tactics, and risk management, let's bring it all together and discuss the overall process of executing a trade.

From your daily routine, which we will discuss in Chapter 9, each day you will have a focus list of the very top ideas to trade. This will be a handful of stocks that meet all of your criteria, are forming setups, and could complete entry tactics that day.

Your daily focus list should have a maximum of around five ideas and ideally just one to three. The tighter this list, the better your execution will be.

For each of these stocks you should have a plan prepared for a trade. You should know what your buy point or entry tactic will be, where your likely stop loss will be set, and how many shares you should buy.

The next step is to set alerts for each of these stocks. We like to set alerts, not only at the buy point but also potentially one or two alerts set slightly below that point. This allows us to be notified as the stock is approaching our level of action.

For each stock on your daily focus list, visualize what it will look like if it executes your entry tactic and how you will respond.

When the market opens, your job is to monitor your setups and alerts. As a stock hits your early alerts, prepare your order with your broker. If you are finding that there is still too much going on, limit the number of stocks on your daily focus list even more to just one or two.

As the stock is hitting your early alerts as well, double-check that it is fulfilling the requirements of your setup and entry tactic. Be very restrictive. If you require a certain amount of volume for instance, make sure that volume is running much more than average.

If the stock triggers your entry conditions, place your order with your broker. Also enter your stop loss that you had planned before.

Once you are in the trade, continue to monitor the stock, but there is no need to watch it constantly. Cheering it on won't help it push higher. We like to place alerts just below our entry price as well as just above our stop loss to keep tabs on the stock.

The best trades often make immediate progress and push higher throughout the day. If a stock does not trigger alerts in the morning, there is often a period of opportunity later in the day after lunchtime or in the last hour of trading.

Near the close, check up on any executed trades. Ideally they are closing strong, and we already are at a few percentage points of profit. Determine how the stock is acting and if you will hold it at least until the next day. In choppier markets we may take a trade off if it has not shown much follow-through or if we are down on a position near the close.

Check in with your stop loss and position management rules to see if there are any actions or adjustments that you have to make.

Once the market closes, review your trades for the day and journal any thoughts or potential opportunities for improvement. We will dive deeper into this process in later chapters.

TRADER'S HANDBOOK CHALLENGE 5

Annotate a full trade of a market leader of your choice from a breakout to where you would sell into strength or weakness. Label key price and volume characteristics. Be sure to share your work on twitter and tweet at us @TraderLion_ and #THChallenge

KEY TAKEAWAYS

Here are five key takeaways from this chapter:

1. Your sell rules should match your goals and trading style.
2. Early stage traders should focus on building consistency with a set of sell rules.
3. Selling into weakness and selling into strength both have pros and cons.
4. The goal is to capture the majority of the trend that is relevant to your time frame.
5. You should have defined steps for trade execution and position management.

BONUS RESOURCE

We recorded a webinar on sell rules, selling into weakness, and selling into strength.

You can watch it today at traderlion.com/handbook.

CHAPTER 8
MARKET CYCLES

"At least 50% of the whole game is the general market."

—William O'Neil, Market Wizard

WHEN YOU LOOK back at your trading results, are there periods where you have found tremendous success with your trading style?

Have there also been periods where you felt like even the most perfect setups failed and you couldn't seem to make a winning trade?

This all has to do with market cycles—the natural shifts in market environments that lead to uptrends, downtrends, and choppy sideways markets.

In this chapter we will show you how to develop a system to identify the current market environment so that you can know with clarity how aggressive you should be when trading.

The best traders can clearly identify when market factors align, and their system will be extremely profitable. Similarly, they have the awareness to scale back their trading when the opportunity period is over, and their style will not be as effective.

This is one of the keys to becoming a Stage 3 and Stage 4 trader, and being able to make progress and protect it, experiencing only minimal drawdowns.

In this chapter we will:

- Further define a market cycle.
- Cover how to pick the criteria to define yours.
- Create an example system designed for swing traders.
- Cover how you should trade during a cycle including coming from cash.
- Provide examples of long-term and short-term cycles for you to study.

This is one of the most important chapters. Being able to identify where you are in your market cycle will ensure that you are always able to trade with the wind at your back. This reduces stress, frustration, drawdowns, and better yet, helps you make and keep profits more easily.

Let's dive in!

WHAT IS A MARKET CYCLE?

The patterns we see in the market are a reflection of human psychology. Based on this, the market and its leadership follow a template that is cyclical which, if you study history, occurs again and again.

These cycles, where we see uptrends and downtrends, can be identified using systems that allow us to maximize our profits and exposure in positive environments, and tailor back exposure and protect profits during negative environments.

The market cycle is composed of two different layers. The first is the technical layer, which involves the amount of liquidity available in the marketplace. This drives the longer-term cycles we see in the market, from bull to bear markets.

The second layer is the human psychology layer, which causes shorter-term fluctuations in the market. This layer is driven by fear and greed as market participants either accumulate or distribute stock.

After a strong short-term move up, some market participants will take profits, locking in gains and causing a pullback. These uptrends and downtrends within the longer-term cycle are important for traders to recognize in order to determine how aggressive and exposed they should be.

Throughout history, market cycles have played out over and over again. To trade sustainably, you need to develop a system that can identify and weather the market's movements.

WHAT CRITERIA DOES A MARKET CYCLE SYSTEM REQUIRE?

To create a market cycle system—which we will show you how to do in short order—you need to define specific criteria that combine to both start and end a market cycle.

These criteria should be based on factors that create a conducive environment for you to trade within. They should also be easy to interpret and provide a clear signal.

The criteria should also line up with your time frame. Long-term position traders should not create a market cycle system that provides them with signals every other week. Instead you should design one that captures the longer-term trends in the market. Swing traders, on the other hand, should design a system that is nimble enough to identify shorter-term uptrends and downtrends.

A market cycle system is a guide for your trading, letting you know when it is appropriate to become more aggressive, and when it would likely be best to pump the brakes and focus on capital protection.

When your cycle turns on, it does not mean that you should go 200% long immediately, but instead you should begin the process of testing the waters and then listening to market feedback.

Similarly, if your market cycle turns off, focus on each of your positions and how they are acting. You can listen to that feedback to decide if you would like to cut exposure.

Key reminder: Remember that like any trading system, your market cycle will not be perfect. It will provide false positives and false negatives. Treat it as confirmation or a sign to change your mindset and encourage you to take the appropriate action that the market is indicating.

HOW SHOULD I PICK THE CRITERIA TO INCORPORATE?

To pick the criteria you will use, study past environments where you felt that your style produced strong results.

With these environments selected, consider how to define it:

Were key indexes trending above certain moving averages on different time frames?

Which breadth indicators helped identify the start and end of this opportunistic environment?

As we will discuss below, you can also use key stocks—market gauges—that are representative of institutional appetite to serve as gauges of overall market health.

The bottom line for when you are creating your system is that the criteria should matter to *you*. Think about what factors you look at on a daily and weekly basis to analyze the market and incorporate those.

HOW DO MARKET GAUGES HELP US IDENTIFY MARKET CYCLES?

In addition to market indexes and breadth metrics, you may choose to add market gauges to your toolset for determining market cycles.

Market gauges are key stocks that institutions are currently supporting/accumulating. We choose these stocks by identifying key growth names as well as the best stocks in the current market leadership.

TSLA and GOOGL are good stalwarts because of their status as institutional favorites and also their weighting in the indexes. We also choose the top stocks in the current potential leadership groups. For instance, in 2023 and 2024, NVDA was very representative of the semiconductor group which was leading.

The process is somewhat subjective, but the key point is that these gauges are leading indicators of the risk appetite of institutions. If they are being supported and holding key psychological levels such as round numbers, the environment is positive and other trades will work well. However, if they are breaking below levels, that shows that the environment is deteriorating, and you have a reason to be more conscious.

To write a rule around your market gauges, you could add a point if they are above a moving average.

TRADING THE MARKET CYCLE

Let's now go through the full cycle and the actions you should be taking during each part.

First, when the market is in a downcycle, you should be limiting exposure or taking select shorts. Keep an eye out for stocks that are showing Relative Strength and holding up well. However, especially for Stage 1 and 2 traders, you should primarily be sitting on your hands and in cash until an uptrend begins. Trying to trade these properly in downward or choppy markets is like trying to sail a boat upwind.

As a downtrend persists, start looking for signs that it is losing downside momentum. One of the first signs to look for is that the indexes will begin to hold support, and may start to turn up on daily charts with a rounded bottom look. Or they may show capitulatory action with a sharp drop that recovers quickly after the market has already become extended to the downside.

The second sign you should look for is decoupling between the market and key stocks/market gauges. Keep a close eye on your watchlists for an indication that they are beginning to ignore the actions of the general market.

When we are in a downcycle and the indexes make new lows or gap down severely into the red, be on alert for the watchlists to be performing significantly better. This shows that even though the market indexes are being pushed downward, institutions are stepping in and accumulating promising stocks.

CREATING A SWING TRADING MARKET CYCLE SYSTEM

To bring these concepts to life, let's build a simple market cycle system for swing traders where the goal is to capture intermediate-term trends. We will then discuss how to trade each part of the cycle.

Although our example is geared toward swing and position traders, you can use a similar method for each shorter-term or longer-term trading, just switch out the criteria to what is logical.

To create our system, we will use the 21 EMA and the QQQ as our reference. Looking back in history the 21 EMA does an excellent job of identifying strong upcycles lasting a few weeks to a few months. Here is a period from Fall 2019 to Fall 2020.

QQQ Fall 2019 – Fall 2020

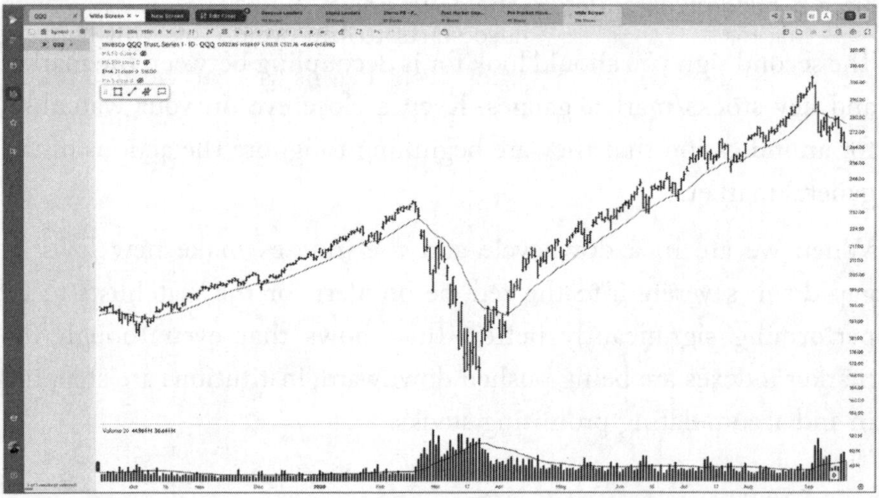

To begin a market cycle, our criteria will be a close above the moving average. To end a cycle we will require two closes below the 21 EMA with the second close being below the prior day's low. Here is the same period marked with the start and end to the two cycles.

QQQ Fall 2019 - Fall 2020

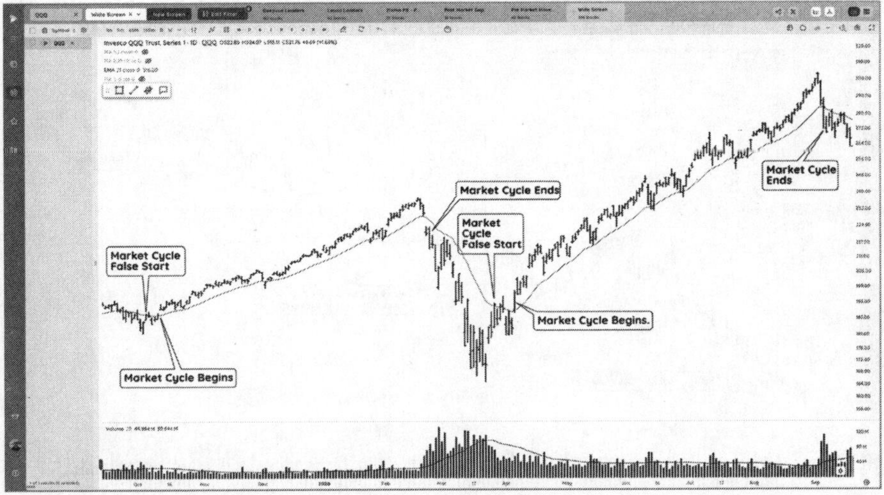

You'll notice with these two simple rules you would have been encouraged to participate during strong uptrends and encouraged to be defensive during the worst of sharp pullbacks.

In both cases, and this will be true for most sensitive market cycle systems, there were a few false starts to the cycle. This will happen; what's key for when a market cycle begins is that we get follow through up, and that leading stocks are also signaling a change with strong action, gap ups, breakouts, and multiple mature bases.

Remember a market cycle turning on does not mean you should go pedal to the metal immediately, but it should be a mindset shift to start testing the waters.

The strongest cycles occur after more significant corrections or extended bear markets. After such periods most will feel tentative about the market. However, these uptrends, when they take hold, can lead to the strongest performance and longest moves.

This criteria is designed to give QQQ the benefit of the doubt when it is in trend. Here are examples of this market cycle applied to 2023.

QQQ Jan 2023

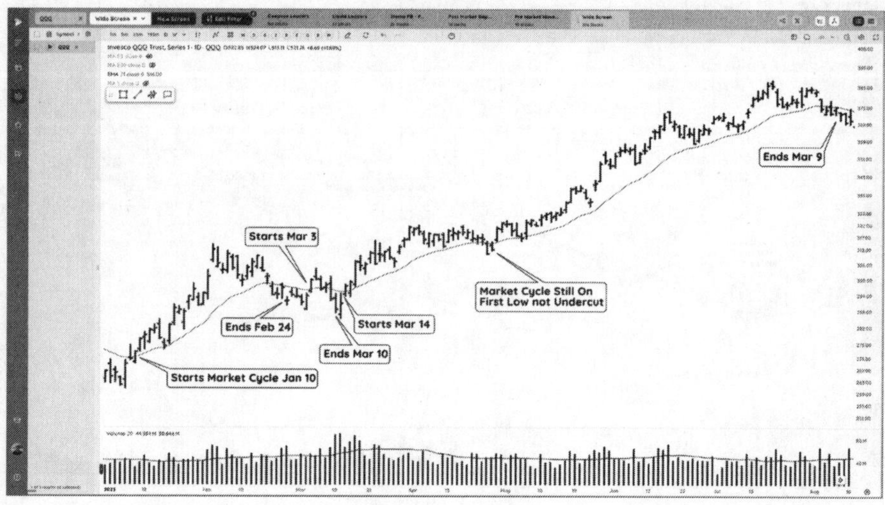

QQQ Fall 2023

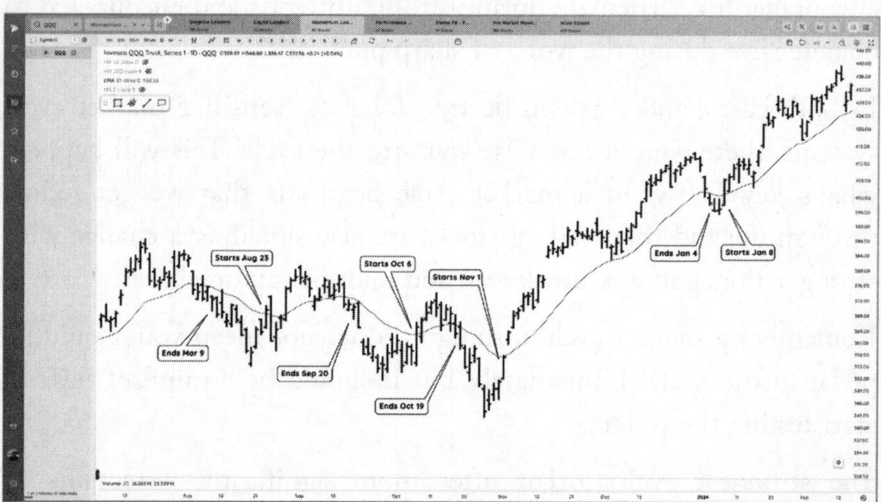

You can see that although there may be false starts during choppier periods, this system does an excellent job of capturing the meat of intermediate-term trends.

Here's 2024:

QQQ Spring 2024

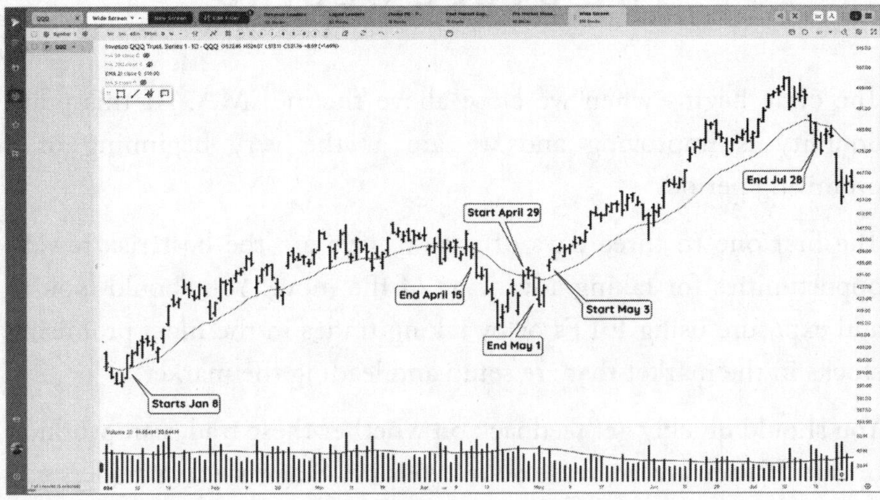

QQQ Summer 2024

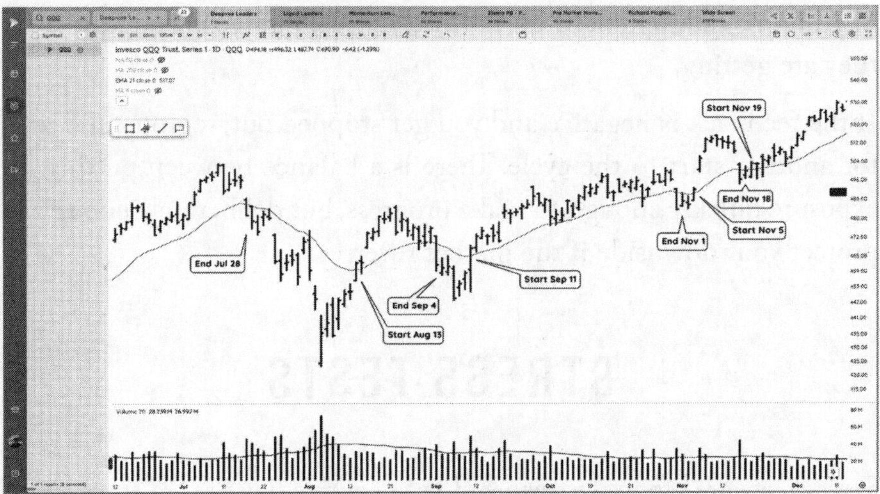

So now that we've defined our system, how do we actually trade it?

THE CYCLE BEGINS

The cycle begins when we close above the 21 EMA. At this point liquidity is improving and we are at the very beginning of a promising period.

The first one to three days of a new cycle are the best risk/reward opportunities for taking advantage of the move. You should look to add exposure using ETFs or by taking trades in the most promising stocks in the market that are setup and leading the market.

You should quickly get feedback on whether these trades are working or not. If they are, increase your exposure. Stage 1 and 2 traders can start with half their normal position size, building up to full size after positive traction in their first few trades. Stage 3 and 4 traders can work more quickly based on intuition as well as how much traction they are getting.

If the feedback is negative and you get stopped out, regroup and wait for another start to the cycle. There is a balance between putting on exposure quickly enough to make progress, but deliberately enough to protect your downside if the market reverses.

STRESS TESTS

Stress tests are when we see a sudden negative day within the start of a new uptrend. These are a natural part of the cycle where profit taking takes hold and we see the market test the strength of the rally.

The first stress test generally occurs on days four to six of the cycle. How your portfolio, watchlists, the leaders, and the market as a whole respond to this bout of selling provides valuable information about the strength of the rally.

If the market holds firm and recovers from the initial weakness, we should expect the rally to extend further.

When days four to six roll around, you want to be ready for the stress test and be in a winning position risk and stops wise.

Even if all your positions at that point are stopped out, you want to ensure that you will be making a higher low on your equity curve.

In general, traders in Stage 1 and 2 should focus on interpretation of the cycle, while Stage 3 and 4 traders should look to anticipate this.

TRADER'S HANDBOOK CHALLENGE 6

Bring up a chart of QQQ in your trading software and go to 2019. Label the market cycles through using the 21 EMA system we covered in the chapter. Be sure to share your work on twitter and tweet at us @ TraderLion_ and #THChallenge.

TRADING LATER IN THE CYCLE

After the first stress test your portfolio should continue to progress, and you can continue to take fresh trades.

There will be continuation stress tests every so often, so never get complacent in managing your risk and listen to the market for feedback.

After a few weeks, keep an eye out for longer consolidation periods or even the end of the cycle. Trends last longer than we think, but stay focused on the best stocks and low-risk entry points, becoming stricter as the trend progresses.

The risk/reward is not as good so you should adjust accordingly. You can think about this in the same way that you don't want to add too heavy a position far above the proper pivot point. Keep your portfolio cost basis low and add less size later in the trend.

Stocks that are just now breaking out multiple months into a cycle are laggards and more prone to failure. Stick with the leaders and remember that the goal is to have enough of a profit cushion that the moving average rises above your cost basis.

When this is the case you can let the trend work for you and let the stock fluctuate naturally. In strong cycles this allows your swing trades to transition into position trades to maximize profit.

KEY TAKEAWAYS

Correctly identifying the current market cycle is one of the most important aspects of trading. It will help you trade with the market at your back and position in promising stocks as the market becomes conducive to your style.

Look back on your trades and determine certain periods where you made a lot of progress. What did the market look like during these times? Distill criteria that define a good trading environment for you and create a system that will turn on during these periods.

Remember that this cycle is a guide, and that you should ultimately listen to trade feedback to determine how to regulate exposure.

The goal is to get from a state of interpretation to anticipation. Stage 1 and 2 traders should focus on identifying cycles, while more advanced traders can look to anticipate and position earlier as they notice the environment changing.

Market cycles will help you become more fluid in your interpretation of the market health. Instead of labels like bull or bear market, you will develop for yourself a more refined way to identify when there is easy money to be made, or if you would be better off going fishing.

Identifying the market cycle should be a part of your routine as a trader. We'll help you create this routine in the next chapter.

See you there!

BONUS RESOURCE

We recorded a webinar on market cycles and how to trade during different parts of them.

You can watch it today at traderlion.com/handbook.

CHAPTER 9

STOCK SELECTION, SCREENING, AND TRADING ROUTINES

"A good company doesn't always mean it's a good stock. The first rule to superperformance is... all stocks are bad unless they are going up."

—Mark Minervini, 2x US Investing Champion

EVERYONE WANTS TO own a stock that can double or triple in a short amount of time. But how do you find them? And more importantly, how do you set up a system so that you can do it consistently each market cycle?

This is what we will cover in this chapter—stock selection, screens, and routines that save you time and help you find and focus on high-potential stocks.

We've already discussed the edges and price/volume characteristics in previous chapters. Now we will talk about how to make use of technology to find stocks easily that fit those criteria.

We will share the screens that we use daily and weekly to stay in tune with the market and find high-potential stocks, as well as how you can design your own screens that are tailored to your specific approach.

THE THEORY OF STOCK SELECTION

We want to be focused on in demand names that have the potential to double or more in the right market environment.

How do we find these? The answer is to follow the template that the market has created for us. If you study history, many of the strongest performing stocks shared both fundamental and technical characteristics.

Many of the characteristics we look for are neatly described in William O'Neil's CANSLIM methodology, which we encourage all our readers to study in his book *How to Make Money in Stocks*.

However, we do have our own spin on things. Our own acronym that summarizes what we are looking for is TIGERS:

- **Theme**—The stock is riding a strong growth theme.
- **Innovation**—The company has a standout product, service, or element that separates it from its peers.
- **Growth**—The company is currently growing its earnings and sales rapidly, or is projected to in upcoming quarters. Quarterly triple-digit growth year over year and acceleration are preferred.
- **Edges**—The chart is displaying at least one of the chart edges we described in Chapter 3.
- **Relative strength**—The stock is displaying unusual strength, outperformance, momentum, and trend.
- **Setup**—The stock is forming an actionable setup.

THEME

Each market cycle (and year) there are distinct themes created by the driving forces of the world and technology.

Within these themes there will be specific companies that ride their waves and grow extremely fast. This growth leads institutions to build positions, driving prices higher, and creating extraordinary moves that we can join as retail traders.

There are two main types of themes: transformative and cyclical.

Transformative themes are largely created by the development of new technology that significantly changes how we live. Some examples of driving factors would be locomotives, steel, electricity, radio, television, rockets, semiconductors, the internet, smartphones, and, currently, artificial intelligence. These themes can be long lasting, and multiple waves of innovation can continue to create fantastic opportunities for new companies to grow.

Cyclical themes are more driven by the economic cycle and macro conditions. Examples are energy, construction, banks, and airlines. These themes may have their day when conditions line up, but often these themes are shorter lived and produce less meaningful opportunities.

During each market cycle, there will be a handful of themes that propel the best stocks higher. If you can track these themes, and notice group moves, you will be well on your way to identifying the top stocks of the cycle.

Think of it this way. When the market is healthy it creates a strong wave that lifts stocks and creates trends. When a larger disruptive theme is emerging and thriving, institutions will look to accumulate positions in the stocks from that theme. This creates another wave.

And if a particular company is extremely well poised to profit from a larger theme, for example if they have the best product, then they will create their own personal tailwind.

When these three waves combine and are all working together, that is when you can find a special stock that can rapidly appreciate in price. Although all the stocks in the theme may do very well, and even laggards within the group may do better than the best stocks outside of the theme, the leader will be head and shoulders above the others.

Your goal should be to identify the top one to three stocks within the current transformative theme of the cycle. We can't predict what they will be, but they will be standing out in terms of momentum, Relative Strength, orderly price action, and edges.

INNOVATION

The leaders of a theme will often have a unique value proposition that is leading them to rapidly grow and take up market share. This could be a new product that leverages a proprietary technology, or a unique approach to solving the most important problems of their customers.

When you discover a theme, try to get a feel for which companies are really on the edge and bringing forward the technology. Read articles, listen to podcasts, but remember to try to avoid sensationalist perspectives.

Everyone will try to say that their product will change the world. Try to take a step back and see what the majority of subject matter experts are agreeing upon.

If possible, try to experience the company and product for yourself, which can give you a unique insight into what sets it apart.

One thing to remember is that even a supposedly great theme, technology, or product does not matter if the market does not care about it. It should be obvious based on the price action that institutions are taking notice and are believers.

So remember, however in-depth your research is, if the price action does not fit your thesis, don't fight it. Look elsewhere and maybe return once the market has started taking notice.

GROWTH

We look for strong and significant earnings and revenue growth. Revenue growth in particular is extremely promising since, in today's markets, more companies seem to be focused on growth at all cost and may forgo profits momentarily.

However, there should be a sense that profits are on the near horizon, and occasionally markets, especially during tighter monetary cycles, may focus almost solely on companies that are making money. Stay fluid and look for growth.

You'll see in the screens we share later a few ways that we incorporate these criteria. In short, however, we like to see at least quarterly growth in earnings or sales of 25% when compared to the same quarter a year prior. The higher the better, with triple digits preferred.

Additionally, we like to see acceleration in growth, meaning we like to see growth trend for instance from 25% EPS growth to 40% to 80% in sequential quarters.

In November 2023 NVDA reported earnings growth of 566%. The previous quarter it also showed strong growth of +440%. The prior quarters were negative but were becoming less so, and NVDA was posting earnings and sales surprises with each report. This showed rapid demand and growth in market share as the leader in the semiconductor/AI theme.

In Deepvue, we highlight growth trends like this by underlining the earnings data in the table with a blue bar.

NVDA Accelerating Earnings Growth Trend

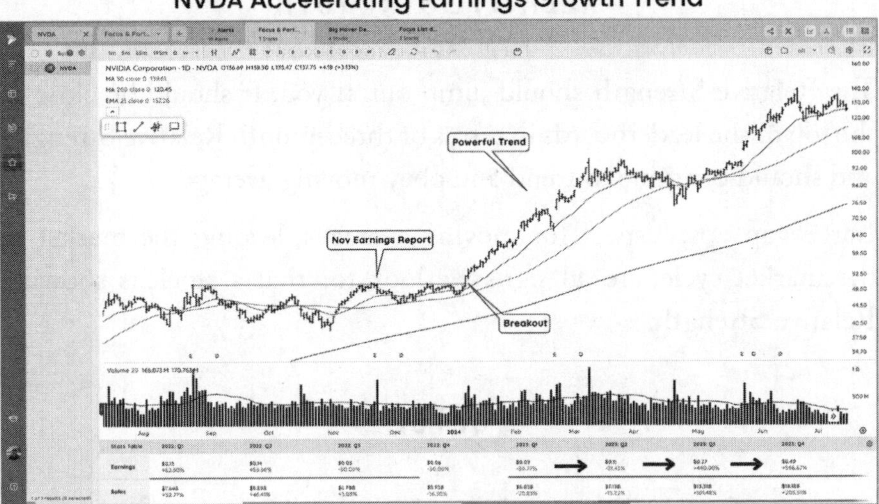

EDGES

Although the fundamentals of a stock are important, the accumulation of the company must ultimately show up in the charts in the form of edges and unique technical characteristics.

We discussed these previously in Chapter 4, but as a reminder we are looking for clear signs that the stock is in high demand by large players.

The stock will show the ability to trend in an orderly fashion when the market is strong. It will seem to fight downtrends and/or bounce quickly up after market corrections end. It will gap up on earnings and breakout and trend from base patterns.

We are not looking for a beaten down stock that nobody wants. We are looking for a rising leader that has already caught the eye of institutions and is already showing outperformance. We are looking for a stock near the beginning of its move, but don't feel the need to "guess" that a stock is under accumulation.

RELATIVE STRENGTH

The Relative Strength should jump out at you. It should be close to the top of the leaderboards in terms of three-month Relative Strength, and should continue to trend and obey moving averages.

Large gap ups, respect for moving averages, leading the market in the market cycle, are all signs we look for that a stock is showing Relative Strength.

SETUP

In terms of stock selection, this is the last piece of the puzzle. Once you've identified a potential leader in a theme, keep track of it on your watchlists and wait until it develops a setup that you have studied and can trade effectively.

This will look different for each trader, but we've covered many options in Chapters 4 and 5.

COMMON STOCK SELECTION QUESTIONS

DO YOU ONLY TRADE LEADERS?

Not necessarily, there are times when secondary stocks in the theme may be outperforming for even weeks on end as the leader's base. These stocks, which may not quite have the fundamental story or liquidity, can still make great trades, but they may be more volatile and better suited for swing trades and treated as "performance enhancers."

DO YOU TRADE STOCKS OUTSIDE OF THEMES?

Yes! Some stocks may lack a larger group theme but still in their own right be forming great trends and growing fast. However, the odds are more in your favor if an idea is part of a larger wave.

DO YOU BUY AND HOLD LEADERS?

Although leadership stocks may make fantastic moves over a span of a few years of several hundred % or more, nothing is known for certain ahead of time, and therein lies the opportunity. You never know if a leader is about to break down for good as it forms a base.

However, leaders can be traded multiple ways with different time frames. Because of their extended outperformance, day traders, swing traders, position traders, and active investors can all look to enter the trends and ride them during the periods that match their strategy.

The advantage is that these leaders have an underlying institutional bid that makes them respect support and key levels which helps traders of all styles manage a trade more effectively and sit with the trends.

Eventually, all great stocks will lose their momentum and either start a longer-term downtrend or base for an extended period of time. Many leaders decline significantly off their peak and are best avoided until they reset and start a new Stage 2 uptrend.

WHAT IF A STOCK HAS A STELLAR CHART BUT DOES NOT HAVE EARNINGS OR SALES GROWTH?

This can still be traded to great effect but may be treated more as a secondary name. However, investigate the stock and see if it is part of a different type of theme, or if EPS and sales growth is expected in the near future.

For instance, a recent theme has emerged where heavily shorted stocks can go on tremendous moves, led by social media interest. The best recent example is GameStop (GME).

These moves have a different type of underlying driving factor and are often more short-lived, albeit spectacular. You can trade them, but you just have to be aware of the dynamics at play and maybe recognize it's more of a swing trade type situation.

BUILDING SCREENS

Now that we have discussed the high-level frameworks of what we look for, let's discuss specifically how to find these types of stocks.

We will walk through our process for creating screens (including a lot of examples) and we will also discuss a weekly and daily routine that you can use to apply them.

GENERAL VERSUS SPECIFIC SCREENS

Let's cover on a high level what we as traders are looking to accomplish with screening.

Then to close, we'll build a high-quality screen that in seconds can help you find top growth stock trading ideas.

THE GOALS OF SCREENING

What are we actually trying to accomplish when it comes to screening? Well, there are two main objectives:

1. Consistently find high-quality and actionable trade ideas.
2. Gain a feel for the health and breadth of market action.

Let's dive into each one.

OBJECTIVE 1: CONSISTENTLY FIND HIGH-QUALITY IDEAS

When it comes to point number 1, it is extremely important to remember that although screens can be very helpful in narrowing your focus, as a final step, you will have to review charts manually to find the best ideas.

However, screening can save you quite a bit of time and allow you to review dozens or only a few hundred high-potential charts instead of painstakingly going through thousands.

Think of screening as a funnel. You start with all the potential stocks in the market and then add restrictions and filters.

This squeezes down the pool of potential stocks until you are left with only the best that meet your trading style's criteria.

OBJECTIVE 2: GAIN A FEEL FOR THE HEALTH AND BREADTH OF MARKET ACTION

This is the second objective of screening and is very underrated in our opinion.

By screening and reviewing charts regularly, you will get a sense of what to expect from the stocks that pass through your filters, and you will also build intuition around the total number of results and setups.

This will help inform you about whether there are a lot of trade ideas working, or if you are seeing a lot less than usual as the market weakens.

Say you are a trend follower and have a general screen that looks for stocks trending over the 21 EMA, 50 SMA, and 200 SMA.

Typically, this particular screen returns about 200 names in a healthy market. Then, one week, you notice that only about 77 names are showing up and looking around you see a lot of stocks breaking down. This is valuable information that you've gained through your routine that tells you that a negative change is starting in the market.

Similarly, if a screen like this provides a lot more results than normal, it can be a sign of a broadening market with many great opportunities developing.

STRUCTURING A SCREEN

Creating screens is an art form, and often many tweaks and updates are required to get them right.

However, we do have a framework that we use consistently to speed up the process. We'll talk through the major steps and also create a live example here with you.

Here are the major steps we will cover:

1. Planning and analysis:
    a. Define the purpose of the screen
    b. Identify your model stock (the textbook result for your desired screen).
    c. Define its characteristics:
        - Break down the fundamental data points
        - Break down the technical data points.
2. Screen development:
    a. Create a prototype
    b. Analyze the results

c. Update the criteria

d. Repeat until satisfied.

These steps can be used to design any screen for any style. They create a loop that you can repeat to create new screens or tweak existing ones.

Now let's put them to work.

DEFINE THE PURPOSE OF THE SCREEN

One key point to remember as you are designing the purpose of your screen is that you should decide upfront whether this screen will cast a wide net or look for very specific situations.

General screens are great for general idea sourcing and building situational awareness, while specialist screens look for unique opportunities or patterns that appear only every so often.

With general screens your goal should be to come up with around 75–400 strong candidates. With specialist screens the results should ideally be less than 50 and fit a very specific situation and setup.

Let's create a screen that identifies strong, liquid stocks that are in uptrends and have strong earnings growth in the most recent quarter.

IDENTIFY YOUR MODEL STOCK

With this purpose and scope in mind, NVDA in early 2023 is a good avatar to think of when designing this screen.

DEFINE THE CHARACTERISTICS

FUNDAMENTAL

We want the stock to have strong earnings growth last quarter and be liquid, so let's choose these data points:

- Average dollar volume (Price of the stock * Average daily volume)
- EPS growth last quarter.

TECHNICAL

We want the stock to be in an uptrend and have strong Relative Strength. With this in mind let's use these technical data points:

- Relative strength rating three-month (ranks the price performance in the last three months of all stocks on a percentile scale)
- Above the 50 SMA
- Above the 200 SMA.

CREATE THE FIRST ITERATION

With these data points in mind, here is the first iteration of the screen in Deepvue.

NVDA Prototype Screen – 1st Iteration

ANALYZE THE RESULTS

Looking at these results we realize that we also want strong EPS growth estimates for the next quarter, so let's add this data point.

UPDATED SCREEN

NVDA Prototype Screen – 2nd Iteration

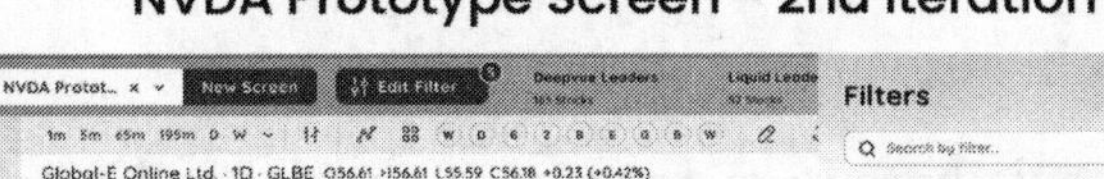

There we go, that looks a lot better. These are liquid stocks that are growing rapidly and have a good runway for the next quarter.

We can also note the number of results we see and keep an eye on how that fluctuates based on market conditions.

We hope you have a good sense of these steps, but remember, we will revisit them until you have mastered this process and become a pro at designing and analyzing screens.

This is a crucial part of becoming a top trader.

TRADING ROUTINES

In trading, we may not be able to control the outcome after we place our order, but we can control the quality of our decision making with thorough preparation.

Routines are crucial in order to help us create trading plans and stay on top of the markets. If you often feel like you are missing obvious setups, or are out of sync with the market, your routines should be on the top of your list to review and improve.

For stock trading, there are two main routines that you will have to define for yourself:

> The first is the daily routine, the steps you take each trading day to prepare for the open, execute during trading hours, and then build your plan for the next day once the market closes.
>
> The second is the weekly routine where you analyze the markets, your own trading, and find ideas for the next week.

In the following pages we will share the outlines of our personal routines. As always, take what works for you and make it your own. Remember also to keep it simple. The best routine is the one you can be consistent with. Start with as few steps as possible and iterate as you go.

THE DAILY TRADING ROUTINE

A daily routine, coupled with weekly analysis, allows you to stay in tune with developing themes and jump on trends early.

Here's a framework that you can use as your foundation.

ONE HOUR BEFORE MARKET OPEN

Review premarket price action and finalize your daily focus list of one to five names. Add alerts on your positions, market gauges, focus list stocks, and other key names that you want to monitor. For focus list stocks we like to set early alerts as well that will let us know to watch the stock as it is approaching our buy area.

If it's within your style, screen or sort for premarket high % movers, high volume, gaps… as you can do in Deepvue or similar software.

Pre Market Chart Setup

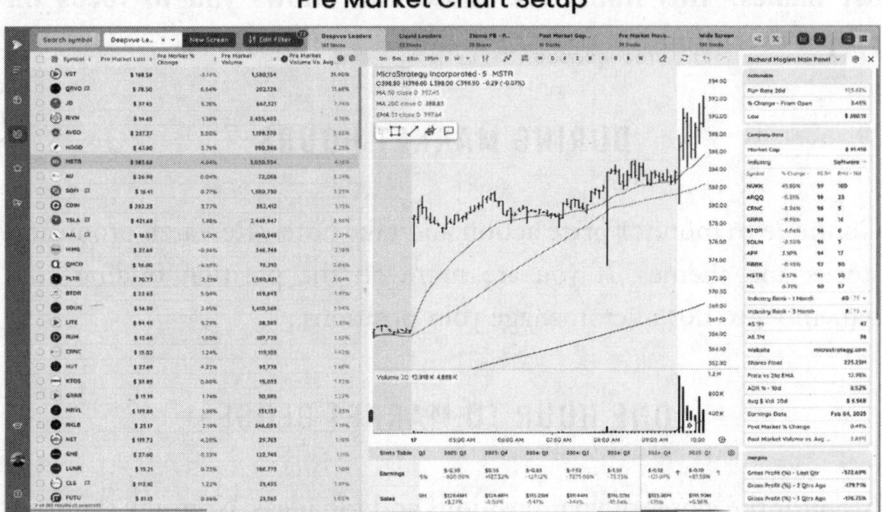

Also be sure to review your existing positions and see if any maintenance will be required.

Visualize possibilities for how the day may resolve and prepare a game plan for each possibility.

MARKET OPEN

Track the price action of your positions and top ideas. Sort your main watchlists looking for:

- High relative volume movers
- High closing ranges
- Strong % movers
- Strong moves from the open.

Make any planned entries or sales. Be sure to monitor and reset alerts as they go off.

Quick tip: If the market open feels very hectic to you, consider only setting alerts on your positions and top one-to-three focus list names. This limits the noise and allows you to focus on proper execution.

DURING MARKET HOURS

Continue to monitor price action and take notes. Research promising stocks and themes. If you are more on the position trading end, remember to not micromanage your positions.

ONE HOUR TO MARKET CLOSE

Monitor the closes of your positions and top ideas. Note any standout names from your lists and screens.

Stocks may surge upward or downward in the last hour, so be ready for any actions you may have to take. For any newly opened positions check on your profit cushion and make a decision on whether you will hold it overnight.

AFTER MARKET HOURS

1. Review your actions and complete a daily trade journal.
2. Monitor any earnings reports if applicable.
3. Run your daily screens and prepare your watchlist for the next day.

With this high-level framework in mind, let's dive deeper into how you can sort and screen intraday.

SORTING SCREENS AND WATCHLISTS INTRADAY

During the day, you should be monitoring your stocks, ideas, and taking notes about rotation, strong groups, weak groups, and any other trends you see.

Here are a few helpful data points that you can use to sort your screens and watchlists:

- Volume run rate
- Price % gain
- Daily closing range
- Above volume weighted average price (VWAP).

VOLUME RUN RATE

Volume run rate is a representation of how volume is tracking versus normal at that instant in time. In Deepvue, we have both a 20-day and 50-day variation.

Our volume run rate data points will let you see how abnormal volume is at any moment in time, even right at 9.30 am after the market opens.

In the first hour, relative volume will let you know which stocks are moving on significant volume, a key indicator that institutions are behind a move and that breakouts may be more likely to hold, as well as breakdowns may be more detrimental.

This will give you a step up versus traders who have to guess by just looking at the raw volume to see if it looks abnormal.

PRICE % CHANGE

Price % change is an obvious but powerful data point that can point you toward the top and worst performing stocks of the day.

In Deepvue, you can sort by this (or price % change from the open) to quickly see the strongest stocks in your watchlists and screens.

On an upside reversal day, where the market and most stocks are rallying strongly from lows, it may also be helpful to sort lists and screens by price % change from lows to see which ones are bouncing the strongest.

DAILY CLOSING RANGE (DCR)

DCR is what top traders use to identify Relative Strengths and strong stocks. It represents the location of the close relative to the range from high to low.

On a negative day in the markets, the strongest stocks that day will have high DCRs near 100, even if they may be red on the day.

ABOVE VWAP

VWAP is commonly used by institutions to enter and manage positions. Stocks under accumulation will consistently trend above this level.

HOW TO USE THESE DATA POINTS

By adding these data points as columns in Deepvue, you can quickly sort your watchlists and screen results throughout the day to monitor leading names and analyze rotation.

Intraday Data Points

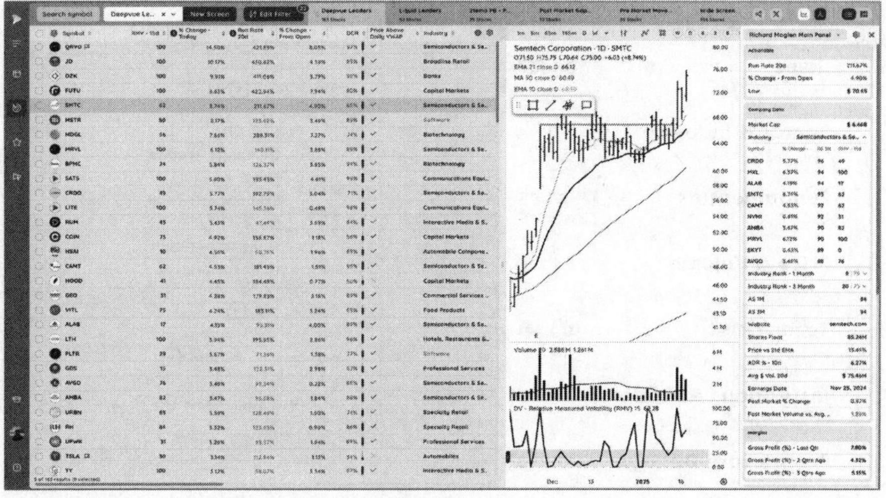

INTRADAY SCREENS

Let's cover three screens that you can run during the trading day to help fund new ideas and track rotation.

UP ON VOLUME

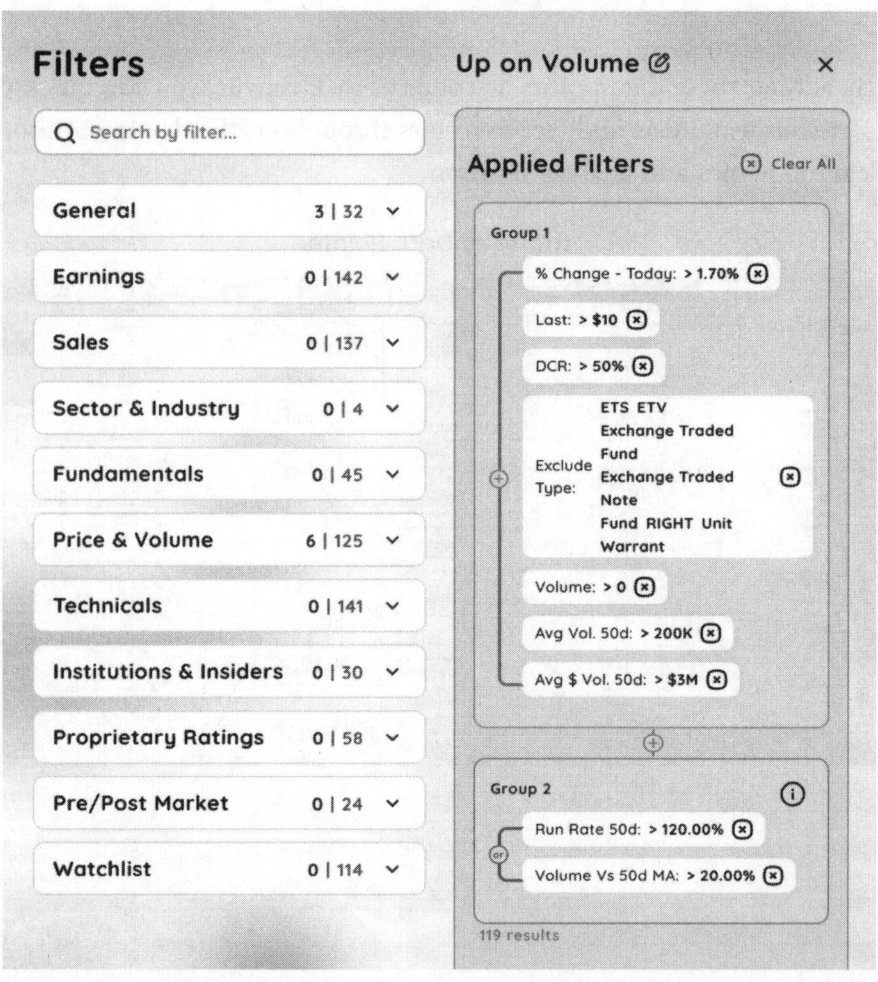

This is Ross Haber's go-to scan. Simply sorting through stocks that are acting well will enable you to read the pulse of the market.

GAP UPS

Gap on Volume

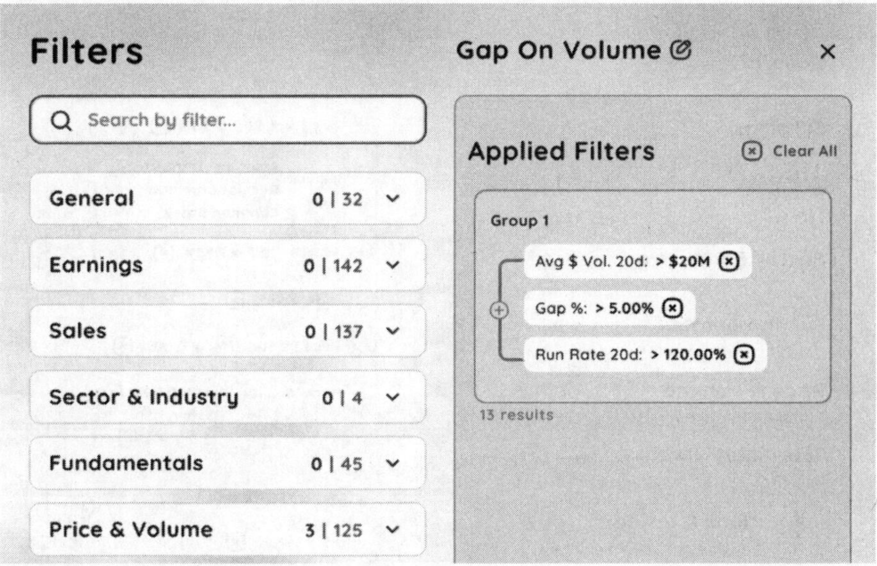

This screen looks for stock with a gap of at least 5% on at least 25% above average volume run rate.

Each day you should track gap ups, especially on earnings. These may or may not be directly actionable, but having them on your radar will allow you to watch for the next setup.

POWER DCR

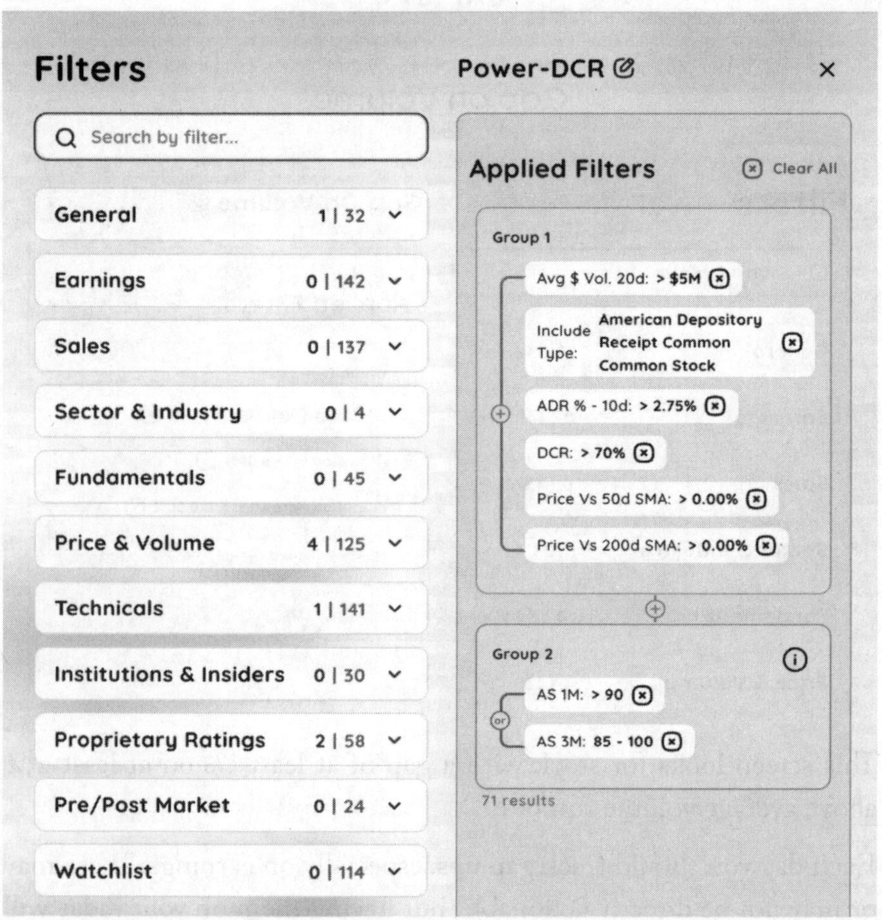

This screen is especially good on down days. It looks for strong stocks in a trend with high closing ranges. Tracking high DCR stocks points you toward the Relative Strength, especially if a whole group is standing out.

POST-MARKET SCREENS

After the market has closed, you should run a subset of your weekly screens that will find any big movers to include on your watchlists.

Then, you should run through your weekly and wide watchlists and build your daily focus list for the next day, jotting down any trends or situational awareness thoughts.

The key thing is that you develop a solid plan for the day surrounding your positions and top ideas.

Remember, even if you work full time and are unable to watch the market, you can do unbelievably well. In fact, in many ways, it is extremely helpful to be away from the noise of intraday price action as it can suck you in and swing your emotions.

THE WEEKLY TRADING ROUTINE

In addition to a daily routine, we also recommend defining a routine that you complete each weekend. It's useful to take a step back and reflect on how you have been trading and any new market developments.

Here is the general framework for a weekly routine:

1. Analyze your actions from the past week. Write down any lessons and mistakes.
2. Analyze the general market indexes.
3. Go through your universe screens:
    e. Save any ideas to your watchlists.
    f. Note any trends and themes developing.

1. Refine your watchlists.
2. Build your weekly focus list.
3. Go enjoy your weekend.

There are many ways to tweak this template to suit your style, but we hope that this general framework serves as a good foundation for you.

We will be discussing post analysis and step 1 in the next chapter and in step 2 you want to apply your market cycle rules to determine the health and breadth of the current market.

With those covered let's go into more detail on how to screen the market and refine your watchlists, which is a common pain point among the traders we've mentored.

BUILDING YOUR STOCK UNIVERSE

What is a stock universe? Well it is generally a list of all the stocks that meet your widest criteria for a potential trade.

You should look to have around 400–500 names that form your universe. Much more than that and the work becomes tedious, and you are likely looking at many subpar charts. Much less than that and you will be eliminating promising charts.

Once you have this universe, you want to either spacebar through each of the charts or run tighter screens on this list.

USING SCREENS TO BUILD YOUR UNIVERSE

Let's now cover some excellent universe screens that you can use for growth style trading. We'll share the specific criteria we use and why.

STAGE ANALYSIS LEADERS' SCREEN

Stage Analysis Leaders

This screen looks for stocks in early Stage 2 uptrends that are in leading groups and either among the strongest stocks this month or over the past three months.

The idea is to incorporate Stan Weinstein's Stage Analysis methodology and look for leading stocks in leading groups. It typically returns around 100 stocks.

WILLIAM O'NEIL CANSLIM GROWTH SCREEN

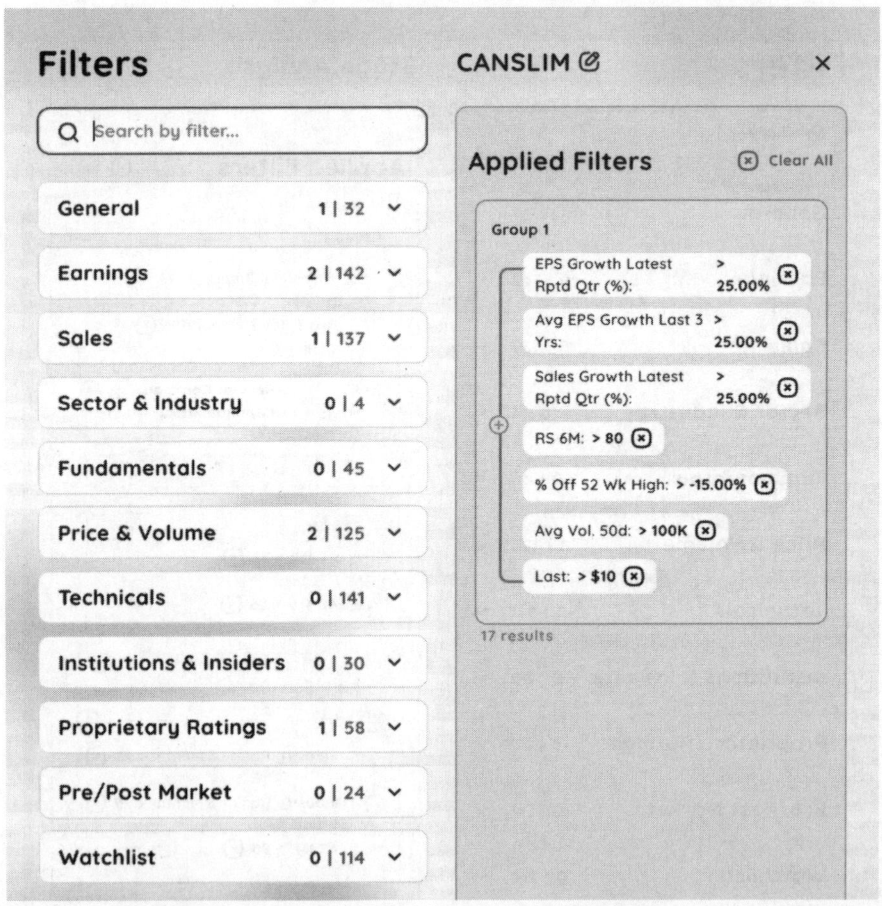

This screen incorporates the criteria that William O'Neil used to find true market leaders. It looks for stocks with strong earnings growth, Relative Strength, and near highs.

It typically returns less than 50 stocks to go through. This is a built-in preset in Deepvue.

MINERVINI TREND TEMPLATE SCREEN

Mark Minervini Inspired Trend Screen

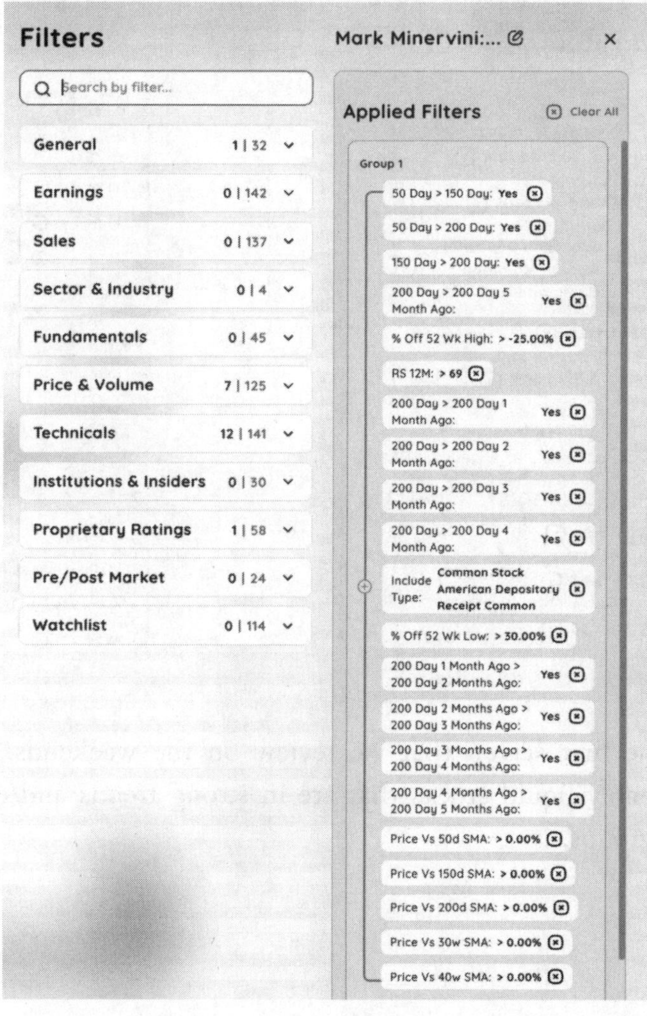

This screen is inspired by Mark Minervini's Trend Template criteria. It looks for strong stocks that are in trend. There are preset variations that look for early-to-established trends.

THE DEEPVUE LEADERS SCREEN

The Deepvue Leaders Screen

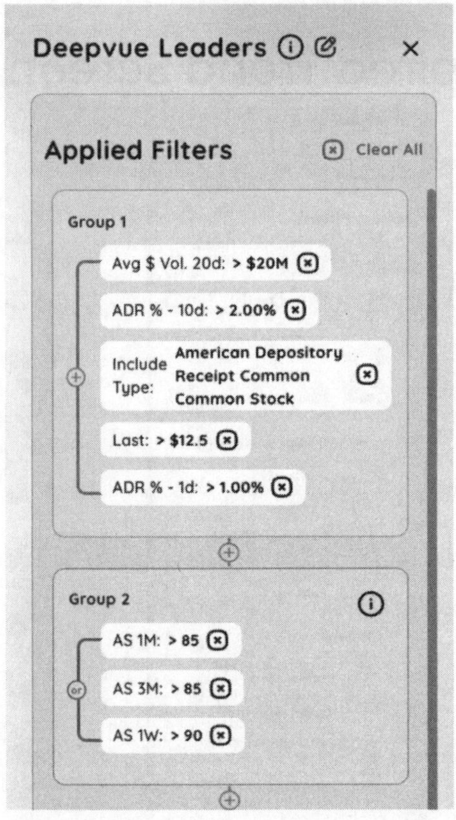

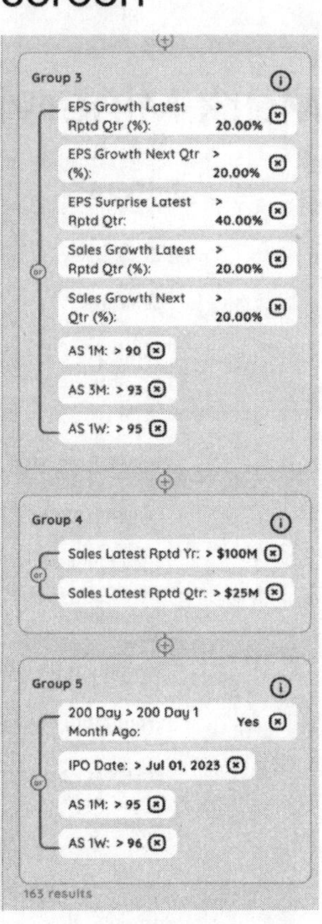

This is the first screen that we review on the weekends. It looks for reasonably liquid stocks that are in strong trends and/or in top industry groups.

This screen makes use of the and/or filters in Deepvue. These allow for added flexibility when screening since you can add "or" conditions where only one criterion needs to be true for a stock to pass through.

CREATING AND REFINING YOUR WATCHLISTS

As you go through your screen results, select stocks that look promising for the next week and are close to completing a setup and are showing your edges.

This first pass should yield about 75 stocks to your weekly universe list.

Next, combine this list with a watchlist where you are tracking the highest quality stocks of the cycle. These are the leaders of the market that are trending and riding larger themes.

Now you should go through this larger list and only select the most actionable and highest potential stocks to add to your weekly focus list. Existing leaders should be added if they are setting up again.

Be very selective here. At the end of the process you should have a maximum of around 15 names on this weekly focus list.

Many traders initially have difficulty arriving at a final list. Our recommendation would be to prioritize stocks that are:

- In the strongest theme of the market cycle
- Have shown the most edges and Relative Strength
- Are most actionable and closest to completing a setup.

With your focus list set don't forget step number 6!

Time away from the screens is extremely valuable, not only for your life but to reset your mind, increase energy and focus, and to trade effectively the next week.

TRADER'S HANDBOOK CHALLENGE 7

List out the key steps of your trading routines. Be specific and describe the screens and processes you will use. Be sure to share your work on twitter and tweet at us @TraderLion_ and #THChallenge.

KEY TAKEAWAYS

Here are two key takeaways from this chapter:

1. Use the TIGERS acronym to remember what to look for in a stock.

   1 **Theme**—The stock is riding a strong growth theme.

   2 **Innovation**—The company has a standout product, service, or element that separates it from its peers.

   3 **Growth**—The company is currently growing its earnings and sales rapidly, or is projected to in upcoming quarters. Quarterly triple digit growth year over year and acceleration are preferred.

   4 **Edges**—The chart is displaying at least one of the chart edges we described in Chapter 3.

   5 **Relative strength**—The stock is displaying unusual strength, outperformance, momentum, and trend.

   6 **Setup**—The stock is forming an actionable setup.

2. The two goals of screening are:
   - Consistently find high-quality and actionable trade ideas.
   - Gain a feel for the health and breadth of market action.

BONUS RESOURCE

We recorded a webinar about stock selection and how to create a trading routine.

You can watch it today at traderlion.com/handbook.

CHAPTER 10
POST ANALYSIS AND TRADING RULES

"The single most important advice I can give anybody is: Learn from your mistakes. That is the only way to become a successful trader."

—David Ryan, 3x US Investing Champion

SO FAR IN this handbook we've focused on building your trading system. However, like with any system, it needs maintenance and a feedback loop to stay up to date with the times and increase its performance.

This will be the focal point of this chapter—how to analyze your system and trading performance on both a single trade and portfolio level, as well as how to analyze that information, draw conclusions, and make updates and improvements.

This chapter will show you how to build a clear picture of your trading and allow you to identify both your strengths and weaknesses.

There is a reason that professional athletes watch film of their previous performances, especially in games where they made crucial mistakes. It's because although that particular game may be over, they can learn from it and improve for the next match, series, or tournament. The athletes don't dwell that they had maybe a bad game or embarrassing moment. Instead they recognize that they will likely experience that same situation again and can improve how they handle it.

It is the same for trading. By analyzing past trades, you will notice patterns of mistakes as well as common strengths.

Trading is excellent for this type of post analysis because you will likely have a large sample size of data each month and year. Although it may be painful to look back on your past trades, especially the losses, it is likely the single most impactful exercise that you can do to improve your performance.

Approach it from a mindset that if you had a winner, then great, you can study what you did right and do more of that. And if you are analyzing a loser, then it's more likely you will be able to identify a mistake that you can avoid in the future.

On my high-school baseball team, before each game our coach would emphasize that we had to minimize the amount of "free bases" that we gave the other team. To count the number of free bases, he would add up the number of walks our pitchers gave up, the number of fielding errors, extra bases that runners took on us after bad throws… any action by us that gave the other team a bonus base.

After each game was over, we would go over each free base and discuss how we could avoid it next time. Some would be unavoidable, but in a game of inches where the difference in scoring could just be one run, free bases became the key metric for us as a team that we worked to improve.

Over the course of the season we gradually gave up fewer and fewer free bases, and ended up playing some of our best baseball and winning the league. Simply by focusing on and trying to improve the fundamental mistakes that we were making, we naturally performed quite a bit better.

Even though it hurt sometimes to discuss overthrows or communication mistakes that led to free bases, we recognized as a team how important it was.

In this chapter we will discuss the equivalent of "free bases" for your trading—key metrics that will help you identify your common weaknesses. In addition to this higher-level view, we will share our frameworks for analyzing single trades as well as how to complete a daily journal to stay in touch with your trading.

Finally, we will cover how you should create trading rules based off your experience and what you have learned from this book in order to codify your trading system.

For Stage 2 traders who feel they are right on the edge of achieving Stage 3, this post-analysis chapter can provide you with just the breakthroughs you need. Take the past six months of your trading data and complete the processes that we will cover, and you will no doubt identify exactly what you need to fix to improve your equity curve.

Now let's dive in!

HOW TO ANALYZE YOUR TRADES

A crucial part of post analysis is analyzing your best and worst trades over a period. This helps you identify not only your biggest trading issues but also the strengths and aspects that you should lean into more.

PICKING TRADES TO ANALYZE

In an ideal world you would analyze every single trade that you take. However, this can take quite a lot of time, so we want to make sure we prioritize trades that will likely provide the best insights.

Over a trading period, sort your trades by the % return. To start with, pick your five top-performing trades as well as your bottom ten. If you have more time, analyze the next top five and next ten worst performing trades.

Likely in just this small sample size you will notice tendencies that you make. With these post analyses, depth is more important than the total number of trades that you look at.

ANALYZING A SINGLE TRADE

To analyze a specific trade, the first step is to collect information about the trade that is relevant to your process.

This includes a stock chart, the screen/routine you used to find the stock, any journal entries about your trading actions, fundamental information, key news events… whatever you used in the moment to make decisions about the trade.

You can create a trade log sheet to help systematize this process. Once you've created one that you like, it's best practice to fill out as much information as you can in real time.

We have a sample trade log that you can use here.

Sample questions that you can use:

Symbol:

Date:

Why did you take this trade? Be specific. What edges was this stock showing?

What setup and entry tactic did you use?

What position sizing are you using? How did you arrive at that amount? How did you manage initial risk?

How did you manage your position after your entry?

How would you rate your trade execution out of ten? Why? What are your key takeaways from this trade?

This log's goal is to capture the most important information in the shortest amount of time. If you find yourself forgetting to fill it out, eliminate as many questions as you can until it takes under two minutes to complete.

ANALYZING YOUR TRADE ON THE CHART

The first step to analyzing a trade is to go back to your entry point.

In your charting software, go back in time to what the stock looked like at the moment in time that you decided to buy.

Label the chart and analyze the quality of the setup/chart. Note any relevant price and volume characteristics.

Here are some sample questions that you can ask yourself:

What was the template setup/entry tactic I was using with this trade? How would I grade this example of the setup/entry tactic?

Were there clear signs of accumulation before my entry?

Was there a lower-risk buy point prior to my actual entry? Why did I not look to enter there?

What was the trend of the stock on multiple time frames? Was I trading with the longer-term context of the setup?

How was the market/sector/group performing at the time of entry into the stock? Where in the market cycle did you take this trade?

When looking at your trading execution, judge your actual entry point and where ideally you would have wanted to buy for the best perceived risk/reward.

> How different was your entry point compared to the ideal? Why was that the case? What would you change going forward?

For each stock case study, after reviewing all your actions, think about what you did well, what you did poorly, and anything else of note about the trade that could help you improve going forward.

It can be difficult looking back on your trades, especially the losers, but remember that the past has already happened and the best thing you can do is study it so that you can trade better in the future.

Consistent 1% improvements over time can lead to dramatic changes in your performance and process.

These improvements are only possible after post analysis that leads you to rule changes and routine tweaks.

EXAMPLE TRADE REVIEW

To walk through this process, let's examine an example trade in RDDT. The example trader in mind here is a swing trader who looks to hold from base to base for weeks to months. When a position is trending, they like to use 2 closes below the 21 EMA as their final sell rule.

They are looking to risk maximum about 0.75% of their portfolio on a given trade. This trade was one of their best of 2024, but they felt like they left some on the table. The trader made 2 trades of RDDT.

The first was a 10% size trade entering at 61.93, exiting the next day at 58.20 for around 6% loss on the position or .6% of their total portfolio. The second was a 10% size position entering at 66.87 and exiting at 134.77 for around a 100% gain or 10% of their total portfolio.

STEP 1: GATHER TRADE LOG INFORMATION ON THE TRADES

The trader checked his notes and found the information he gathered on the trades. It's also good practice to grab any screenshots you have of the chart at key actions like buys and sells.

Here is what the trader noted before Trade 1.

The reason for focusing on RDDT was that it was a liquid recent ipo that had been consolidating for a while and had recently made higher lows in a consolidation while the market was making lower lows.

Reddit Before Trade 1

STEP 2: MARK UP THE CHART WITH BUYS AND SELLS

Reddit Post Analysis Example

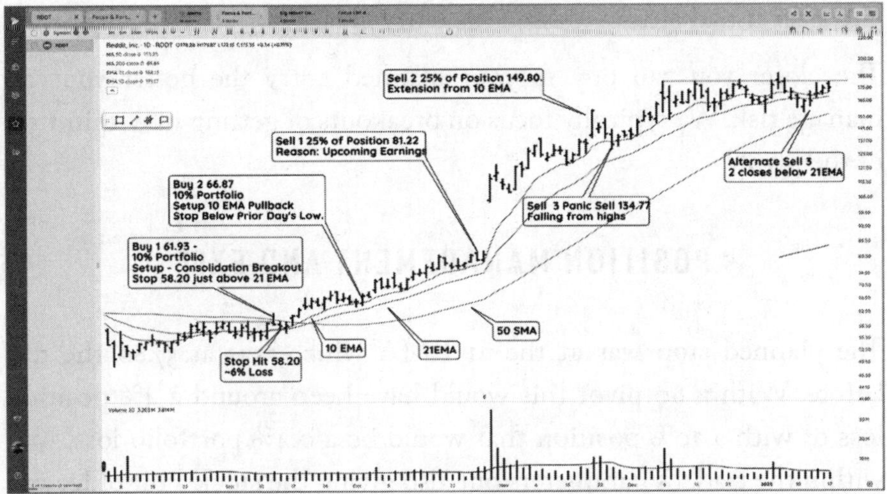

STEP 3: GO ACTION BY ACTION AND GRADE YOUR PLAN AND EXECUTION OF THAT PLAN

Remember that in the moment you only have the information available to you at the time. It's important to be as intellectually honest with yourself about what you did, why, and what you could do better next time.

For the first trade the reason for purchasing was that it was breaking above the two-week consolidation and the 50 day moving average.

Entry Buy 1:

The plan was to enter on a break above the consolidation pivot of 60.

Looking at his entry the trader noted that he entered late, about 3% above the pivot of the consolidation. He had not placed alerts below the pivot and entered only after noticing it later in the session and not wanting to miss out on the move.

Grading: 6/10

The plan was solid, however the trader noted that he did not follow his routine to set alerts to properly execute, and therefore he entered too late after it had already passed his entry area.

The closer you can buy to your planned entry the better you can manage risk. We typically focus on breakouts of getting in within 1.5% of the pivot.

POSITION MANAGEMENT AND EXIT

The planned stop was at the 21 EMA which was at 57.80 the day before. With a 60 pivot this would have been around a 4% position loss or with a 10% position that would be a 0.4% portfolio loss, well within the trader's parameters but also giving the stock a bit of leeway to get going at the pivot.

The next day the 21 EMA had risen to around 58, however, with the poor entry execution the updated stop loss was closer to a 6% loss.

The stock faded sharply right after the trader's entry and closed near the low of the day. The trader adjusted his stop slightly higher to try to manage his risk a bit tighter.

The next day it followed through down and stopped him out, but ultimately closed off of the 21 EMA.

Grading: 8/10

Risk was managed at the original planned spot of the 21 EMA but the trader moved up their stop early.

Reddit Trade 1

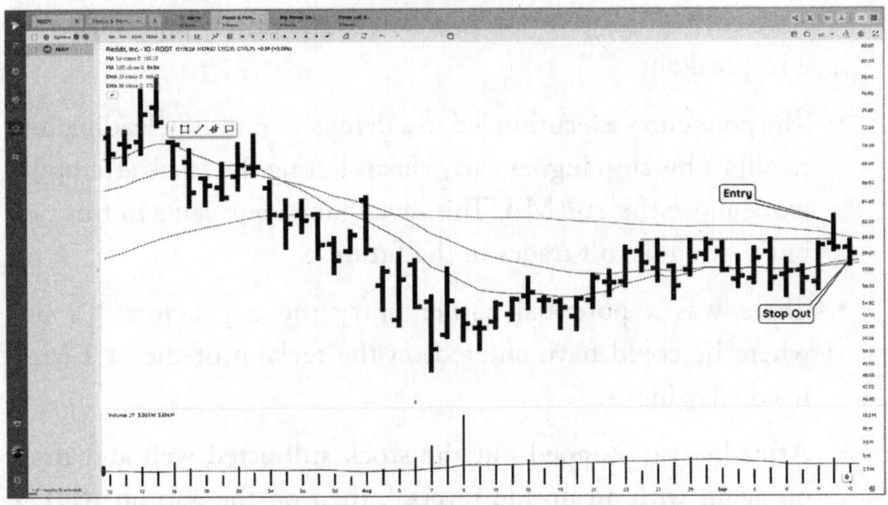

STEP 4: OVERALL TRADE OBSERVATIONS

Reddit Trade 1 Observations

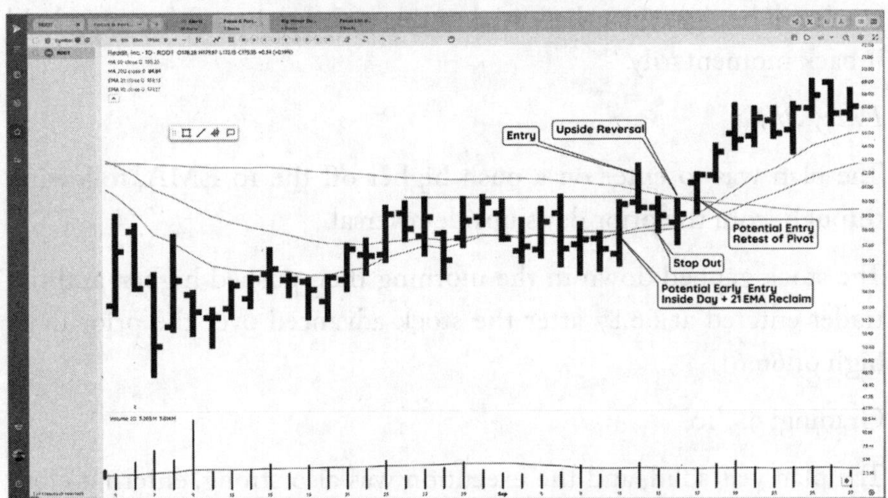

After analyzing this trade the trader made the following observations:

- The poor entry execution led to a larger than expected loss.

- The day of entry with the poor close broke expectations, he could have cut half his position or taken it off entirely and waited for a re-breakout.
- The poor entry execution led to a defensive mindset, leading him to adjust his stop higher early versus letting the stock attempt to work above the 21 EMA. This saved him a few cents in this case but may choke off trades in the future.
- There was a potential earlier entry the day before his buy where he could have entered on the reclaim of the 21 EMA/ inside day highs.
- After he was stopped out the stock still acted well and it set up again with an upside reversal, then on the gap up RDDT retested the pivot and closed well, another good entry where risk could have been managed at the low of the day.

Key Point – when analyzing a trade always look out into the future a few weeks past your exit and see if the stock set up again. Often the stock will be right, just the initial timing or even the market cycle held it back momentarily.

Entry Buy 2:

The plan was to enter on a push higher off the 10 EMA, following through from the prior day's upside reversal.

The stock gapped down in the morning then pushed higher, and the trader entered at 66.87 after the stock advanced over the prior day's high of 66.61.

Grading: 9.5/10

The plan was solid, and the execution was also strong, entering close to the pivot. Advanced traders could have looked to enter a bit sooner after the opening weakness as it formed up.

POSITION MANAGEMENT AND EXIT

From this entry RDDT trended cleanly above the moving averages.

Sell 1 was due to upcoming earnings and was 25% of the position. This is prudent to lock in solid profits while holding a core for a larger move. Earnings are binary events, you always want to make sure you are accepting a large gap either way and have adequate cushion.

Reddit Trade 2: Sell 1 Ahead of Earnings

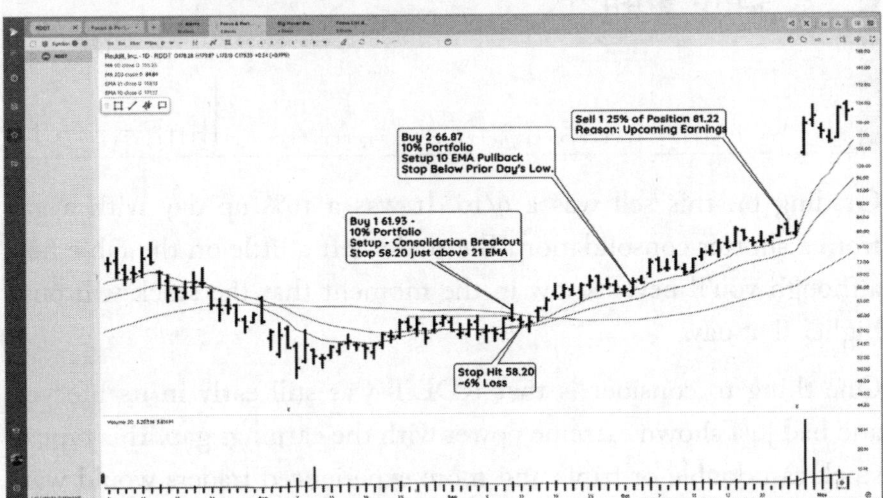

Grading on this sell was a 10/10. Often top traders like to wait for the week prior to earnings to sell a portion if they are planning to. Exactly when or how much is up to the individual.

Sell 2 was into strength as RDDT got stretched from the 10 EMA. Selling into strength on extensions and when to do so is a learned tactic that requires feel. More advanced traders can look to trade around their positions and add back sold portions at the next entry area.

Reddit Trade 2: Sell 2 Extension

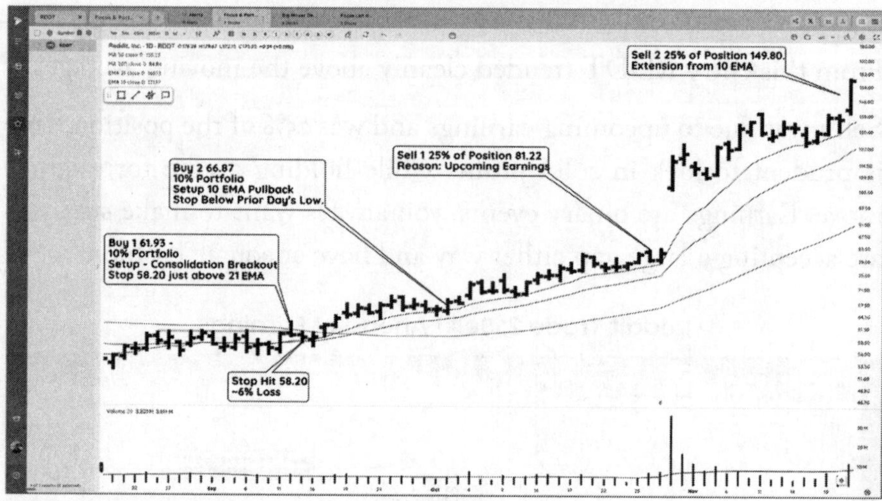

Grading on this sell was a 9/10. It was a 16% up day with a gap from a shorter consolidation. The trader left a little on the table here although you'll never know in the moment that the stock will push higher that day.

One thing to consider is that RDDT was still early in its lifecycle and had just shown extreme power with the earnings gap. This type of stock can double or triple and more experienced traders would want to recognize this and look to hold as much of their core for as long as they can.

Sell 3 was the key one, the trader sold after the stock had pulled back sharply from the extension but still above the 21 EMA. This was a sell based on emotion as the trader had gone from excited and near euphoric on the strong gap and go move up to now, panicked as RDDT had gapped lower and was following through down.

Reddit Trade 2: Sell 3 Panic Sell

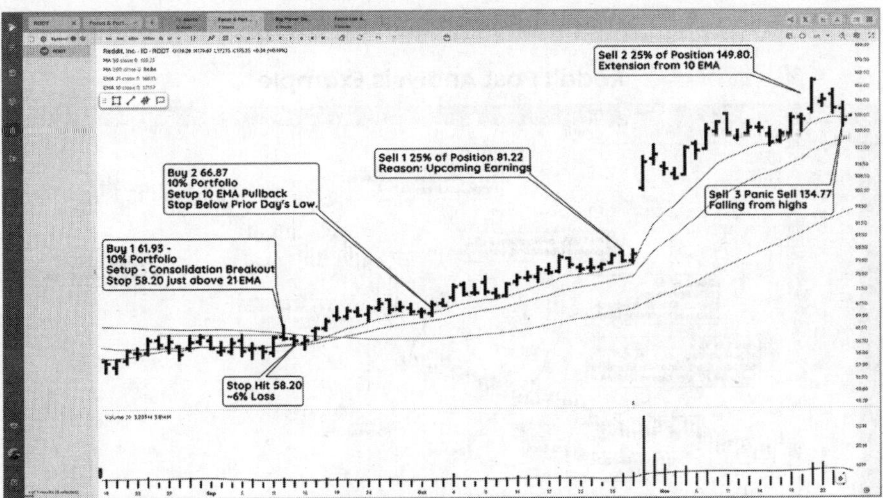

This type of day is why traders need to have rules and be vulnerable to their system.

Grading for Sell 3 is a 2/10. The stock had not triggered the 2 closes below the 21 EMA. At this point the stock was making higher highs and higher lows.

OVERALL TRADE OBSERVATIONS

Reddit Post Analysis Example

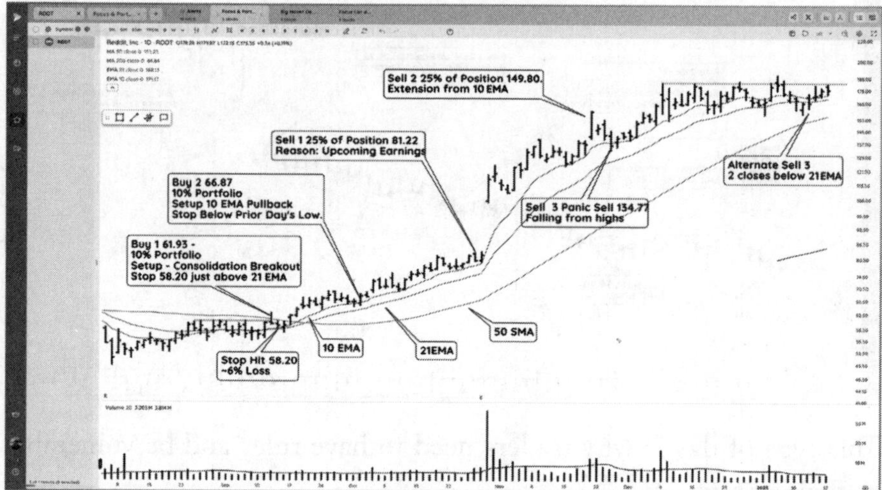

After analyzing Trade 2 the traders made the following observations:

- A strong entry helped build a cushion right away, allowing them to hold a core position through earnings.
- The final sell was due to emotion, if they can't stomach a 15% drawdown above the 21 EMA they need to be more proactive with selling into strength, **or** they need to accept the wiggles and jiggles that will happen above uptrending moving averages.
- RDDT respected the 10 EMA after the entry, the trader could have switched to 2 closes below that moving average after the respect was clear.
- The sell signal if the trader had followed his rules would have been weeks later and 20% higher. However, an advanced trader especially with that type of cushion may have decided to wait another day before selling here, as the second close was higher than the low of the first and RDDT was simply consolidating in a base.

Key Points when analyzing a single trade:

First, analyzing your trades will be the most effective way of determining your weaknesses and areas of improvement as a trader. They will help you refine your entries, exits, and position management. However, remember to be stern but forgiving of yourself. We are human and will make errors. The goal is to incrementally improve over time and post analysis is the path to do so.

Analyze your trades objectively and try to come up with system level action/rules to improve your trading. Instead of saying I need to just buy closer to the pivot, implement a rule and change to your routine so that you are aware of the stock even before it breaks through.

Also, each series of trades will be impacted by the market. Some markets reward fast sells into strength while others reward holding for long moves. Remember to take this into account and don't change your rules too fast simply because of the data of one market cycle.

CREATING A TRADING JOURNAL

WHY IS JOURNALING IMPORTANT?

Journaling is the process of taking notes on your actions in the market and your thoughts, feelings, and analysis.

Just like a stock chart is a record of a company's price action history and contains important clues signaling accumulation or the starts and ends of trends, a trade journal contains clues about the strengths and weaknesses of your trading.

Trading is also a personal journey.

A journal can help you reflect on successes, or problems you are experiencing. If you can be truly honest with yourself, by reading your trading journal in retrospect, you can diagnose and solve many of your faults.

It can also serve as a time capsule—you'll be able to look back on past years' notes and see how far you've come.

DAILY TRADE JOURNAL SECTIONS

Your daily journal should not feel like a huge task to complete each day. Around 15 minutes should be plenty of time to fill out the sections. You can set up a Google form that you can fill out each day which stores your data in a spreadsheet.

OVERALL TRADING PERFORMANCE CHECK-IN

It can be helpful to include an overall trading performance check-in at the start of your journal. Out of ten, how do you rank your execution and trading?

MARKET TREND AND THOUGHTS

Include a chart of the market indexes. What are your current thoughts on the trend? How does it fit into your market cycle?

NEW POSITIONS WITH CHARTS AND THOUGHTS

List out any new positions you took, and thoughts on their performance and your execution. Include your setup, rationale for each trade, and how well you followed your plan.

ACTIVE TRADES AND THOUGHTS

Also include your thoughts on your existing positions. Are any of them close to needing management? Which are your strongest positions?

KEY NOTES

Include any additional notes or thoughts in this section. Check in on how you are feeling currently about your trading performance and psychology.

That's it!

This should be a quick check-in that you can consistently complete. This allows you to reference how you were thinking and feeling in different moments of the market cycle and trades during post analysis.

TRADE ANALYTICS

The next step of post analysis is to analyze your performance and trade analytics. This should be completed regularly, ideally every few months.

You can do this manually or there are different journaling services out there that can automate calculating the statistics.

This process allows you to objectively step back and analyze your edge. The following is inspired by Mark Minervini as well as Dr. Eric Wish.

The key metrics that we suggest you track are:

- Batting average—the % of trades which are winners
- Average gain $, %, equity contribution—your average gain on winners in terms of dollars, % gain per position, and equity contribution

- Average loss $, %, equity contribution—your average loss on losers in terms of dollars, % loss per position, and equity contribution
- Your risk/reward ratio—the ratio of your average gain/average loss
- Max gain $, %, equity contribution—your maximum gain in terms of dollars, % gain per position, and equity contribution
- Max loss $, %, equity contribution—your largest loss in terms of dollars, % loss per position, and equity contribution
- Average trade length for winners—the number of days on average of winning trades
- Average trade length for losers—the number of days on average of losing trades.

Let's walk through each metric and how you can use it to draw conclusions about your trading.

BATTING AVERAGE

The batting average is calculated by dividing the number of winners by the total number of trades losers. If you want to take this a step further, you can eliminate trades near 0% return say -1% to 1%. These are scratched trades and may skew the perception of the final number.

Your batting average is important to track personally but is a lot less important as a performance indicator than traders believe.

Many market wizards and traders we've met actually have win rates of around 40% on average. This may seem low, but in reality what this means is that they are excellent at cutting the losers short. They have a lot of small losses but make up for all of them with large gains when they do have winners.

However, the batting average or win % is helpful to track on a personal level to see how it fluctuates in different market environments. If you notice your average dipping, it's a sign to take the foot off the gas and pump the brakes. The market could be weakening, or your style simply could not be working as effectively as usual.

AVERAGE GAIN

Your average gain is calculated by taking the average of all your winning trades. You should calculate it three ways: dollar amount, % gain on the position, and equity contribution. This is because you could have a trade that was a huge winner, but it was also a tiny position. That will skew the % gain calculation but not the equity contribution. To calculate the equity contribution, multiply the % gain on the position by the position size. A 30% gain on a trade that was 20% of your portfolio was a 6% equity contribution.

Tracking this over time gives a similar view to the batting average. It can help you identify the best trading periods as you see it trending upwards, and then in choppier periods it will contract.

AVERAGE LOSS

Your average loss is calculated by taking the average of all your losing trades. Like the average gain you should calculate it three ways: dollar amount, % gain on the position, and equity contribution.

To really excel at trading this should be one of the key metrics that you focus on improving. Just a small tweak in your average loss can dramatically improve your risk/reward ratio and your overall performance.

This is also one of the metrics that we have the most control over through the methods discussed in the risk management chapter.

RISK/REWARD RATIO

The risk/reward ratio is calculated by dividing the average gain by the average loss. You should do this for all three ways.

This is the key metric that shows how effective you are as a trader. You should shoot for a 2:1 or more ratio.

Swing traders may have a lower ratio but make up for it with a higher win % while position traders may have 4:1, 6:1, or even higher but a lower win %.

All these combinations can be effective; it's about finding the style that suits you. All styles must keep their losses small, but they can differ in terms of the amount of trades they are taking to turn over their edge.

MAX GAIN

The max gain is the maximum gain you made over the period. This can help you know what's possible with your style.

MAX LOSS

Your max loss is the maximum loss you made over the period. Ideally this is nearly the same as your average loss. If you have a much larger max loss, make sure to identify what mistake you made and take steps to avoid it in the future.

You should also analyze any loss significantly higher than your average loss. Simply improving the tail end of the distribution of your losses can significantly improve your performance.

AVERAGE TRADE LENGTH FOR WINNERS

This is the average number of days from entry to exit of your winning trades. It can help tell you if you are letting your winners run. Ideally this is much longer than the average duration of your losers.

AVERAGE TRADE LENGTH FOR LOSERS

This is the average number of days from entry to exit of your losing trades. We want to minimize this as much as possible to make sure we are cutting losses fast and moving that capital toward the next potential winner.

EQUITY CURVE ANALYSIS

Your equity curve is the plot of your account value over time. It provides the truth about your trading. We ideally want it to resemble a staircase from bottom left to top right and avoid a lot of erratic moves up and down.

If you plot your equity curve and there are a lot of boom and bust periods, it means that you really need to work on your risk and position management.

Looking at your equity curve, pay special attention to large jumps and strong uptrends. These are your difference maker periods. Look back at your trades during these periods and your journals to identify what setups you were using, what stocks you traded, and any other important factors.

Study yourself at your best and try to replicate those actions as much as possible. Your performance will be somewhat correlated to the market, so don't forget how much of an impact that can have. The key is to try to flatten drawdowns in your equity curve which were caused by market corrections and pullbacks.

STUDYING YOUR TRADES

As we discussed above, in addition to calculating these metrics, you should review your best and worst trades on charts. You should do this with as many as you can, but to start with we recommend taking your top five to ten best and worst trades and marking them up.

Look for common factors in the trades to identify your strengths and weaknesses. This can be a game-changer in your performance.

With regular post analysis, you will start to notice tendencies. Once you do, use that feedback and analysis to adjust your trading rules to target your weaknesses and enhance your strengths.

If for example you notice all your biggest losses come from one type of setup, limit the use of that setup for a month or two and see how that impacts your data. Iterate, analyze, adjust, repeat.

Of course, you can't adjust your rules if you don't have any. This is a serious endeavor and is worthy of you spending the time to think through your system. Let's cover the process below and get your started.

THE IMPORTANCE OF BUILDING A TRADING RULE SET

What is the key to longevity in the markets? Certainly keeping losses small and allowing winners to run is part of it, but what does that really mean? How small will you cut losses and why? And how do you find stocks to trade in the first place? And how do you size them so a winner will actually have an impact?

The answer to these questions (and many others) should lie within your own personal set of trading rules. Your rules may look very different than ours, but they should still address the most important questions that govern your personal trading system.

And why is it important to have rules in the first place? Consistency in process and in actions will ultimately lead to success, with the caveat that you establish a feedback loop which constantly re-evaluates the system, makes adjustments and improvements, leading to continuous improvement.

Random actions lead to random inputs to the system, causing impulses which can bypass important protections and cause serious damage to your account and confidence.

So how do you become more disciplined? How can you make sure you avoid random actions and follow a strong plan? The answer is developing a robust rule set and actually following it.

WHY YOU NEED A SET OF TRADING RULES

If you are reading this and do not have a set of trading rules, then the most important thing you need to do to improve your performance is read through this entire section and spend a weekend or two outlining exactly how you will trade.

Similarly, if you have some rules but sometimes fail to abide by them, or often make trades outside of your system, then you need to put in more work, and make a rule set that you will actually follow 99% of the time.

And by the way, if your rules are not written down and outlined so clearly that someone with similar knowledge could follow them to a T, then you need to put in more time until it gets to that point. Rules in your head don't count, especially if you are in the first three or even five years of your journey. You haven't earned the right by successfully trading and managing risk through multiple market cycles to say you don't need written rules.

So we need rules, rules to manage risk, rules to govern our trading, rules to ensure that we protect our capital over time and can benefit from a long career of compounding.

As you read this section remember as we do so that everyone's rule set will look slightly different, and it will be catered toward their own personal situation, skills, interests, goals, style, and time frame. Feel free to get creative with this—add sections, add subsections, and even remove parts if you find it necessary. At the end of the day, your rules are for you.

Value yourself and spend significant time on this, revisit and revise occasionally, and you'll find that it will help answer key questions you may have, make you more confident, and improve your execution.

BUILDING YOUR RULE SET

As you write your rules, the focus should be on clarity, specificity, and depth.

A trader of similar skill and knowledge as yourself should be able to follow your process. This ensures that you are fully thinking through each aspect of your rules and are clarifying it enough for the rule to be usable.

For example, don't just say: "If the market is in an uptrend I will buy good stocks."

What is the market? How do you define an uptrend? What makes a good stock? How will you buy them? How much?

Instead it should look similar to something like this: If the Nasdaq Composite is above a rising 21 EMA I will look to buy 5% positions in five stocks with YoY EPS quarterly growth > 25% on breakouts from sound bases.

You don't have to define every little thing, but like we said you should define it well enough that a trader of similar experience level and style could follow.

Here are the sections that we encourage you to start with:

- Section 1: Market analysis
- Section 2: Stock selection and routines
- Section 3: Edges, setups, and entry tactics
- Section 4: Risk management and position sizing
- Section 5: Sell rules and position management
- Section 6: Post analysis and journaling
- Section 7: Contingency planning

We've covered each of these sections throughout this book, so as you define your rules, it may be helpful to re-read those parts of the handbook.

SECTION 1: MARKET ANALYSIS

Assessing the market, and really here we mean the larger context and current environment, is a key aspect of trading and reaching higher levels of performance.

MARKET AND TRENDS

The first part of the section should describe how you will analyze the larger market and determine the relevant trends for your time frame.

For instance, you can use a key moving average on an index or index ETF to define these trends. Using QQQ as an example, you can say that the market is in a short-term uptrend if it is above a rising 10 SMA, an intermediate-term uptrend if it is above a rising 21 EMA, and a long-term uptrend if it is above a rising 200 SMA.

You can use these definitions of trend later on in your rule set. For example:

> If the market is in a long-term downtrend but in an intermediate-term and short-term uptrend. I will look to increase exposure to 40% by purchasing strong stocks with 5% size.

GROUP AND THEME ANALYSIS

In addition to analyzing the general market, you also should have rules which help define your process for identifying both leading and lagging groups.

For instance, you can sort thematic ETFs by performance over different time frames to see what groups are performing well.

QUALITATIVE ANALYSIS OF THE PERFORMANCE OF CURRENT MARKET LEADERS

Speaking of leadership, it is extremely helpful to define what that means to you:

- How do you determine leadership?
- How will you add/remove stocks to your leadership list?

- How will you assess the health and breadth of leadership?
- How will your market analysis inform your actions?

Having written rules to identify the market environment and the status of leadership. You need to next determine how this will impact your trading decisions. You may find it helpful to come up with rule variations for the following market types.

- Uptrends on all time frames, strong leadership.
- Long-term uptrend, short-term downtrend, leaders weakening.
- Long-term downtrend, lack of leadership.
- Long-term downtrend, short-term uptrends, developing leadership.
- Choppy short- and medium-term trends, mixed leadership.

In these different situations you should be clear about position sizing, types of setups you will take, risk management rules, and general aggressiveness.

SECTION 2: STOCK SELECTION AND ROUTINES

STOCK SELECTION

Stock selection is an important aspect of trading. However, remember that even a great stock, when traded poorly, can lead to mediocre results. We want to focus on great stocks, but don't get so lost in the search for the absolutely perfect stock that you degrade the quality of your execution.

When it comes to stock selection, you want to create a universe of ideas that meet your criteria for a "high potential stock." How you define that specifically is up to your strategy.

In general, however, this should be a decent definition:

> A high-potential stock is a stock that has shown a display of power and strength, and has now setup in a repeatable pattern that provides the opportunity for an asymmetric reward to risk.

We are looking for stocks that through price and volume, have shown recent Relative Strength, have shown the character of a leader that can trend in the past, and are now presenting a setup where you can manage risk tightly and logically.

The stock should also ideally be part of an emerging theme where a group of stocks are together showing signs of accumulation. They will have a large runway in terms of new and developing products, and strong earnings, sales growth, and/or the anticipation of future growth through excellent estimates.

ROUTINES

In order to consistently find high-potential stocks at the correct moment, you need to develop routines to screen and manage watchlists as well as analyze the markets.

Review Chapter 9 for an in-depth walkthrough of what to include here.

SECTION 3: EDGES, SETUPS, AND ENTRY TACTICS

In this section of your rules, you should define the specific edges, setups, and entry tactics you will use to trade high-potential stocks.

This goes hand in hand with stock selection as you should be focusing your watchlist on stocks that are showing many edges, and presenting chart patterns that are constructive and tradable.

For further detail and guidance on this section of your rules, review Chapters 4 and 5.

You should include in this section a database with chart examples of the edges, setups, and entry tactics you will use. Creating this database not only provides you with precedents that you can refer back to, but it also helps build intuition and clarifies exactly what you are looking for.

SECTION 4: RISK MANAGEMENT AND POSITION SIZING

This section should outline your process for managing risk for the different setups and tactics you trade. This includes how you will set and adjust stop losses.

You should also define for yourself the amount of total risk you will have in different market conditions and situations, as well as when you might go on margin and by how much.

You should also define your process for sizing positions, including what your starting size is, and if and how you would increase your size. This includes defining a maximum position size.

Review Chapter 6 for help with this section.

SECTION 5: SELL RULES AND POSITION MANAGEMENT

In this section you should define how you will manage positions. This includes trade execution, selling into weakness, and selling into strength.

Chapter 7 should be a helpful resource here.

SECTION 6: POST ANALYSIS AND JOURNALING

In this section you should lay out how often you will analyze your trading and what you will do each time.

You should also cover your process for journaling and also when/how you will update your rules based on your post-trade analysis. The early part of this chapter should be reviewed as you plan out these rules.

SECTION 7: CONTINGENCY PLANNING

There are a lot of special cases and potentially devastating scenarios associated with trading. Thousands of dollars are on the line, and you should try to plan for anything that can happen.

> How will you handle it if one of your positions gaps down huge on earnings or news?
>
> How will you trade if you lose power or internet?

Where and how will you store important passwords to your broker?

What will you do if you are locked out of your accounts?

What are important numbers that you should have quick access to just in case?

These are some examples of situations that you should address in this section.

TRADER'S HANDBOOK CHALLENGE 8

Write your trading rules.

For this exercise, write or revise your trading rule set. Take your time with this and think things through. Your trading rules are for your benefit; they are part of your contract with yourself that you will be taking trading seriously. Be sure to share your work on twitter and tweet at us @TraderLion_ and #THChallenge.

KEY TAKEAWAYS

Here are five key takeaways from this chapter:

1. Post analysis of your trading will allow you to understand your strengths and weaknesses.
2. Analyzing your worst performing stock can help you dramatically improve your performance.
3. Journaling can help you stay in tune with your thoughts and actions.

4. Your trading statistics reveal the truth about your trading, and can help you understand which parts of your system to focus on improving.
5. Trading rules define our system. They are a living document you will update over time as you evolve as a trader.

BONUS RESOURCE

We recorded a webinar about post analysis and we also include a free trade log which can calculate key stats for you.

You can watch it today at traderlion.com/handbook.

CHAPTER 11
FINDING NEW EDGES, SETUPS, AND ENTRY TACTICS

"Once you stop learning you start dying."

—Albert Einstein

HOW CAN YOU find new edges and setups, and adapt your trading as the markets change over time? That's the question that we aim to answer in this chapter.

We will answer it in two parts. First we will cover our process for studying the market and running experiments to test out new ideas. Then we will discuss how you can create model books: Resources that are focused on studying the top-performing stocks to build references for future trades.

If you are newer to trading, this chapter will be a great way for you to structure a deep dive into an edge/setup/entry tactic that you learned in this book or elsewhere, and to build confidence in that setup.

If you are more advanced, the same blueprint can help you investigate observations that you have noticed during your trading, and you can then create your own setups and structure.

This chapter is where your passion for the markets comes alive as you can put on your scientist hat and explore new ideas.

Here's a quick outline of what we will cover:

- Trading studies:
  - coming up with ideas
  - defining a study
  - collecting examples and data
  - analyzing the results
  - drawing conclusions.
- Building model books.

Now let's dive in!

TRADING STUDIES

COMING UP WITH IDEAS

The first step to completing a trading study is being motivated to start one. This may sound a bit funny, but in order to complete a trading study you need to be passionate enough about the particular topic to really spend the time collecting and analyzing data.

The ideas you pick to study should be reasonably focused, and it can be anything that you are curious about with respect to the markets or trading.

A great place to start is a trading setup or pattern that you wish to learn more about and add to your arsenal. You can also find ideas by reading trading books, listening to what other traders have studied or how they trade, or by analyzing previous model book stock moves.

Here are some questions that can help you find a topic:

- If there was one setup that you wanted to learn more about, what would it be?
- What part of trading do you think is your weakness? What specifically do you need to work on?
- When you look at past stocks, what stands out to you that they all seem to share?
- When you listen to market wizards, what stands out to you as the reason for their success? Is it something that you can investigate further to learn more about?
- Is there a very unique model book stock that you have noticed recently? What made it different?
- What are some commonly accepted truths about the market that you've found are not always the case with real trading?
- Are there any strategies that you've learned about from traders of other time frames that you think could apply to your style?
- How would your personal performance have changed if you tweaked your entries or exit rules, say only sold if a stock closed twice below the 21ema?

You can study a setup, an indicator signal, dive deep into a particular model book stock, or anything else that you would love to learn more about.

Once you have a few ideas, think about which of them you want to focus on. There will be plenty of downtime during market corrections or after market hours to get to all of them eventually.

DEFINING A STUDY

Once you have your topic in mind, verify that it is focused enough that you could reasonably expect to complete the study in about a month.

We've found through personal experience that most studies take a lot longer to complete than we expect, especially if we are very ambitious from the start.

A month-long study will likely turn into two to three months, so make sure you set reasonable expectations with yourself about how much time you can commit to the study.

Also make sure that the topic is feasible, meaning that you have access to the data or programs needed to complete it. Excel can get most people pretty far once they learn to use a few formulas, but data is not always available.

Once you have your scope set, you should be able to phrase it in a similar format to this:

> I will complete a trading study on ____________ with the goal of ____________________. To do this I will ____________________ and then ________________ to come up with my conclusion.

An example would be:

> I will complete a trading study on large gap downs with the goal of defining a tradable setup. To do this I will collect many examples of gap downs that successfully rebounded as well as failed and then analyze them to find common characteristics and patterns.

or

I will complete a trading study of Google's IPO move with the goal of identifying entry points as well as characteristics that led to its success. To do this I will analyze the price and volume data as well as research news catalysts during the time and then create a detailed case study with my findings.

Gap Down Study Example

Google IPO Base Study Example

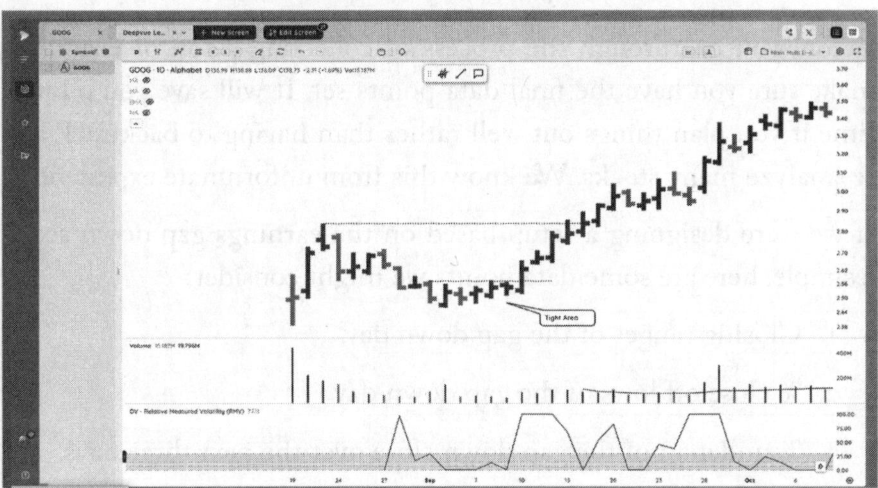

We also highly recommend at this point that you try to find a few friends who would also be interested in this study. This can split up the workload going forward and invite different perspectives and questions.

COLLECTING EXAMPLES AND DATA

The next step is to define the exact data you need and how you will use it. Be very specific and again remember to try to keep the study as focused as possible.

Motivation is high at the beginning of a study, but you want to make sure that you are not biting off more than you can chew later. You can always do follow-up studies later based on your findings and expand the scope.

Next, you will want to create a data table and add a few examples. Collect the data you want from these examples and analyze them completely.

Going through this process with just a few examples will show you any blind spots you may have in your scope or study design. Make any adjustments necessary to your study design.

Before you go through the process of collecting a ton of examples, make sure you have the final data points set. It will save you a lot of time if you plan things out well rather than having to backtrack and re-analyze many stocks. We know this from unfortunate experiences.

If we were designing a setup based on the earnings gap down scope example, here are some data points we might consider:

1. Closing ranges of the gap down day.
2. % close off lows of the gap down day.
3. % undercut of the gap down close over the next three days.
4. Volume compared to average of the gap down day.

5. % the gap down low is below the 50 SMA.
6. % from the gap down low after five days.
7. Trends of the ten day, 21 EMA, 50 SMA, 200 SMA before the gap down.
8. QQQ versus the 21 EMA.
9. Performance from the gap down one month later.
10. Performance from the gap down three months later.
11. Performance from the gap down six months later.

If you have an example of the setup that worked particularly well, really analyze its chart and the characteristics that defined the move. This can help you come up with important data points.

Especially when studying a pattern or setup, we find it is very important to collect examples from different time periods and market environments. You can even track these as data points and be able to come up with very interesting conclusions (if you have a statistically relevant sample size). As an example: "Earnings gap ups have a 70% success rate when the QQQ is above the 21 EMA but only a 40% success rate when it is below."

These numbers are just examples, but you can see how that kind of information can give you a real edge and deeper understanding of a setup.

ANALYZING THE RESULTS

Once you have the data, make sure it is organized, and you are not missing anything. You will be amazed at how annoying it can be to have to redo analysis after finding that you pasted in a column incorrectly.

Next write down a handful of hypotheses after collecting all the examples and looking at their charts. They should be testable based on the data you have.

Some examples:

- I hypothesize that stocks which are higher than the gap down close three days later are more likely to outperform over the next few months.
- I hypothesize that stocks whose gap down lows were more than 30% below the 50 SMA are more likely to outperform over the next few months.

The benefit of having the data is that you can always come up with new questions to answer.

The next step is to make plots of your data. Plot characteristics of the setup versus their performance over the next few months, and note any trends or interesting observations you see.

You can also look to group your examples based on similar data points or outcomes. Think about what characteristics the most successful examples share.

It's also very helpful to analyze outliers in the data. How are they different than the others? How did that impact things?

You should also remember to be open-minded. You may not find any commonalities or key results and that's OK! Or you may find that your hypotheses were completely wrong. Let the data guide your thinking.

DRAWING CONCLUSIONS

Once you have analyzed the data and jotted down any initial observations, organize your findings in a document and summarize your key takeaways.

Include any relevant plots or charts for quick access in the future. You can also have a section that contains key statistics that you found from your data.

These questions can help you with the final report:

- What was the most significant finding from the study?
- Which of your hypotheses were definitely true or false? Which were ambiguous?
- What key statistics did you find that could help your trading?
- How did the market environment impact the performance of the setup?
- What was the most interesting plot of your data? Why?
- What was the most surprising thing you learned?
- What would you like to investigate in a follow-up study?

Once you have completed your study, we recommend you share the findings with others to get their perspectives.

That's it! You've now completed your first study and taken a definitive step toward expanding your trading knowledge.

BUILDING MODEL BOOKS

THE IMPORTANCE OF BUILDING MODEL BOOKS

A crucial step in a trader's journey is when they focus on studying the past to analyze what factors led to winning trades and what repeatable setups existed in the market.

During these studies, you should build repositories of examples grouped by market cycle, type of setup, or other similarity.

You can then use these model books to search precedents from the past that can help you perform in future market cycles.

But first, let's define a model book even further.

WHAT IS A MODEL BOOK?

A model book is a compilation of the highest quality, best-performing stocks over any particular period or cycle. For each stock, both fundamental and technical data relevant to that period are included and then "marked up" with detailed notes.

Model books serve two purposes:

1. They serve as a reference of historical precedent which can be referred back to and applied to a relevant, current situation.
2. Going through the process of creating your own model book gives you a deep, detailed understanding of what these stocks look like, time after time, cycle after cycle, as well as some of the inherent differences, based on things such as a particular stock's personality, liquidity, size, etc.

BUILDING MODEL BOOKS AT O'NEIL

When I was a portfolio manager at O'Neil I was tasked with building the 1998–2000 model book with Mike Webster and Charles Harris.

This was certainly a very interesting market cycle to study. I learned a lot from this experience, especially working with Bill to select the top stocks from this time period.

One of the first things I noticed about Bill is that he was incredibly selective with the stocks we included in the book. They had to be textbook CANSLIM and fit his model of the greatest performing stocks of all time.

Many of the stocks that I and the other portfolio managers traded in our personal accounts most definitely did not fit the bill.

O'Neil focused on the highest quality stocks with standout earnings and sales growth as well as the N-factor in CANSLIM.

Personally, when building my own model books, I do not require every single CANSLIM criteria to be met. However, I do focus on liquid stocks which trade tightly in an organized manner, since that is what I prefer to trade.

THE STEPS OF BUILDING A MODEL BOOK

There are six main steps to building a model book:

1. Determine the scope of the model book.
2. Building a larger list.
3. Finalizing a smaller list.
4. Researching fundamental drivers.
5. Annotating the charts.
6. Building the model book.

Let's dive into each one with more detail.

STEP 1: DETERMINE THE SCOPE OF THE MODEL BOOK

The first step of the process is to determine the scope of the model book. This depends on the type of reference you wish to create.

The model books that I built for the firm and now for TraderLion focus on different market cycles or years. However, you could also build a model book organized around studying a particular setup or group of stocks such as IPOs or Stage 2 Breakouts.

The bottom line is that a model book should help you study winners and be able to serve as a reference for future trades. I like building them covering full market cycles because it will show how leaders break out, make their moves, and then ultimately break down.

STEP 2: BUILD A LARGER LIST

Once you have determined the scope of the model book, the next step is to start to source ideas and build a larger list of stocks to choose from.

Cast a wide net at first as this will help you study history and determine a better idea of what you are looking for.

For building yearly or market cycle model books I like to start with looking at the best-performing stocks each year. You can use a screening software for this or simply google top-performing stocks for 202x.

STEP 3: FINALIZE A SMALLER LIST

After you have created a larger universe of stocks to sort through, it's time to be extremely selective and only accept the best examples.

This could be based on % moves, liquidity, trading style… based on your preferences. I would suggest focusing on only a select few stocks, especially if this is your first model book. Some very strong years, like in 2020, you may have a large list of market leaders, but most years won't have quite so many prime model book stocks.

I consider acceleration in earnings and sales, institutional sponsorship, and last but not least, the N in CANSLIM, meaning the story, key driver, or metric behind each stock.

The final list should be both representative of the leading themes of the market cycle and contain excellent charts to study.

STEP 4: RESEARCH FUNDAMENTAL DRIVERS

After you have your final list, the next step is to start analyzing the stocks from both a fundamental and technical perspective.

I like to include a summary of the business and a description of the company. Then I note how the group and sector of the stock performed over the course of the year. Finally, I look at the earnings growth, sales growth, fund sponsorship, and any other standout CANSLIM fundamentals.

I suggest looking into any other fundamental factors that could have contributed to the stock's performance, such as a new product announcement or significant change in management.

STEP 5: ANNOTATE THE CHARTS

The next step is to analyze the stock's chart throughout its entire move. You want to highlight any important price and volume characteristics for your trading style as well as potential entry and exit points.

One key aspect of my annotations is looking at the Relative Strength line to watch for periods of outperformance and Relative Strength new highs before price. This is a key characteristic that I have noticed in market leaders cycle after cycle.

Here is an example of chart annotations and the Relative Strength line new high before price from the TraderLion 2020 model book. You can access this for free at TraderLion.com.

Model Book Annotation Example: DOCU 2020 TraderLion Model Book

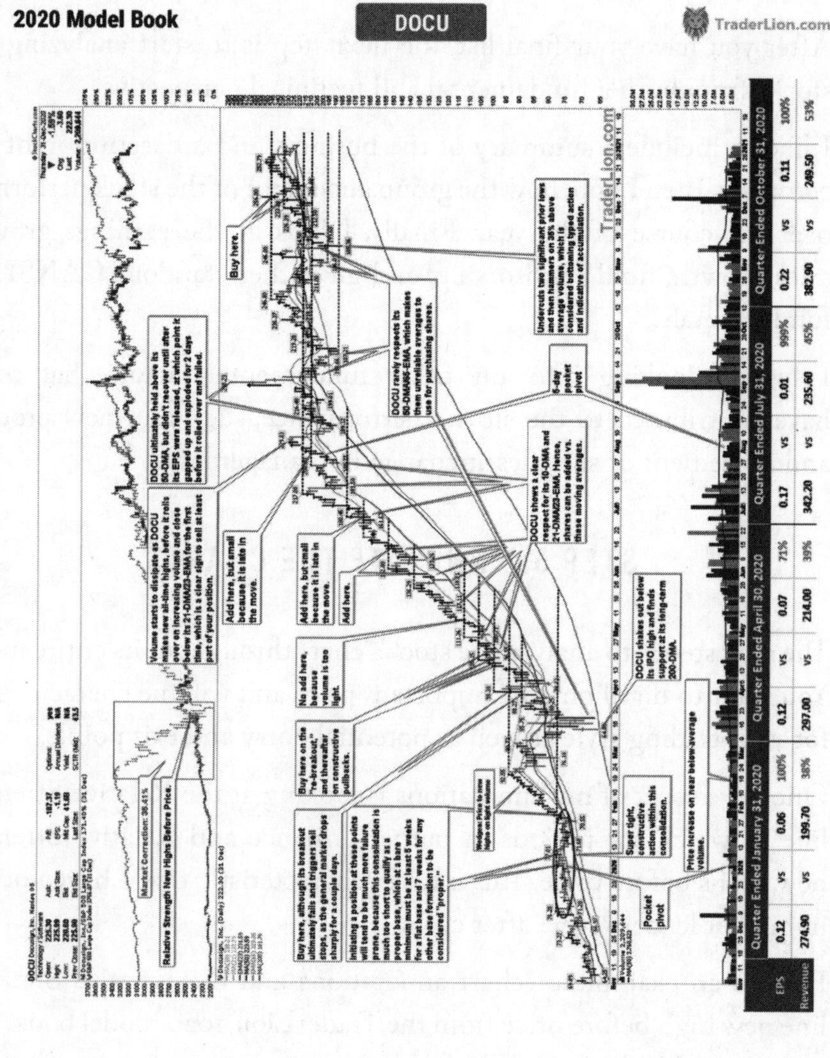

STEP 6: BUILD THE MODEL BOOK

To build the final model book we use a graphic design tool like Canva (several are available online) to organize both the fundamental and technical information into one document. On one page I include the fundamental information and then on the next the annotated chart with earnings and sales growth.

KEY TAKEAWAY

As I have mentioned in the past, one of the most important takeaways from building model books has been the consolidation pivot entry. It allows you to begin your position at low-risk entry points up the right side of a promising stock's base, much earlier than waiting for a traditional base breakout to occur.

I've also noticed that even when you think you have missed a true market leader's move, it will almost always present another low-risk entry point, such as a pullback to a pivot or key moving average. As you build your own model books, you will come up with your own takeaways that you can apply to future trades and market cycles.

ADVICE FOR BUILDING MODEL BOOKS

I strongly believe that every trader should build model books of winning stocks. It is one of the best ways to study and build a strong intuition/conviction surrounding different setups.

As I mentioned before, traders should focus on a small set of stocks at first and analyze them deeply. Then as you become more familiar with the process and gain experience, you can expand your focus.

TRADER'S HANDBOOK CHALLENGE 9

Construct your own model book using stocks from the most recent year. Be sure to share your work on twitter and tweet at us @TraderLion_ and #THChallenge.

KEY TAKEAWAYS

Here are five key takeaways from this chapter:

1. Trading studies are an excellent way to continue to improve your performance as a trader.
2. You should choose ideas that you are passionate about studying.
3. Refine the scope of your trading study to ensure that it is manageable.
4. Model books allow you to learn the template for winning trades.
5. A model book is a compilation of the highest quality, best-performing stocks over any particular period or cycle. For each stock, both fundamental and technical data relevant to that period are included and then "marked up" with detailed notes.

BONUS RESOURCE

Looking for inspiration or just want to study our model books? They are available for free 2018 onward on TraderLion.com.

You can find them linked at traderlion.com/handbook.

CHAPTER 12
CHARTS WORTH STUDYING

> "The first step in learning to pick stock market winners is for you to examine leading winners of the past to learn all the characteristics of the most successful stocks."
>
> —***William O'Neil***

TO GIVE YOU a head start on studying top performing stocks, we wanted to include this bonus chapter of many market leaders from the recent past.

We've compiled over 120 annotated stocks for your review. Each has important lessons that you can apply to your own trading.

Take your time and study how they set up, break out, trend, and ultimately pullback and breakdown.

With enough careful analysis, you will start to recognize the commonalities and phases among these stocks that you will be able to identify in real time going forward.

We've broken down these charts into different sections:

- Base Breakouts
- Failed Base Breakouts
- Gaps
- Failed Gaps
- 2016 and Earlier Market Leaders
- 2017 Market Leaders
- 2018 Market Leaders
- 2019 Market Leaders
- 2020 Market Leaders
- 2021 Market Leaders
- 2022 Market Leaders
- 2023 Market Leaders
- 2024 Market Leaders

TRADER'S HANDBOOK CHALLENGE 10

After going through all of these charts, pick three of your own and annotate them in a similar manner. Label key price and volume characteristics, entries, exits, and any other relevant details.

Be sure to share your work on twitter and tweet at us @TraderLion_ and #THChallenge.

BASE BREAKOUTS

This section focuses on textbook examples of trading up the right side of a base and finally the base breakout.

This includes highlighting early entries such as upside reversals, range breakouts, inside days and more.

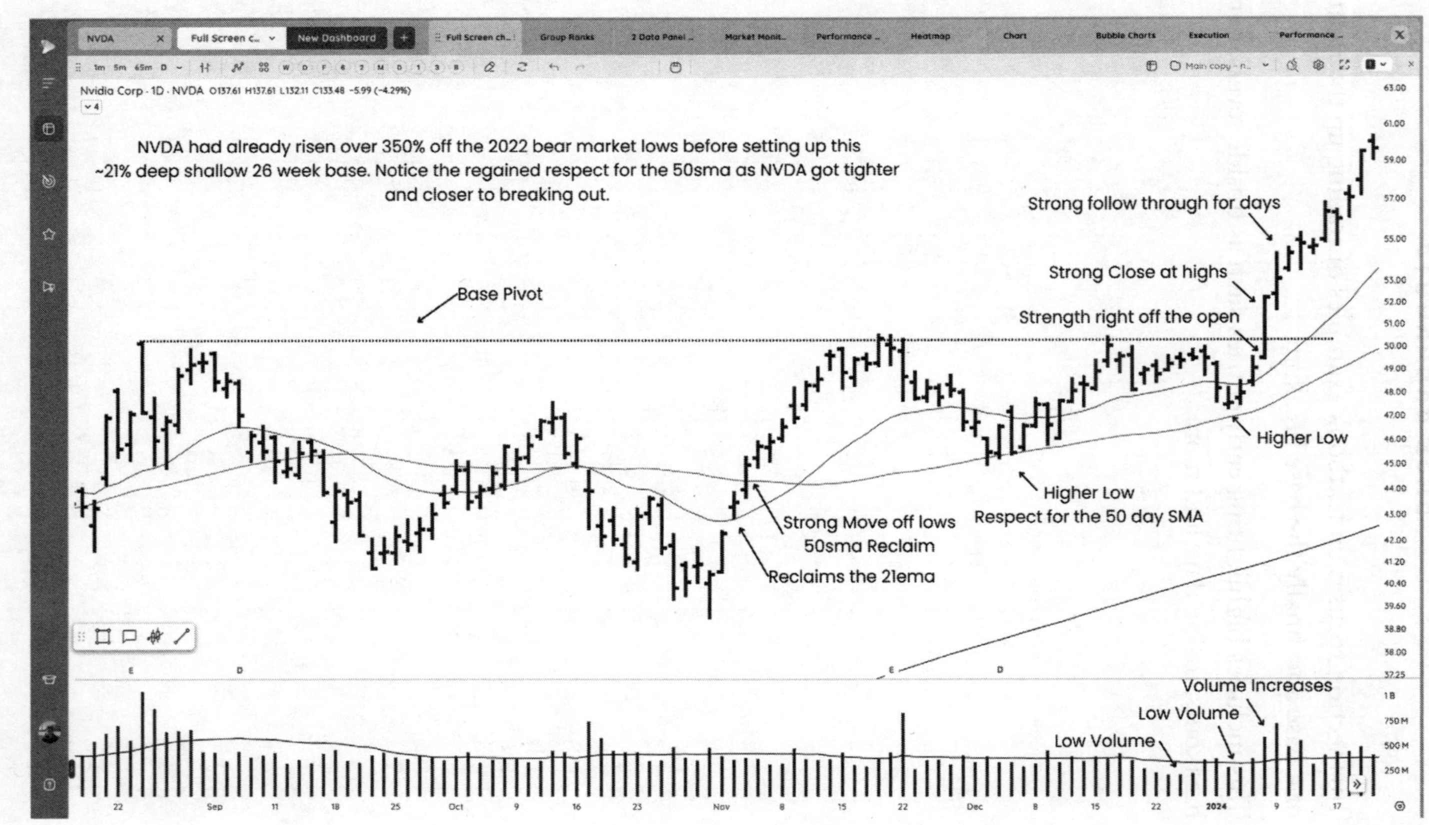
NVDA 2024 Daily Base Breakout – 180% in 23 Weeks
Nvidia Corp · 1D · NVDA O137.61 H137.61 L132.11 C133.48 −5.99 (−4.29%)
NVDA had already risen over 350% off the 2022 bear market lows before setting up this
~21% deep shallow 26 week base. Notice the regained respect for the 50sma as NVDA got tighter
and closer to breaking out.
Base Pivot
Strong follow through for days
Strong Close at highs
Strength right off the open
Higher Low
Higher Low
Respect for the 50 day SMA
Strong Move off lows
50sma Reclaim
Reclaims the 21ema
Volume Increases
Low Volume
Low Volume

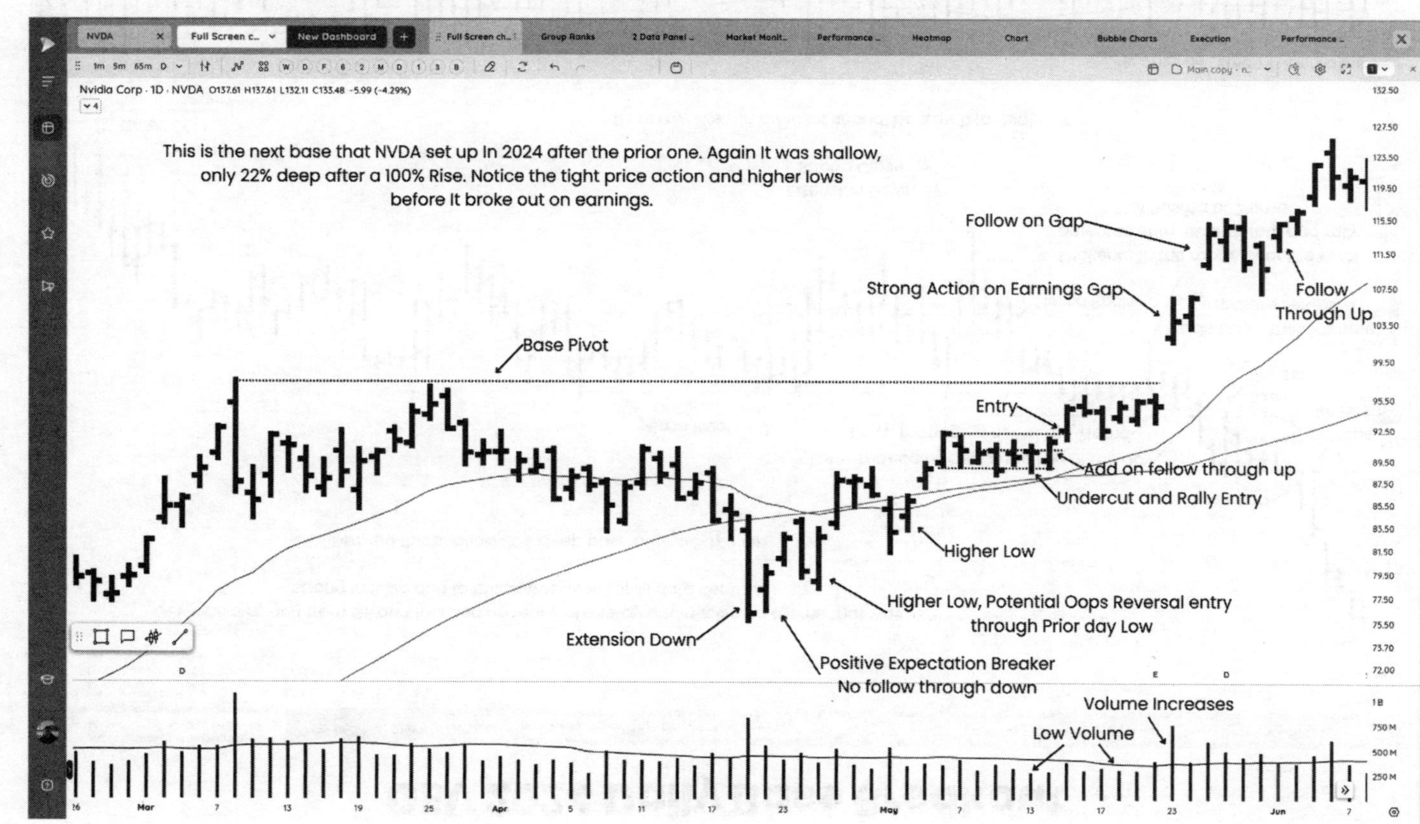
NVDA 2024 Daily Base Breakout- 50% Rise In 24 Days
Nvidia Corp · 1D · NVDA O137.61 H137.61 L132.11 C133.48 -5.99 (-4.29%)
This is the next base that NVDA set up in 2024 after the prior one. Again it was shallow, only 22% deep after a 100% Rise. Notice the tight price action and higher lows before it broke out on earnings.
Follow on Gap
Strong Action on Earnings Gap
Follow Through Up
Base Pivot
Entry
Add on follow through up
Undercut and Rally Entry
Higher Low
Higher Low, Potential Oops Reversal entry through Prior day Low
Extension Down
Positive Expectation Breaker No follow through down
Volume Increases
Low Volume

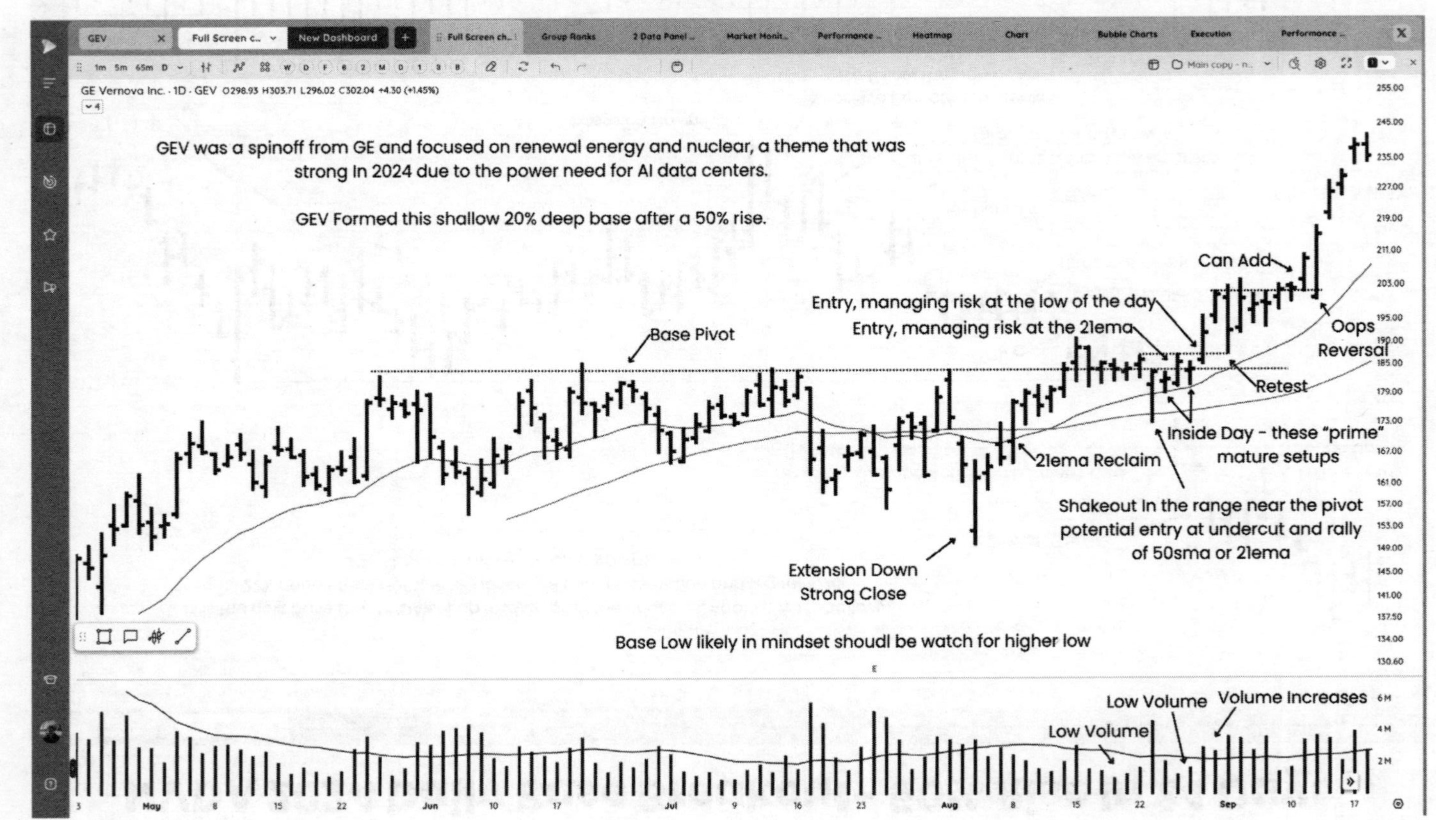
GEV 2024 Daily Base Breakout
GE Vernova Inc. · 1D · GEV O298.93 H303.71 L296.02 C302.04 +4.30 (+1.45%)
GEV was a spinoff from GE and focused on renewal energy and nuclear, a theme that was strong in 2024 due to the power need for AI data centers.
GEV Formed this shallow 20% deep base after a 50% rise.
Base Pivot
Entry, managing risk at the low of the day
Entry, managing risk at the 21ema
Can Add
Oops Reversal
Retest
Inside Day - these "prime" mature setups
21ema Reclaim
Shakeout In the range near the pivot potential entry at undercut and rally of 50sma or 21ema
Extension Down Strong Close
Base Low likely in mindset shoudl be watch for higher low
Low Volume
Low Volume
Volume Increases

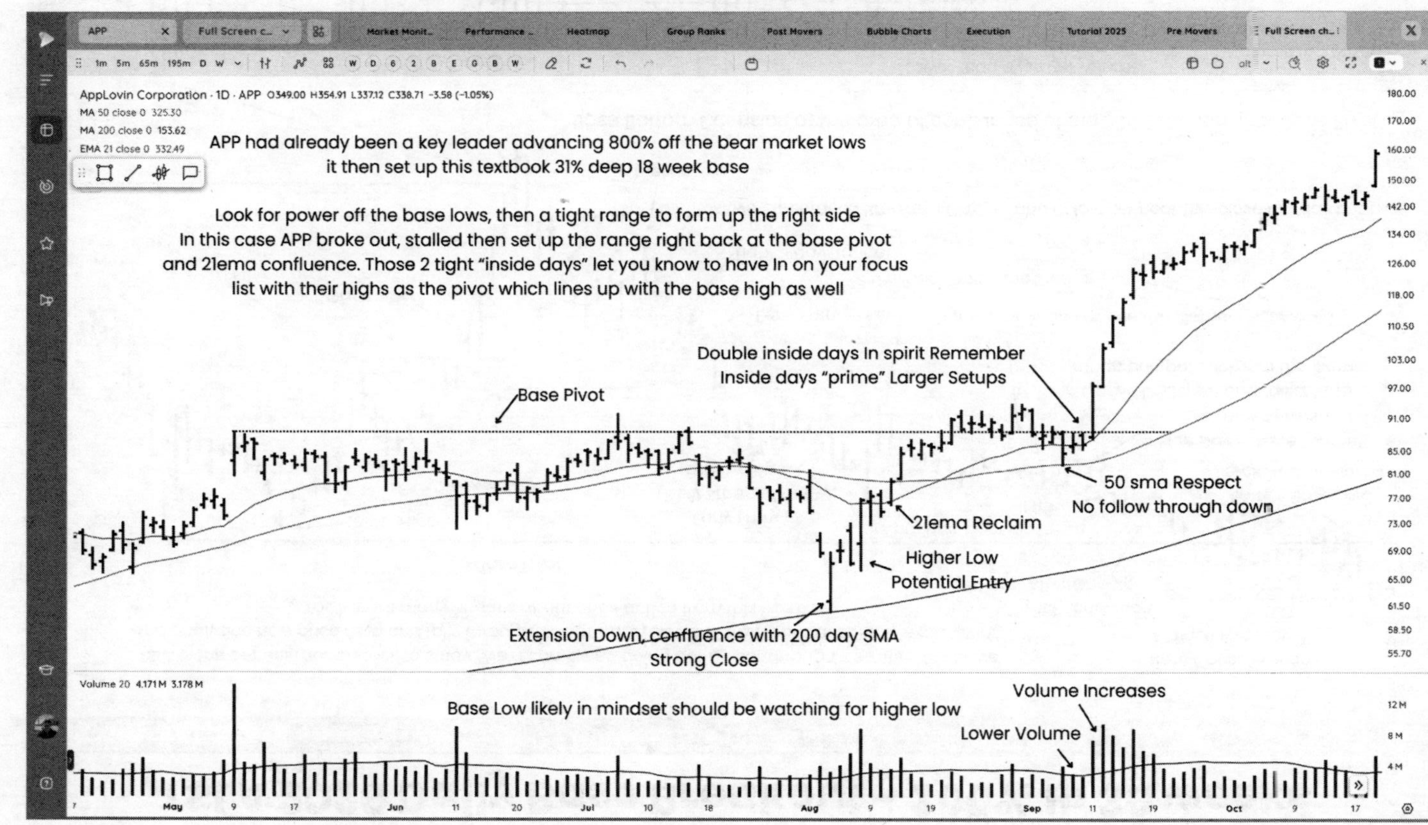
APP 2024 Daily Base Breakout
AppLovin Corporation · 1D · APP O349.00 H354.91 L337.12 C338.71 −3.58 (−1.05%)
MA 50 close 0 325.30
MA 200 close 0 153.62
EMA 21 close 0 332.49
APP had already been a key leader advancing 800% off the bear market lows
it then set up this textbook 31% deep 18 week base
Look for power off the base lows, then a tight range to form up the right side
In this case APP broke out, stalled then set up the range right back at the base pivot
and 21ema confluence. Those 2 tight "inside days" let you know to have In on your focus
list with their highs as the pivot which lines up with the base high as well
Base Pivot
Double inside days In spirit Remember
Inside days "prime" Larger Setups
50 sma Respect
No follow through down
21ema Reclaim
Higher Low
Potential Entry
Extension Down, confluence with 200 day SMA
Strong Close
Volume 20 4.171M 3.178M
Base Low likely in mindset should be watching for higher low
Volume Increases
Lower Volume
May
Jun
Jul
Aug
Sep
Oct

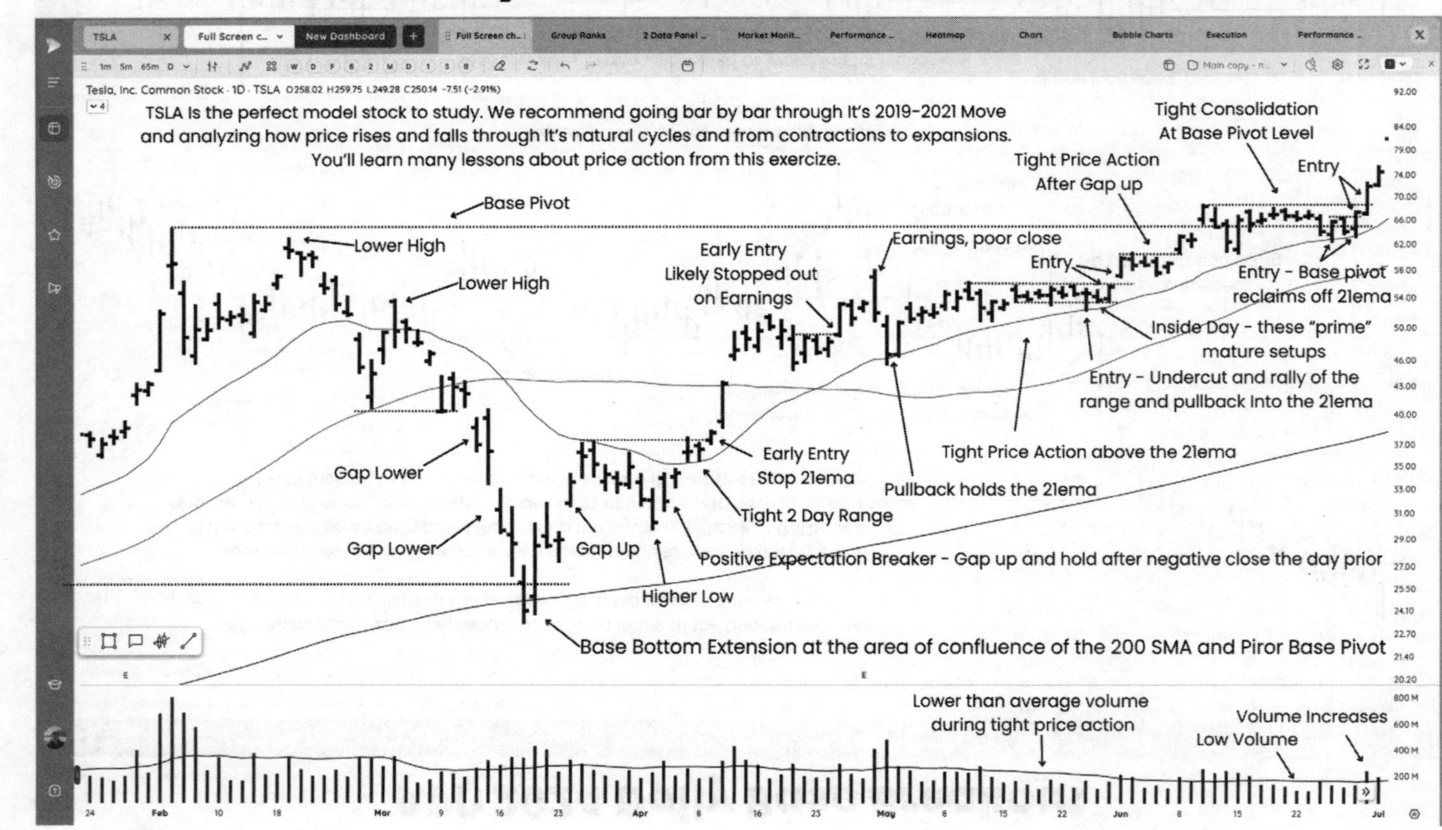
TSLA 2020 Daily Base Breakout – 300% In 30 weeks
TSLA Is the perfect model stock to study. We recommend going bar by bar through It's 2019-2021 Move
and analyzing how price rises and falls through It's natural cycles and from contractions to expansions.
You'll learn many lessons about price action from this exercize.
Base Pivot
Lower High
Lower High
Gap Lower
Gap Lower
Early Entry
Likely Stopped out
on Earnings
Earnings, poor close
Tight Price Action
After Gap up
Tight Consolidation
At Base Pivot Level
Entry
Entry
Entry – Base pivot
reclaims off 21ema
Inside Day – these "prime"
mature setups
Entry – Undercut and rally of the
range and pullback Into the 21ema
Tight Price Action above the 21ema
Pullback holds the 21ema
Early Entry
Stop 21ema
Tight 2 Day Range
Gap Up
Positive Expectation Breaker – Gap up and hold after negative close the day prior
Higher Low
Base Bottom Extension at the area of confluence of the 200 SMA and Piror Base Pivot
Lower than average volume
during tight price action
Low Volume
Volume Increases

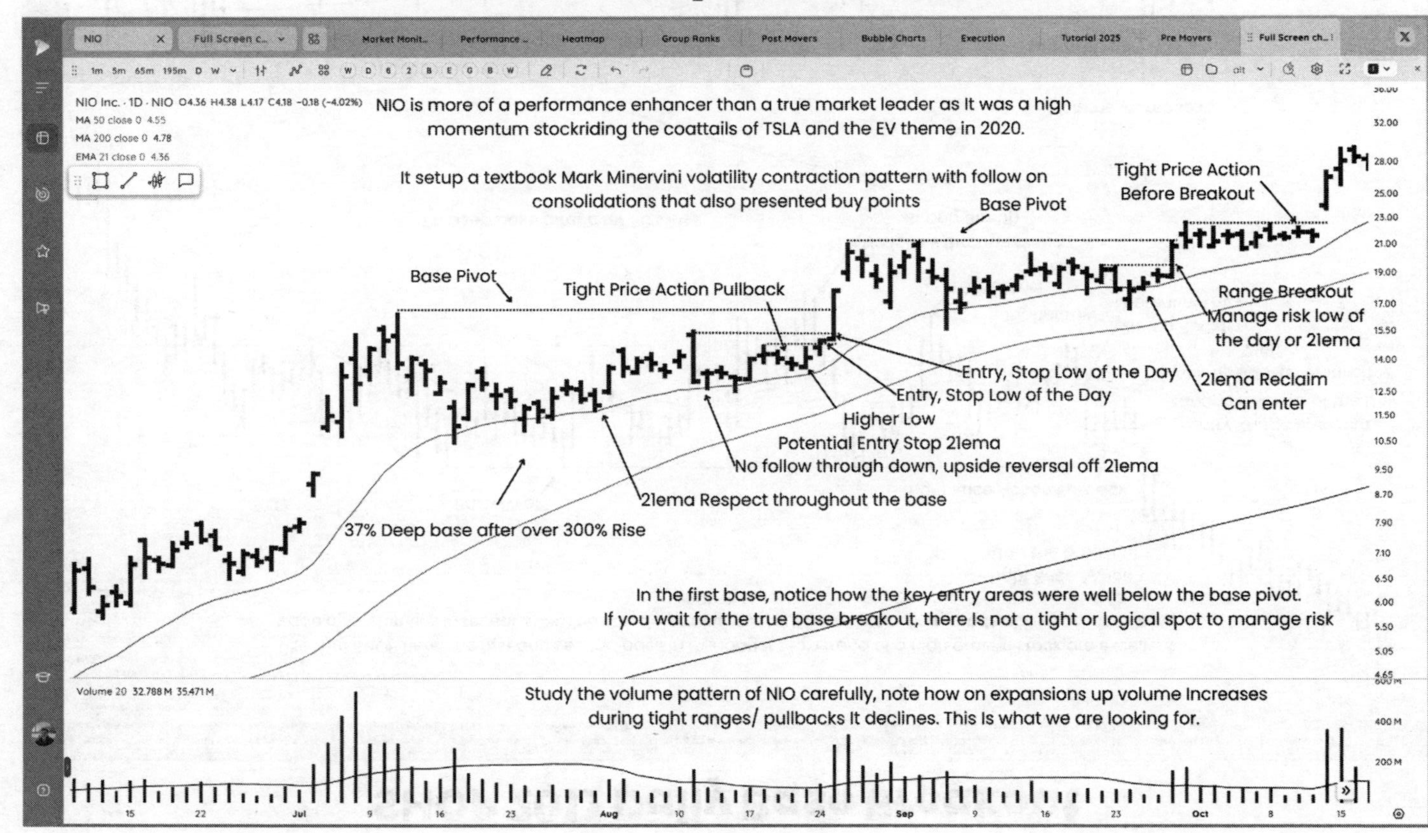
NIO 2020 Daily Base Breakout
NIO Inc. · 1D · NIO O4.36 H4.38 L4.17 C4.18 −0.18 (−4.02%)
MA 50 close 0 4.55
MA 200 close 0 4.78
EMA 21 close 0 4.36
NIO is more of a performance enhancer than a true market leader as It was a high momentum stockriding the coattails of TSLA and the EV theme in 2020.
It setup a textbook Mark Minervini volatility contraction pattern with follow on consolidations that also presented buy points
Base Pivot
Tight Price Action Pullback
Base Pivot
Tight Price Action Before Breakout
Range Breakout
Manage risk low of the day or 21ema
21ema Reclaim Can enter
Entry, Stop Low of the Day
Entry, Stop Low of the Day
Higher Low
Potential Entry Stop 21ema
No follow through down, upside reversal off 21ema
21ema Respect throughout the base
37% Deep base after over 300% Rise
In the first base, notice how the key entry areas were well below the base pivot.
If you wait for the true base breakout, there Is not a tight or logical spot to manage risk
Study the volume pattern of NIO carefully, note how on expansions up volume Increases during tight ranges/ pullbacks It declines. This Is what we are looking for.
Volume 20 32.788 M 35.471 M

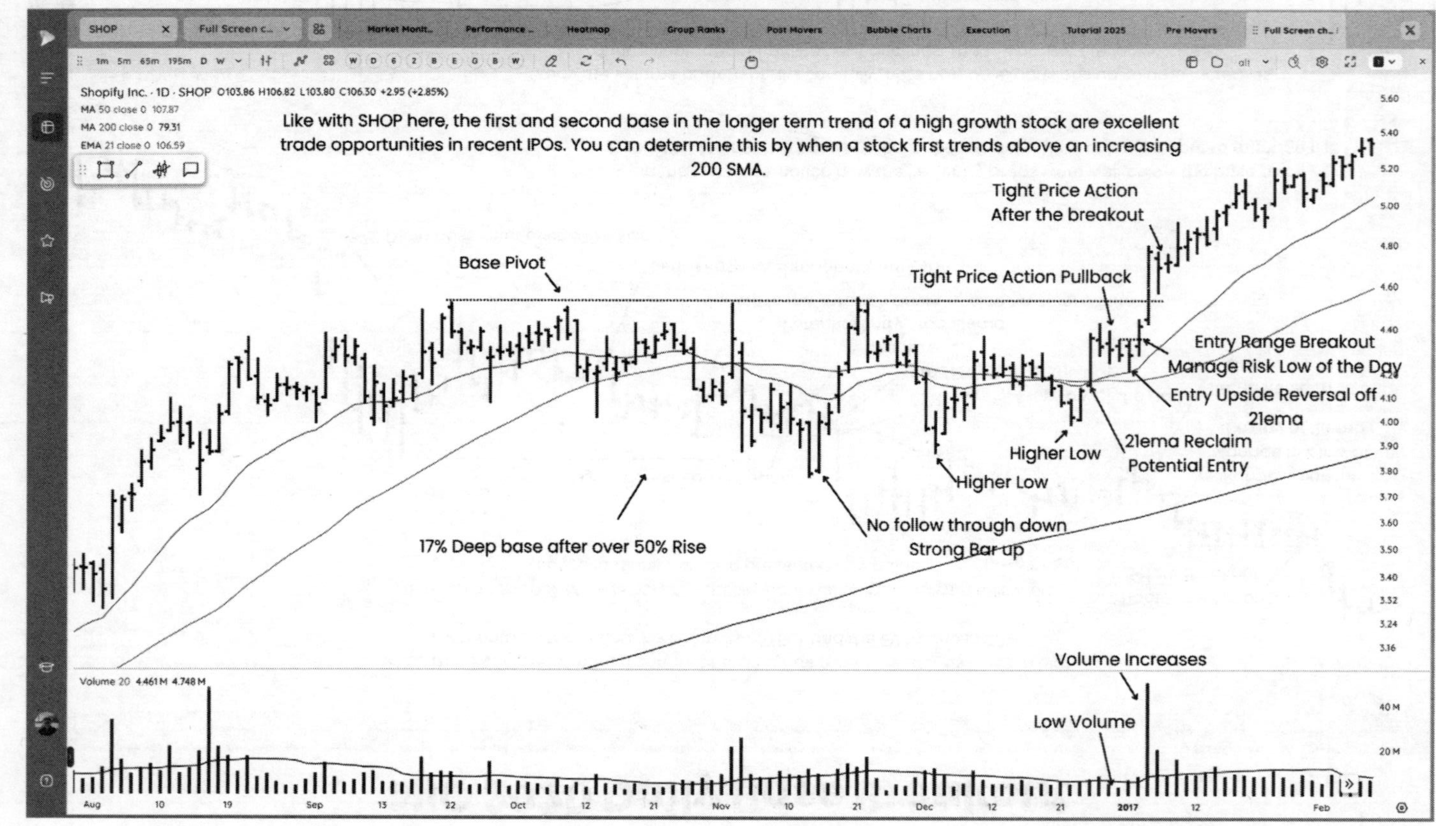
SHOP 2017 Daily Base Breakout
Shopify Inc. · 1D · SHOP O103.86 H106.82 L103.80 C106.30 +2.95 (+2.85%)
MA 50 close 0 107.87
MA 200 close 0 79.31
EMA 21 close 0 106.59
Like with SHOP here, the first and second base in the longer term trend of a high growth stock are excellent trade opportunities in recent IPOs. You can determine this by when a stock first trends above an increasing 200 SMA.
Tight Price Action
After the breakout
Base Pivot
Tight Price Action Pullback
Entry Range Breakout
Manage Risk Low of the Day
Entry Upside Reversal off
21ema
21ema Reclaim
Potential Entry
Higher Low
Higher Low
No follow through down
Strong Bar up
17% Deep base after over 50% Rise
Volume Increases
Low Volume

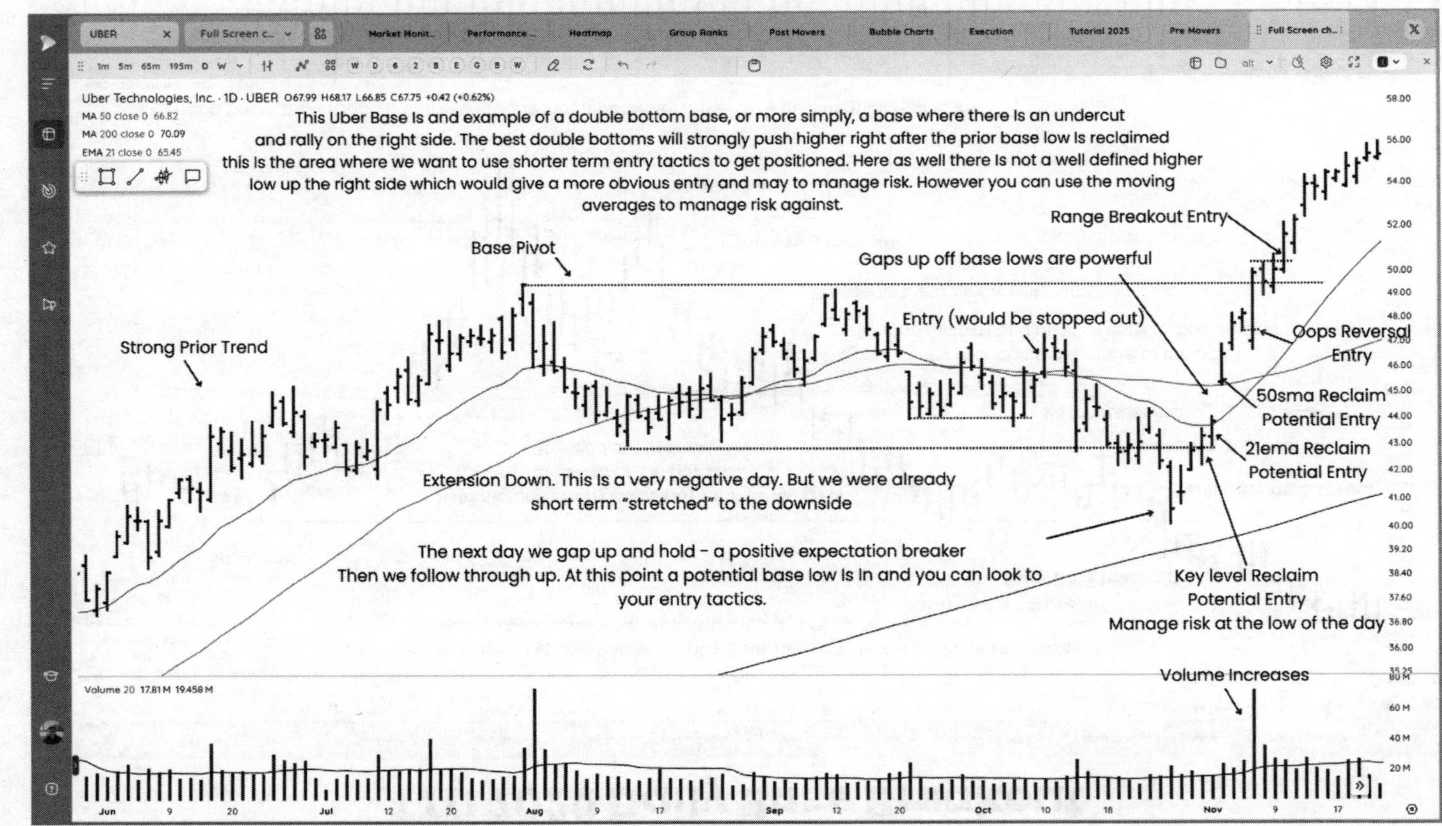
UBER 2023 Daily Base Breakout
Uber Technologies, Inc. · 1D · UBER O67.99 H68.17 L66.85 C67.75 +0.42 (+0.62%)
MA 50 close 0 66.82
MA 200 close 0 70.09
EMA 21 close 0 65.45
This Uber Base is and example of a double bottom base, or more simply, a base where there is an undercut
and rally on the right side. The best double bottoms will strongly push higher right after the prior base low is reclaimed
this is the area where we want to use shorter term entry tactics to get positioned. Here as well there is not a well defined higher
low up the right side which would give a more obvious entry and may to manage risk. However you can use the moving
averages to manage risk against.
Strong Prior Trend
Base Pivot
Range Breakout Entry
Gaps up off base lows are powerful
Entry (would be stopped out)
Oops Reversal
Entry
50sma Reclaim
Potential Entry
21ema Reclaim
Potential Entry
Extension Down. This is a very negative day. But we were already
short term "stretched" to the downside
The next day we gap up and hold - a positive expectation breaker
Then we follow through up. At this point a potential base low is in and you can look to
your entry tactics.
Key level Reclaim
Potential Entry
Manage risk at the low of the day
Volume Increases

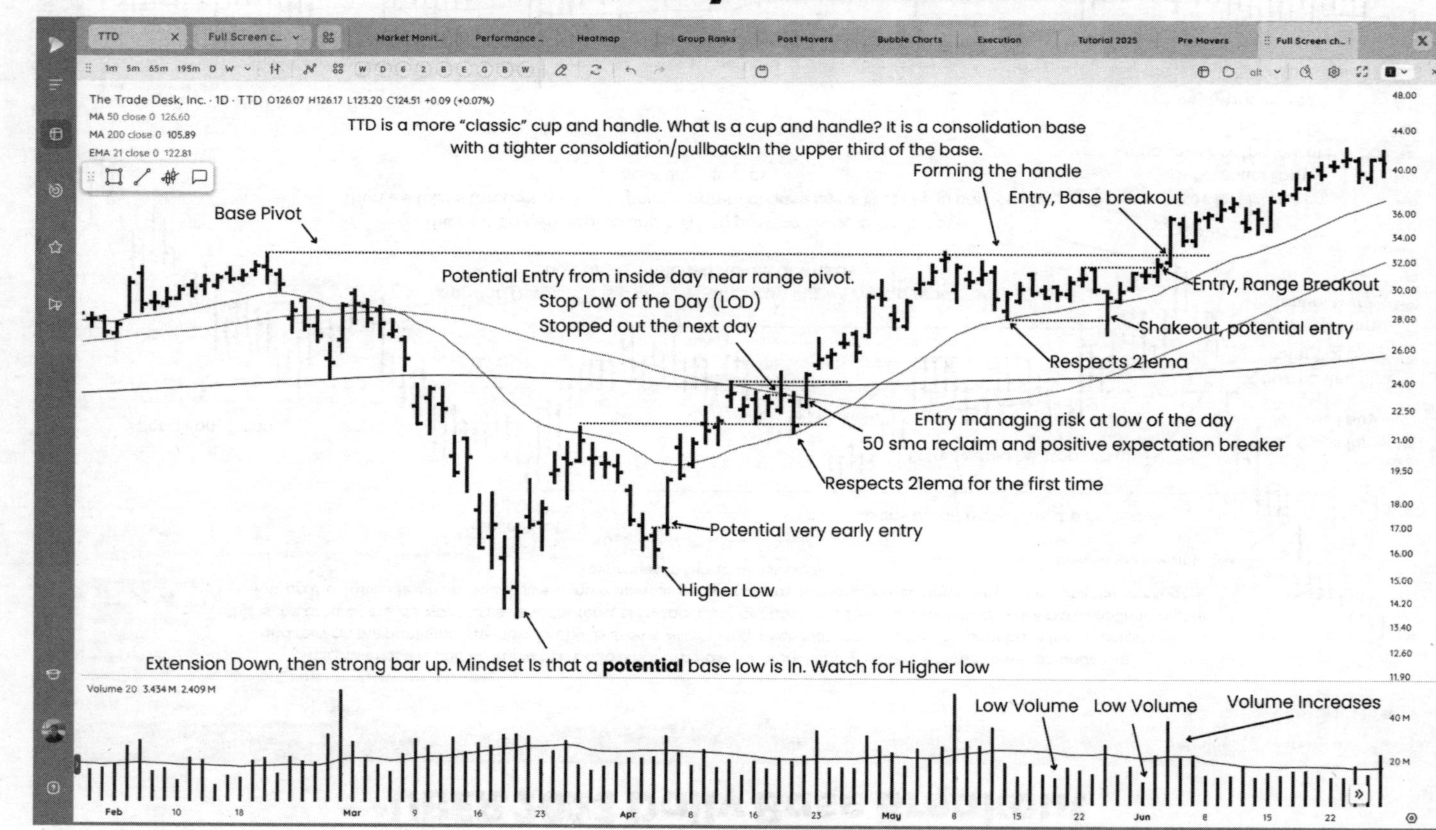
TTD 2020 Daily Base Breakout
The Trade Desk, Inc. · 1D · TTD O126.07 H126.17 L123.20 C124.51 +0.09 (+0.07%)
MA 50 close 0 126.60
MA 200 close 0 105.89
EMA 21 close 0 122.81
TTD is a more "classic" cup and handle. What is a cup and handle? It is a consolidation base
with a tighter consoldiation/pullbackin the upper third of the base.
Forming the handle
Entry, Base breakout
Base Pivot
Potential Entry from inside day near range pivot.
Stop Low of the Day (LOD)
Stopped out the next day
Entry, Range Breakout
Shakeout, potential entry
Respects 21ema
Entry managing risk at low of the day
50 sma reclaim and positive expectation breaker
Respects 21ema for the first time
Potential very early entry
Higher Low
Extension Down, then strong bar up. Mindset is that a potential base low is in. Watch for Higher low
Volume 20 3.434 M 2.409 M
Low Volume
Low Volume
Volume Increases

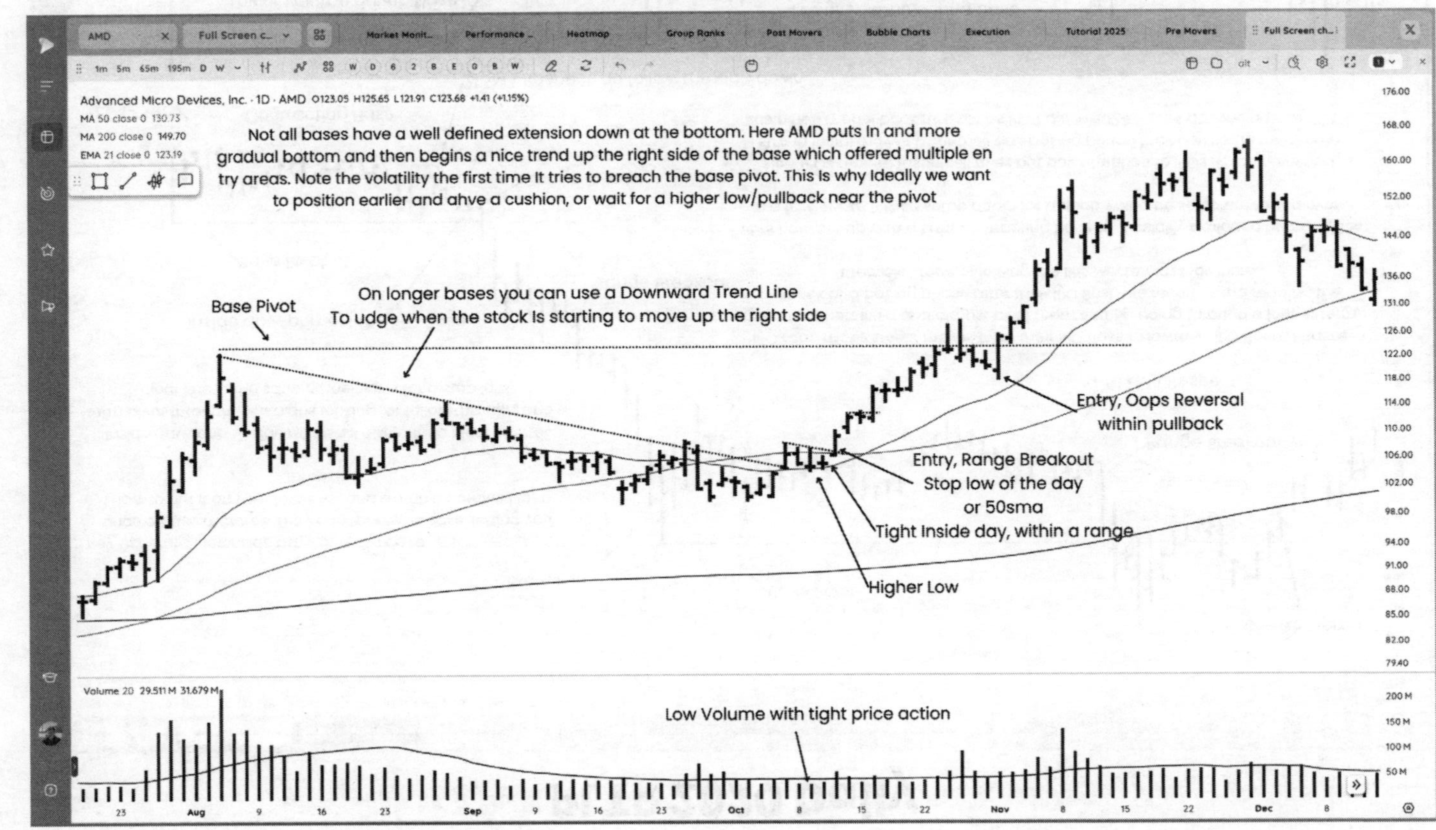
AMD 2021 Daily Base Breakout
Advanced Micro Devices, Inc. · 1D · AMD O123.05 H125.65 L121.91 C123.68 +1.41 (+1.15%)
MA 50 close 0 130.73
MA 200 close 0 149.70
EMA 21 close 0 123.19
Not all bases have a well defined extension down at the bottom. Here AMD puts In and more gradual bottom and then begins a nice trend up the right side of the base which offered multiple en try areas. Note the volatility the first time It tries to breach the base pivot. This is why Ideally we want to position earlier and ahve a cushion, or wait for a higher low/pullback near the pivot
Base Pivot
On longer bases you can use a Downward Trend Line
To udge when the stock Is starting to move up the right side
Entry, Oops Reversal within pullback
Entry, Range Breakout Stop low of the day or 50sma
Tight Inside day, within a range
Higher Low
Low Volume with tight price action
Volume 20 29.511 M 31.679 M

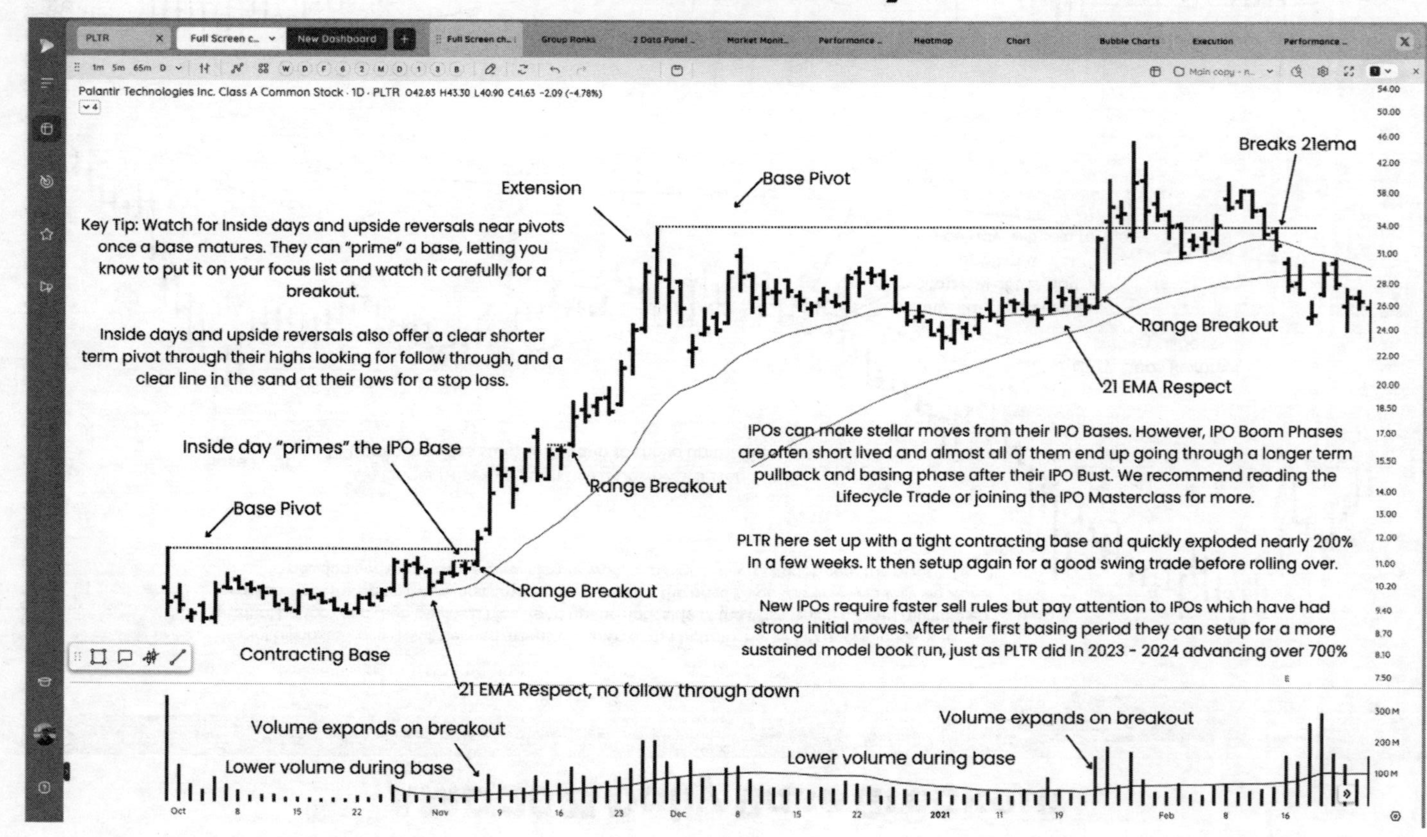
PLTR 2020 Daily
Palantir Technologies Inc. Class A Common Stock · 1D · PLTR O42.83 H43.30 L40.90 C41.63 −2.09 (−4.78%)
Key Tip: Watch for inside days and upside reversals near pivots once a base matures. They can "prime" a base, letting you know to put it on your focus list and watch it carefully for a breakout.
Inside days and upside reversals also offer a clear shorter term pivot through their highs looking for follow through, and a clear line in the sand at their lows for a stop loss.
Extension
Base Pivot
Breaks 21ema
Range Breakout
21 EMA Respect
Inside day "primes" the IPO Base
Range Breakout
Base Pivot
Range Breakout
Contracting Base
21 EMA Respect, no follow through down
IPOs can make stellar moves from their IPO Bases. However, IPO Boom Phases are often short lived and almost all of them end up going through a longer term pullback and basing phase after their IPO Bust. We recommend reading the Lifecycle Trade or joining the IPO Masterclass for more.
PLTR here set up with a tight contracting base and quickly exploded nearly 200% In a few weeks. It then setup again for a good swing trade before rolling over.
New IPOs require faster sell rules but pay attention to IPOs which have had strong initial moves. After their first basing period they can setup for a more sustained model book run, just as PLTR did in 2023 - 2024 advancing over 700%
Volume expands on breakout
Lower volume during base
Volume expands on breakout
Lower volume during base

FAILED BASE BREAKOUTS

Breakouts do not always succeed. This section focuses on examples of later stage base failures or bases that simply rolled over. The goal here is to analyze how to identify a failure and logical spots to exit to protect yourself.

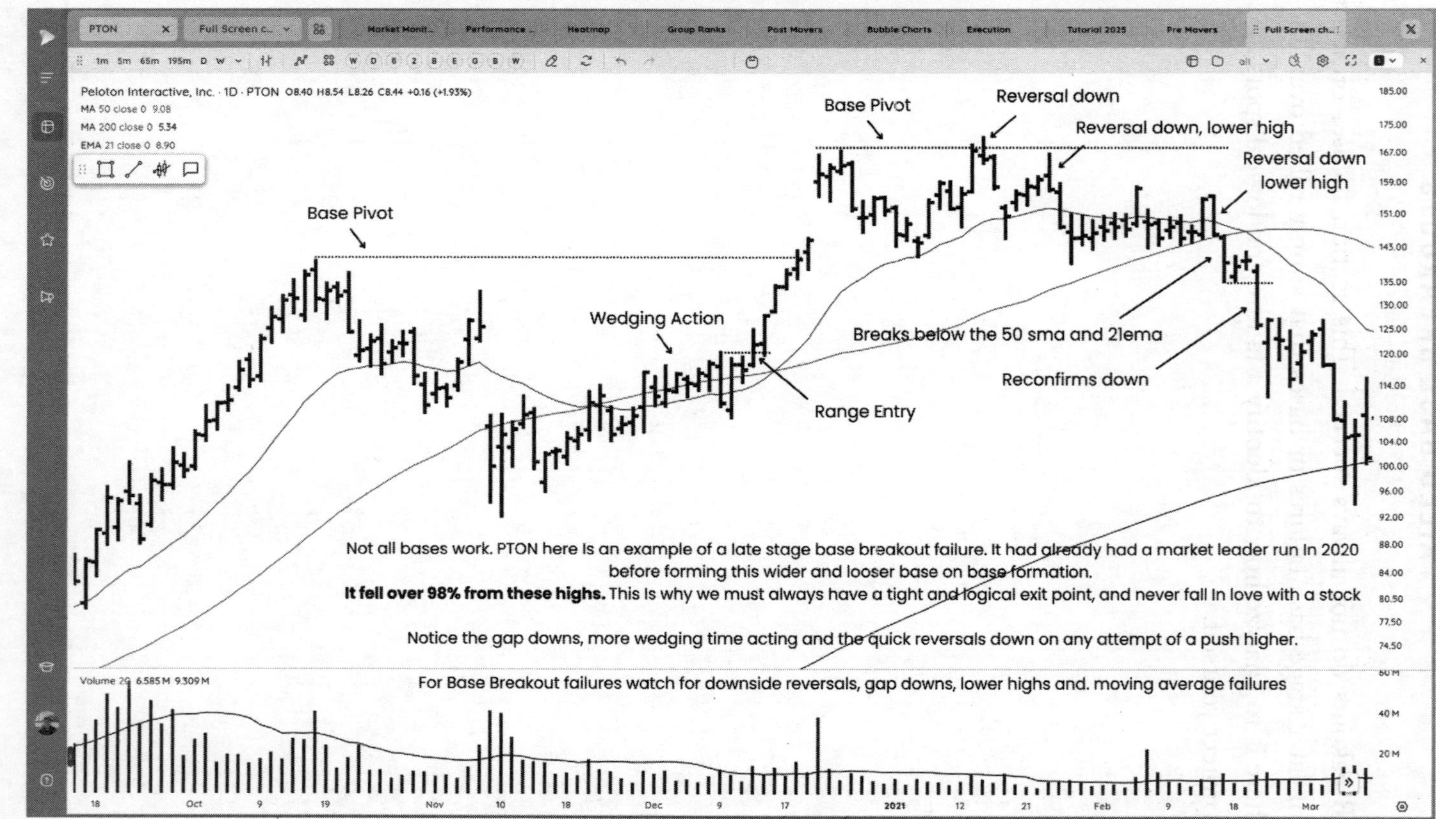
PTON 2021 Daily Base Breakout Failure
Peloton Interactive, Inc. · 1D · PTON O8.40 H8.54 L8.26 C8.44 +0.16 (+1.93%)
MA 50 close 0 9.08
MA 200 close 0 5.34
EMA 21 close 0 8.90
Base Pivot
Wedging Action
Range Entry
Base Pivot
Reversal down
Reversal down, lower high
Reversal down
lower high
Breaks below the 50 sma and 21ema
Reconfirms down
Not all bases work. PTON here is an example of a late stage base breakout failure. It had already had a market leader run in 2020
before forming this wider and looser base on base formation.
It fell over 98% from these highs. This is why we must always have a tight and logical exit point, and never fall in love with a stock
Notice the gap downs, more wedging time acting and the quick reversals down on any attempt of a push higher.
For Base Breakout failures watch for downside reversals, gap downs, lower highs and. moving average failures

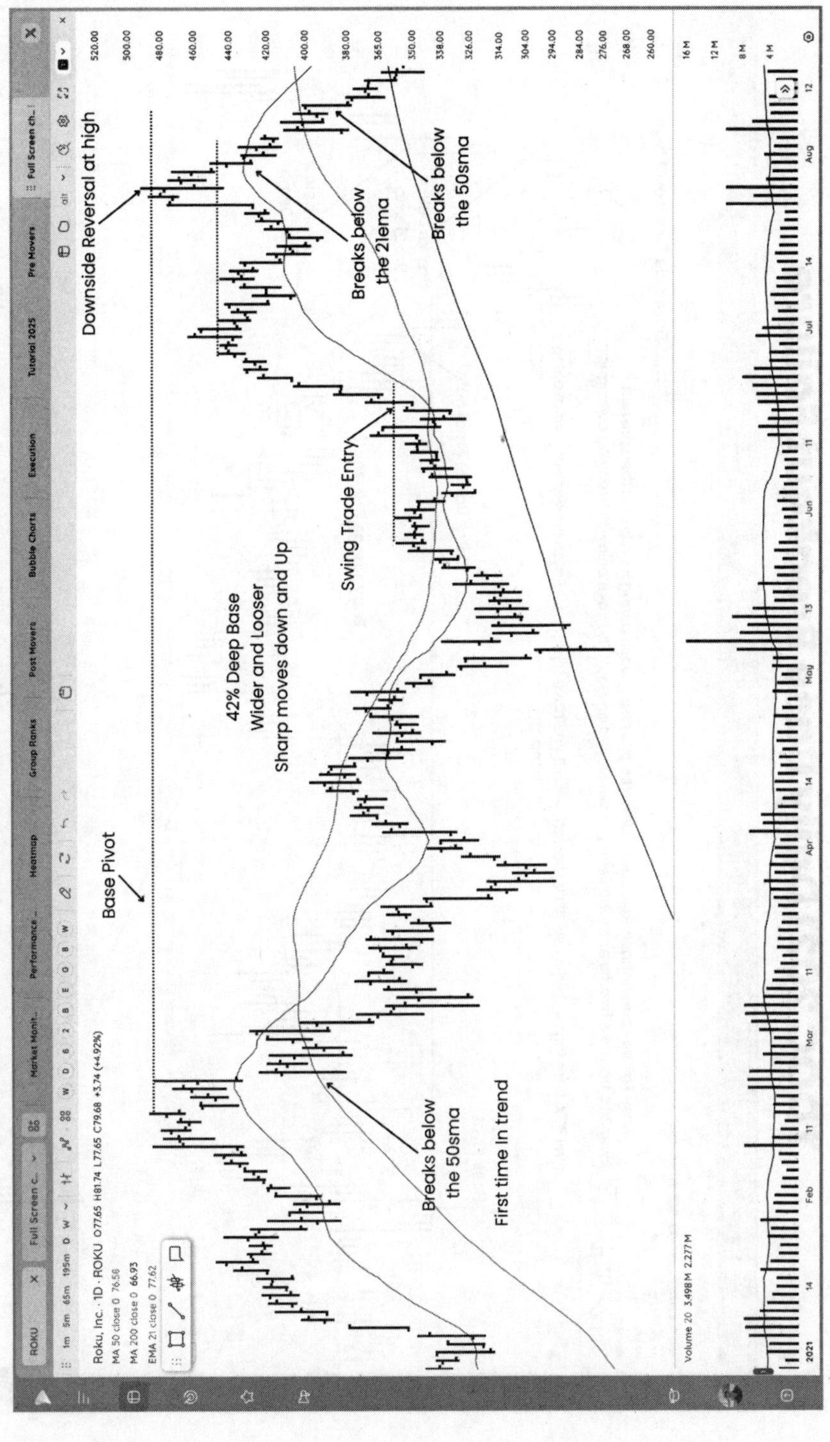
ROKU 2021 Daily Base Breakout Failure
Base Pivot
Downside Reversal at high
42% Deep Base
Wider and Looser
Sharp moves down and Up
Swing Trade Entry
Breaks below the 21ema
Breaks below the 50sma
Breaks below the 50sma
First time in trend

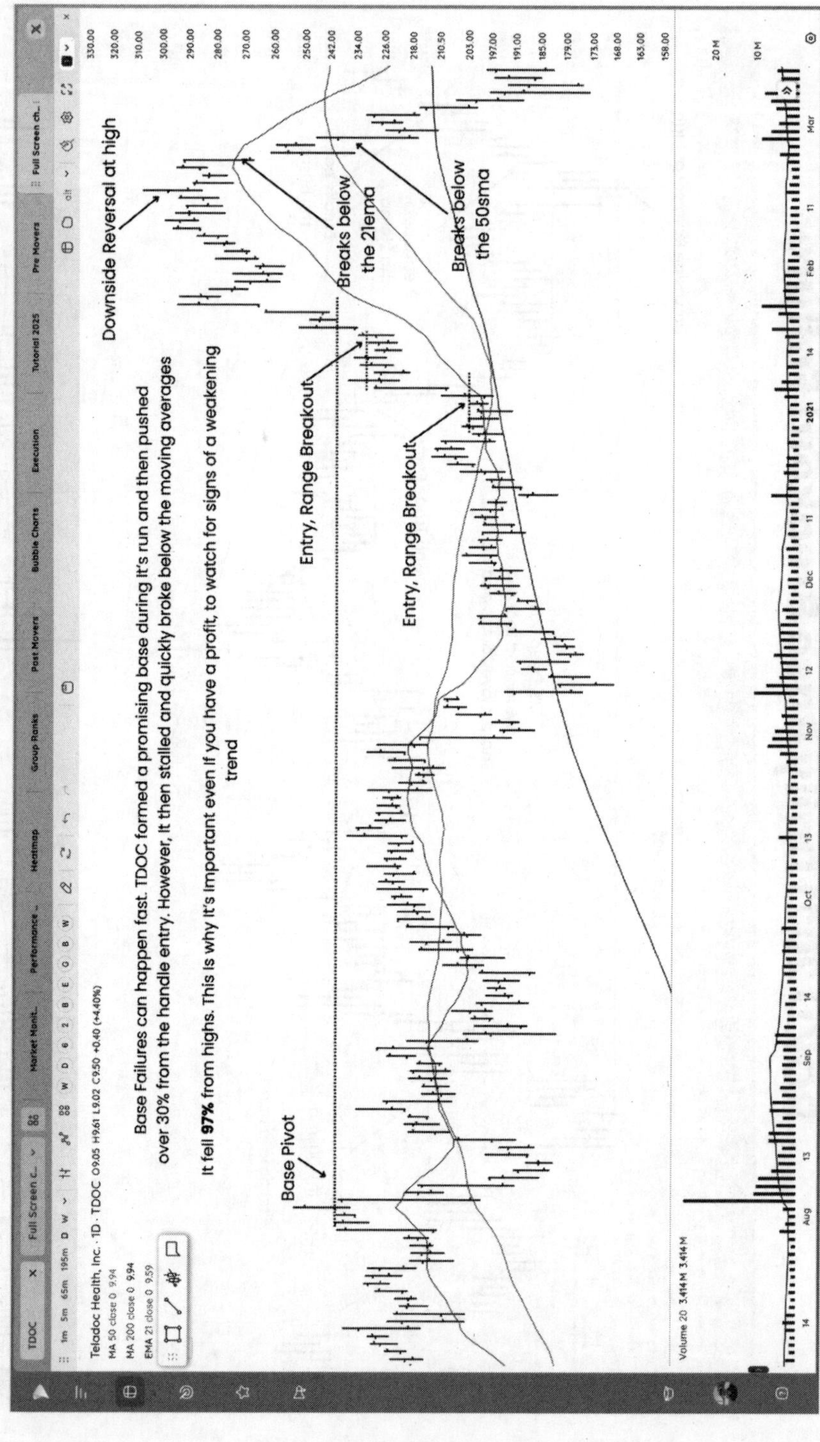
TDOC 2021 Daily Base Breakout Failure
Base Failures can happen fast. TDOC formed a promising base during it's run and then pushed over 30% from the handle entry. However, it then stalled and quickly broke below the moving averages
It fell **97%** from highs. This is why it's important even if you have a profit, to watch for signs of a weakening trend
Downside Reversal at high
Breaks below the 21ema
Breaks below the 50sma
Entry, Range Breakout
Entry, Range Breakout
Base Pivot

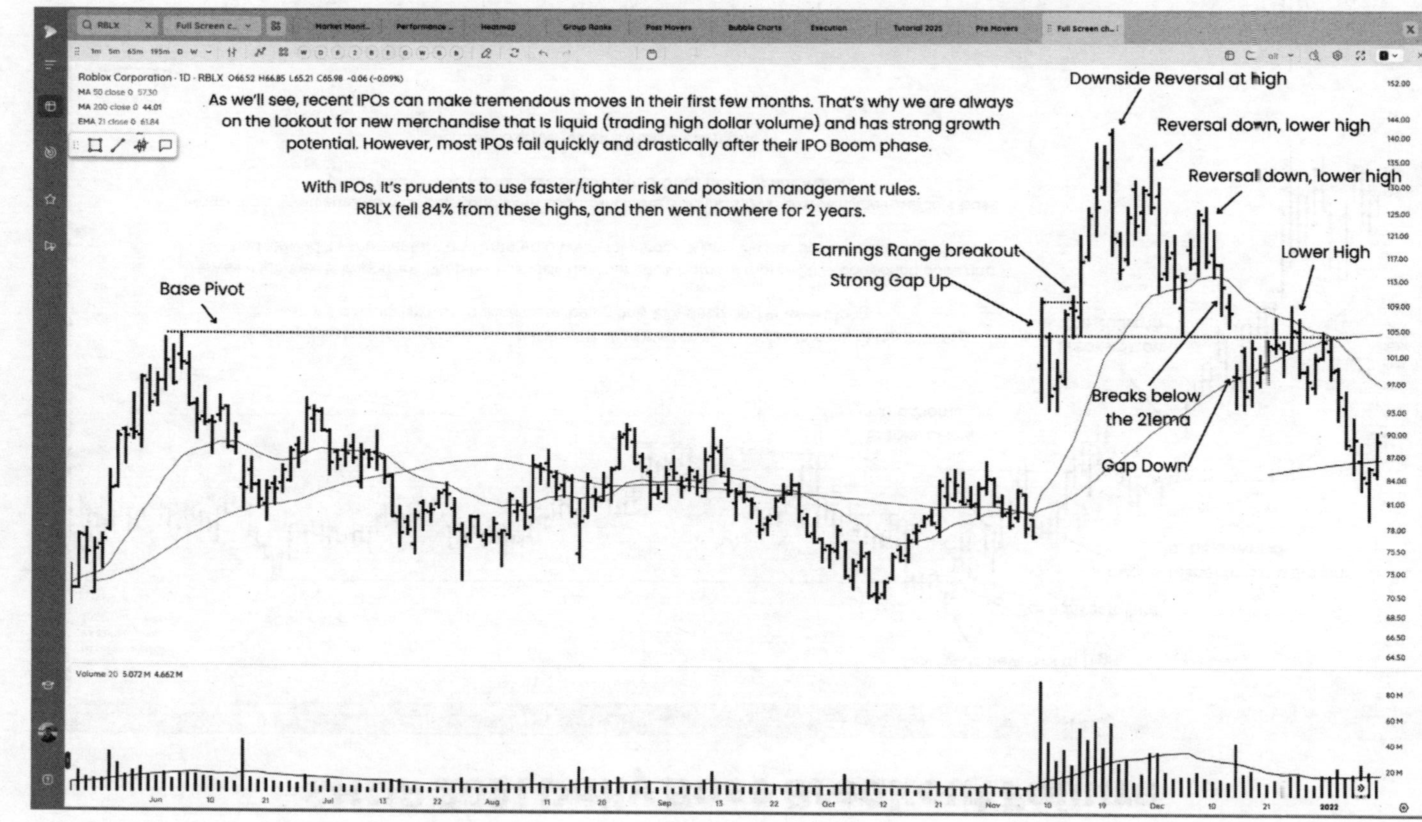
RBLX 2021 Daily Base Breakout Failure
Roblox Corporation · 1D · RBLX O66.52 H66.85 L65.21 C65.98 −0.06 (−0.09%)
MA 50 close 0 57.30
MA 200 close 0 44.01
EMA 21 close 0 61.84
As we'll see, recent IPOs can make tremendous moves in their first few months. That's why we are always on the lookout for new merchandise that is liquid (trading high dollar volume) and has strong growth potential. However, most IPOs fail quickly and drastically after their IPO Boom phase.
With IPOs, it's prudents to use faster/tighter risk and position management rules.
RBLX fell 84% from these highs, and then went nowhere for 2 years.
Downside Reversal at high
Reversal down, lower high
Reversal down, lower high
Lower High
Earnings Range breakout
Strong Gap Up
Base Pivot
Breaks below the 21ema
Gap Down
Volume 20 5.072 M 4.662 M

SHOP 2021 Daily Base Breakout Failure
Shopify Inc. · 1D · SHOP O107.34 H107.79 L105.75 C106.37 +0.07 (+0.07%)
MA 50 close 0 108.36
MA 200 close 0 79.47
EMA 21 close 0 106.57
Base Pivot
Downside Reversal at high
Base pivot failure
begins respecting the 21ema to the downside
Breaks below the 21ema
Breaks below the 200sma
SHOP is a great stock to study going all the way back to It's IPO. Here we are looking at the 2021 Top. It's a relatively nice looking base, being only 22% deep and 18 weeks long.
However, context Is Important. Shop had already run over 200% from It's march 2020 correction base and had slowed It's momentum and entered a Weinstein Stage 3 with the 200 day MA catching up.
Notice how If you entered a bit early and were cognizant If the watning sides like downside reversals, base pivot failures, you woudl have exited with a small profit or breakeven.
Meanwhile **SHOP fell 86% from these highs**
Volume 20 3.228M 4.418M

GAPS

This section focuses on strong examples from the past that were tradeable and resulted in strong trends and market leading moves. Gaps, most often caused by news catalysts such as earnings reports, offer a great setup in the right environment.

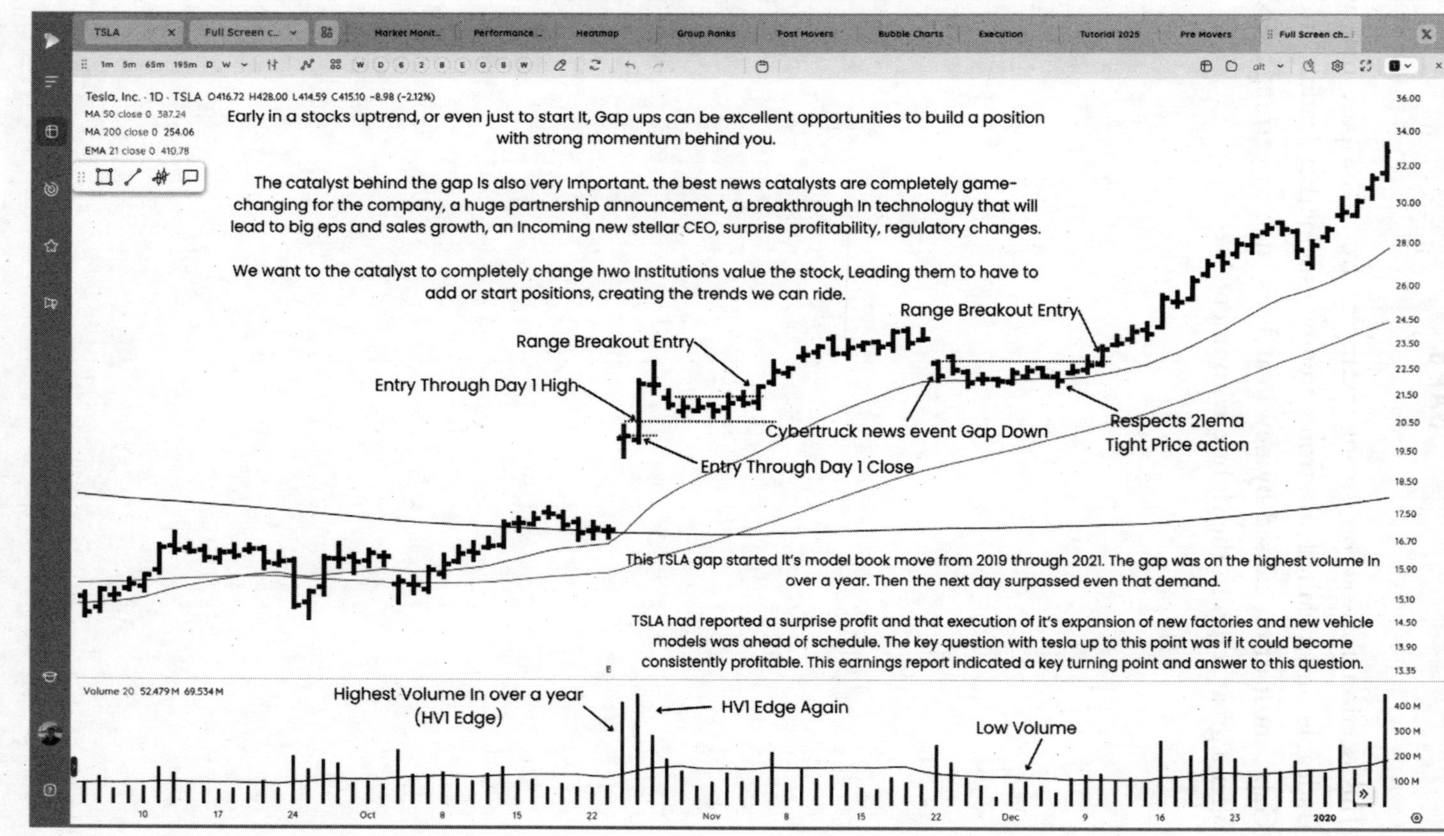
TSLA GAP 2019 DAILY
Early in a stocks uptrend, or even just to start It, Gap ups can be excellent opportunities to build a position with strong momentum behind you.
The catalyst behind the gap Is also very Important. the best news catalysts are completely game-changing for the company, a huge partnership announcement, a breakthrough In technologuy that will lead to big eps and sales growth, an Incoming new stellar CEO, surprise profitability, regulatory changes.
We want to the catalyst to completely change hwo Institutions value the stock, Leading them to have to add or start positions, creating the trends we can ride.
Range Breakout Entry
Range Breakout Entry
Entry Through Day 1 High
Cybertruck news event Gap Down
Respects 21ema
Tight Price action
Entry Through Day 1 Close
This TSLA gap started It's model book move from 2019 through 2021. The gap was on the highest volume In over a year. Then the next day surpassed even that demand.
TSLA had reported a surprise profit and that execution of it's expansion of new factories and new vehicle models was ahead of schedule. The key question with tesla up to this point was if it could become consistently profitable. This earnings report indicated a key turning point and answer to this question.
Highest Volume In over a year (HV1 Edge)
HV1 Edge Again
Low Volume

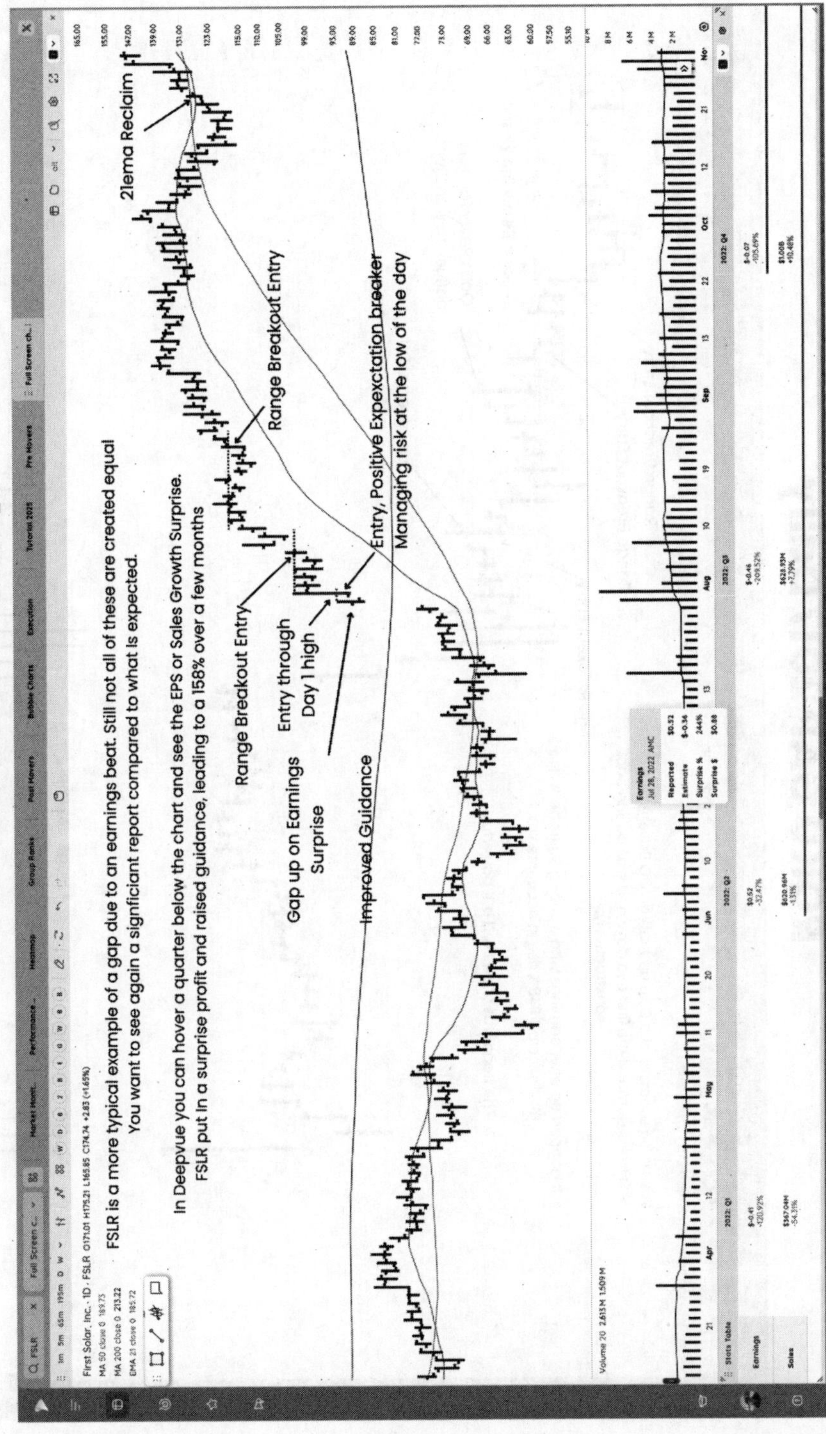
FSLR GAP 2022 Daily
FSLR is a more typical example of a gap due to an earnings beat. Still not all of these are created equal
You want to see again a signficiant report compared to what is expected.
In Deepvue you can hover a quarter below the chart and see the EPS or Sales Growth Surprise.
FSLR put In a surprise profit and raised guidance, leading to a 158% over a few months
21ema Reclaim
Range Breakout Entry
Range Breakout Entry
Entry through
Day 1 high
Entry, Positive Expexctation breaker
Managing risk at the low of the day
Gap up on Earnings
Surprise
Improved Guidance

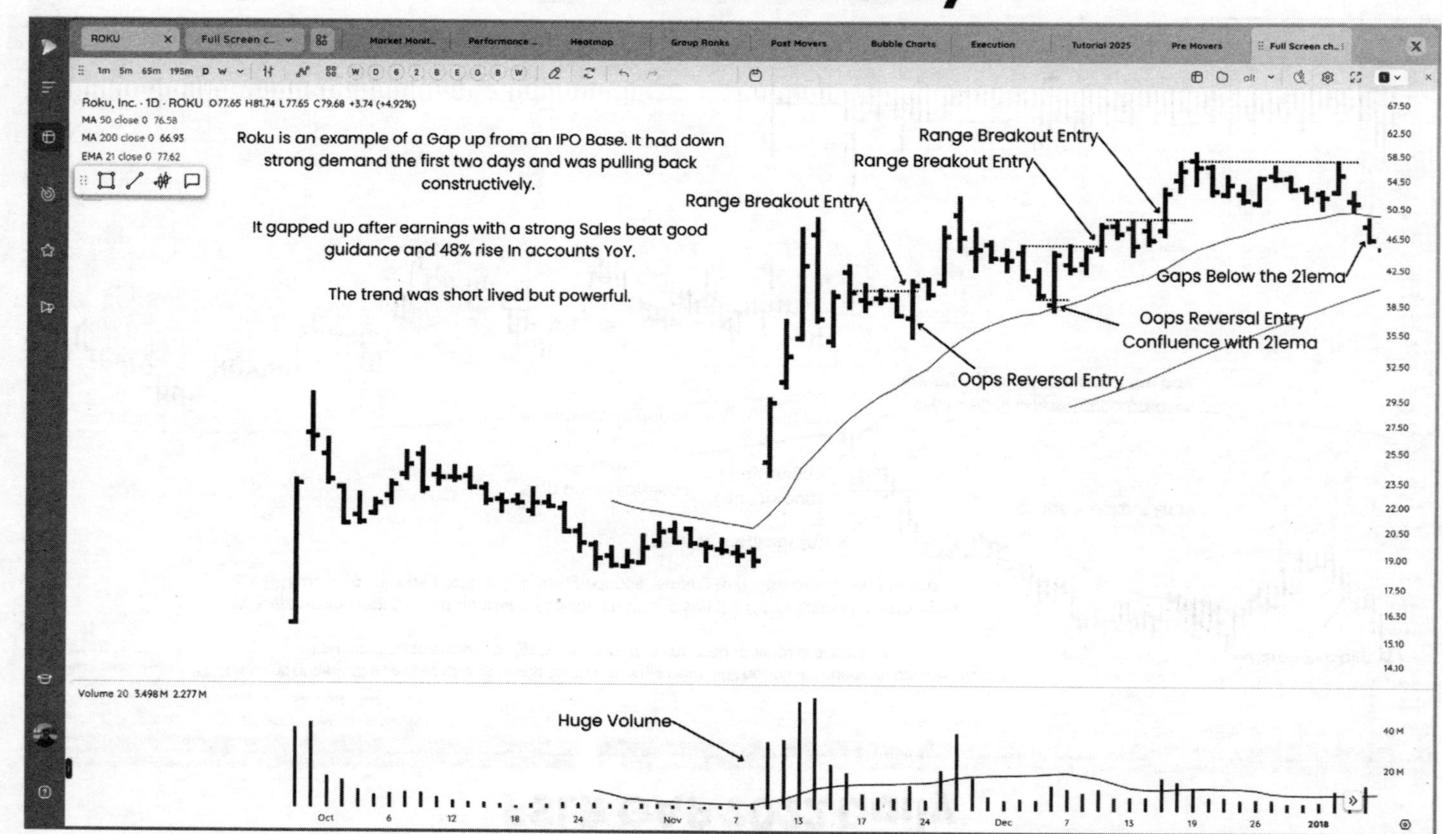
ROKU GAP 2017 Daily
Roku, Inc. · 1D · ROKU O77.65 H81.74 L77.65 C79.68 +3.74 (+4.92%)
MA 50 close 0 76.58
MA 200 close 0 66.93
EMA 21 close 0 77.62
Roku is an example of a Gap up from an IPO Base. It had down strong demand the first two days and was pulling back constructively.
It gapped up after earnings with a strong Sales beat good guidance and 48% rise in accounts YoY.
The trend was short lived but powerful.
Range Breakout Entry
Range Breakout Entry
Range Breakout Entry
Gaps Below the 21ema
Oops Reversal Entry
Confluence with 21ema
Oops Reversal Entry
Volume 20 3.498 M 2.277 M
Huge Volume

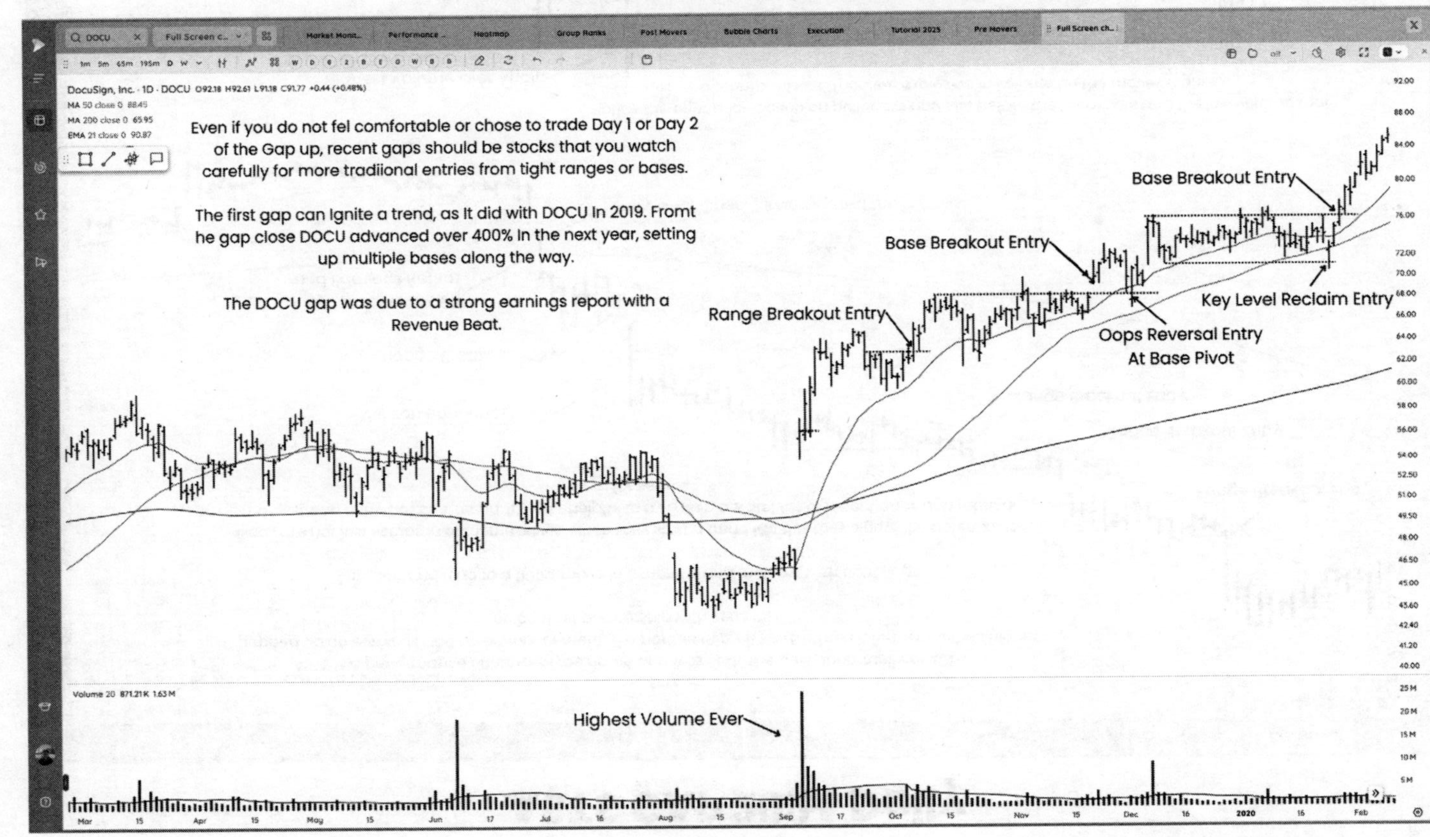
DOCU GAP 2019 Daily
DocuSign, Inc. · 1D · DOCU O92.18 H92.61 L91.18 C91.77 +0.44 (+0.48%)
MA 50 close 0 88.45
MA 200 close 0 65.95
EMA 21 close 0 90.87
Even if you do not fel comfortable or chose to trade Day 1 or Day 2
of the Gap up, recent gaps should be stocks that you watch
carefully for more tradiional entries from tight ranges or bases.
The first gap can ignite a trend, as it did with DOCU in 2019. Fromt
he gap close DOCU advanced over 400% in the next year, setting
up multiple bases along the way.
The DOCU gap was due to a strong earnings report with a
Revenue Beat.
Range Breakout Entry
Base Breakout Entry
Oops Reversal Entry
At Base Pivot
Base Breakout Entry
Key Level Reclaim Entry
Volume 20 871.21K 1.63M
Highest Volume Ever

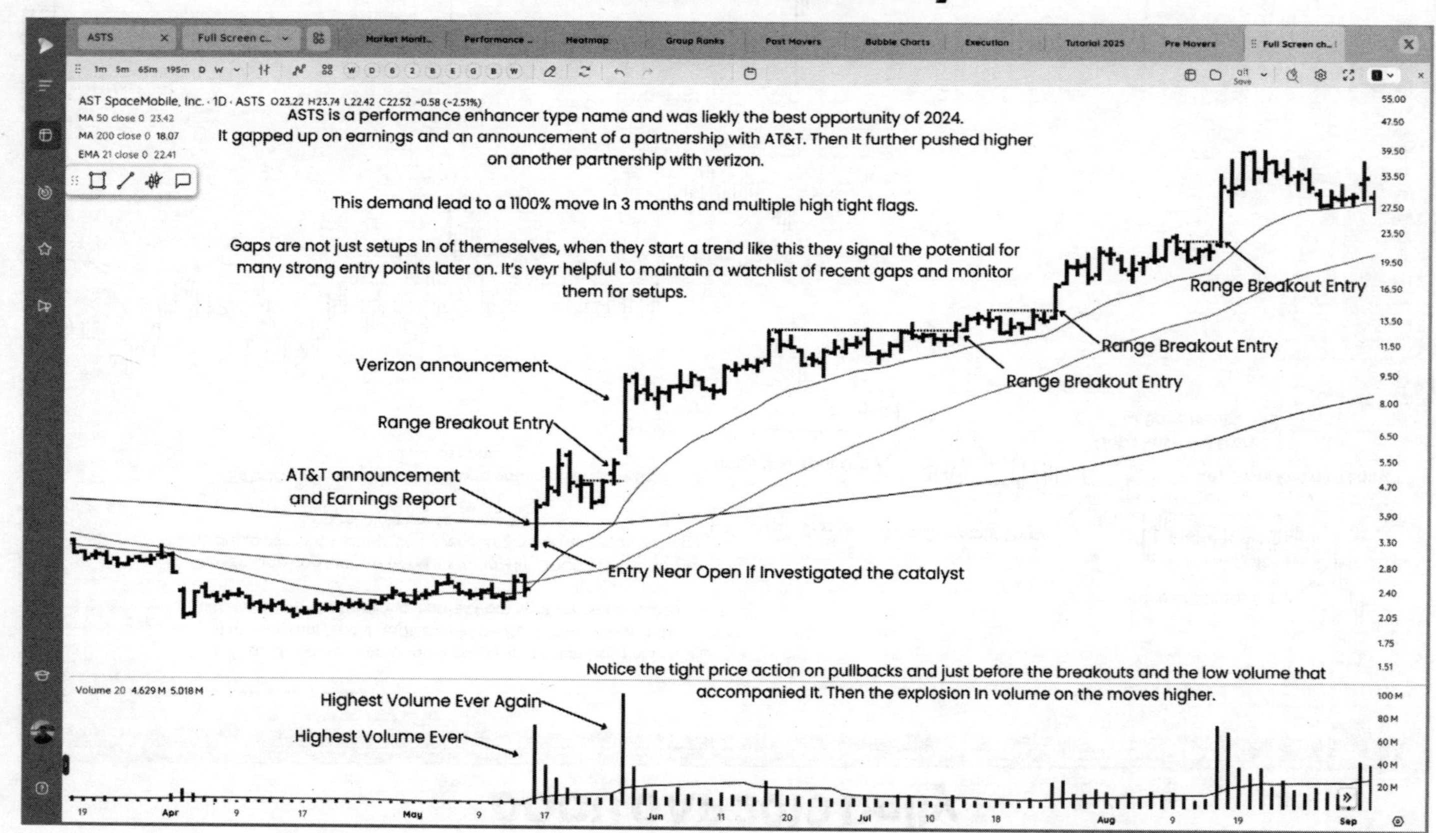
ASTS GAP 2024 Daily
AST SpaceMobile, Inc. · 1D · ASTS O23.22 H23.74 L22.42 C22.52 −0.58 (−2.51%)
MA 50 close 0 23.42
MA 200 close 0 18.07
EMA 21 close 0 22.41
ASTS is a performance enhancer type name and was liekly the best opportunity of 2024.
It gapped up on earnings and an announcement of a partnership with AT&T. Then it further pushed higher on another partnership with verizon.
This demand lead to a 1100% move in 3 months and multiple high tight flags.
Gaps are not just setups in of themeselves, when they start a trend like this they signal the potential for many strong entry points later on. It's veyr helpful to maintain a watchlist of recent gaps and monitor them for setups.
Verizon announcement
Range Breakout Entry
AT&T announcement and Earnings Report
Entry Near Open If Investigated the catalyst
Range Breakout Entry
Range Breakout Entry
Range Breakout Entry
Notice the tight price action on pullbacks and just before the breakouts and the low volume that accompanied it. Then the explosion in volume on the moves higher.
Volume 20 4.629M 5.018M
Highest Volume Ever Again
Highest Volume Ever

ASTS GAP 2024 Daily Alternative View

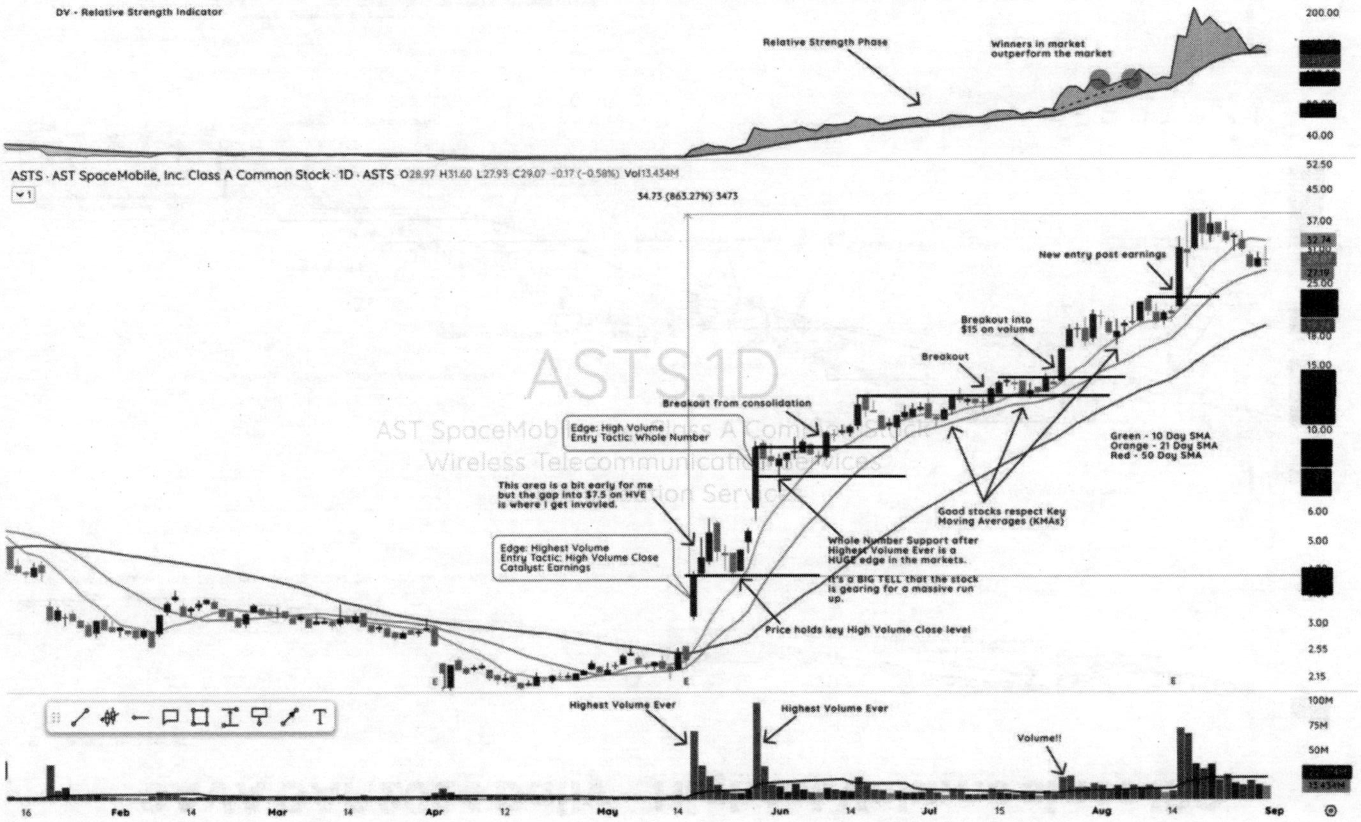

DV - Relative Strength Indicator

Relative Strength Phase

Winners in market outperform the market

ASTS · AST SpaceMobile, Inc. Class A Common Stock · 1D · ASTS O28.97 H31.60 L27.93 C29.07 −0.17 (−0.58%) Vol13.434M

34.73 (863.27%) 3473

ASTS, 1D

AST SpaceMobile, Inc. Class A Common Stock

Wireless Telecommunication Services

New entry post earnings

Breakout into $15 on volume

Breakout

Breakout from consolidation

Edge: High Volume
Entry Tactic: Whole Number

This area is a bit early for me but the gap into $7.5 on HVE is where I get invovled.

Edge: Highest Volume
Entry Tactic: High Volume Close
Catalyst: Earnings

Good stocks respect Key Moving Averages (KMAs)

Whole Number Support after Highest Volume Ever is a HUGE edge in the markets.

It's a BIG TELL that the stock is gearing for a massive run up.

Price holds key High Volume Close level

Green - 10 Day SMA
Orange - 21 Day SMA
Red - 50 Day SMA

Highest Volume Ever

Highest Volume Ever

Volume!!

200.00 40.00 52.50 45.00 37.00 32.74 27.19 25.00 18.00 15.00 10.00 6.00 5.00 3.00 2.55 2.15

100M 75M 50M 13.434M

16 Feb 14 Mar 14 Apr 12 May 14 Jun 14 Jul 15 Aug 14 Sep

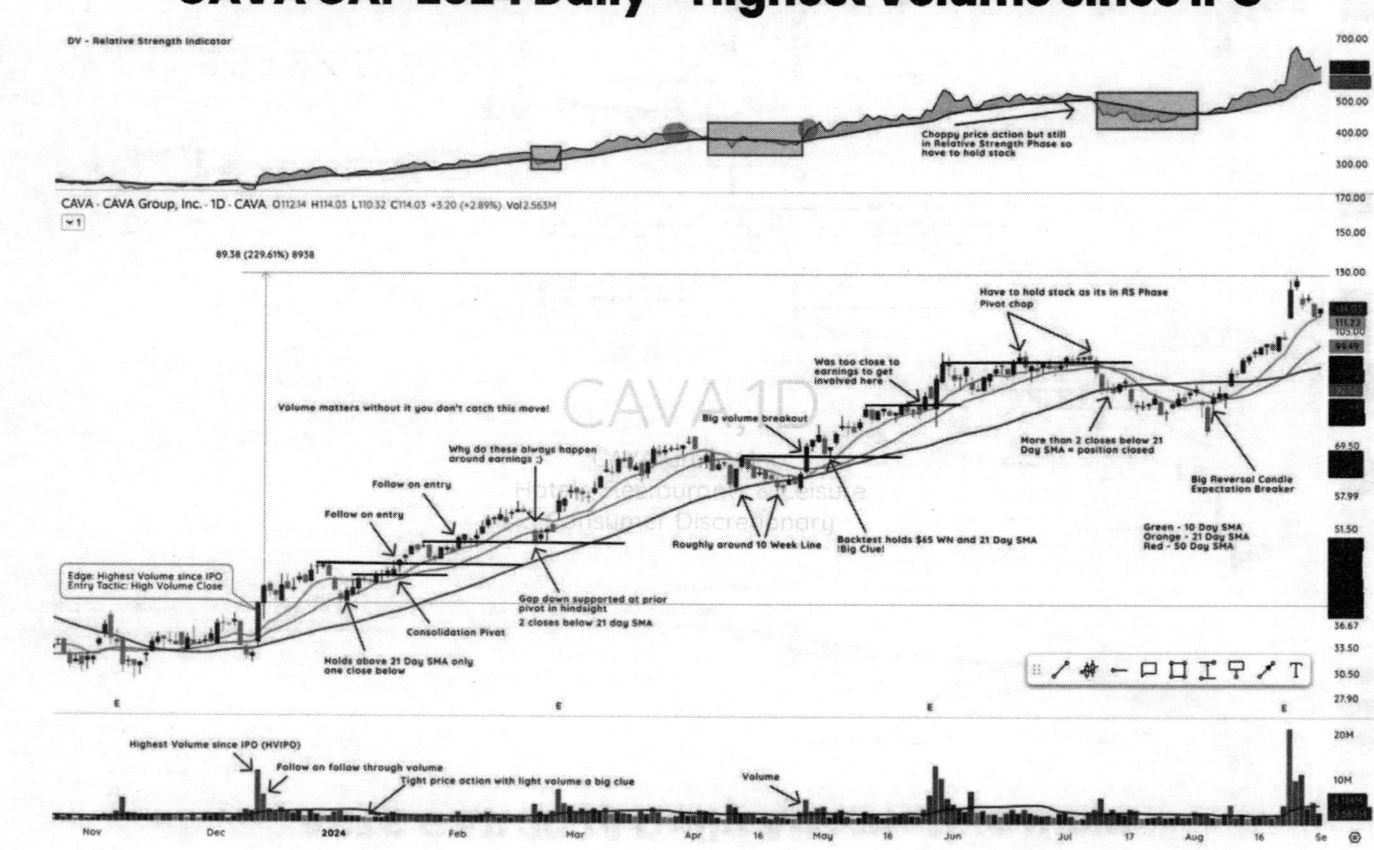
CAVA GAP 2024 Daily - Highest Volume since IPO
DV - Relative Strength Indicator
Choppy price action but still in Relative Strength Phase so have to hold stock
CAVA · CAVA Group, Inc. · 1D · CAVA O112.14 H114.03 L110.32 C114.03 +3.20 (+2.89%) Vol 2.563M
89.38 (229.61%) 8938
Volume matters without it you don't catch this move!
Edge: Highest Volume since IPO
Entry Tactic: High Volume Close
Follow on entry
Follow on entry
Why do these always happen around earnings :)
Holds above 21 Day SMA only one close below
Consolidation Pivot
Gap down supported at prior pivot in hindsight
2 closes below 21 day SMA
Big volume breakout
Roughly around 10 Week Line
Backtest holds $65 WN and 21 Day SMA
!Big Clue!
Was too close to earnings to get involved here
Have to hold stock as its in RS Phase
Pivot chop
More than 2 closes below 21 Day SMA = position closed
Big Reversal Candle
Expectation Breaker
Green - 10 Day SMA
Orange - 21 Day SMA
Red - 50 Day SMA
Highest Volume since IPO (HVIPO)
Follow on follow through volume
Tight price action with light volume a big clue
Volume
Nov
Dec
2024
Feb
Mar
Apr
May
Jun
Jul
Aug

WGS GAP 2024 Daily – Highest Volume EVER

Indicator: Deepvue Relative Strength

Relative Strength Phase Ends

Remains in Relative Strength Phase

WGS · GeneDx Holdings Corp. Class A Common Stock · 1D · WGS O32.73 H32.73 L31.30 C31.90 −0.57 (−1.76%) Vol126.184K

19.84 (116.39%) 1984

116% from High Volume Close Entry Tactic after High Volume Edge Day 2 Entry

Breakout from second CP

Highest Volume Ever
Edge: High Volume
Entry Tactic: High Volume Close

Breakout from Consolidation

Expectation breaker / reversal day

Price respects 21 DMA

HVC

Price holds KMAs
Key Moving Averages

2 closes below the 21 Day SMA
Not in Relative Strength Phase
Sold position

CP

CP

Significance of this High Volume Bar

1. Gaps up into $15 area - big number in the markets
2. Registers Highest Volume Ever at $15 is a big deal (historically a big clue of a winner)
3. Closing Range is STRONG so demand remained high from open to close
4. Catalyst: Earnings
5. Float: < 50M shares

Key Moving Averages

Green - 10 DMA
Orange - 21 DMA
Red - 50 DMA

High Volume Ever on Gap Up = HVE

Follow on Follow Through Volume

Pullback volume is low

Breakout on volume

12 Apr 10 19 May 10 21 Jun 12 Jul 11 22 Aug 12 21 Sep

FAILED GAPS

Just like not all base breakouts work out, gaps, like any setup can fail. Here we cover a few types of examples to look out for.

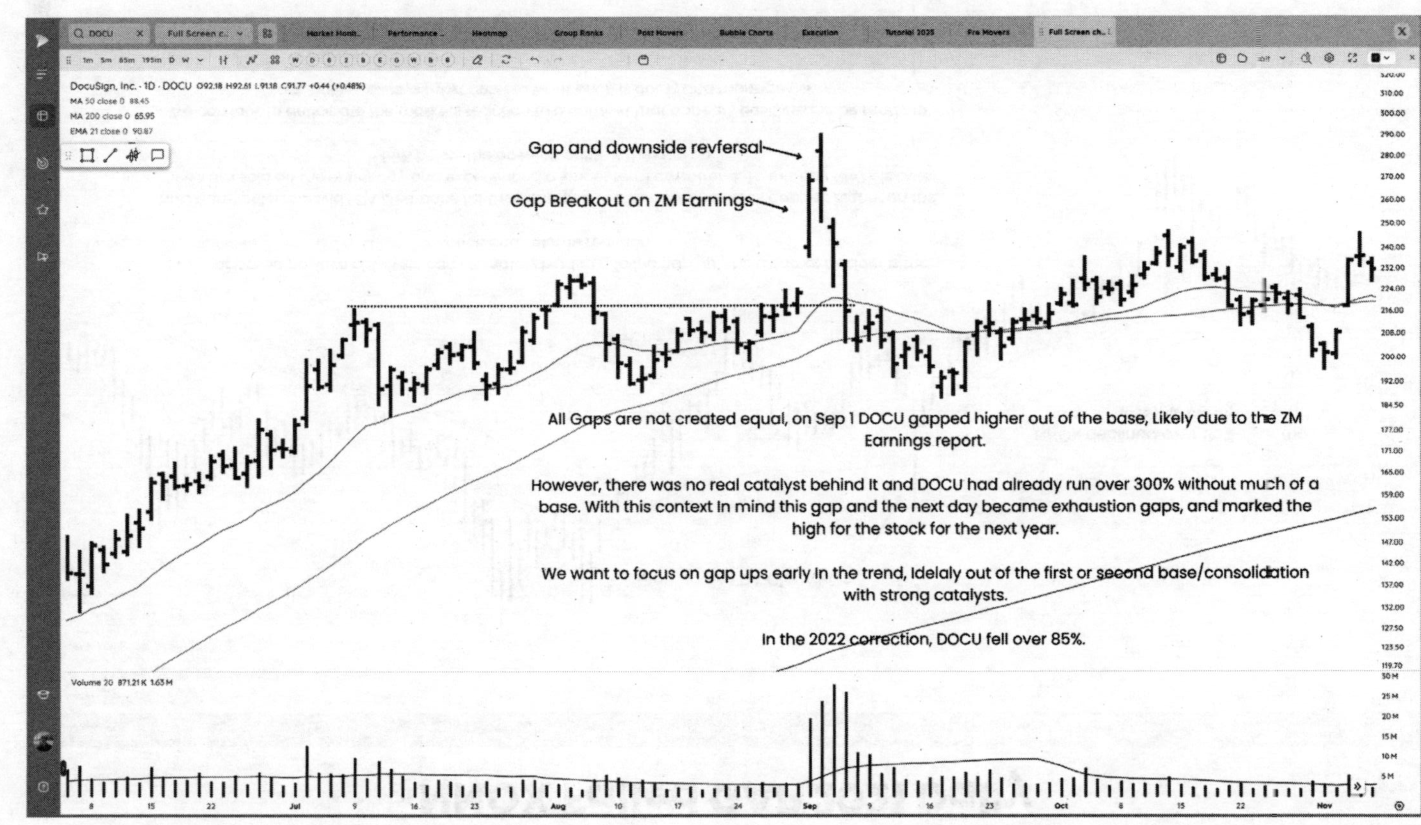
DOCU Failed GAP 2020 Daily
DocuSign, Inc. · 1D · DOCU
Gap and downside revfersal
Gap Breakout on ZM Earnings
All Gaps are not created equal, on Sep 1 DOCU gapped higher out of the base, Likely due to the ZM Earnings report.
However, there was no real catalyst behind it and DOCU had already run over 300% without much of a base. With this context in mind this gap and the next day became exhaustion gaps, and marked the high for the stock for the next year.
We want to focus on gap ups early in the trend, Idelaly out of the first or second base/consolidation with strong catalysts.
In the 2022 correction, DOCU fell over 85%.

NNOX Failed GAP 2021 Daily
Nano-X Imaging Ltd. · 1D · NNOX O8.60 H9.20 L8.46 C8.99 +0.62 (+7.40%)
MA 50 close 0 7.21
MA 200 close 0 7.47
EMA 21 close 0 8.09
Gap up on FDA Clearance
NNOX declined over 85% over the next few years
Even supposed positive catalysts can ultimately lead to a failed gap up. The ultiamte decider is the price and volume reaction
NNOX on April 5 receivid FDA clearance for their Imaging technology. The Stock gapped higher on the news but sold off the entire day and experienced a longer term downtrend. To this day NNOX is over 80% below the opening price of the gap up.
We can look to anticipate the markets reaction to a catalyst that appears positive and be ready to act, but we always must defer to what price is doing and manage risk.

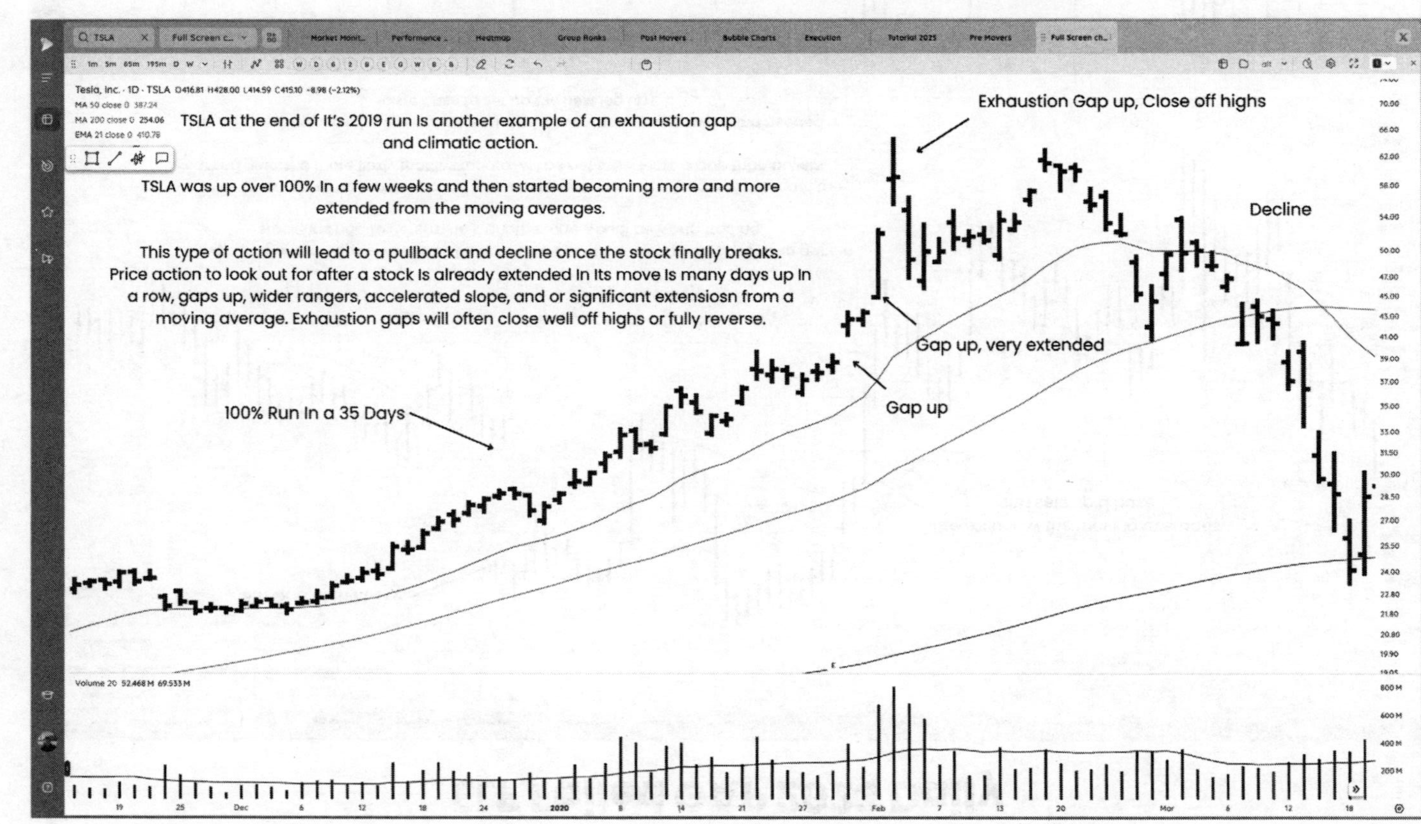
TSLA Failed GAP 2020 Daily
Tesla, Inc. · 1D · TSLA
TSLA at the end of It's 2019 run Is another example of an exhaustion gap and climatic action.
TSLA was up over 100% In a few weeks and then started becoming more and more extended from the moving averages.
This type of action will lead to a pullback and decline once the stock finally breaks. Price action to look out for after a stock Is already extended In Its move Is many days up In a row, gaps up, wider rangers, accelerated slope, and or significant extensiosn from a moving average. Exhaustion gaps will often close well off highs or fully reverse.
Exhaustion Gap up, Close off highs
Decline
Gap up, very extended
Gap up
100% Run In a 35 Days

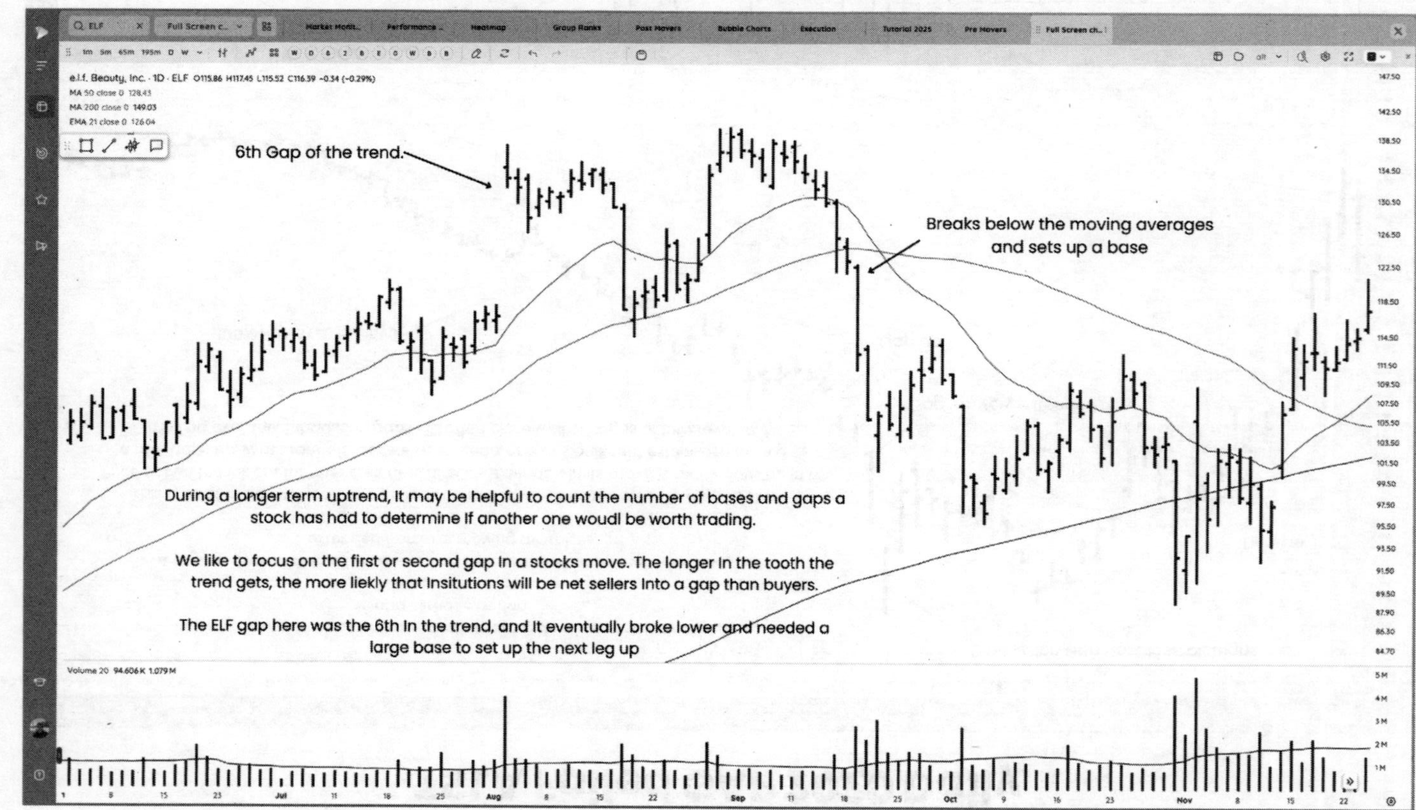
ELF Failed GAP 2023 Daily
e.l.f. Beauty, Inc. · 1D · ELF O115.86 H117.45 L115.52 C116.39 −0.34 (−0.29%)
MA 50 close 0 128.43
MA 200 close 0 149.03
EMA 21 close 0 126.04
6th Gap of the trend.
Breaks below the moving averages
and sets up a base
During a longer term uptrend, It may be helpful to count the number of bases and gaps a
stock has had to determine If another one woudl be worth trading.
We like to focus on the first or second gap In a stocks move. The longer In the tooth the
trend gets, the more liekly that Insitutions will be net sellers Into a gap than buyers.
The ELF gap here was the 6th In the trend, and It eventually broke lower and needed a
large base to set up the next leg up
Volume 20 94.606 K 1.079 M

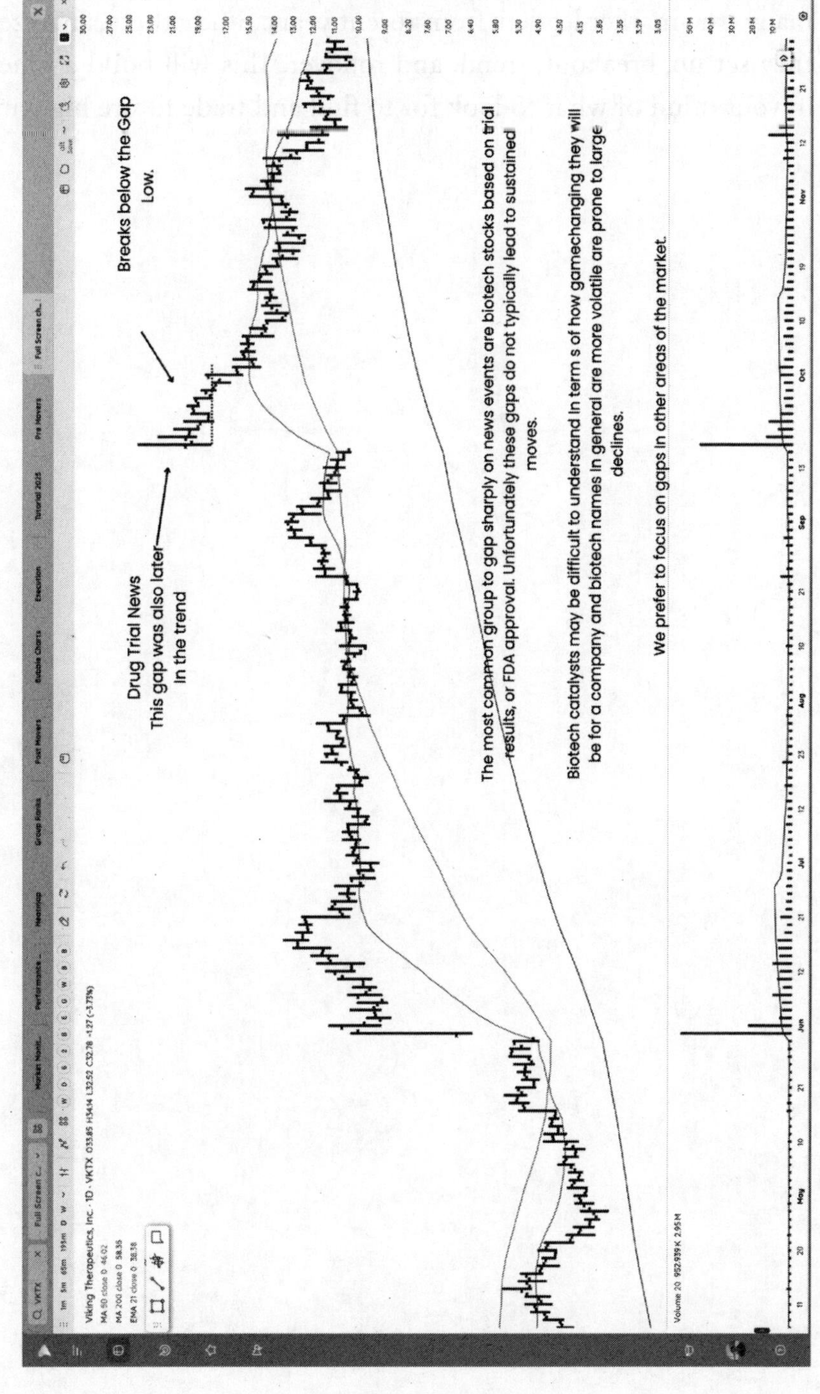
VKTX Failed GAP 2018 Daily
Drug Trial News
This gap was also later
In the trend
Breaks below the Gap
Low.
The most common group to gap sharply on news events are biotech stocks based on trial results, or FDA approval. Unfortunately these gaps do not typically lead to sustained moves.
Biotech catalysts may be difficult to understand in term s of how gamechanging they will be for a company and biotech names in general are more volatile are prone to large declines.
We prefer to focus on gaps in other areas of the market.

The next section of this model book chapter shares annotated charts of many true market leaders from recent years. Study these, analyze how they set up, breakout, trend, and rollover. This will build a blueprint in your mind of what to look for to find and trade future big winners.

2016 AND EARLIER MARKET LEADERS

TSLA 2013 DAILY 1/2

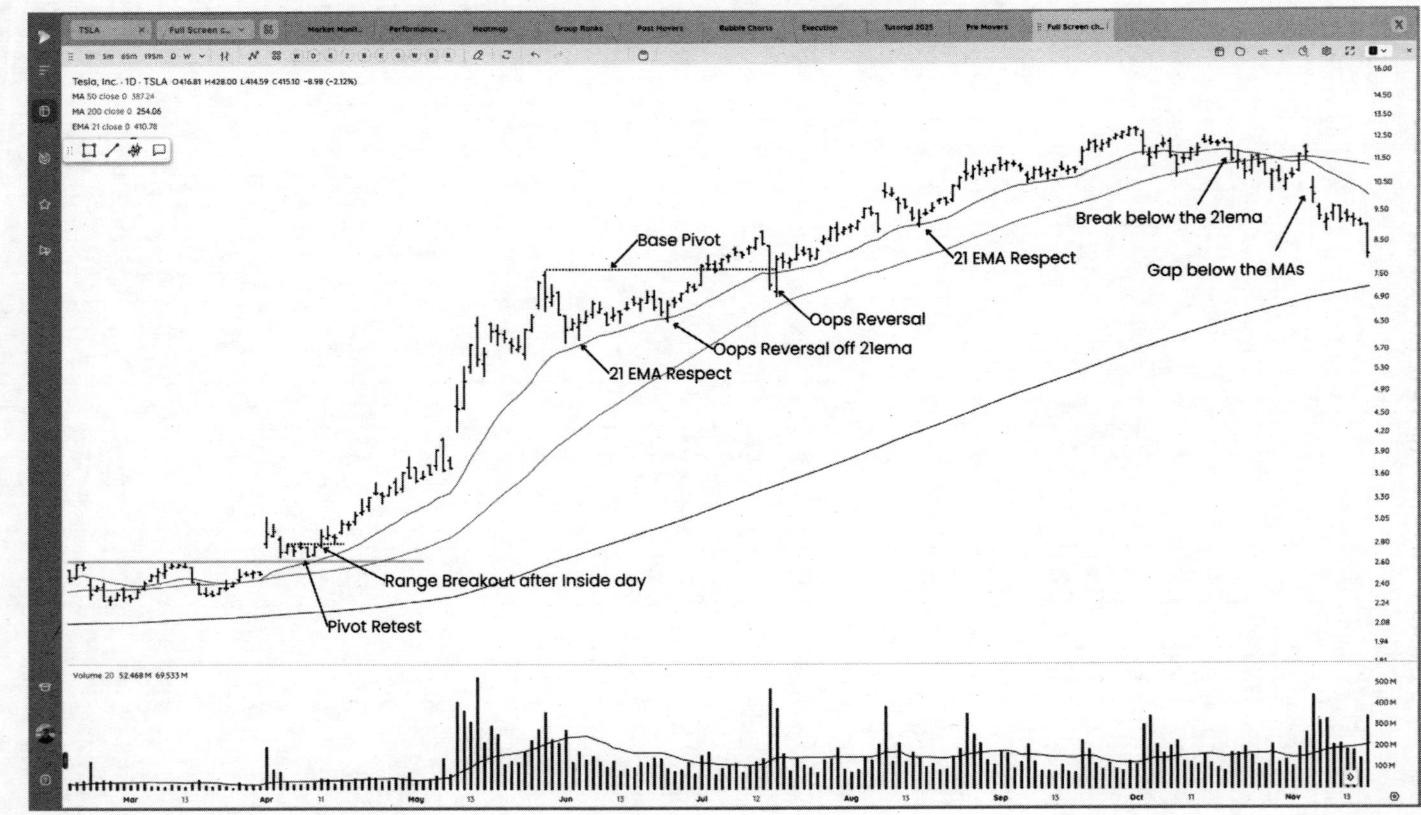

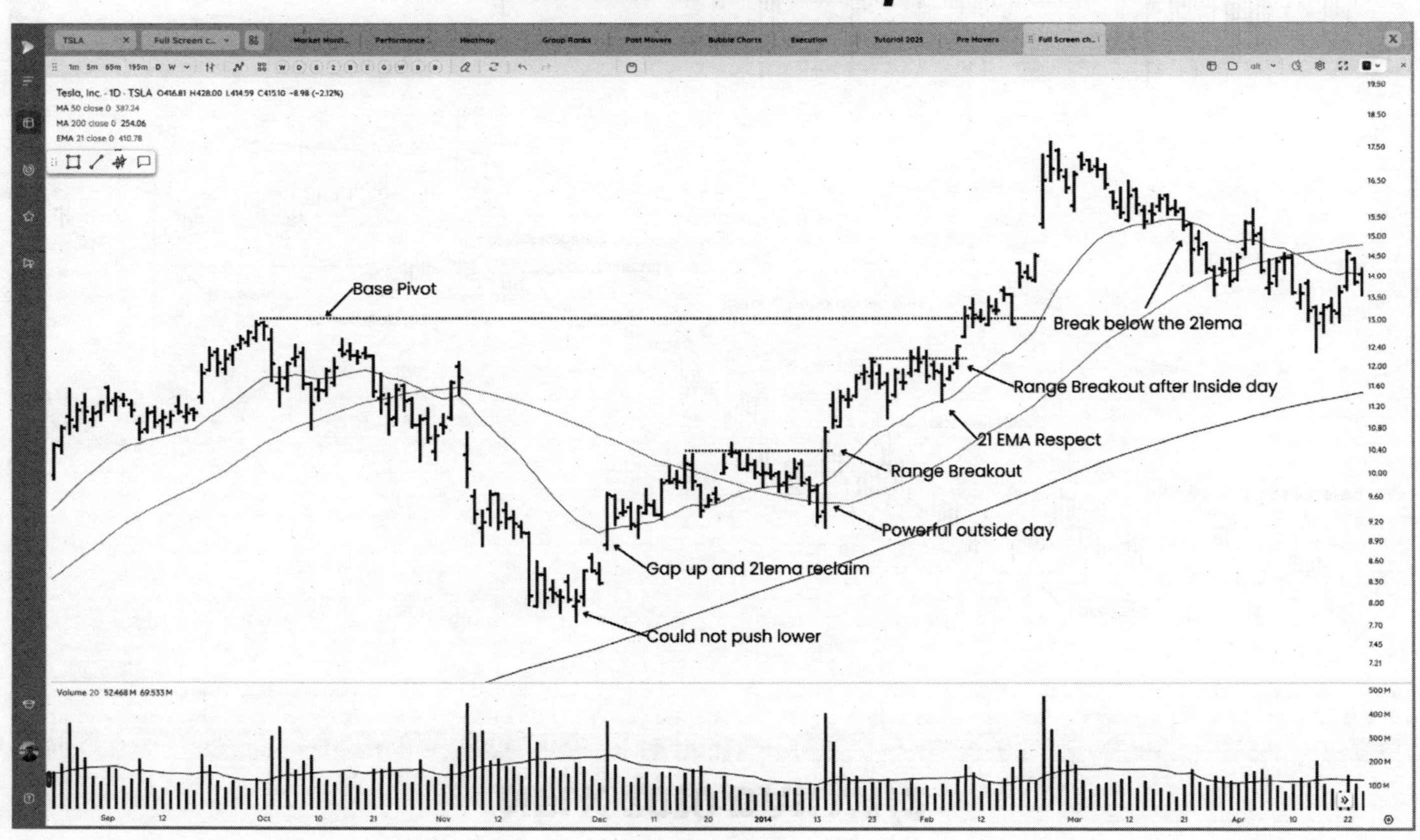
TSLA 2013 DAILY 2/2
Tesla, Inc. · 1D · TSLA
MA 50 close 0 387.24
MA 200 close 0 254.06
EMA 21 close 0 410.78
Base Pivot
Break below the 21ema
Range Breakout after Inside day
21 EMA Respect
Range Breakout
Powerful outside day
Gap up and 21ema reclaim
Could not push lower

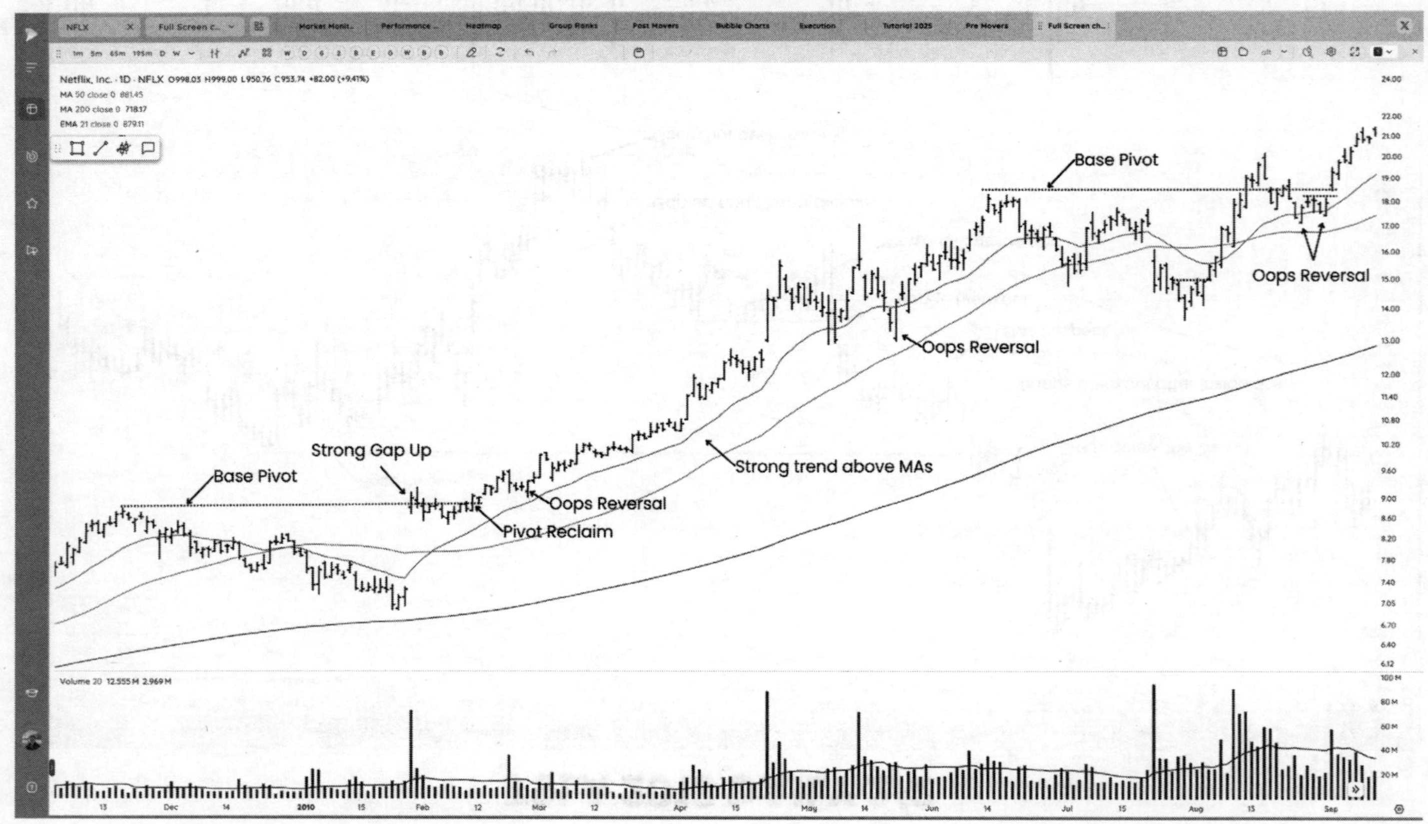
NFLX 2010 DAILY 1/2
Netflix, Inc. · 1D · NFLX O998.03 H999.00 L950.76 C953.74 +82.00 (+9.41%)
MA 50 close 0 881.45
MA 200 close 0 718.17
EMA 21 close 0 879.11
Base Pivot
Strong Gap Up
Pivot Reclaim
Oops Reversal
Strong trend above MAs
Oops Reversal
Base Pivot
Oops Reversal
Volume 20 12.555M 2.969M

NFLX 2010 DAILY 2/2

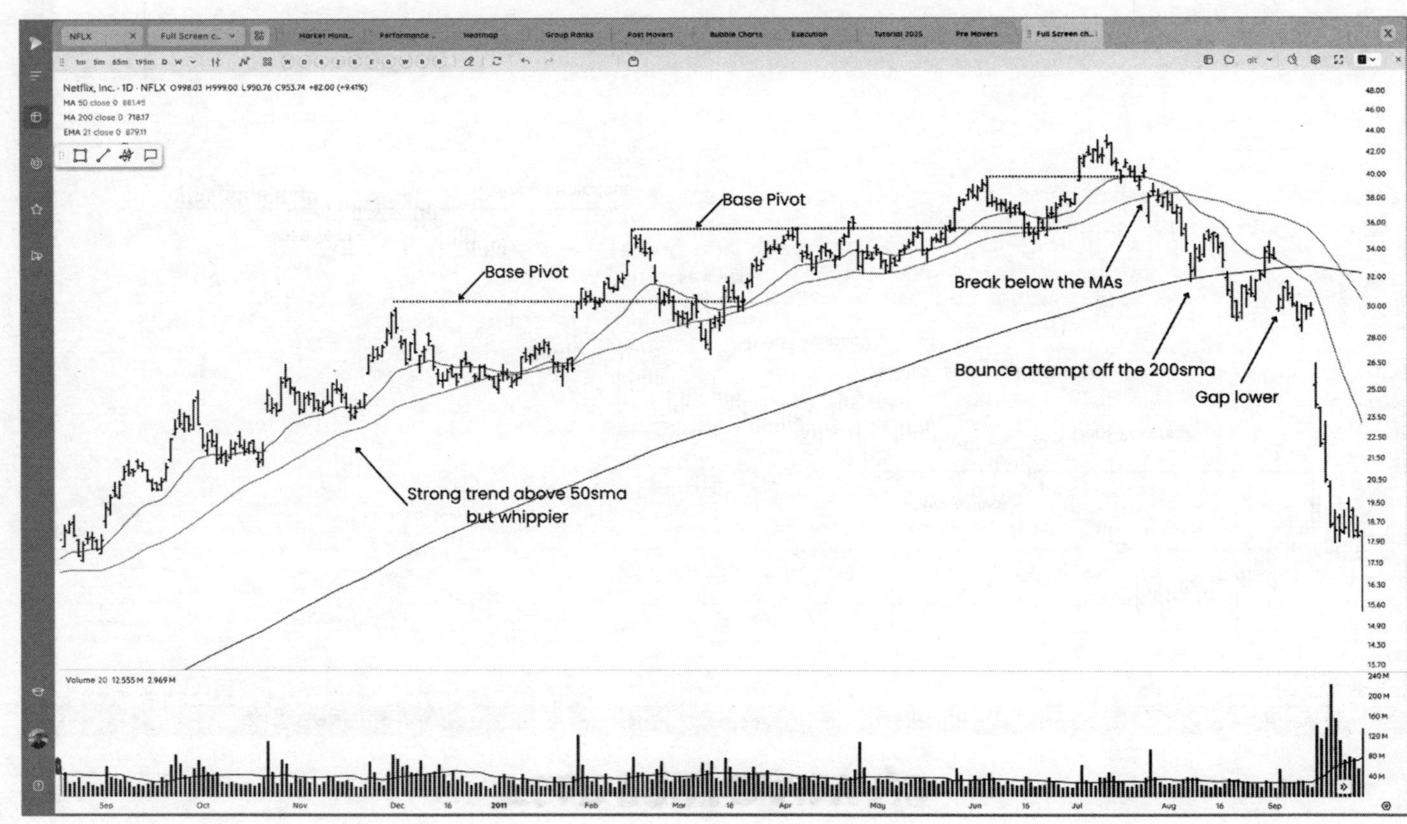

FSLR 2007 DAILY 1/2

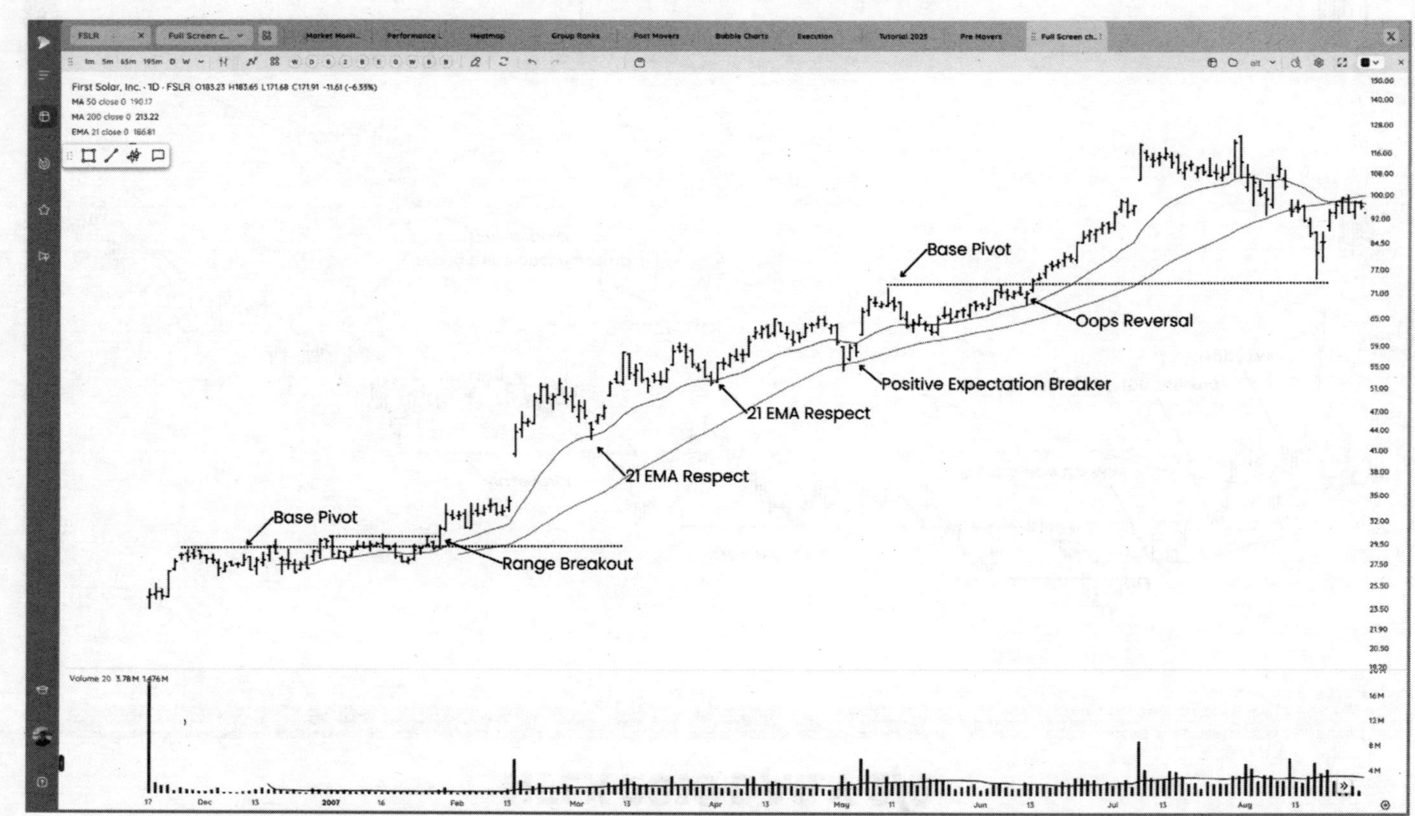

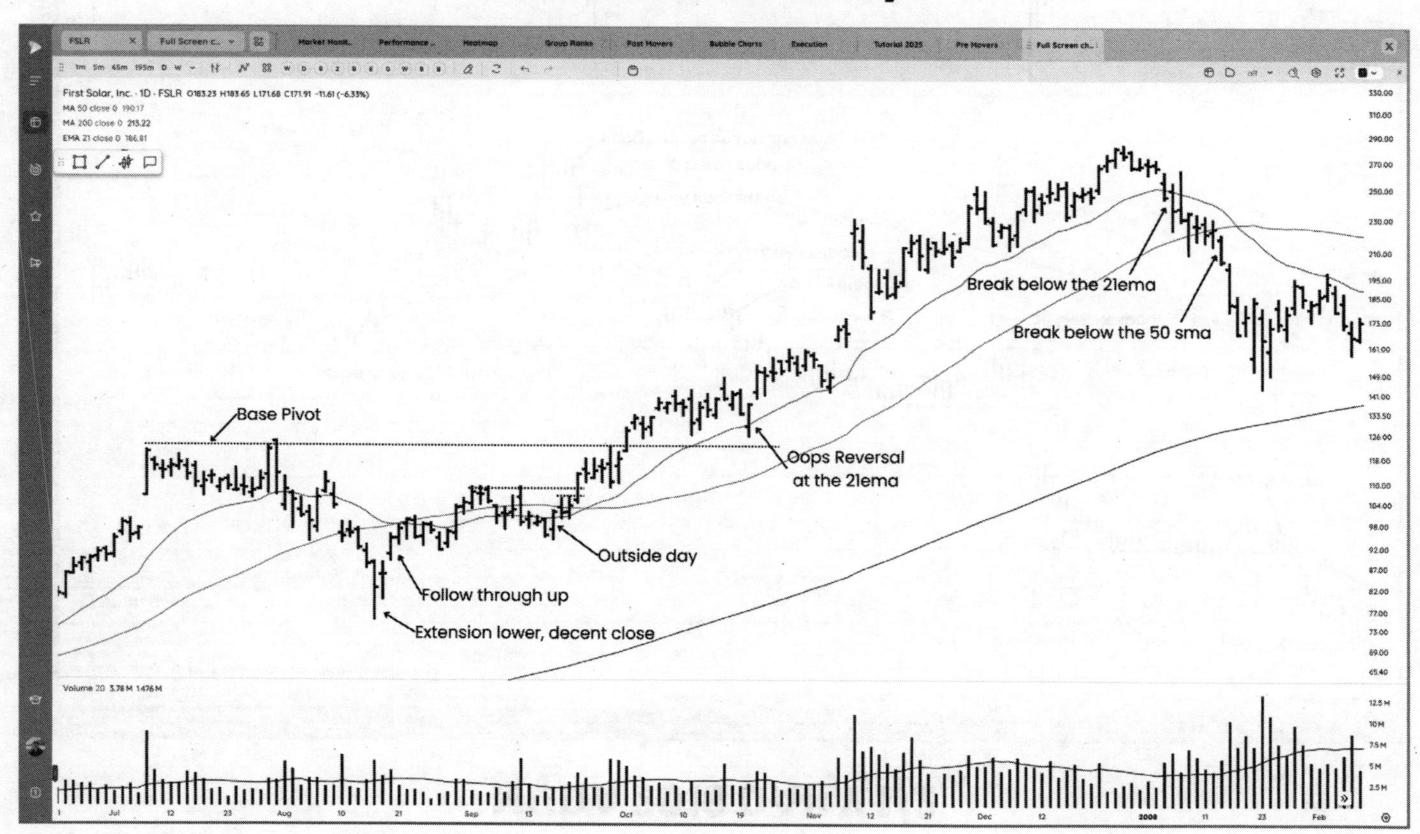
FSLR 2007 DAILY 2/2
First Solar, Inc. · 1D · FSLR O183.23 H183.65 L171.68 C171.91 −11.61 (−6.33%)
MA 50 close 0 190.17
MA 200 close 0 213.22
EMA 21 close 0 186.81
Base Pivot
Follow through up
Extension lower, decent close
Outside day
Oops Reversal
at the 21ema
Break below the 21ema
Break below the 50 sma
Volume 20 3.78 M 1.476 M

NVDA 2016 DAILY 1/2

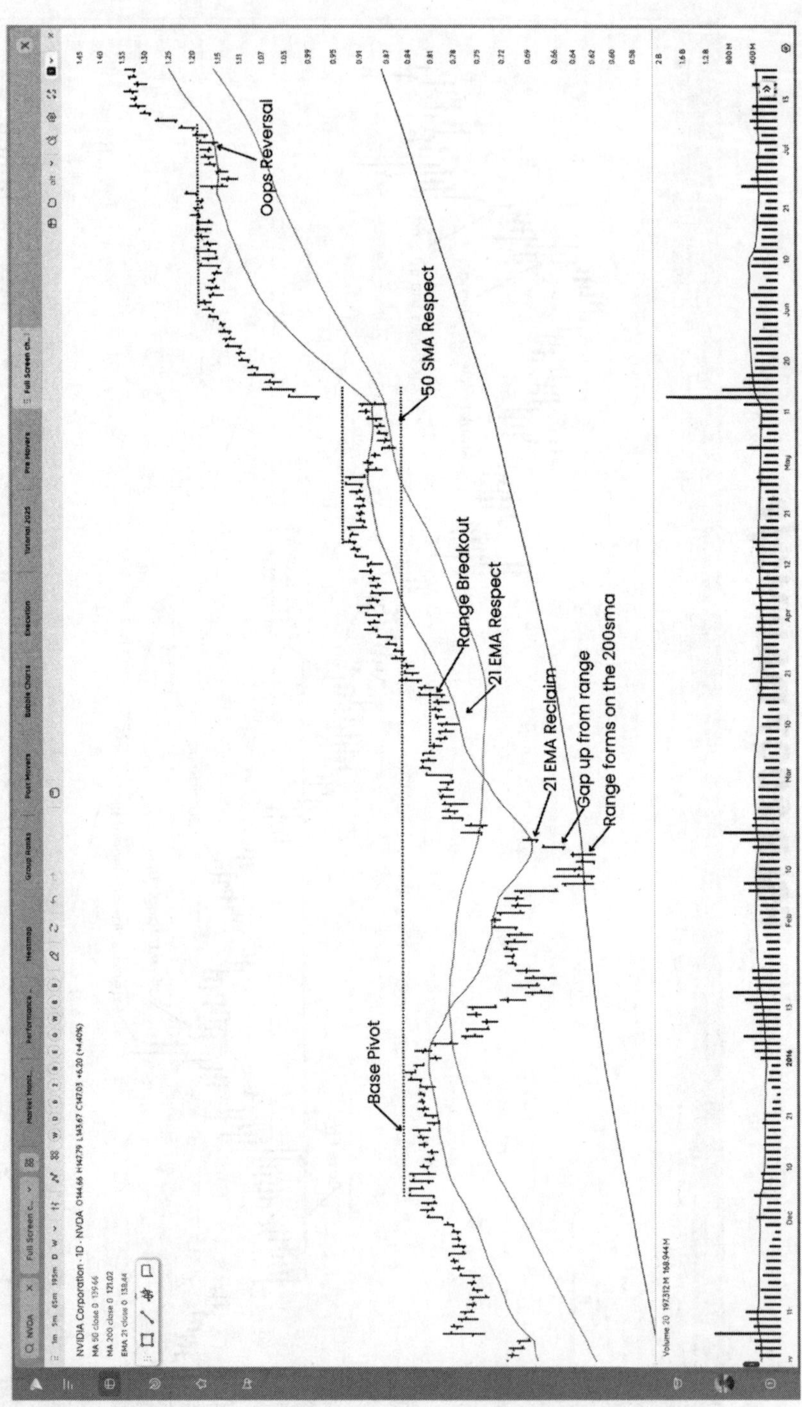

NVDA 2016 DAILY 2/2
NVIDIA Corporation · 1D · NVDA O144.66 H147.79 L143.67 C147.03 +6.20 (+4.40%)
MA 50 close 0 139.66
MA 200 close 0 121.02
EMA 21 close 0 138.44
Base Pivot
Break lower from tight range
contained by 21ema
21 EMA Reclaim
Base low respect
50 SMA Respect
Volume 20 197.312 M 168.944 M

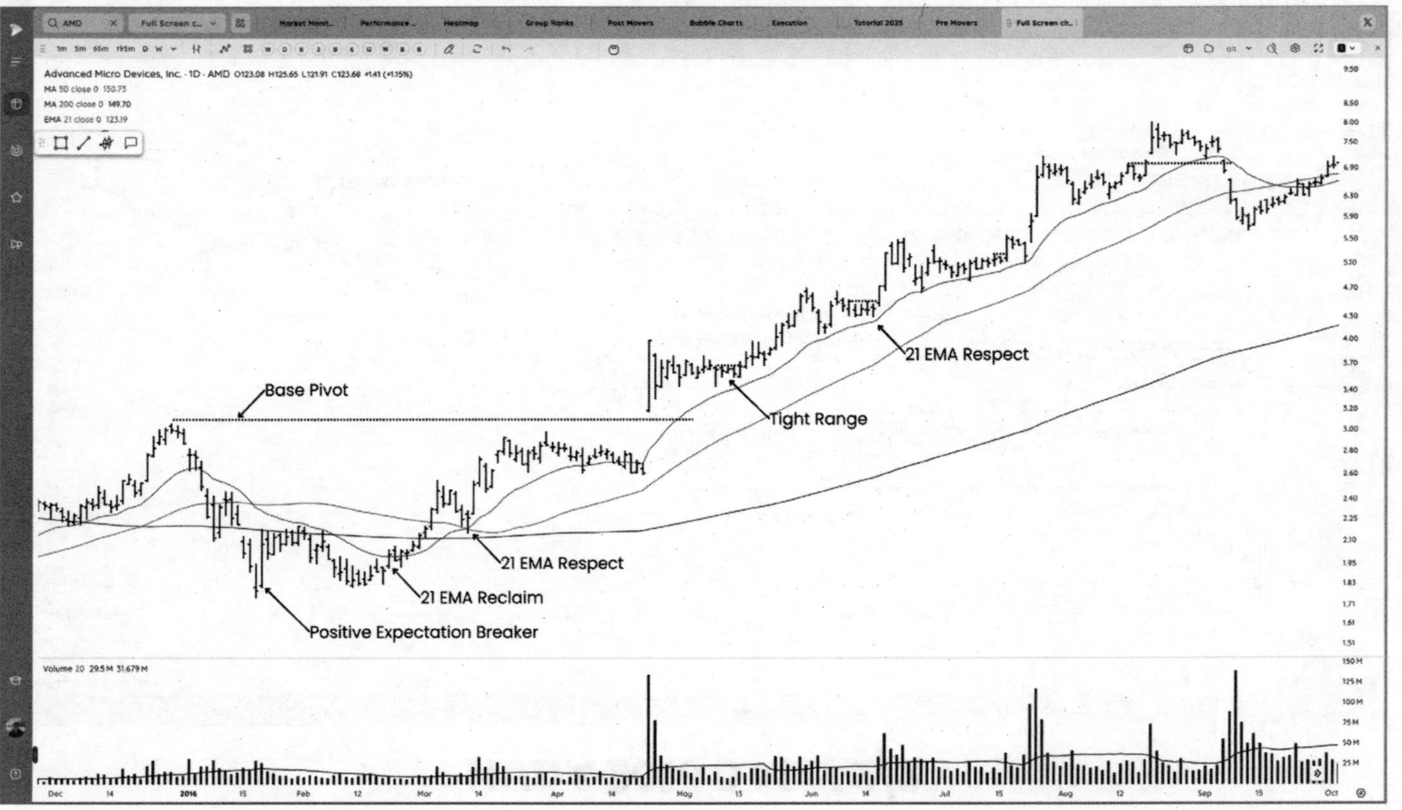
AMD 2016 DAILY 1/2
Advanced Micro Devices, Inc. · 1D · AMD O123.08 H125.65 L121.91 C123.68 +1.41 (+1.15%)
MA 50 close 0 130.73
MA 200 close 0 149.70
EMA 21 close 0 123.19
Base Pivot
Tight Range
21 EMA Respect
21 EMA Respect
21 EMA Reclaim
Positive Expectation Breaker
Volume 20 29.5 M 31.679 M

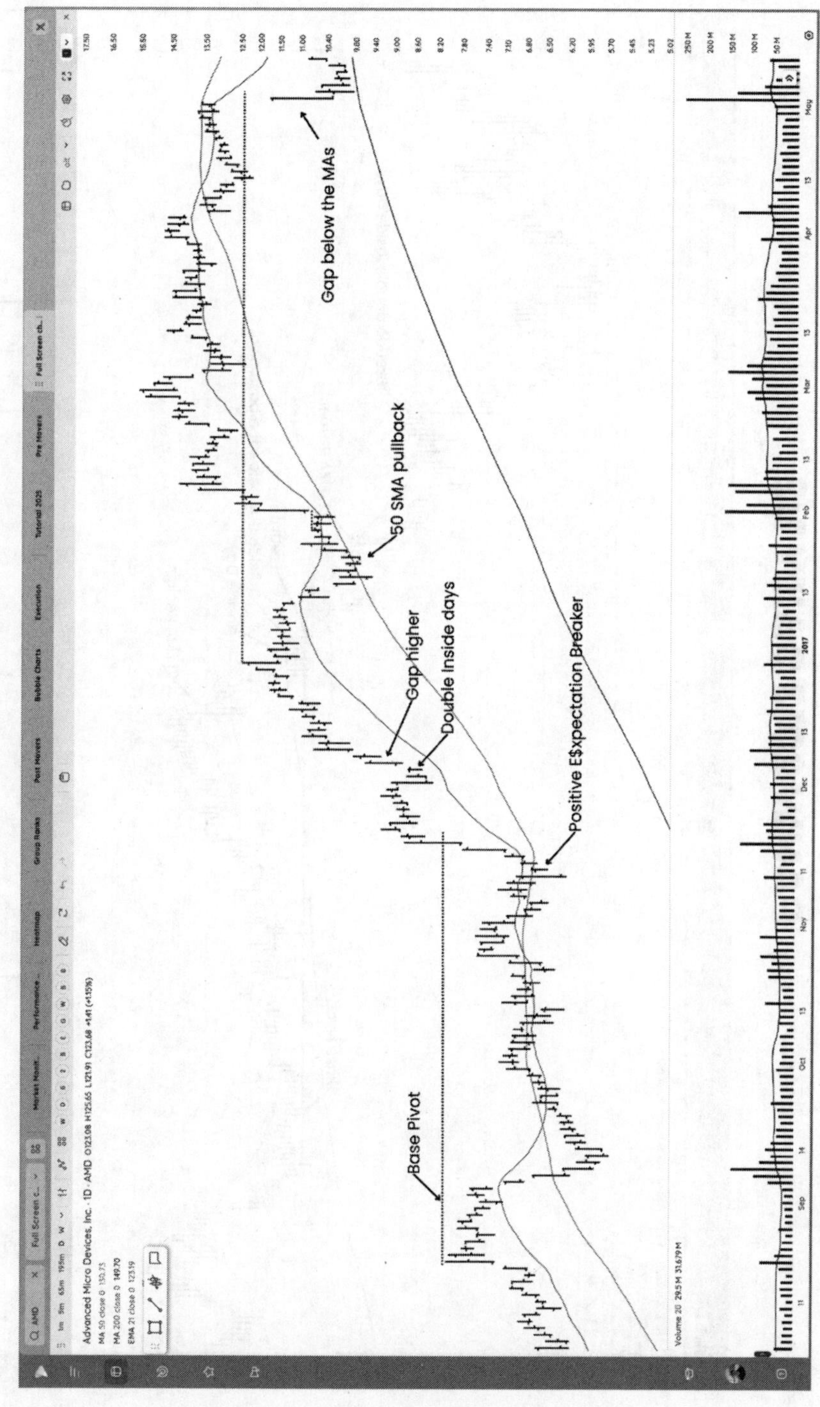
AMD 2016 DAILY 2/2
Base Pivot
Gap higher
Double Inside days
Positive E$xpectation Breaker
50 SMA pullback
Gap below the MAs

PANW 2013 DAILY 1/2

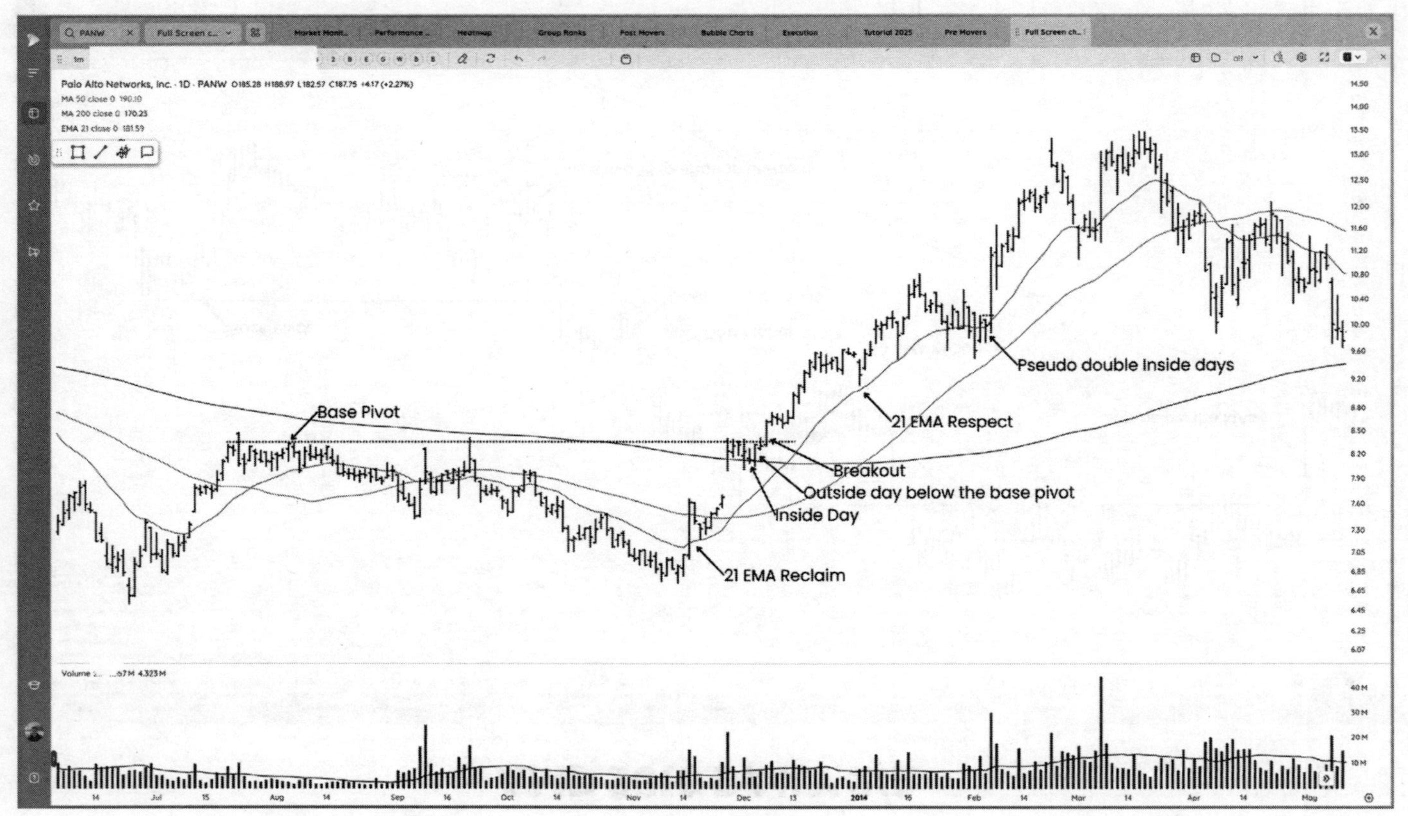

PANW 2013 DAILY 2/2

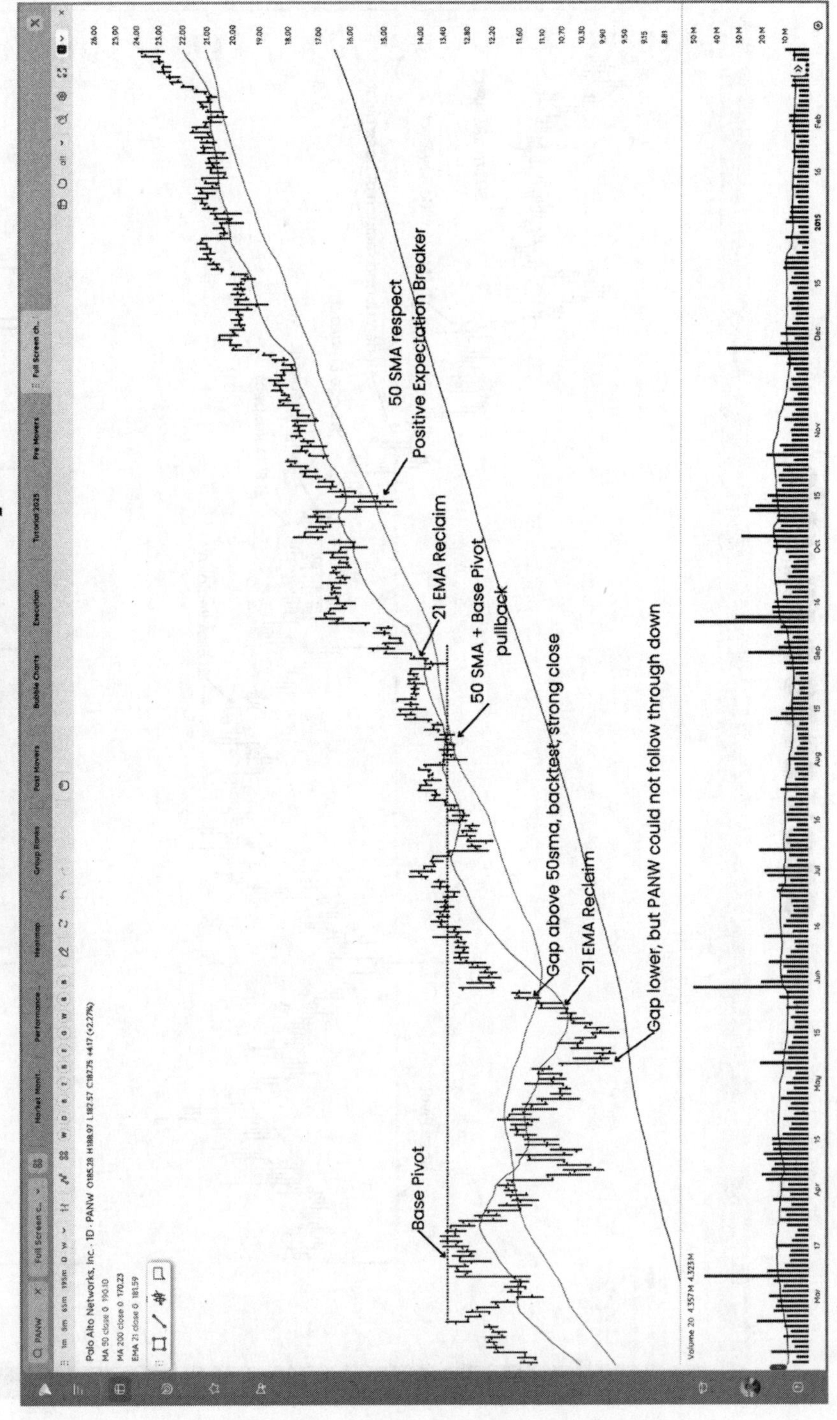

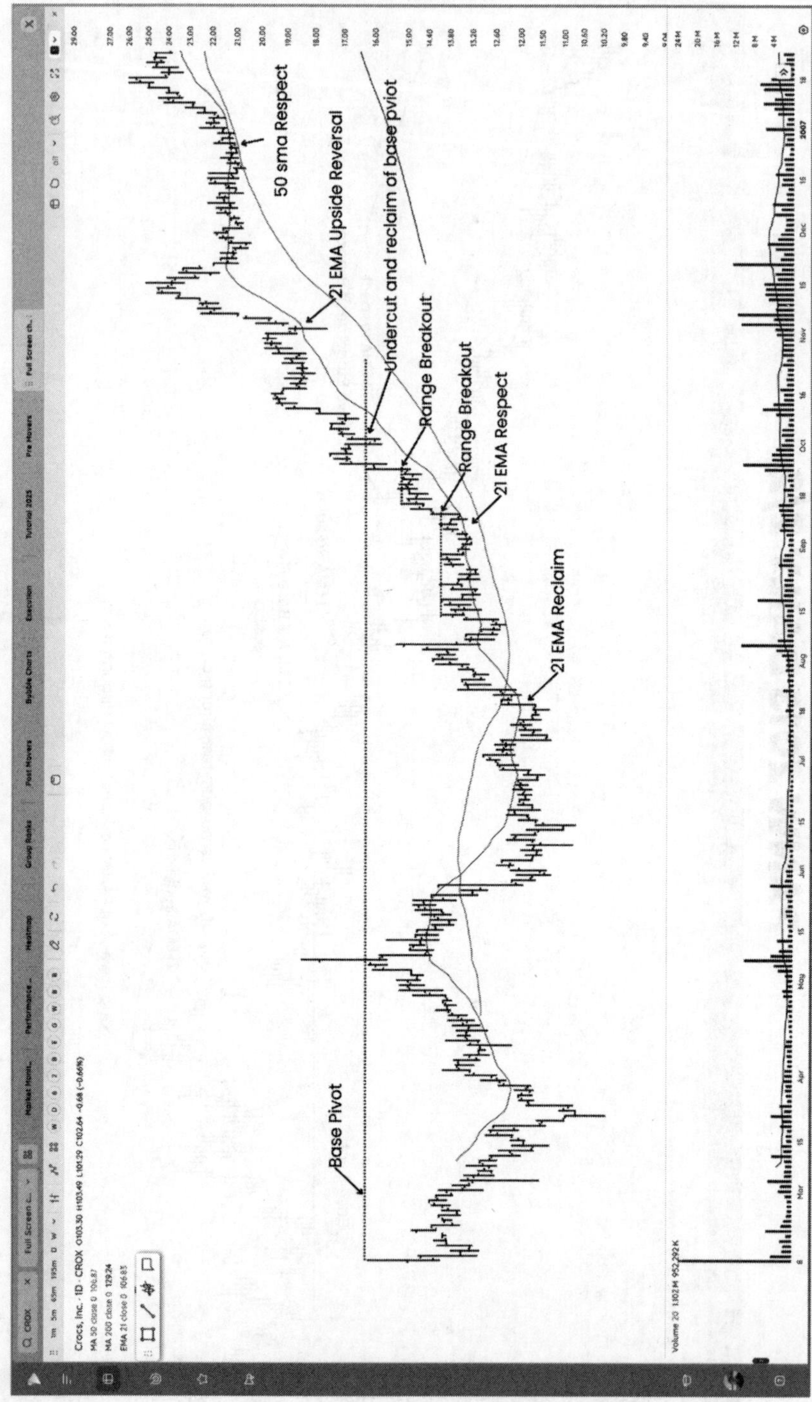
CROX 2006 DAILY1/2
Base Pivot
21 EMA Reclaim
21 EMA Respect
Range Breakout
Range Breakout
Undercut and reclaim of base pviot
21 EMA Upside Reversal
50 sma Respect

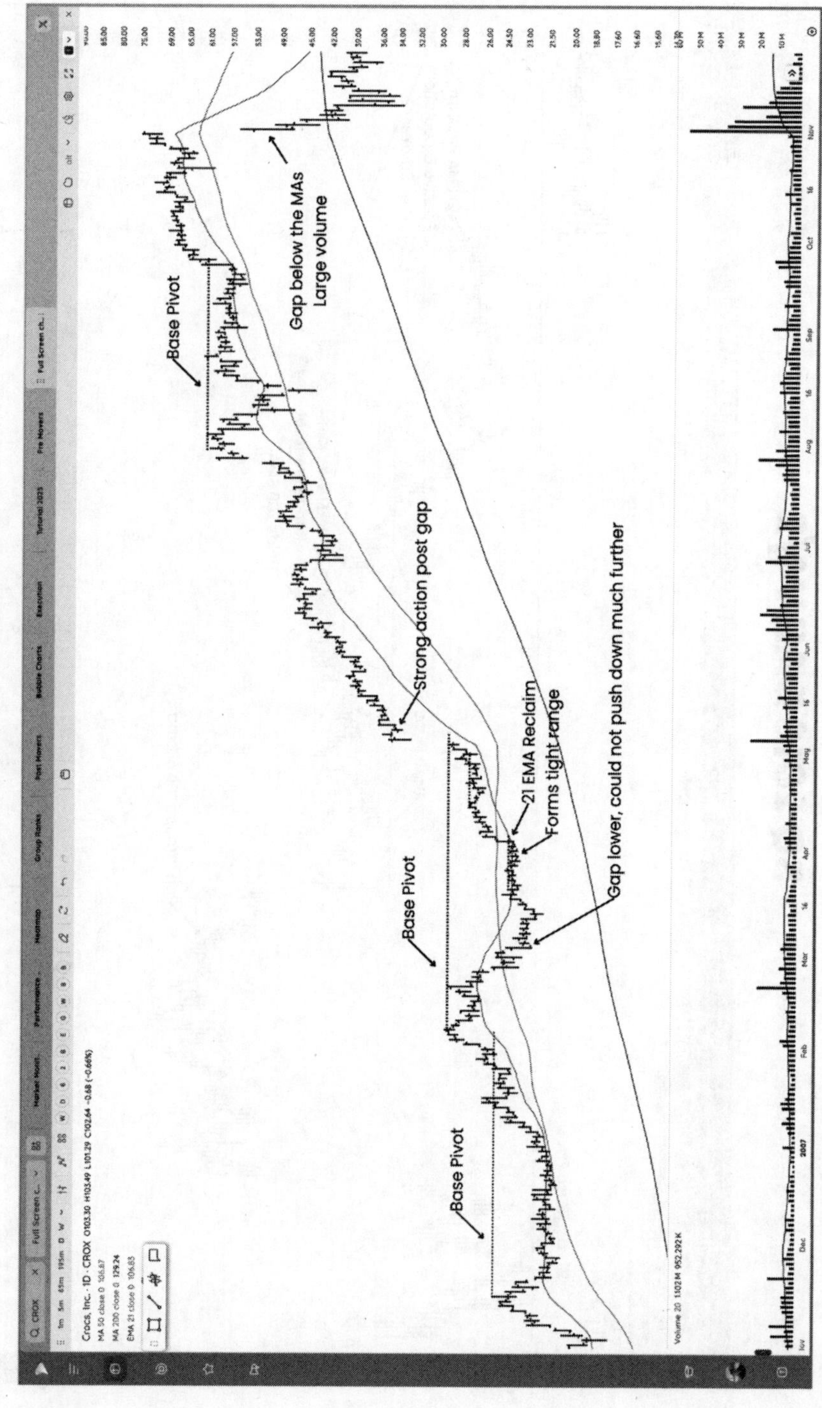
CROX 2006 DAILY 2/2
Base Pivot
Base Pivot
Base Pivot
Strong action post gap
21 EMA Reclaim
Forms tight range
Gap lower, could not push down much further
Gap below the MAs
Large volume

SQ 2016 DAILY 1/2

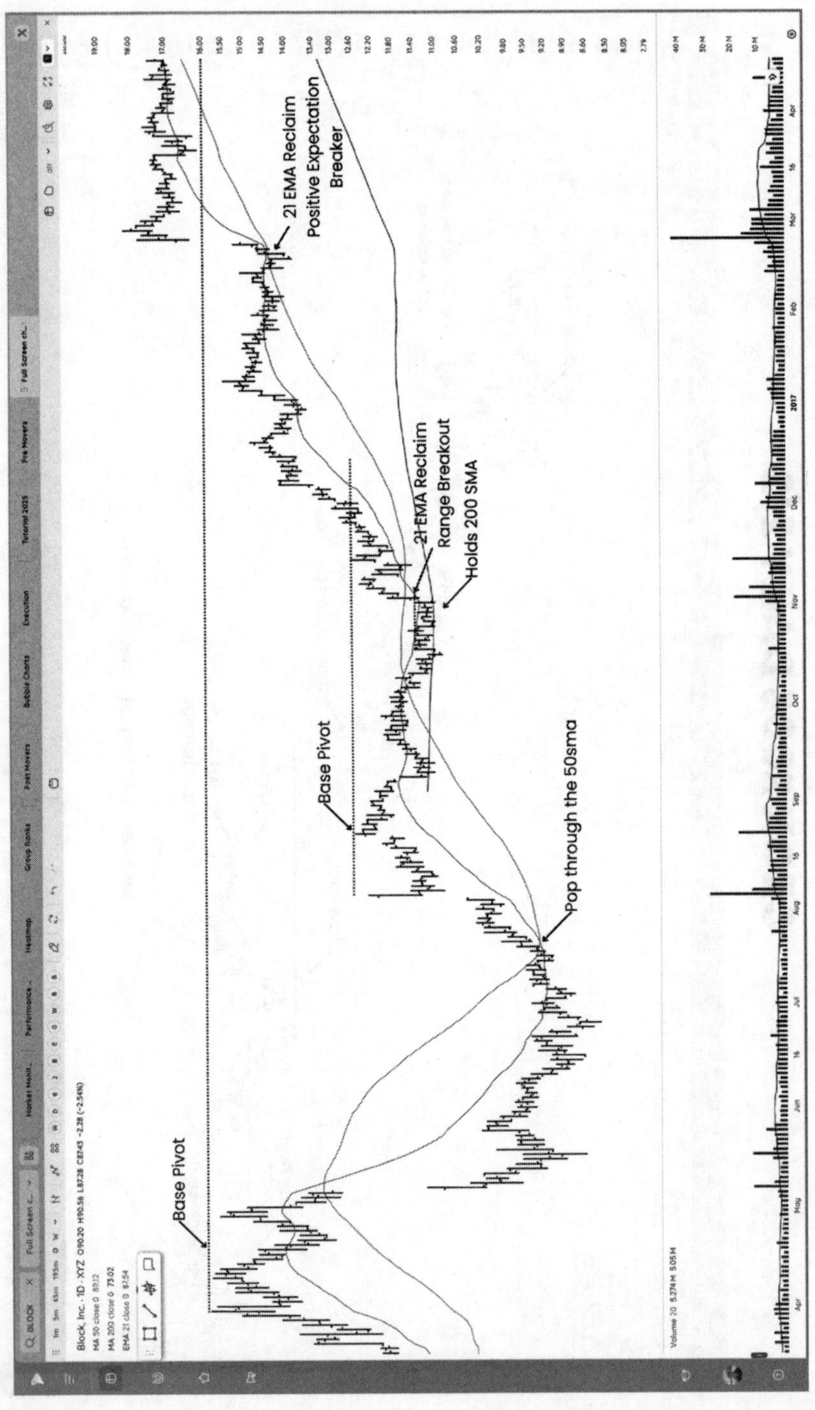

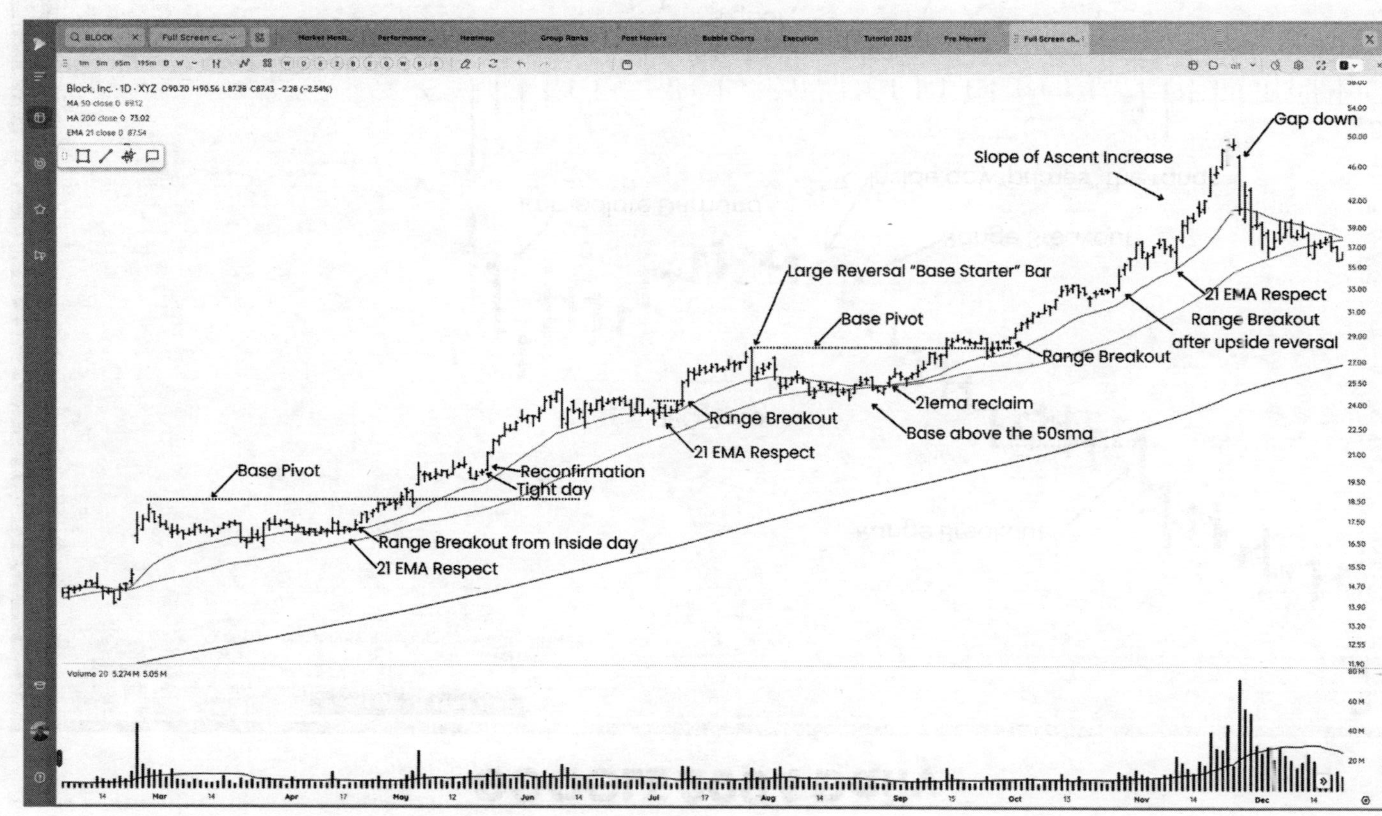
SQ 2016 DAILY 2/2
Block, Inc. · 1D · XYZ O90.20 H90.56 L87.28 C87.43 −2.28 (−2.54%)
MA 50 close 0 89.12
MA 200 close 0 73.02
EMA 21 close 0 87.54
Gap down
Slope of Ascent Increase
Large Reversal "Base Starter" Bar
Base Pivot
21 EMA Respect
Range Breakout
after upside reversal
Range Breakout
21ema reclaim
Base above the 50sma
Range Breakout
21 EMA Respect
Base Pivot
Reconfirmation
Tight day
Range Breakout from Inside day
21 EMA Respect
Volume 20 5.274M 5.05M

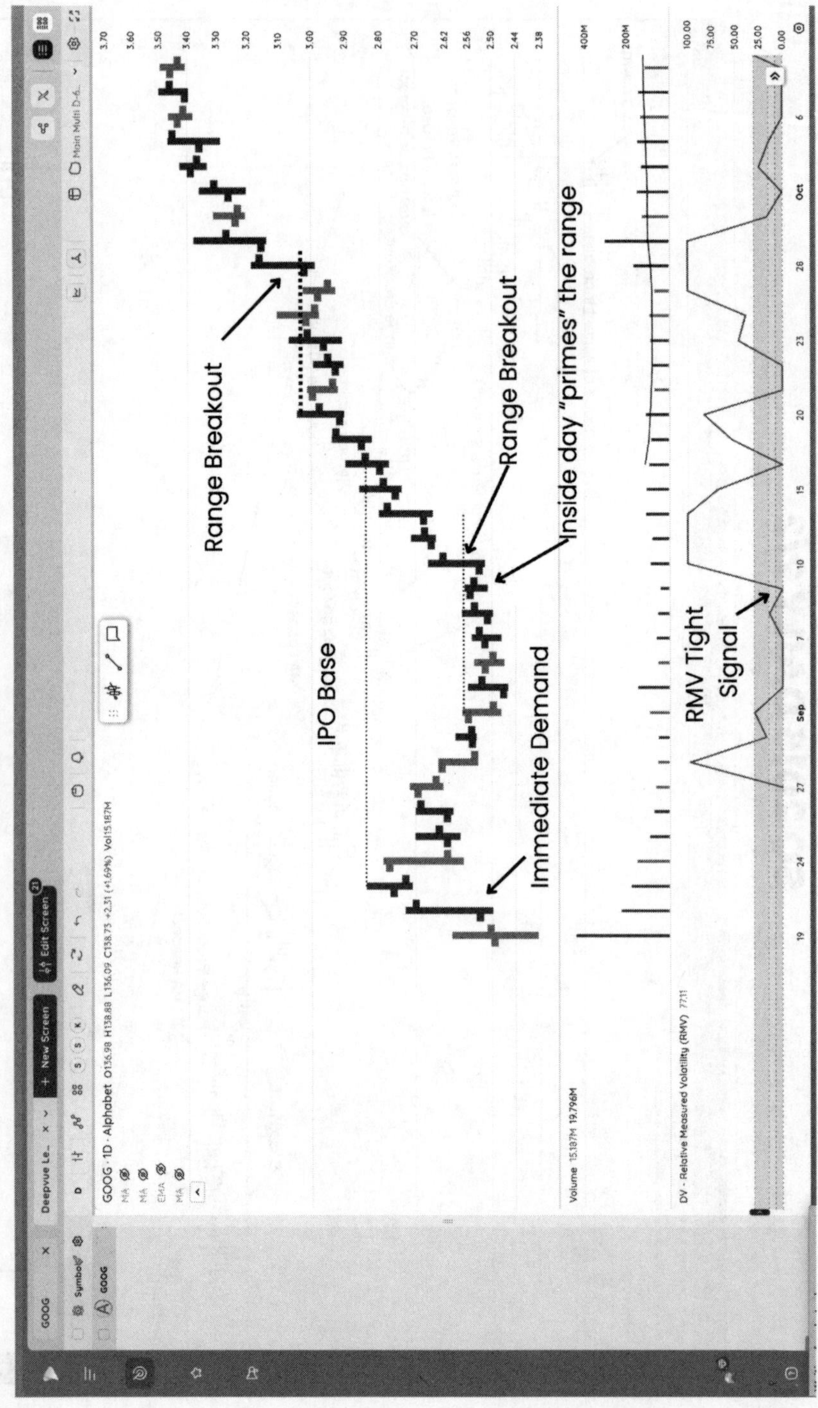
GOOGLE 2004 Daily
Range Breakout
IPO Base
Range Breakout
Inside day "primes" the range
Immediate Demand
RMV Tight Signal

2017 MARKET LEADERS

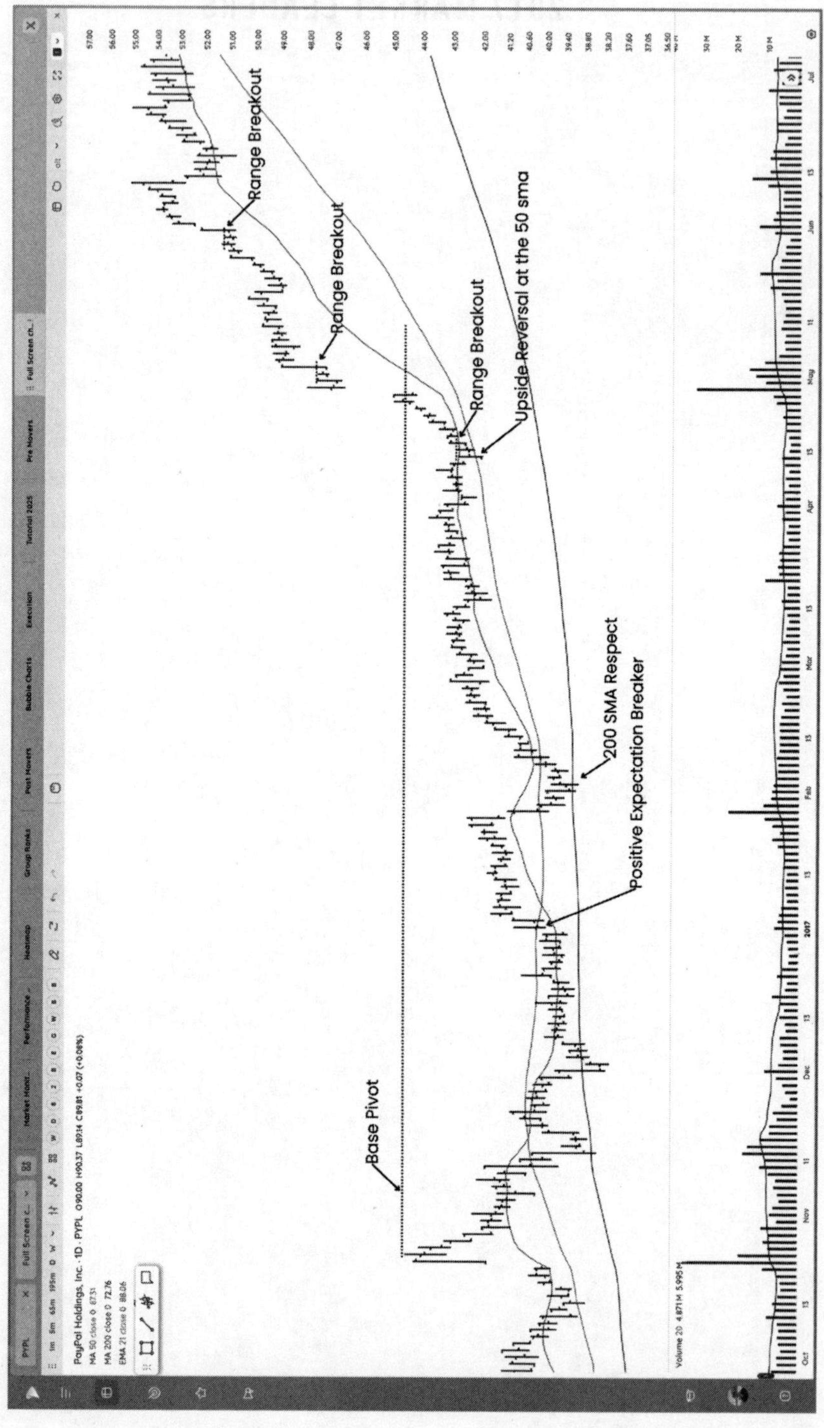
PYPL 2017 DAILY 1/2
Range Breakout
Range Breakout
Range Breakout
Upside Reversal at the 50 sma
200 SMA Respect
Positive Expectation Breaker
Base Pivot

PYPL 2017 DAILY 2/2

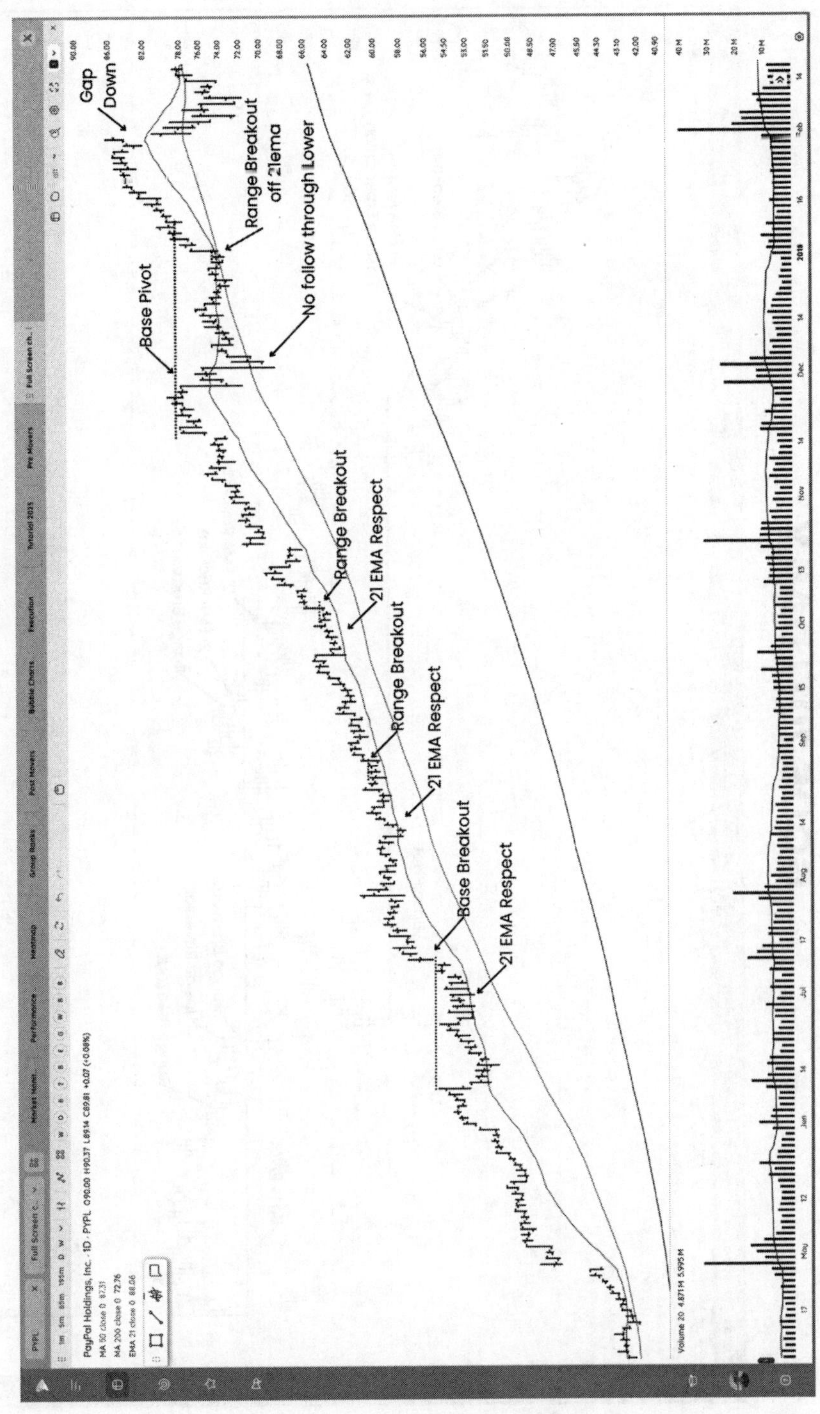

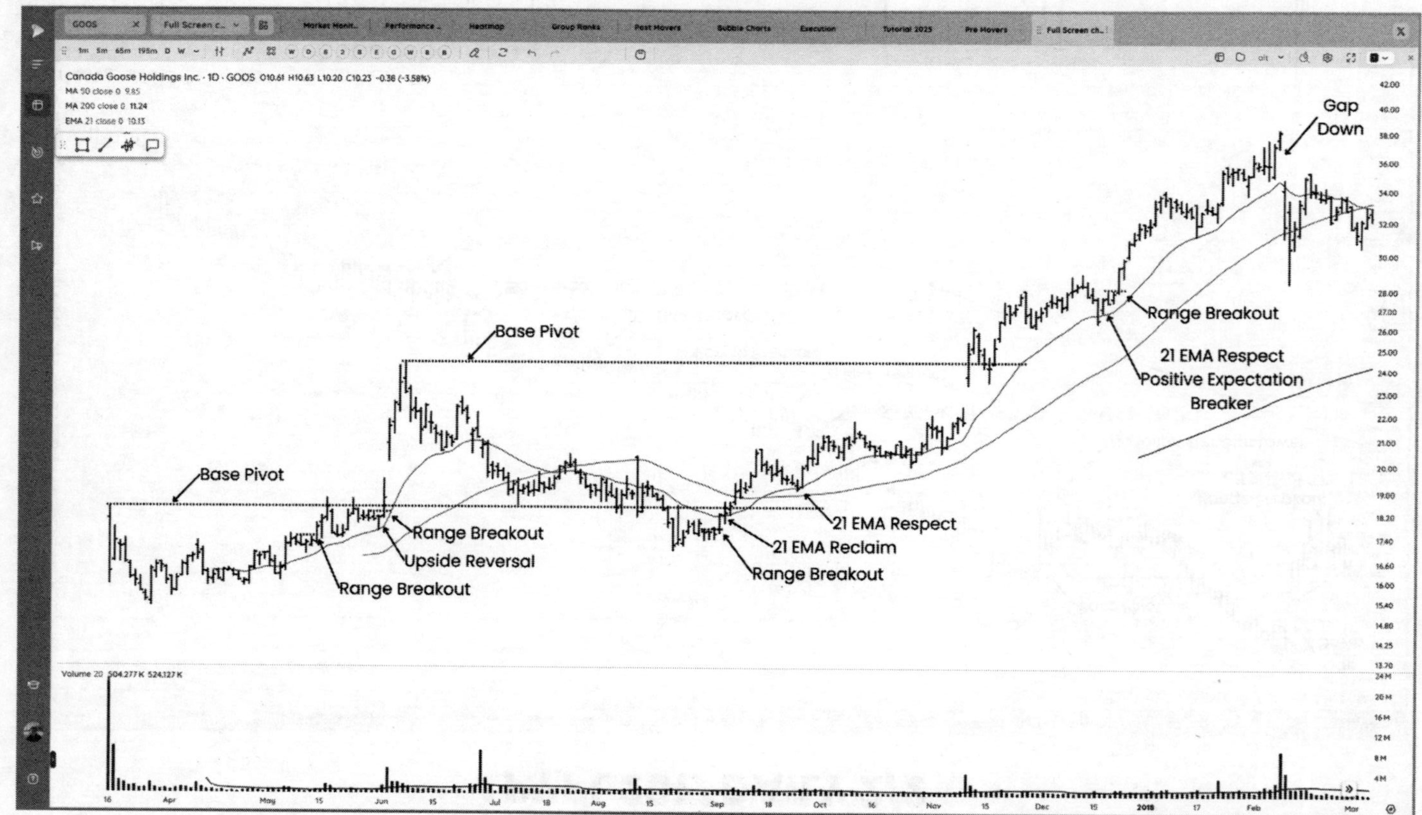
GOOS 2017 DAILY
Canada Goose Holdings Inc. · 1D · GOOS O10.61 H10.63 L10.20 C10.23 −0.38 (−3.58%)
MA 50 close 0 9.85
MA 200 close 0 11.24
EMA 21 close 0 10.13
Gap Down
Range Breakout
21 EMA Respect
Positive Expectation Breaker
Base Pivot
Base Pivot
Range Breakout
Upside Reversal
Range Breakout
21 EMA Respect
21 EMA Reclaim
Range Breakout
Volume 20 504.277 K 524.127 K

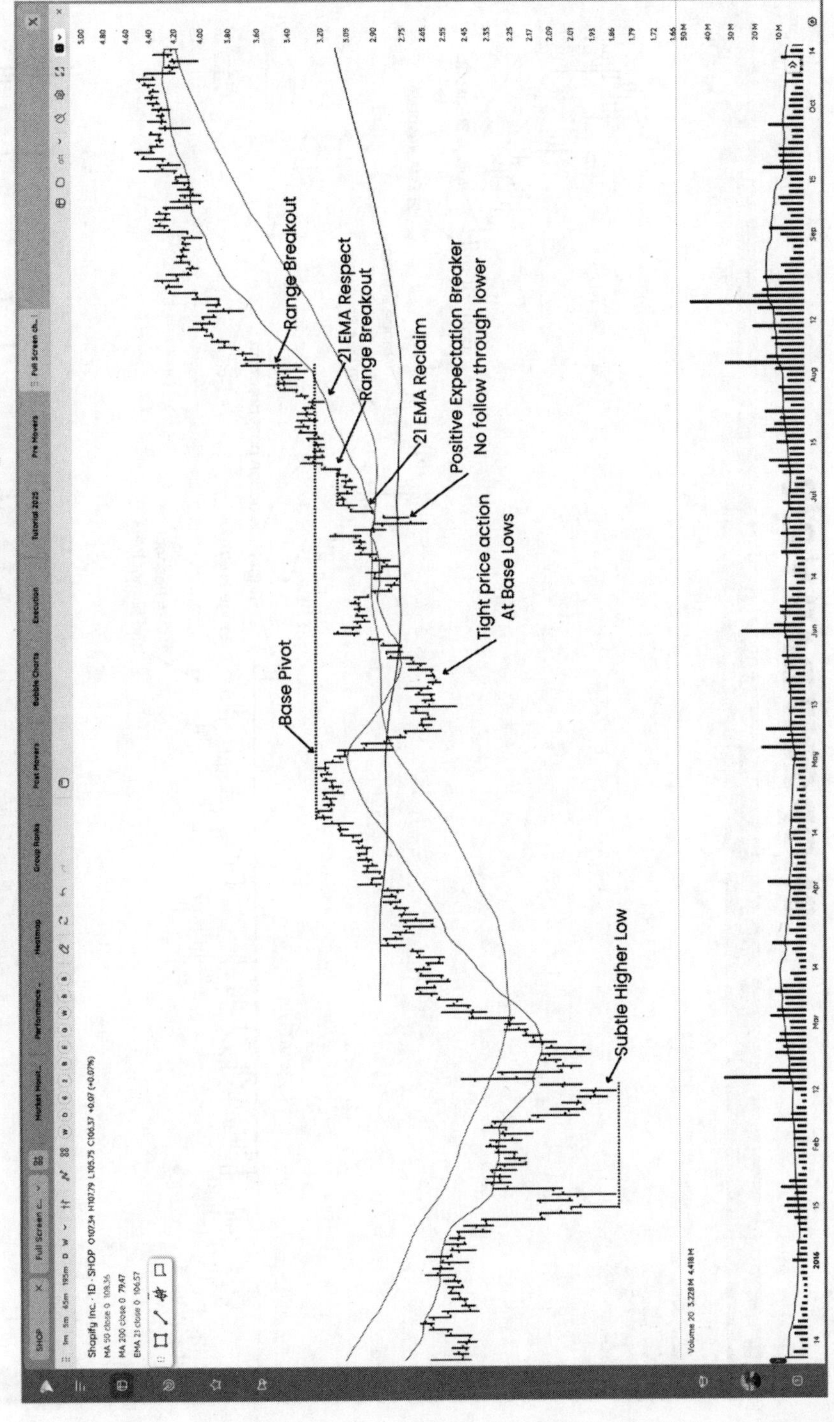
SHOP 2016–2017 DAILY 1/3
Range Breakout
21 EMA Respect
Range Breakout
21 EMA Reclaim
Positive Expectation Breaker
No follow through lower
Base Pivot
Tight price action
At Base Lows
Subtle Higher Low

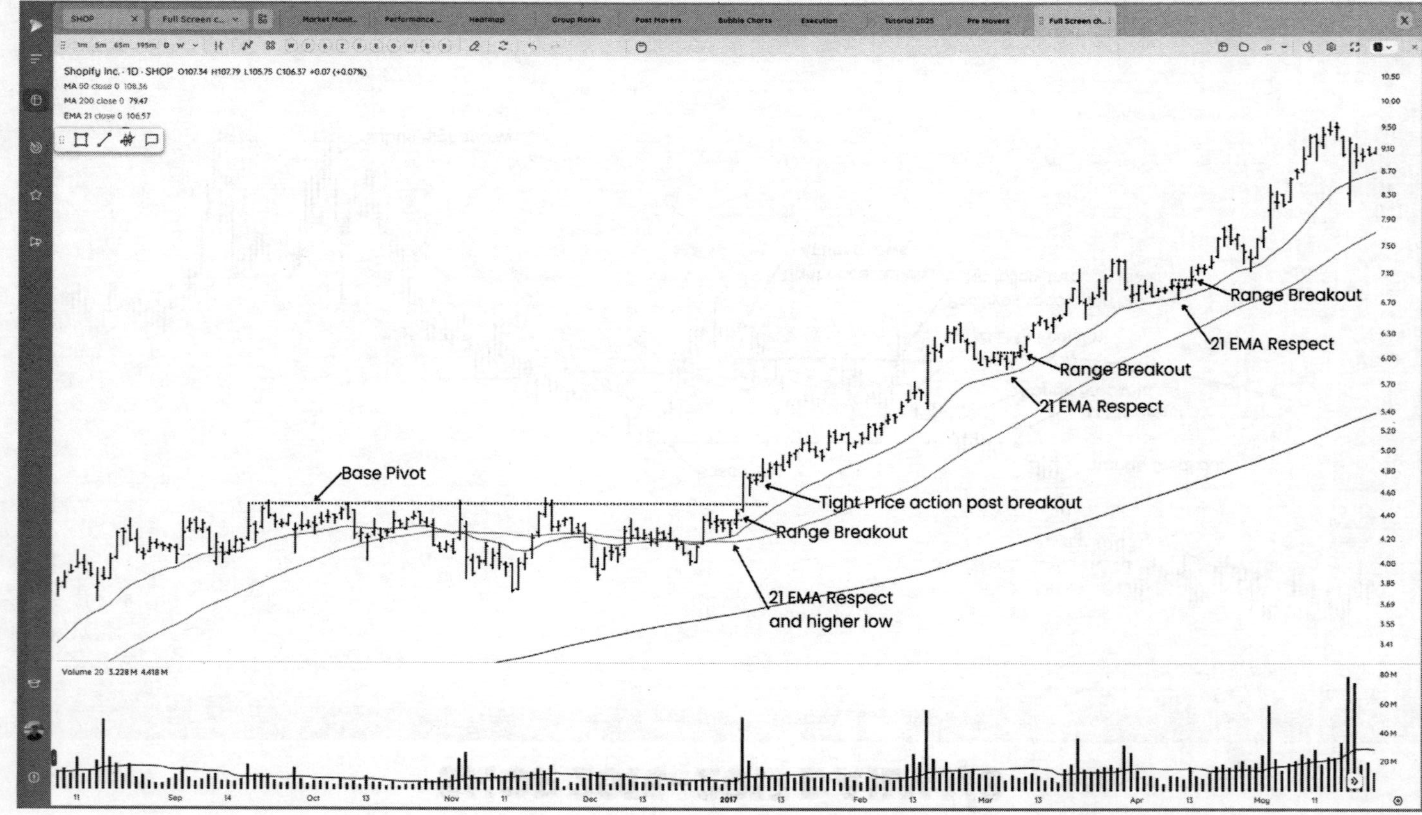
SHOP 2017 DAILY 2/3
Shopify Inc. · 1D · SHOP O107.34 H107.79 L105.75 C106.37 +0.07 (+0.07%)
MA 50 close 0 108.36
MA 200 close 0 79.47
EMA 21 close 0 106.57
Base Pivot
Tight Price action post breakout
Range Breakout
21 EMA Respect
and higher low
Range Breakout
21 EMA Respect
Range Breakout
21 EMA Respect
Volume 20 3.228 M 4.418 M

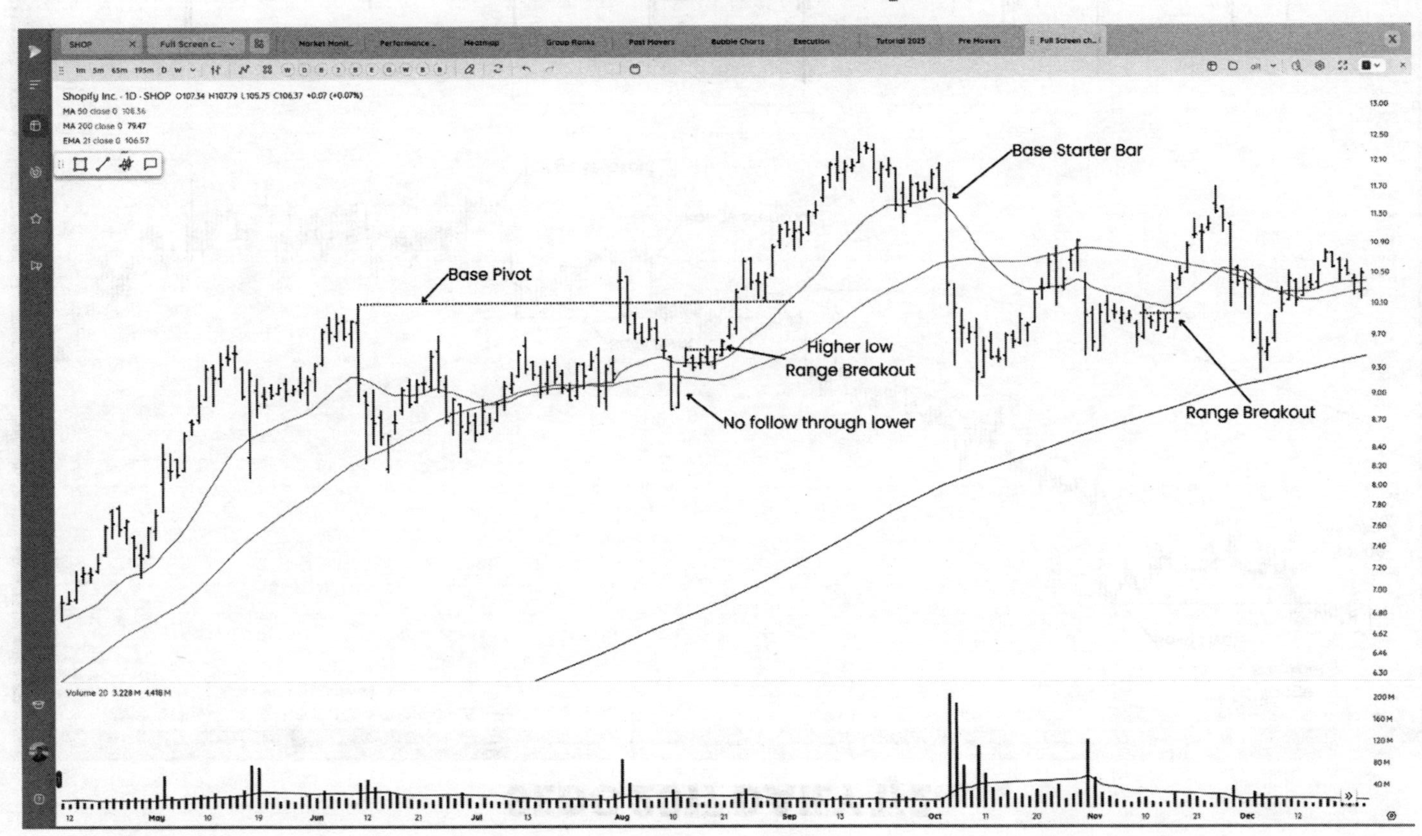
SHOP 2017 DAILY 3/3
Shopify Inc. · 1D · SHOP O107.34 H107.79 L105.75 C106.37 +0.07 (+0.07%)
MA 50 close 0 106.36
MA 200 close 0 79.47
EMA 21 close 0 106.57
Base Pivot
Higher low
Range Breakout
No follow through lower
Base Starter Bar
Range Breakout
Volume 20 3.228 M 4.418 M

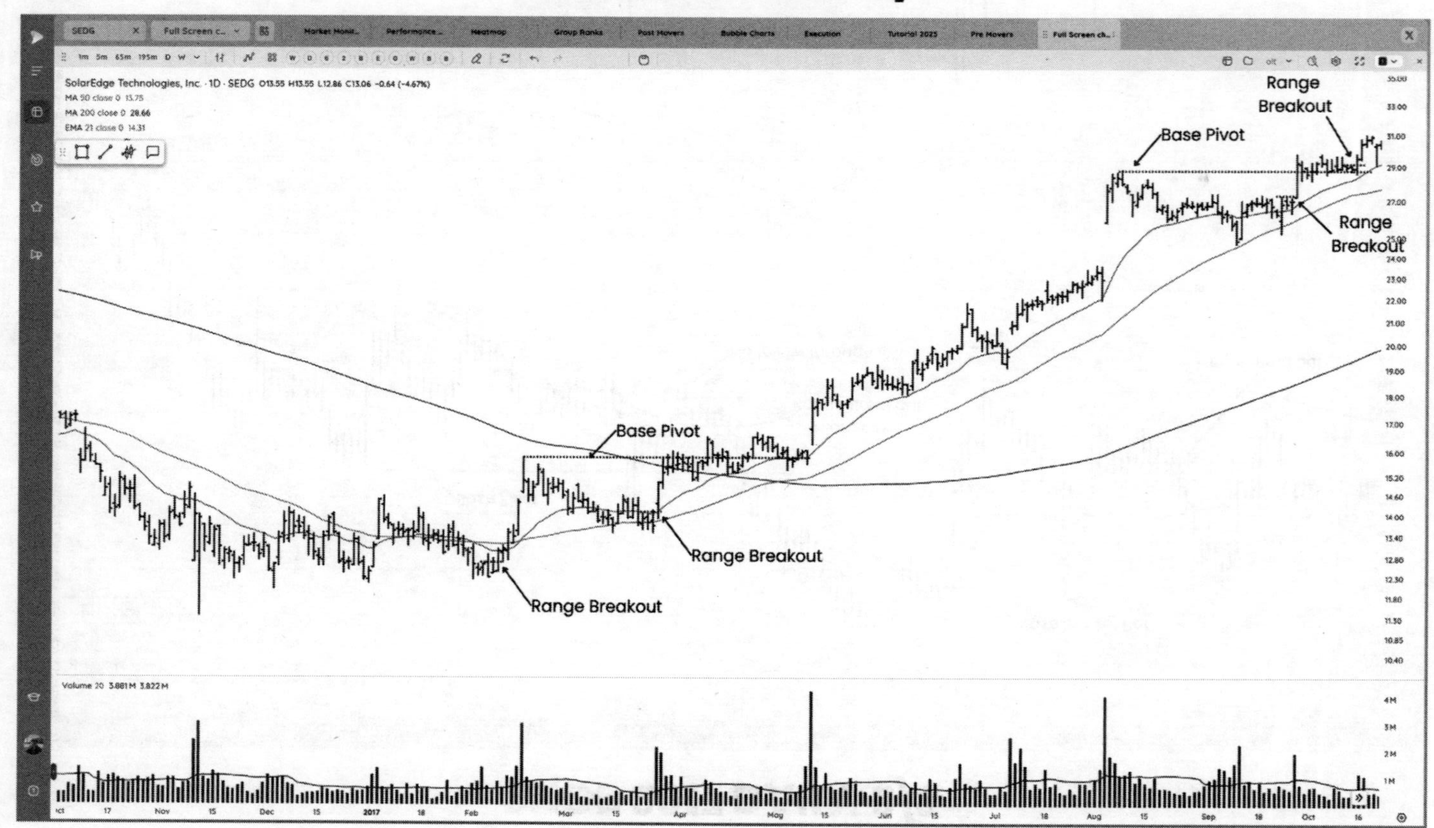
SEDG 2017 DAILY 1/2
SolarEdge Technologies, Inc. · 1D · SEDG O13.55 H13.55 L12.86 C13.06 −0.64 (−4.67%)
MA 50 close 0 13.75
MA 200 close 0 28.66
EMA 21 close 0 14.31
Range Breakout
Base Pivot
Range Breakout
Base Pivot
Range Breakout
Range Breakout
Volume 20 3.881 M 3.822 M

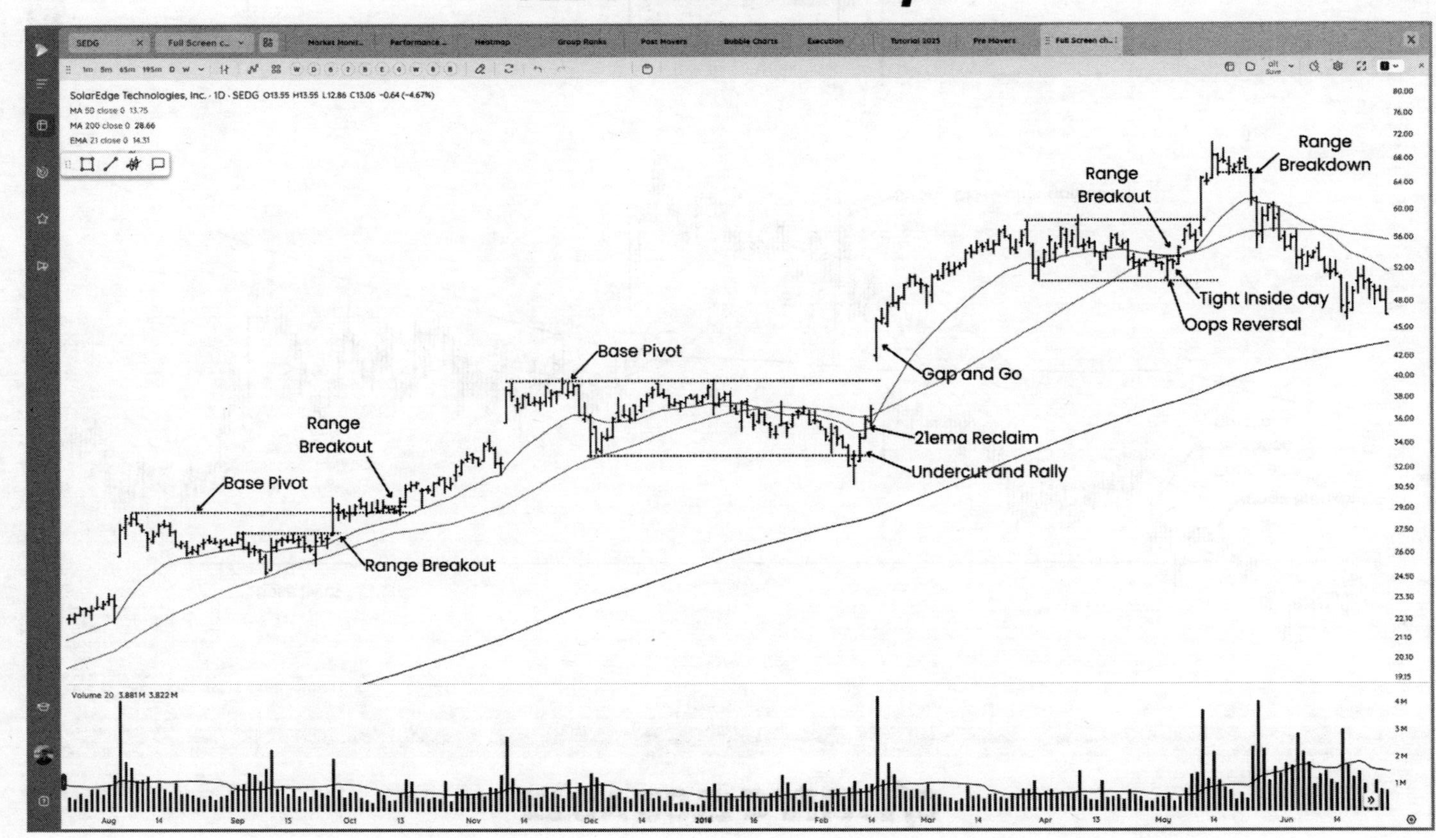
SEDG 2017 DAILY 2/2
SolarEdge Technologies, Inc. · 1D · SEDG O13.55 H13.55 L12.86 C13.06 −0.64 (−4.67%)
MA 50 close 0 13.75
MA 200 close 0 28.66
EMA 21 close 0 14.31
Base Pivot
Range Breakout
Range Breakout
Base Pivot
Gap and Go
21ema Reclaim
Undercut and Rally
Range Breakout
Tight Inside day
Oops Reversal
Range Breakdown
Volume 20 3.881M 3.822M

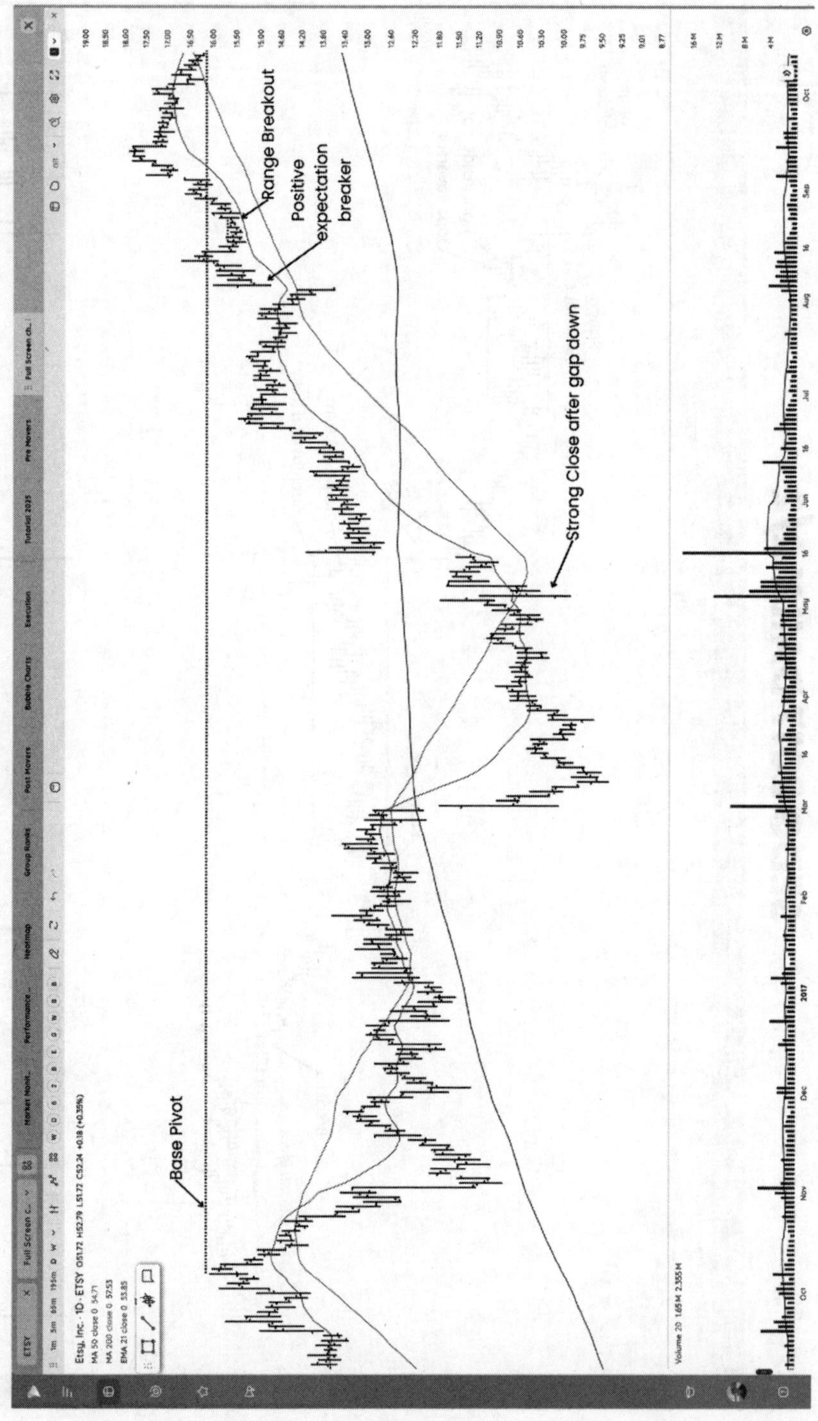

ETSY 2017 DAILY 1/2
Base Pivot
Range Breakout
Positive expectation breaker
Strong Close after gap down

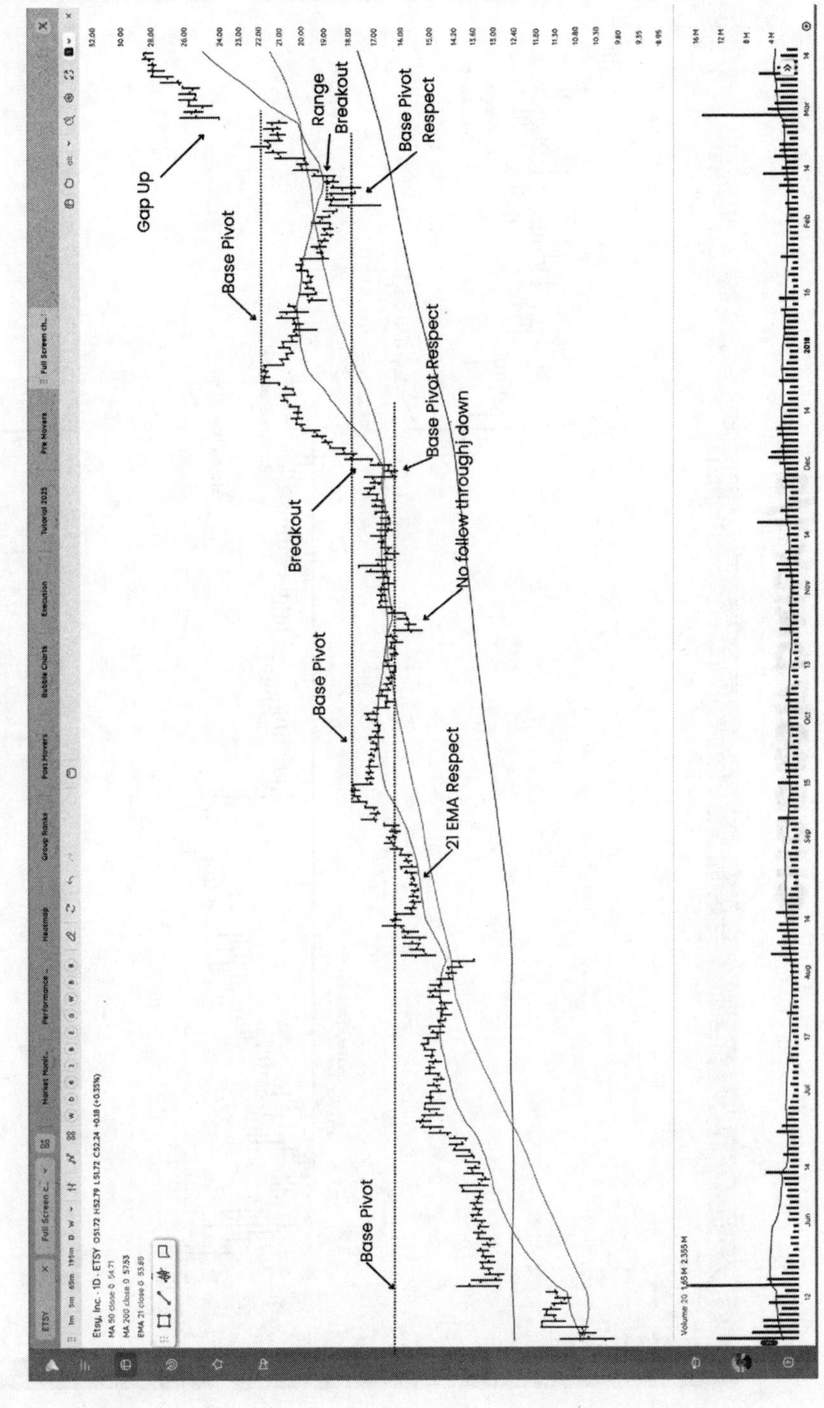
ETSY 2017 DAILY 2/2
Gap Up
Base Pivot
Range
Breakout
Base Pivot
Respect
Breakout
Base Pivot Respect
No follow throughj down
Base Pivot
21 EMA Respect
Base Pivot

CHGG 2017 DAILY 1/2

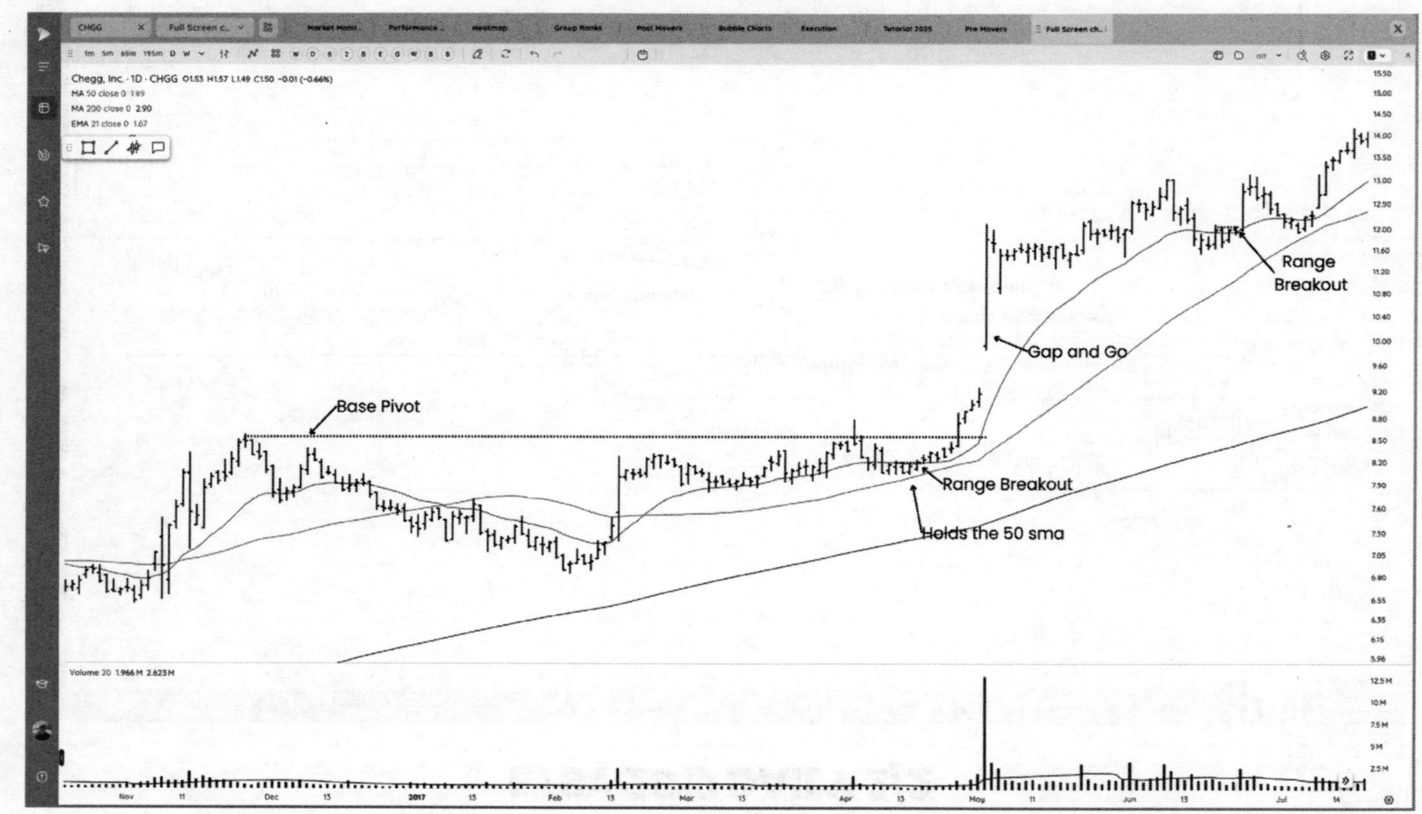

CHGG 2017 DAILY 2/2

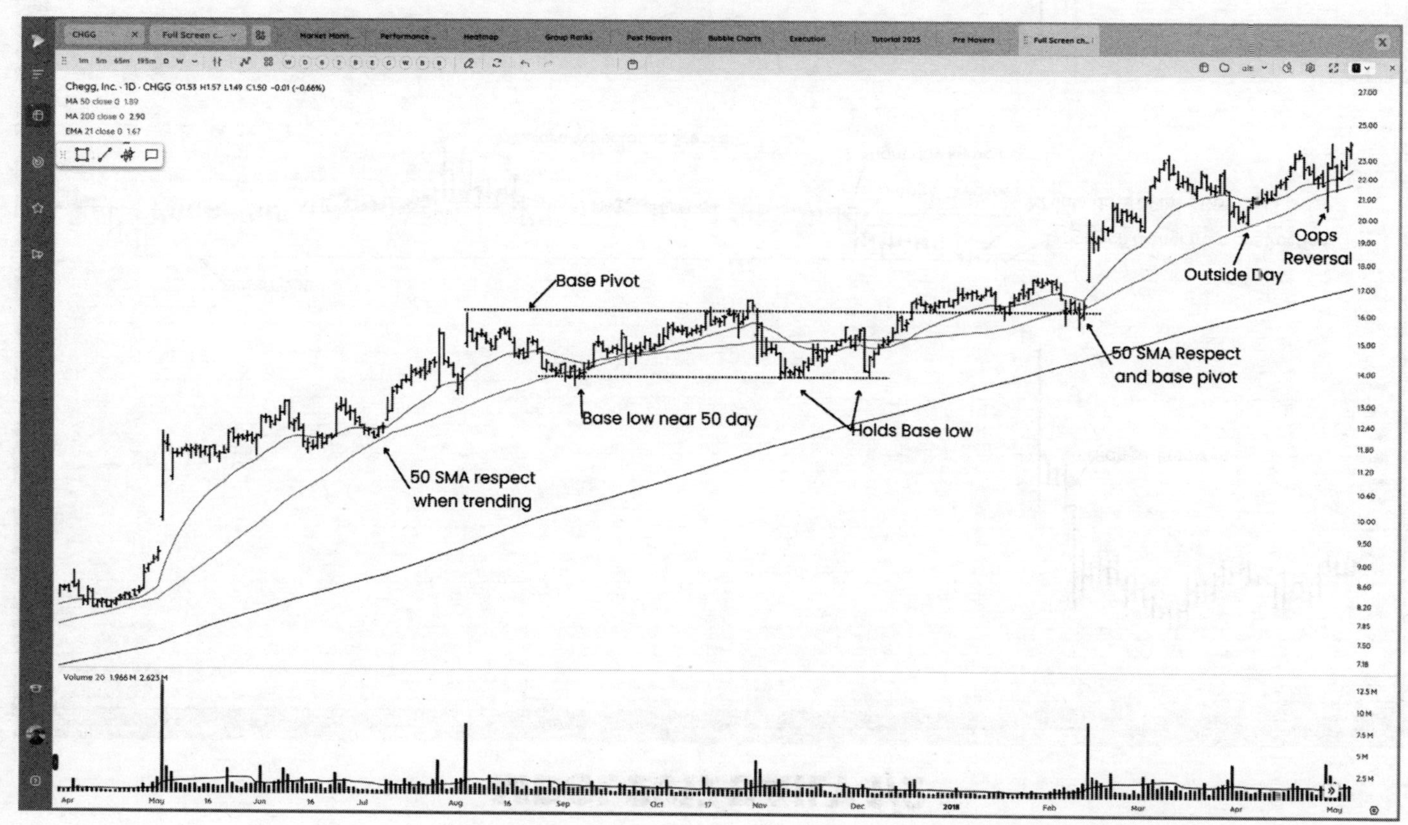

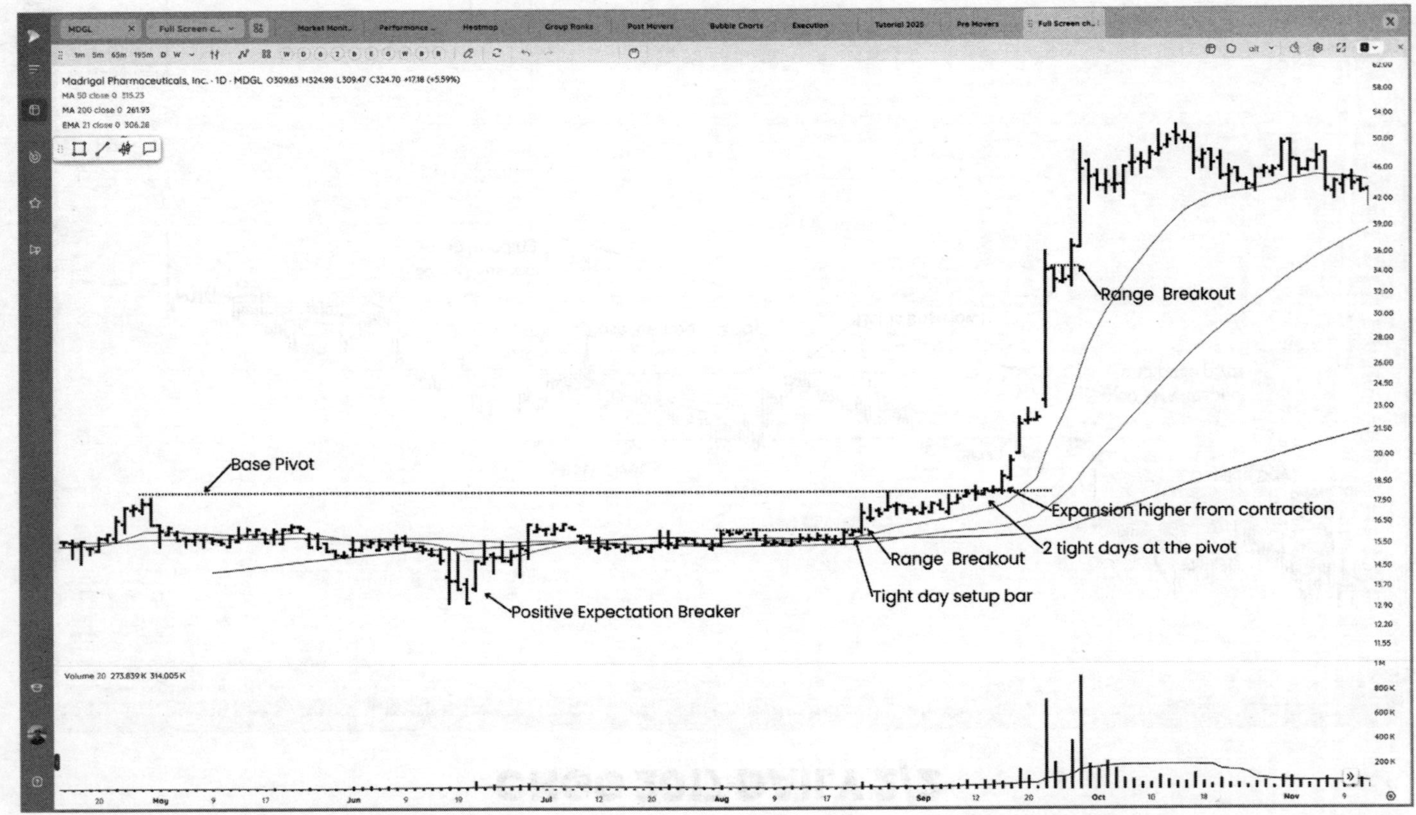
MDGL 2017 DAILY 1/2
Base Pivot
Positive Expectation Breaker
Tight day setup bar
Range Breakout
2 tight days at the pivot
Expansion higher from contraction
Range Breakout

MDGL 2017 DAILY 2/2

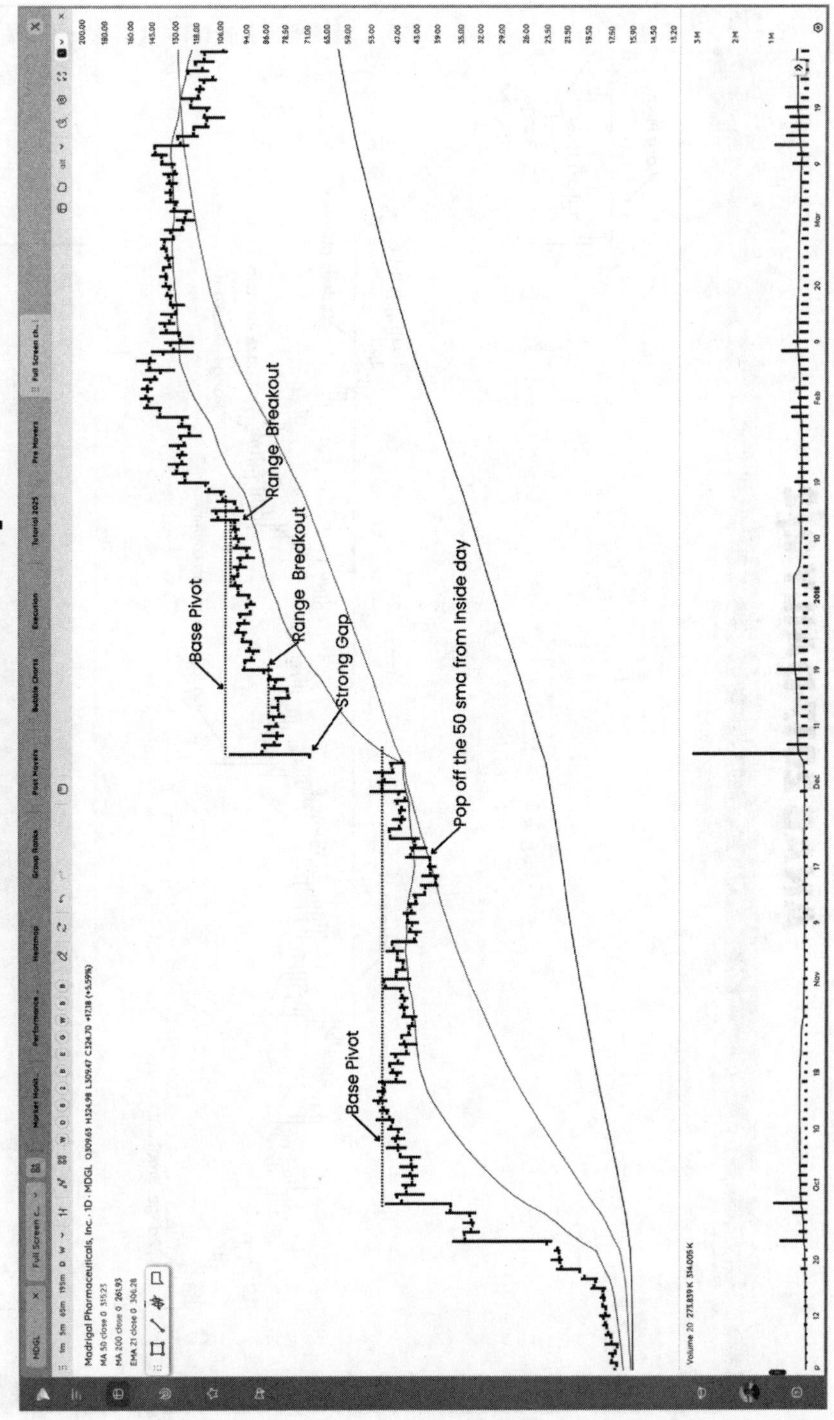

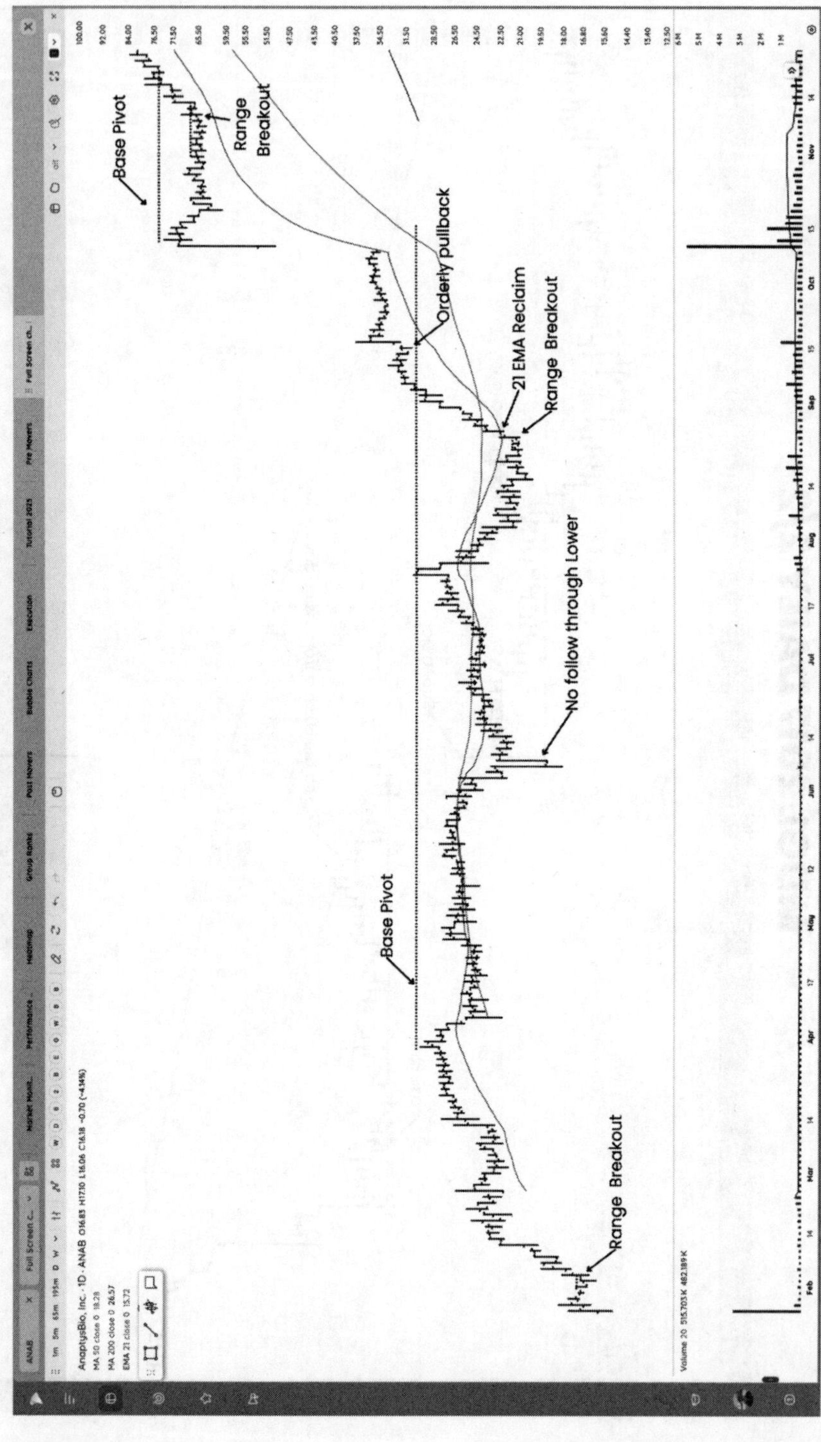
ANAB 2017 DAILY 2/2
Base Pivot
Range Breakout
Orderly pullback
21 EMA Reclaim
Range Breakout
No follow through Lower
Base Pivot
Range Breakout

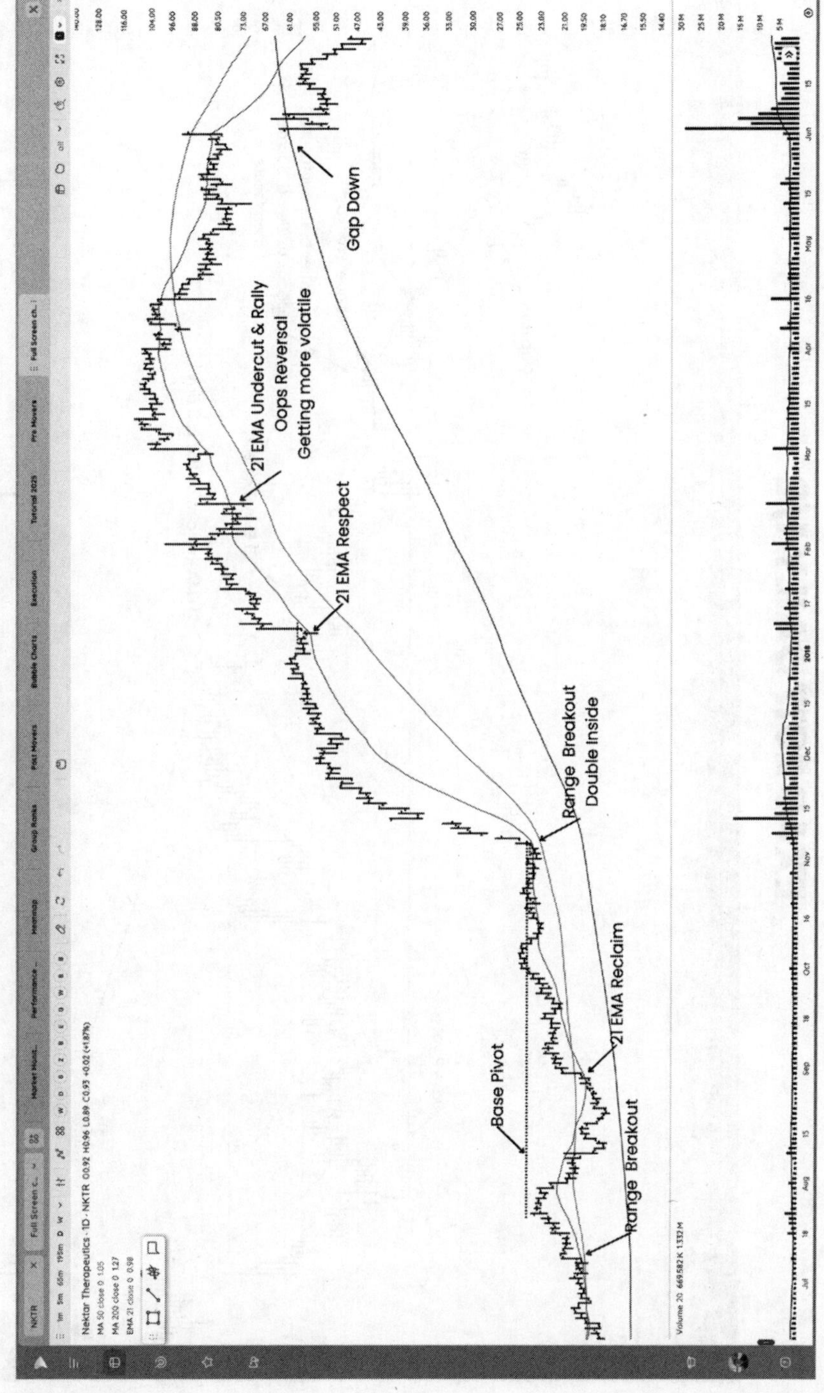
NKTR 2017 DAILY 2/2
Nektar Therapeutics · 1D · NKTR
Base Pivot
Range Breakout
21 EMA Reclaim
Range Breakout
Double Inside
21 EMA Respect
21 EMA Undercut & Rally
Oops Reversal
Getting more volatile
Gap Down

EXAS 2017 DAILY 1/2

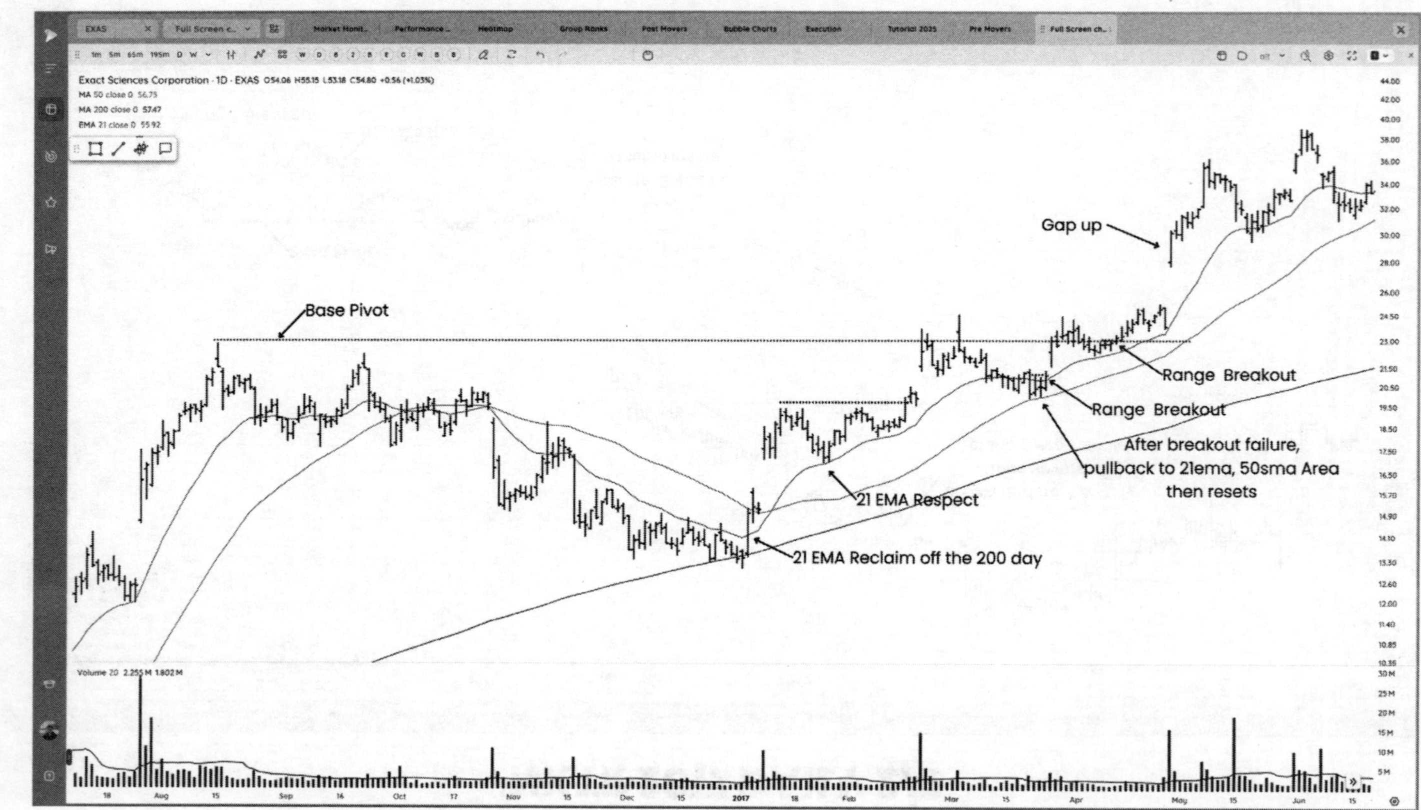

EXAS 2017 DAILY 2/2

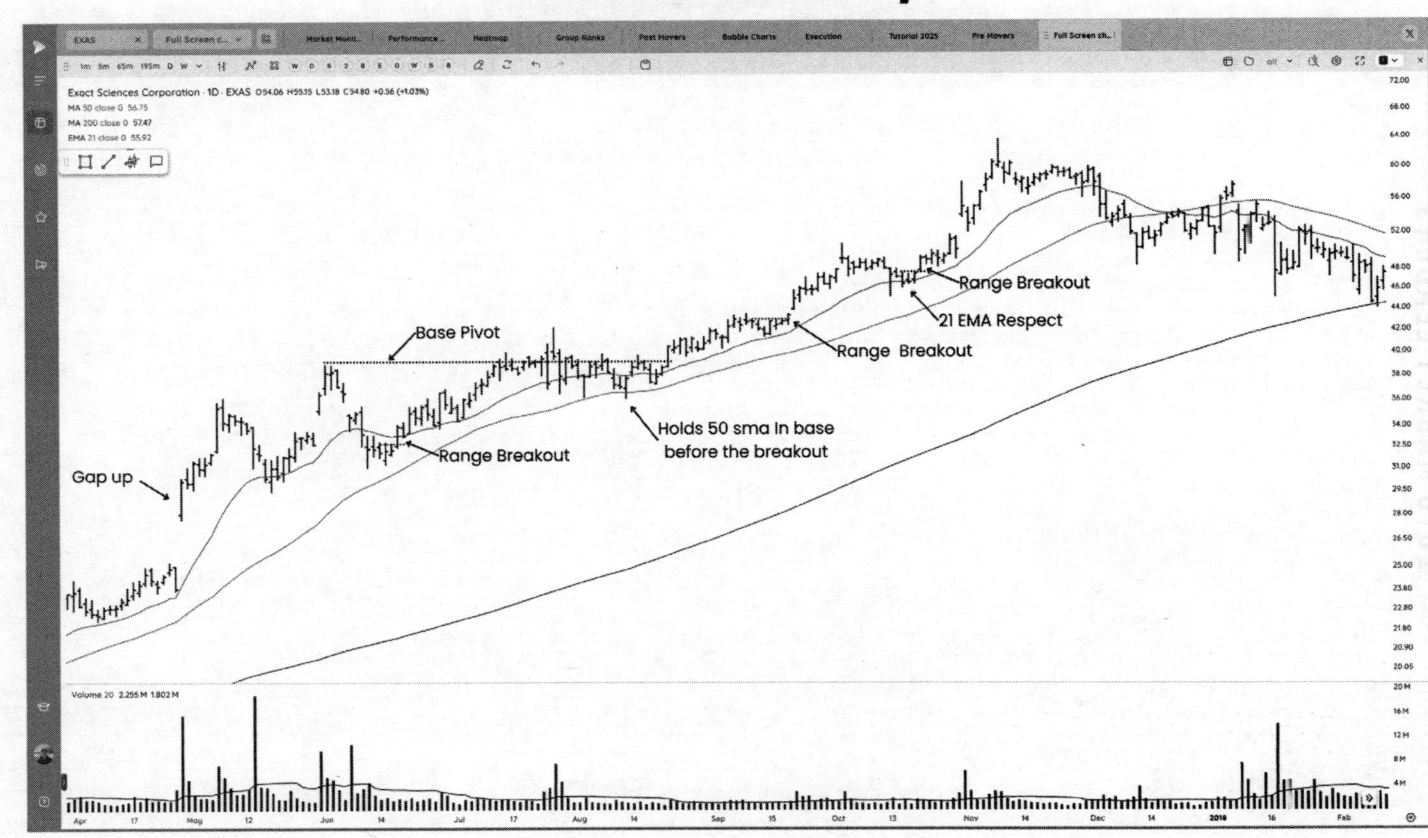

2018 MARKET LEADERS

TLRY 2018 DAILY

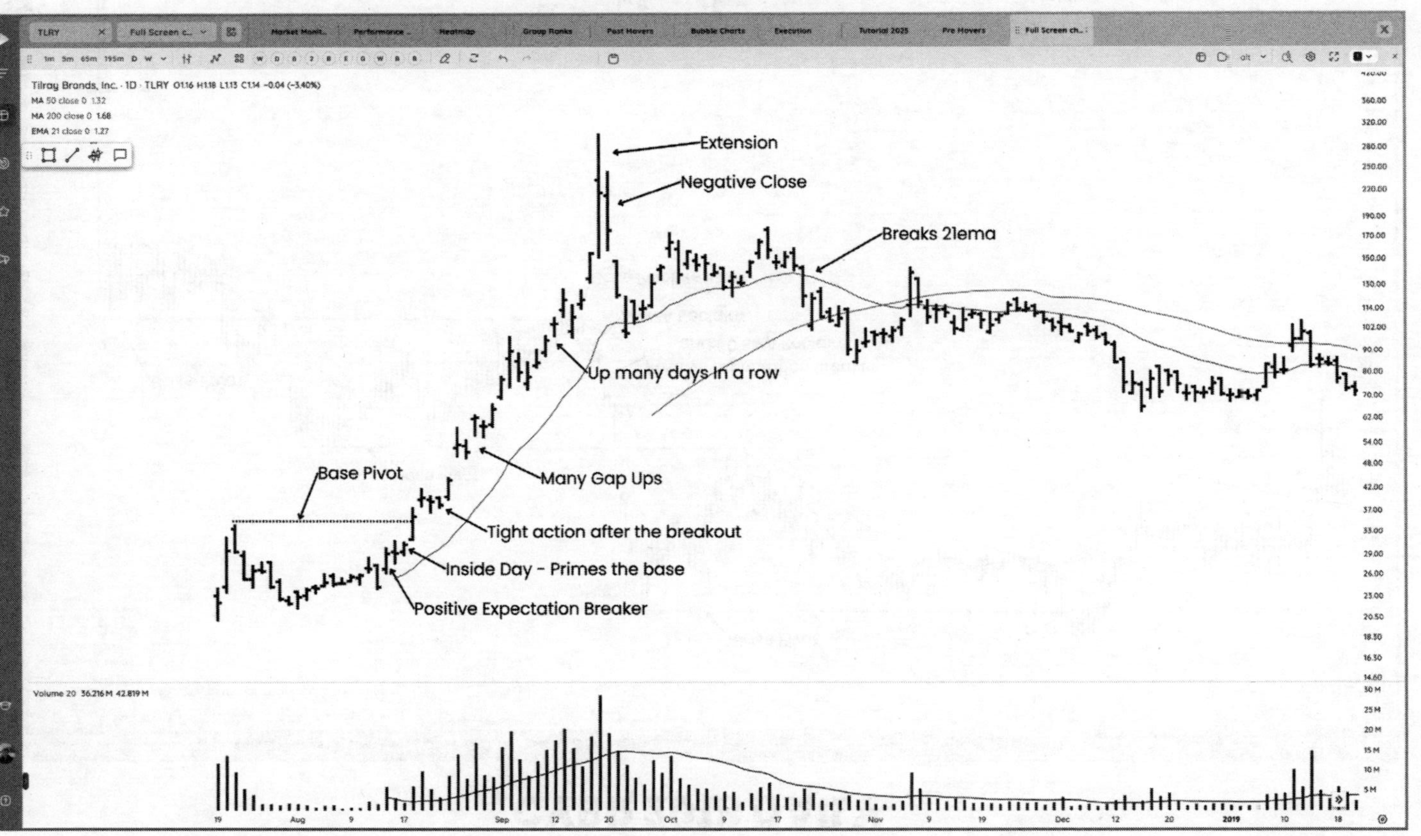

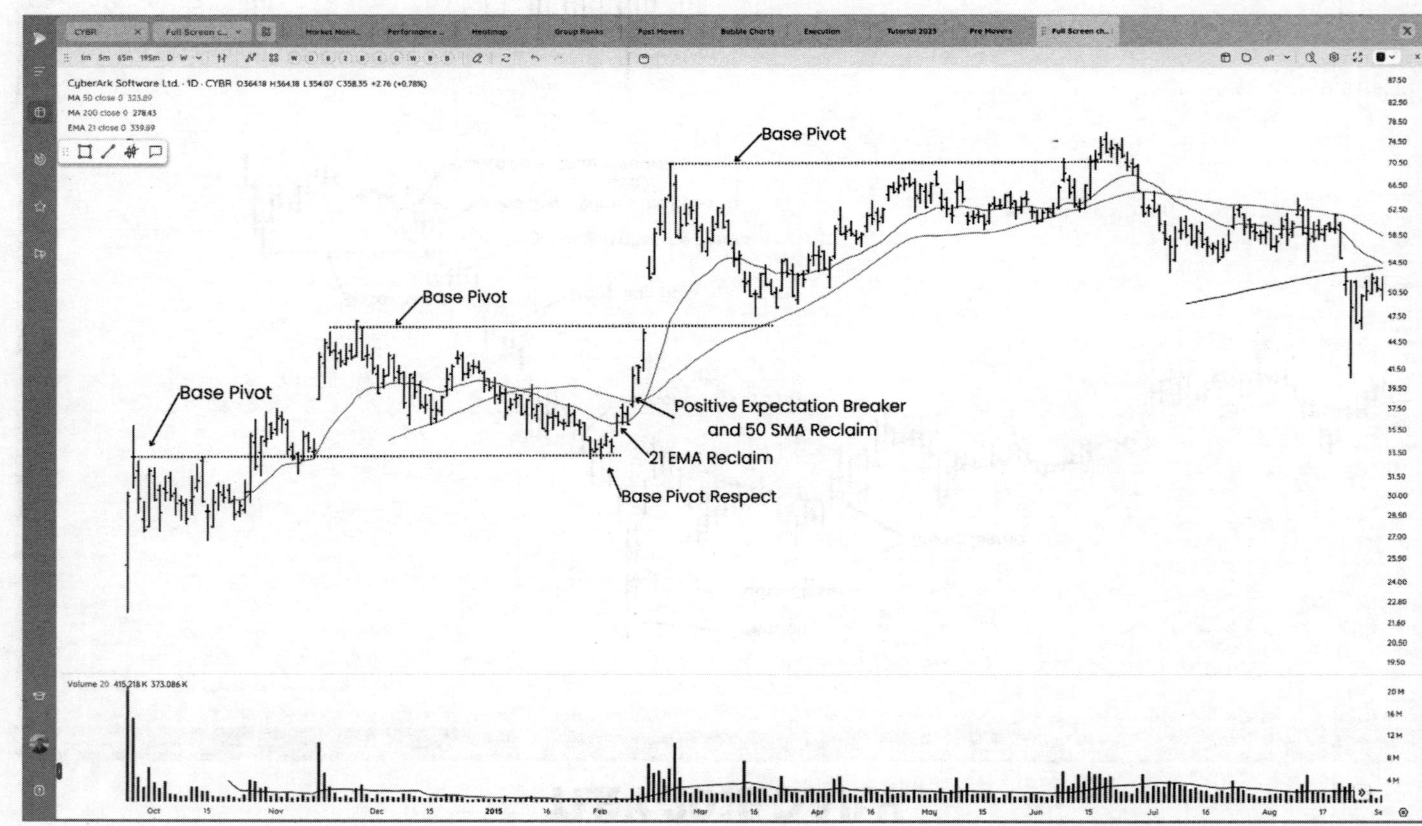
CYBR 2018 DAILY
CyberArk Software Ltd. · 1D · CYBR O364.18 H364.18 L354.07 C358.35 +2.76 (+0.78%)
MA 50 close 0 323.89
MA 200 close 0 278.43
EMA 21 close 0 339.89
Base Pivot
Base Pivot
Base Pivot
Positive Expectation Breaker
and 50 SMA Reclaim
21 EMA Reclaim
Base Pivot Respect

OKTA 2018 DAILY 1/2

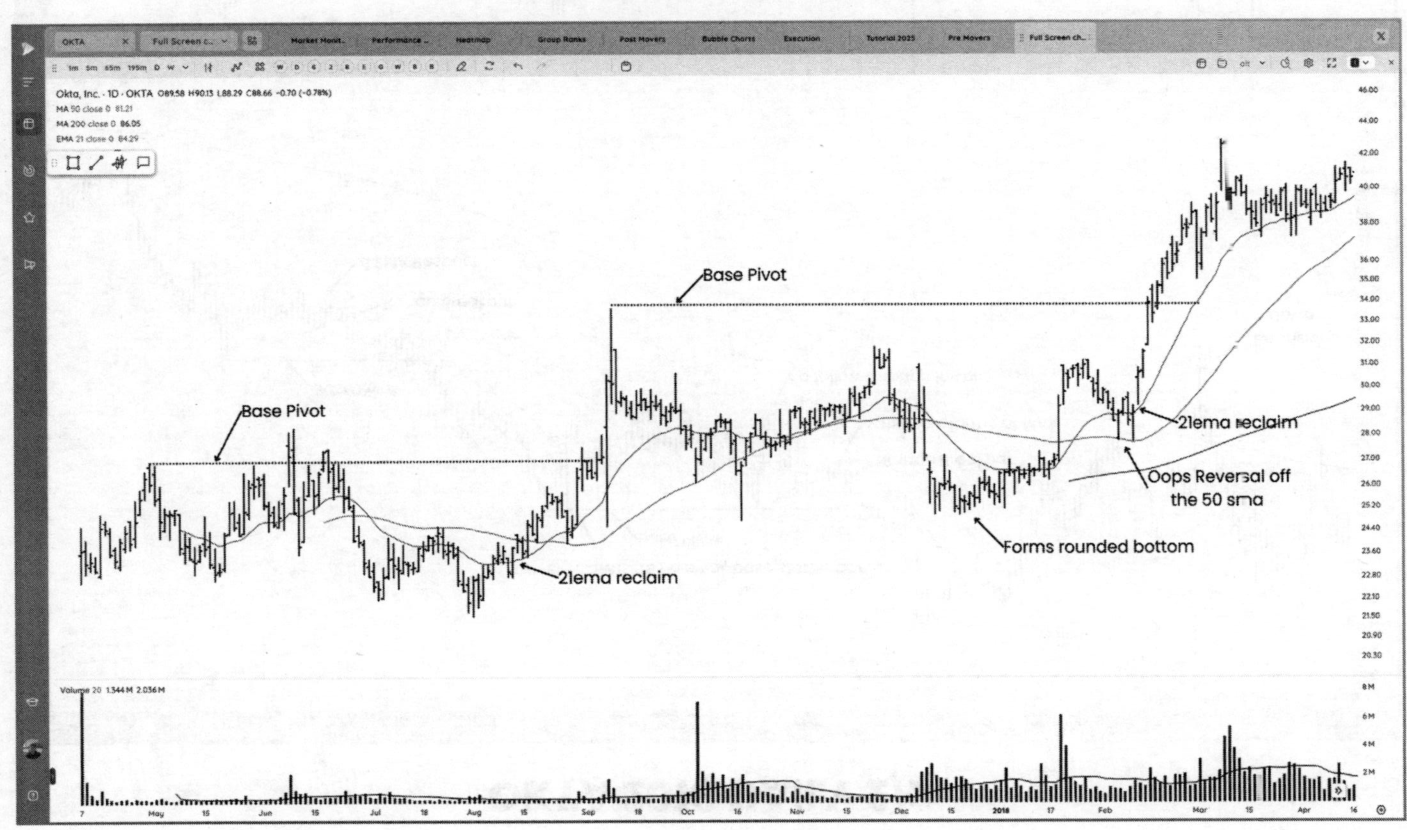

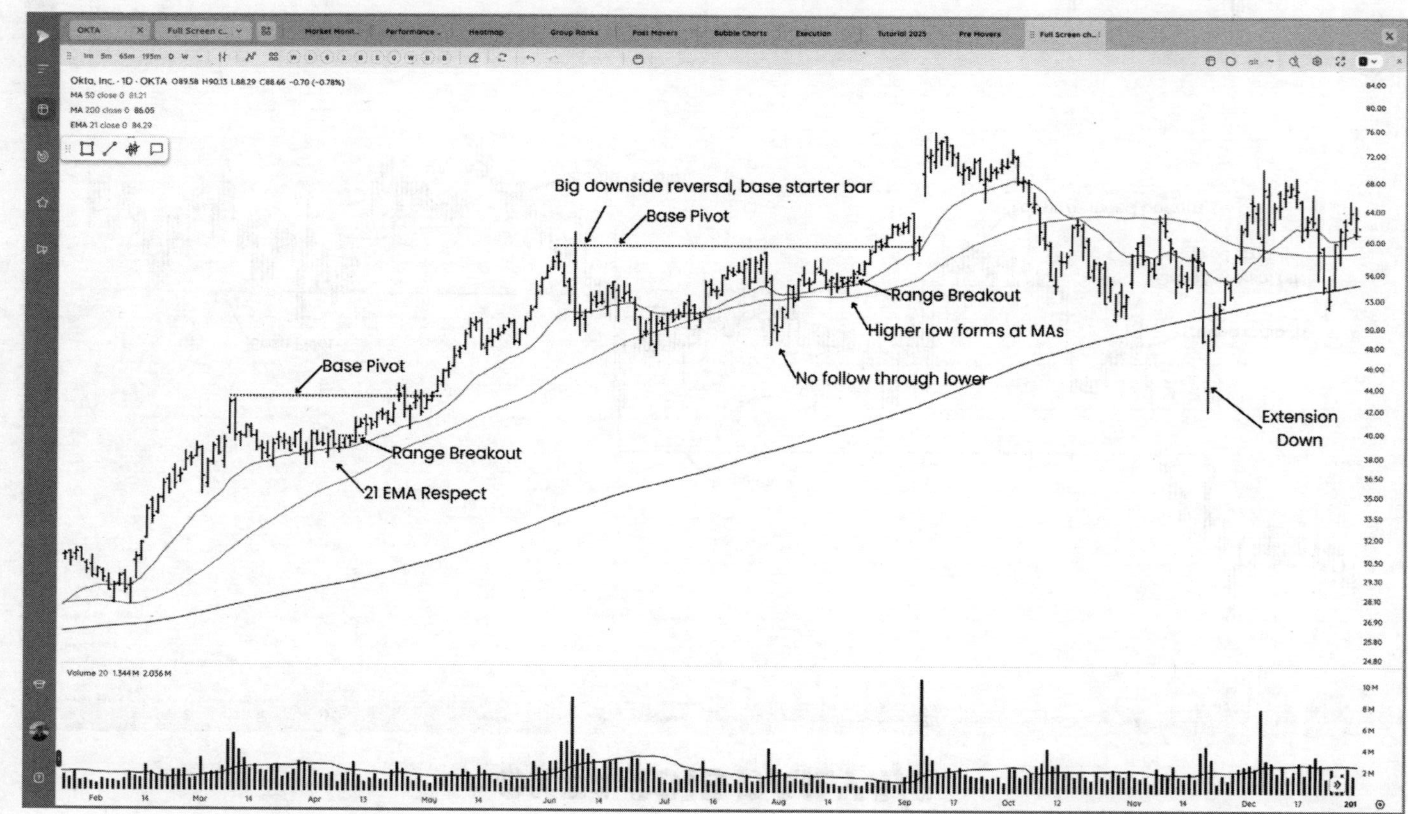
OKTA 2018 DAILY 2/2
Okta, Inc. · 1D · OKTA O89.58 H90.13 L88.29 C88.66 -0.70 (-0.78%)
MA 50 close 0 81.21
MA 200 close 0 86.05
EMA 21 close 0 84.29
Big downside reversal, base starter bar
Base Pivot
Range Breakout
Higher low forms at MAs
No follow through lower
Base Pivot
Range Breakout
21 EMA Respect
Extension
Down
Volume 20 1.344 M 2.036 M

TWLO 2018 DAILY

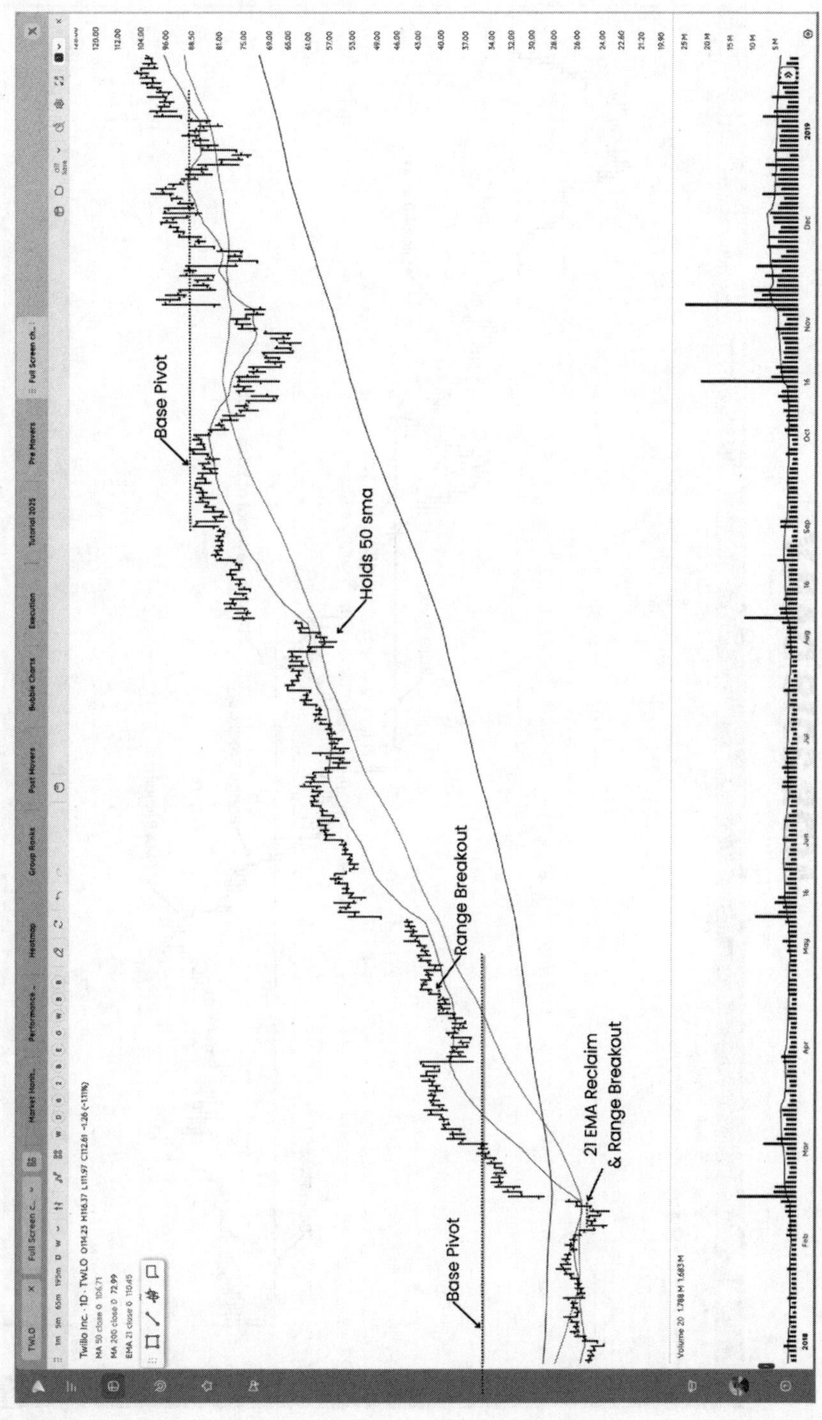

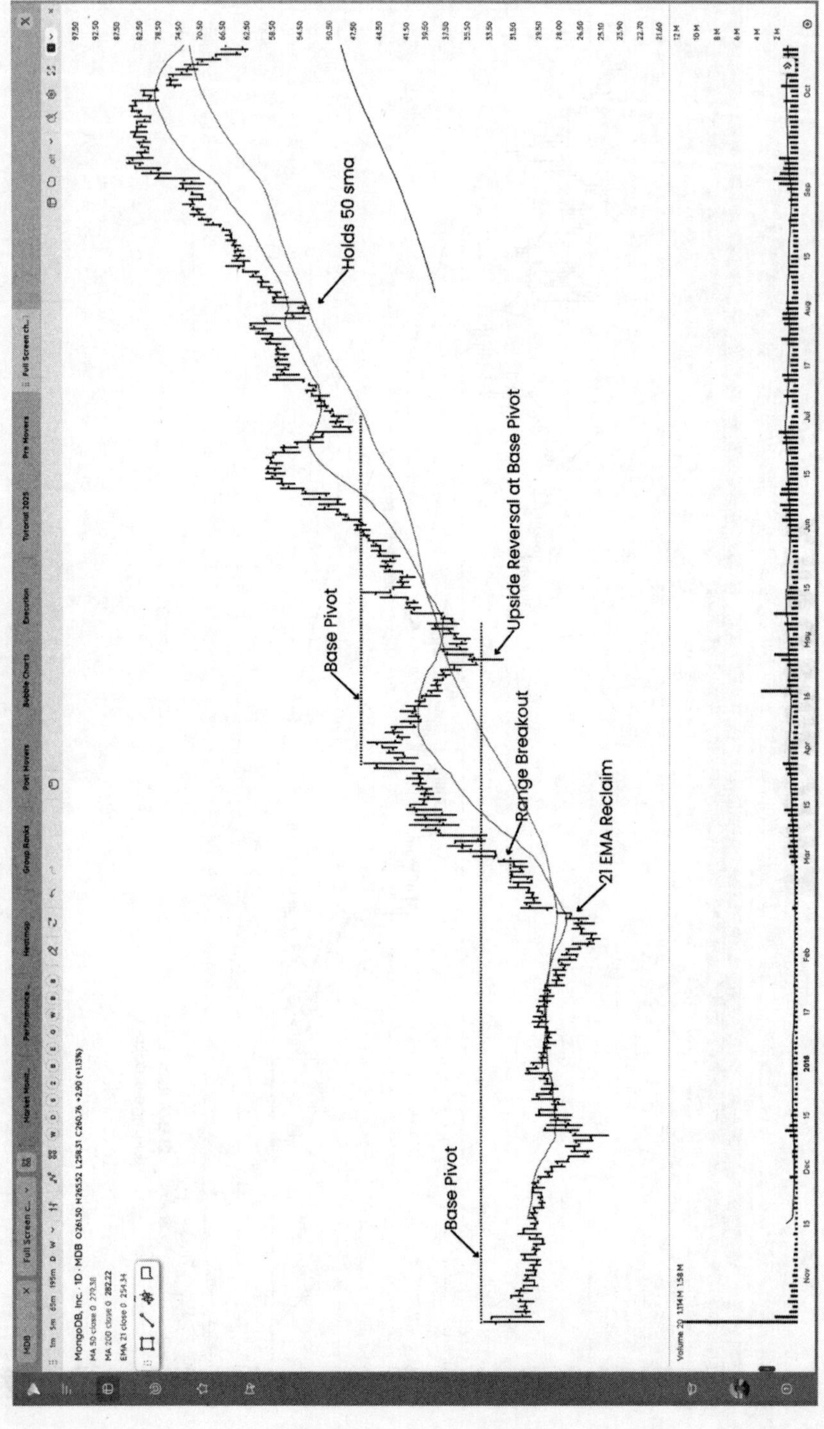
MDB 2018 DAILY
Base Pivot
Range Breakout
21 EMA Reclaim
Base Pivot
Upside Reversal at Base Pivot
Holds 50 sma

GSHD 2018 DAILY

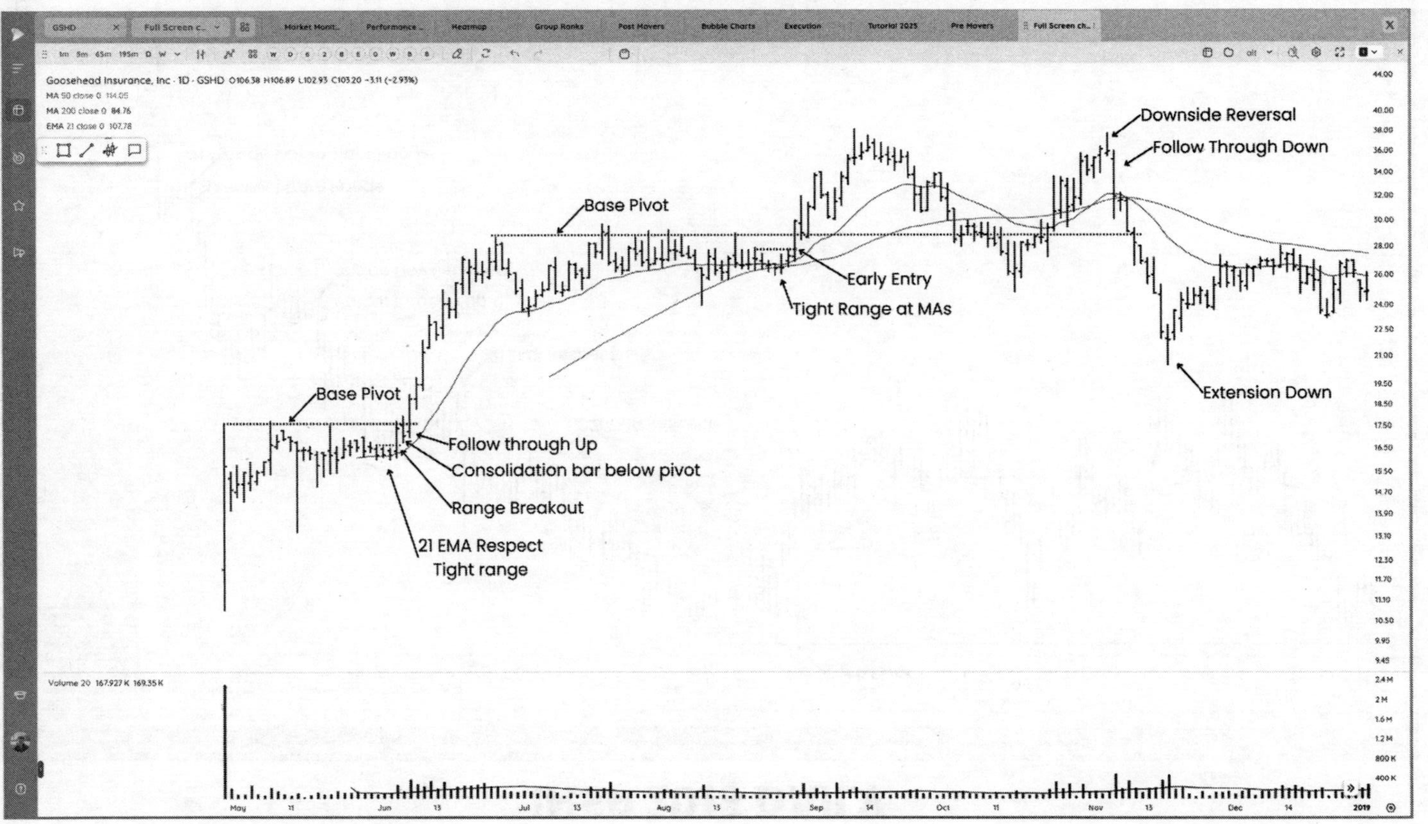

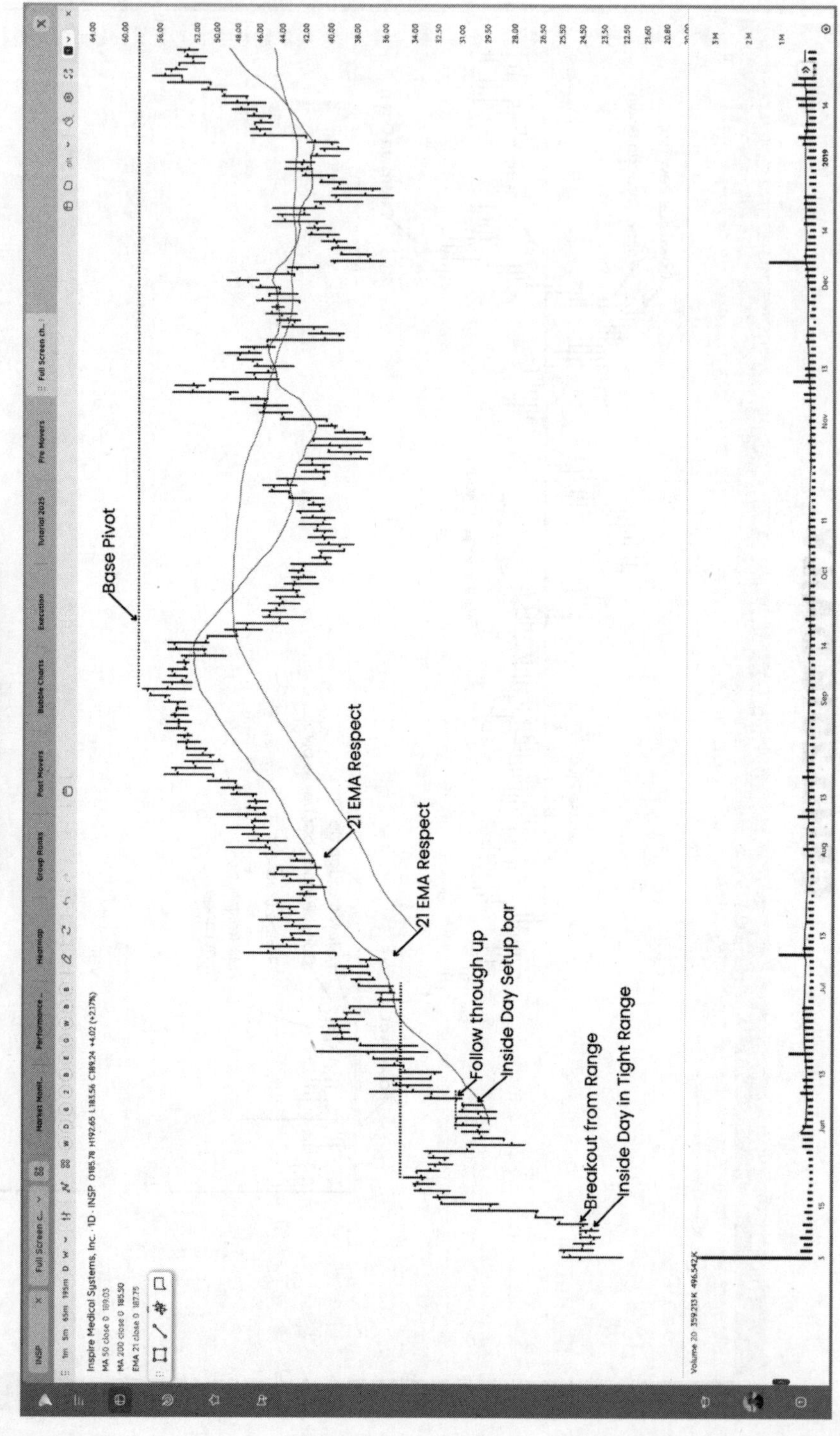
INSP 2018 DAILY
Base Pivot
21 EMA Respect
21 EMA Respect
Follow through up
Inside Day Setup bar
Breakout from Range
Inside Day in Tight Range

CROX 2018 DAILY

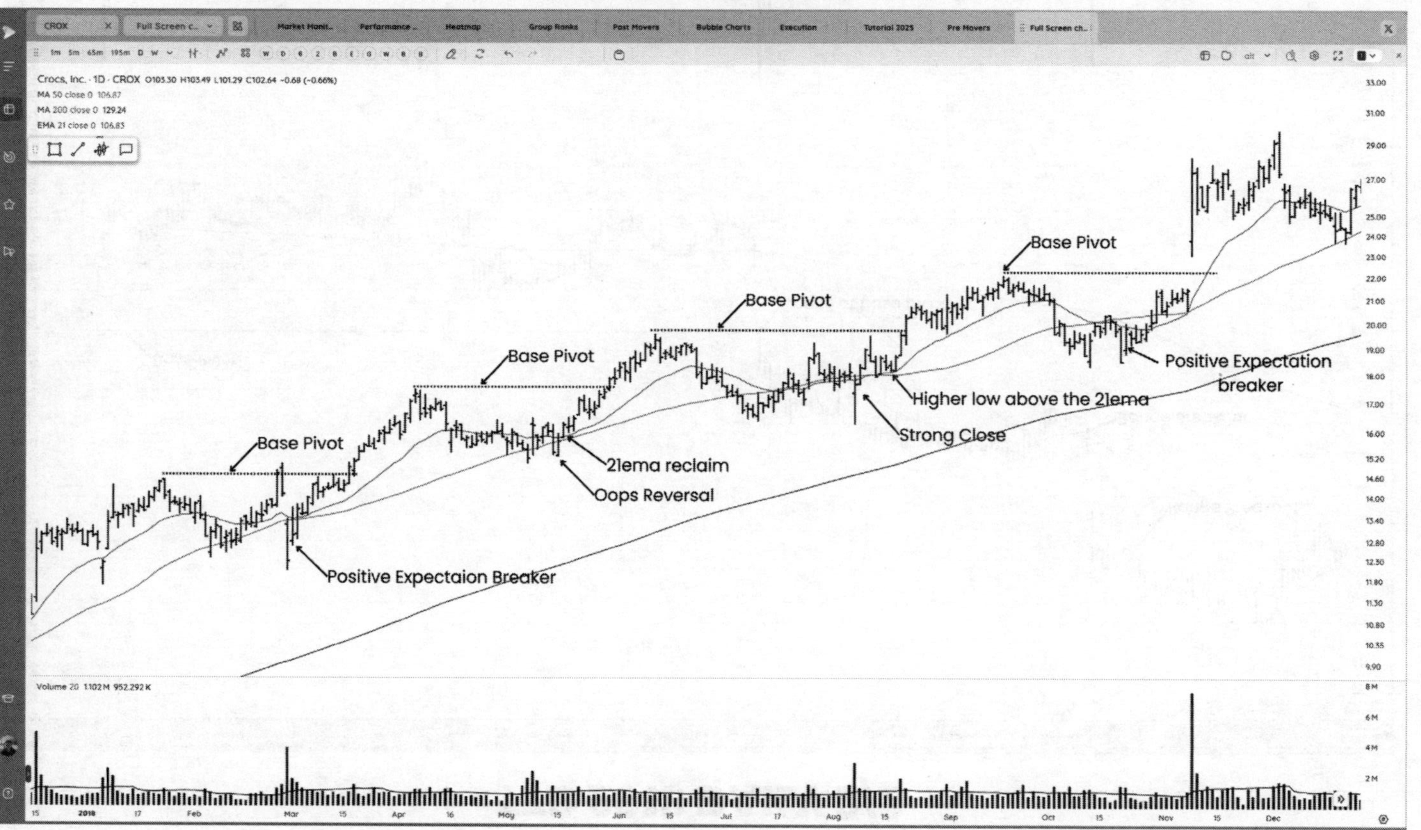

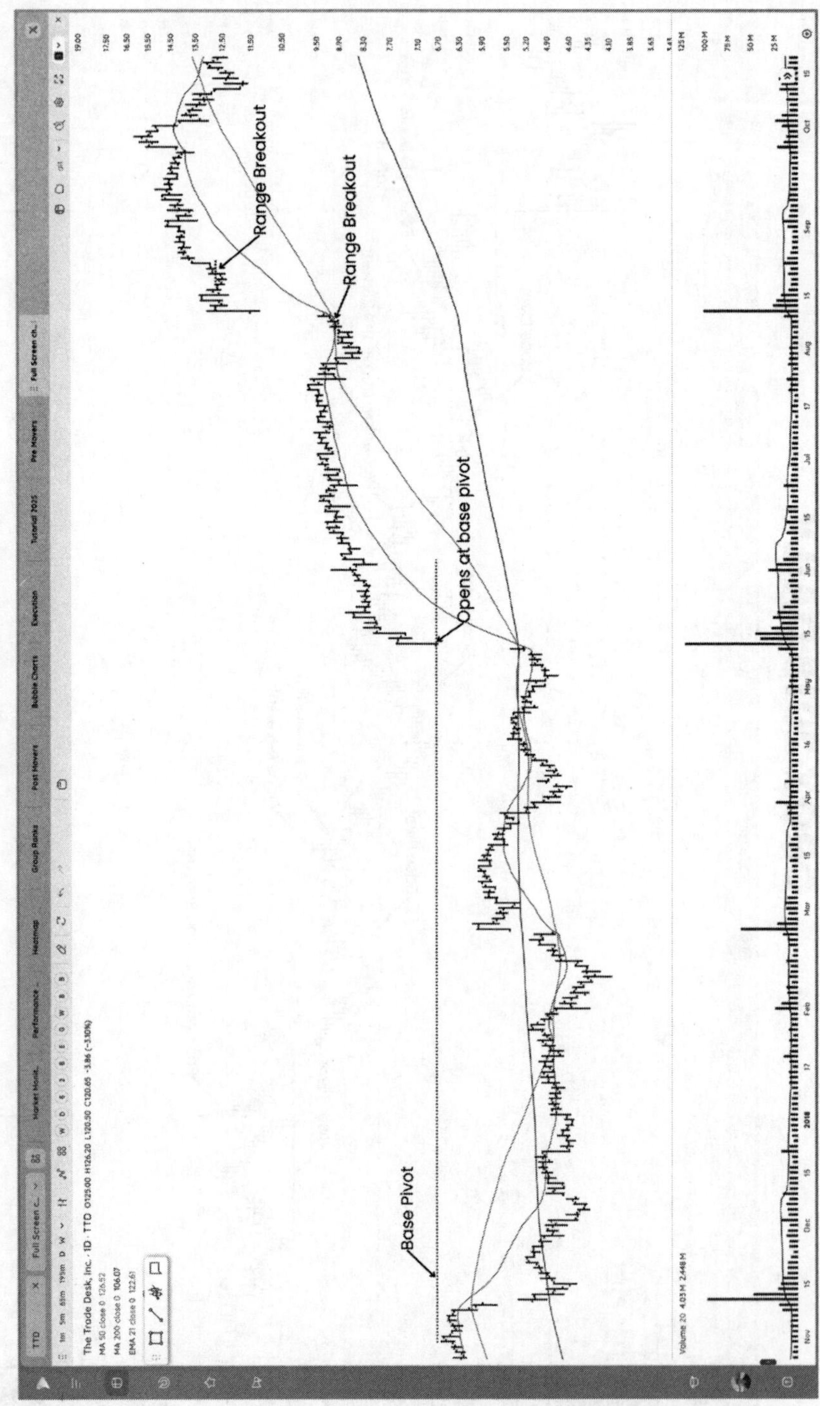
TTD 2018 DAILY 2/2
Base Pivot
Opens at base pivot
Range Breakout
Range Breakout

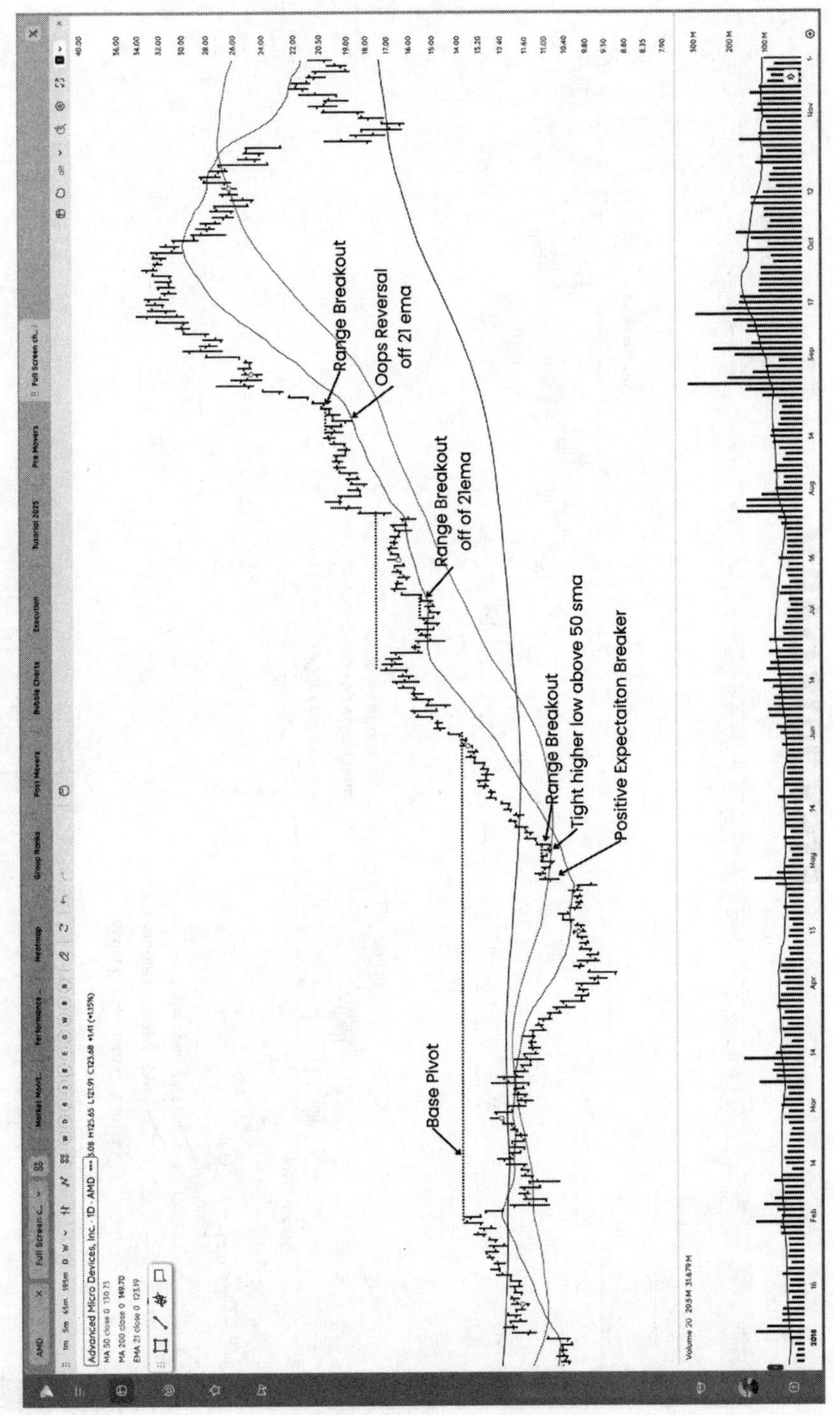
AMD 2018 DAILY
Base Pivot
Positive Expectaiton Breaker
Tight higher low above 50 sma
Range Breakout
Range Breakout
off of 21ema
Oops Reversal
off 21 ema
Range Breakout

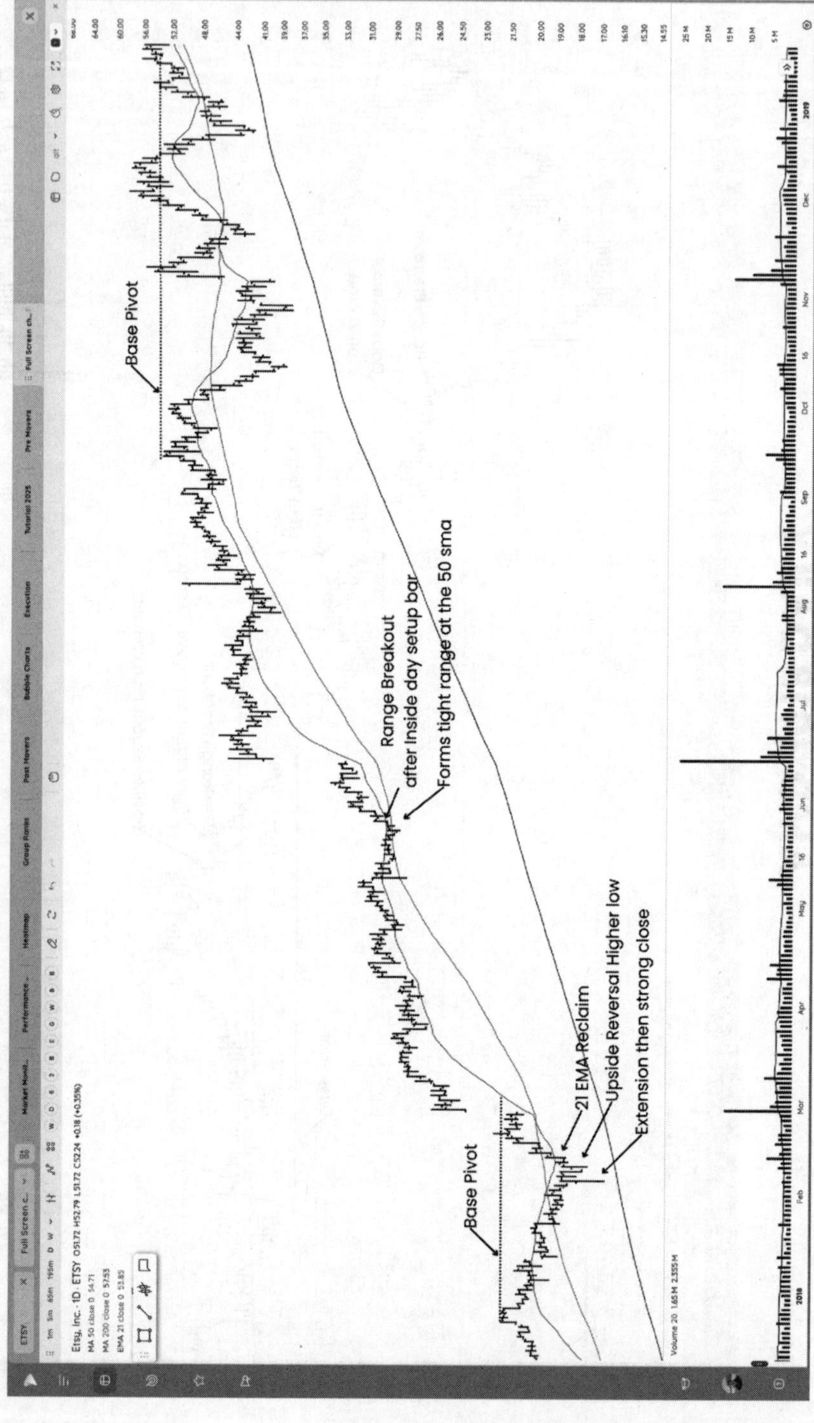
ETSY 2018 DAILY
Base Pivot
21 EMA Reclaim
Upside Reversal Higher low
Extension then strong close
Range Breakout
after Inside day setup bar
Forms tight range at the 50 sma
Base Pivot

2019 MARKET LEADERS

CYBR 2019 DAILYBase Pivot

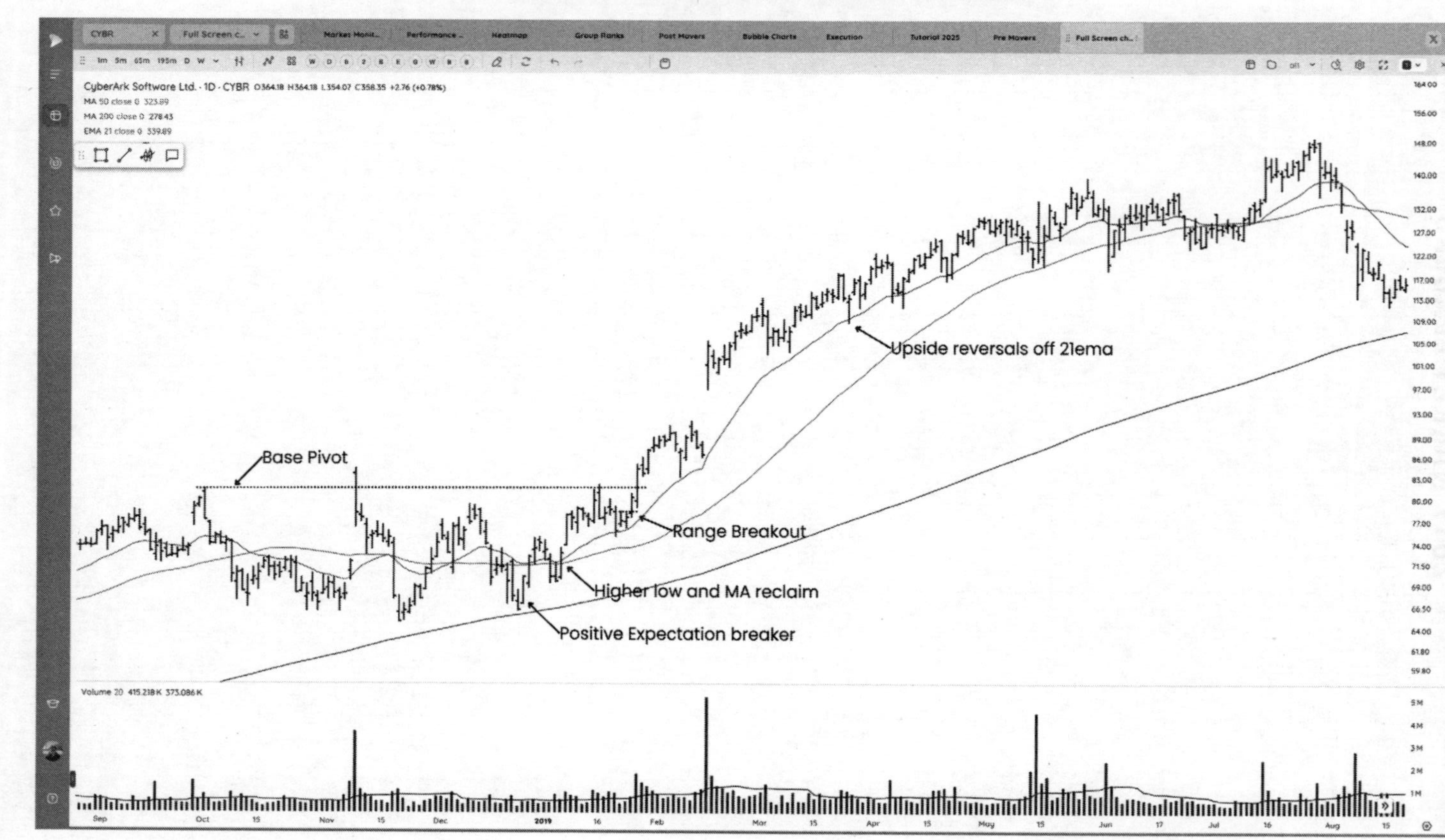

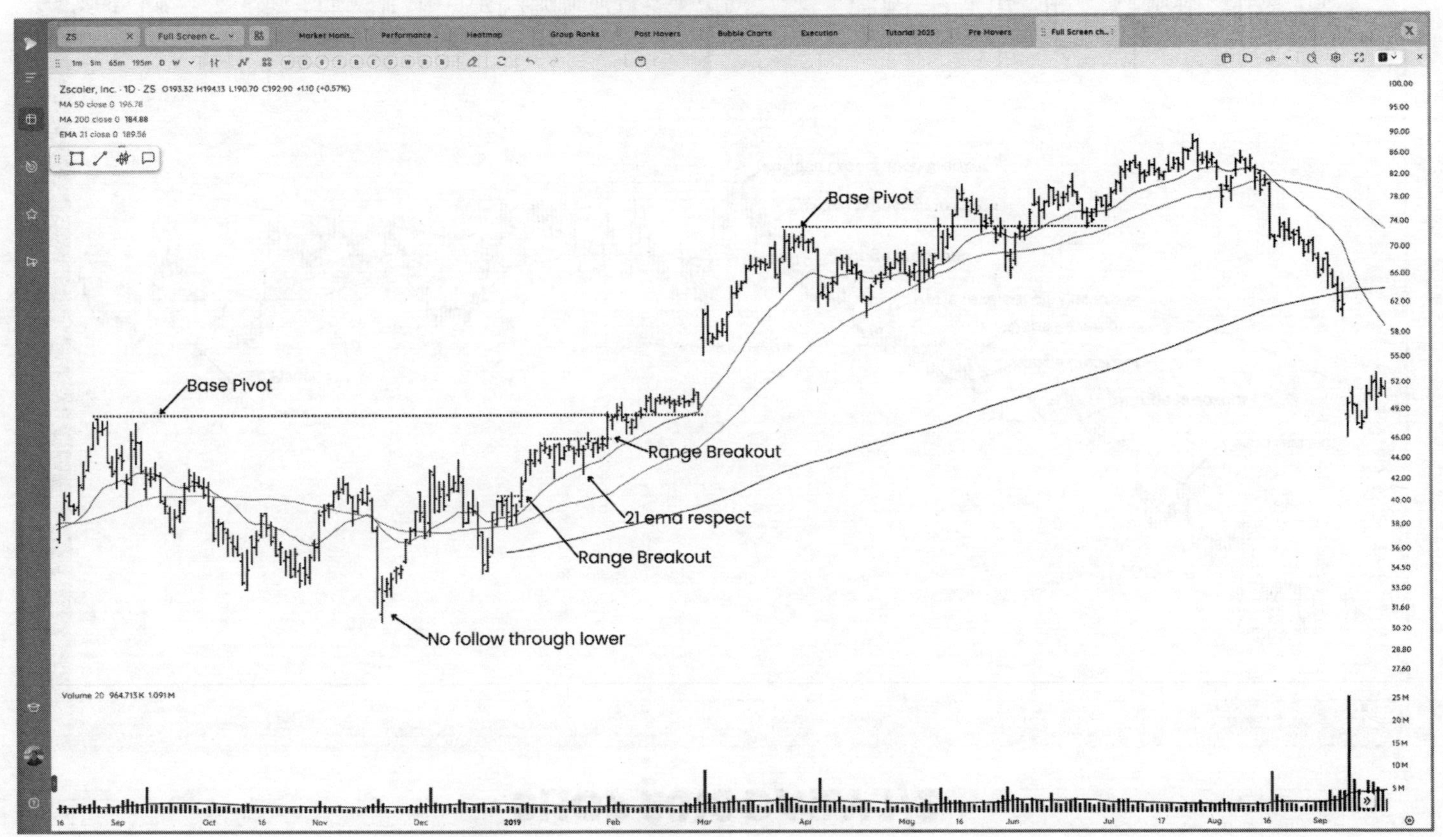
ZS 2019 DAILY
Zscaler, Inc. · 1D · ZS O193.52 H194.13 L190.70 C192.90 +1.10 (+0.57%)
MA 50 close 0 196.78
MA 200 close 0 184.88
EMA 21 close 0 189.56
Base Pivot
Base Pivot
Range Breakout
21 ema respect
Range Breakout
No follow through lower
Volume 20 964.713K 1.091M

SHOP 2019 DAILY 1/2

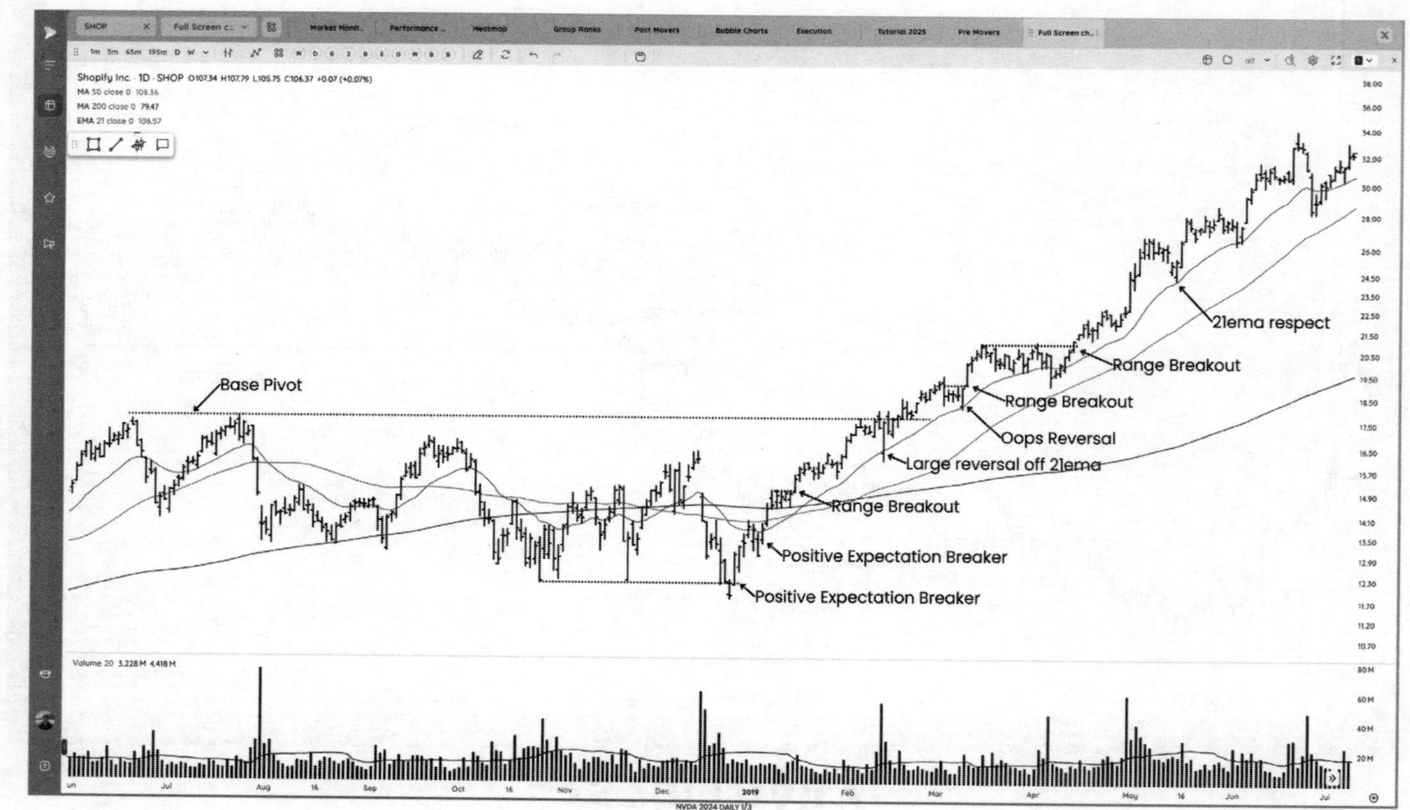

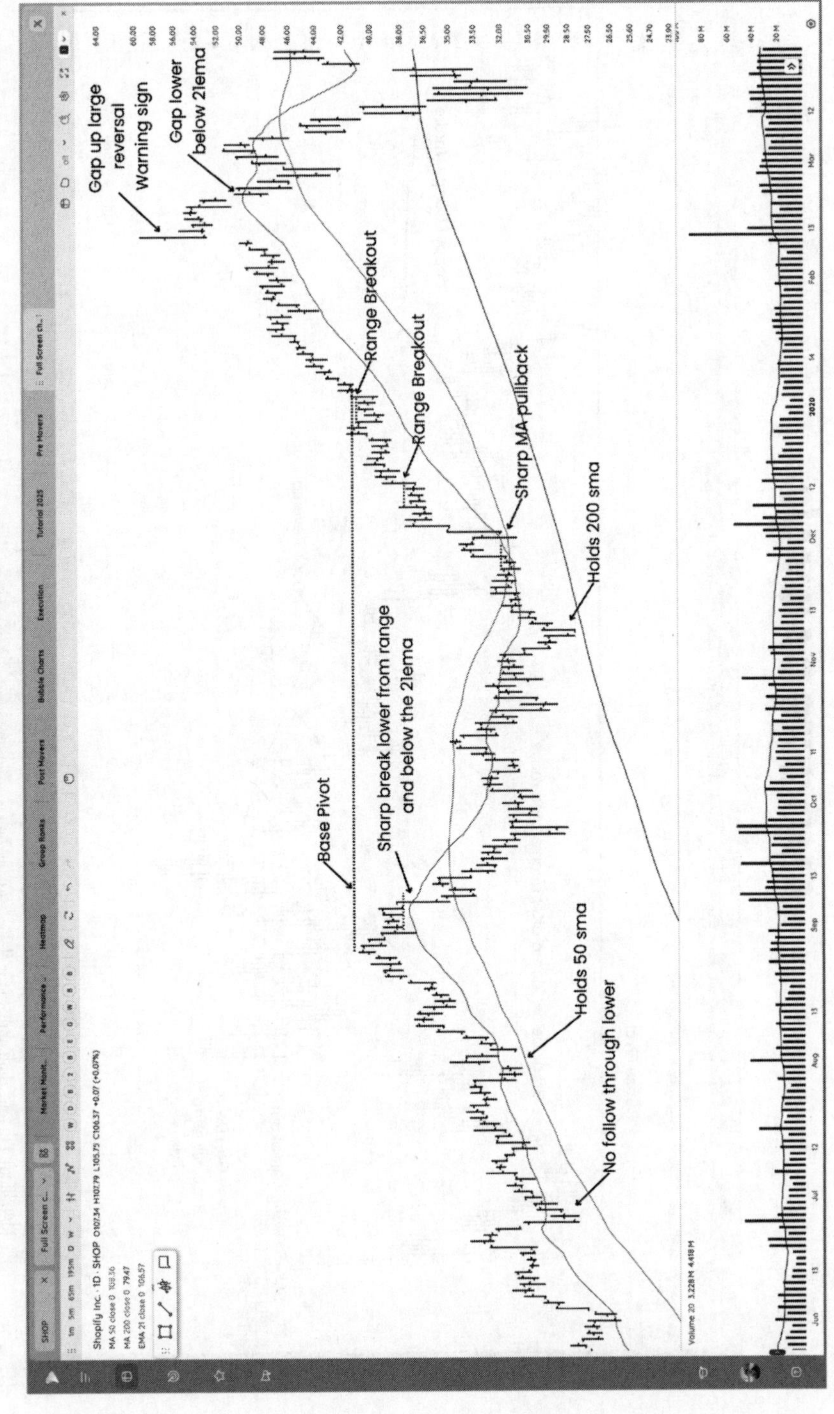
SHOP 2019 DAILY 2/2
Gap up large reversal Warning sign
Gap lower below 21ema
Range Breakout
Range Breakout
Sharp MA pullback
Holds 200 sma
Base Pivot
Sharp break lower from range and below the 21ema
Holds 50 sma
No follow through lower

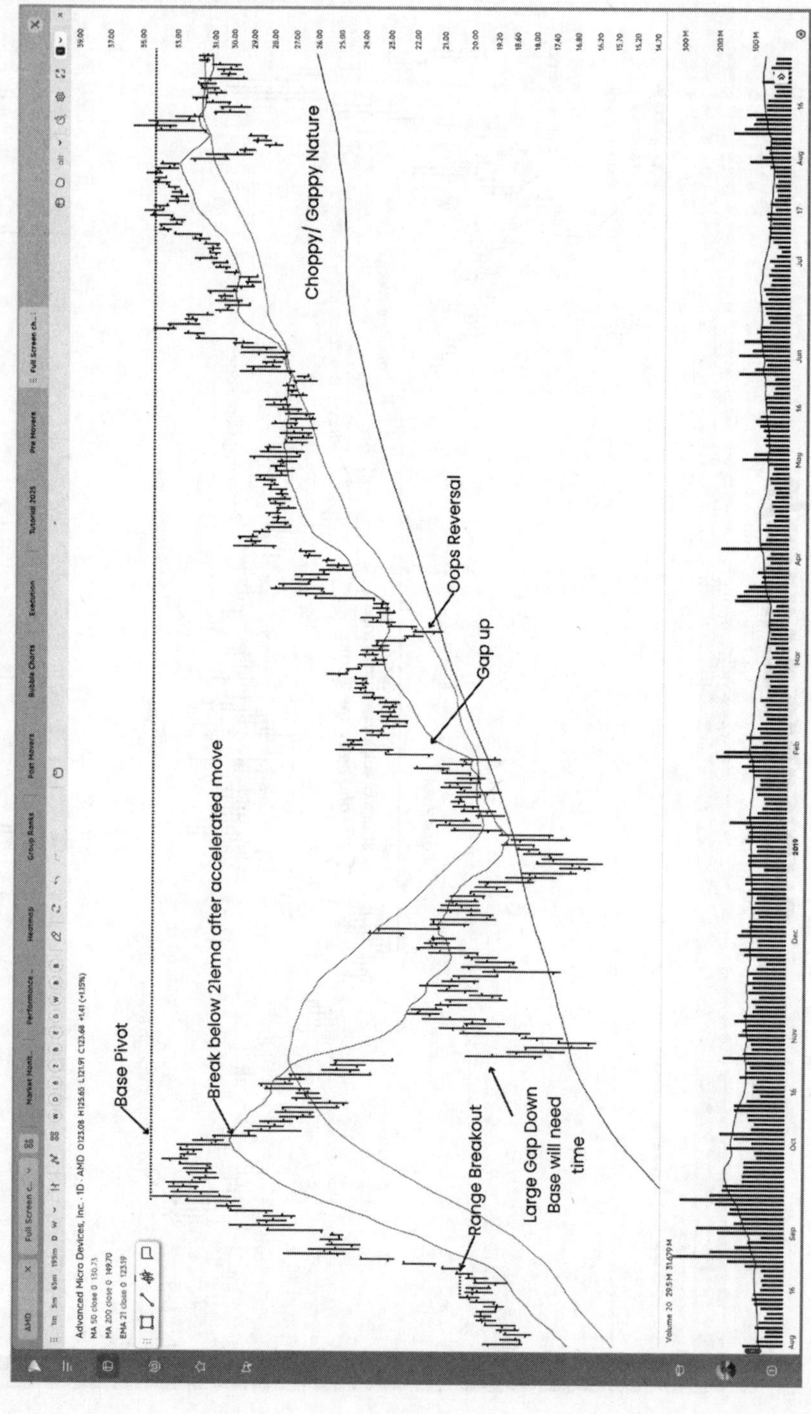
AMD 2019 DAILY 1/2
Base Pivot
Break below 21ema after accelerated move
Range Breakout
Large Gap Down
Base will need
time
Gap up
Oops Reversal
Choppy/ Gappy Nature
Advanced Micro Devices, Inc. · 1D · AMD
MA 50 close 0
MA 200 close 0
EMA 21 close 0

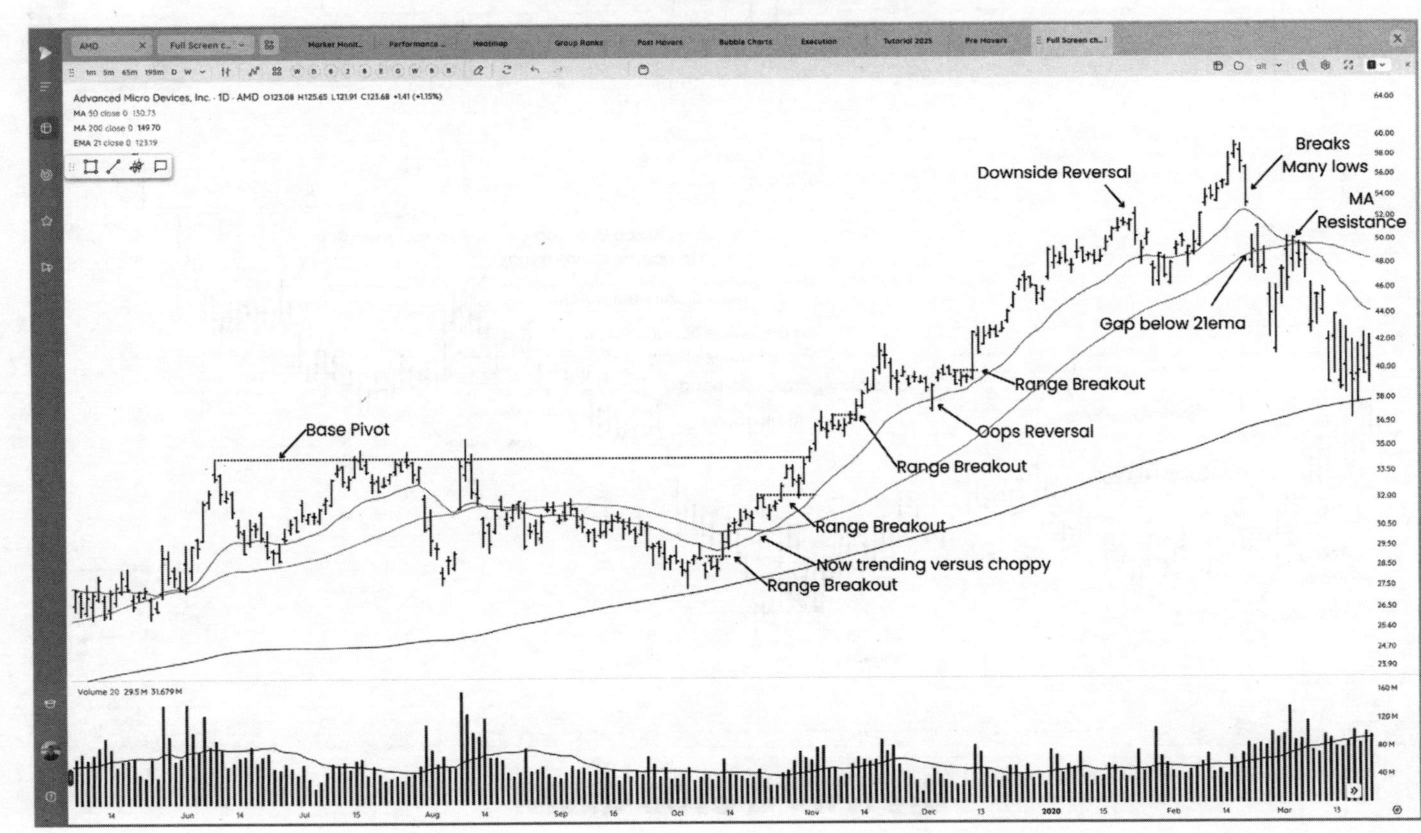
AMD 2019 DAILY 2/2
Advanced Micro Devices, Inc. · 1D · AMD O123.08 H125.65 L121.91 C123.68 +1.41 (+1.15%)
MA 50 close 0 130.73
MA 200 close 0 149.70
EMA 21 close 0 123.19
Base Pivot
Range Breakout
Now trending versus choppy
Range Breakout
Range Breakout
Oops Reversal
Range Breakout
Downside Reversal
Gap below 21ema
Breaks
Many lows
MA
Resistance
Volume 20 29.5 M 31.679 M

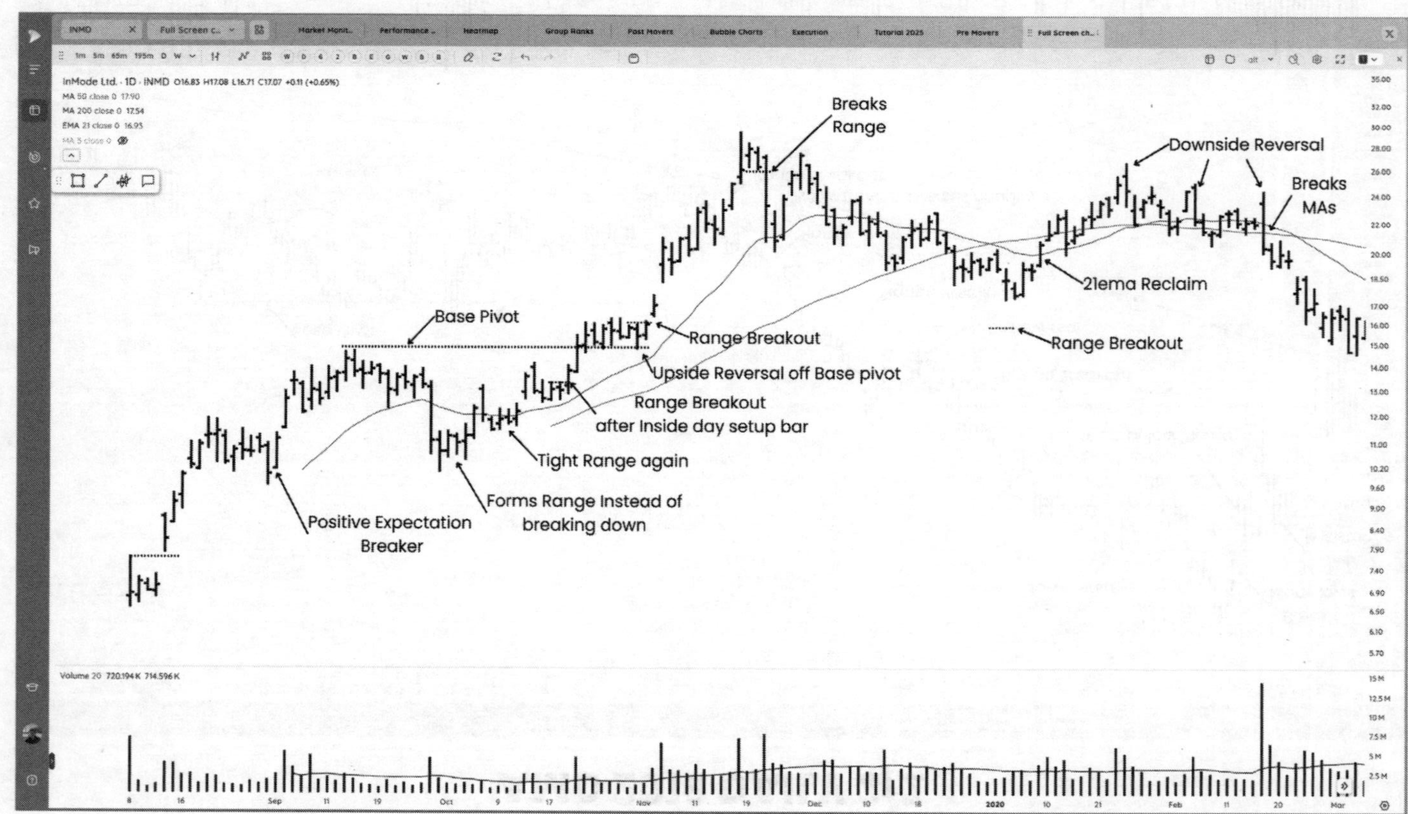
INMD 2019 DAILY 1/2
inMode Ltd. · 1D · INMD O16.83 H17.08 L16.71 C17.07 +0.11 (+0.65%)
MA 50 close 0 17.90
MA 200 close 0 17.54
EMA 21 close 0 16.93
Breaks Range
Downside Reversal
Breaks MAs
21ema Reclaim
Base Pivot
Range Breakout
Range Breakout
Upside Reversal off Base pivot
Range Breakout after Inside day setup bar
Tight Range again
Forms Range Instead of breaking down
Positive Expectation Breaker
Volume 20 720.194K 714.596K

DOCU 2019 DAILY 1/2

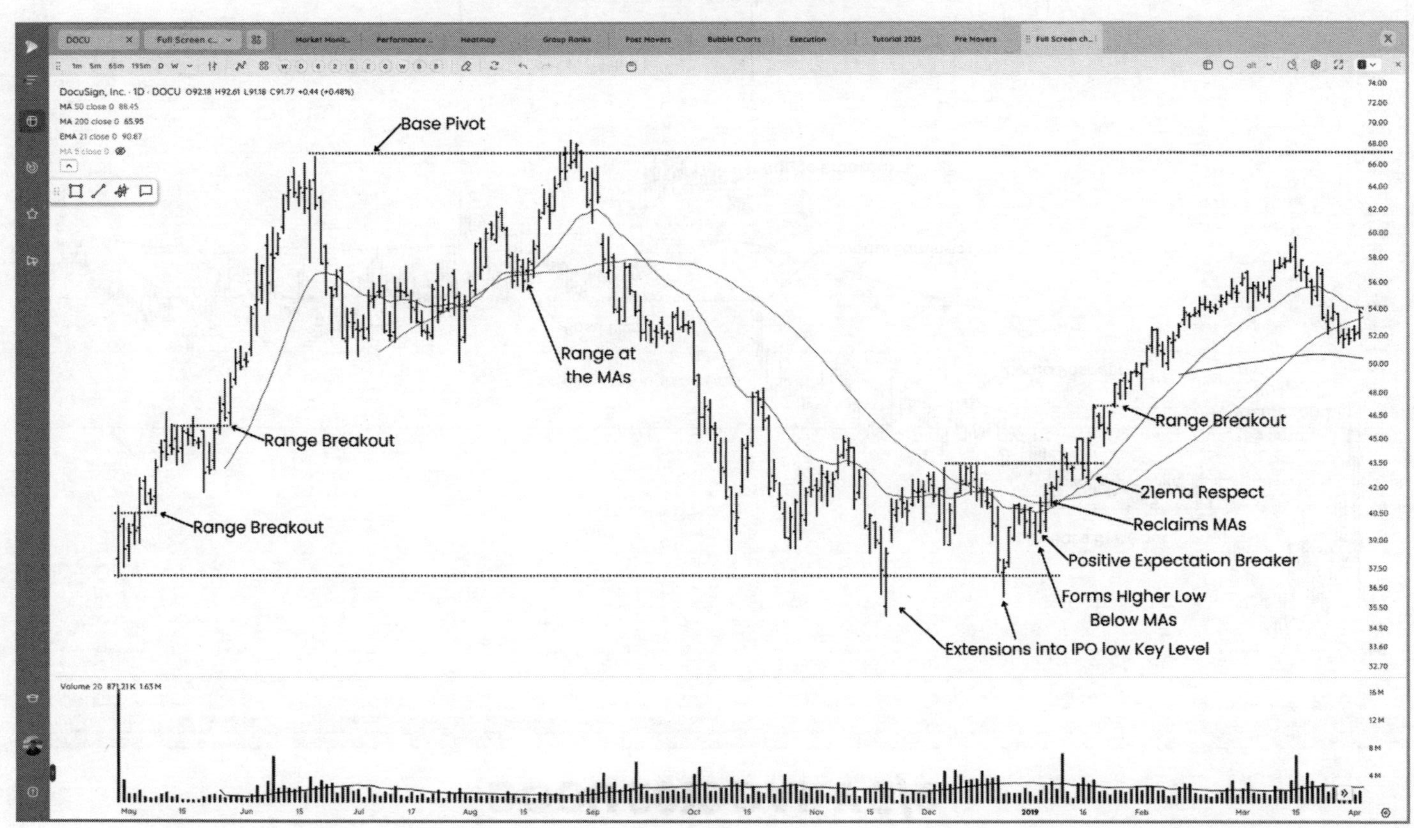

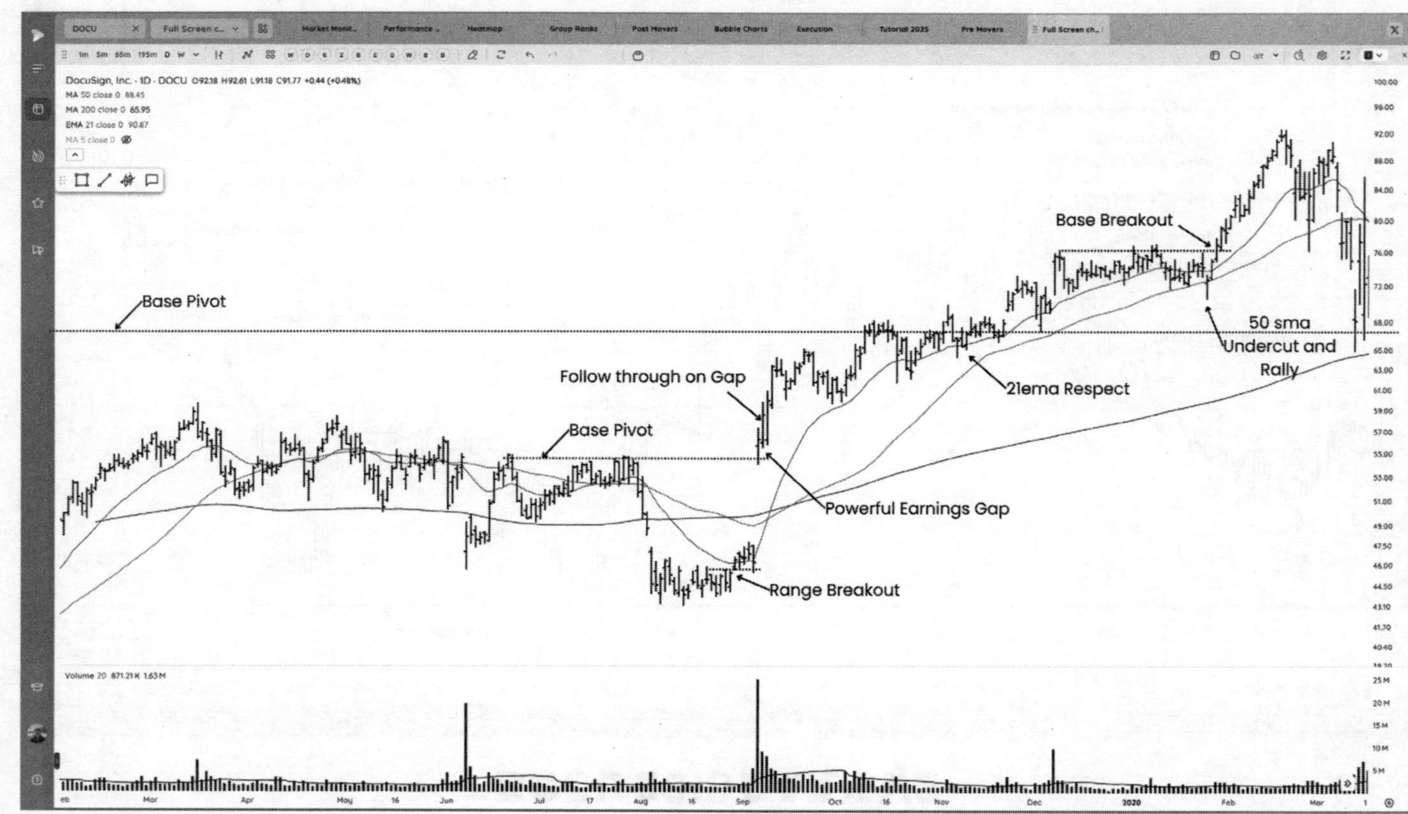
DOCU 2019 DAILY 2/2
DocuSign, Inc. · 1D · DOCU O92.18 H92.61 L91.18 C91.77 +0.44 (+0.48%)
MA 50 close 0 88.45
MA 200 close 0 65.95
EMA 21 close 0 90.87
Base Pivot
Base Pivot
Follow through on Gap
Powerful Earnings Gap
Range Breakout
21ema Respect
Base Breakout
50 sma
Undercut and
Rally
Volume 20 871.21K 1.63M

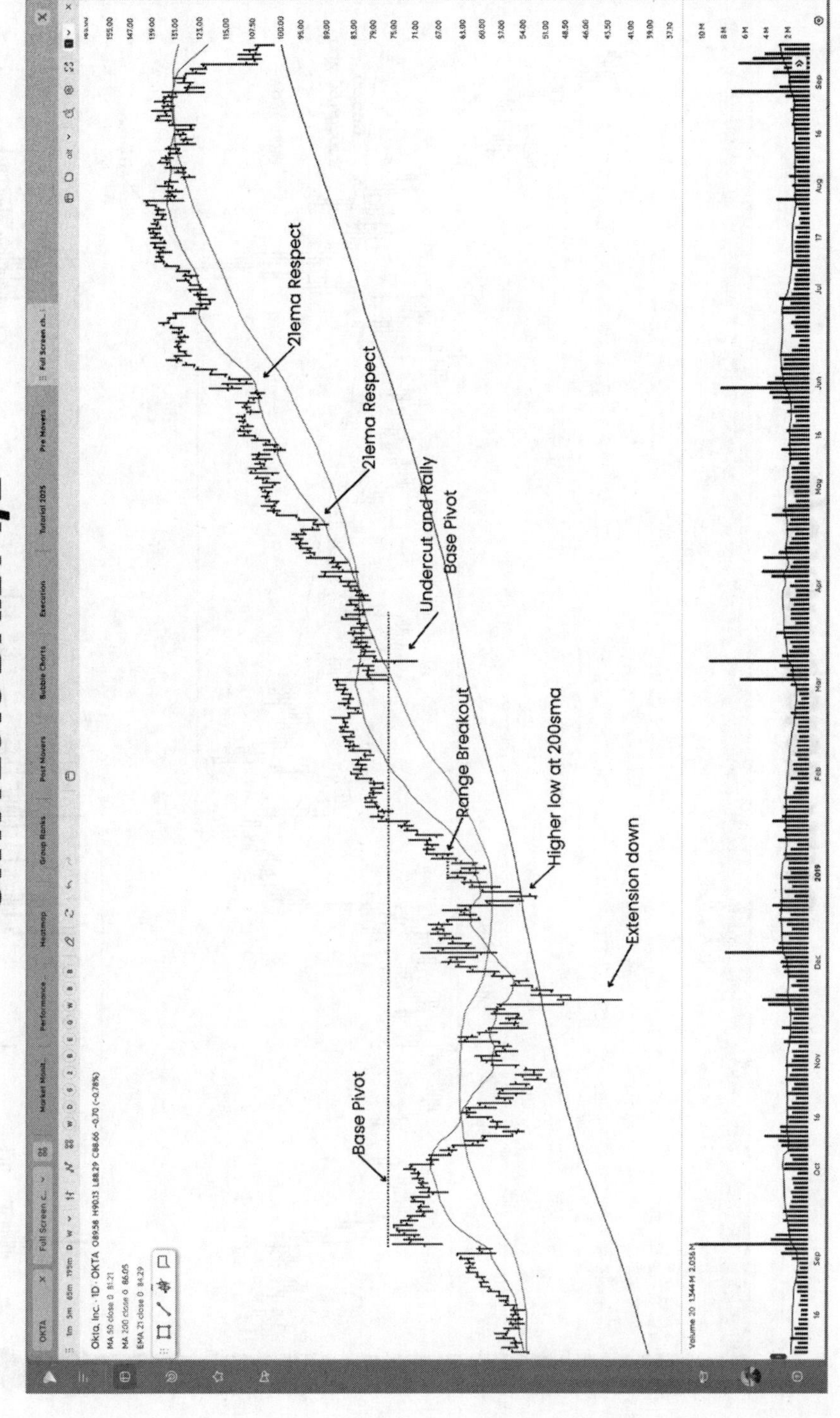
OKTA 2019 DAILY 1/2
Base Pivot
Extension down
Higher low at 200sma
Range Breakout
Base Pivot
Undercut and Rally
21ema Respect
21ema Respect

OKTA 2019 DAILY 2/2

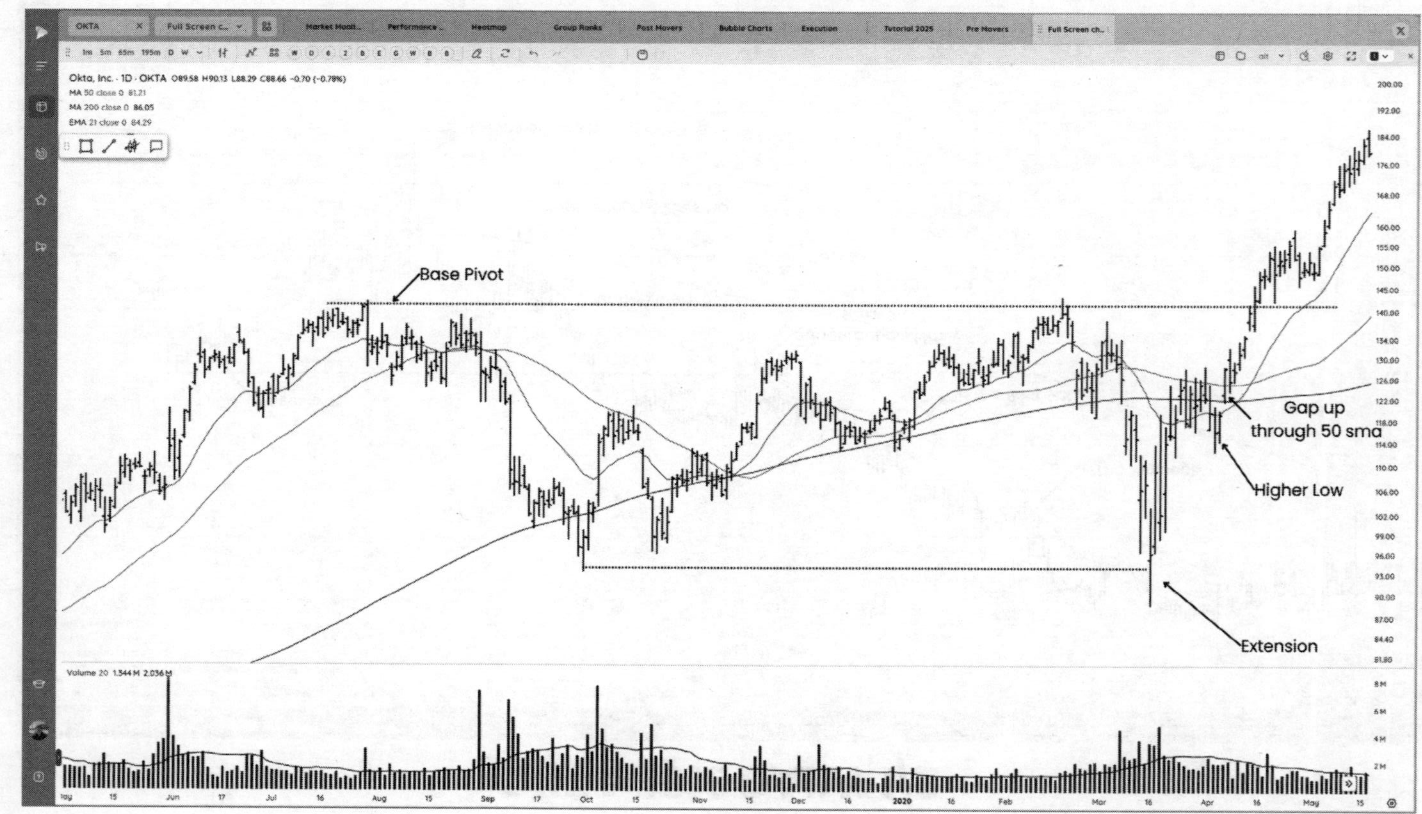

SE 2019 DAILY 1/2

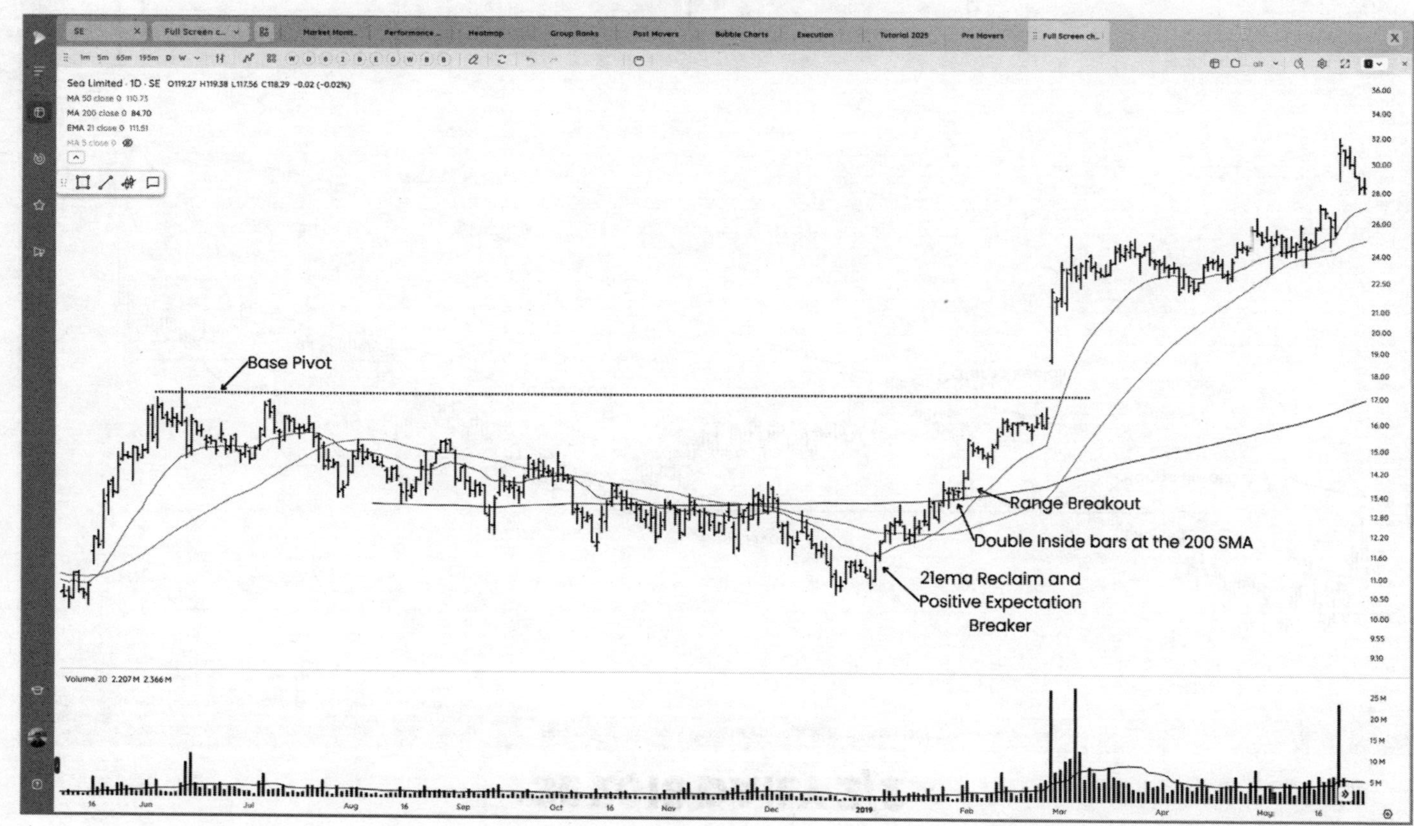

SE 2019 DAILY 2/2

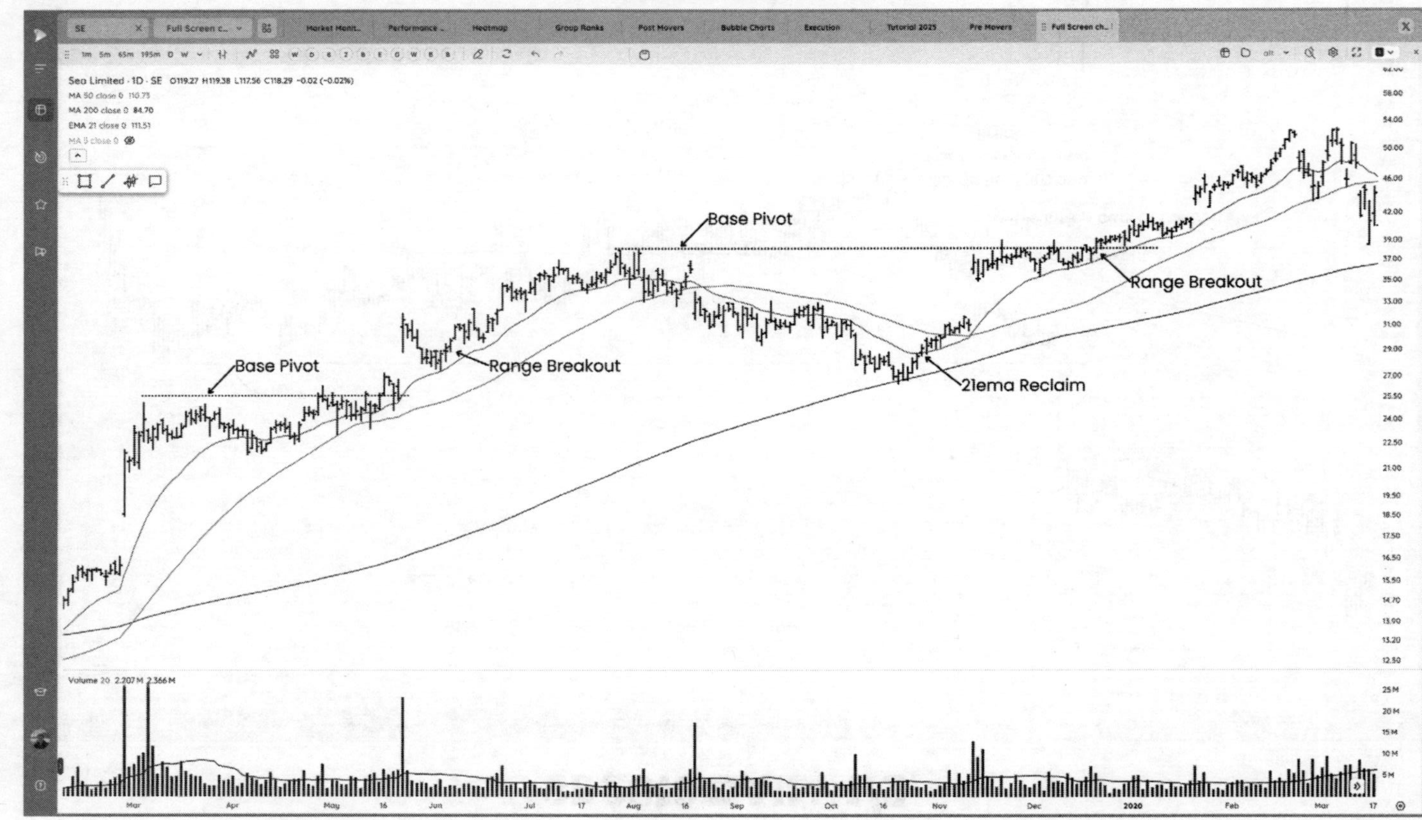

ARWR 2019 DAILY 1/2

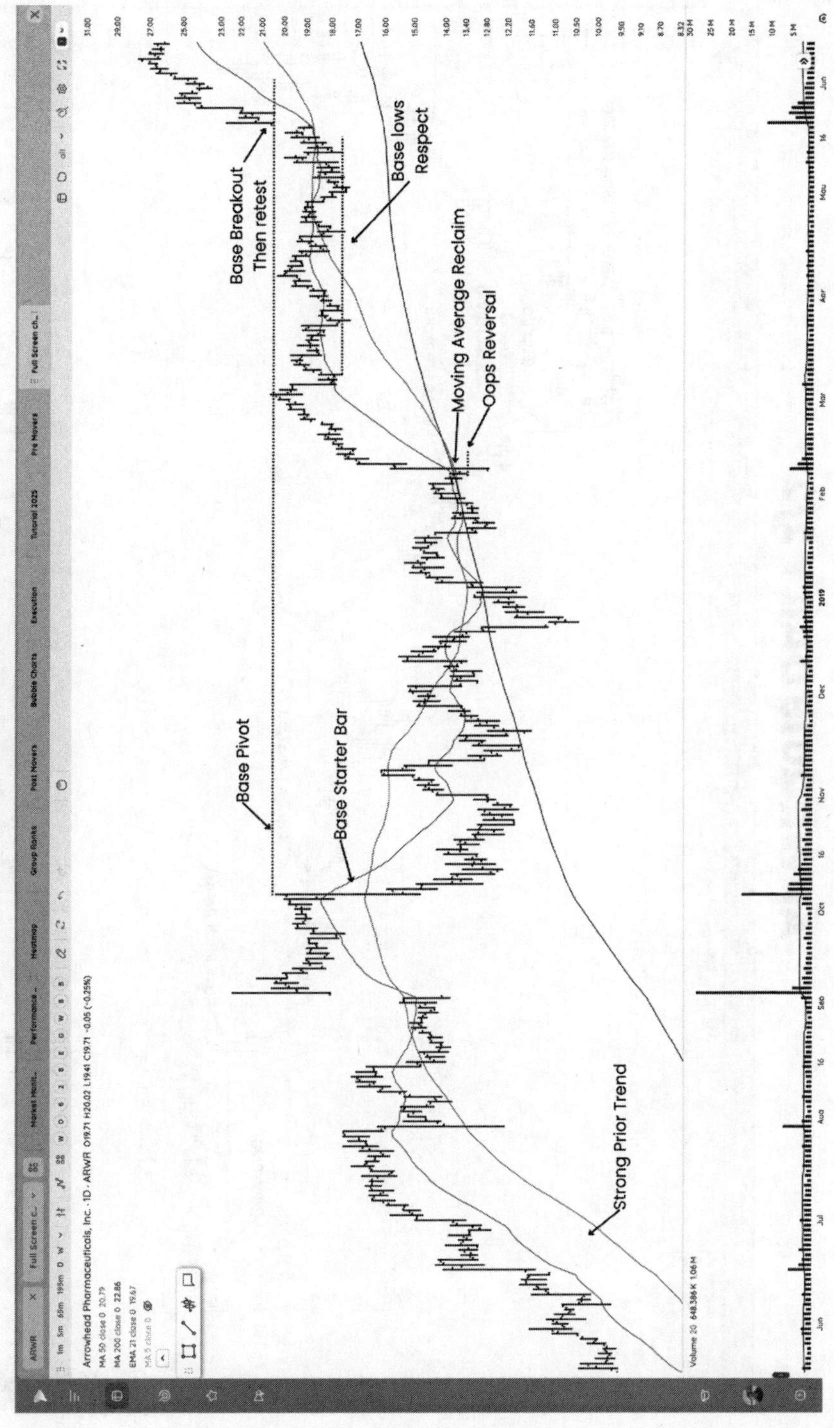

ARWR 2019 DAILY 2/2

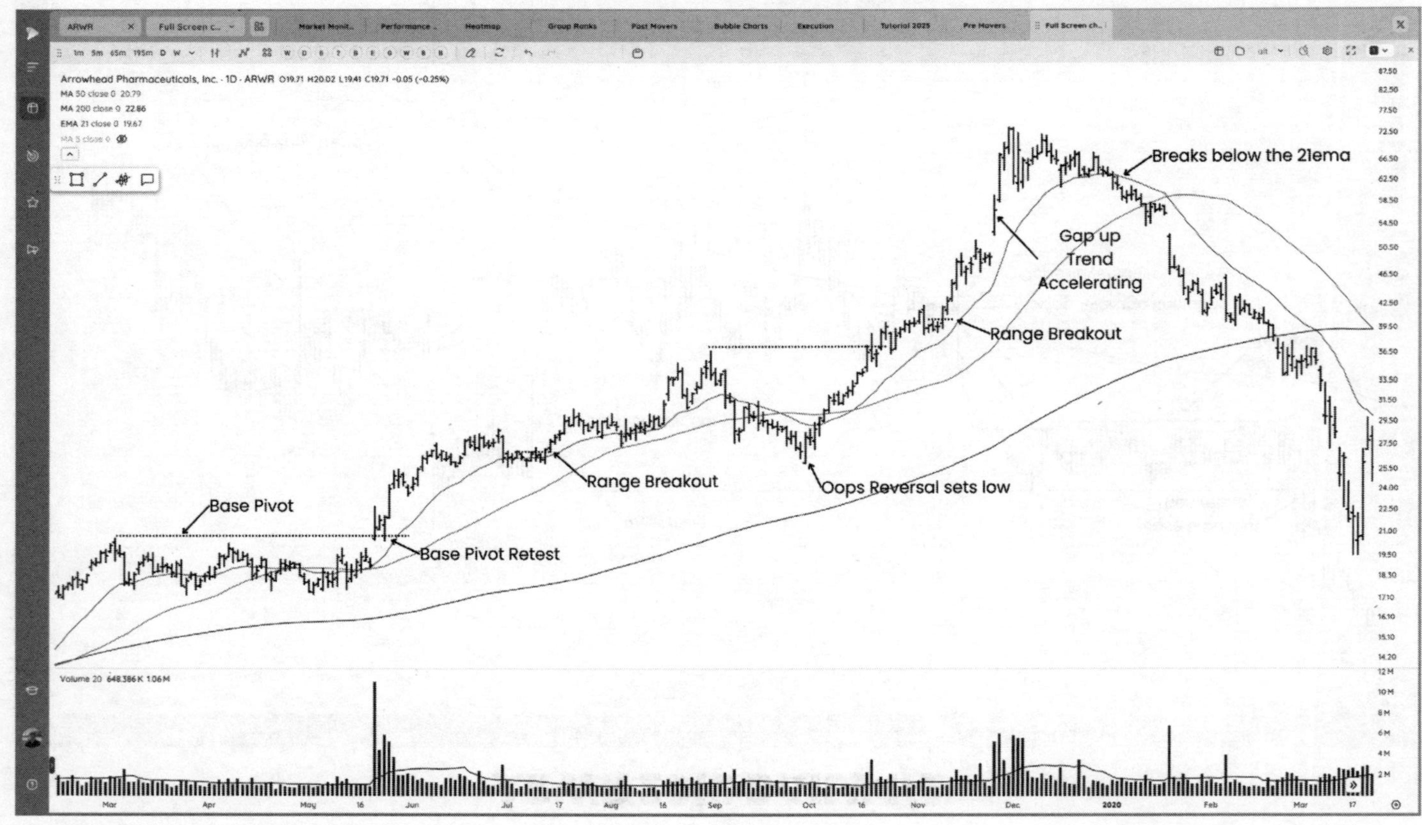

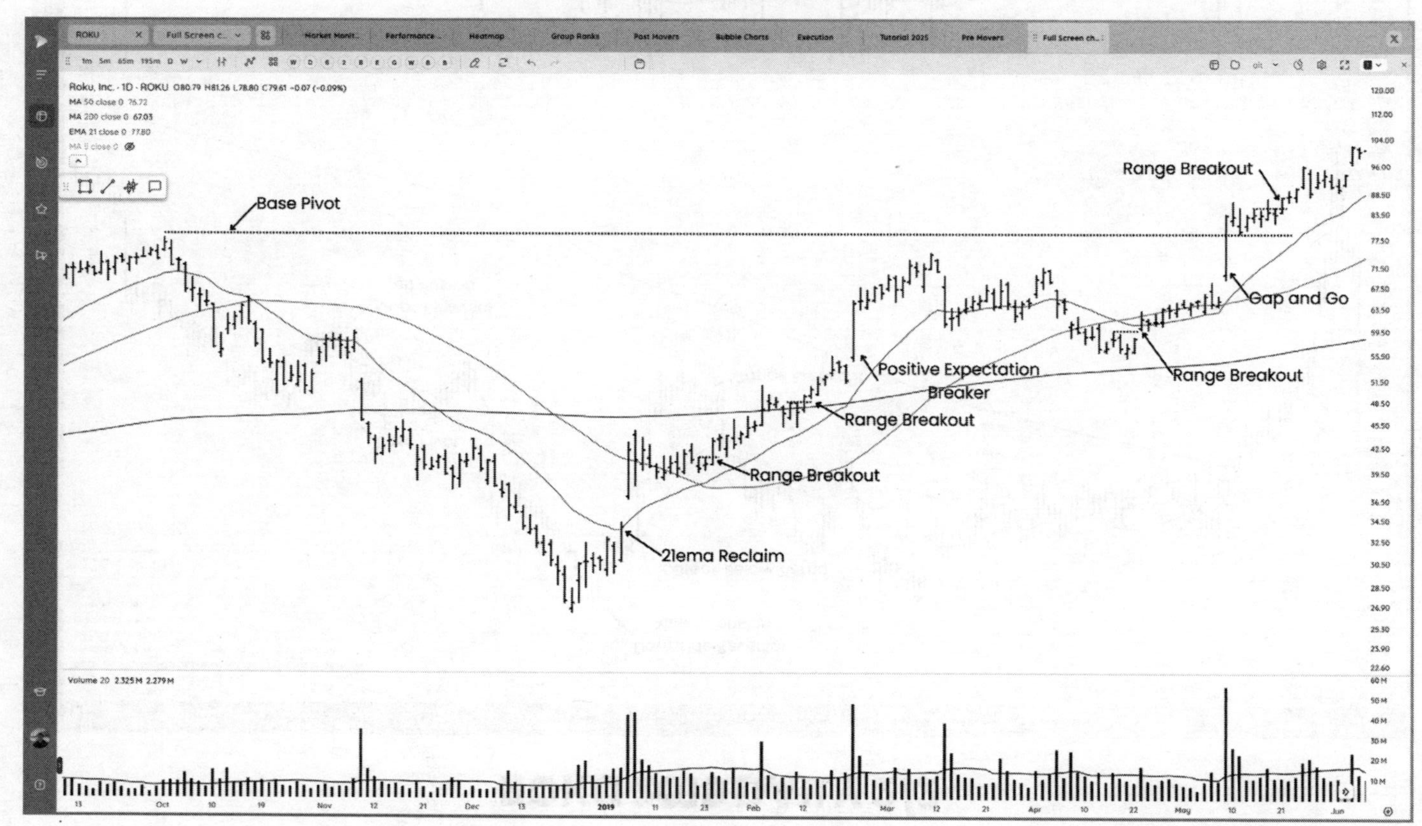
ROKU 2019 DAILY 1/2
Roku, Inc. · 1D · ROKU O80.79 H81.26 L78.80 C79.61 −0.07 (−0.09%)
MA 50 close 0 76.72
MA 200 close 0 67.03
EMA 21 close 0 77.80
Base Pivot
Range Breakout
Gap and Go
Range Breakout
Positive Expectation Breaker
Range Breakout
Range Breakout
21ema Reclaim
Volume 20 2.325M 2.279M

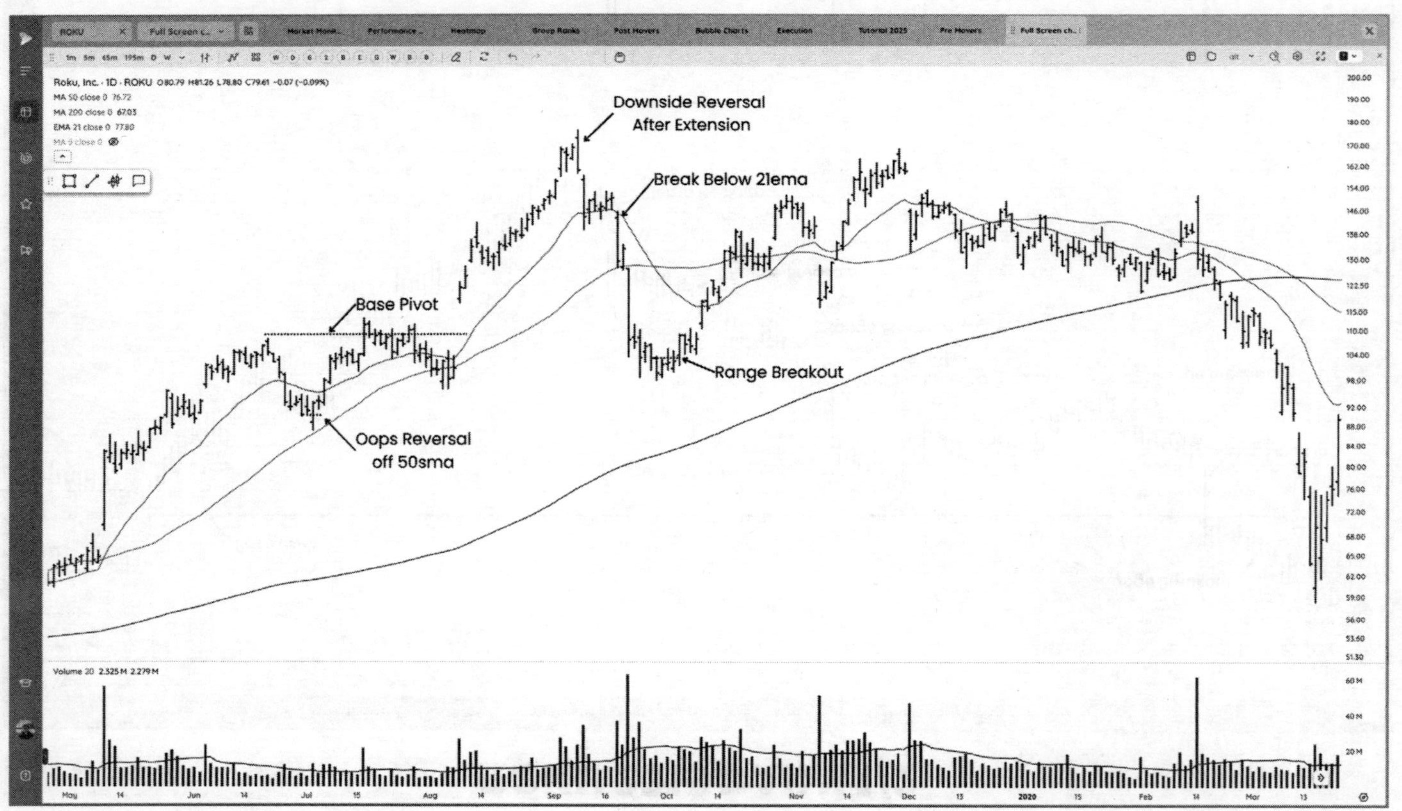
ROKU 2019 DAILY 2/2
Roku, Inc. · 1D · ROKU O80.79 H81.26 L78.80 C79.61 −0.07 (−0.09%)
MA 50 close 0 76.72
MA 200 close 0 67.03
EMA 21 close 0 77.80
Downside Reversal
After Extension
Break Below 21ema
Range Breakout
Base Pivot
Oops Reversal
off 50sma
Volume 20 2.525M 2.279M

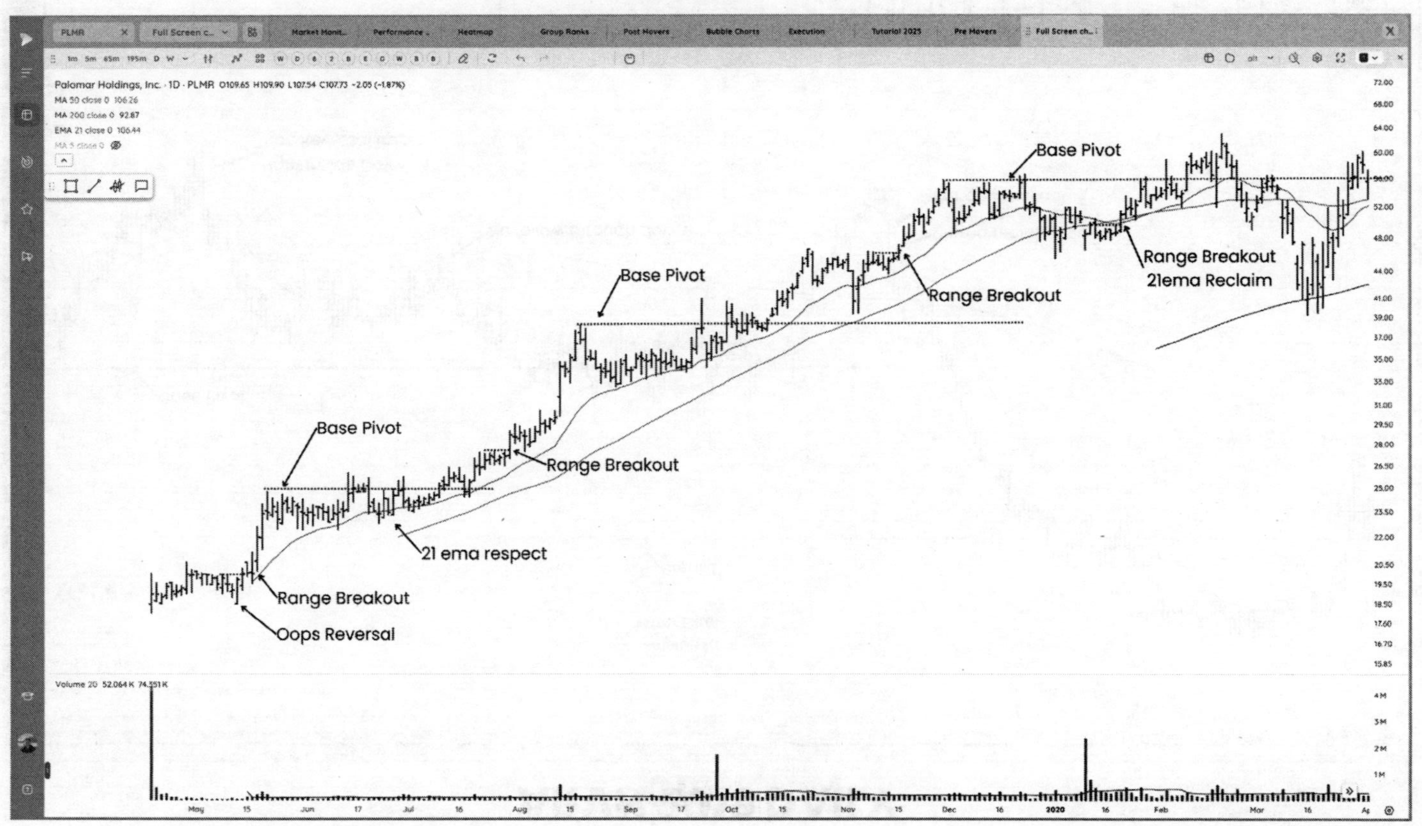
PLMR 2019 DAILY
Palomar Holdings, Inc. · 1D · PLMR O109.65 H109.90 L107.54 C107.73 −2.05 (−1.87%)
MA 50 close 0 106.26
MA 200 close 0 92.87
EMA 21 close 0 106.44
Base Pivot
Range Breakout
Oops Reversal
21 ema respect
Base Pivot
Range Breakout
Base Pivot
Range Breakout
Range Breakout
21ema Reclaim
Volume 20 52.064 K 74.351 K

ARVN 2019 DAILY

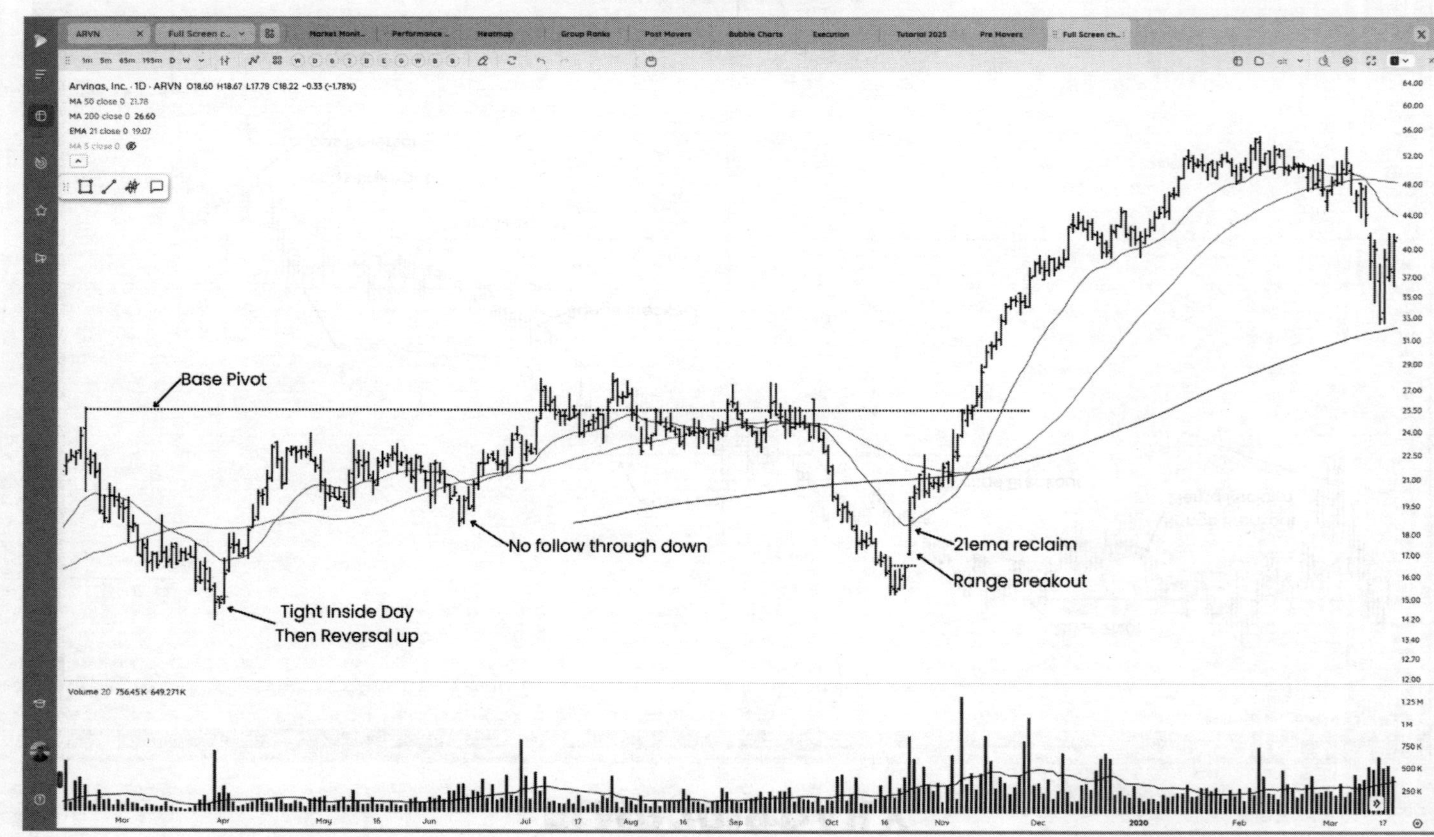

SEDG 2019 DAILY 1/2

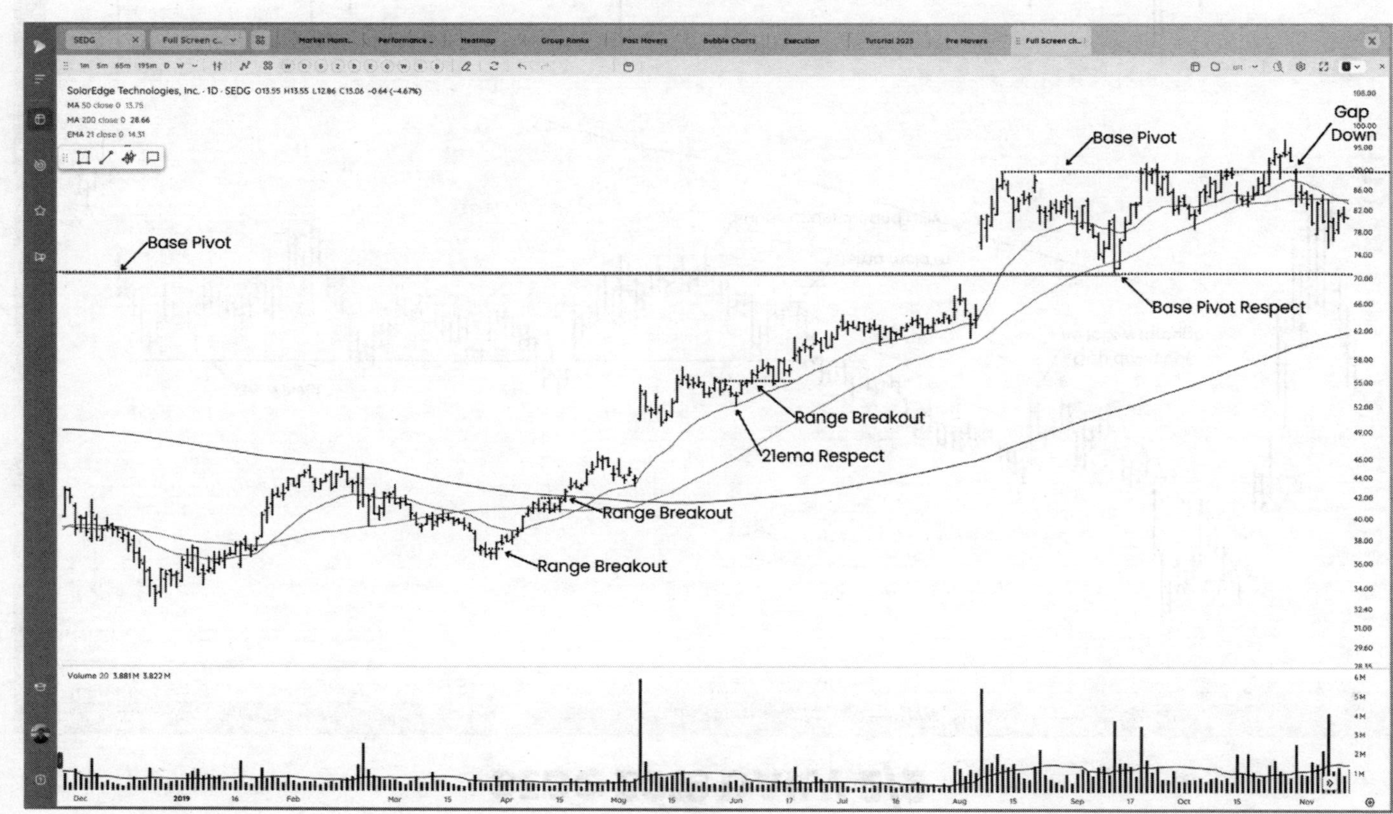

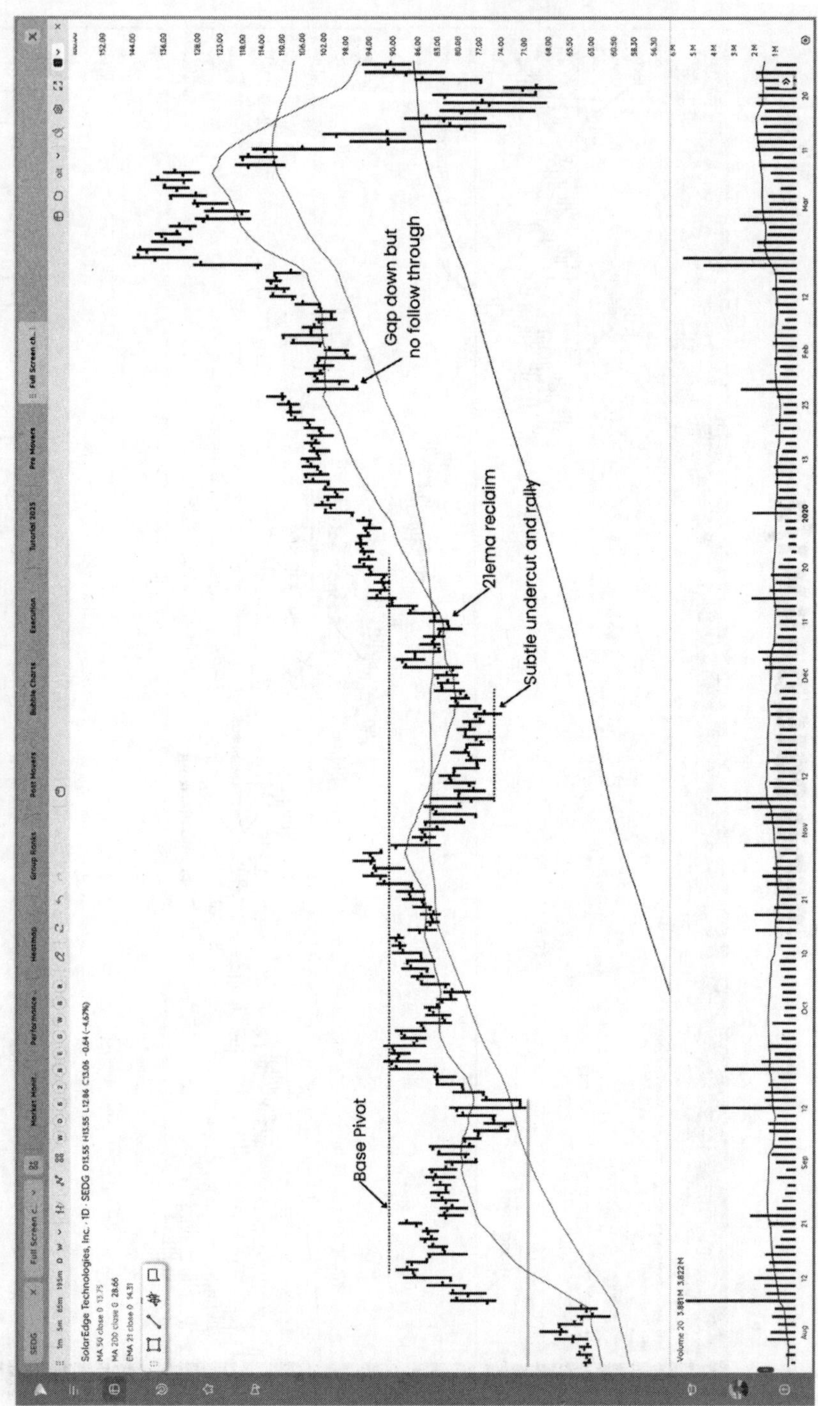
SEDG 2019 DAILY 2/2
Base Pivot
Gap down but
no follow through
21ema reclaim
Subtle undercut and rally

2020 MARKET LEADERS

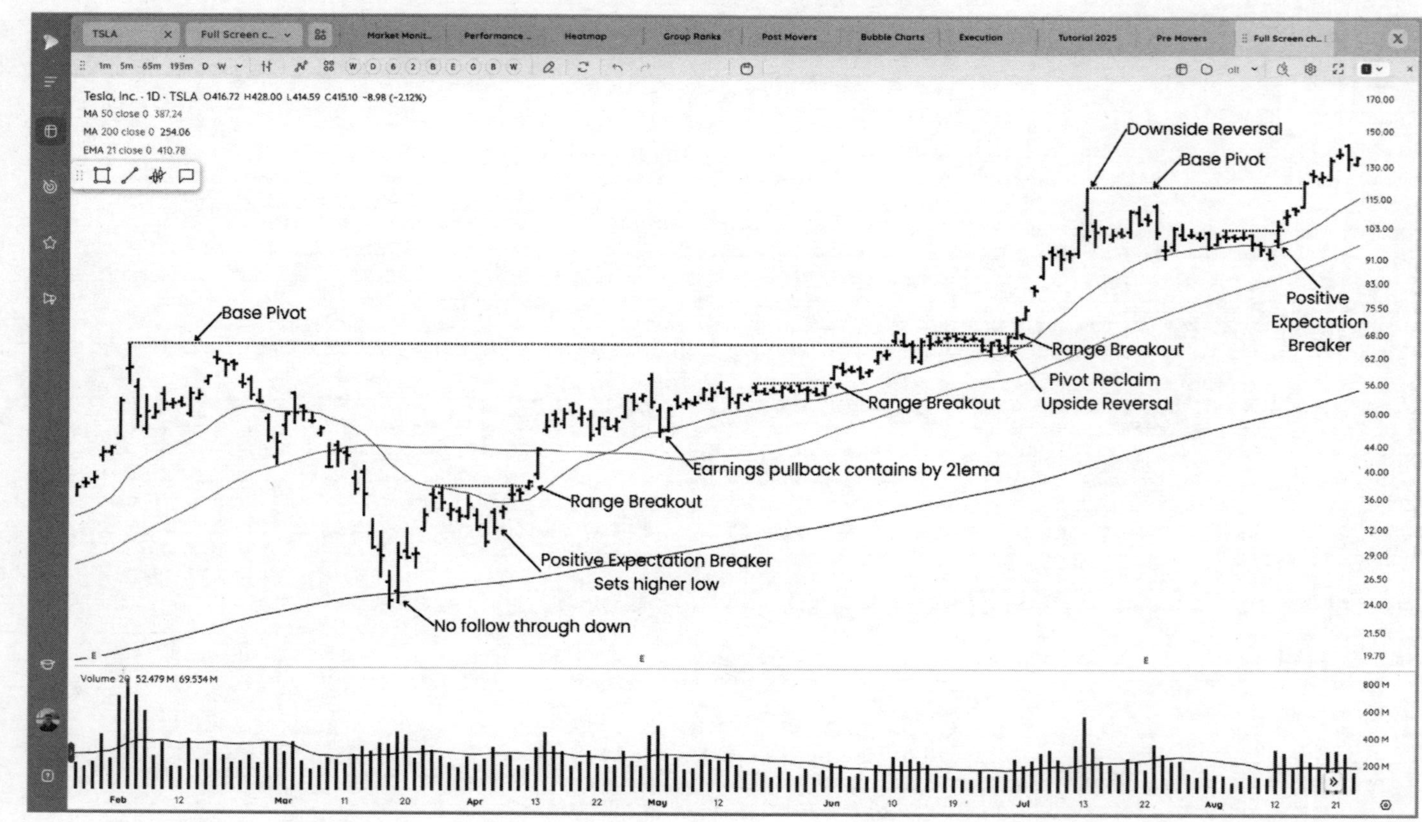
TSLA 2020 DAILY 1/2
Tesla, Inc. · 1D · TSLA O416.72 H428.00 L414.59 C415.10 -8.98 (-2.12%)
MA 50 close 0 387.24
MA 200 close 0 254.06
EMA 21 close 0 410.78
Base Pivot
No follow through down
Positive Expectation Breaker
Sets higher low
Range Breakout
Earnings pullback contains by 21ema
Range Breakout
Range Breakout
Pivot Reclaim
Upside Reversal
Downside Reversal
Base Pivot
Positive
Expectation
Breaker

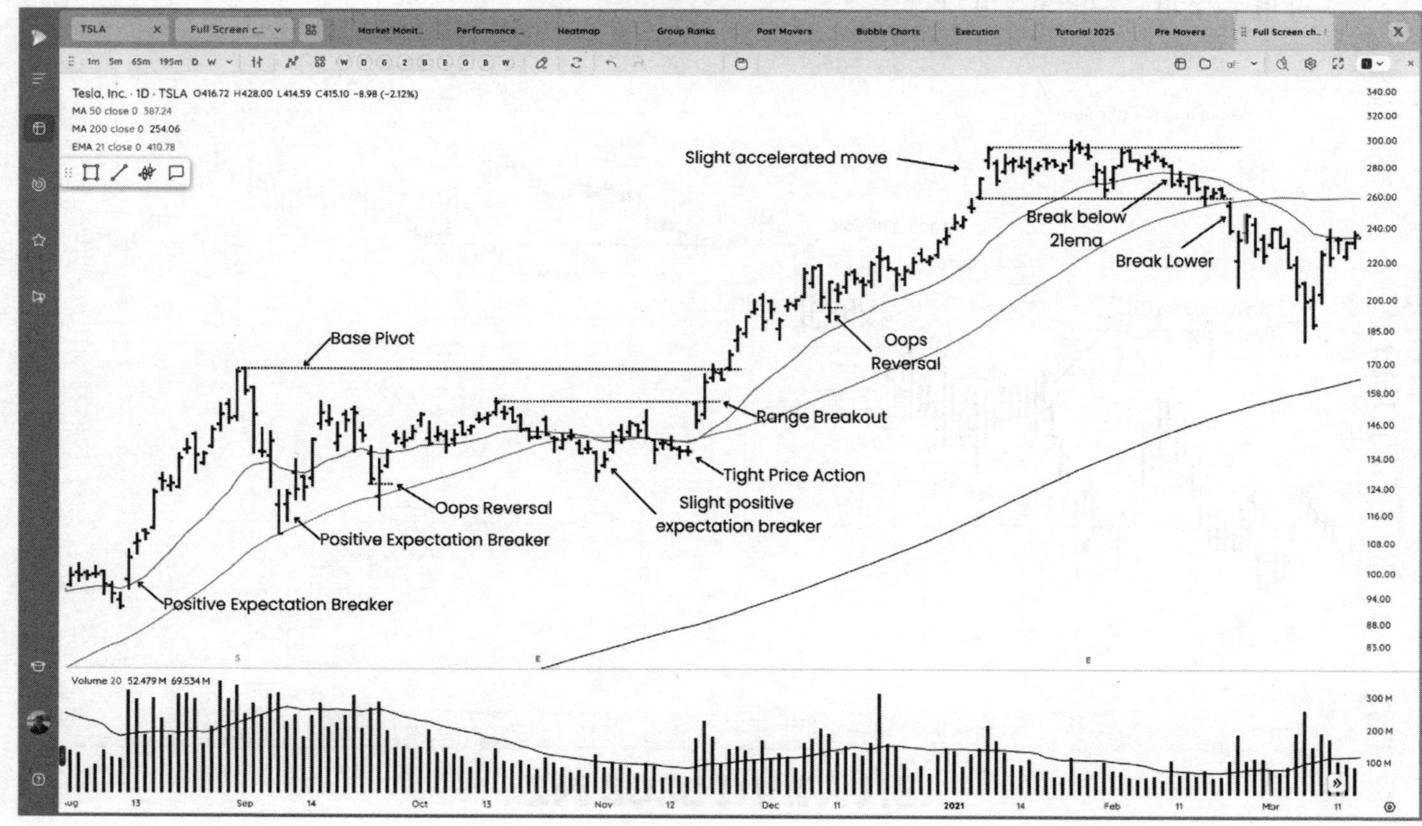
TSLA 2020 DAILY 2/2
Tesla, Inc. · 1D · TSLA O416.72 H428.00 L414.59 C415.10 −8.98 (−2.12%)
MA 50 close 0 387.24
MA 200 close 0 254.06
EMA 21 close 0 410.78
Slight accelerated move
Break below 21ema
Break Lower
Base Pivot
Oops Reversal
Range Breakout
Tight Price Action
Oops Reversal
Slight positive expectation breaker
Positive Expectation Breaker
Positive Expectation Breaker
Volume 20 52.479 M 69.534 M

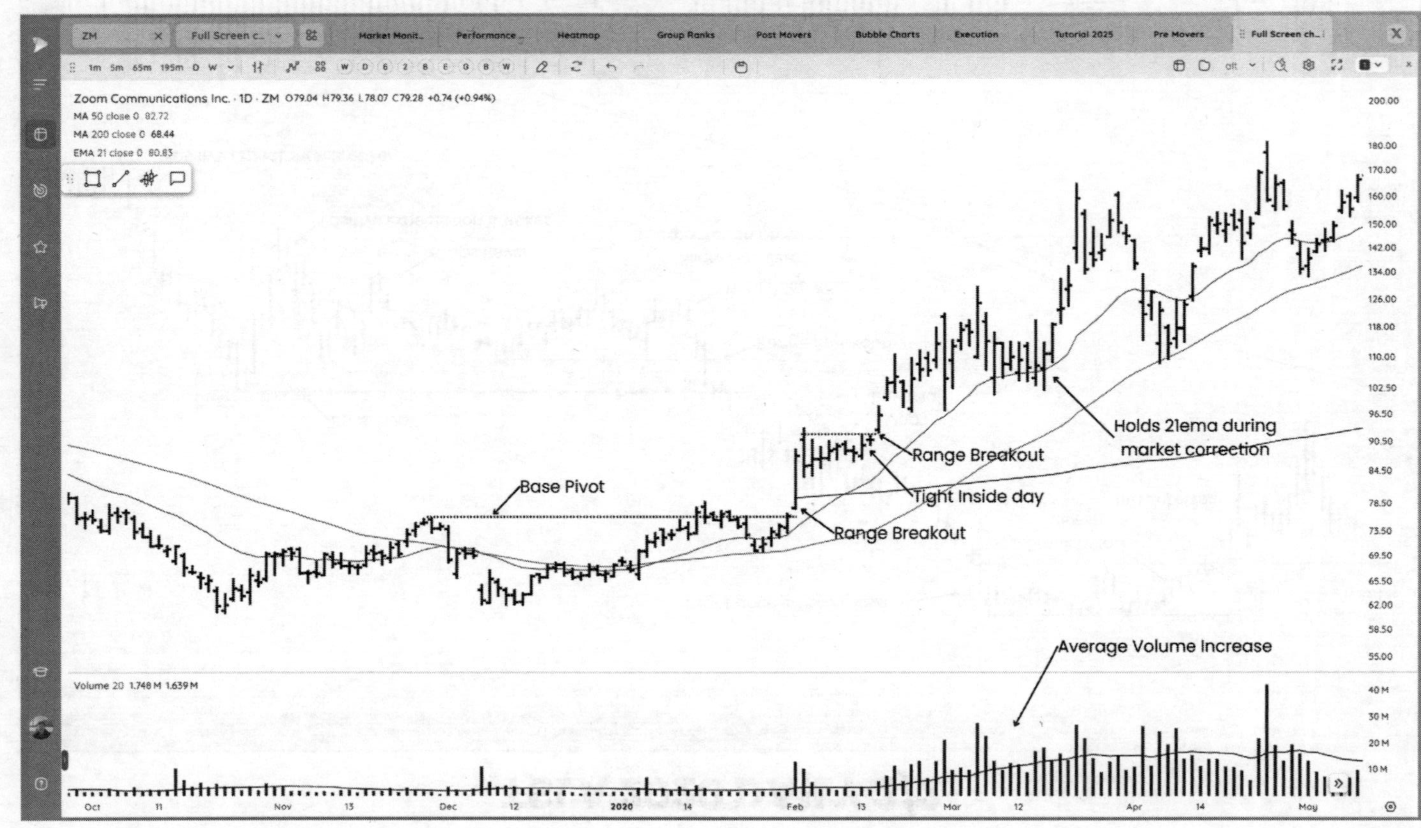
ZM 2020 DAILY 1/2
Zoom Communications Inc. · 1D · ZM O79.04 H79.36 L78.07 C79.28 +0.74 (+0.94%)
MA 50 close 0 82.72
MA 200 close 0 68.44
EMA 21 close 0 80.83
Base Pivot
Range Breakout
Tight Inside day
Range Breakout
Holds 21ema during
market correction
Average Volume Increase
Volume 20 1.748 M 1.639 M

ZM 2020 DAILY 2/2

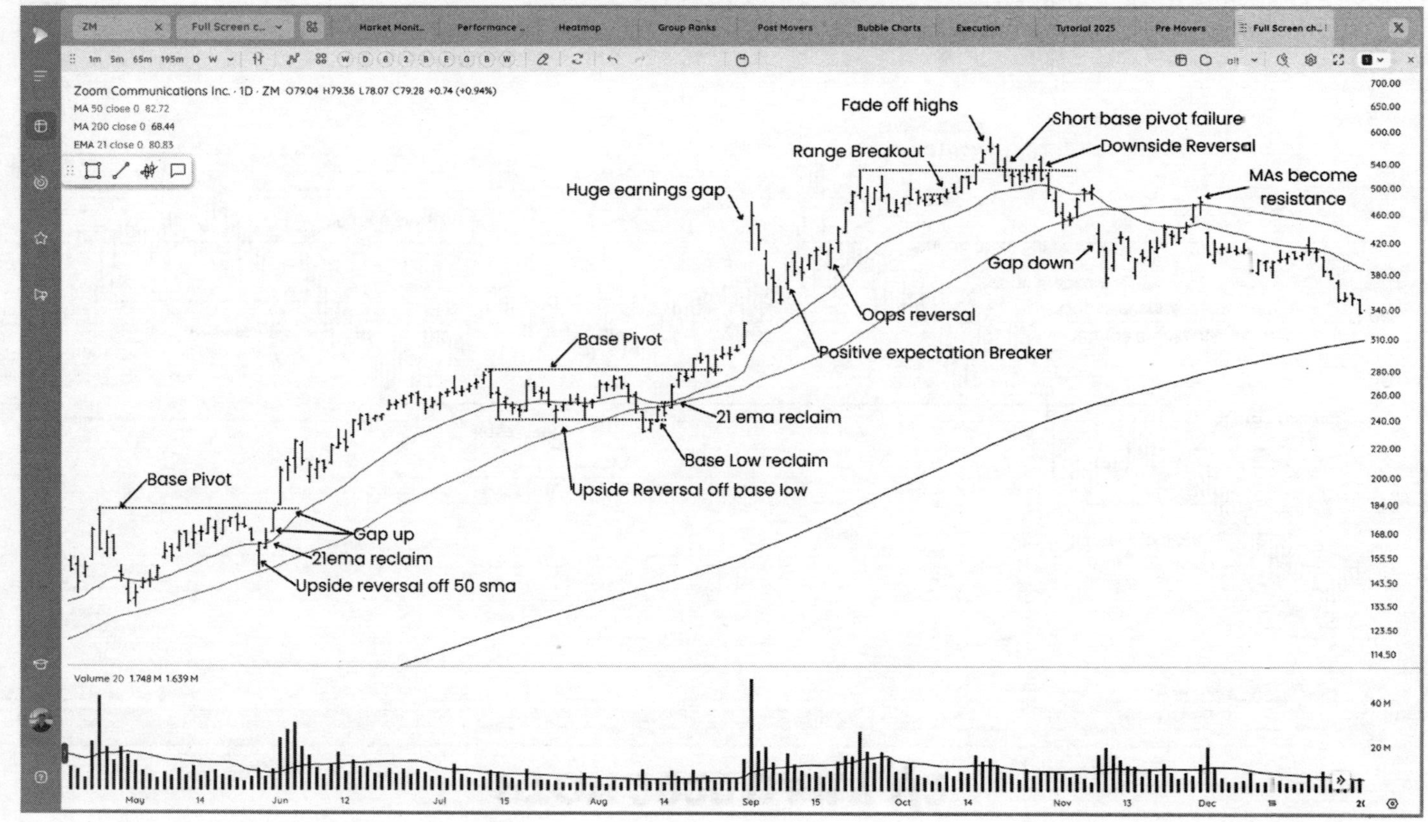

PTON 2020 DAILY 1/2

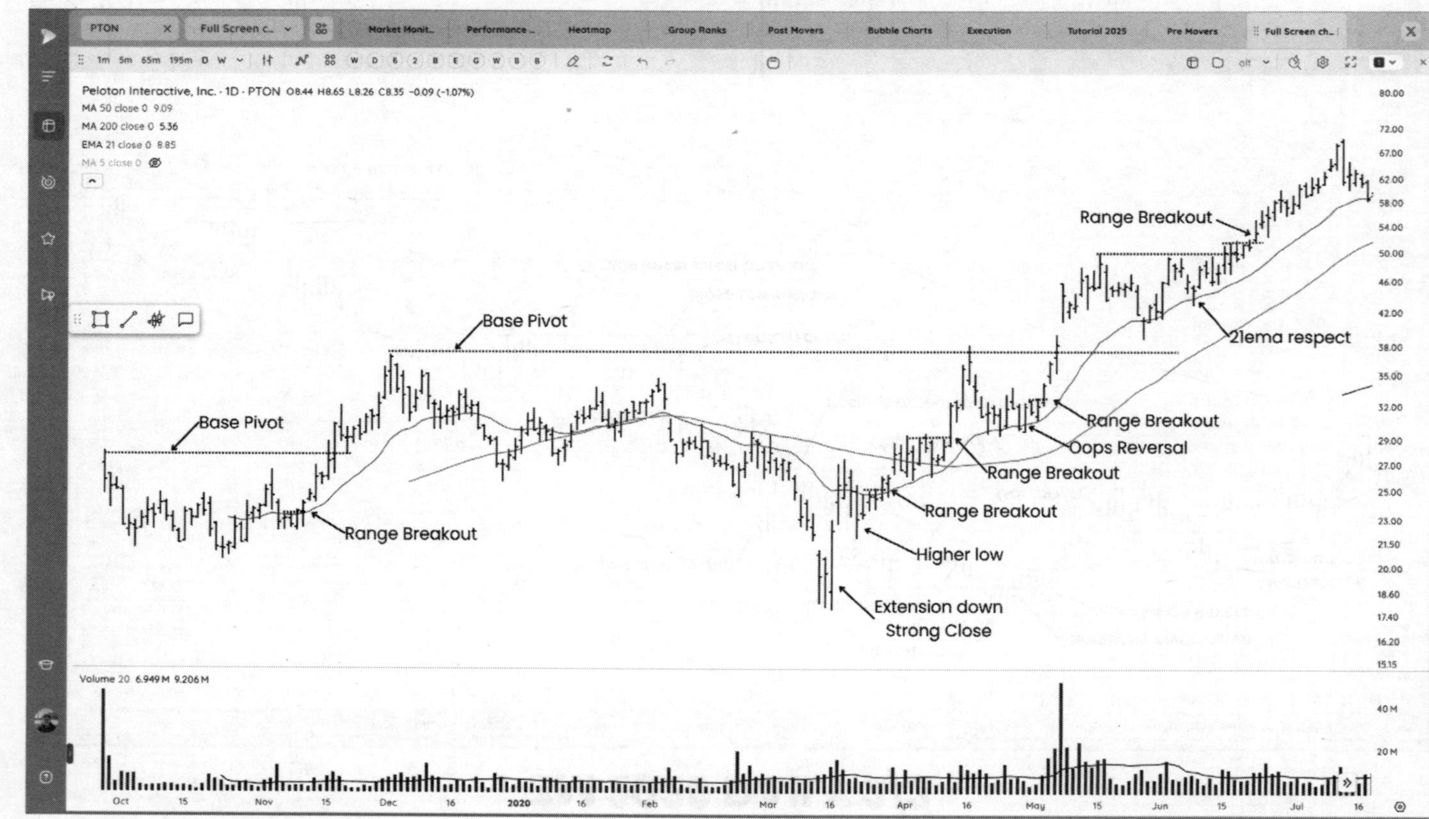

PTON 2020 DAILY 2/2

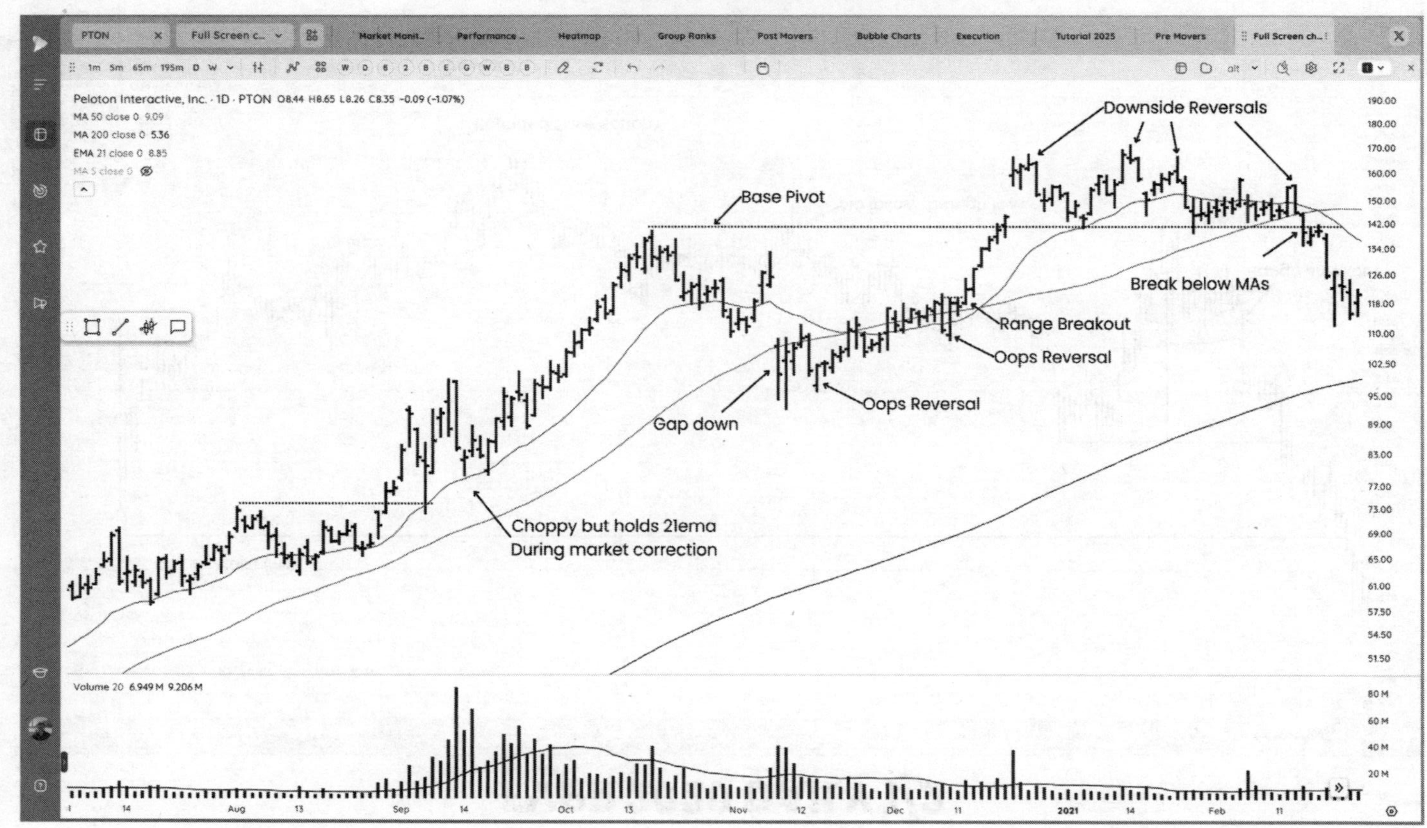

FVRR 2020 DAILY 1/2

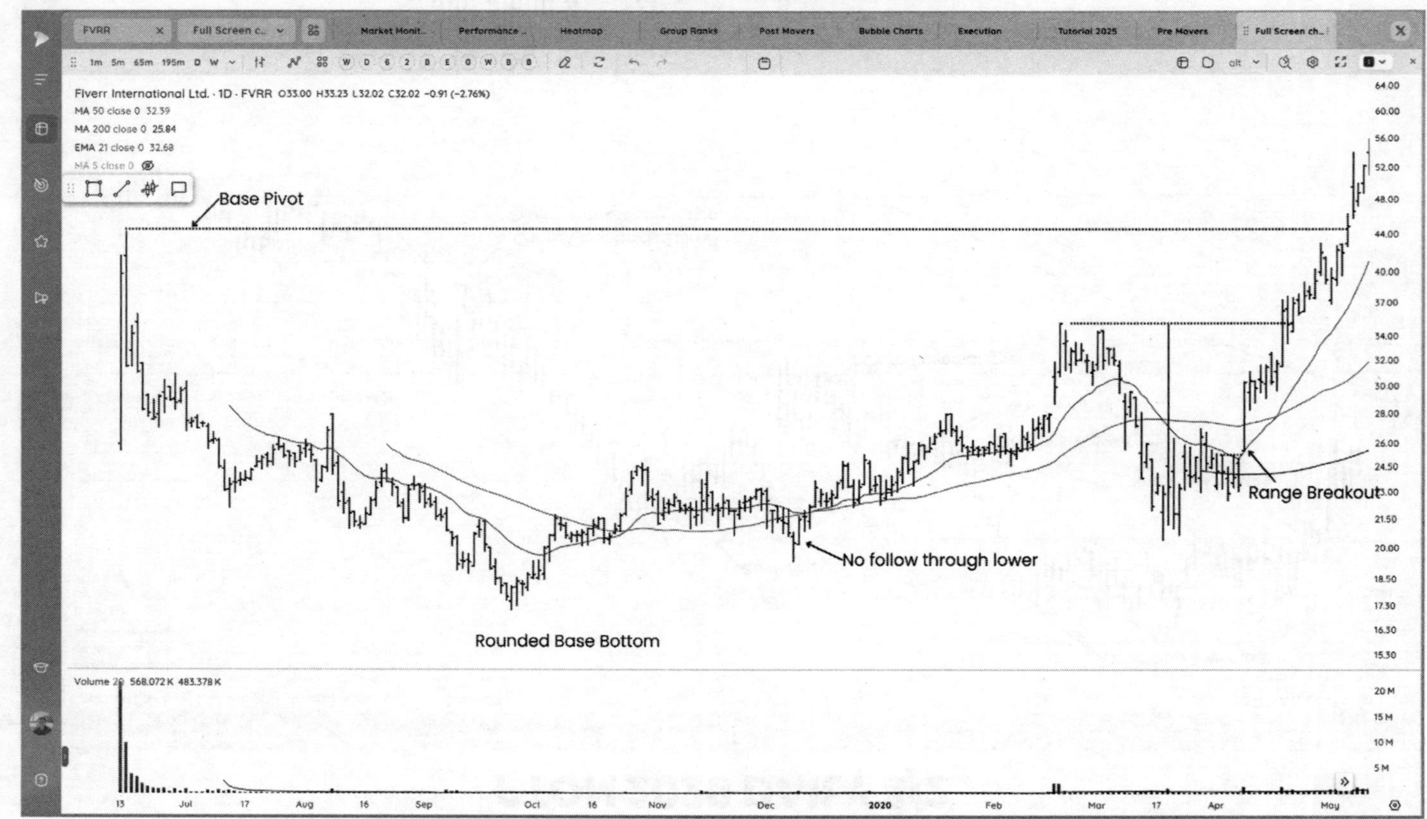

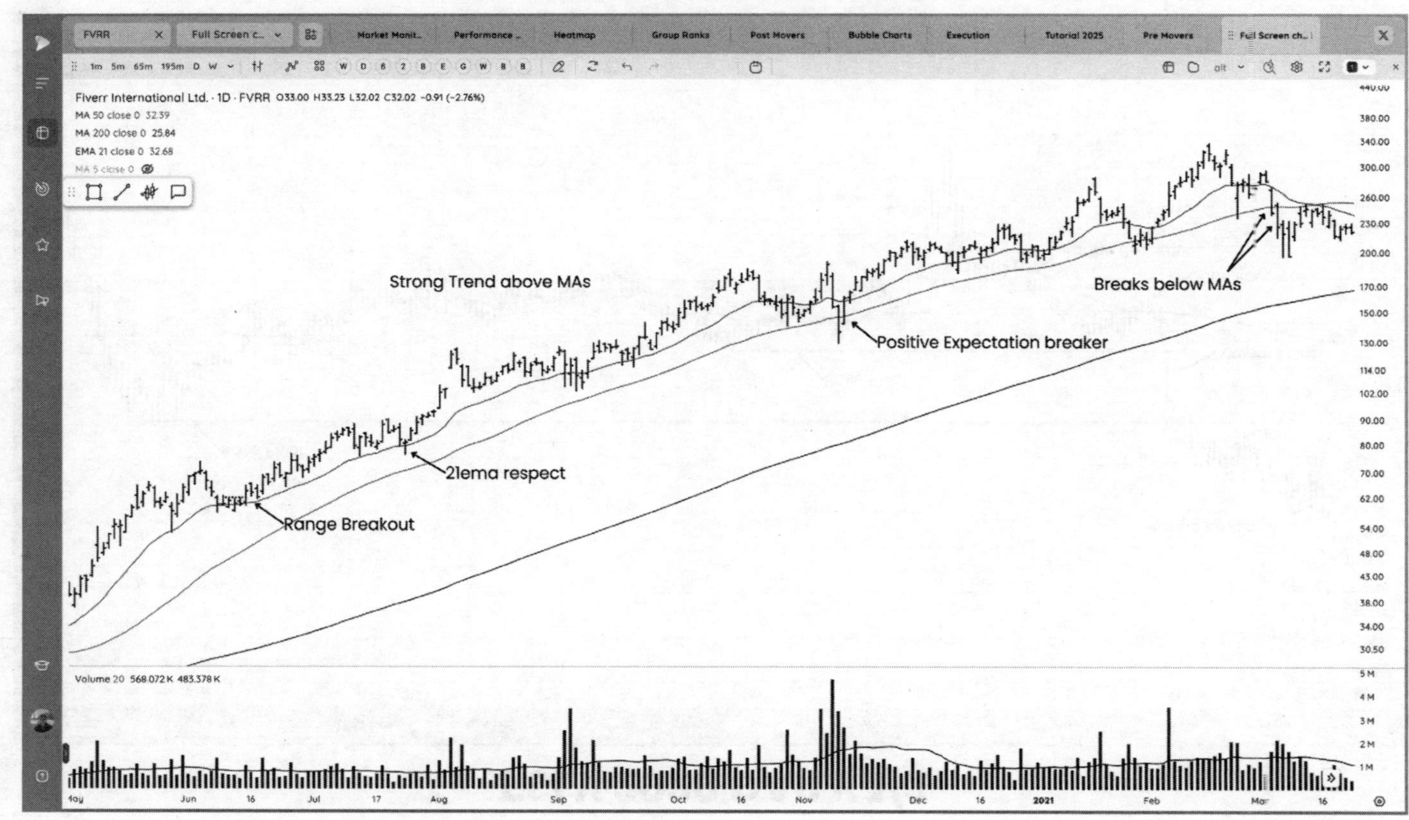
FVRR 2020 DAILY 2/2
Fiverr International Ltd. · 1D · FVRR O33.00 H33.23 L32.02 C32.02 −0.91 (−2.76%)
MA 50 close 0 32.39
MA 200 close 0 25.84
EMA 21 close 0 32.68
Range Breakout
21ema respect
Strong Trend above MAs
Positive Expectation breaker
Breaks below MAs
Volume 20 568.072 K 483.378 K

FSLY 2020 DAILY 1/2

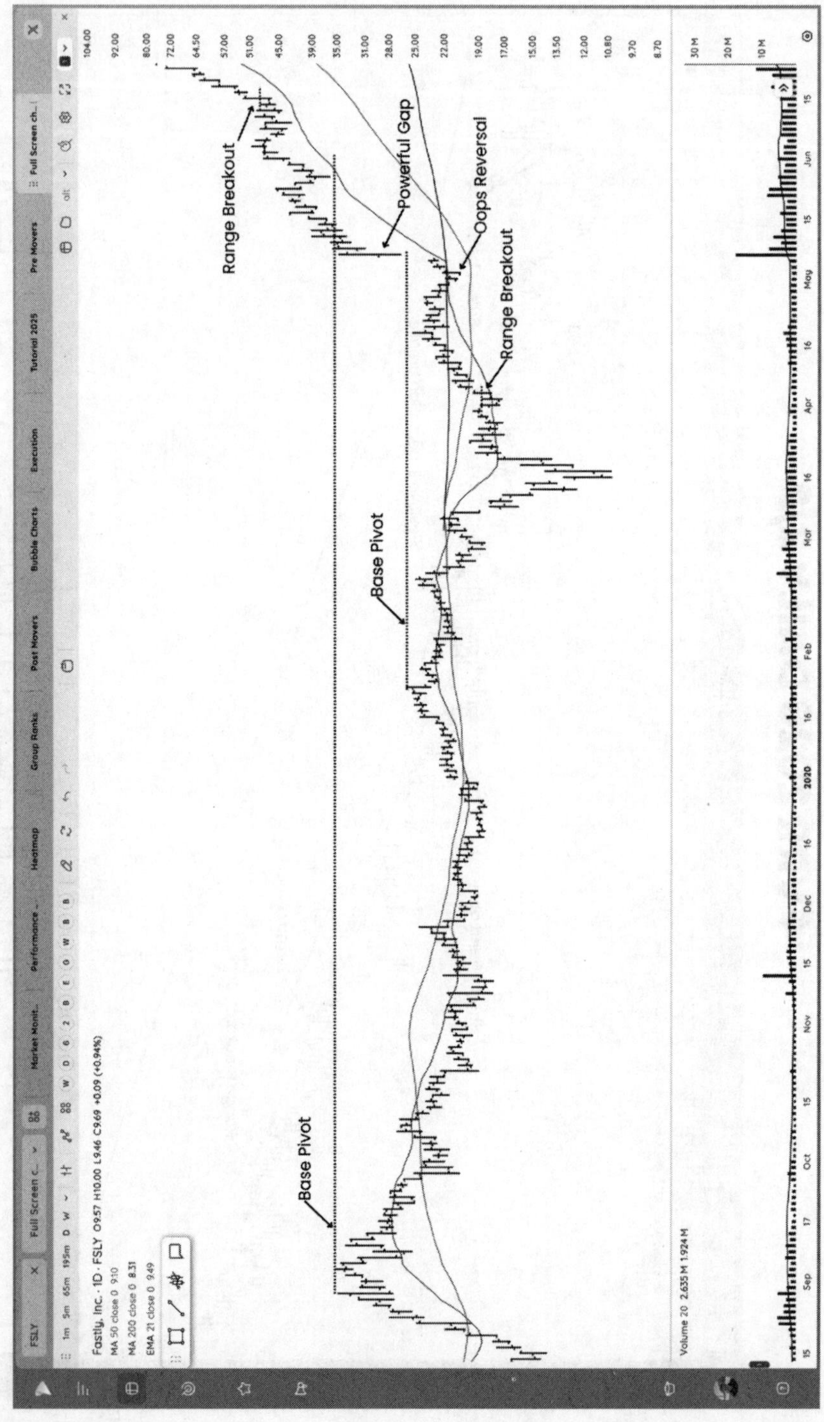

FSLY 2020 DAILY 2/2

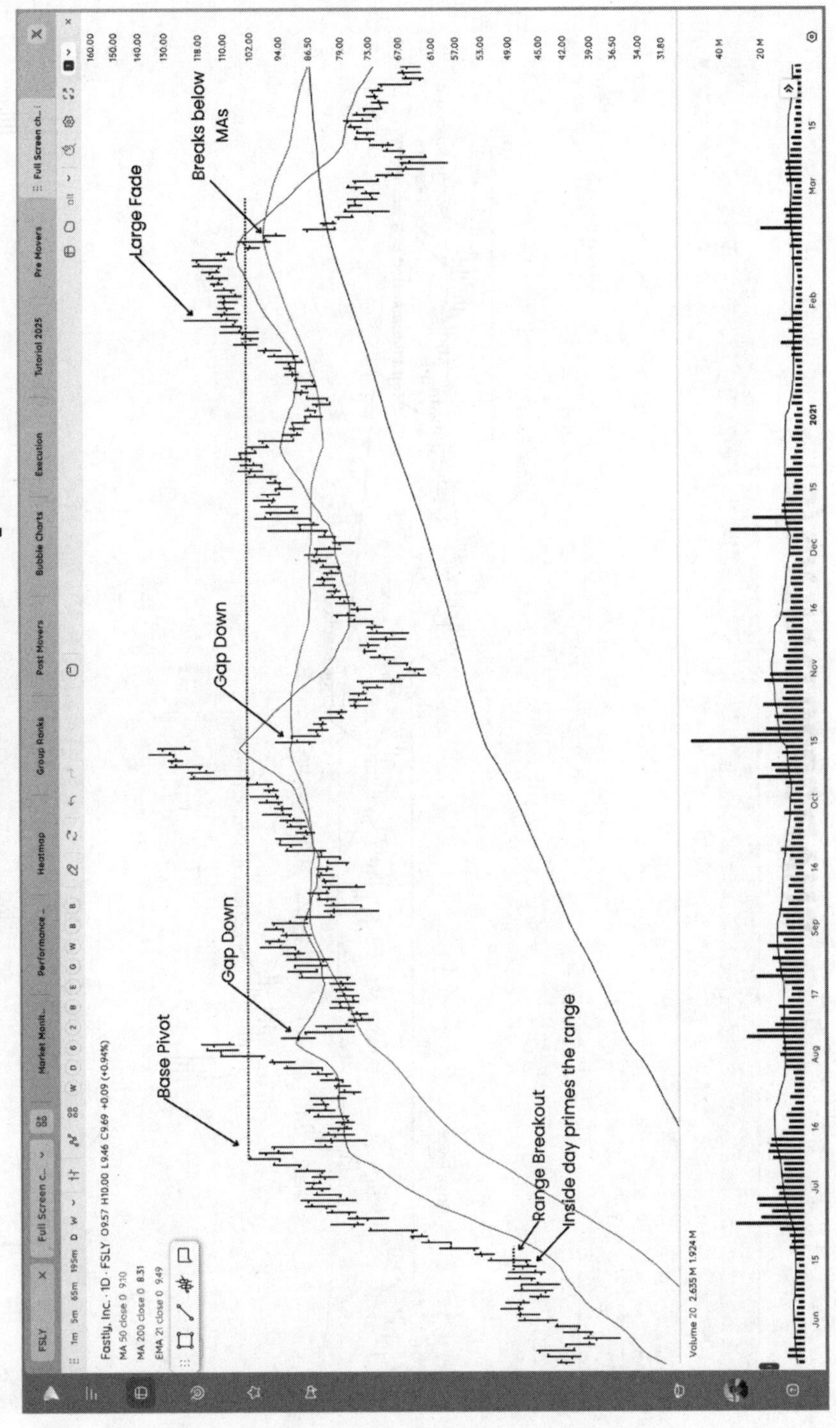

SNAP 2020 DAILY 1/2

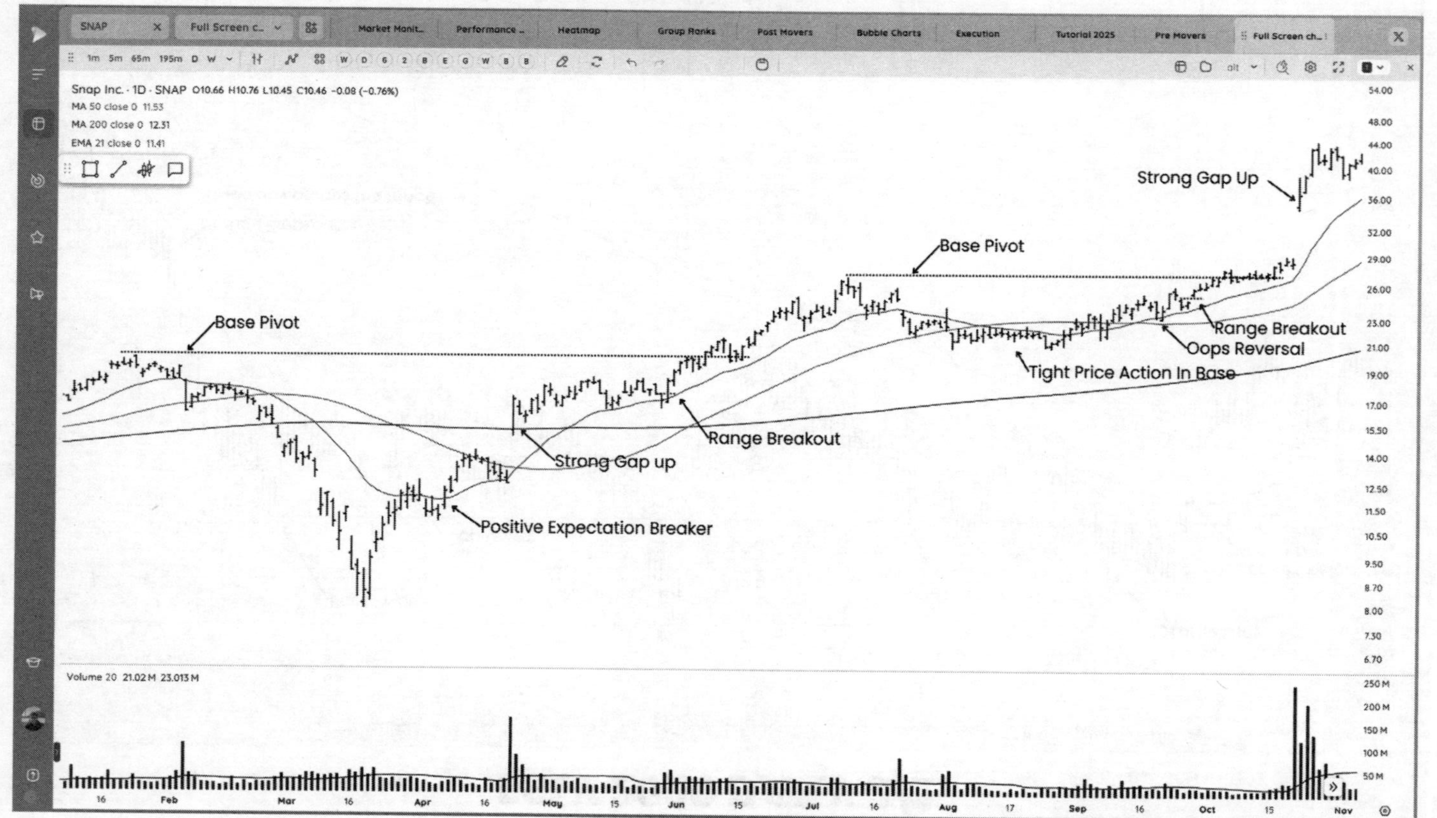

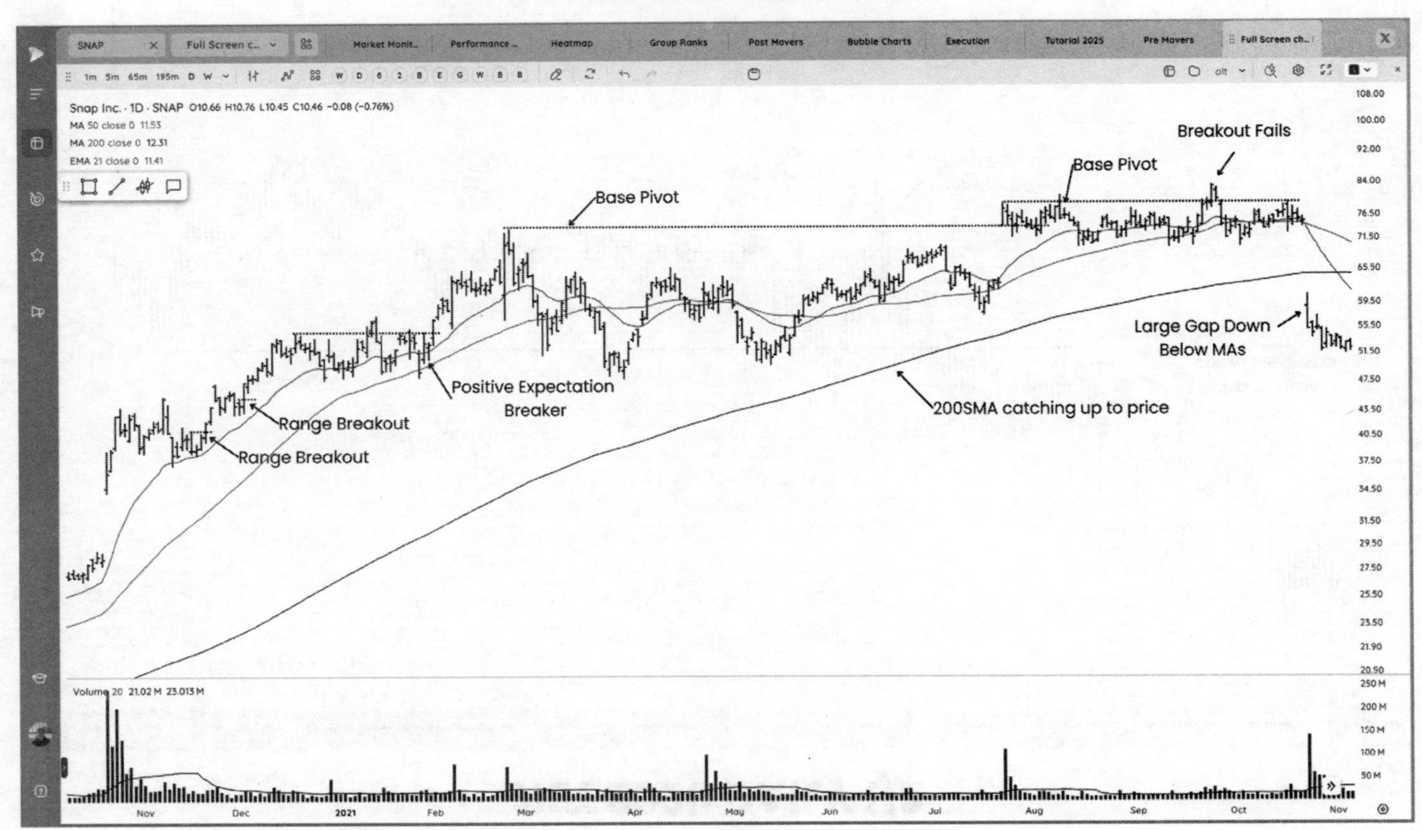
SNAP 2020 DAILY 2/2
Snap Inc. · 1D · SNAP O10.66 H10.76 L10.45 C10.46 −0.08 (−0.76%)
MA 50 close 0 11.53
MA 200 close 0 12.31
EMA 21 close 0 11.41
Base Pivot
Breakout Fails
Base Pivot
Large Gap Down
Below MAs
Positive Expectation
Breaker
200SMA catching up to price
Range Breakout
Range Breakout
Volume 20 21.02 M 23.013 M

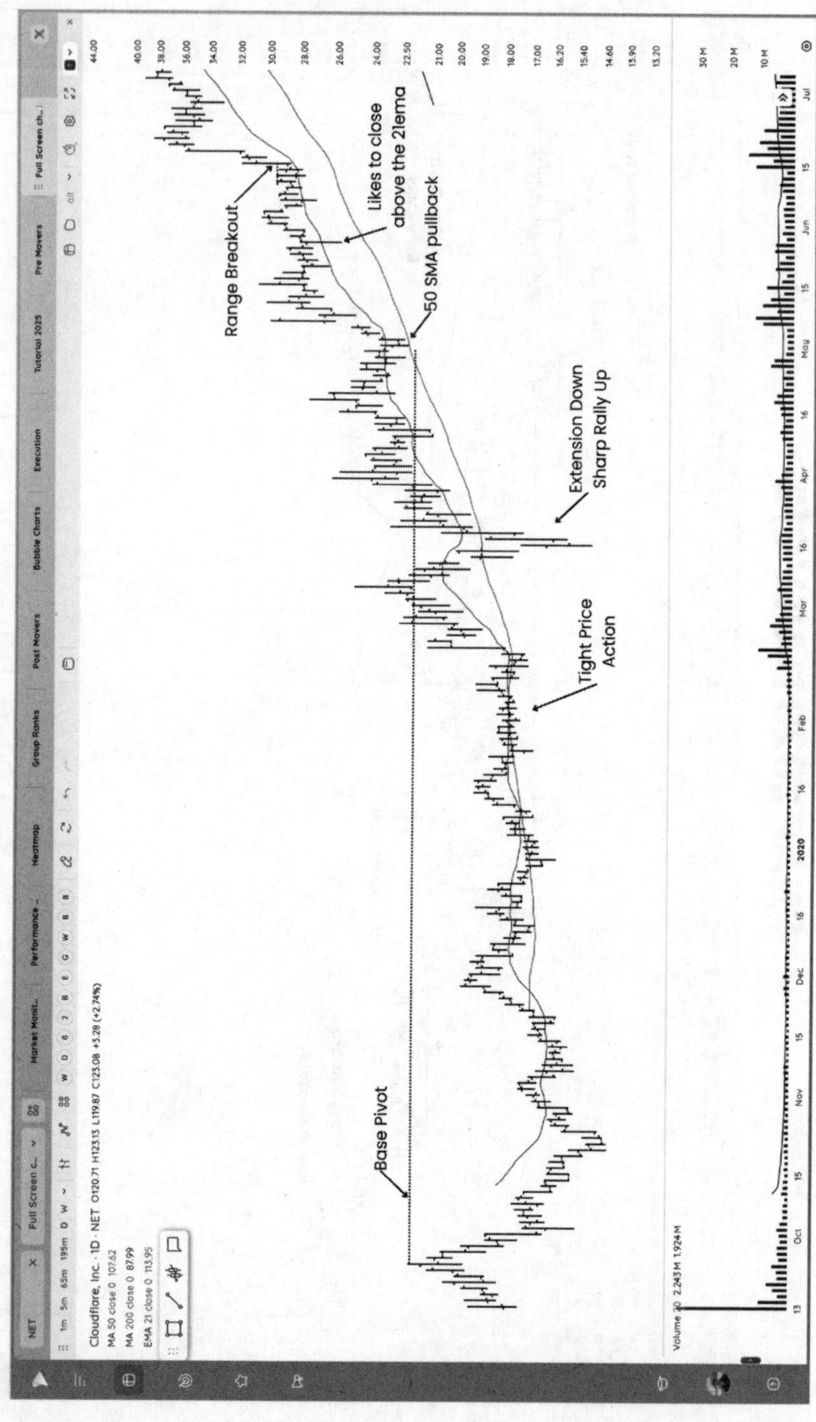
NET 2020 DAILY 1/2
Cloudflare, Inc. · 1D · NET O120.71 H123.13 L119.87 C123.08 +3.28 (+2.74%)
MA 50 close 0 107.62
MA 200 close 0 87.99
EMA 21 close 0 113.95
Base Pivot
Tight Price Action
Extension Down Sharp Rally Up
50 SMA pullback
Likes to close above the 21ema
Range Breakout
Volume 20 2.243 M 1.924 M

NET 2020 DAILY 2/2

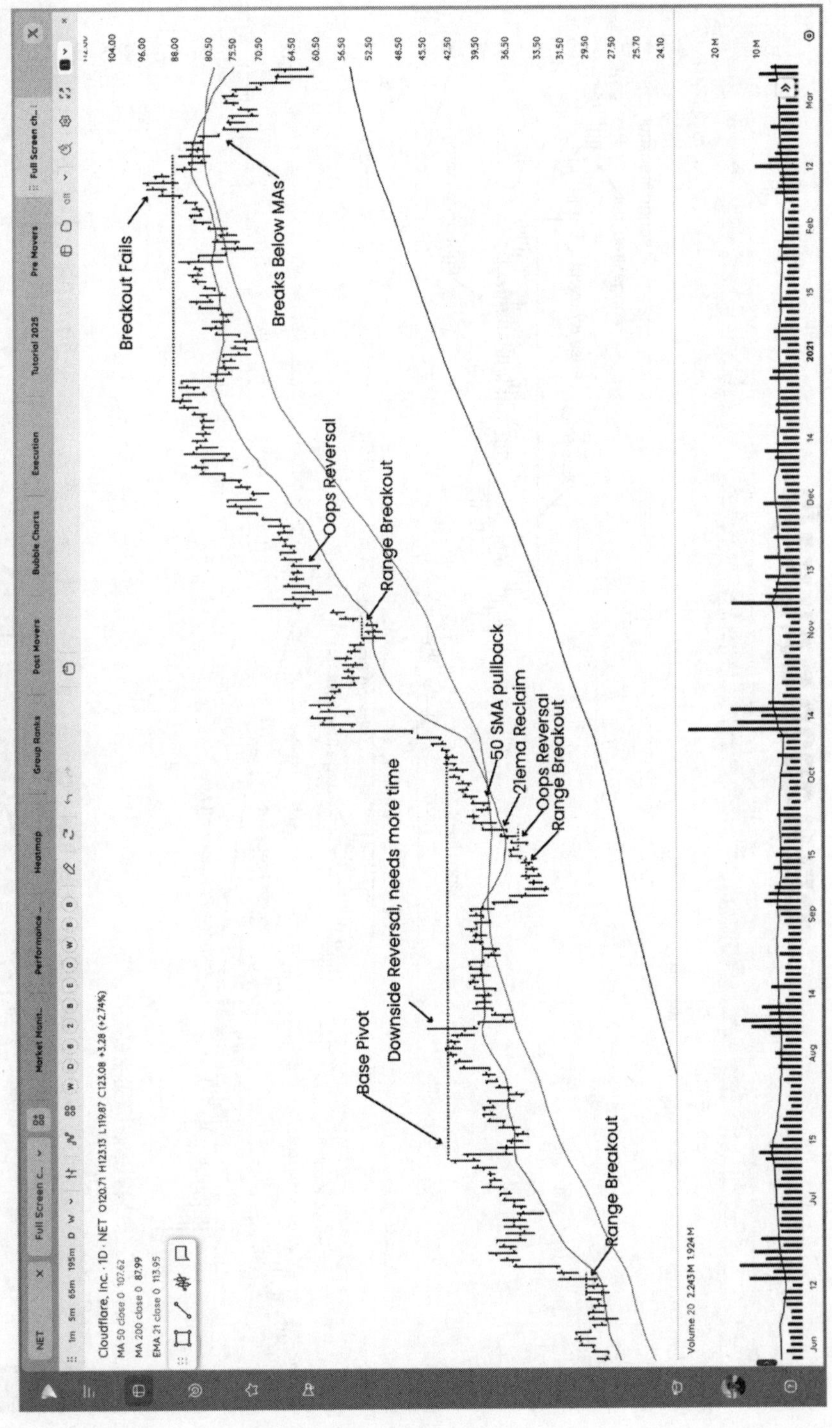

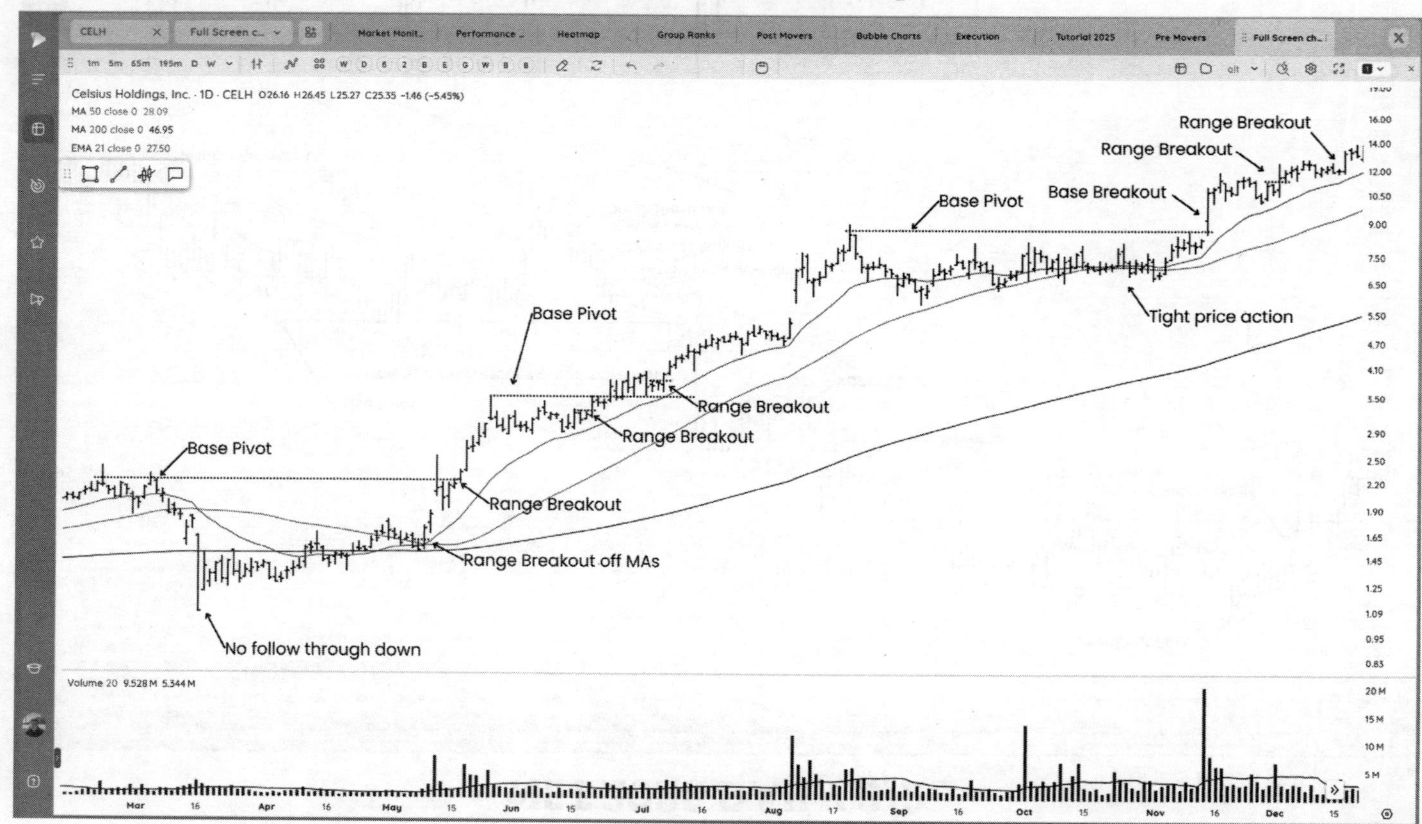
CELH 2020 DAILY 1/2
Celsius Holdings, Inc. · 1D · CELH O26.16 H26.45 L25.27 C25.35 -1.46 (-5.45%)
MA 50 close 0 28.09
MA 200 close 0 46.95
EMA 21 close 0 27.50
Base Pivot
No follow through down
Range Breakout
Range Breakout off MAs
Base Pivot
Range Breakout
Range Breakout
Base Pivot
Tight price action
Base Breakout
Range Breakout
Range Breakout
Volume 20 9.528M 5.344M
Mar
Apr
May
Jun
Jul
Aug
Sep
Oct
Nov
Dec

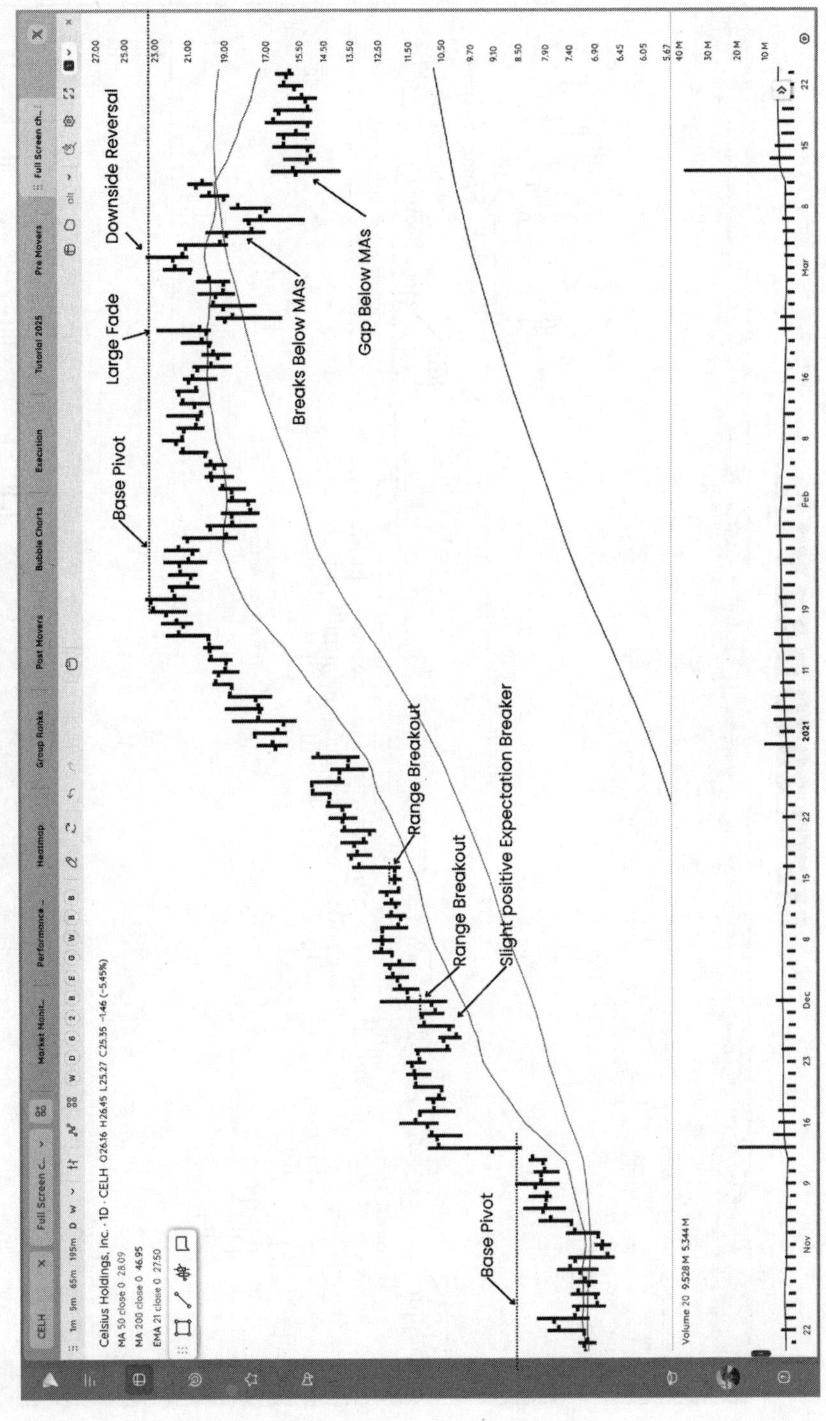
CELH 2020 DAILY 2/2
Celsius Holdings, Inc. · 1D · CELH O26.16 H26.45 L25.27 C25.35 −1.46 (−5.45%)
MA 50 close 0 28.09
MA 200 close 0 46.95
EMA 21 close 0 27.50
Base Pivot
Range Breakout
Range Breakout
Slight positive Expectation Breaker
Base Pivot
Large Fade
Downside Reversal
Breaks Below MAs
Gap Below MAs
Volume 20 9.528 M 5.344 M

MSTR 2020 DAILY 1/2

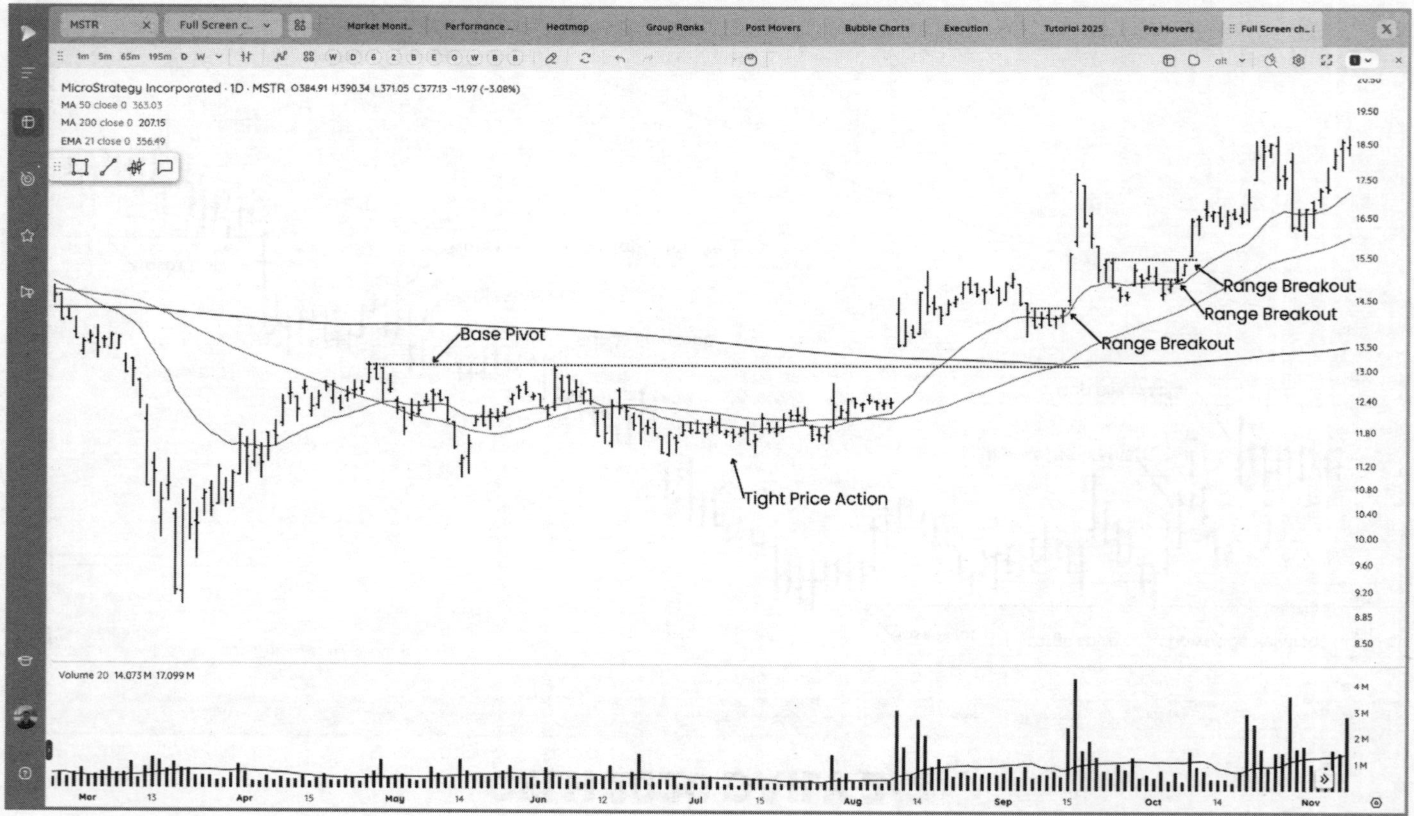

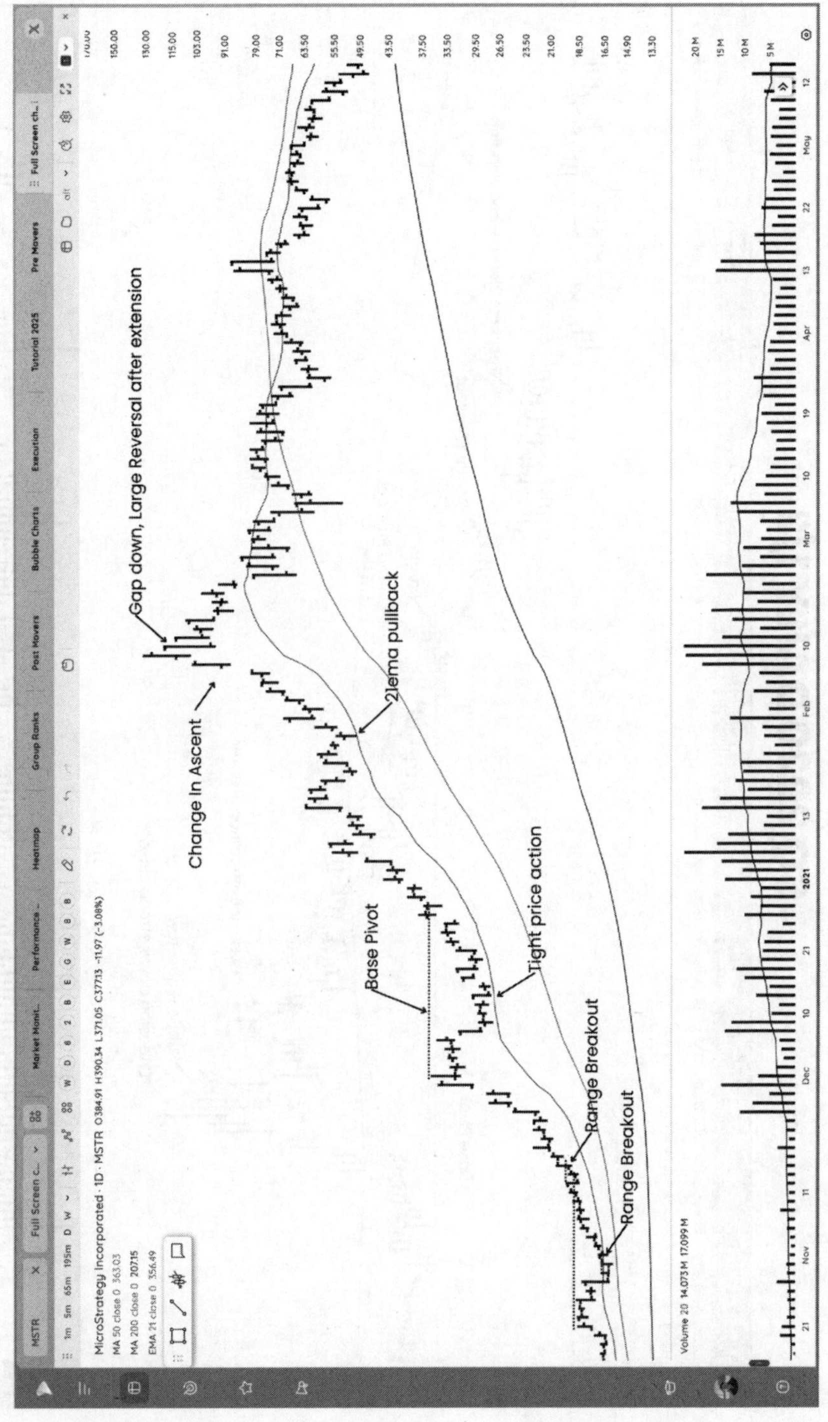
MSTR 2020 DAILY 2/2
Gap down, Large Reversal after extension
Change In Ascent
21ema pullback
Base Pivot
Tight price action
Range Breakout
Range Breakout

SQ 2020 DAILY 1/2

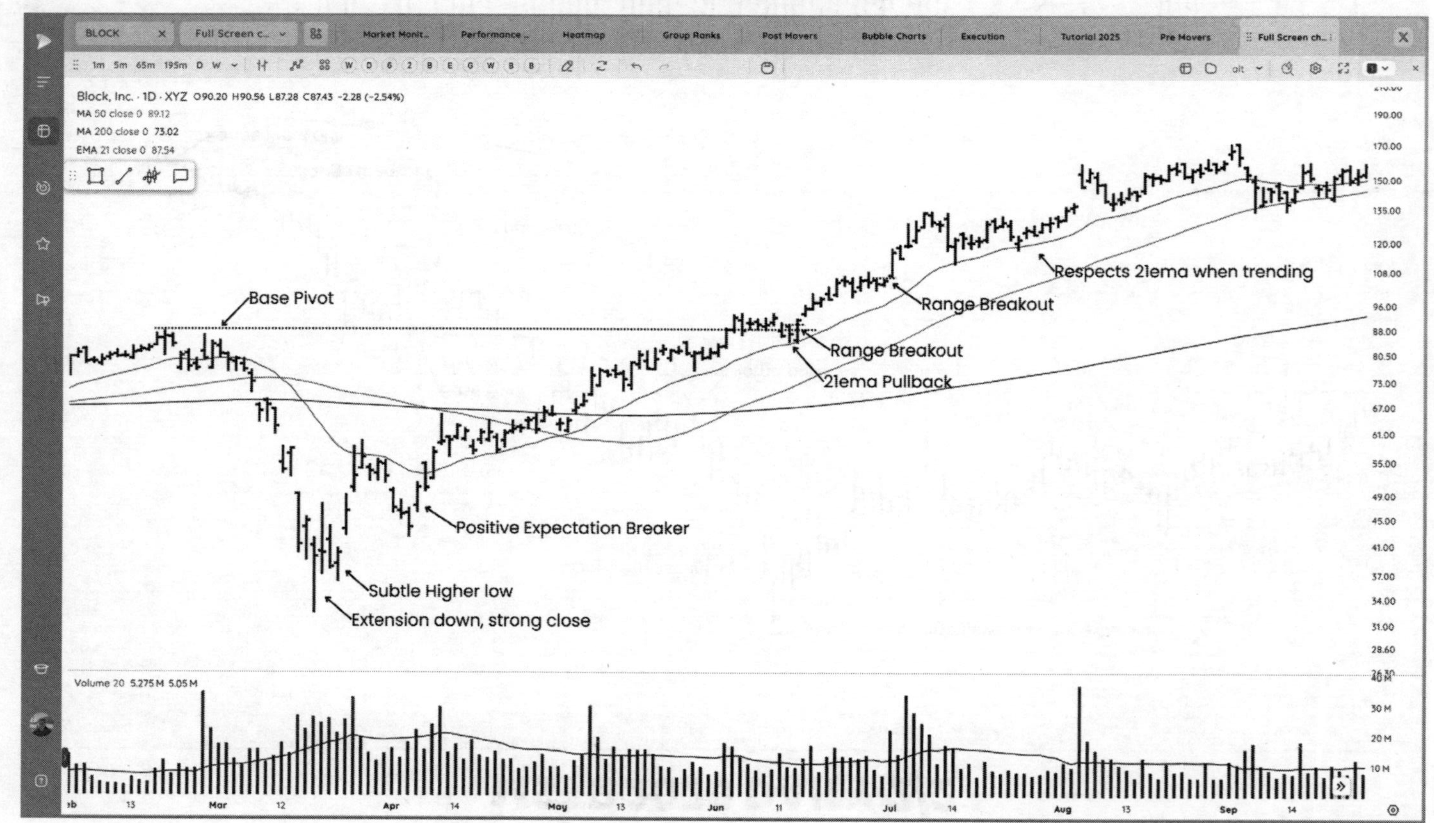

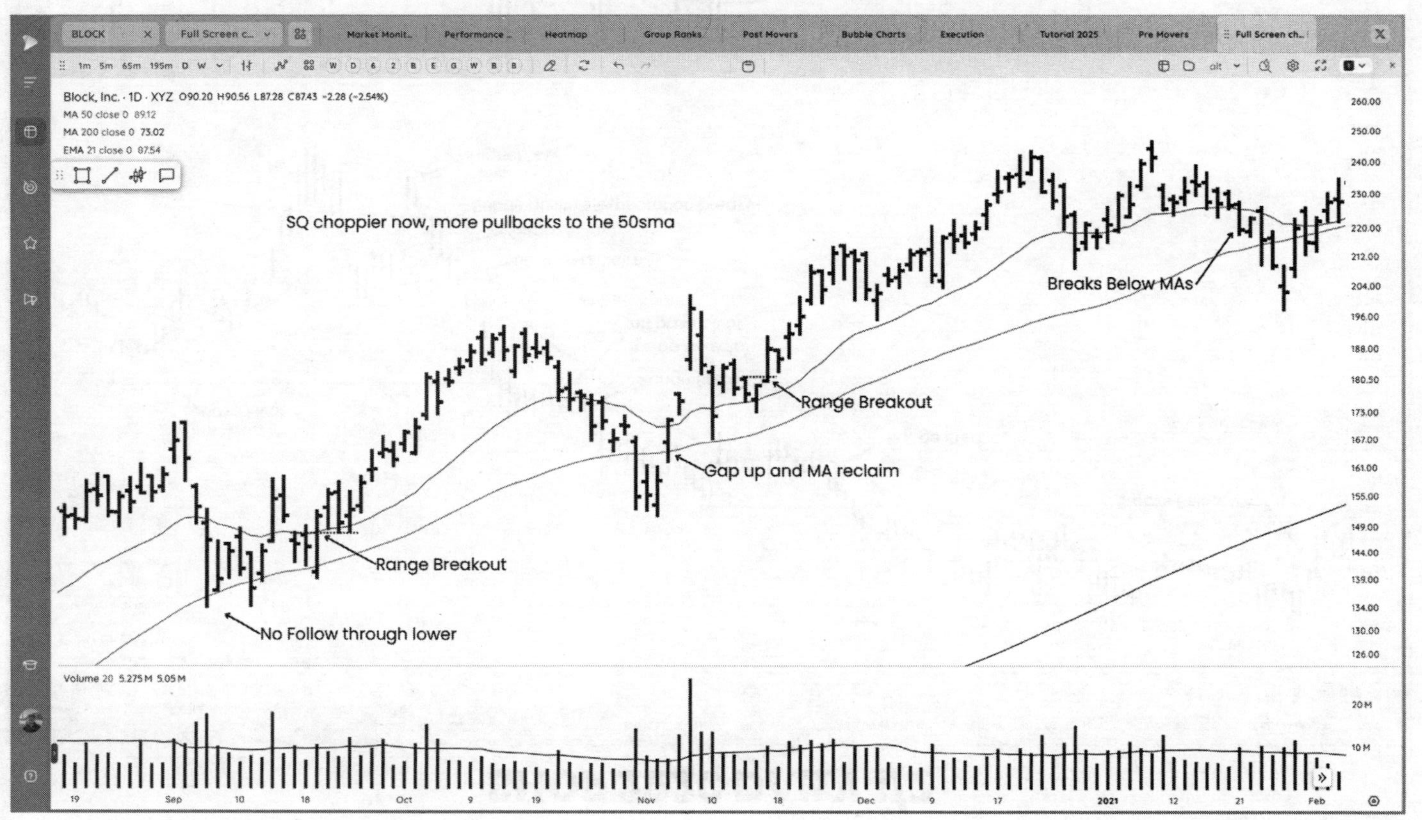

SQ 2020 DAILY 2/2
Block, Inc. · 1D · XYZ O90.20 H90.56 L87.28 C87.43 −2.28 (−2.54%)
MA 50 close 0 89.12
MA 200 close 0 73.02
EMA 21 close 0 87.54
SQ choppier now, more pullbacks to the 50sma
Breaks Below MAs
Range Breakout
Gap up and MA reclaim
Range Breakout
No Follow through lower
Volume 20 5.275M 5.05M

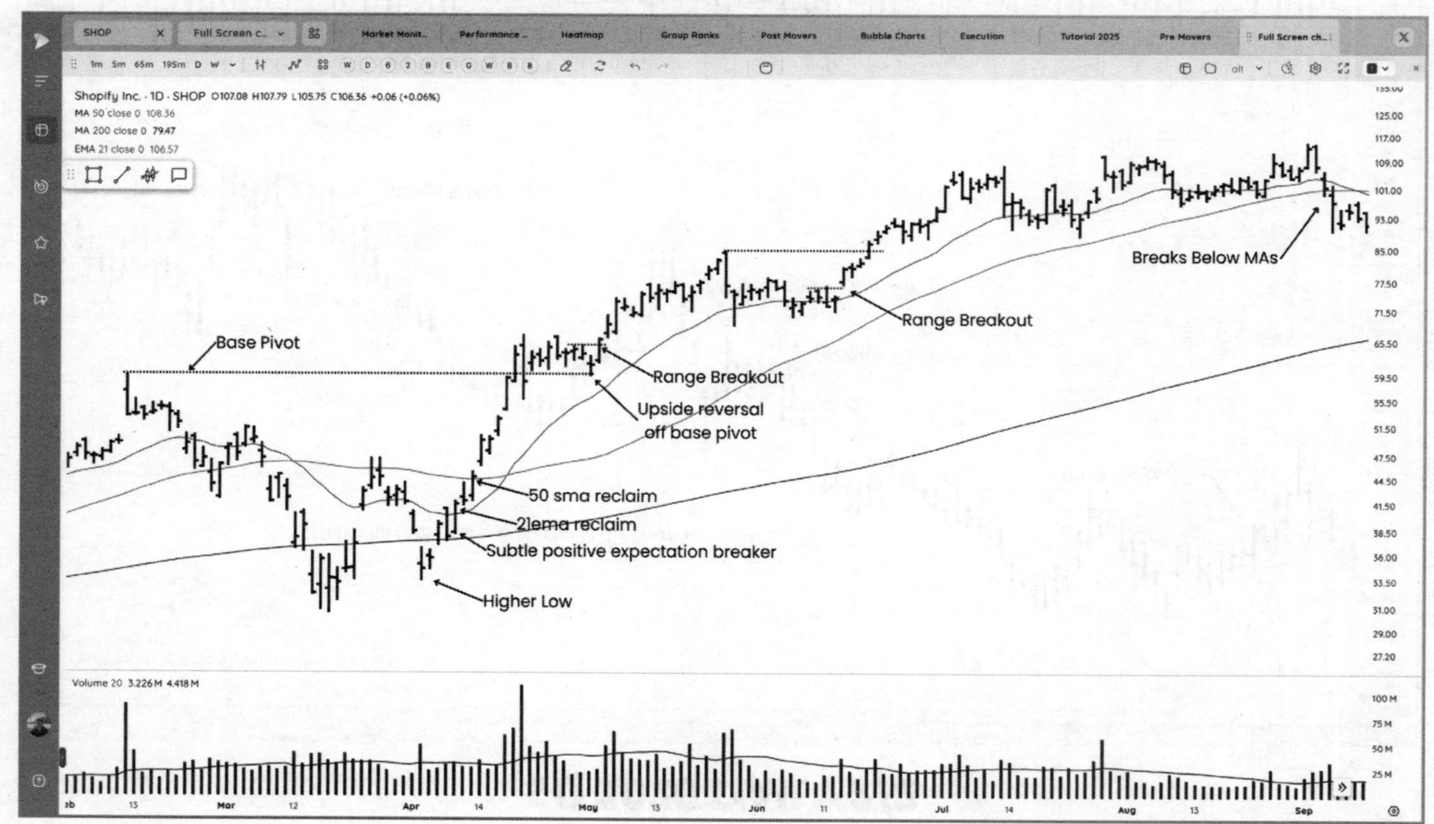
SHOP 2020 DAILY 1/2
Shopify Inc. · 1D · SHOP O107.08 H107.79 L105.75 C106.36 +0.06 (+0.06%)
MA 50 close 0 108.36
MA 200 close 0 79.47
EMA 21 close 0 106.57
Base Pivot
Range Breakout
Upside reversal off base pivot
50 sma reclaim
21ema reclaim
Subtle positive expectation breaker
Higher Low
Range Breakout
Breaks Below MAs
Volume 20 3.226M 4.418M

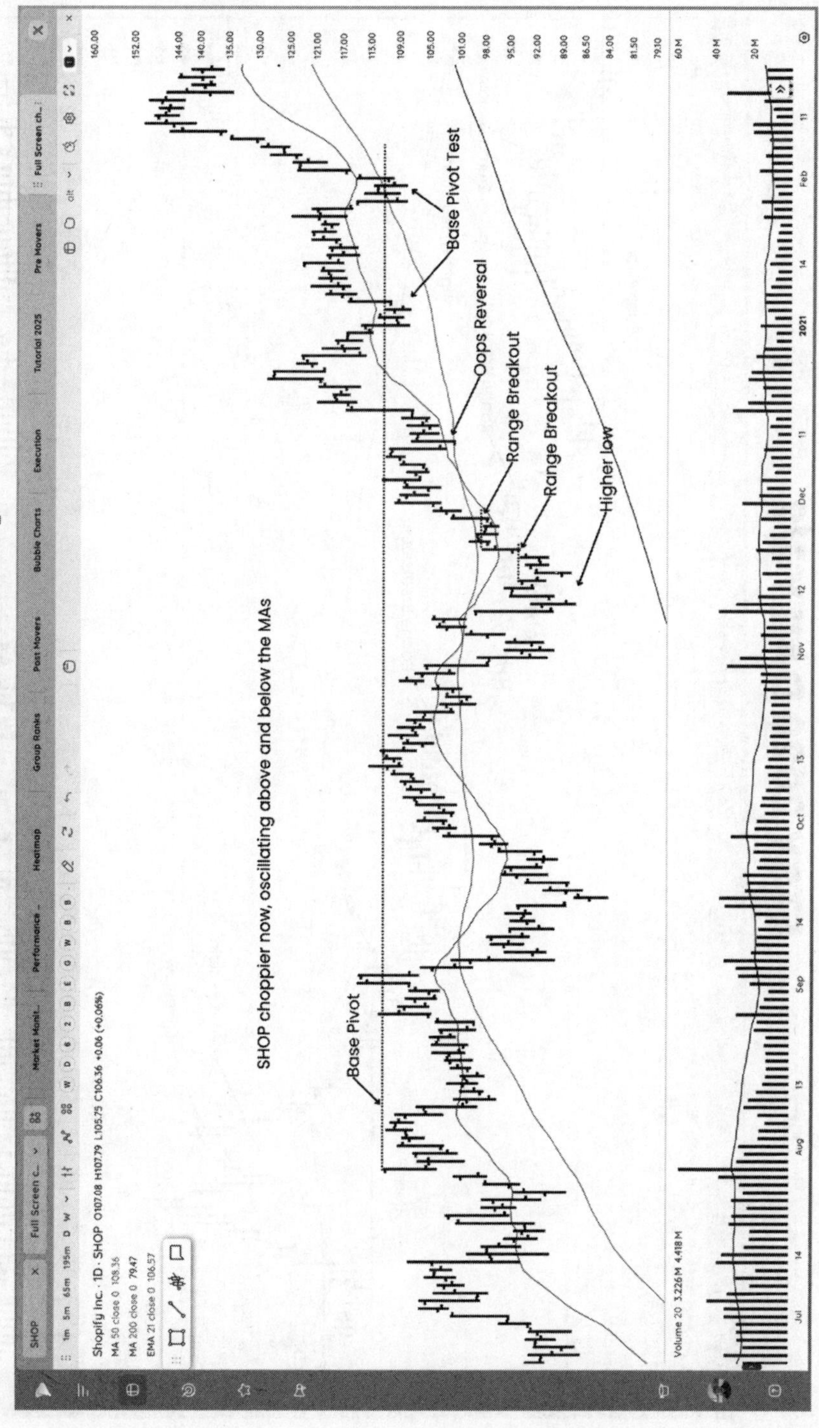
SHOP 2020 DAILY 2/2
Shopify Inc. · 1D · SHOP O107.08 H107.79 L105.75 C106.36 +0.06 (+0.06%)
MA 50 close 0 108.36
MA 200 close 0 79.47
EMA 21 close 0 106.57
SHOP choppier now, oscillating above and below the MAs
Base Pivot
Base Pivot Test
Oops Reversal
Range Breakout
Range Breakout
Higher low
Volume 20 3.226 M 4.418 M

ETSY 2020 DAILY 1/2

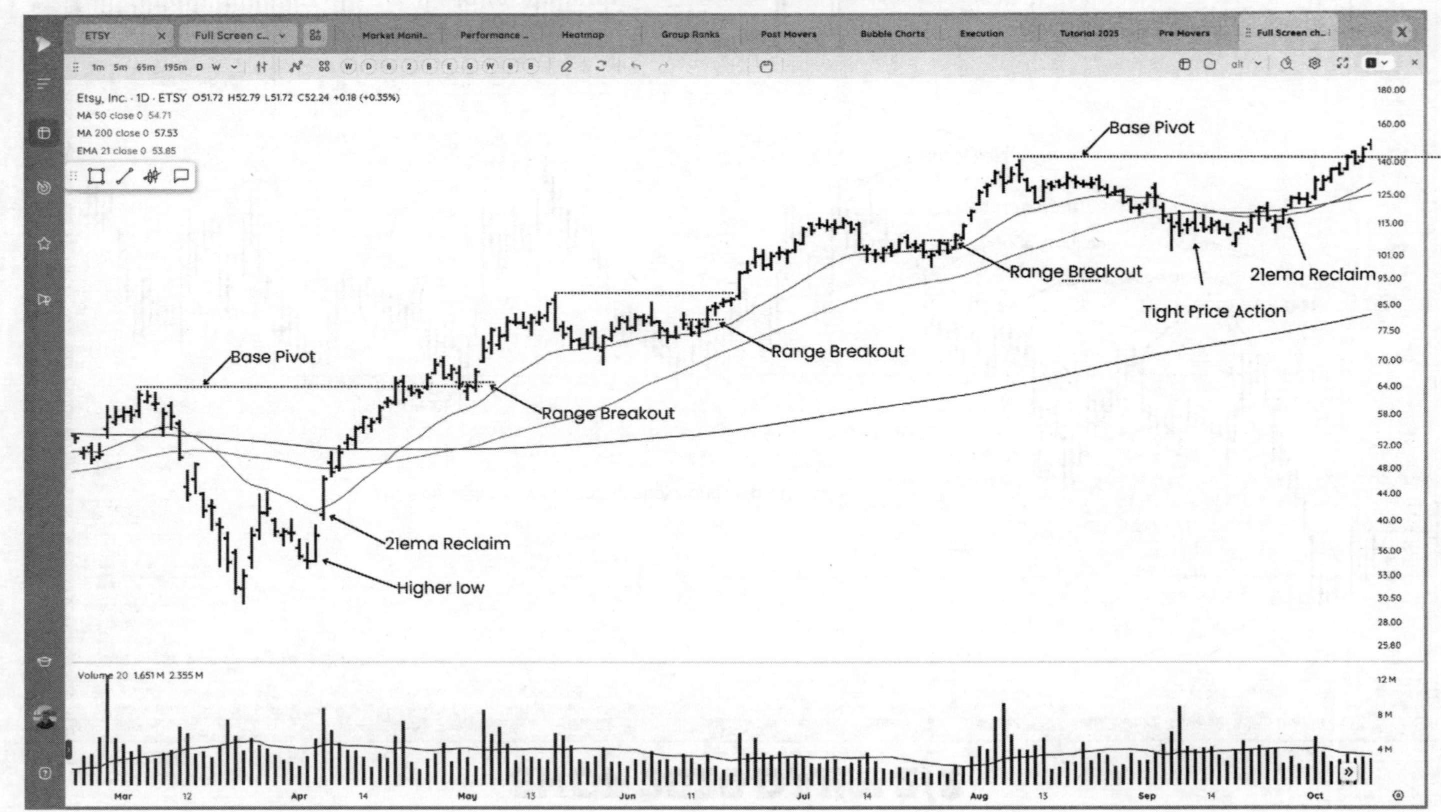

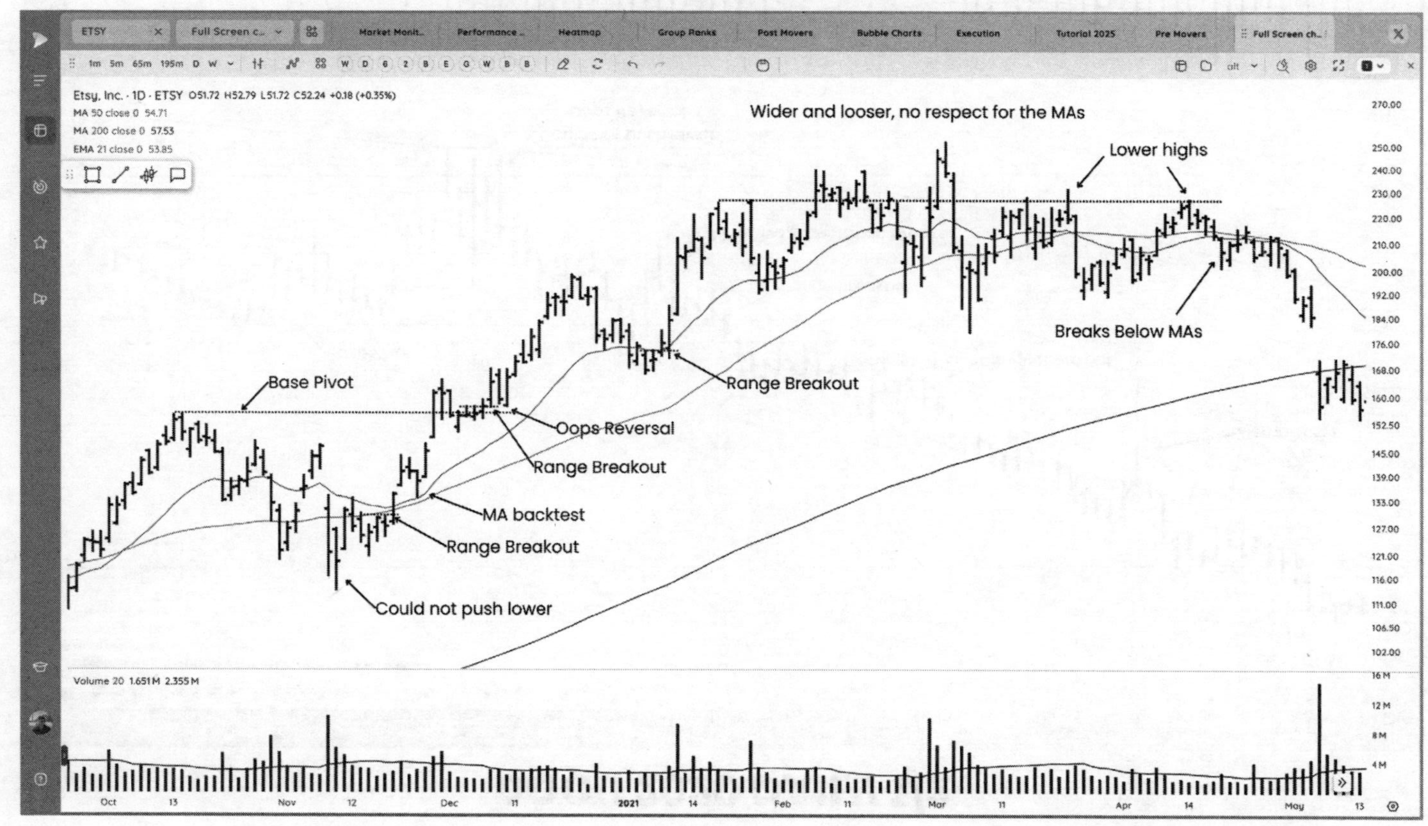
ETSY 2020 DAILY 2/2
Etsy, Inc. · 1D · ETSY O51.72 H52.79 L51.72 C52.24 +0.18 (+0.35%)
MA 50 close 0 54.71
MA 200 close 0 57.53
EMA 21 close 0 53.85
Wider and looser, no respect for the MAs
Lower highs
Breaks Below MAs
Range Breakout
Base Pivot
Oops Reversal
Range Breakout
MA backtest
Range Breakout
Could not push lower
Volume 20 1.651M 2.355M

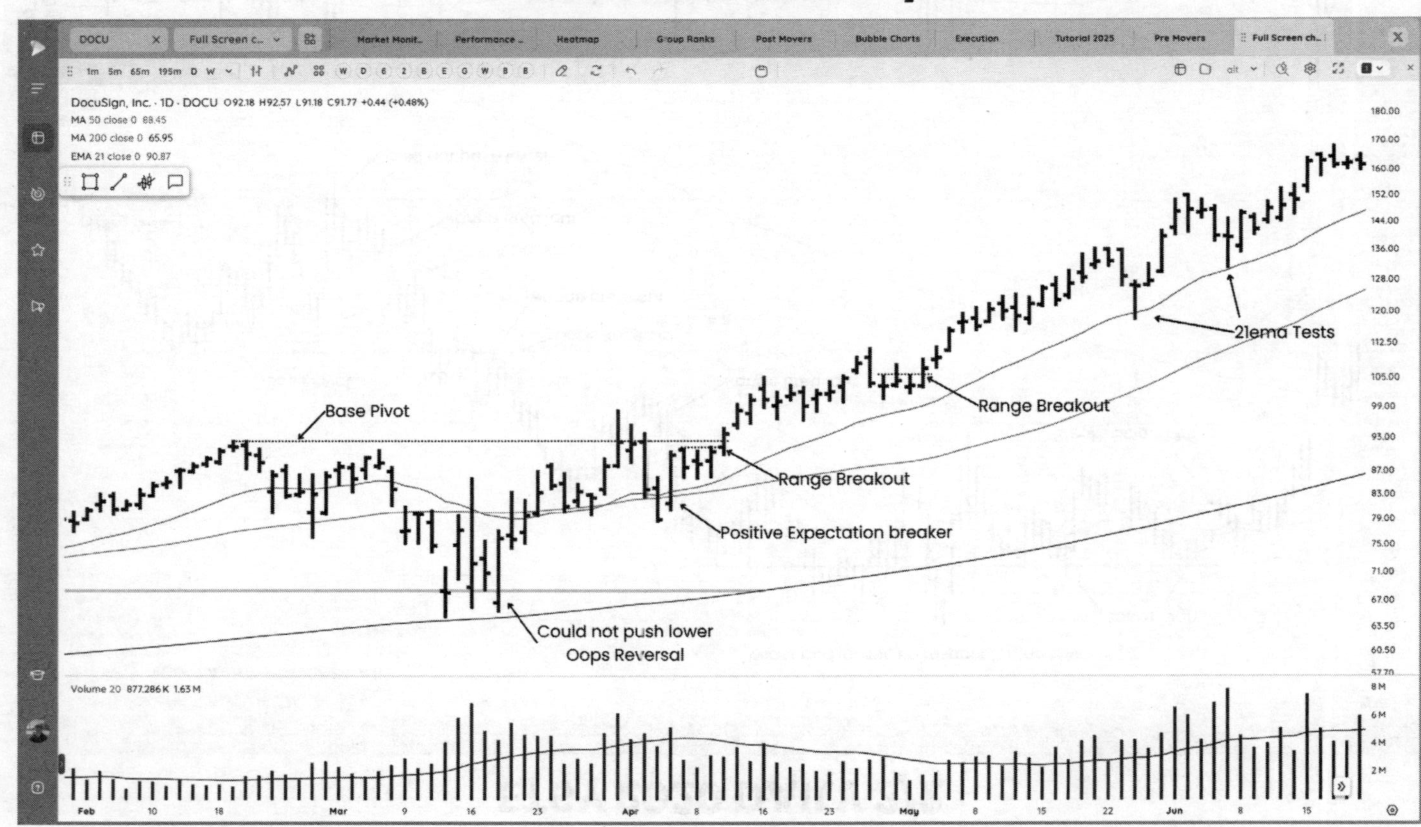
DOCU 2020 DAILY 1/2
DocuSign, Inc. · 1D · DOCU O92.18 H92.57 L91.18 C91.77 +0.44 (+0.48%)
MA 50 close 0 88.45
MA 200 close 0 65.95
EMA 21 close 0 90.87
Base Pivot
Range Breakout
Positive Expectation breaker
Could not push lower
Oops Reversal
Range Breakout
21ema Tests
Volume 20 877.286 K 1.63 M

DOCU 2020 DAILY 2/2

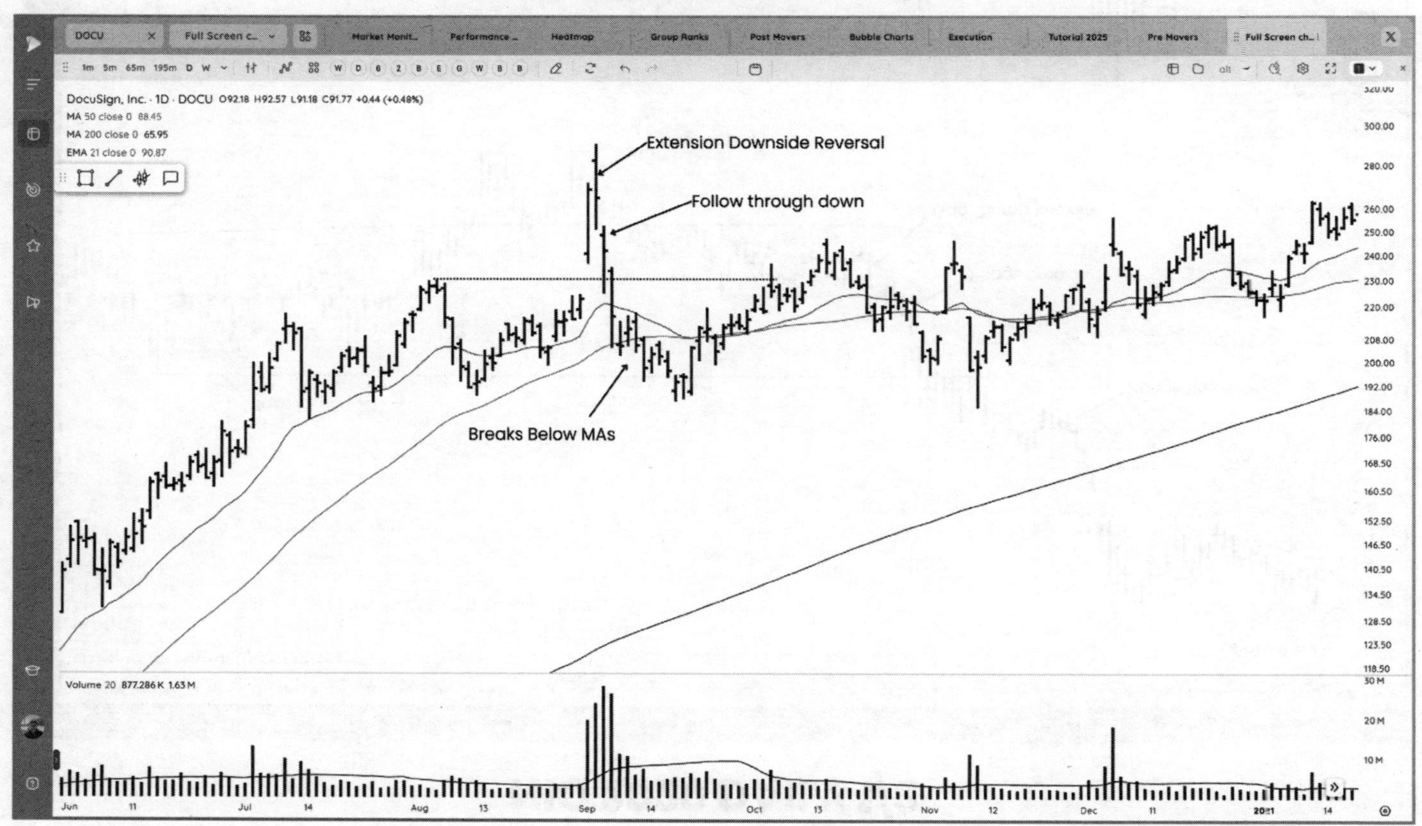

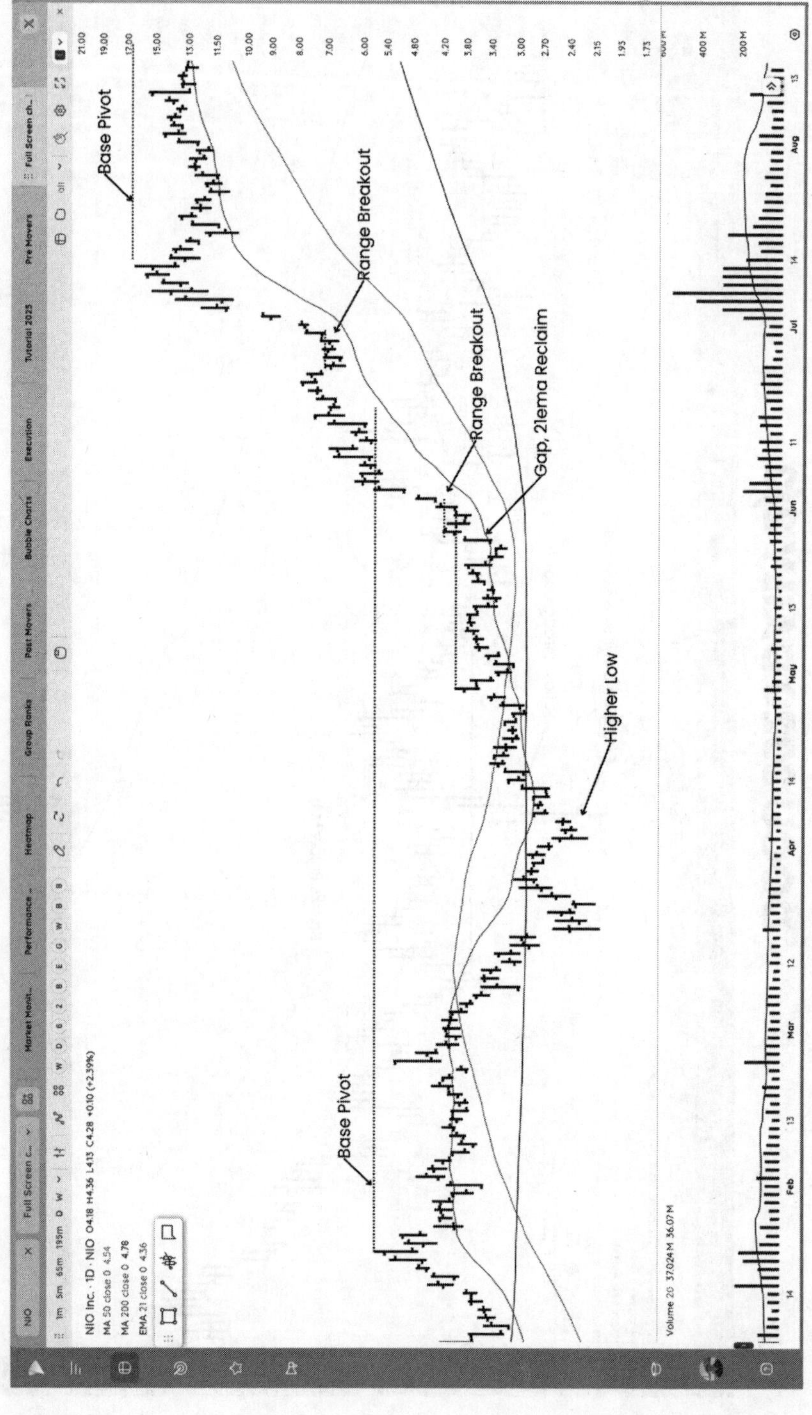
NIO 2020 DAILY 1/3
Base Pivot
Higher Low
Gap, 21ema Reclaim
Range Breakout
Range Breakout
Base Pivot
NIO Inc. · 1D · NIO O4.18 H4.36 L4.13 C4.28 +0.10 (+2.39%)
MA 50 close 0 4.54
MA 200 close 0 4.78
EMA 21 close 0 4.36
Volume 20 37.024 M 36.07 M

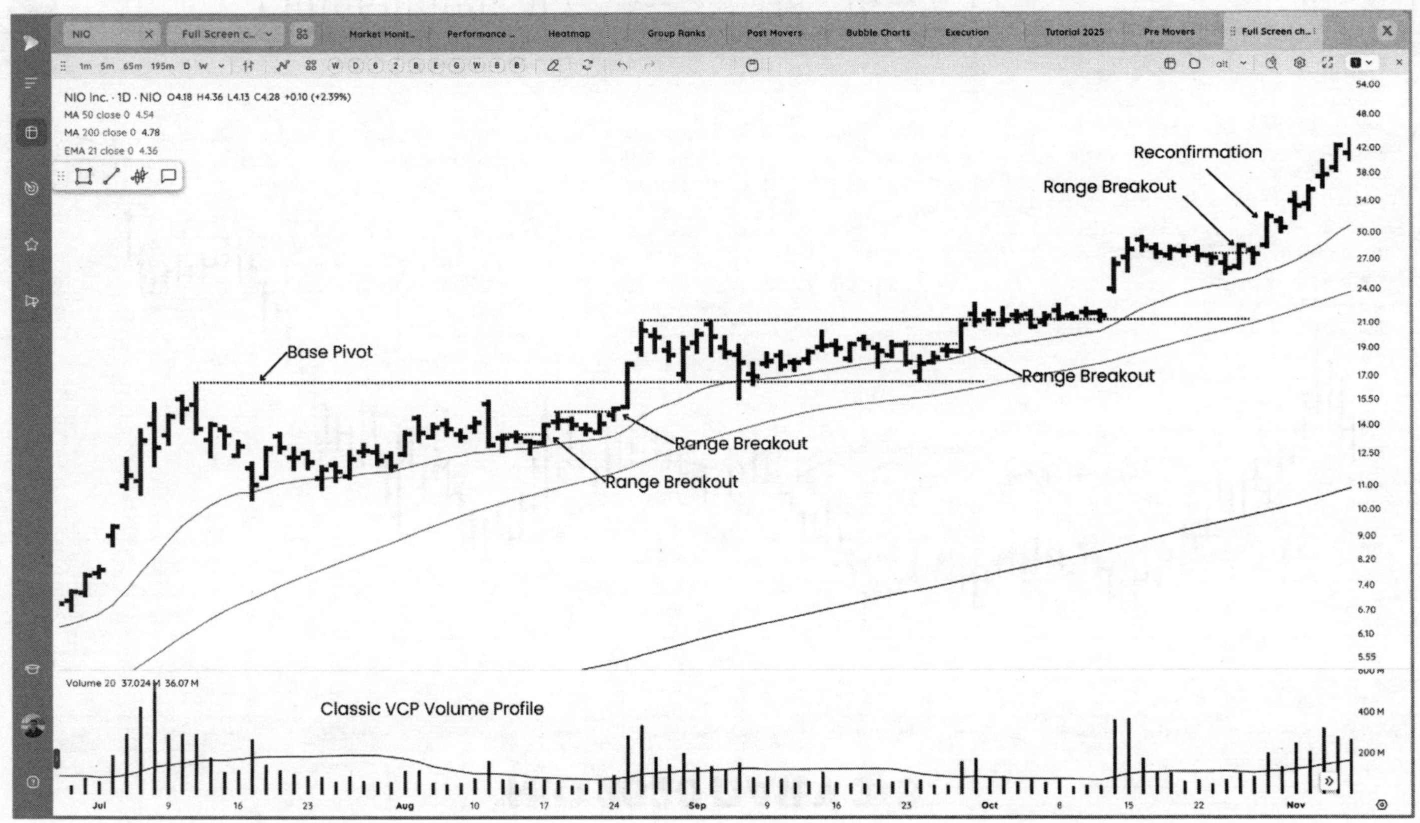
NIO 2020 DAILY 2/3
NIO Inc. · 1D · NIO O4.18 H4.36 L4.13 C4.28 +0.10 (+2.39%)
MA 50 close 0 4.54
MA 200 close 0 4.78
EMA 21 close 0 4.36
Reconfirmation
Range Breakout
Base Pivot
Range Breakout
Range Breakout
Range Breakout
Volume 20 37.024M 36.07M
Classic VCP Volume Profile

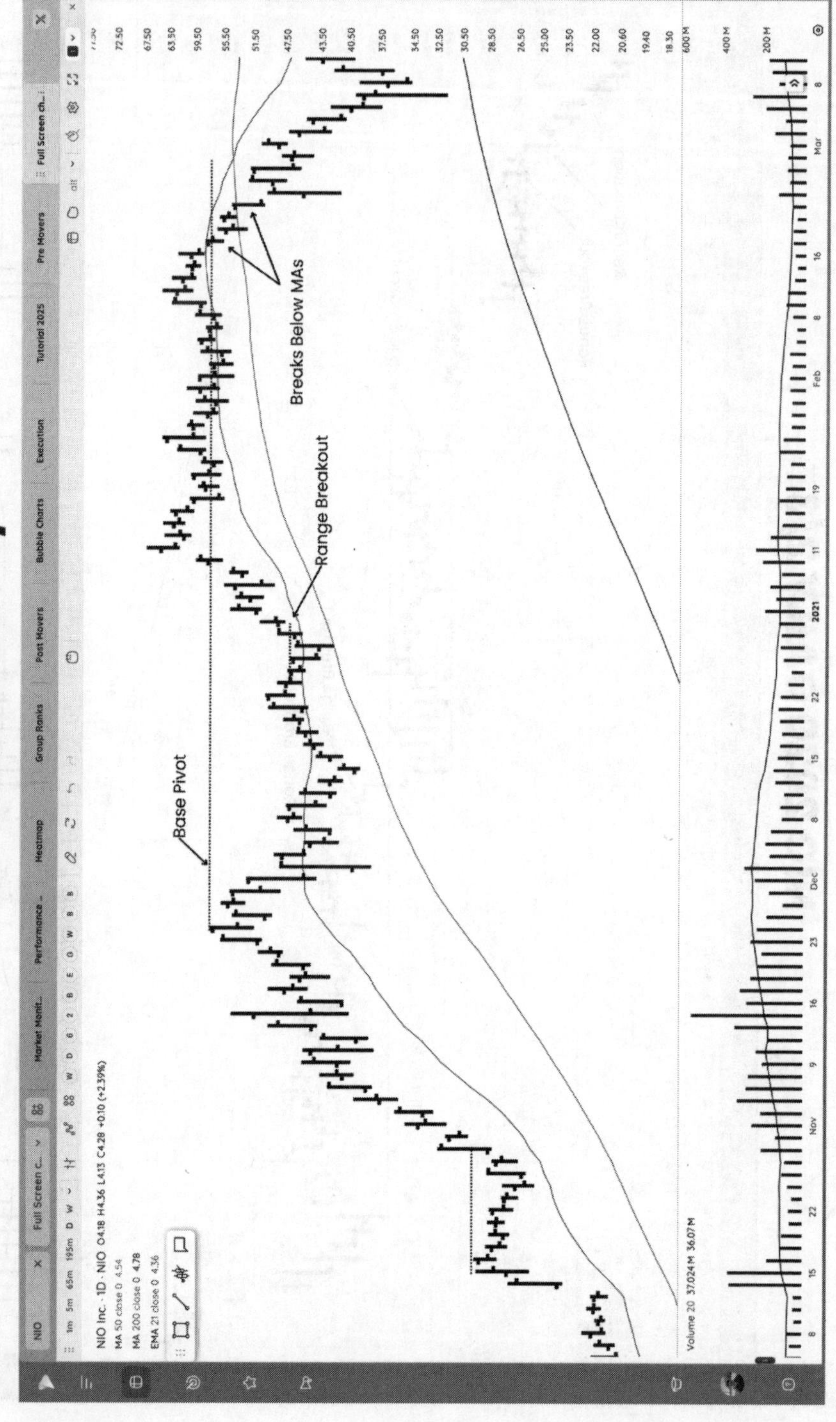
NIO 2020 DAILY 3/3
Base Pivot
Range Breakout
Breaks Below MAs

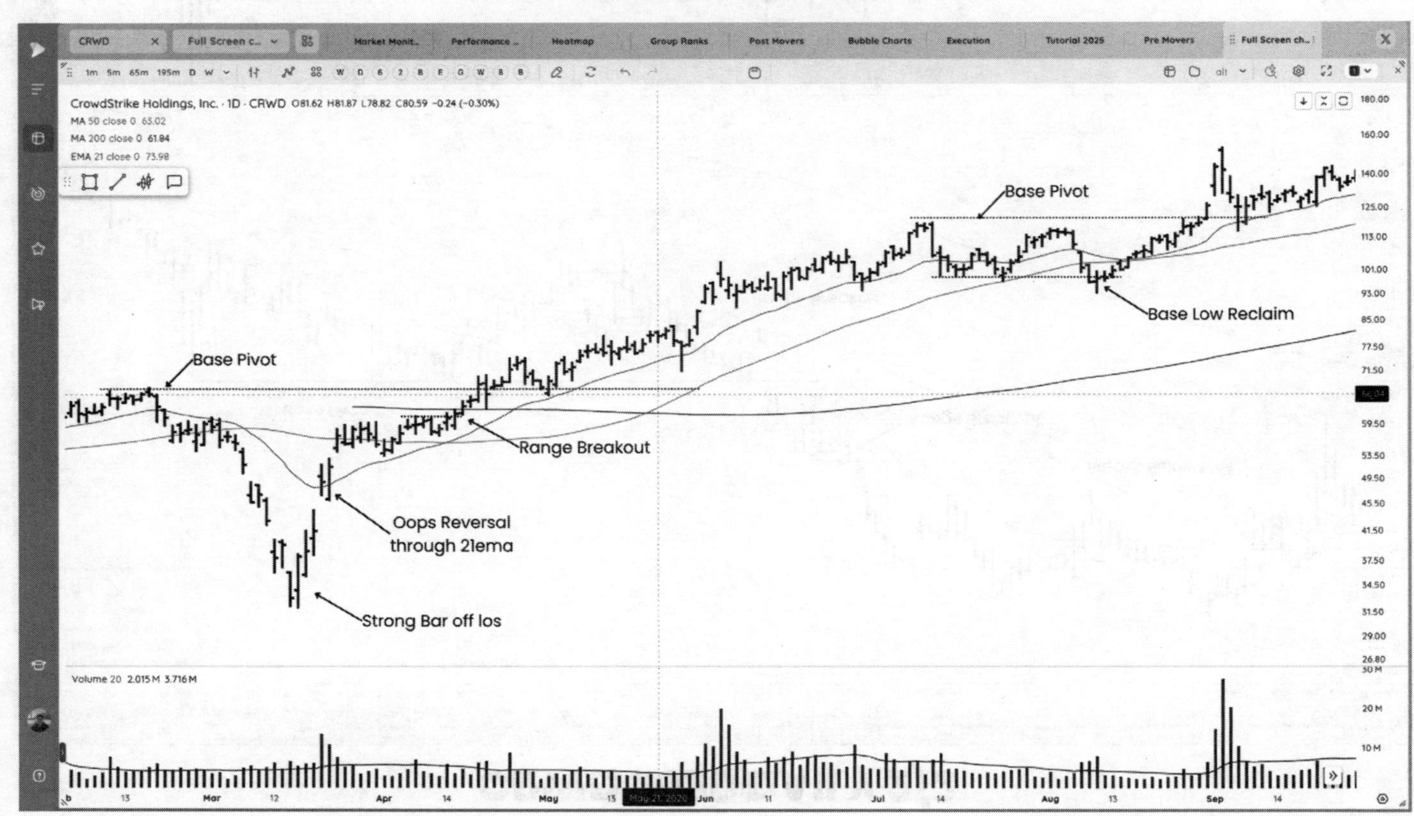
CRWD 2020 DAILY 1/2
CrowdStrike Holdings, Inc. · 1D · CRWD O81.62 H81.87 L78.82 C80.59 −0.24 (−0.30%)
MA 50 close 0 63.02
MA 200 close 0 61.84
EMA 21 close 0 73.98
Base Pivot
Range Breakout
Oops Reversal
through 21ema
Strong Bar off los
Base Pivot
Base Low Reclaim
Volume 20 2.015 M 3.716 M

CRWD 2020 DAILY 2/2

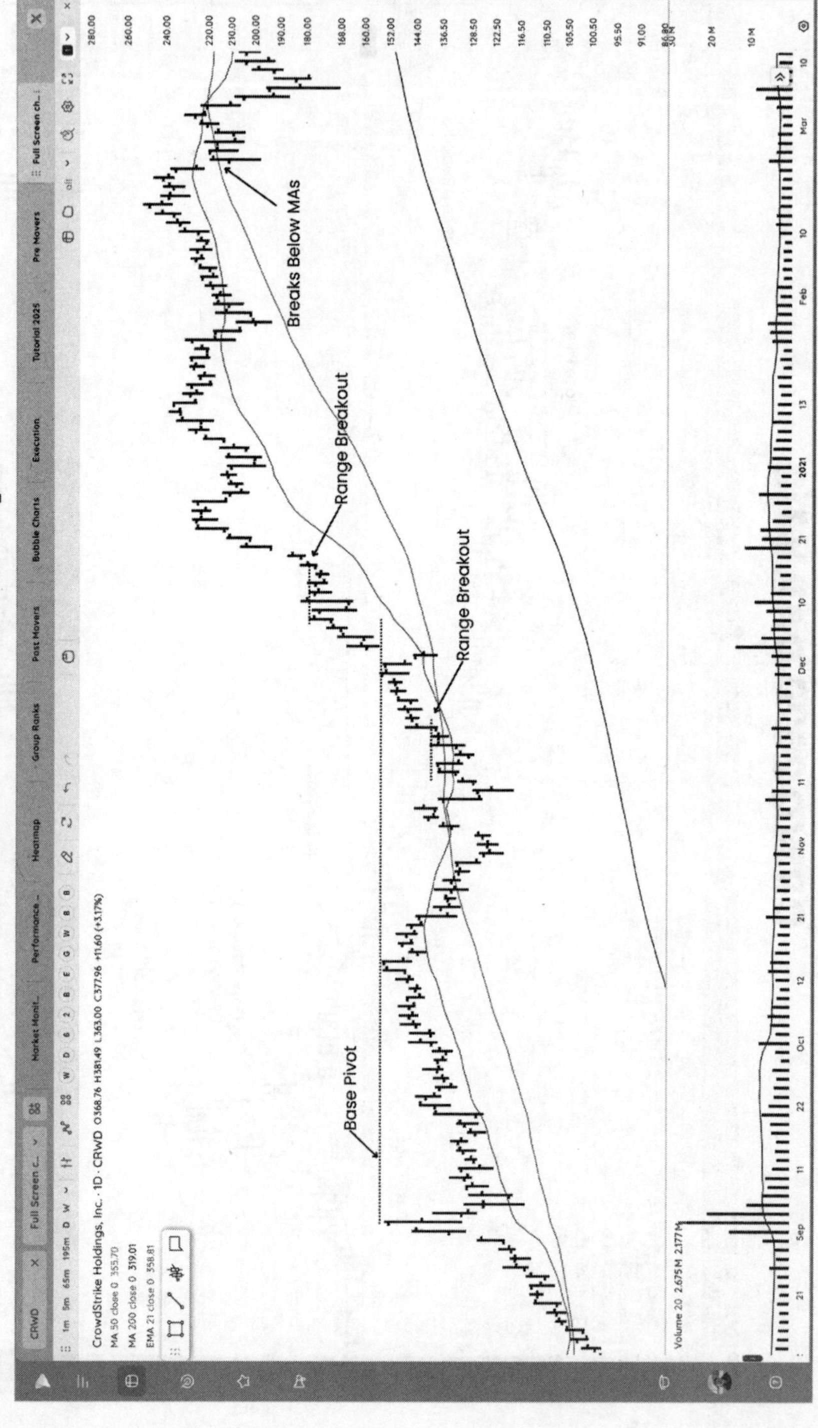

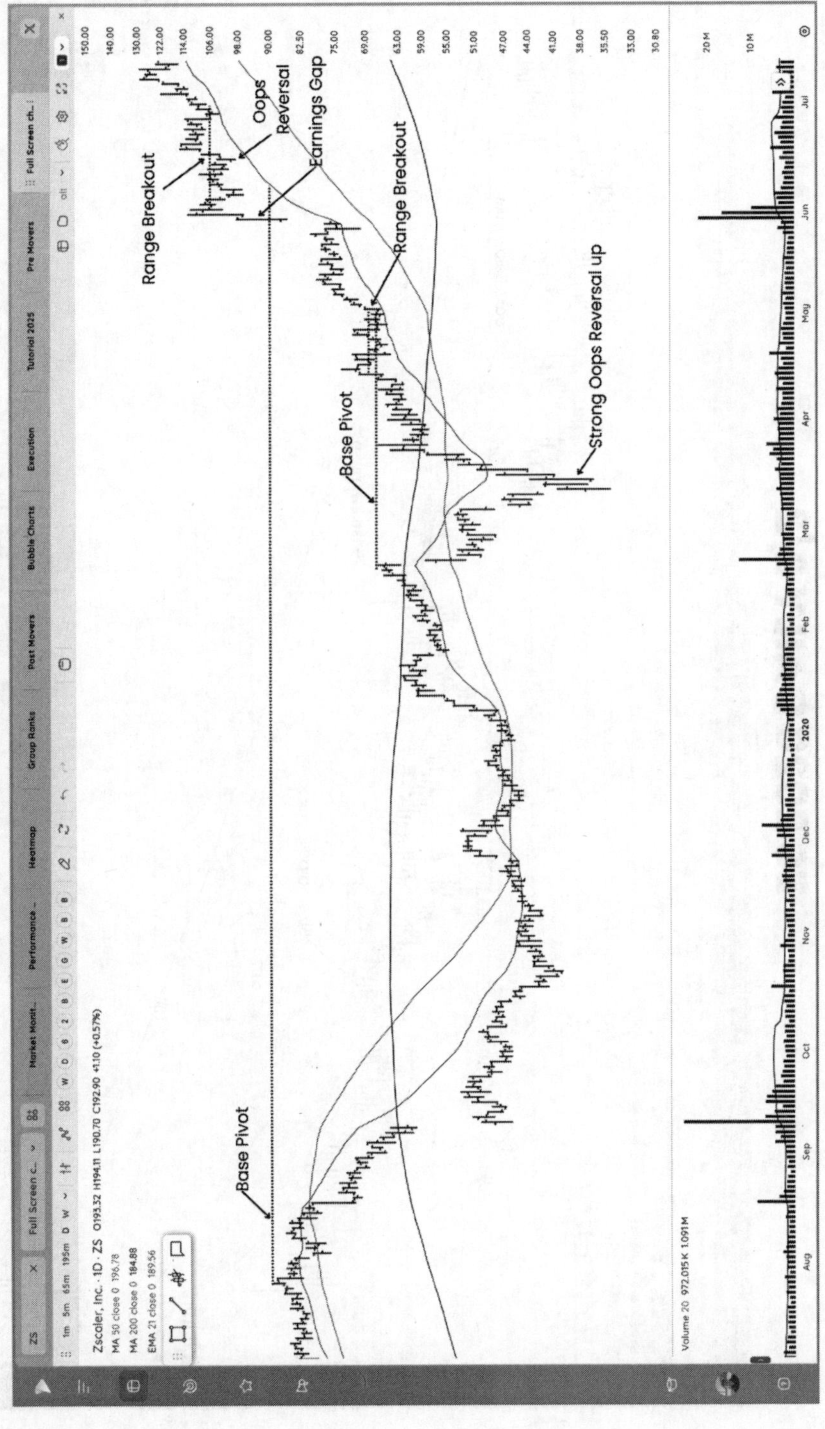
ZS 2020 DAILY 1/2
Zscaler, Inc. · 1D · ZS O193.32 H194.11 L190.70 C192.90 +1.10 (+0.57%)
MA 50 close 0 196.78
MA 200 close 0 184.88
EMA 21 close 0 189.56
Base Pivot
Range Breakout
Oops Reversal
Earnings Gap
Range Breakout
Base Pivot
Strong Oops Reversal up
Volume 20 972.015 K 1.091 M

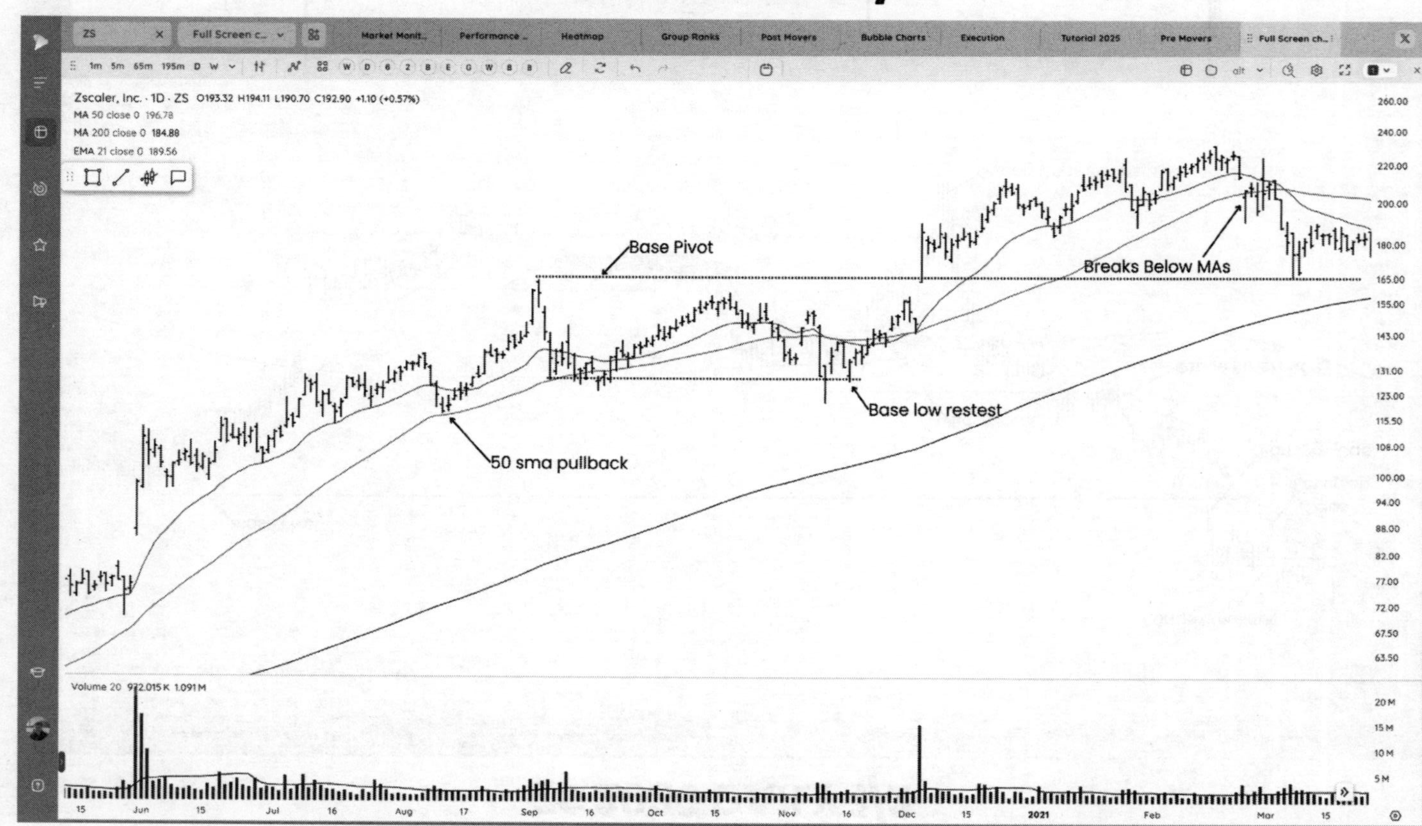
ZS 2020 DAILY 2/2
Zscaler, Inc. · 1D · ZS O193.32 H194.11 L190.70 C192.90 +1.10 (+0.57%)
MA 50 close 0 196.78
MA 200 close 0 184.88
EMA 21 close 0 189.56
Base Pivot
50 sma pullback
Base low restest
Breaks Below MAs
Volume 20 972.015 K 1.091 M

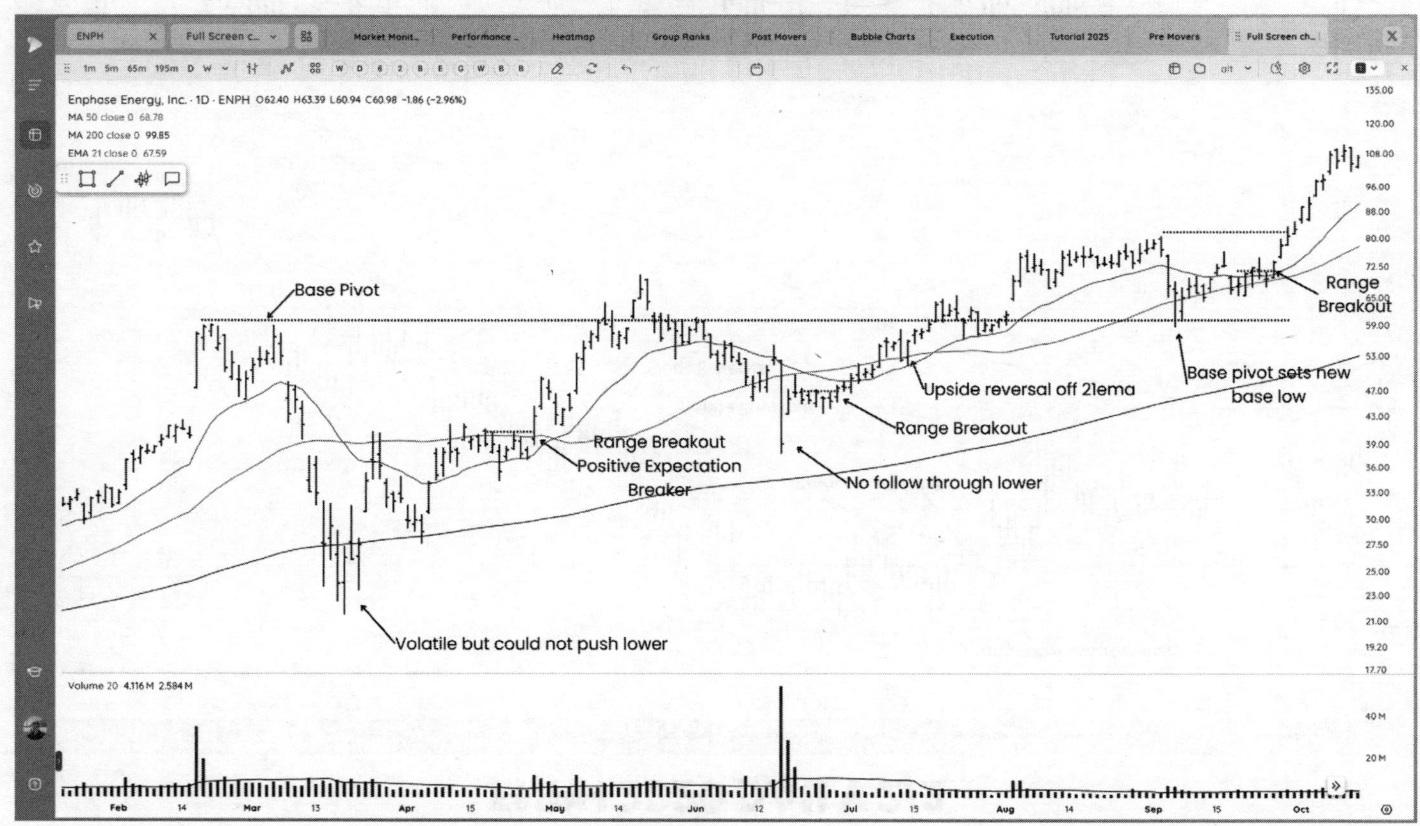

ENPH 2020 DAILY 1/2
Enphase Energy, Inc. · 1D · ENPH O62.40 H63.39 L60.94 C60.98 −1.86 (−2.96%)
MA 50 close 0 68.78
MA 200 close 0 99.85
EMA 21 close 0 67.59
Base Pivot
Volatile but could not push lower
Range Breakout
Positive Expectation
Breaker
No follow through lower
Range Breakout
Upside reversal off 21ema
Base pivot sets new
base low
Range
Breakout
Volume 20 4.116 M 2.584 M

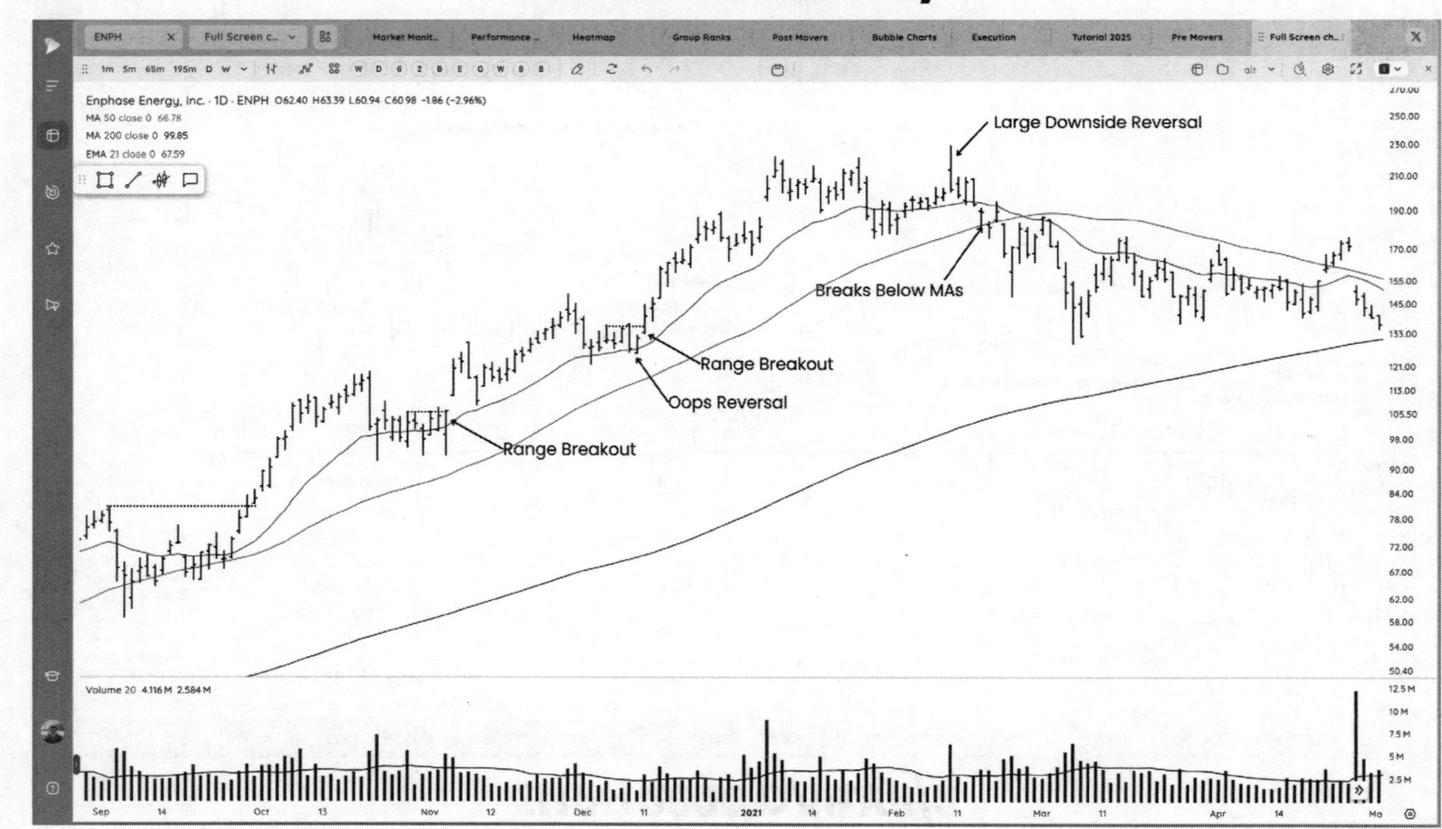
ENPH 2020 DAILY 2/2
Enphase Energy, Inc. · 1D · ENPH O62.40 H63.39 L60.94 C60.98 −1.86 (−2.96%)
MA 50 close 0 68.78
MA 200 close 0 99.85
EMA 21 close 0 67.59
Large Downside Reversal
Breaks Below MAs
Range Breakout
Oops Reversal
Range Breakout
Volume 20 4.116 M 2.584 M

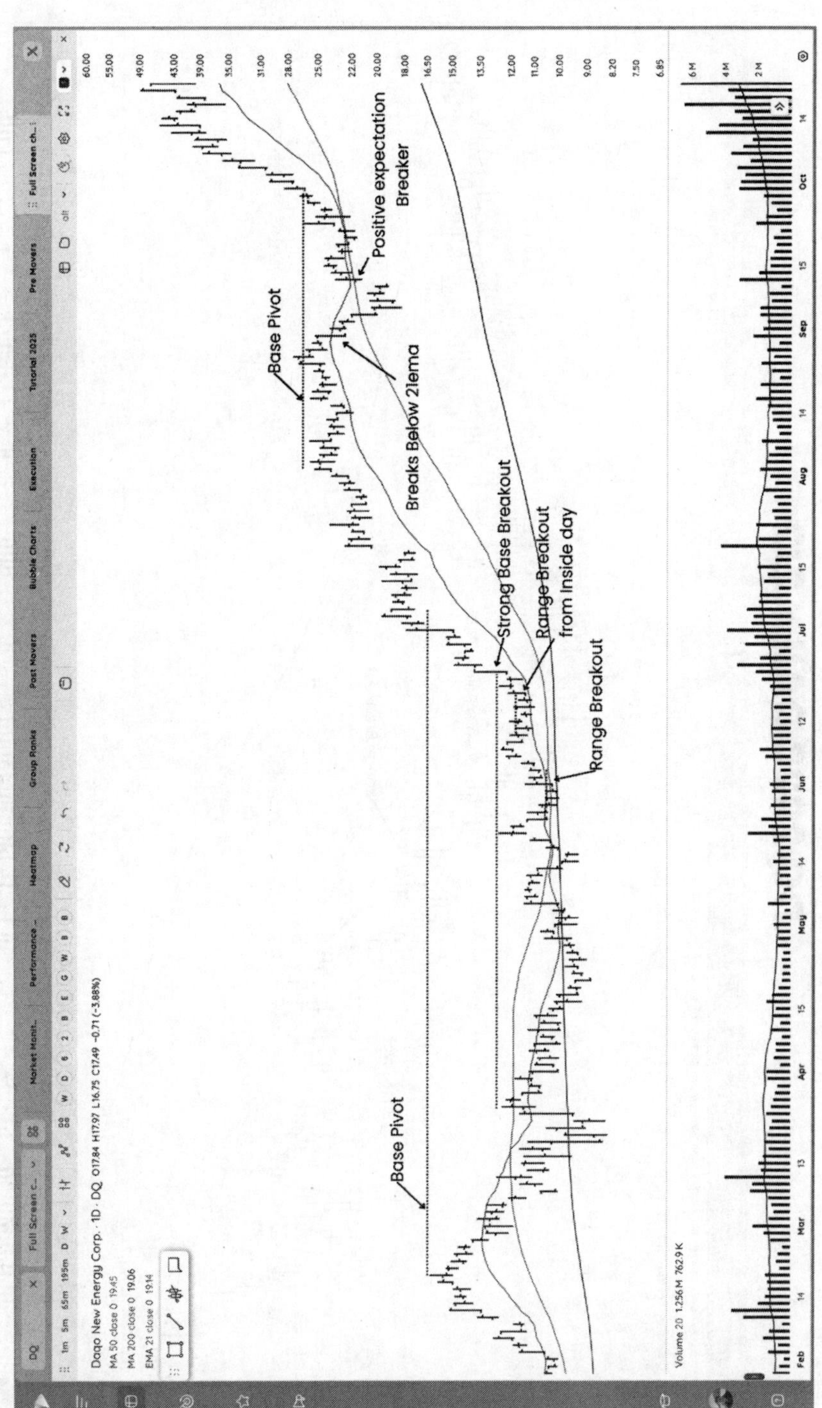
DQ 2020 DAILY 1/2
Daqo New Energy Corp. · 1D · DQ O17.84 H17.97 L16.75 C17.49 −0.71 (−3.88%)
MA 50 close 0 19.45
MA 200 close 0 19.06
EMA 21 close 0 19.14
Base Pivot
Base Pivot
Positive expectation
Breaker
Breaks Below 21ema
Strong Base Breakout
Range Breakout
from Inside day
Range Breakout
Volume 20 1.256 M 762.9 K

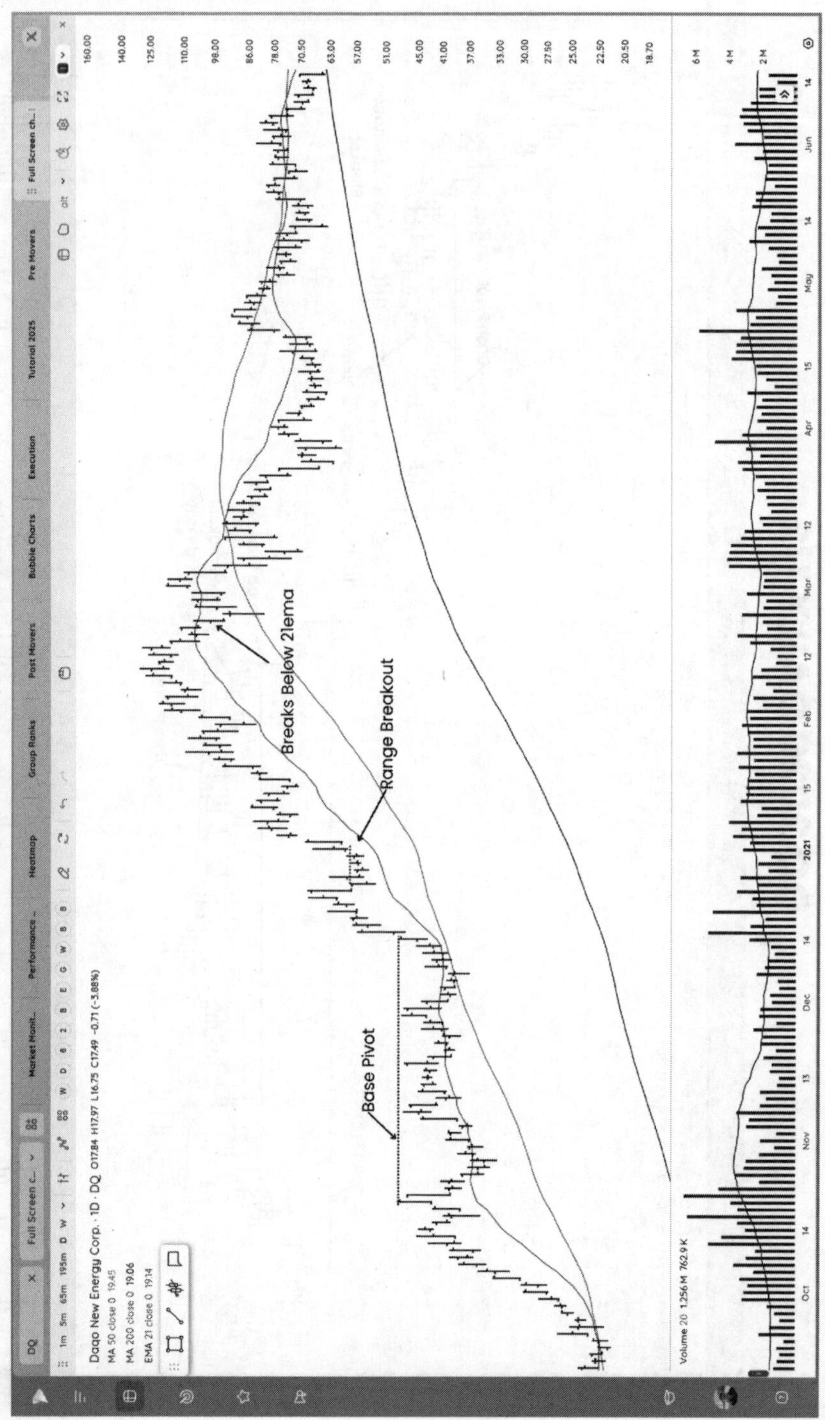
DQ 2020 DAILY 2/2
Daqo New Energy Corp. · 1D · DQ O17.84 H17.97 L16.75 C17.49 −0.71 (−3.88%)
MA 50 close 0 19.45
MA 200 close 0 19.06
EMA 21 close 0 19.14
Base Pivot
Range Breakout
Breaks Below 21ema
Volume 20 1.256 M 762.9 K

SE 2020 DAILY 1/2

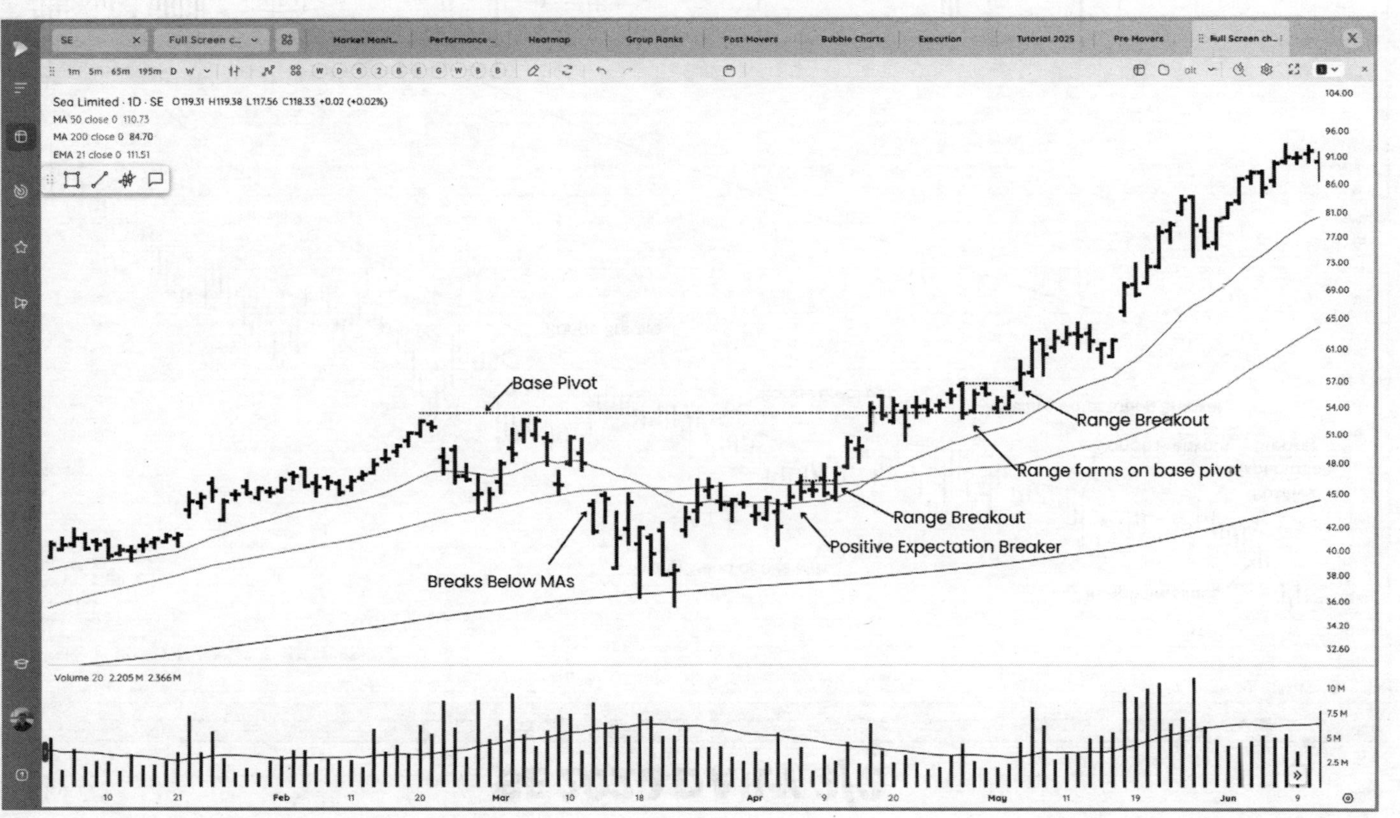

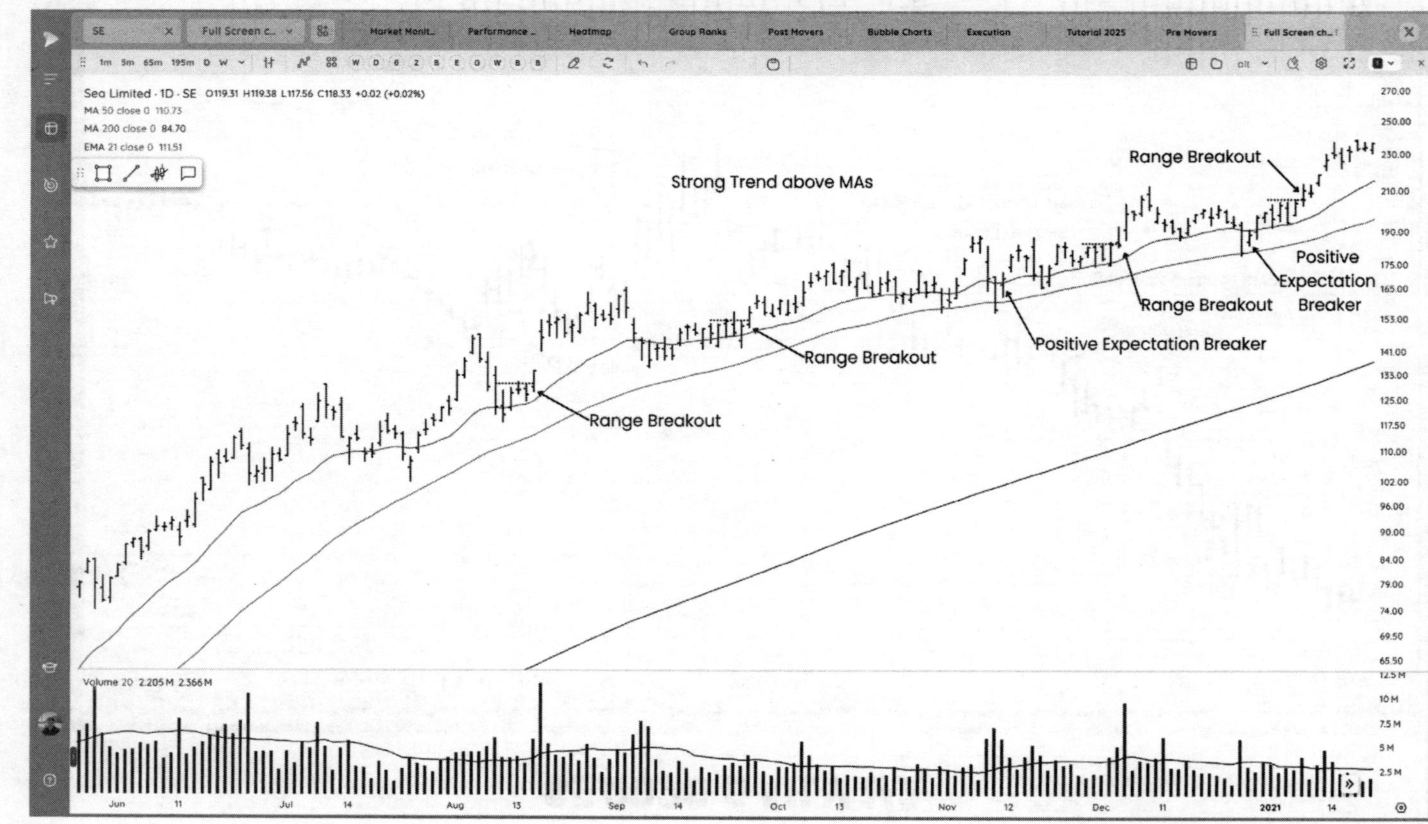
SE 2020 DAILY 2/2
Sea Limited · 1D · SE O119.31 H119.38 L117.56 C118.33 +0.02 (+0.02%)
MA 50 close 0 110.73
MA 200 close 0 84.70
EMA 21 close 0 111.51
Strong Trend above MAs
Range Breakout
Range Breakout
Positive Expectation Breaker
Range Breakout
Positive
Expectation
Breaker
Range Breakout
Volume 20 2.205 M 2.366 M
Jun
Jul
Aug
Sep
Oct
Nov
Dec
2021

TWLO 2020 DAILY 1/2

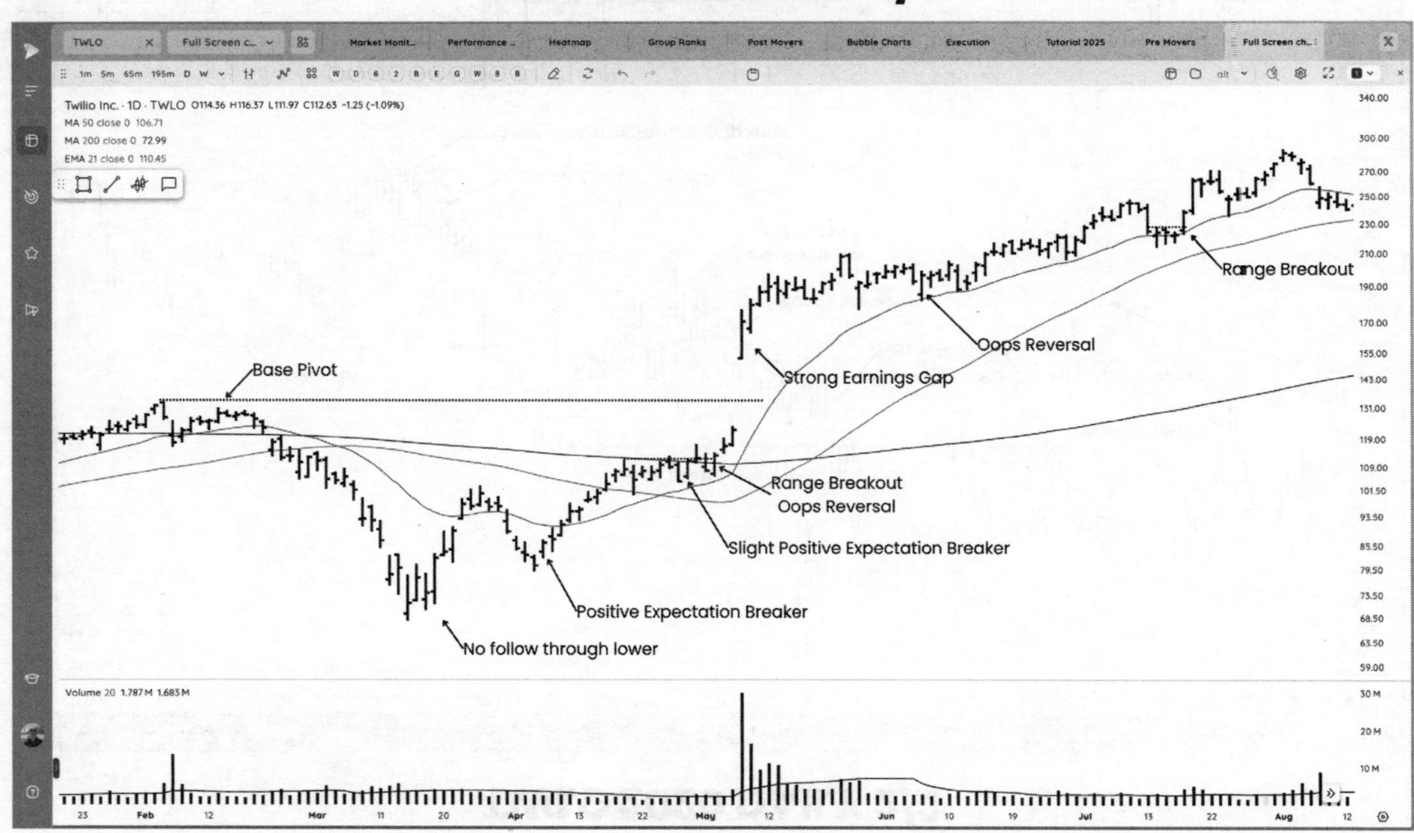

TWLO 2020 DAILY 2/2

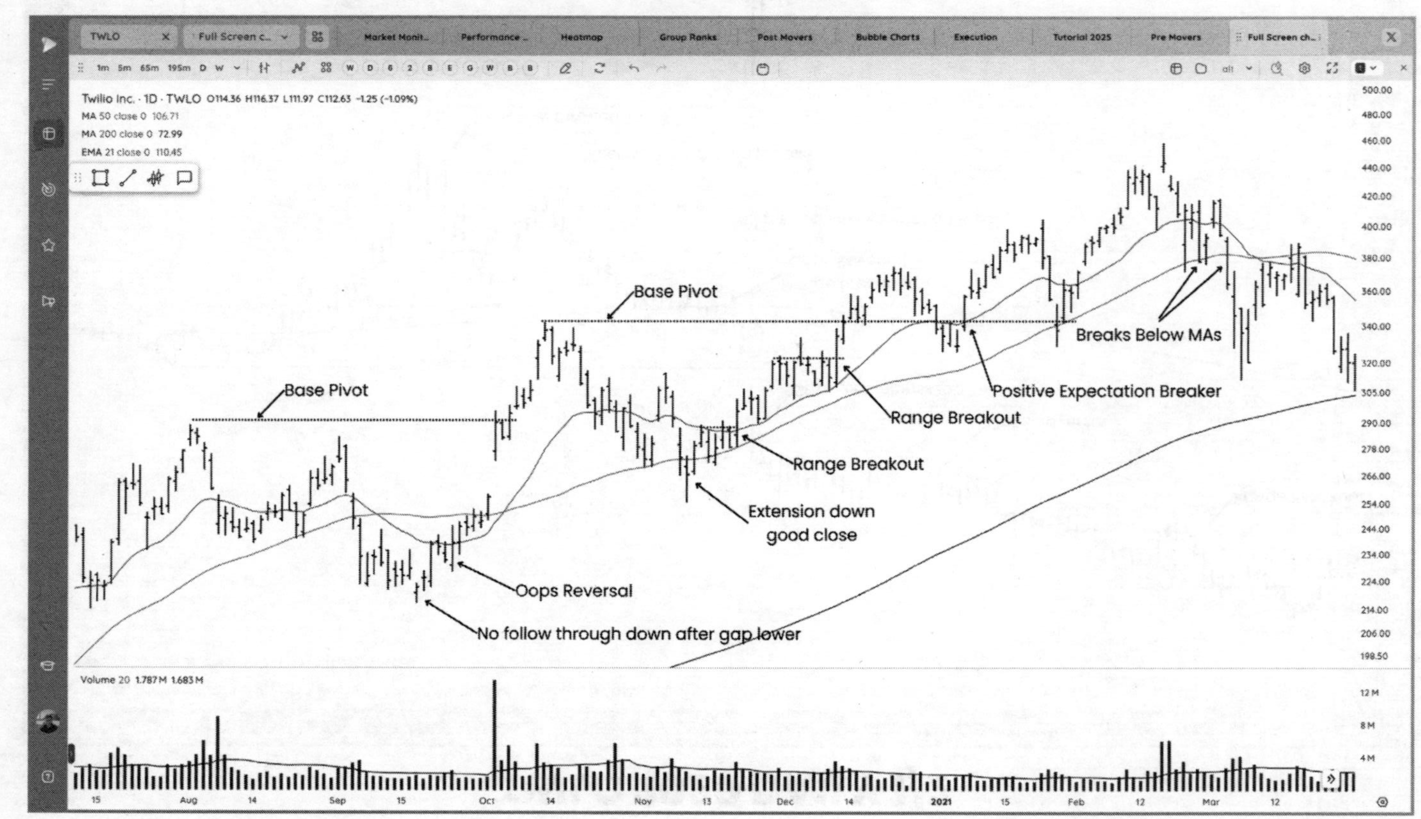

TTD 2020 DAILY 1/2

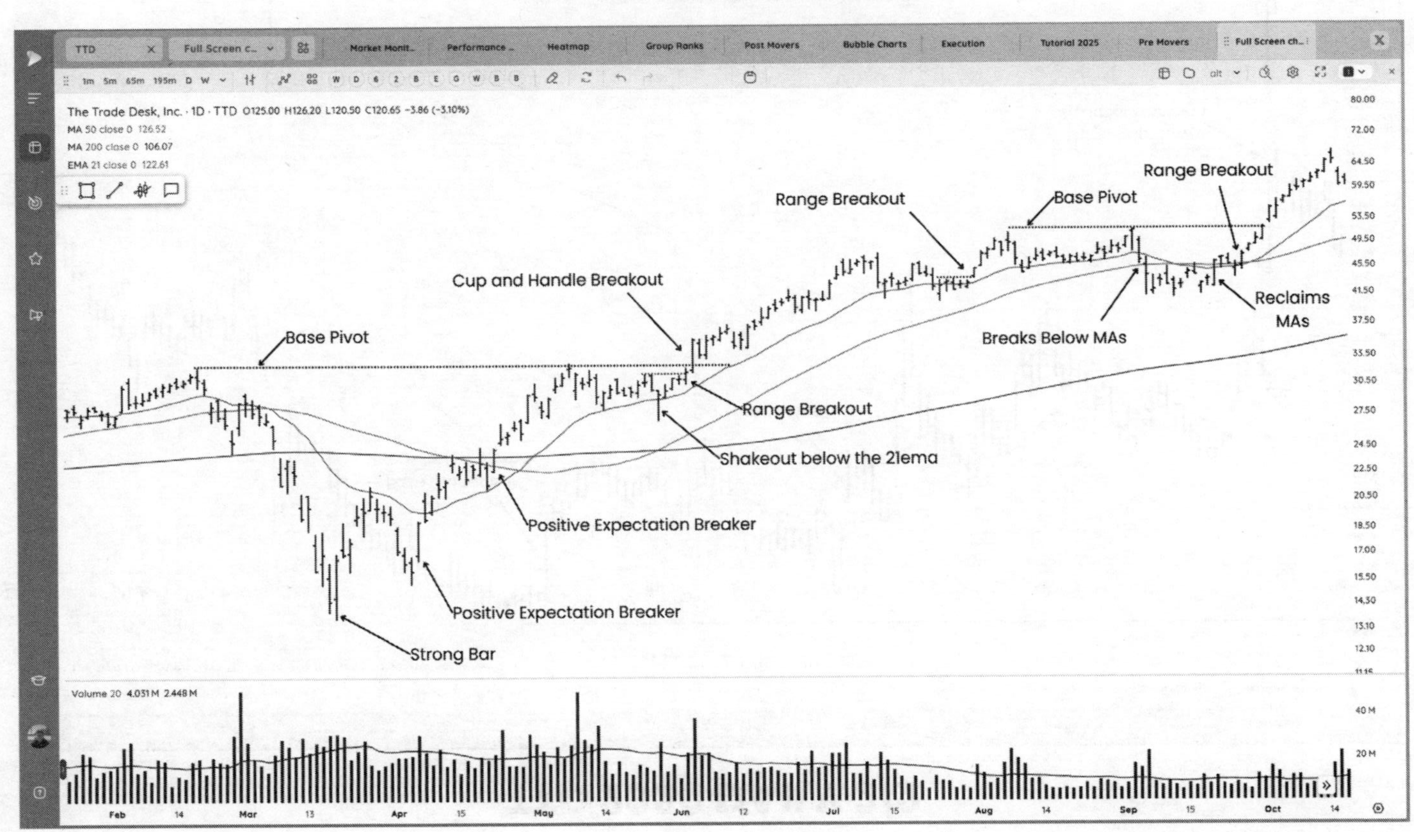

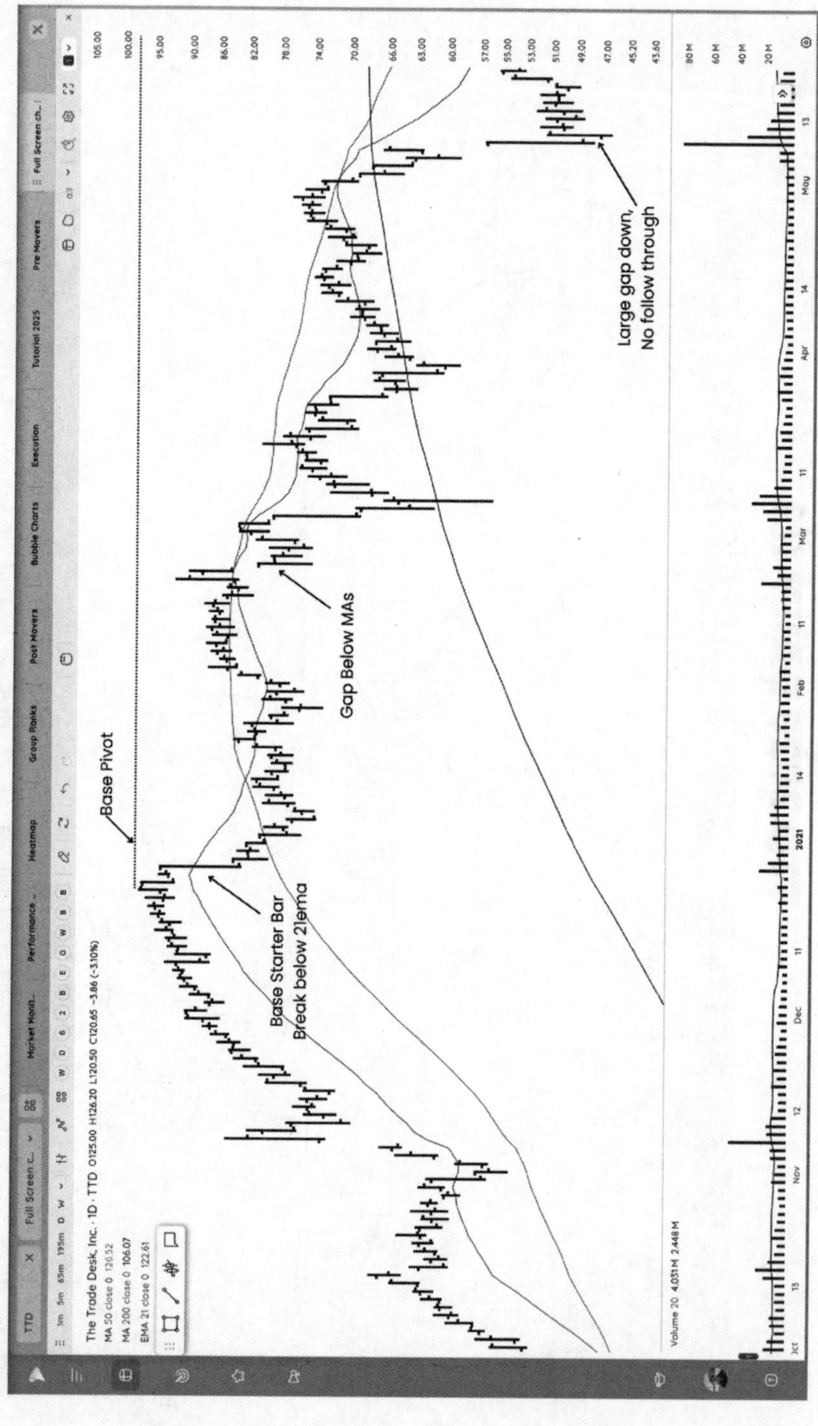

TTD 2020 DAILY 2/2
The Trade Desk, Inc. · 1D · TTD O125.00 H126.20 L120.50 C120.65 −3.86 (−3.10%)
MA 50 close 0 126.52
MA 200 close 0 106.07
EMA 21 close 0 122.61
Base Pivot
Base Starter Bar
Break below 21ema
Gap Below MAs
Large gap down,
No follow through
Volume 20 4.031 M 2.448 M

ZG 2020 DAILY 1/2

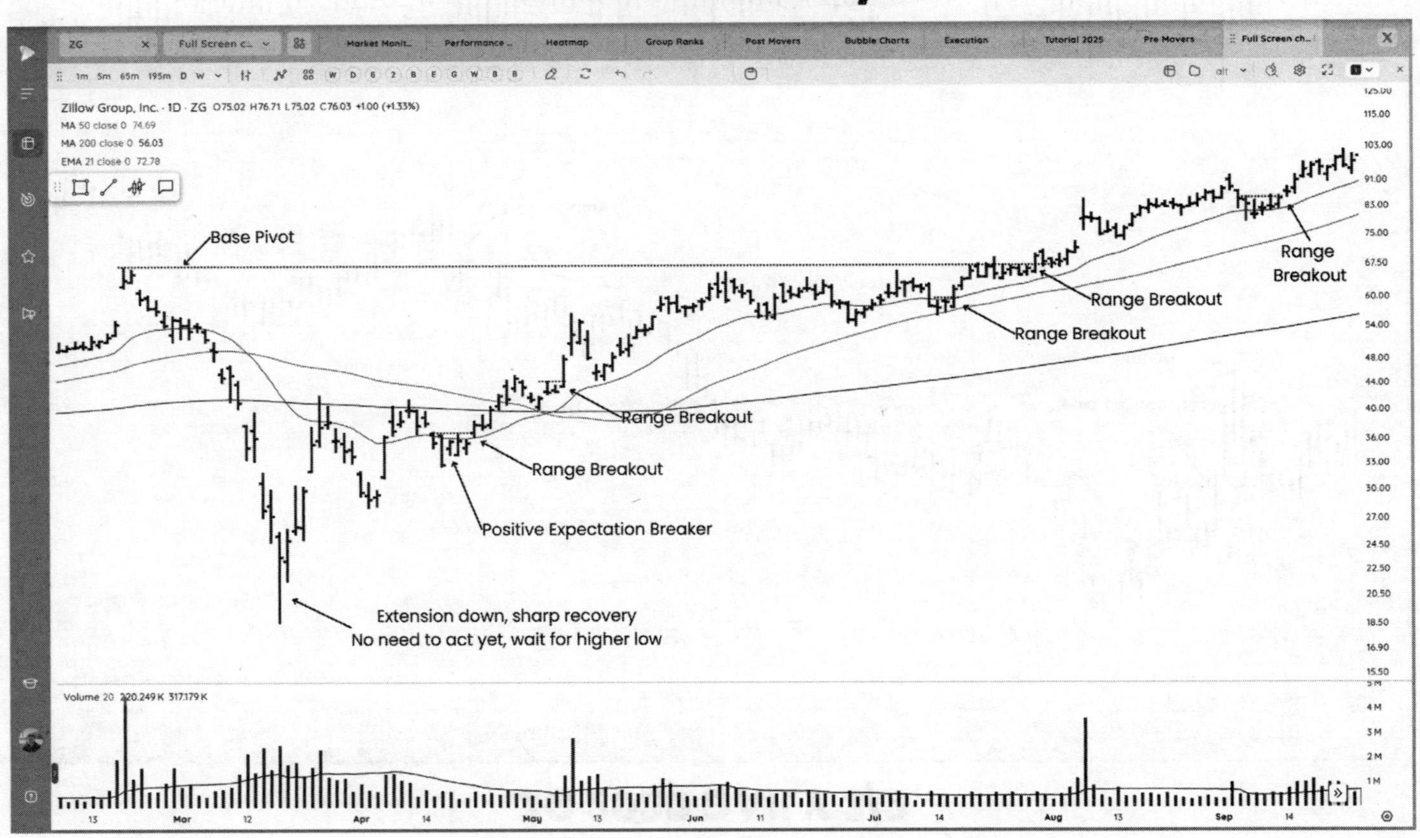

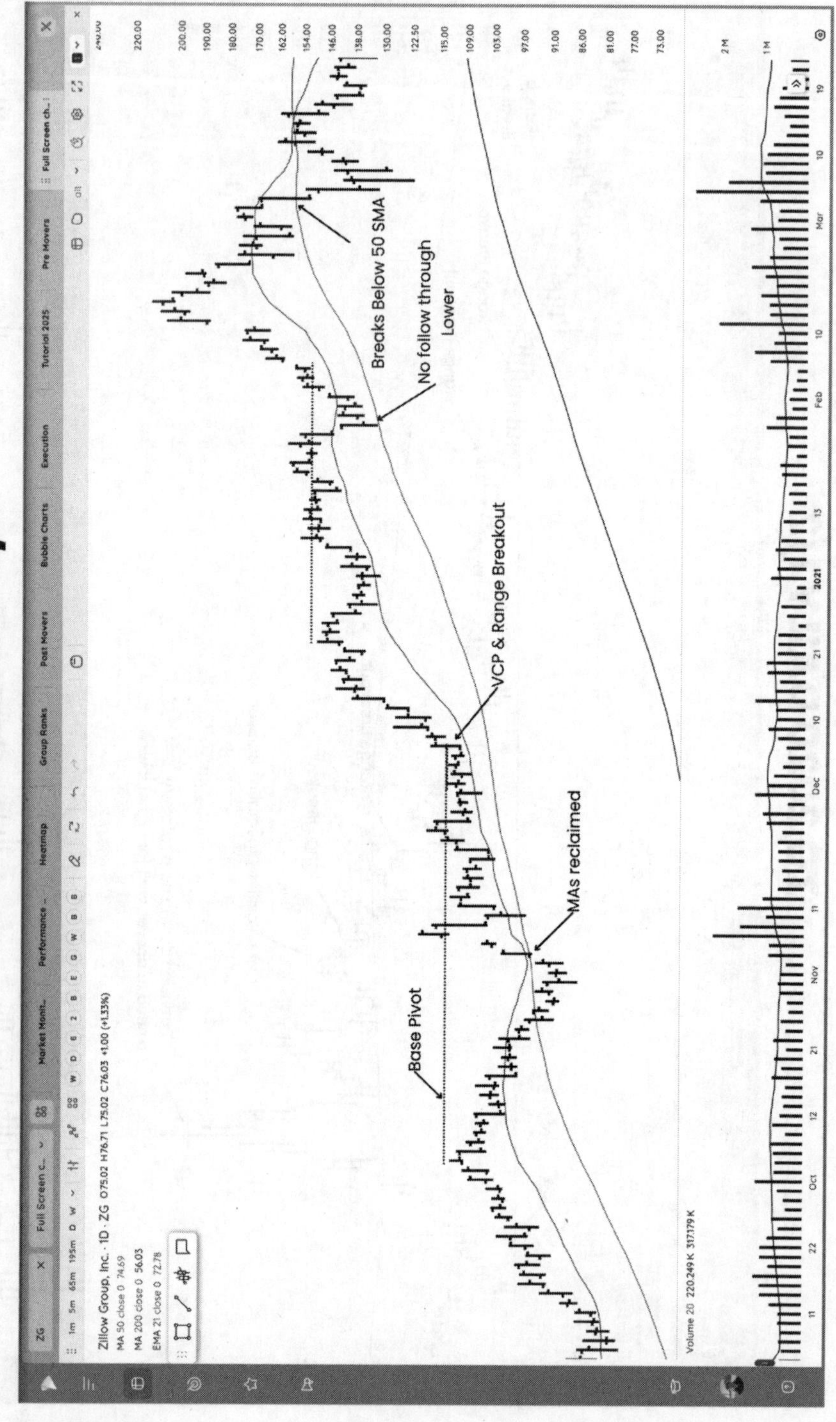
ZG 2020 DAILY 2/2
Zillow Group, Inc. · 1D · ZG
Base Pivot
MAs reclaimed
VCP & Range Breakout
No follow through Lower
Breaks Below 50 SMA

MELI 2020 DAILY 1/2

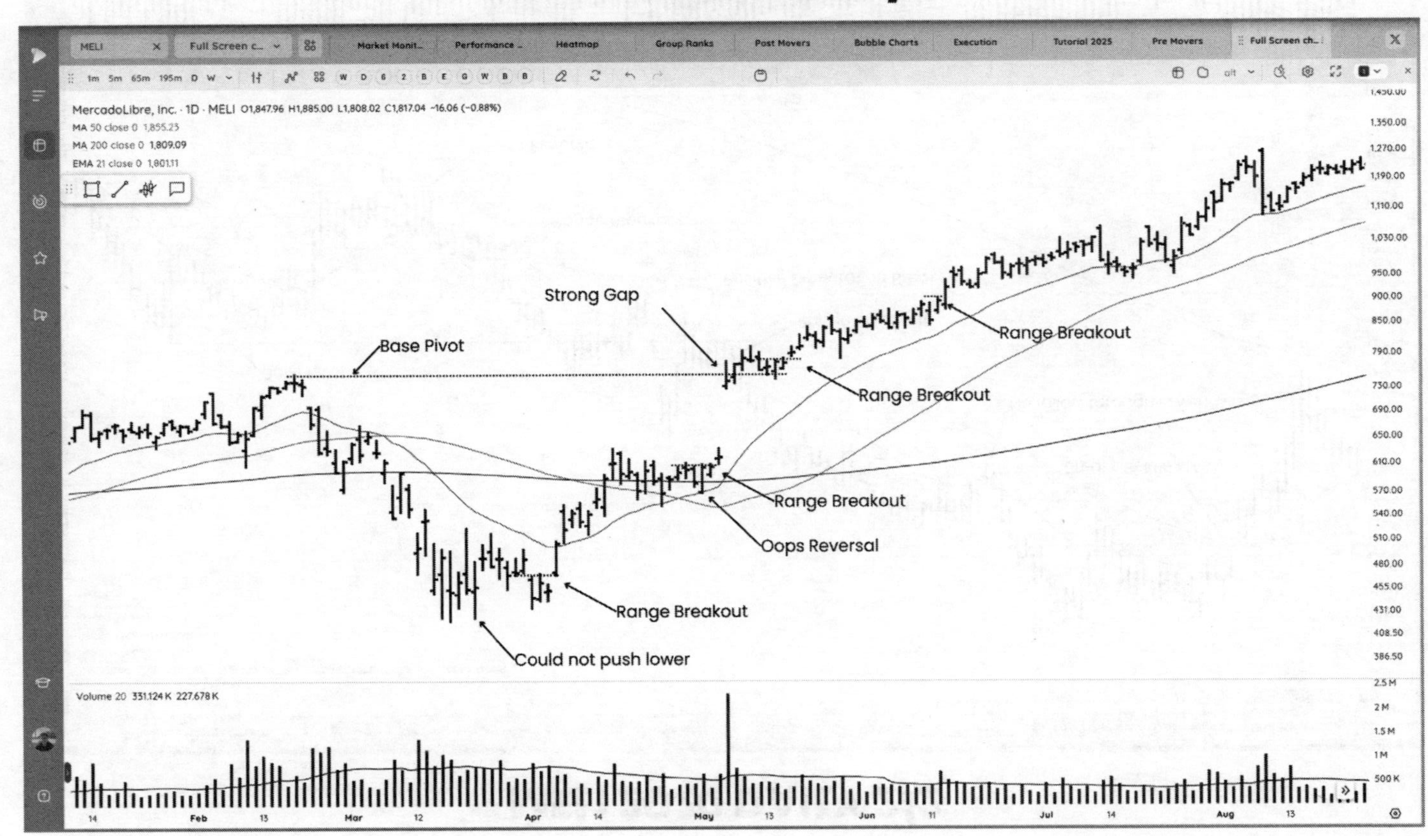

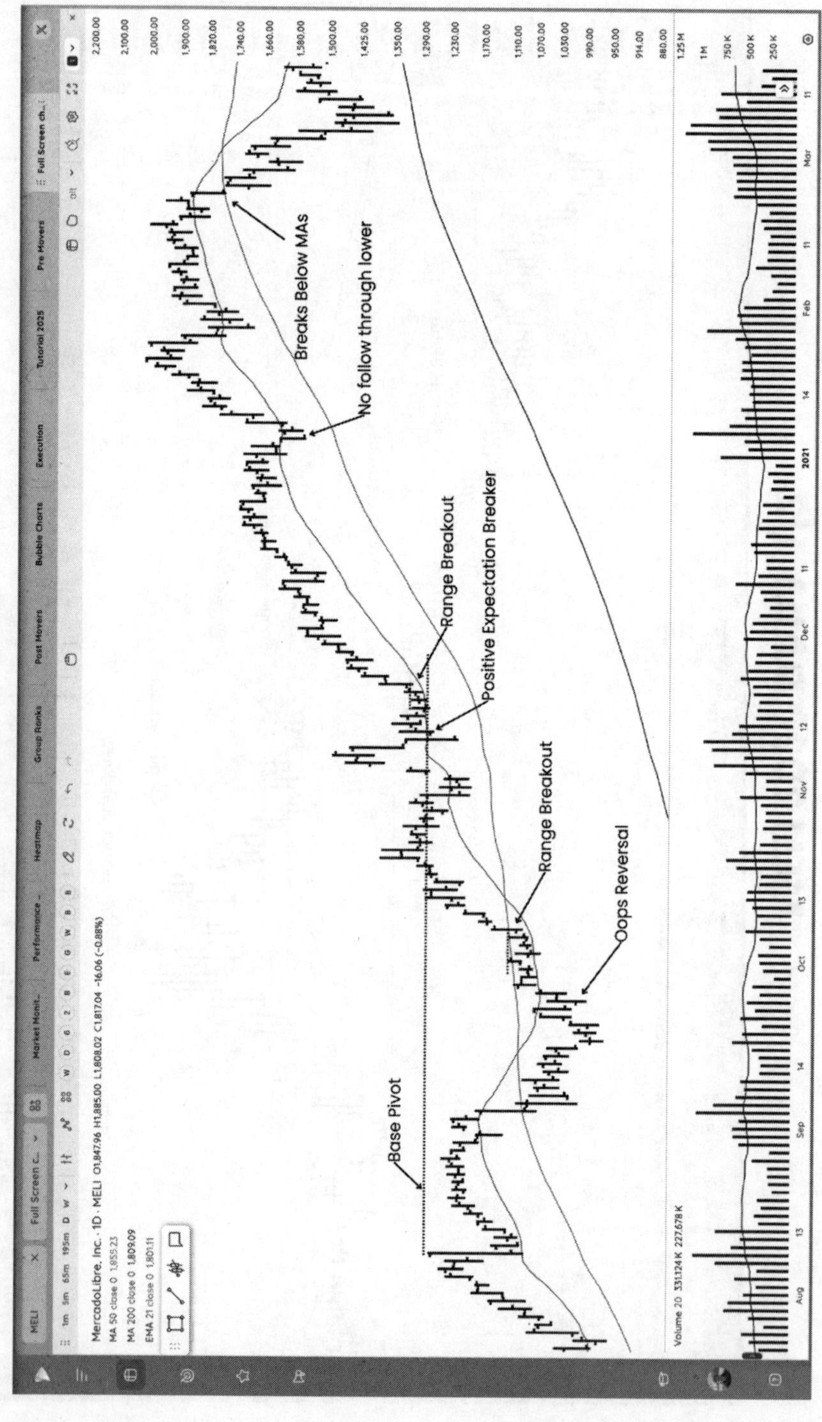
MELI 2020 DAILY 2/2
MercadoLibre, Inc. · 1D · MELI O1,847.96 H1,885.00 L1,808.02 C1,817.04 -16.06 (-0.88%)
MA 50 close 0 1,855.23
MA 200 close 0 1,809.09
EMA 21 close 0 1,801.11
Base Pivot
Oops Reversal
Range Breakout
Positive Expectation Breaker
Range Breakout
No follow through lower
Breaks Below MAs
Volume 20 331.124K 227.678K

PINS 2020 DAILY 1/2

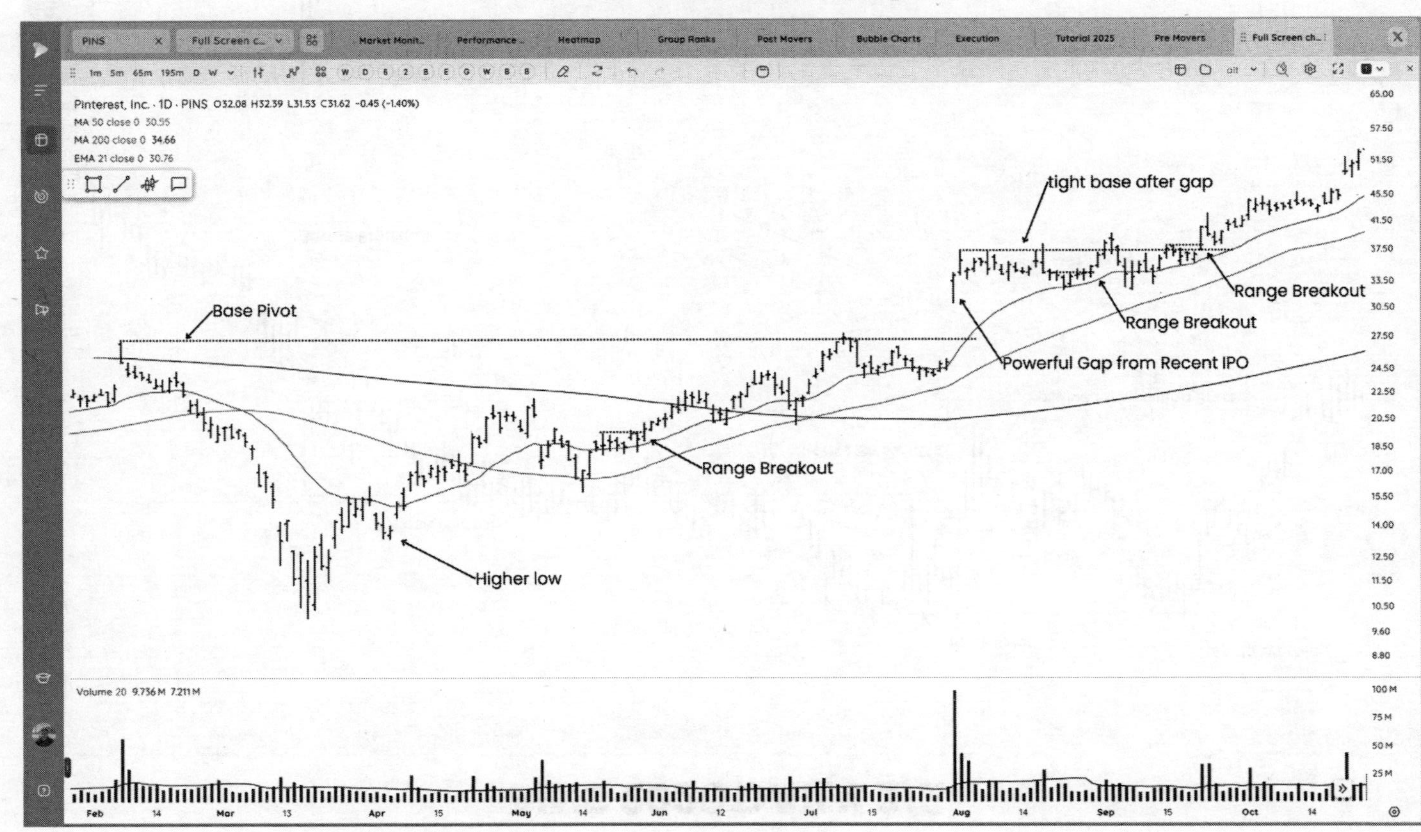

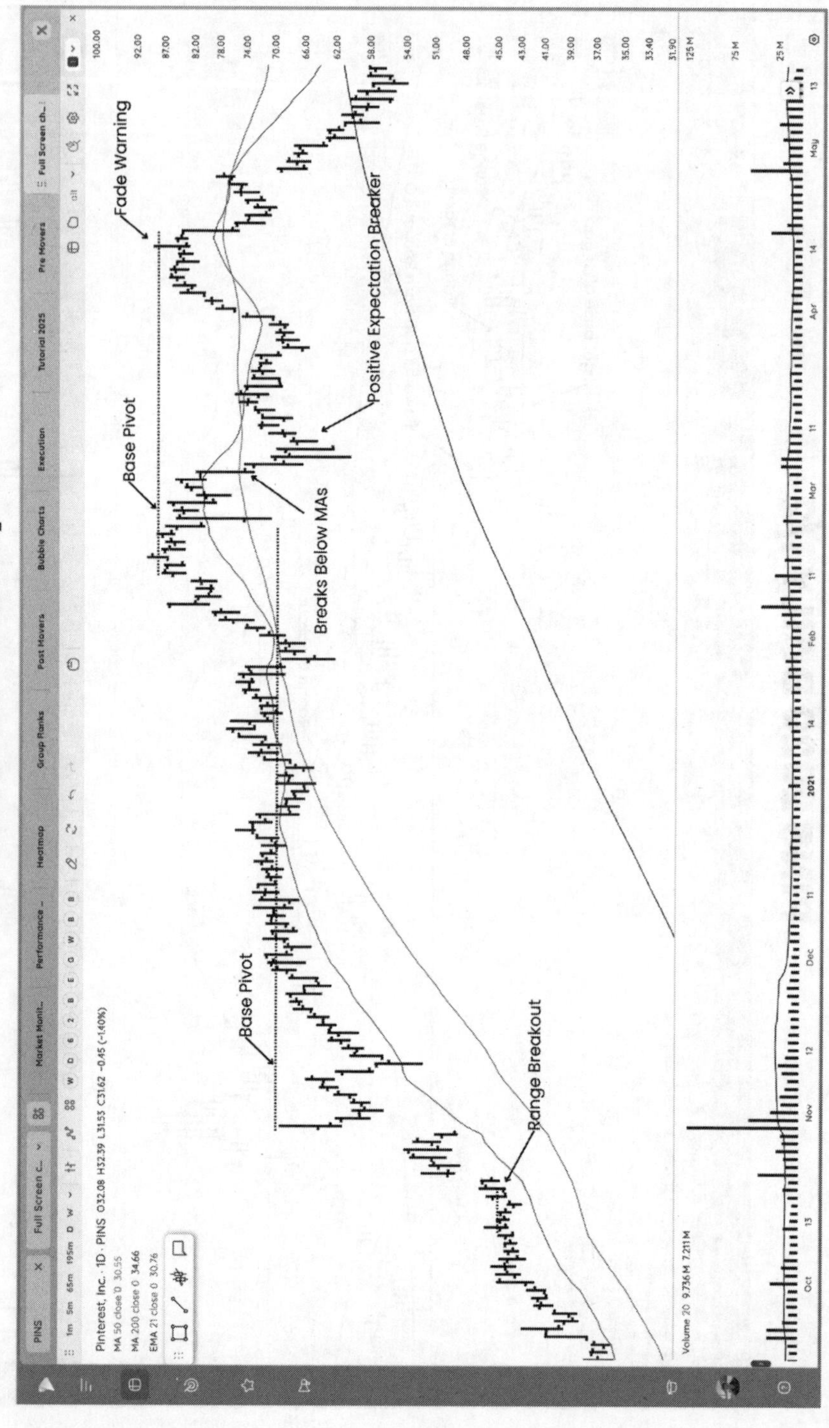
PINS 2020 DAILY 2/2
Range Breakout
Base Pivot
Breaks Below MAs
Base Pivot
Positive Expectation Breaker
Fade Warning

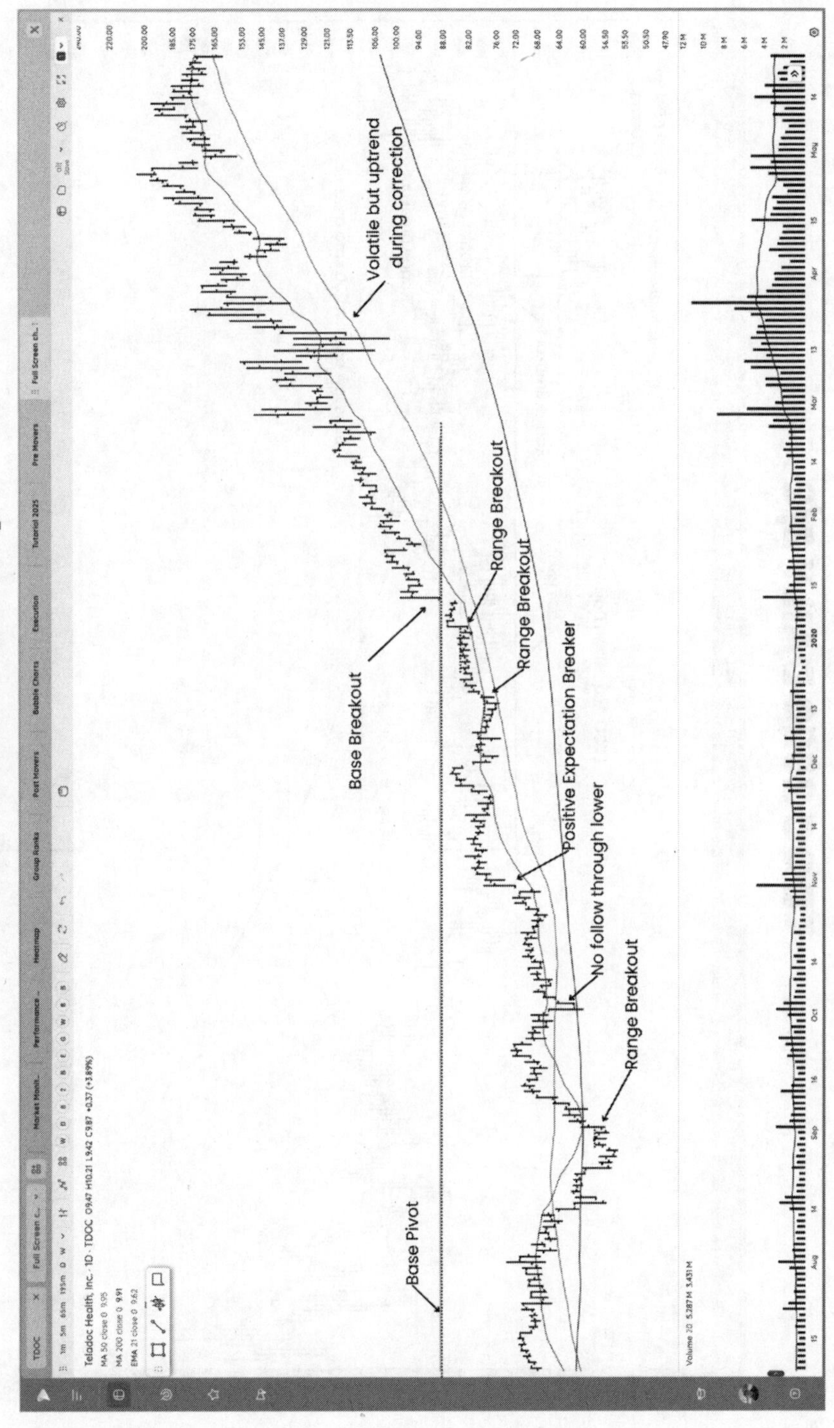
TDOC 2020 DAILY 1/2
Base Pivot
Base Breakout
Volatile but uptrend during correction
Range Breakout
Range Breakout
Positive Expectation Breaker
No follow through lower
Range Breakout

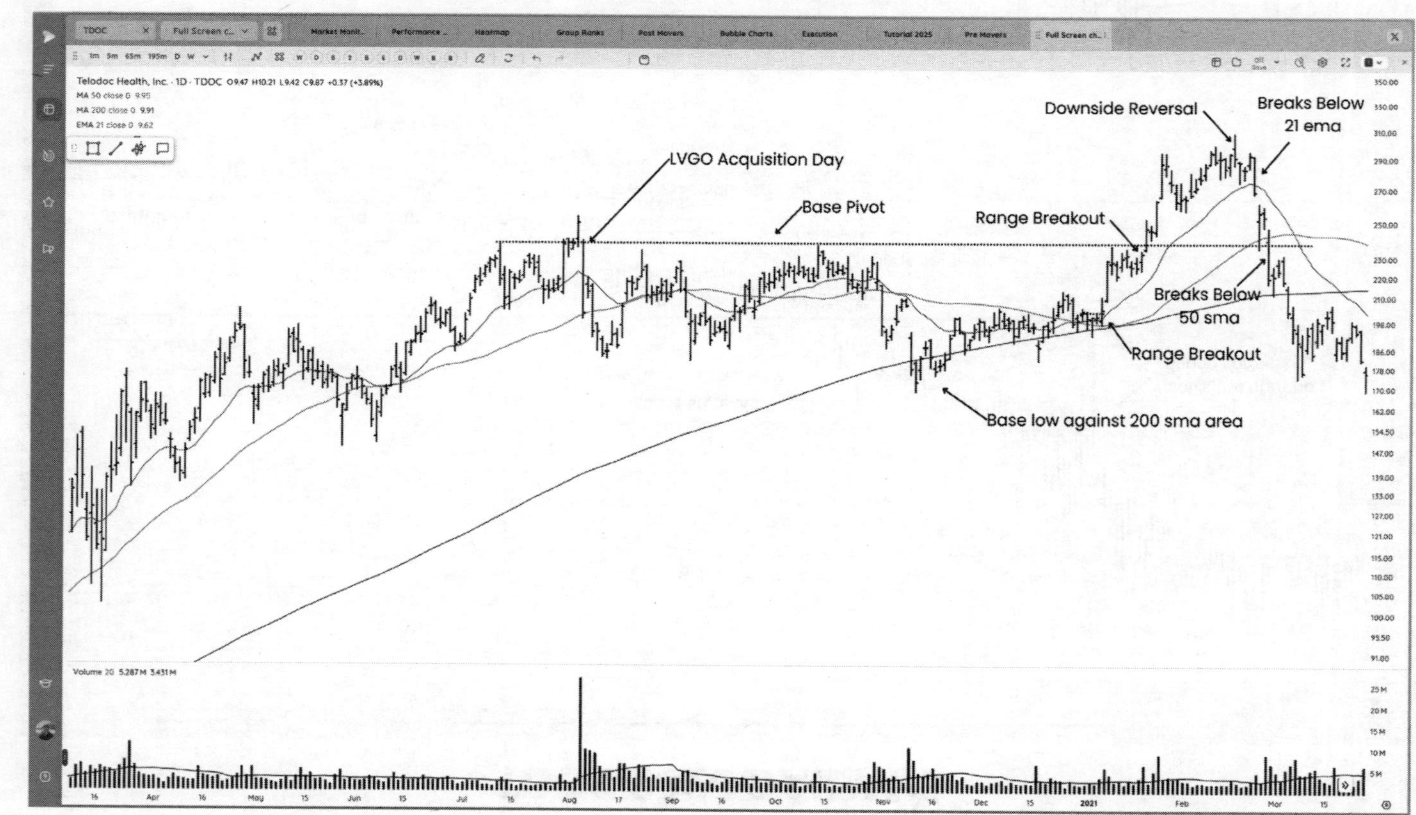
TDOC 2020 DAILY 2/2
Teladoc Health, Inc. · 1D · TDOC O9.47 H10.21 L9.42 C9.87 +0.37 (+3.89%)
MA 50 close 0 9.95
MA 200 close 0 9.91
EMA 21 close 0 9.62
LVGO Acquisition Day
Base Pivot
Range Breakout
Downside Reversal
Breaks Below
21 ema
Breaks Below
50 sma
Range Breakout
Base low against 200 sma area
Volume 20 5.287 M 3.431 M

SPCE 2020 DAILY

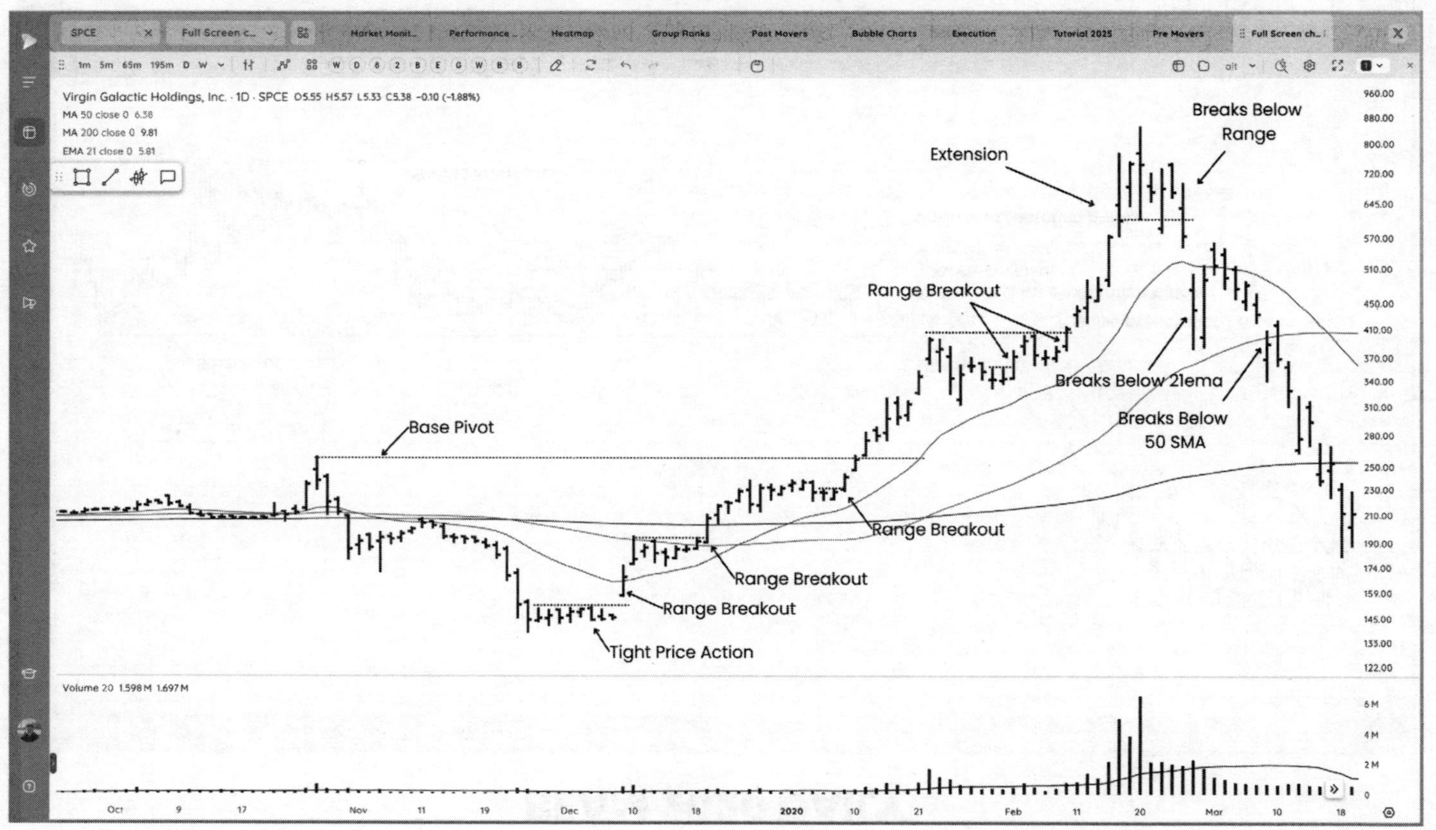

BEAM 2020 DAILY

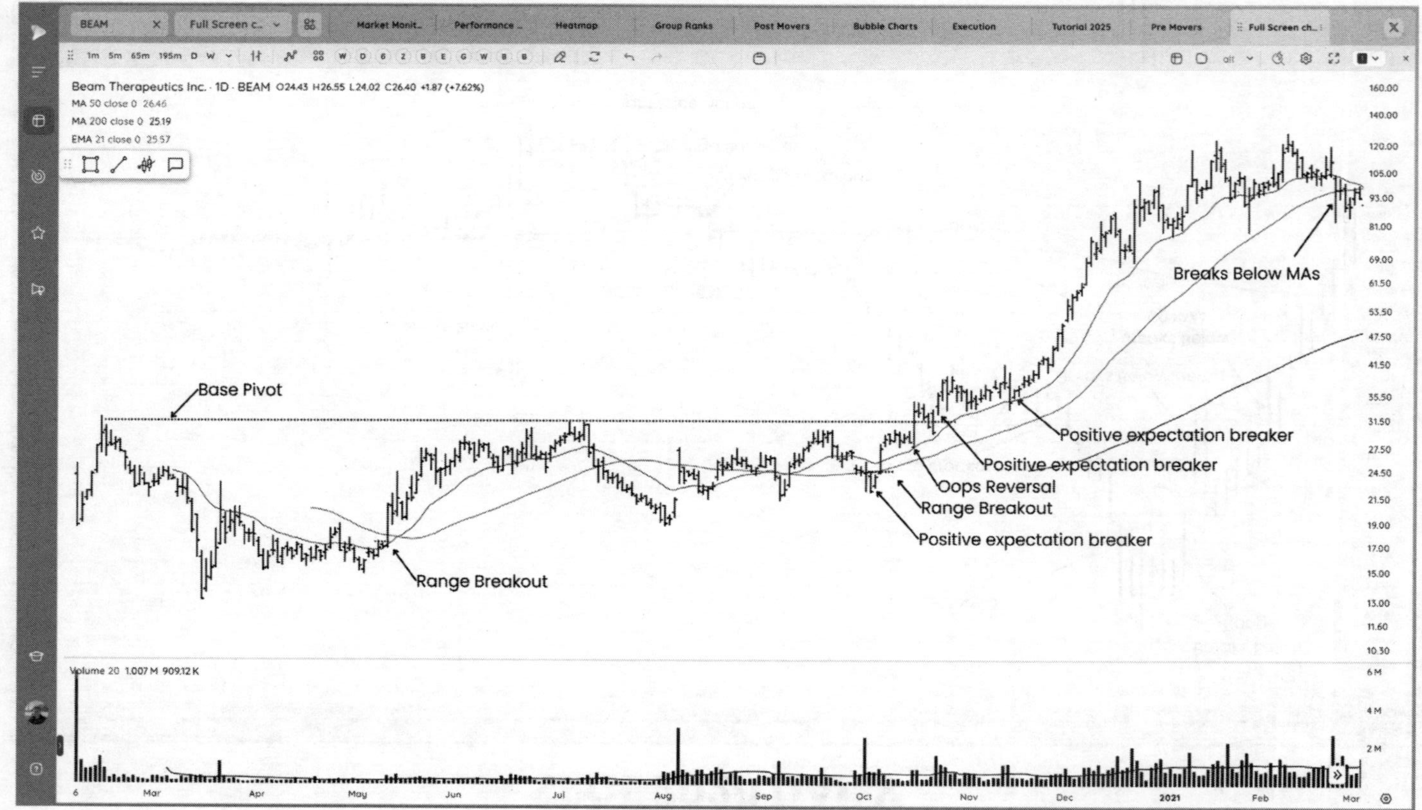

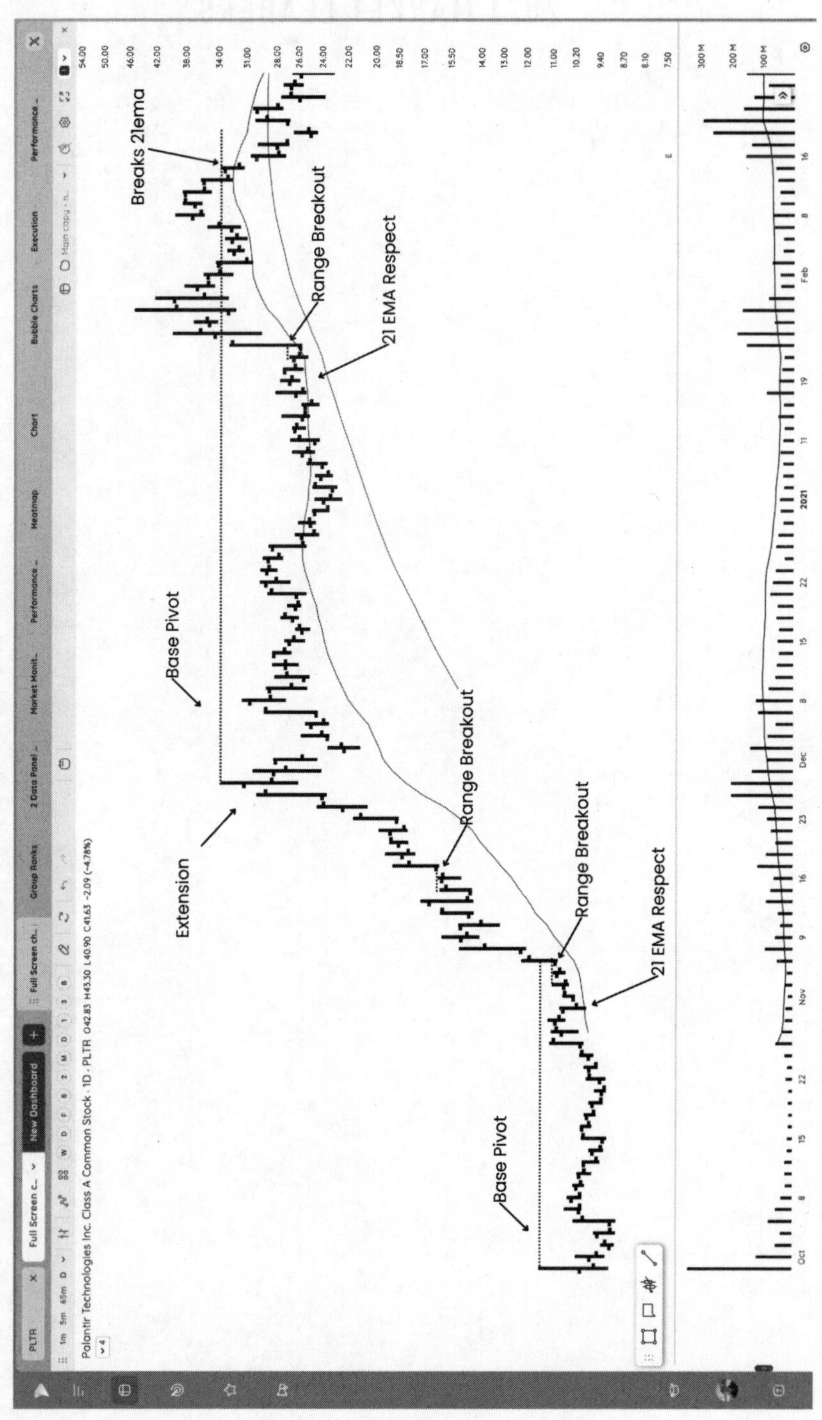
PLTR 2020 Daily
Base Pivot
21 EMA Respect
Range Breakout
Range Breakout
Extension
Base Pivot
21 EMA Respect
Range Breakout
Breaks 21ema

2021 MARKET LEADERS

ASAN 2021 DAILY 1/2
Asana, Inc. · 1D · ASAN O20.68 H20.68 L19.82 C20.21 -0.21 (-1.03%)
MA 50 close 0 18.92
MA 200 close 0 14.77
EMA 21 close 0 20.17
Base Pivot
Breakout
Base Pivot
Breaks Below MAs
Inside day and up at the pivot
Range Breakout
Follow through and 21ema reclaim
Range Breakout
Range Breakout
Oops Reversal
Range Breakout
Range Breakout
Volume Increase
Volume 20 1.82 M 2.645 M

ASAN 2021 DAILY 2/2

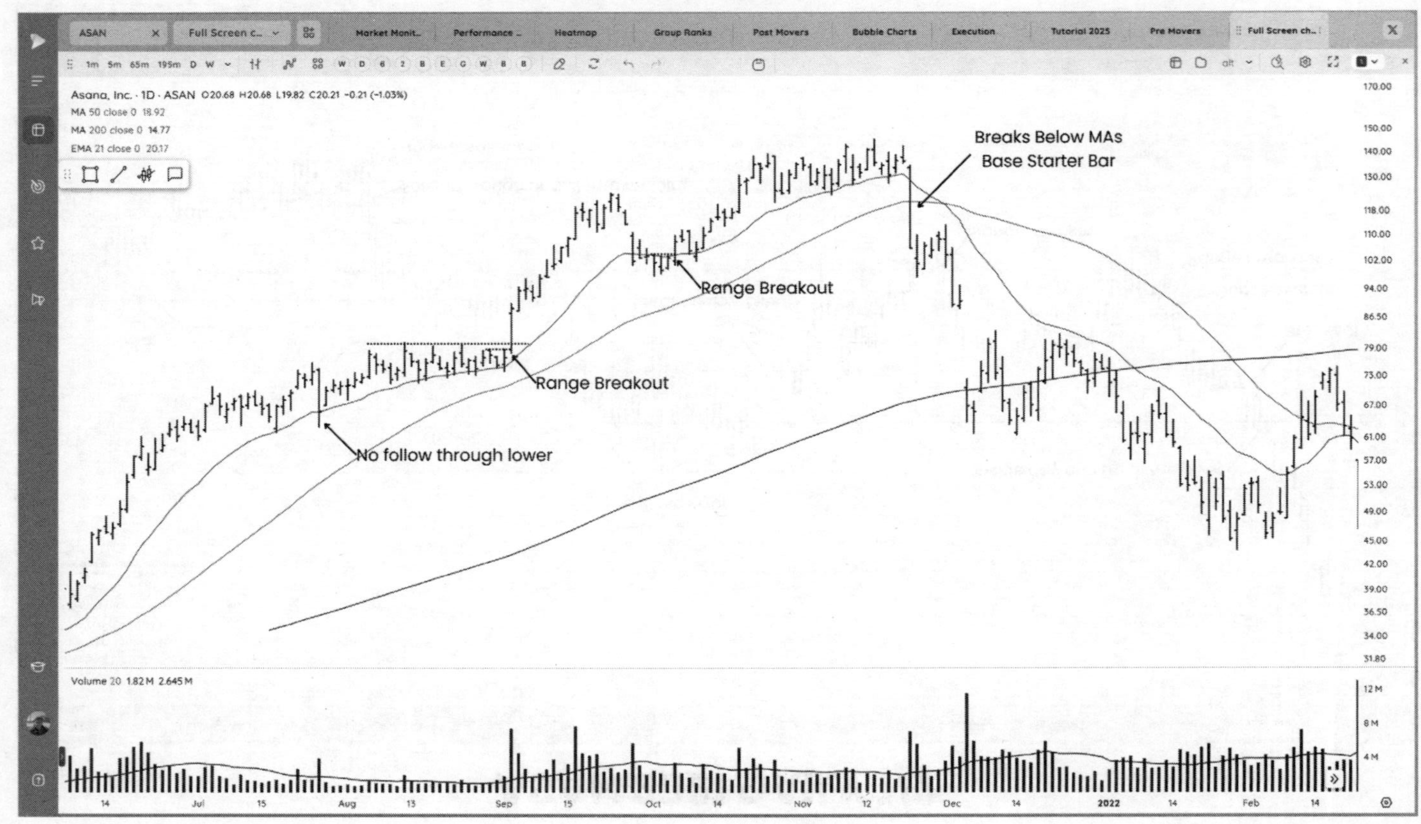

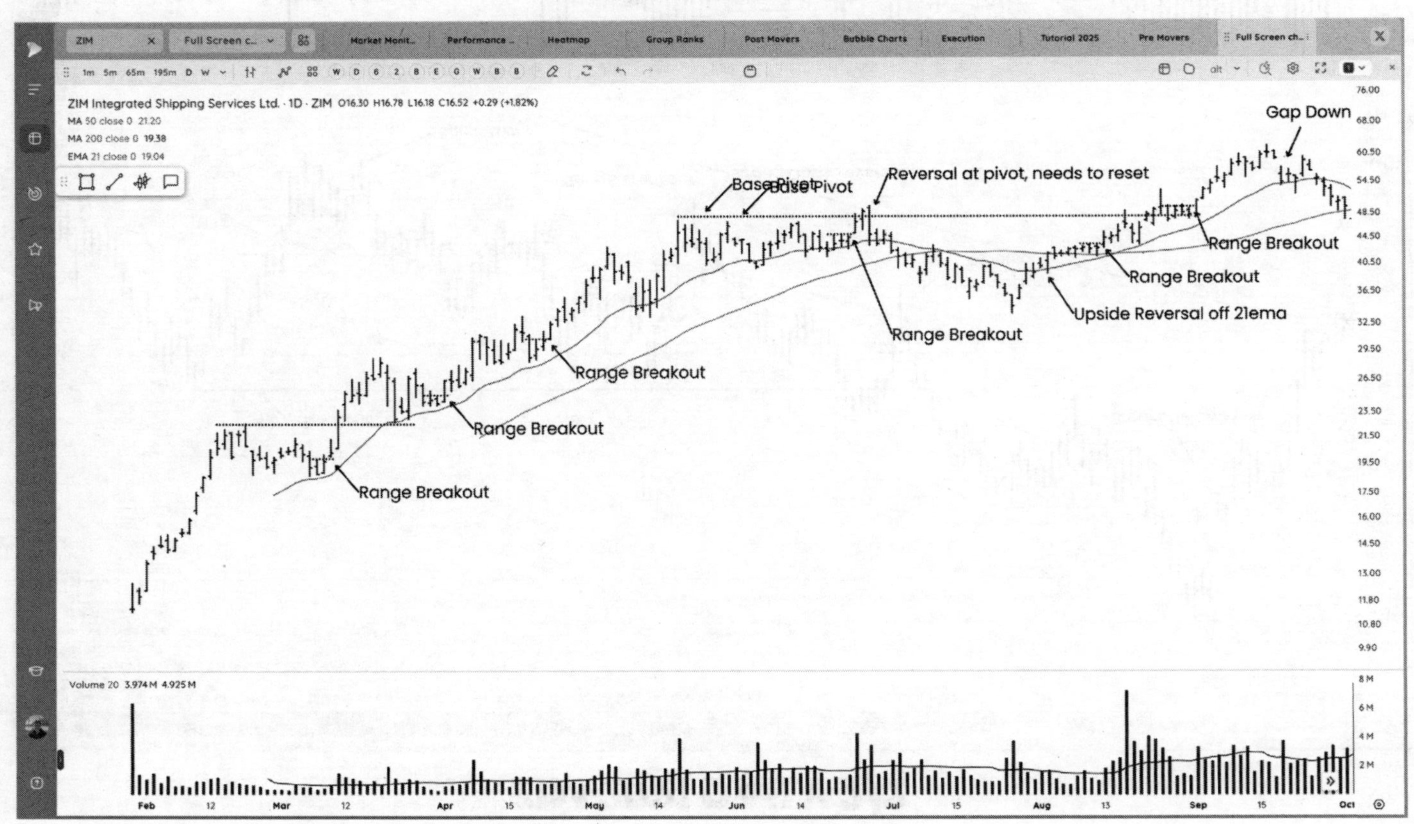
ZIM 2021 DAILY 1/2
ZIM Integrated Shipping Services Ltd. · 1D · ZIM O16.30 H16.78 L16.18 C16.52 +0.29 (+1.82%)
MA 50 close 0 21.20
MA 200 close 0 19.38
EMA 21 close 0 19.04
Base
Pivot
Reversal at pivot, needs to reset
Gap Down
Range Breakout
Range Breakout
Upside Reversal off 21ema
Range Breakout
Range Breakout
Range Breakout
Range Breakout
Volume 20 3.974 M 4.925 M

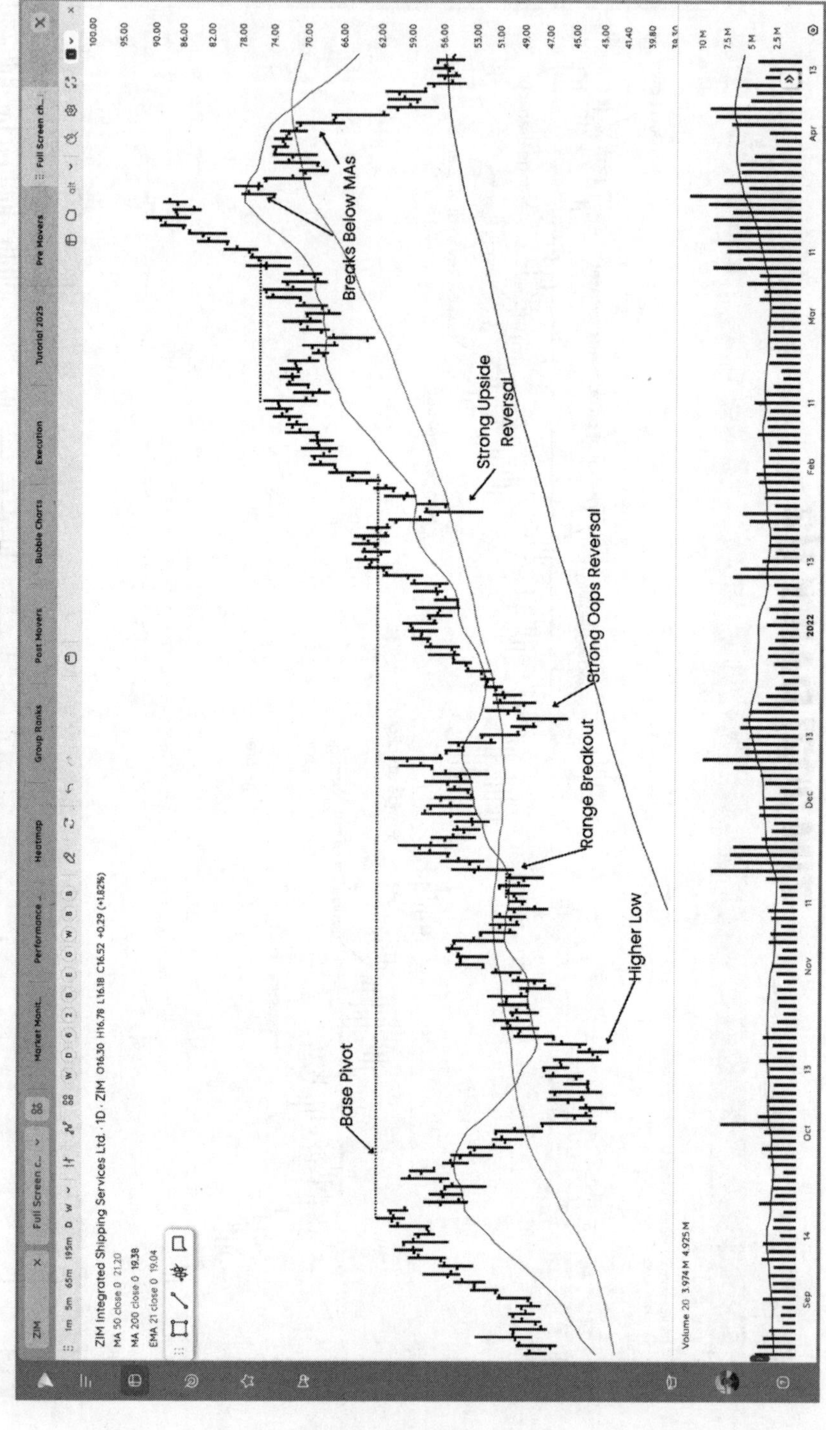
ZIM 2021 DAILY 2/2
ZIM Integrated Shipping Services Ltd. · 1D · ZIM O16.30 H16.78 L16.18 C16.52 +0.29 (+1.82%)
MA 50 close 0 21.20
MA 200 close 0 19.38
EMA 21 close 0 19.04
Base Pivot
Higher Low
Range Breakout
Strong Oops Reversal
Strong Upside Reversal
Breaks Below MAs
Volume 20 3.974 M 4.925 M

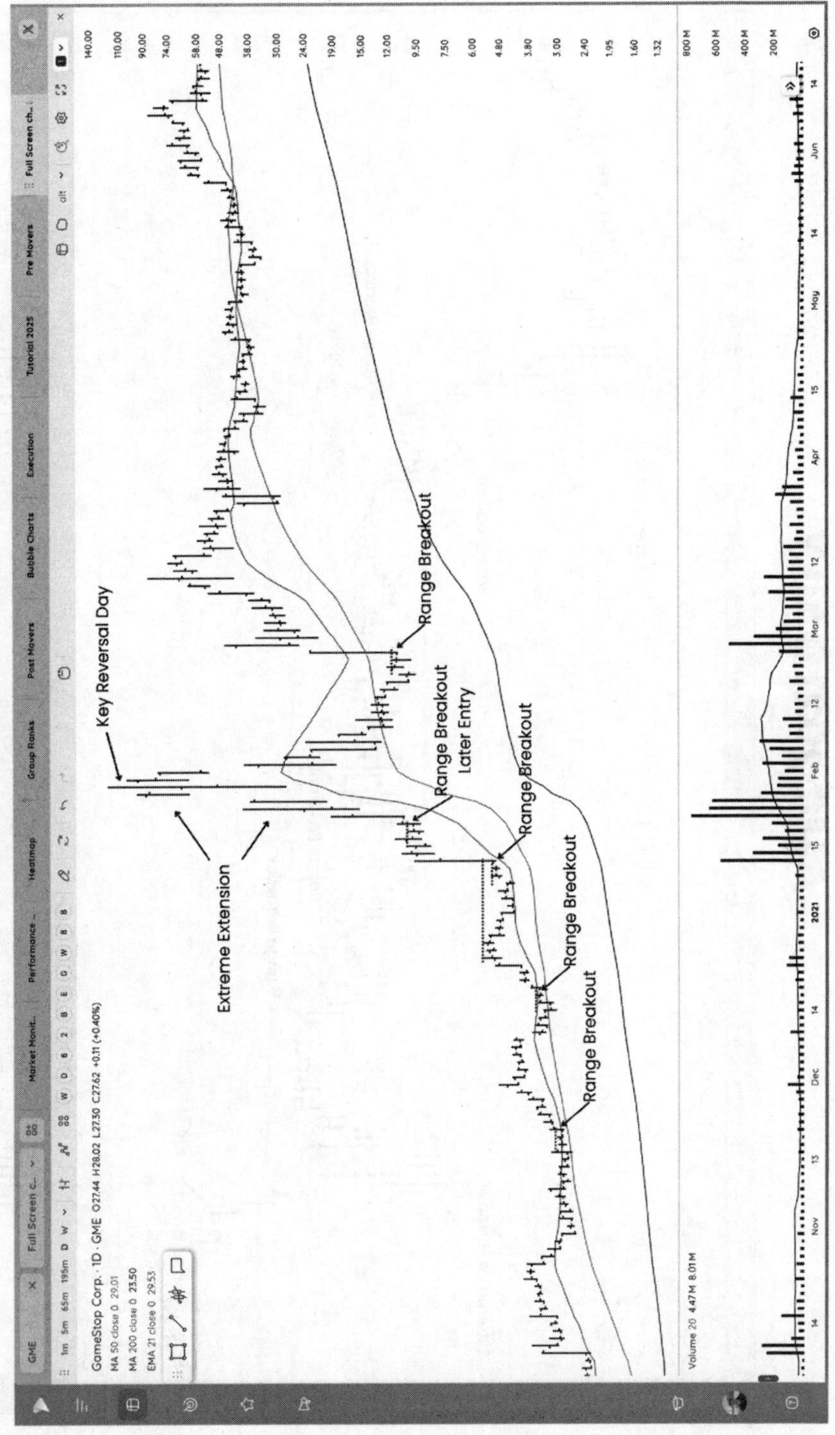
GME 2021 DAILY
Key Reversal Day
Extreme Extension
Range Breakout
Range Breakout
Later Entry
Range Breakout
Range Breakout
Range Breakout
GameStop Corp. · 1D · GME O27.44 H28.02 L27.30 C27.62 +0.11 (+0.40%)
MA 50 close 0 29.01
MA 200 close 0 23.50
EMA 21 close 0 29.53
Volume 20 4.47M 8.01M

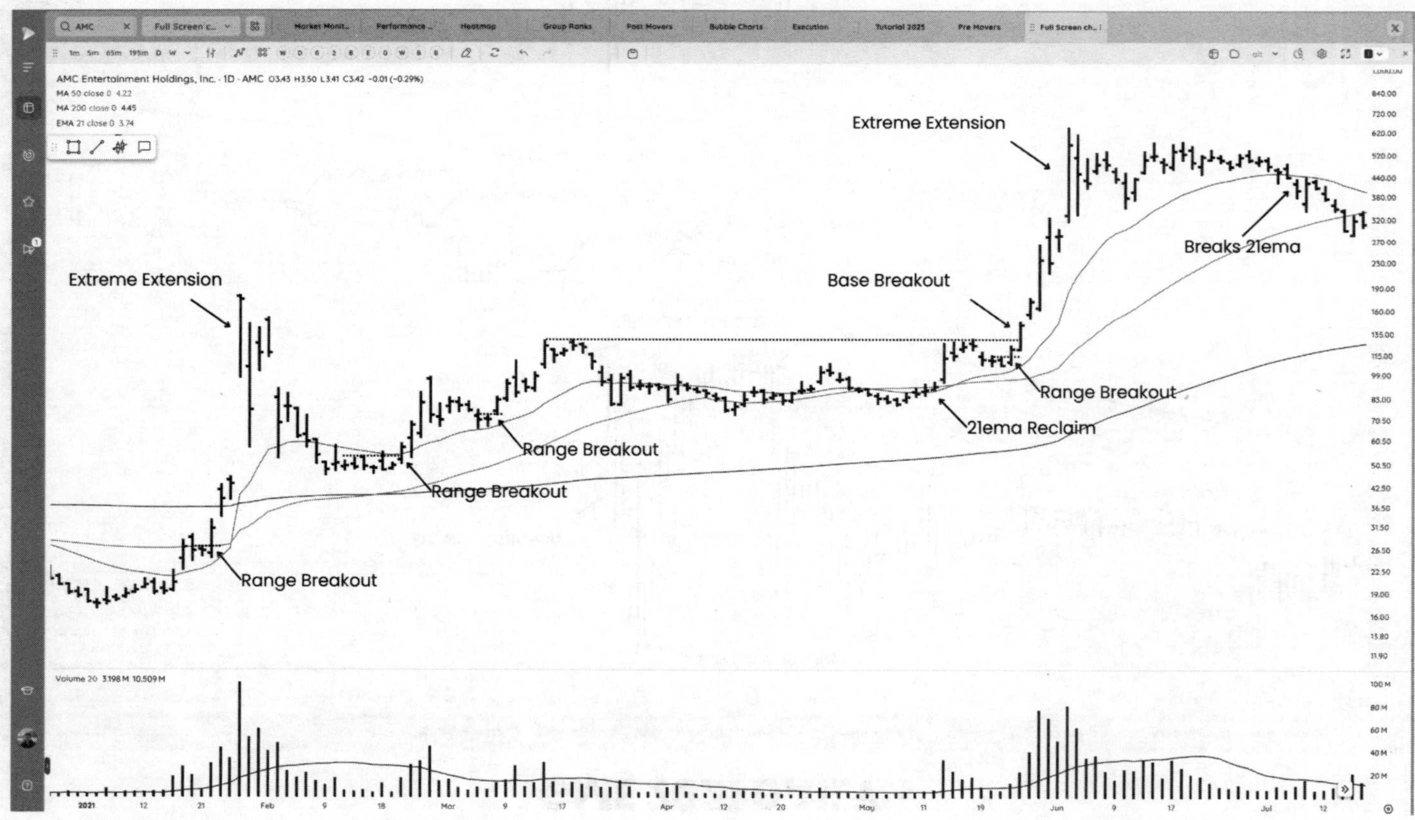
AMC 2021 DAILY
AMC Entertainment Holdings, Inc. · 1D · AMC O3.43 H3.50 L3.41 C3.42 −0.01 (−0.29%)
MA 50 close 0 4.22
MA 200 close 0 4.45
EMA 21 close 0 3.74
Extreme Extension
Range Breakout
Range Breakout
Range Breakout
Extreme Extension
Base Breakout
Range Breakout
21ema Reclaim
Breaks 21ema
Volume 20 3.198 M 10.509 M

CAR 2021 DAILY 1/2

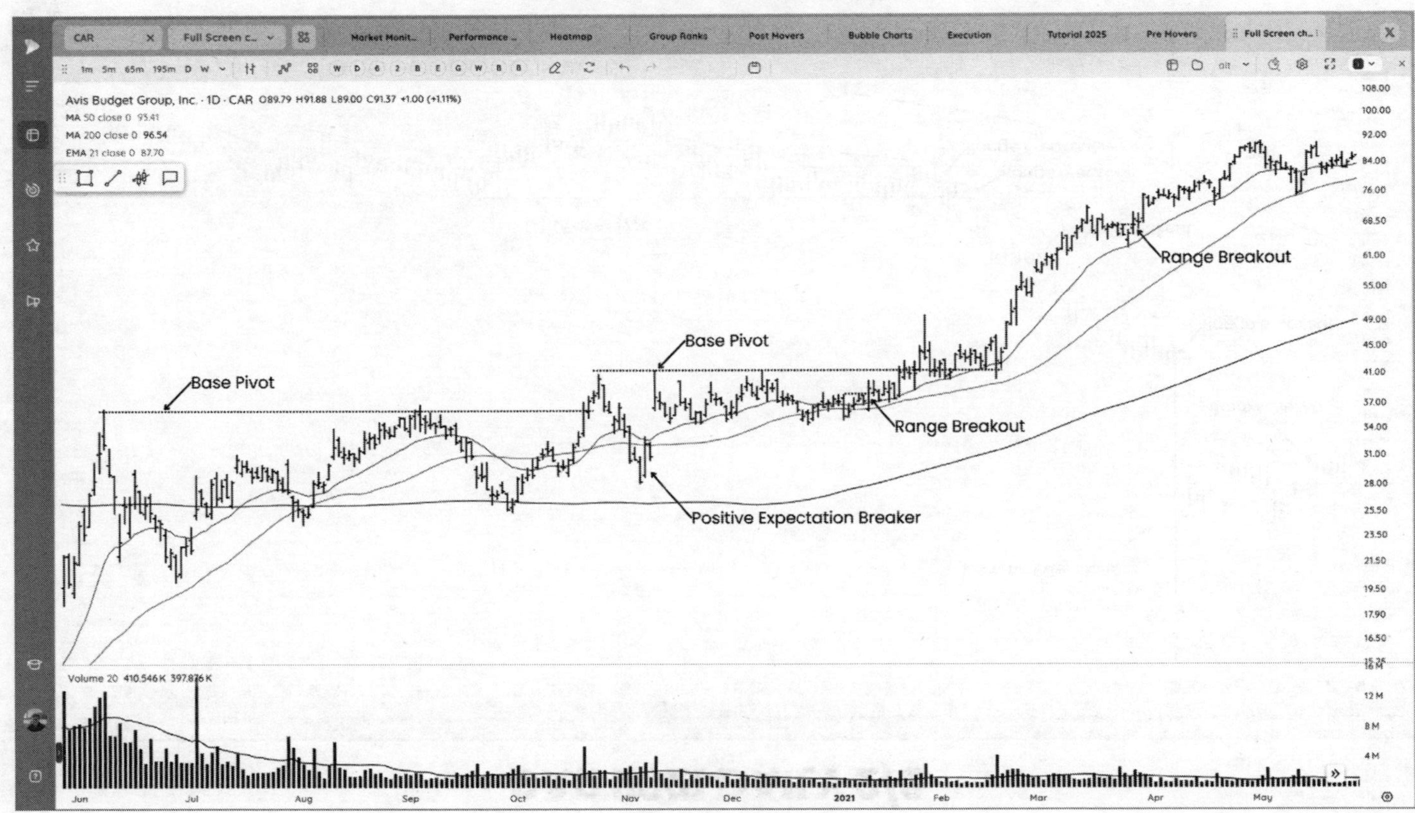

CAR 2021 DAILY 2/2

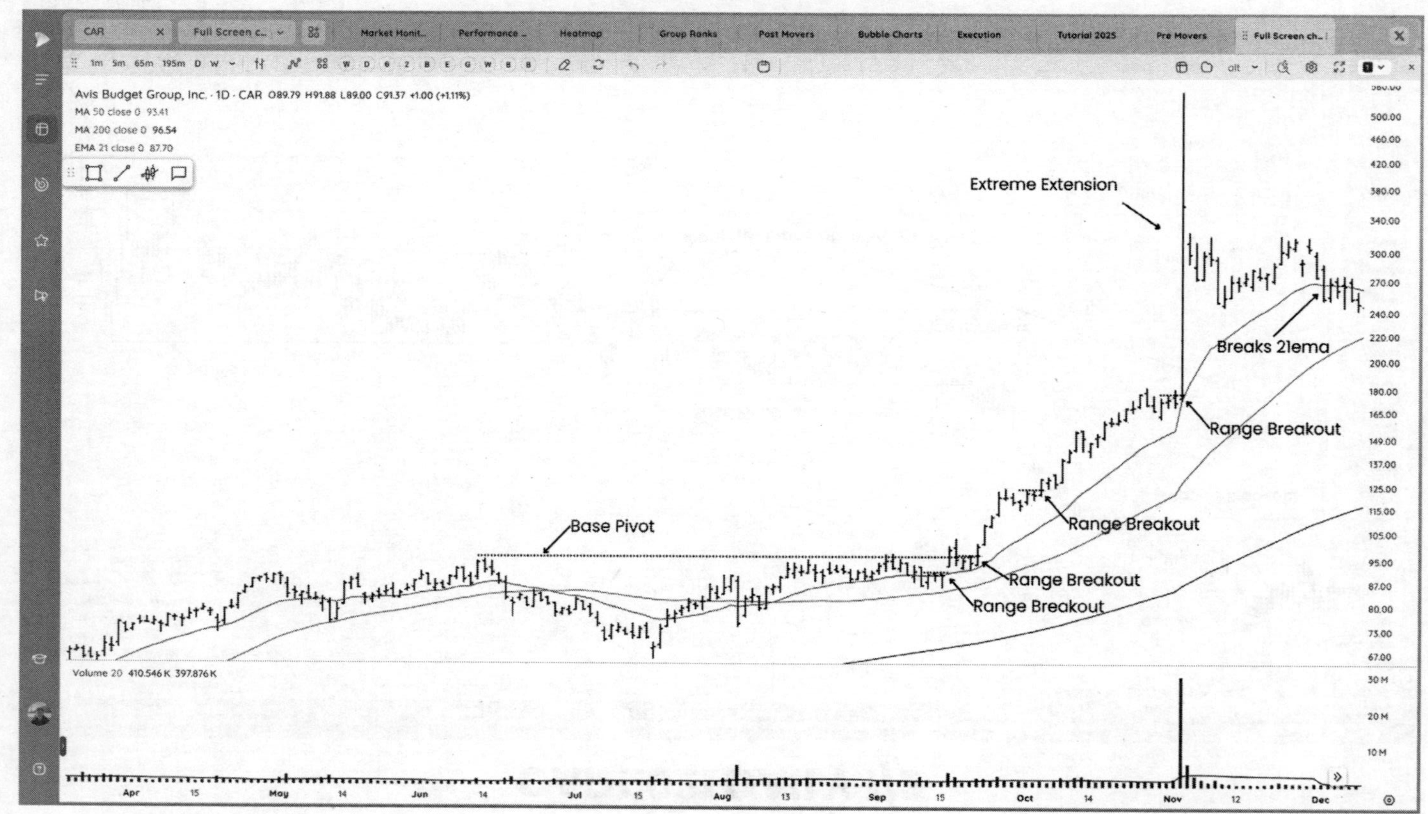

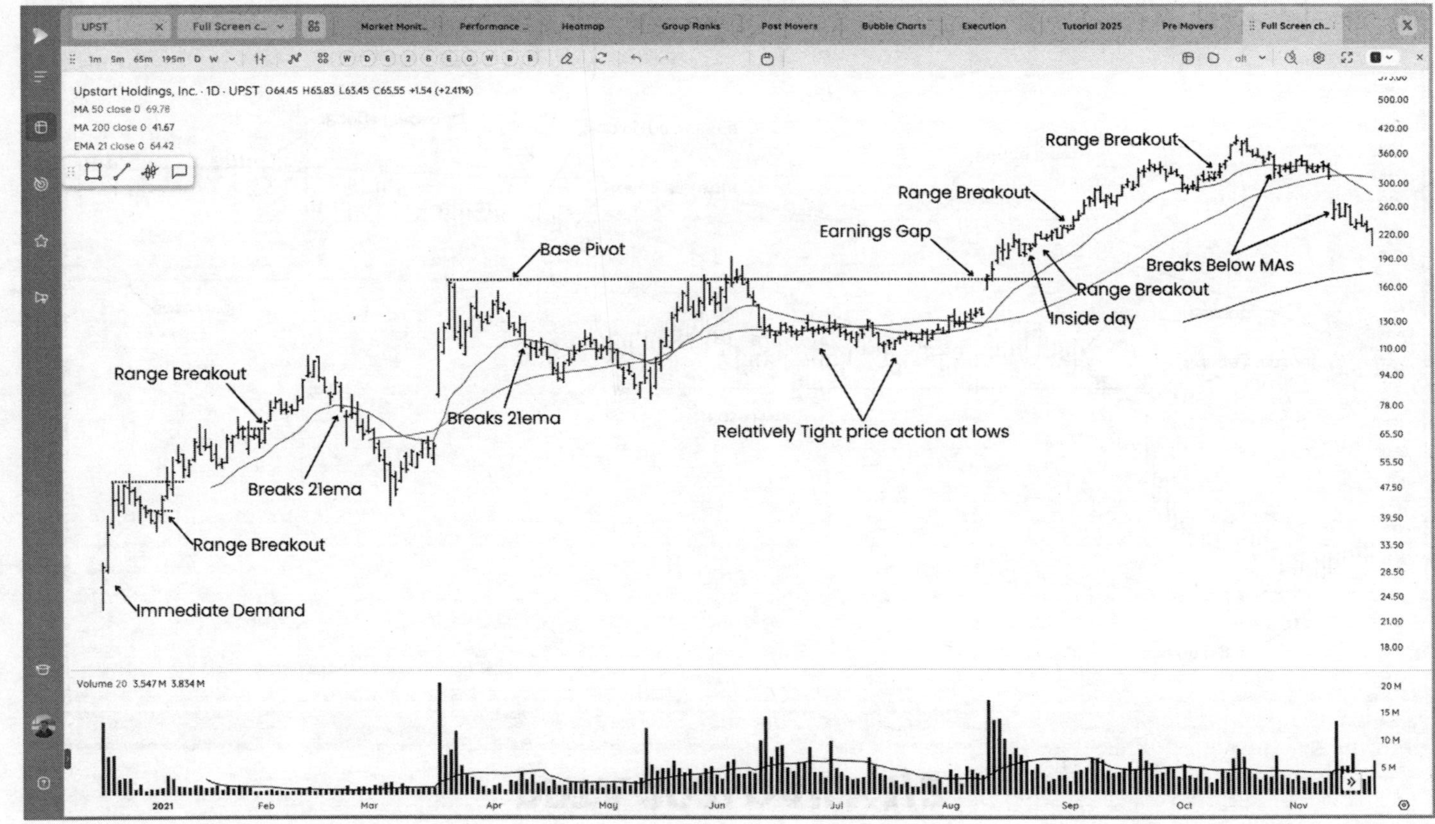
UPST 2021 DAILY
Upstart Holdings, Inc. · 1D · UPST O64.45 H65.83 L63.45 C65.55 +1.54 (+2.41%)
MA 50 close 0 69.78
MA 200 close 0 41.67
EMA 21 close 0 64.42
Immediate Demand
Range Breakout
Range Breakout
Breaks 21ema
Breaks 21ema
Base Pivot
Relatively Tight price action at lows
Earnings Gap
Range Breakout
Inside day
Range Breakout
Range Breakout
Breaks Below MAs
Volume 20 3.547 M 3.834 M

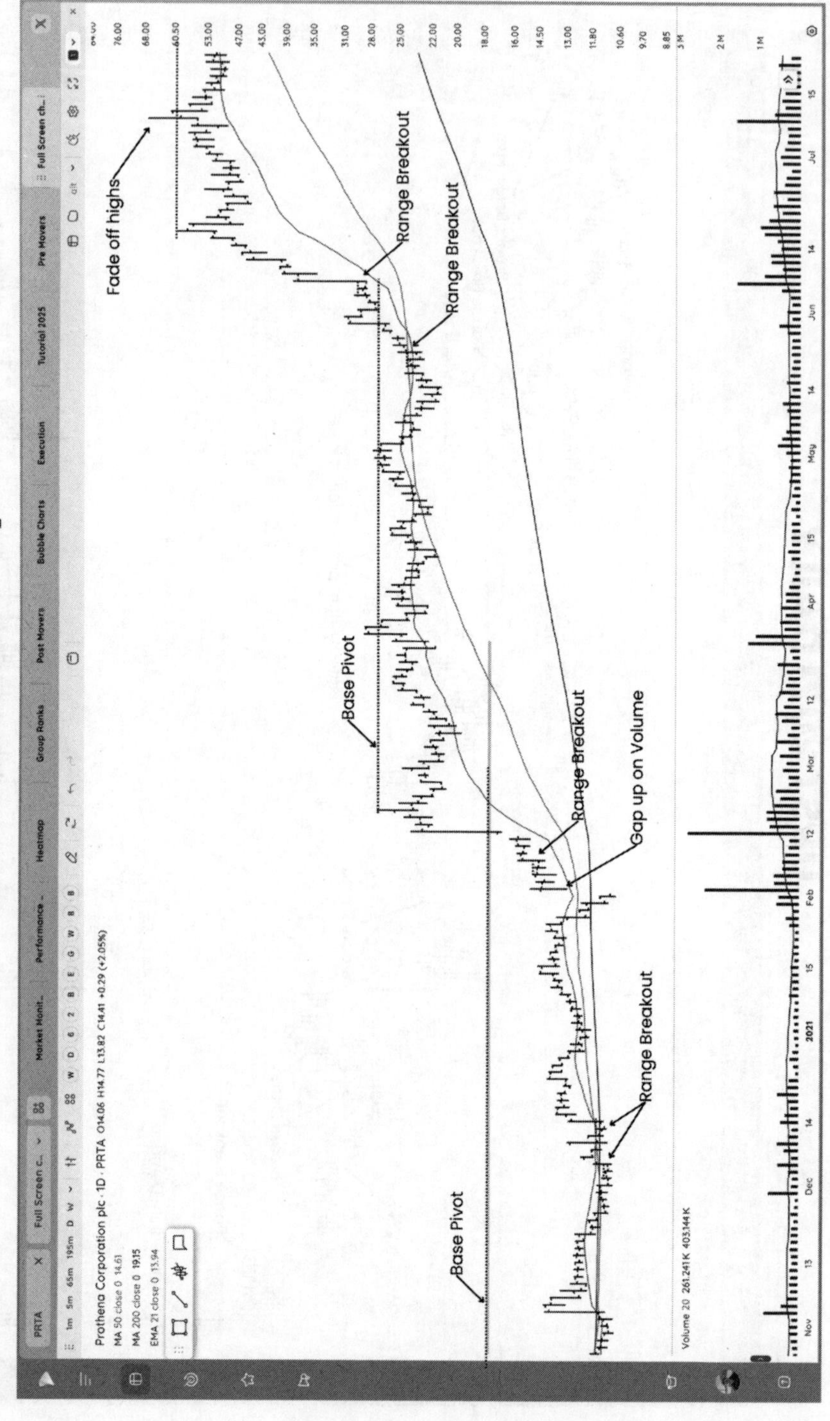
PRTA 2021 DAILY 1/2
Prothena Corporation plc · 1D · PRTA O14.06 H14.77 L13.82 C14.41 +0.29 (+2.05%)
MA 50 close 0 14.61
MA 200 close 0 19.15
EMA 21 close 0 13.94
Base Pivot
Range Breakout
Range Breakout
Gap up on Volume
Range Breakout
Base Pivot
Range Breakout
Range Breakout
Fade off highs
Volume 20 261.241K 403.144K

PRTA 2021 DAILY 2/2

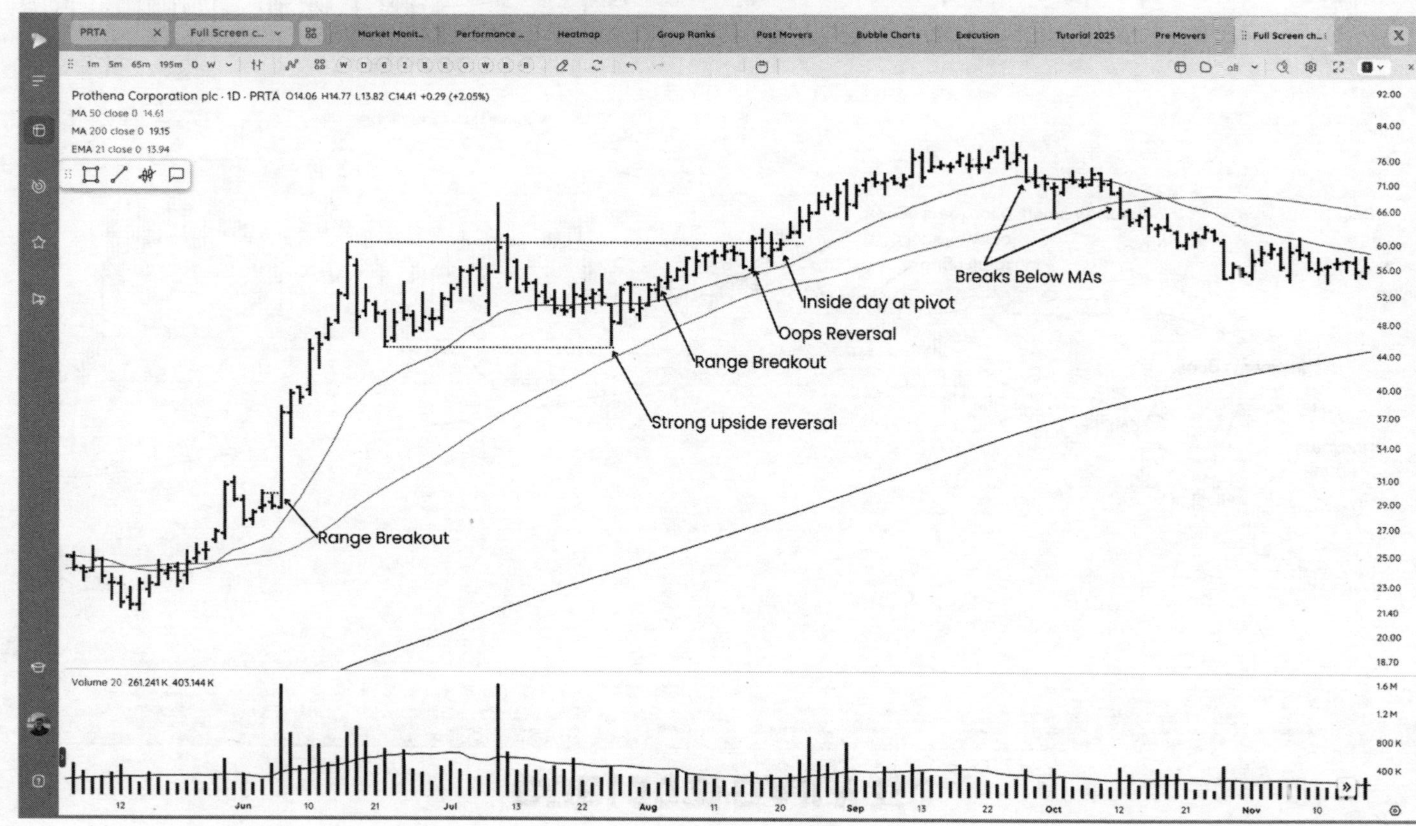

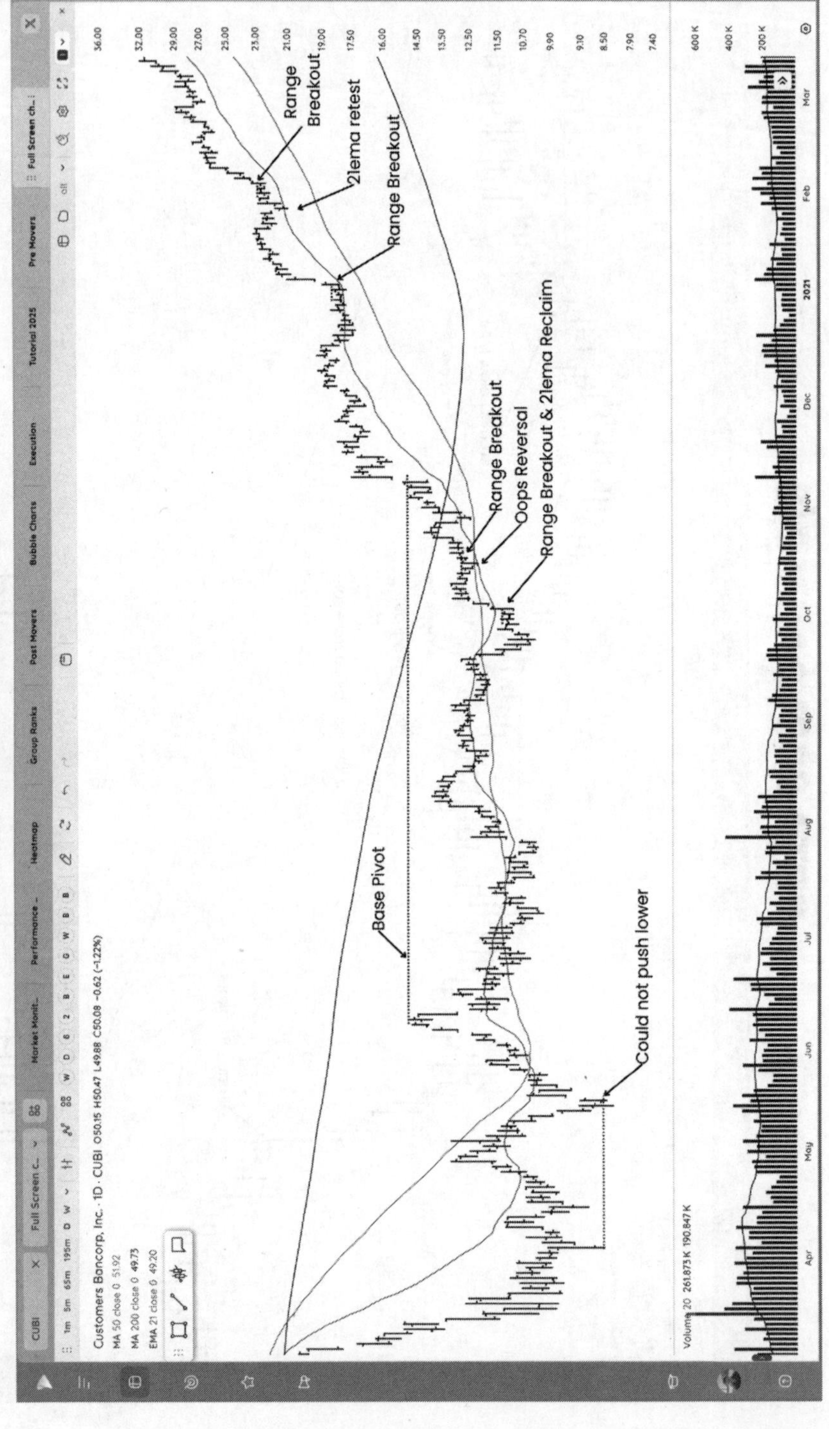
CUBI 2021 DAILY 1/2
Customers Bancorp, Inc. · 1D · CUBI O50.15 H50.47 L49.88 C50.08 −0.62 (−1.22%)
MA 50 close 0 51.92
MA 200 close 0 49.73
EMA 21 close 0 49.20
Range Breakout
21ema retest
Range Breakout
Range Breakout
Oops Reversal
Range Breakout & 21ema Reclaim
Base Pivot
Could not push lower
Volume 20 261.873 K 190.847 K
Apr
May
Jun
Jul
Aug
Sep
Oct
Nov
Dec
2021
Feb
Mar

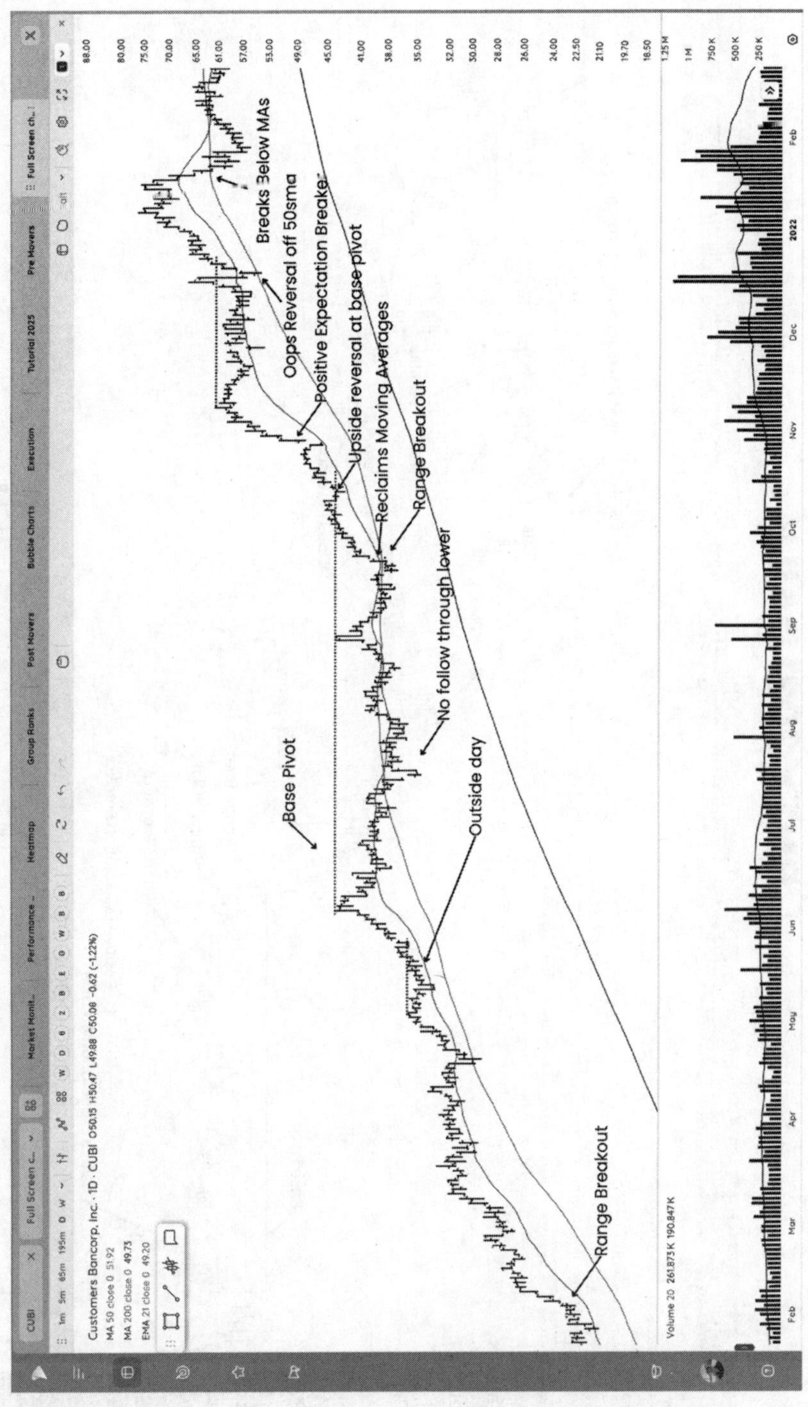
CUBI 2021 DAILY 2/2
Customers Bancorp, Inc. · 1D · CUBI
Range Breakout
Outside day
Base Pivot
No follow through lower
Range Breakout
Reclaims Moving Averages
Upside reversal at base pivot
Positive Expectation Breaker
Oops Reversal off 50sma
Breaks Below MAs

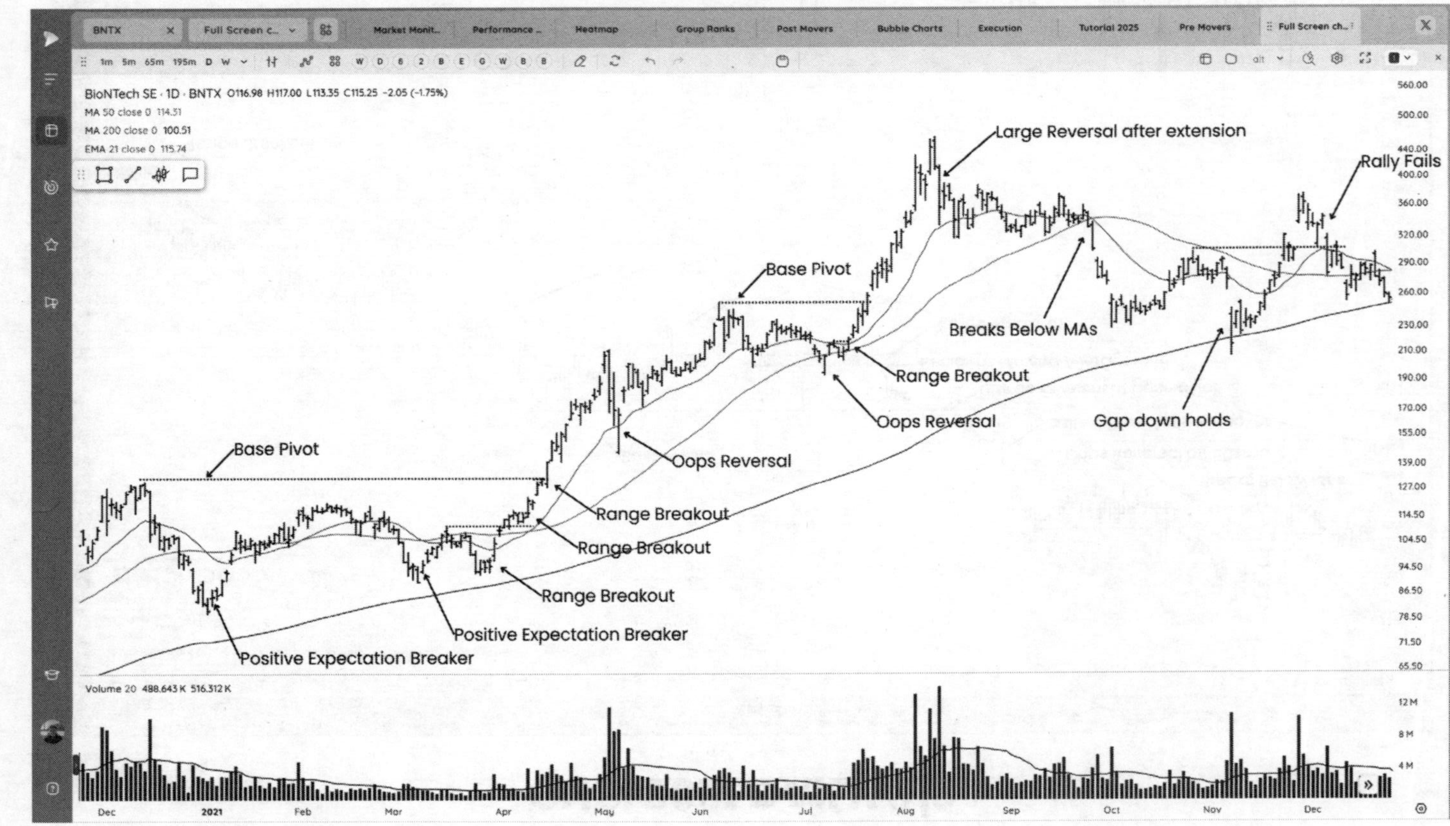

BNTX 2021 DAILY
BioNTech SE · 1D · BNTX O116.98 H117.00 L113.35 C115.25 −2.05 (−1.75%)
MA 50 close 0 114.31
MA 200 close 0 100.51
EMA 21 close 0 115.74
Base Pivot
Positive Expectation Breaker
Positive Expectation Breaker
Range Breakout
Range Breakout
Range Breakout
Oops Reversal
Base Pivot
Range Breakout
Oops Reversal
Large Reversal after extension
Breaks Below MAs
Gap down holds
Rally Fails
Volume 20 488.643 K 516.312 K

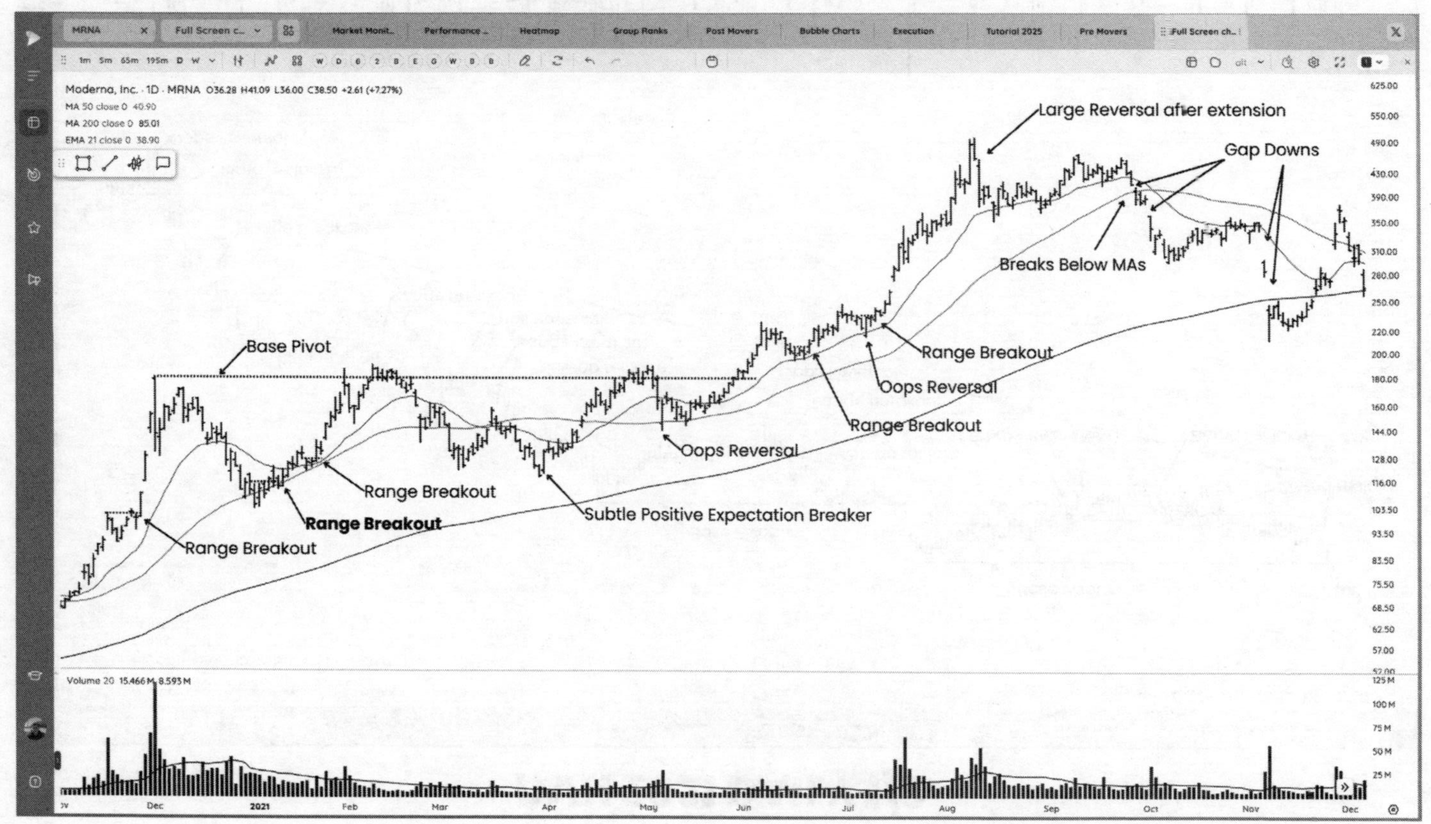
MRNA 2021 DAILY
Moderna, Inc. · 1D · MRNA O36.28 H41.09 L36.00 C38.50 +2.61 (+7.27%)
MA 50 close 0 40.90
MA 200 close 0 85.01
EMA 21 close 0 38.90
Large Reversal after extension
Gap Downs
Breaks Below MAs
Base Pivot
Range Breakout
Oops Reversal
Range Breakout
Oops Reversal
Range Breakout
Range Breakout
Subtle Positive Expectation Breaker
Range Breakout
Volume 20 15.466 M 8.593 M

DVN 2021 DAILY 1/2

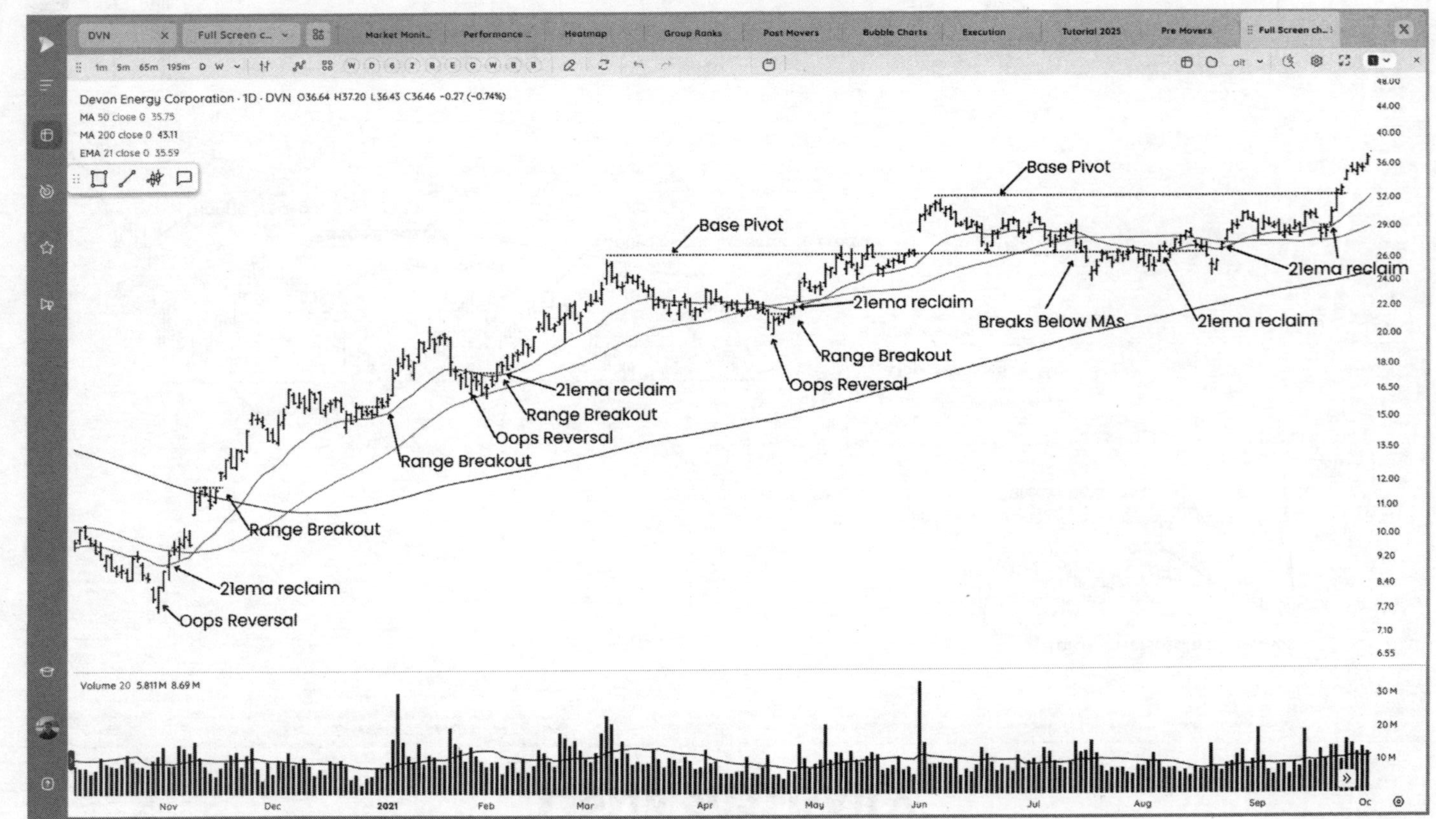

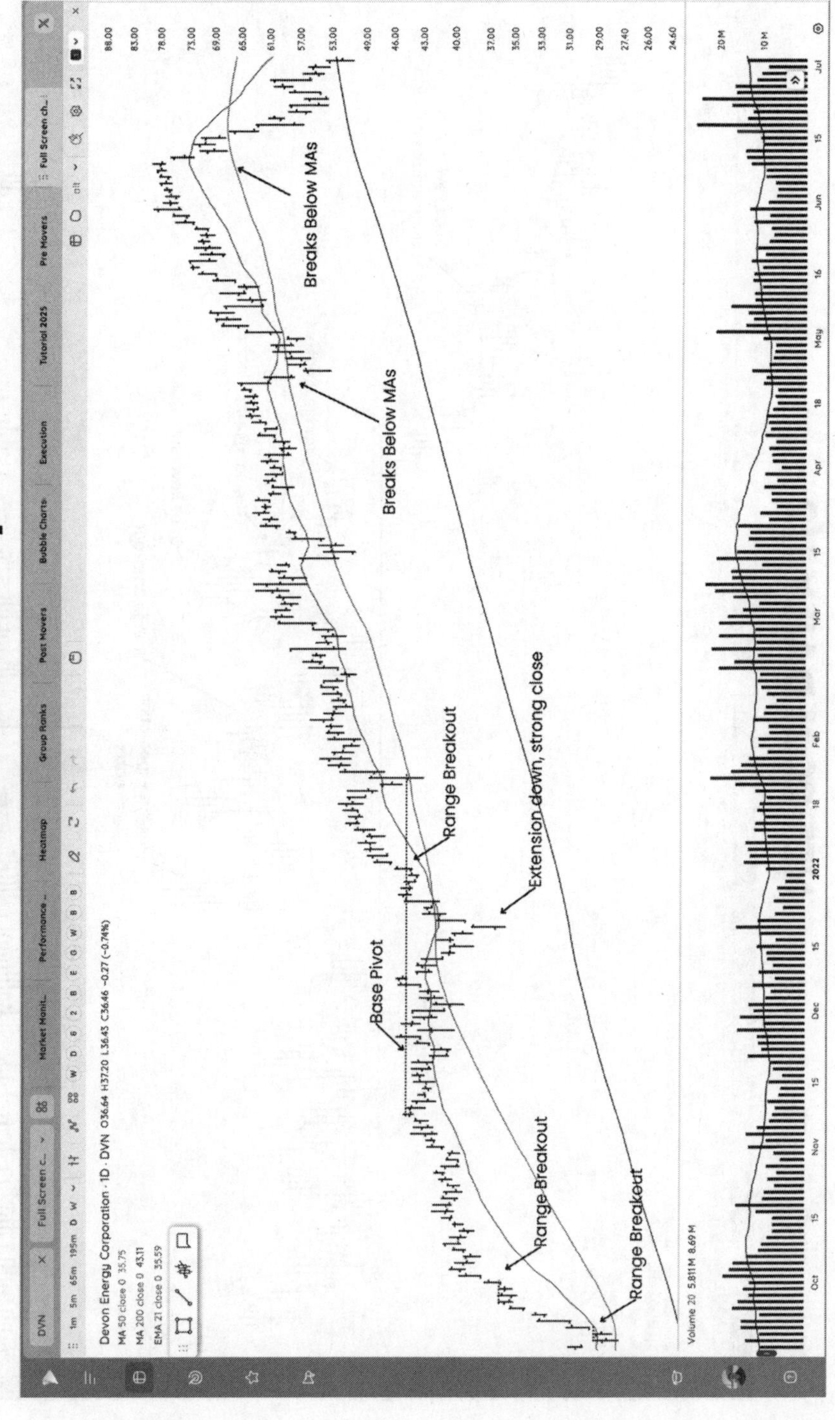
DVN 2021 DAILY 2/2
Devon Energy Corporation · 1D · DVN O36.64 H37.20 L36.43 C36.46 −0.27 (−0.74%)
MA 50 close 0 35.75
MA 200 close 0 43.11
EMA 21 close 0 35.59
Range Breakout
Range Breakout
Base Pivot
Range Breakout
Extension down, strong close
Breaks Below MAs
Breaks Below MAs
Volume 20 5.811 M 8.69 M

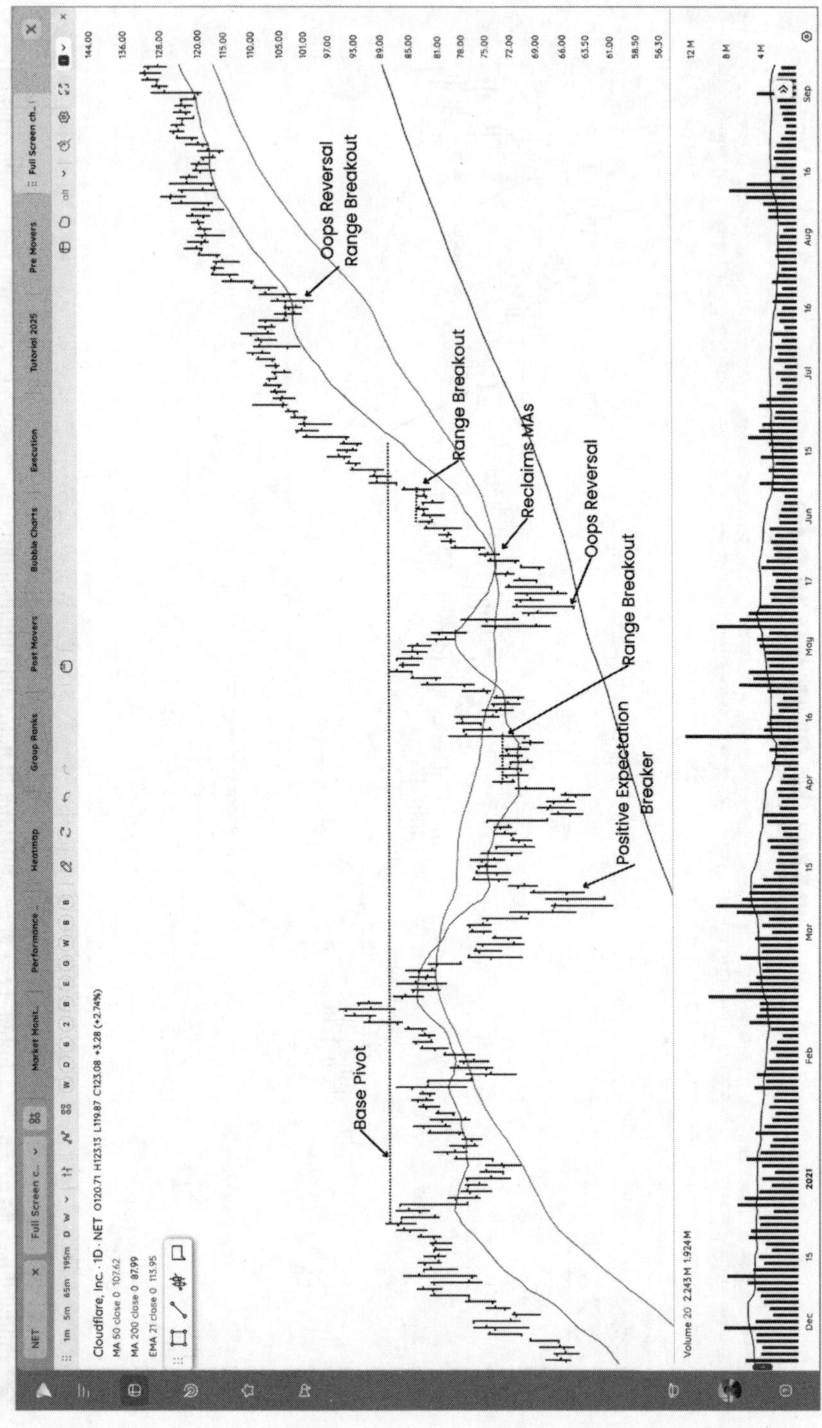
NET 2021 DAILY 1/2
Cloudflare, Inc. · 1D · NET O120.71 H123.13 L119.87 C123.08 +3.28 (+2.74%)
MA 50 close 0 107.62
MA 200 close 0 87.99
EMA 21 close 0 113.95
Base Pivot
Positive Expectation Breaker
Range Breakout
Oops Reversal
Reclaims MAs
Range Breakout
Oops Reversal
Range Breakout
Volume 20 2.243 M 1.924 M

NET 2021 DAILY 2/2

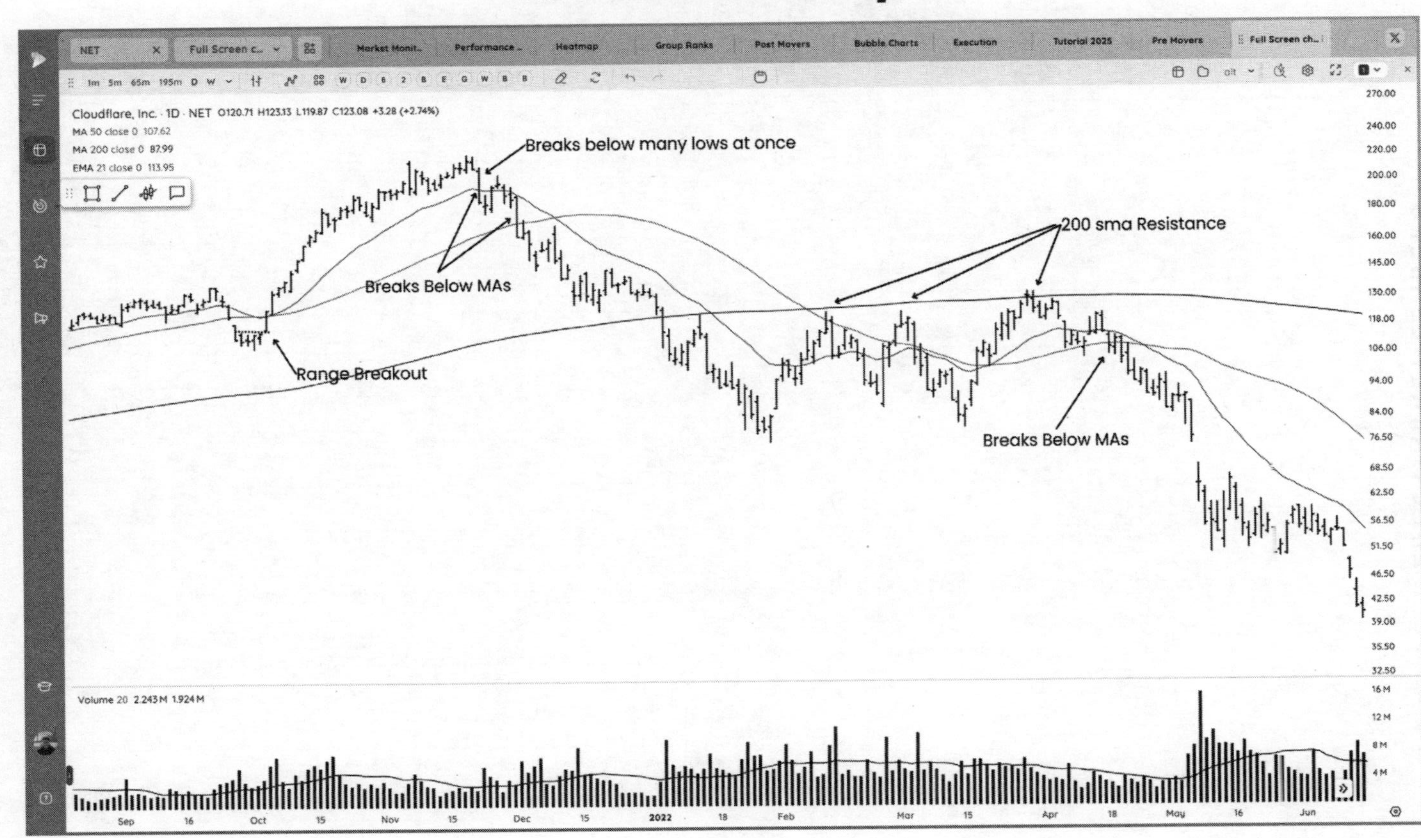

2022 MARKET LEADERS

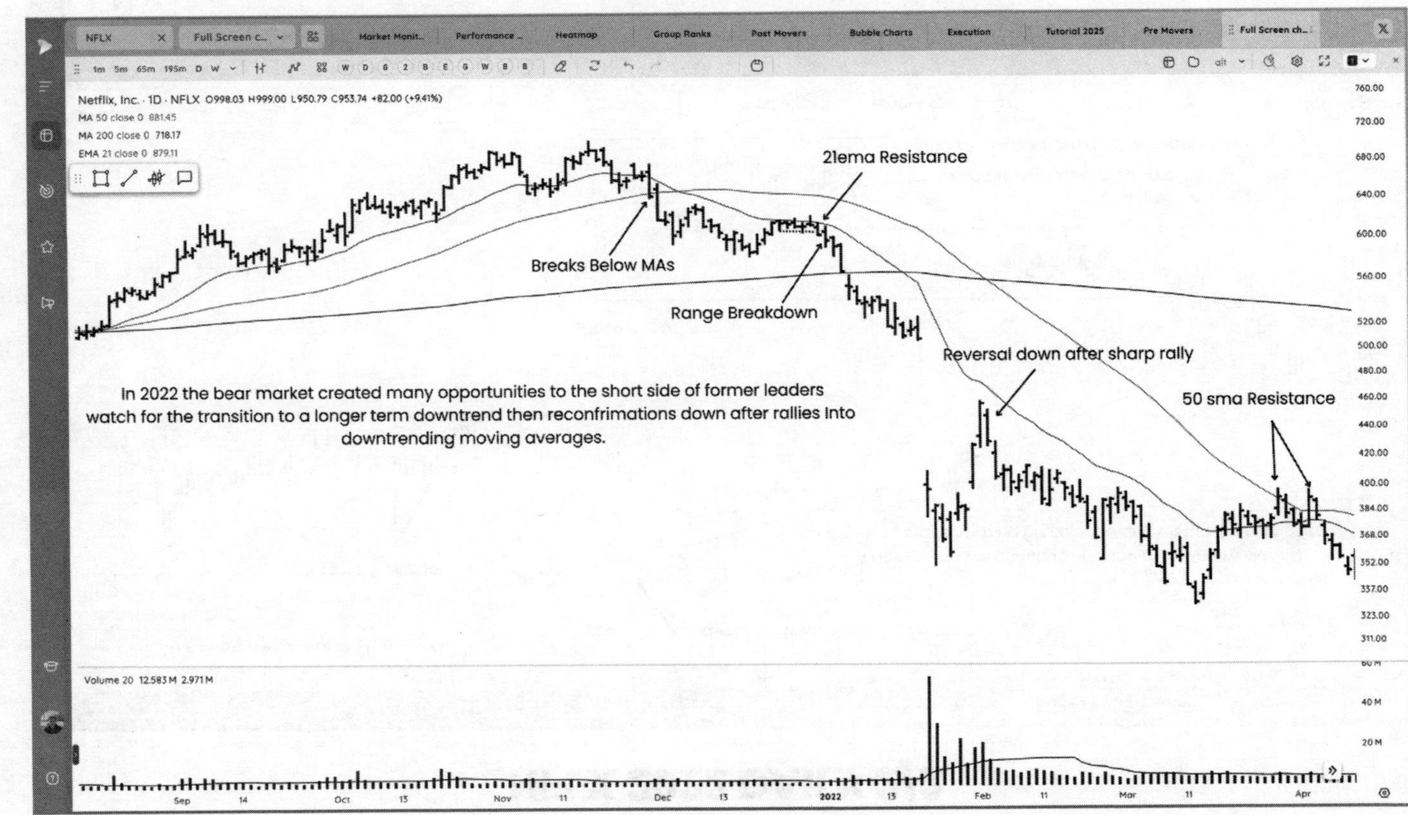
NFLX 2022 DAILY 1/2
Netflix, Inc. · 1D · NFLX O998.03 H999.00 L950.79 C953.74 +82.00 (+9.41%)
MA 50 close 0 881.45
MA 200 close 0 718.17
EMA 21 close 0 879.11
21ema Resistance
Breaks Below MAs
Range Breakdown
Reversal down after sharp rally
50 sma Resistance
In 2022 the bear market created many opportunities to the short side of former leaders
watch for the transition to a longer term downtrend then reconfrimations down after rallies Into
downtrending moving averages.
Volume 20 12.583 M 2.971 M

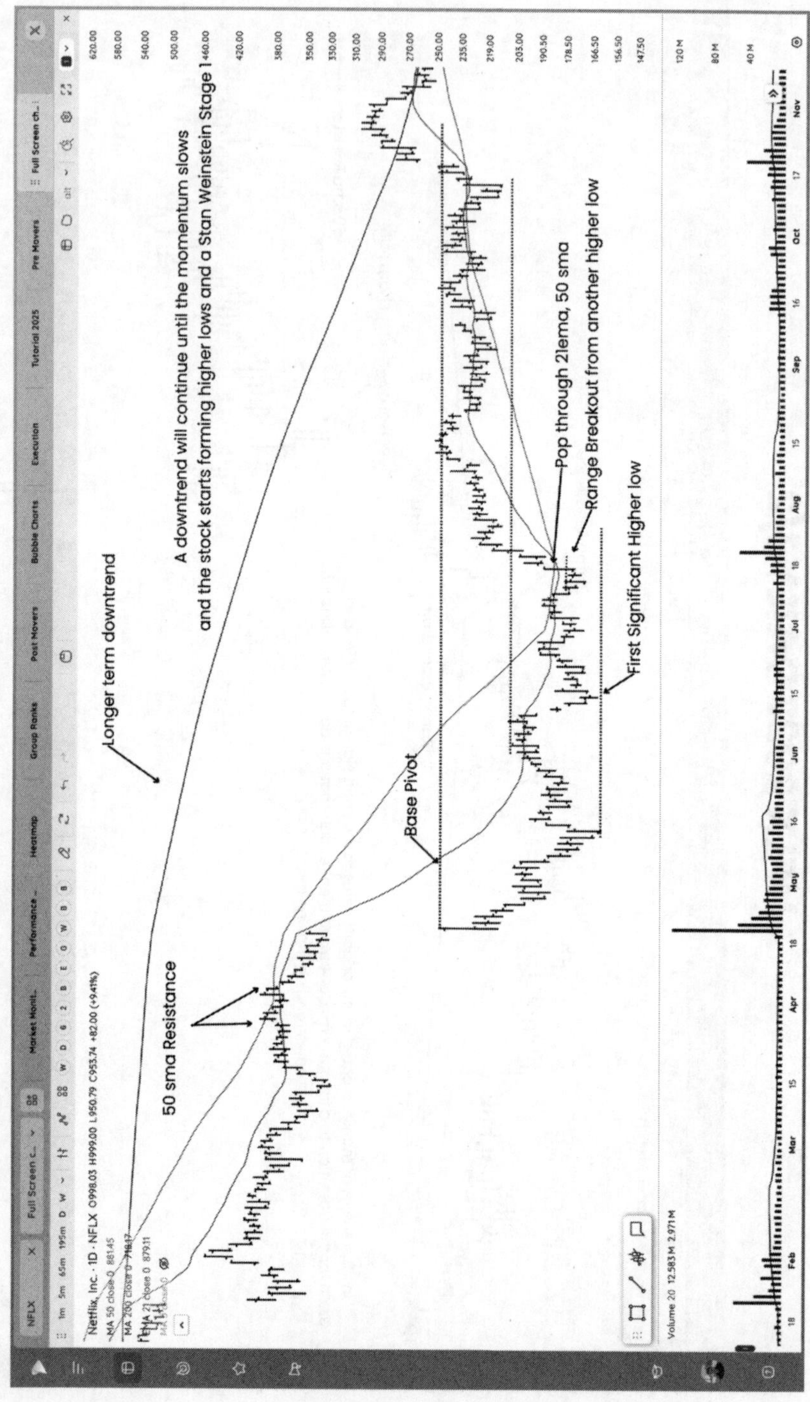
NFLX 2022 DAILY 2/2
Longer term downtrend
A downtrend will continue until the momentum slows
and the stock starts forming higher lows and a Stan Weinstein Stage 1
50 sma Resistance
Base Pivot
Pop through 21ema, 50 sma
Range Breakout from another higher low
First Significant Higher low

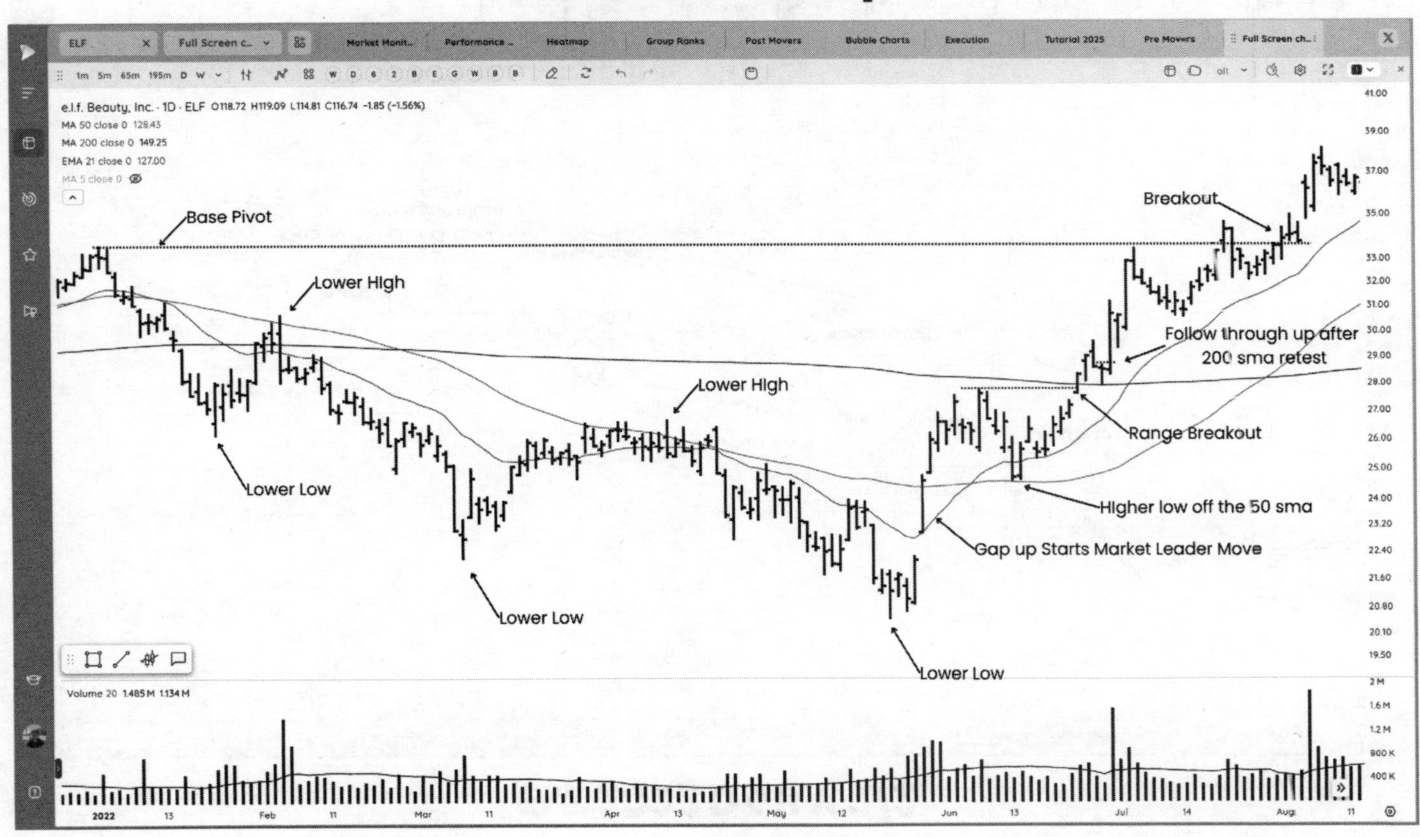
ELF 2022 DAILY 1/2
e.l.f. Beauty, Inc. · 1D · ELF O118.72 H119.09 L114.81 C116.74 −1.85 (−1.56%)
MA 50 close 0 128.43
MA 200 close 0 149.25
EMA 21 close 0 127.00
MA 5 close 0
Base Pivot
Lower High
Lower Low
Lower Low
Lower High
Lower Low
Gap up Starts Market Leader Move
Higher low off the 50 sma
Range Breakout
Follow through up after 200 sma retest
Breakout
Volume 20 1.485 M 1.134 M

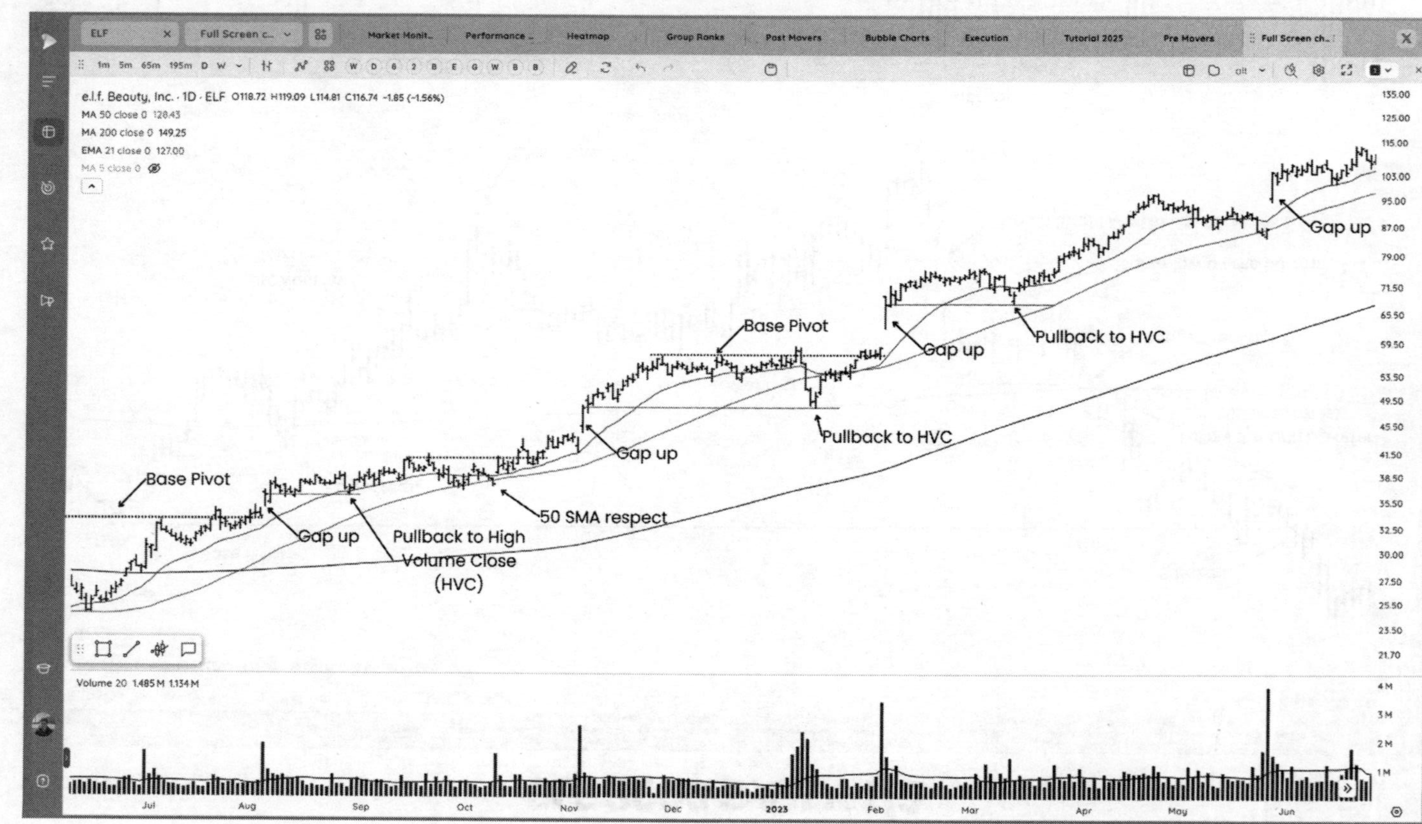
ELF 2022 DAILY 2/2
e.l.f. Beauty, Inc. · 1D · ELF O118.72 H119.09 L114.81 C116.74 -1.85 (-1.56%)
MA 50 close 0 128.43
MA 200 close 0 149.25
EMA 21 close 0 127.00
Base Pivot
Gap up
Pullback to High Volume Close (HVC)
50 SMA respect
Gap up
Base Pivot
Pullback to HVC
Gap up
Pullback to HVC
Gap up
Volume 20 1.485 M 1.134 M
Jul
Aug
Sep
Oct
Nov
Dec
2023
Feb
Mar
Apr
May
Jun

STNG 2022 DAILY 1/2

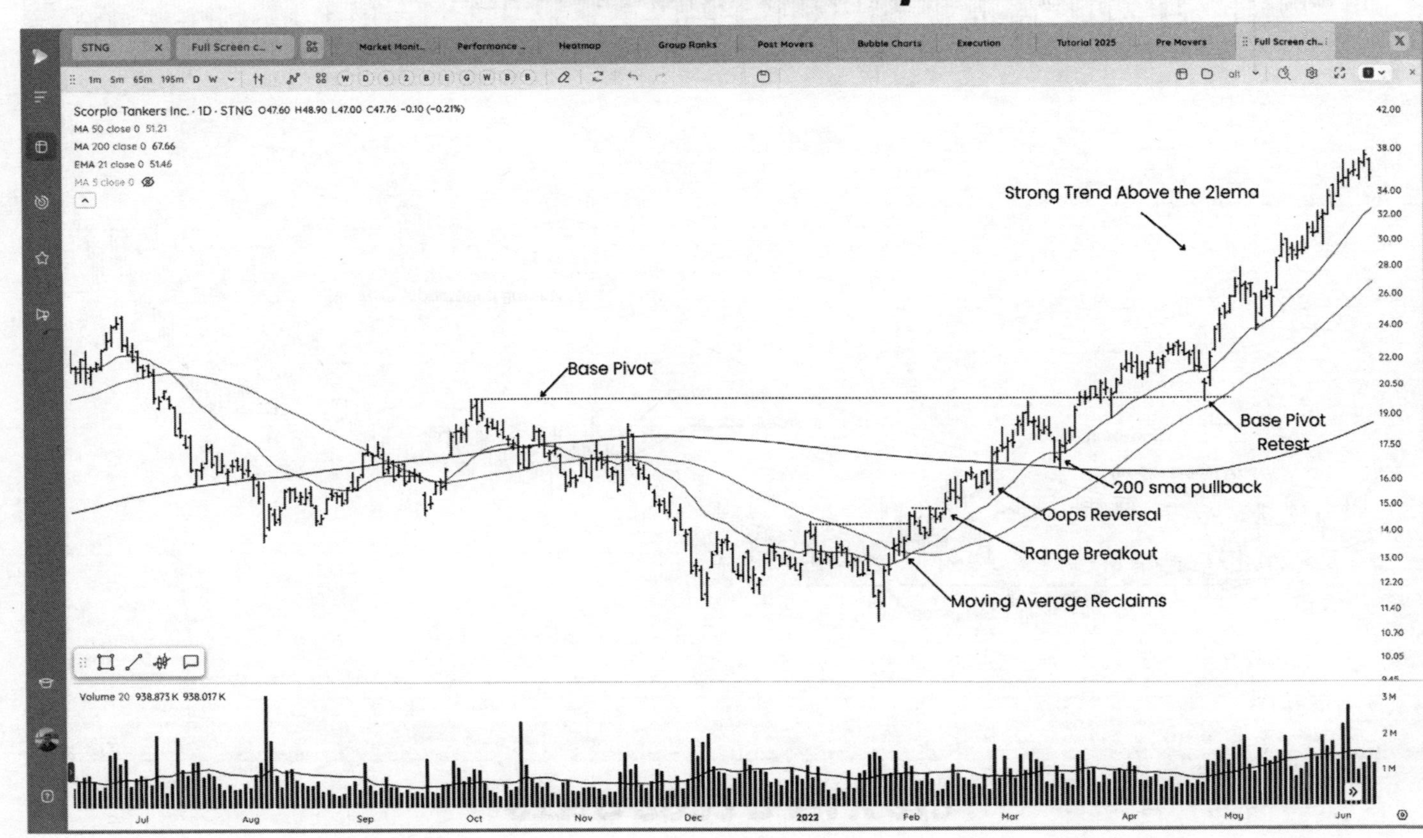

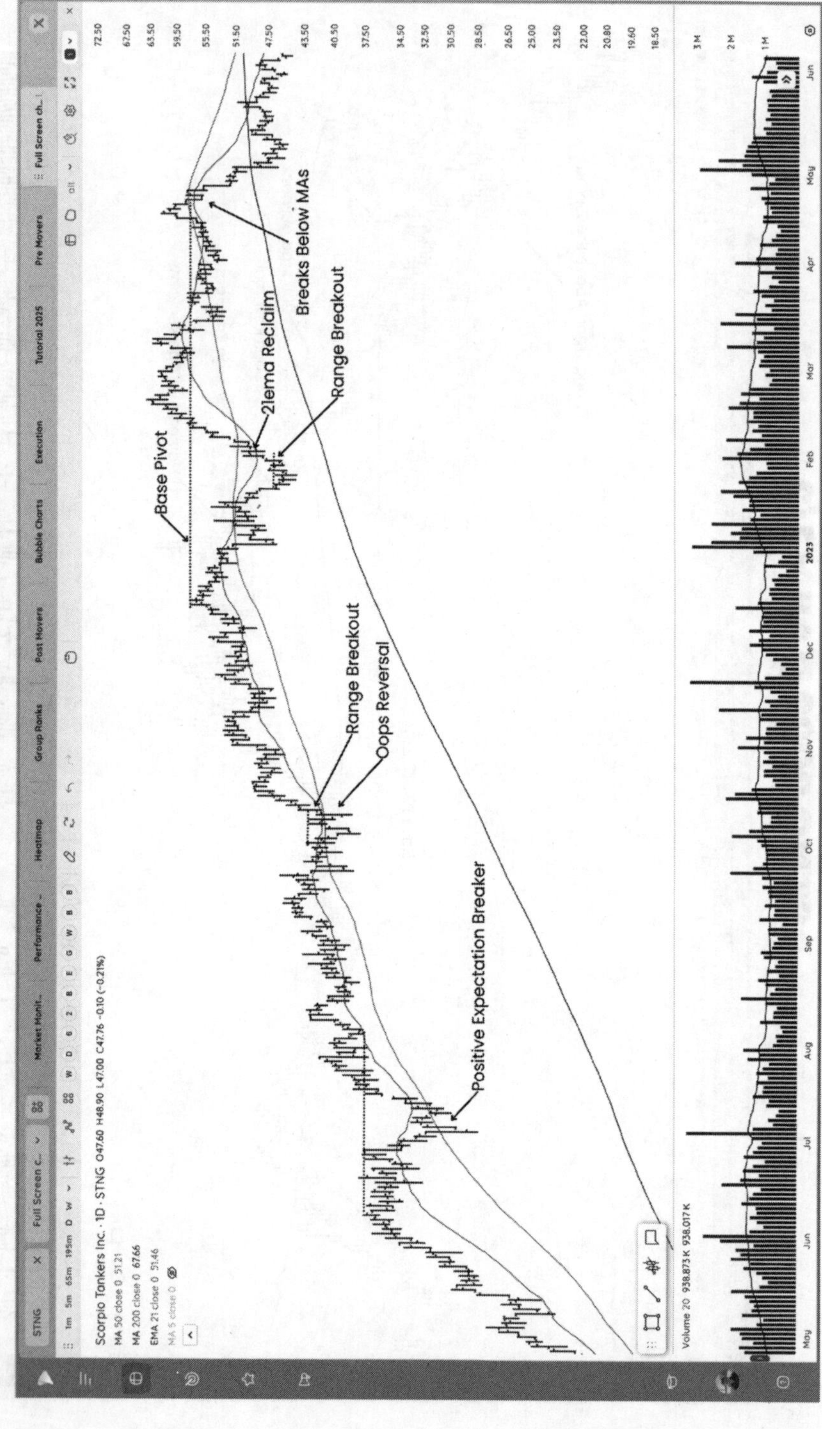
STNG 2022 DAILY 2/2
Scorpio Tankers Inc. · 1D · STNG O47.60 H48.90 L47.00 C47.76 −0.10 (−0.21%)
MA 50 close 0 51.21
MA 200 close 0 67.66
EMA 21 close 0 51.46
Base Pivot
21ema Reclaim
Range Breakout
Breaks Below MAs
Range Breakout
Oops Reversal
Positive Expectation Breaker

TMDX 2022 DAILY 1/2

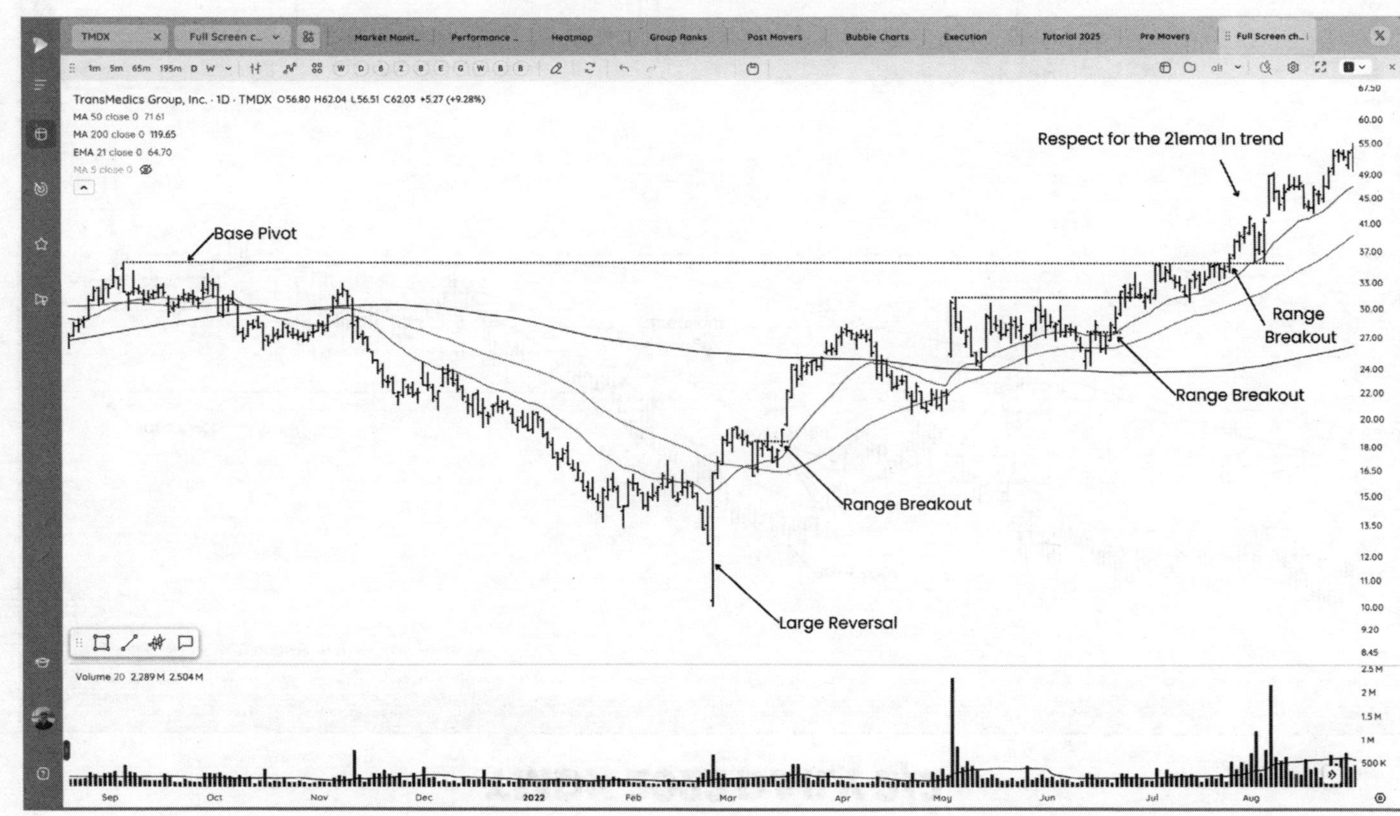

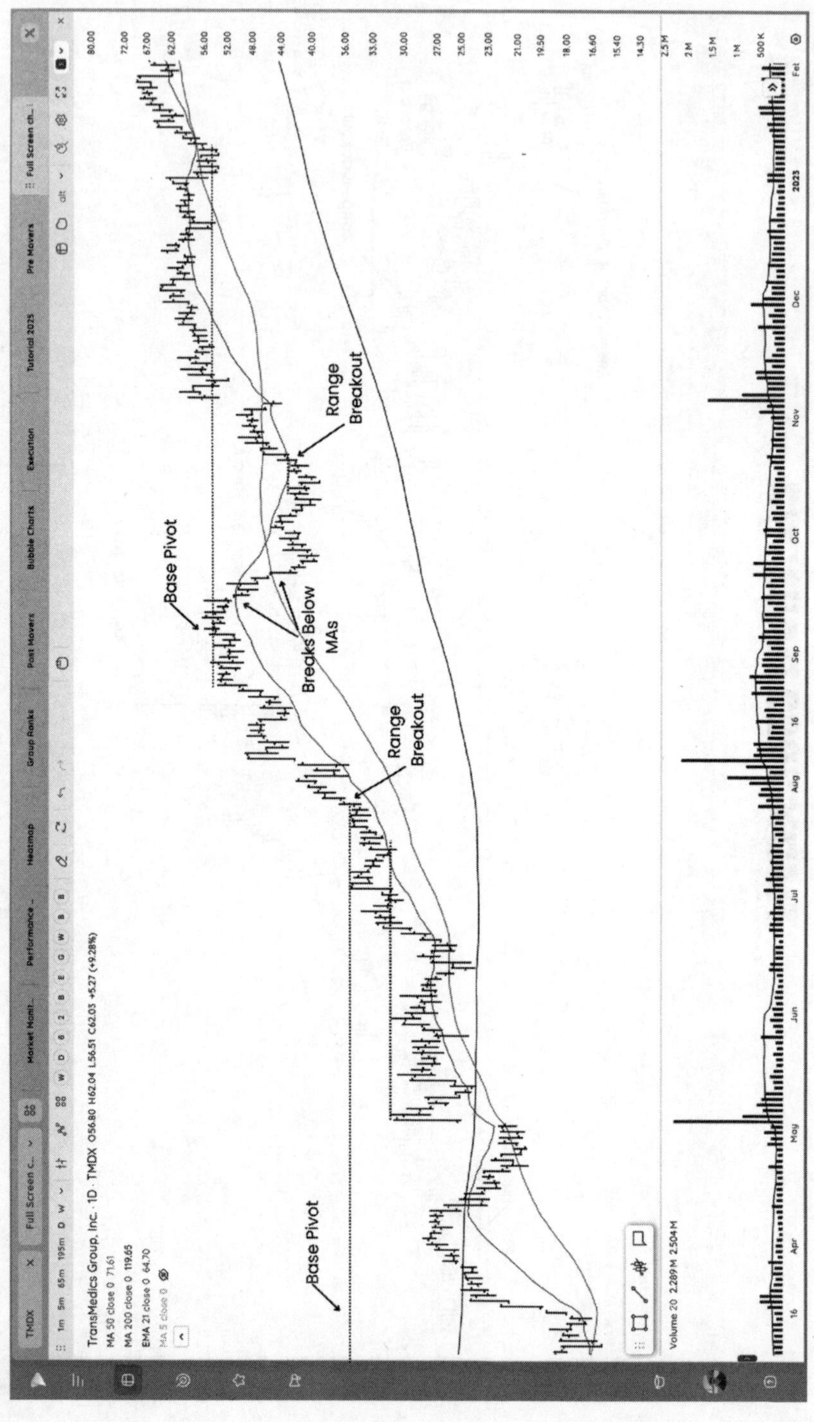
TMDX 2022 DAILY 2/2
TransMedics Group, Inc. · 1D · TMDX O56.80 H62.04 L56.51 C62.03 +5.27 (+9.28%)
MA 50 close 0 71.61
MA 200 close 0 119.65
EMA 21 close 0 64.70
MA 5 close 0
Base Pivot
Range Breakout
Base Pivot
Breaks Below MAs
Range Breakout
Volume 20 2.289 M 2.504 M

AMR 2022 DAILY 1/2

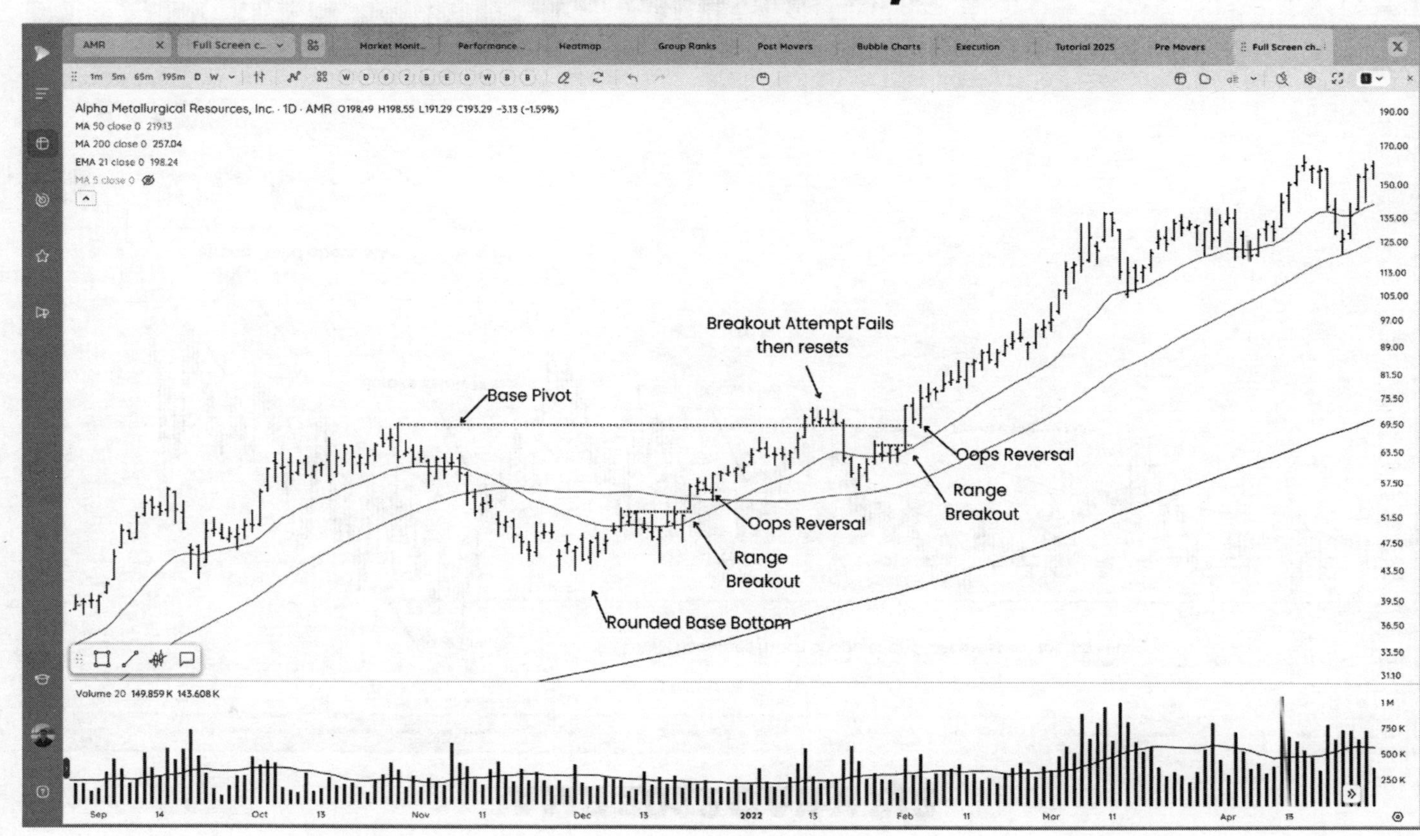

AMR 2022 DAILY 2/2

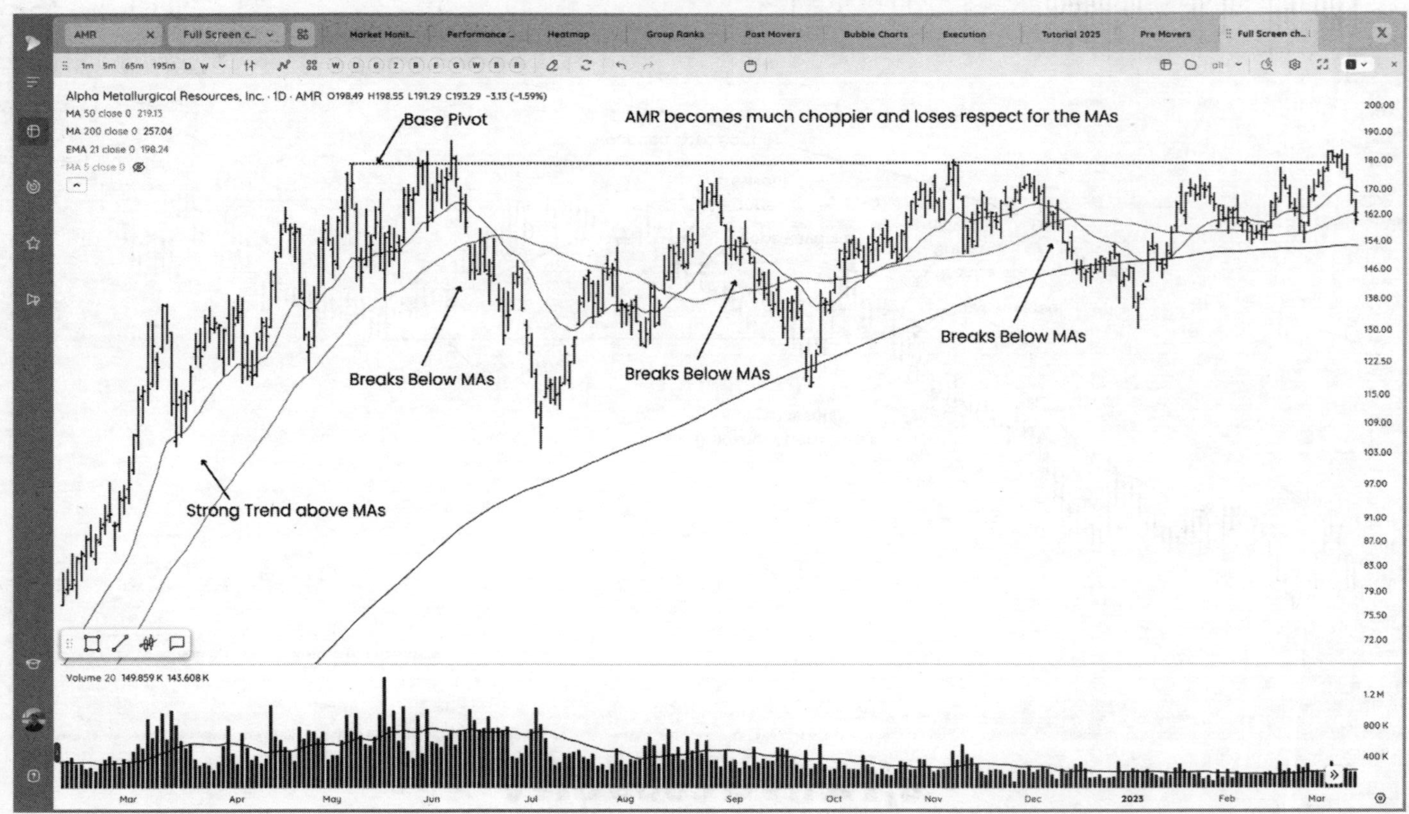

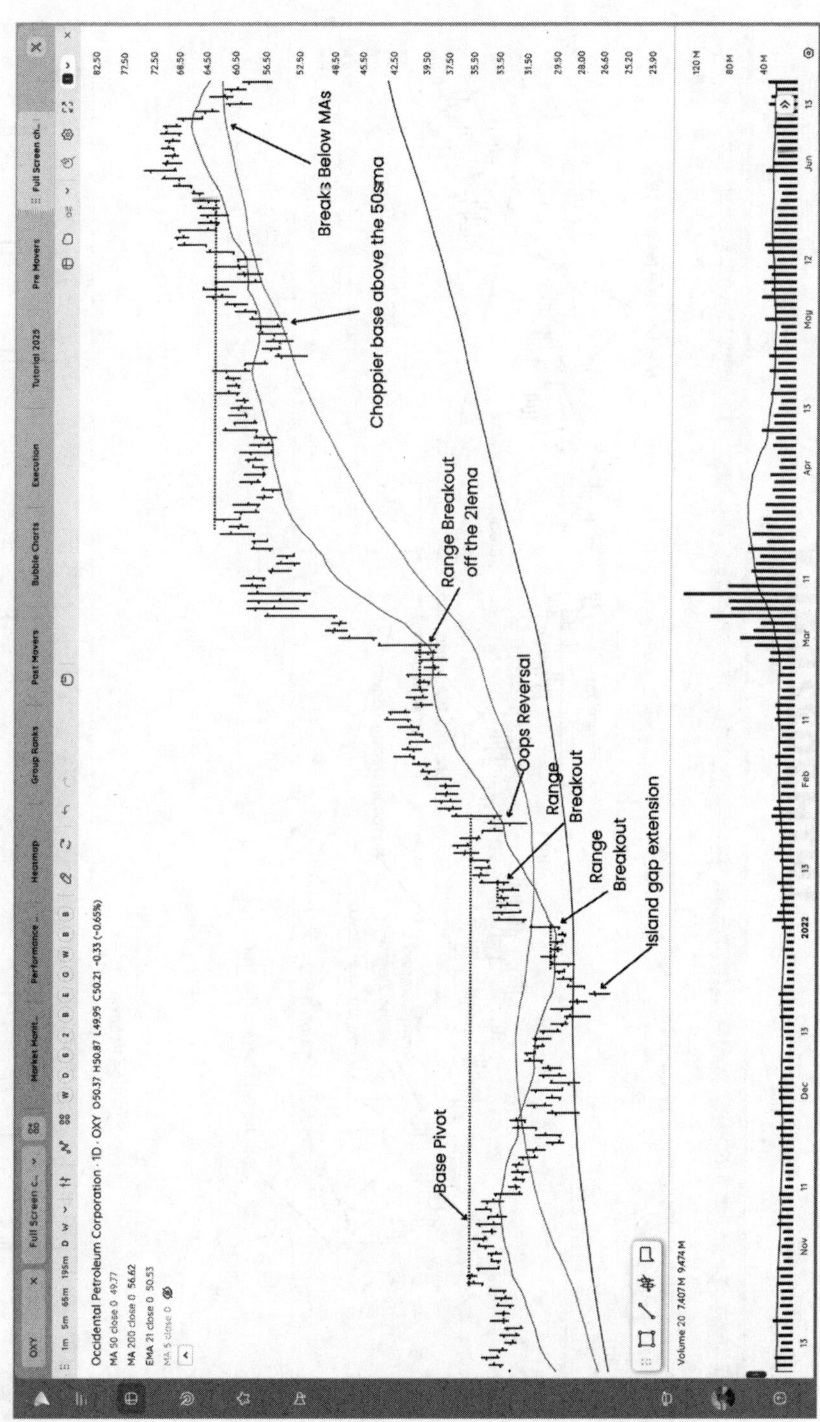
OXY 2022 DAILY
Occidental Petroleum Corporation · 1D · OXY O50.37 H50.87 L49.95 C50.21 −0.33 (−0.65%)
MA 50 close 0 49.77
MA 200 close 0 56.62
EMA 21 close 0 50.53
Base Pivot
Island gap extension
Range Breakout
Range Breakout
Oops Reversal
Range Breakout off the 21ema
Choppier base above the 50sma
Breaks Below MAs
Volume 20 7.407M 9.474M

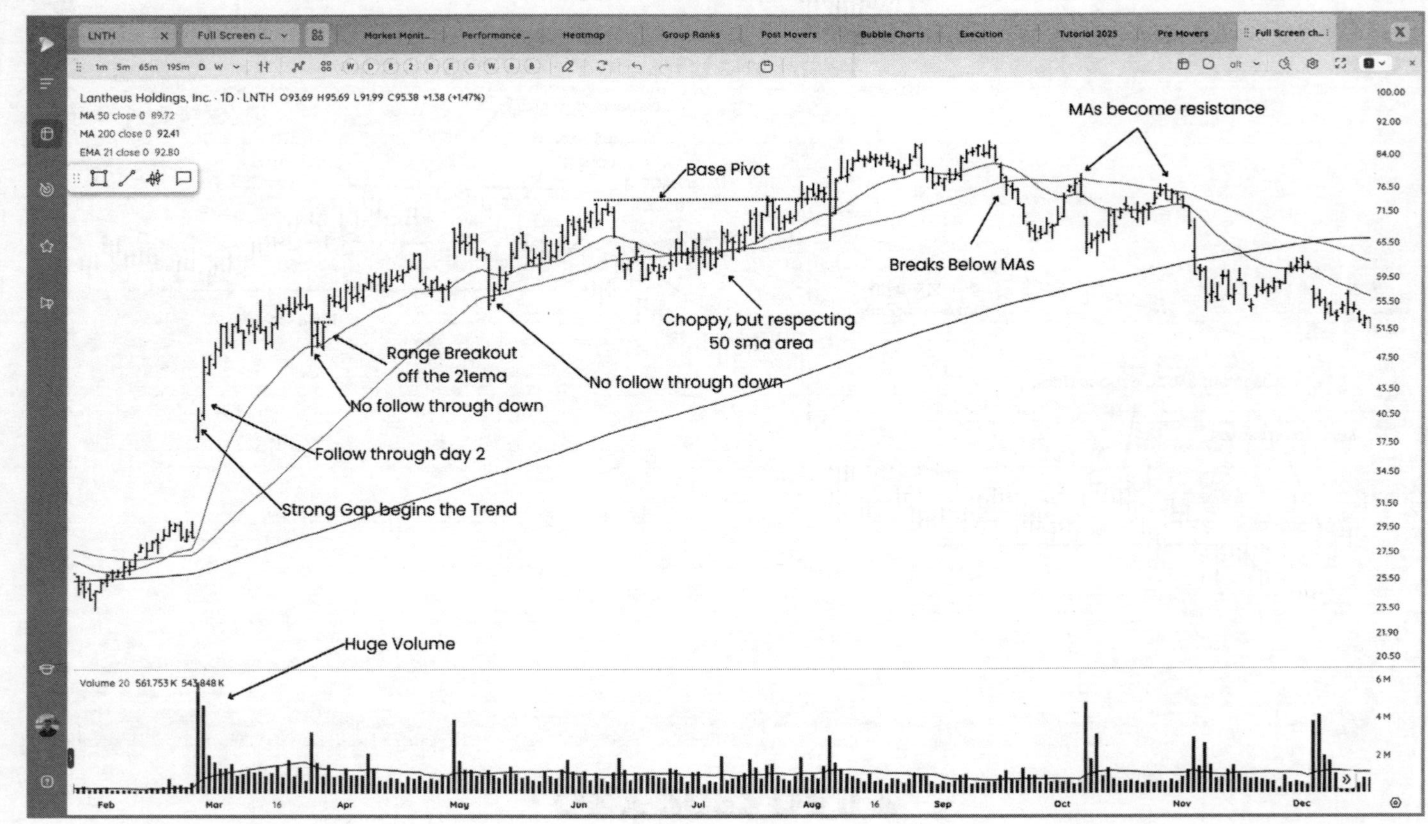

LNTH 2022 DAILY
Lantheus Holdings, Inc. · 1D · LNTH O93.69 H95.69 L91.99 C95.38 +1.38 (+1.47%)
MA 50 close 0 89.72
MA 200 close 0 92.41
EMA 21 close 0 92.80
Base Pivot
MAs become resistance
Breaks Below MAs
Choppy, but respecting 50 sma area
Range Breakout off the 21ema
No follow through down
No follow through down
Follow through day 2
Strong Gap begins the Trend
Huge Volume
Volume 20 561.753 K 543.848 K
Feb
Mar
16
Apr
May
Jun
Jul
Aug
16
Sep
Oct
Nov
Dec

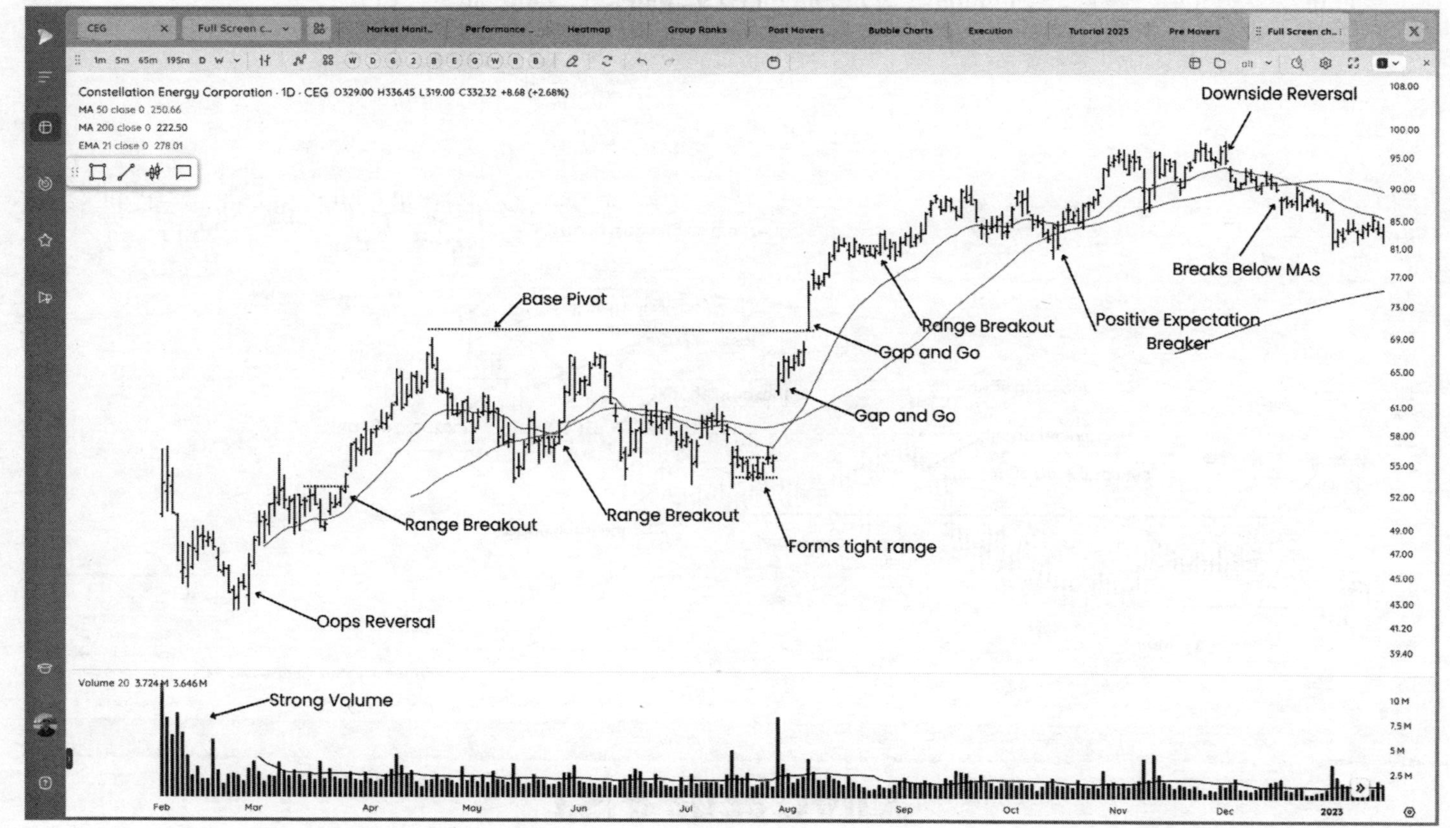
CEG 2022 DAILY
Constellation Energy Corporation · 1D · CEG O329.00 H336.45 L319.00 C332.32 +8.68 (+2.68%)
MA 50 close 0 250.66
MA 200 close 0 222.50
EMA 21 close 0 278.01
Downside Reversal
Breaks Below MAs
Positive Expectation Breaker
Range Breakout
Gap and Go
Gap and Go
Base Pivot
Forms tight range
Range Breakout
Range Breakout
Oops Reversal
Volume 20 3.724M 3.646M
Strong Volume

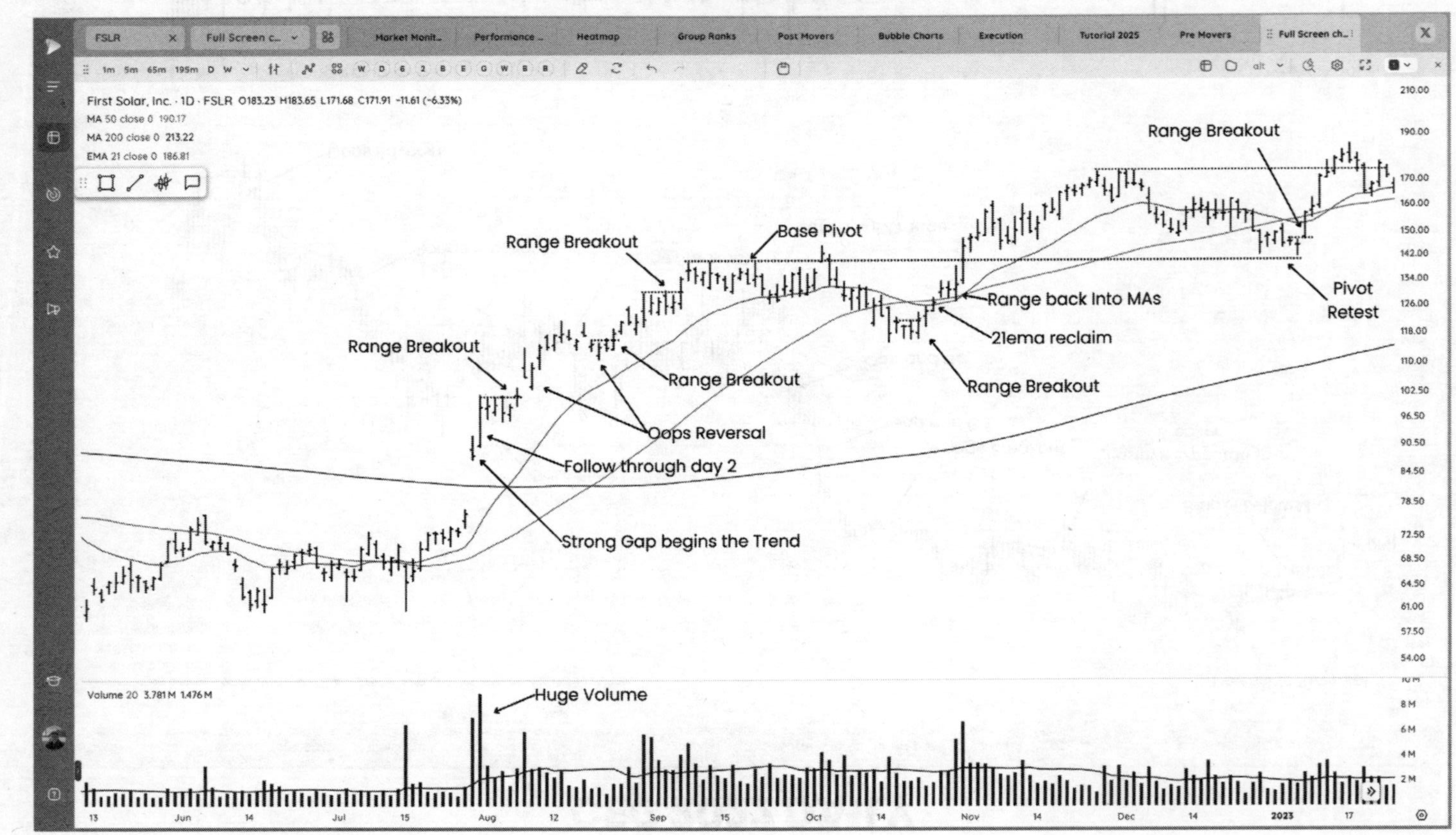
FSLR 2022 DAILY
First Solar, Inc. · 1D · FSLR O183.23 H183.65 L171.68 C171.91 -11.61 (-6.33%)
MA 50 close 0 190.17
MA 200 close 0 213.22
EMA 21 close 0 186.81
Range Breakout
Base Pivot
Range Breakout
Range Breakout
Pivot
Retest
Range back into MAs
21ema reclaim
Range Breakout
Range Breakout
Oops Reversal
Follow through day 2
Strong Gap begins the Trend
Volume 20 3.781M 1.476M
Huge Volume

2023 MARKET LEADERS

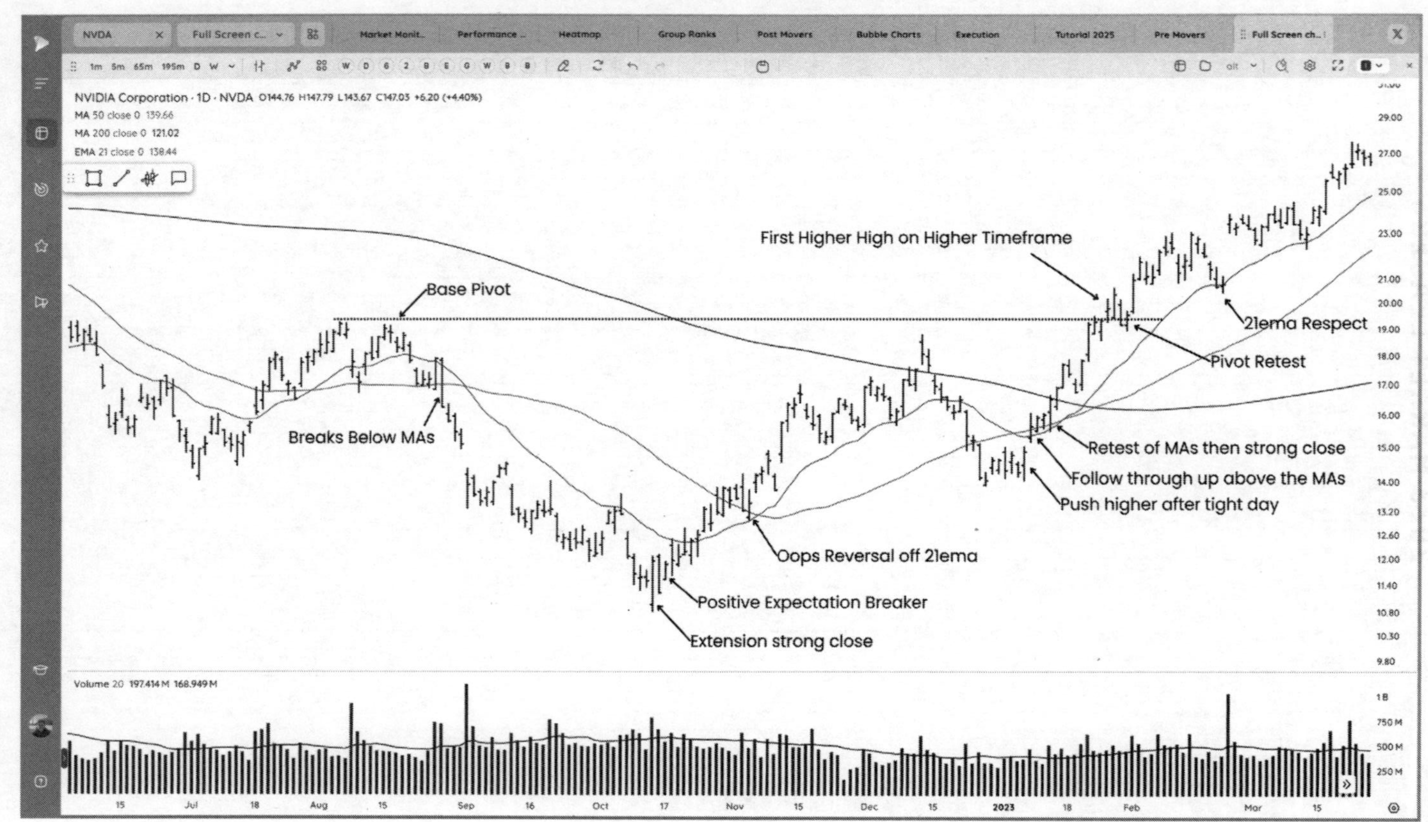
NVDA 2023 DAILY 1/2
NVIDIA Corporation · 1D · NVDA O144.76 H147.79 L143.67 C147.03 +6.20 (+4.40%)
MA 50 close 0 139.66
MA 200 close 0 121.02
EMA 21 close 0 138.44
Base Pivot
Breaks Below MAs
First Higher High on Higher Timeframe
21ema Respect
Pivot Retest
Retest of MAs then strong close
Follow through up above the MAs
Push higher after tight day
Oops Reversal off 21ema
Positive Expectation Breaker
Extension strong close
Volume 20 197.414 M 168.949 M

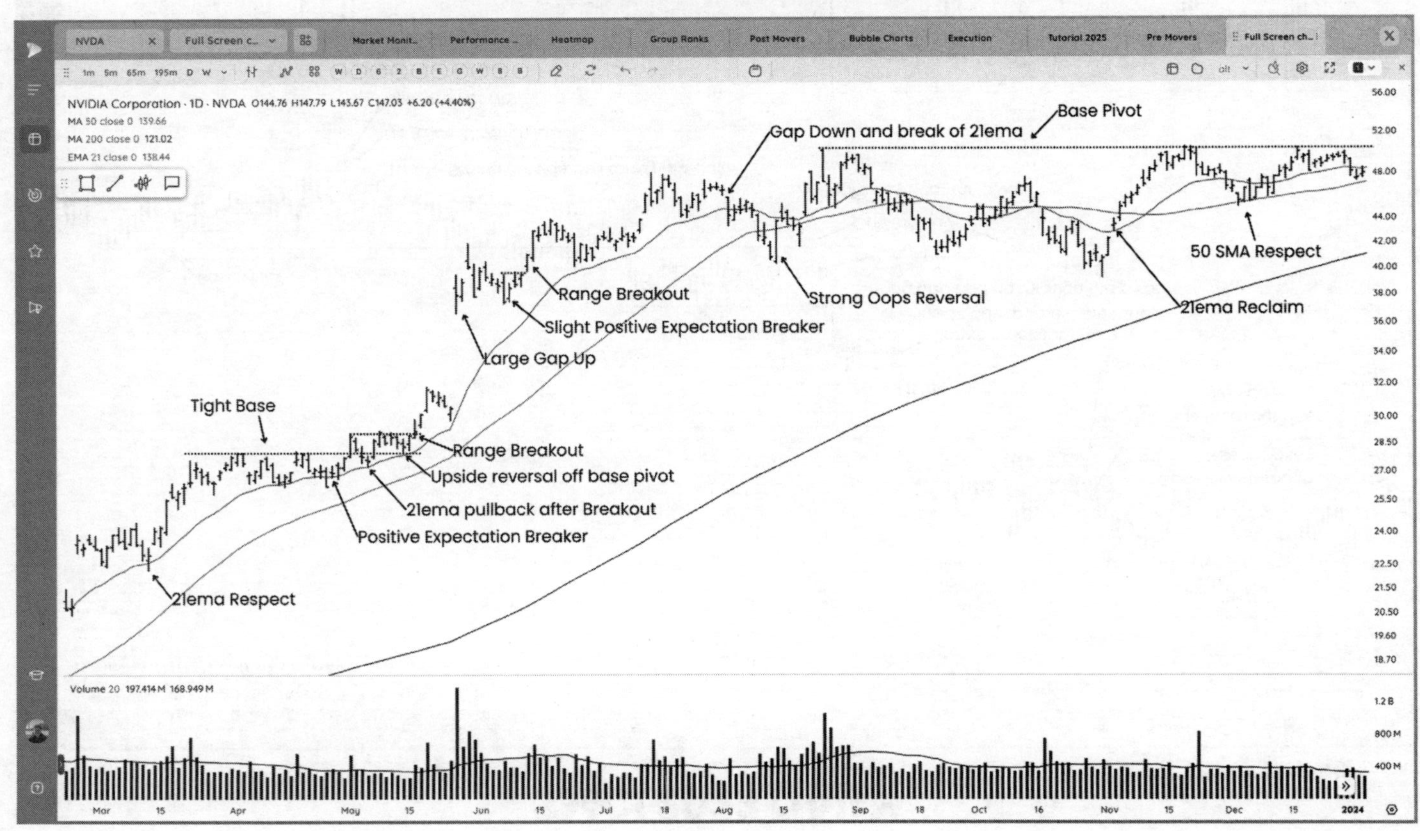
NVDA 2023 DAILY 2/2
NVIDIA Corporation · 1D · NVDA O144.76 H147.79 L143.67 C147.03 +6.20 (+4.40%)
MA 50 close 0 139.66
MA 200 close 0 121.02
EMA 21 close 0 138.44
Tight Base
21ema Respect
Range Breakout
Upside reversal off base pivot
21ema pullback after Breakout
Positive Expectation Breaker
Large Gap Up
Slight Positive Expectation Breaker
Range Breakout
Gap Down and break of 21ema
Strong Oops Reversal
Base Pivot
21ema Reclaim
50 SMA Respect
Volume 20 197.414 M 168.949 M
Mar
15
Apr
May
15
Jun
15
Jul
18
Aug
15
Sep
18
Oct
16
Nov
15
Dec
15
2024

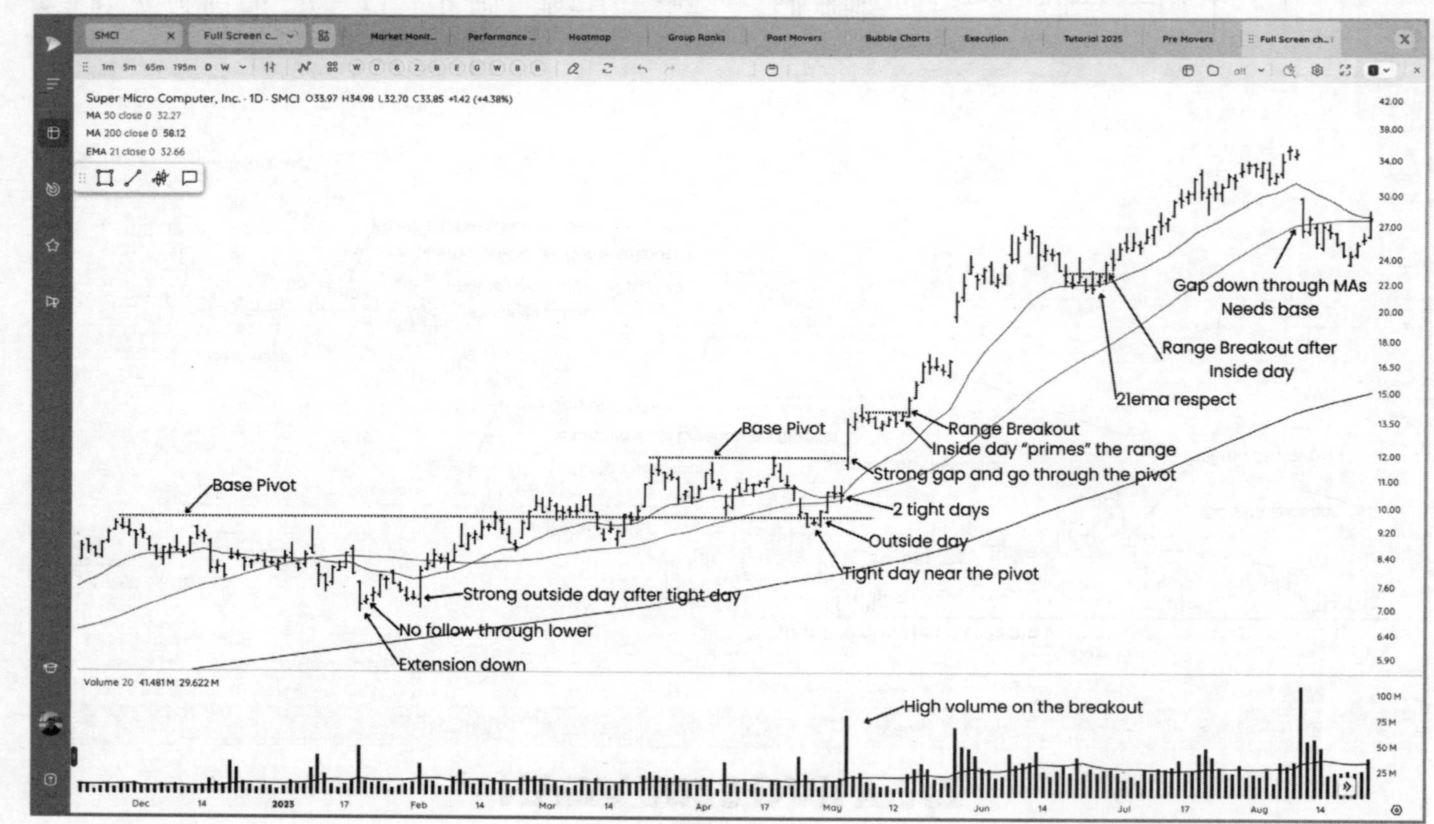
SMCI 2023 DAILY
Super Micro Computer, Inc. · 1D · SMCI O33.97 H34.98 L32.70 C33.85 +1.42 (+4.38%)
MA 50 close 0 32.27
MA 200 close 0 58.12
EMA 21 close 0 32.66
Base Pivot
Strong outside day after tight day
No follow through lower
Extension down
Base Pivot
Range Breakout
Inside day "primes" the range
Strong gap and go through the pivot
2 tight days
Outside day
Tight day near the pivot
High volume on the breakout
Range Breakout after Inside day
21ema respect
Gap down through MAs
Needs base
Volume 20 41.481M 29.622M

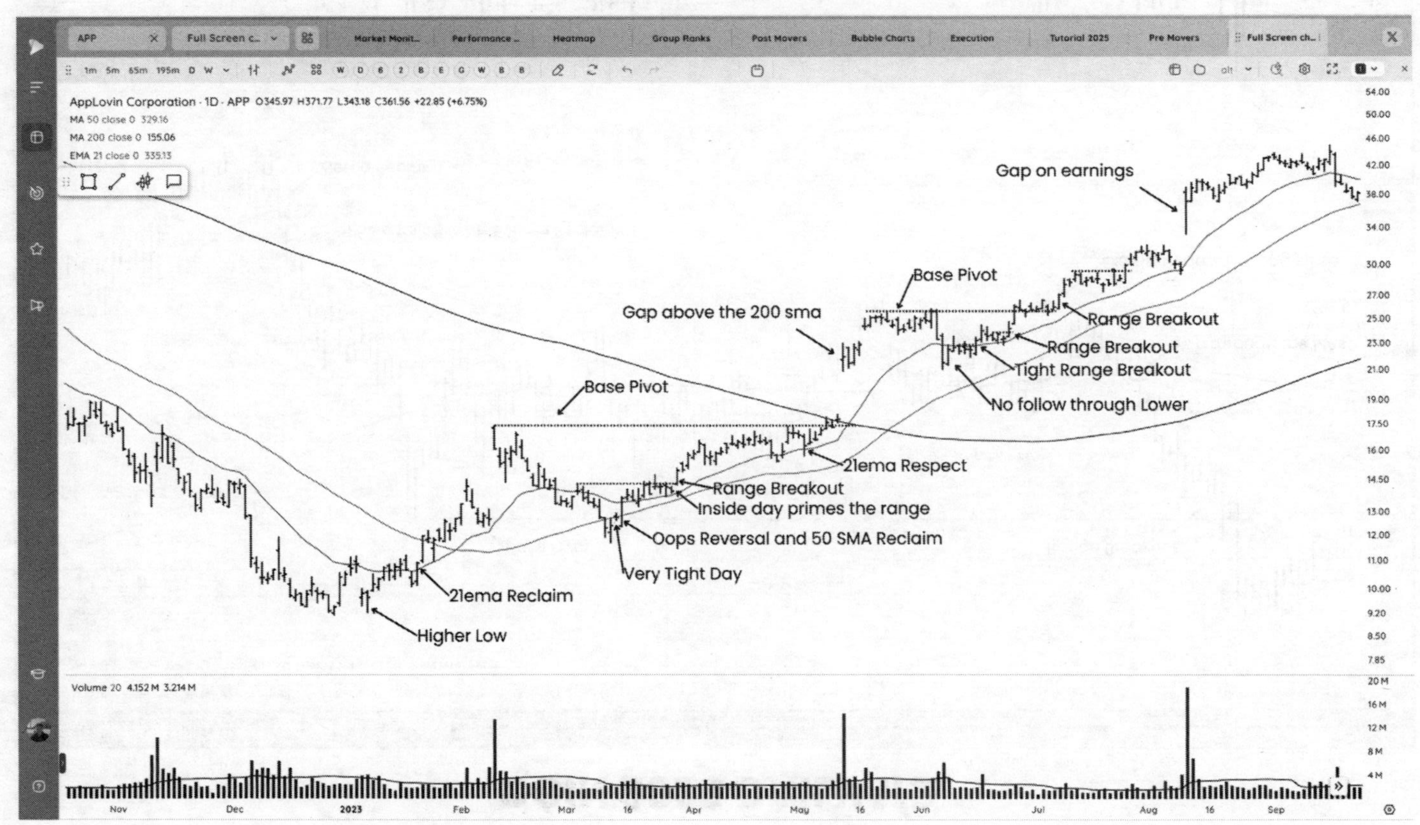
APP 2023 DAILY
AppLovin Corporation · 1D · APP O345.97 H371.77 L343.18 C361.56 +22.85 (+6.75%)
MA 50 close 0 329.16
MA 200 close 0 155.06
EMA 21 close 0 335.13
Gap on earnings
Base Pivot
Gap above the 200 sma
Range Breakout
Range Breakout
Tight Range Breakout
No follow through Lower
Base Pivot
21ema Respect
Range Breakout
Inside day primes the range
Oops Reversal and 50 SMA Reclaim
Very Tight Day
21ema Reclaim
Higher Low
Volume 20 4.152 M 3.214 M

COIN 2023 DAILY 1/2

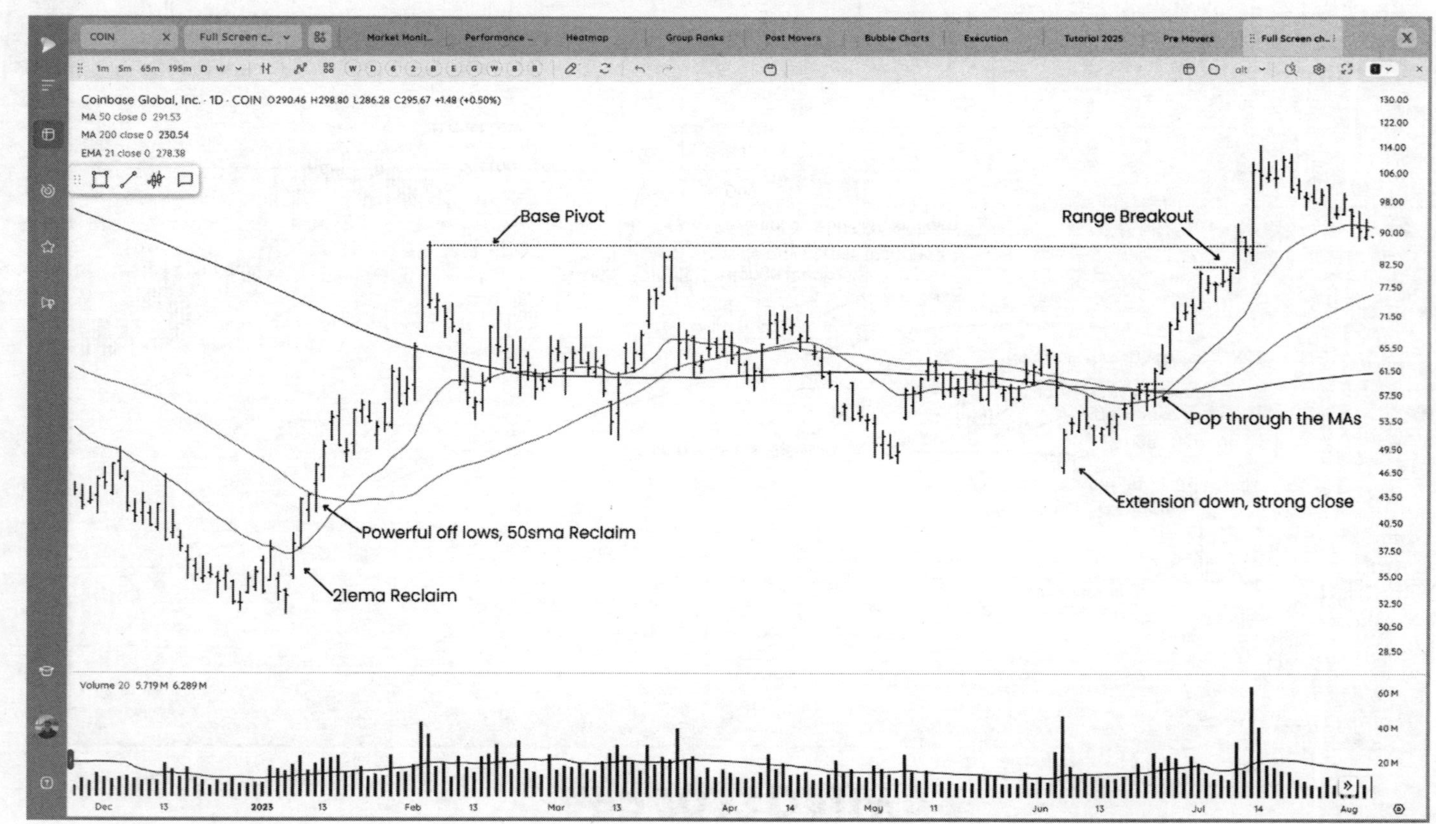

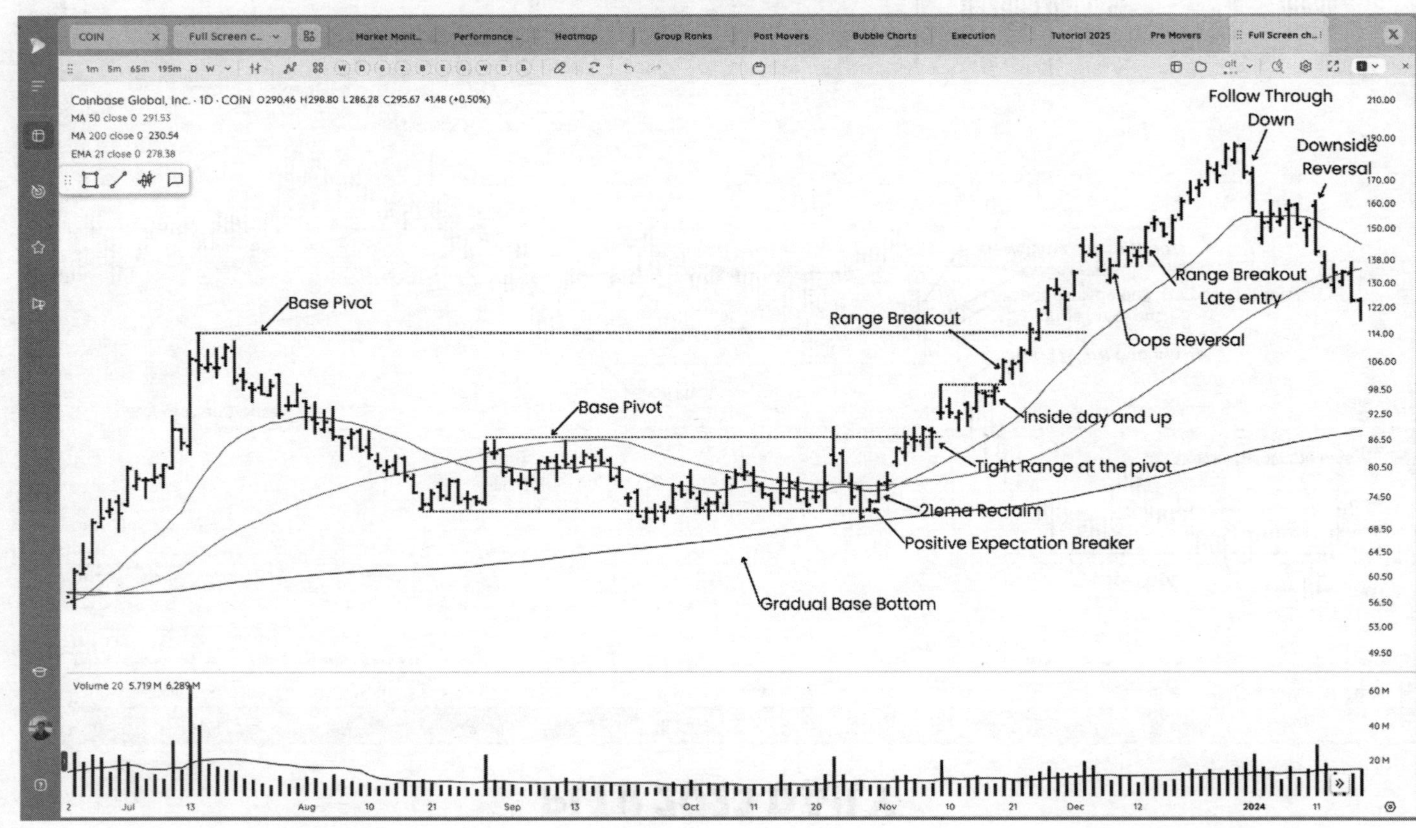
COIN 2023 DAILY 2/2
Coinbase Global, Inc. · 1D · COIN O290.46 H298.80 L286.28 C295.67 +1.48 (+0.50%)
MA 50 close 0 291.53
MA 200 close 0 230.54
EMA 21 close 0 278.38
Base Pivot
Range Breakout
Base Pivot
Gradual Base Bottom
Inside day and up
Tight Range at the pivot
21ema Reclaim
Positive Expectation Breaker
Oops Reversal
Range Breakout
Late entry
Follow Through
Down
Downside
Reversal
Volume 20 5.719 M 6.289 M

PLTR 2023 DAILY

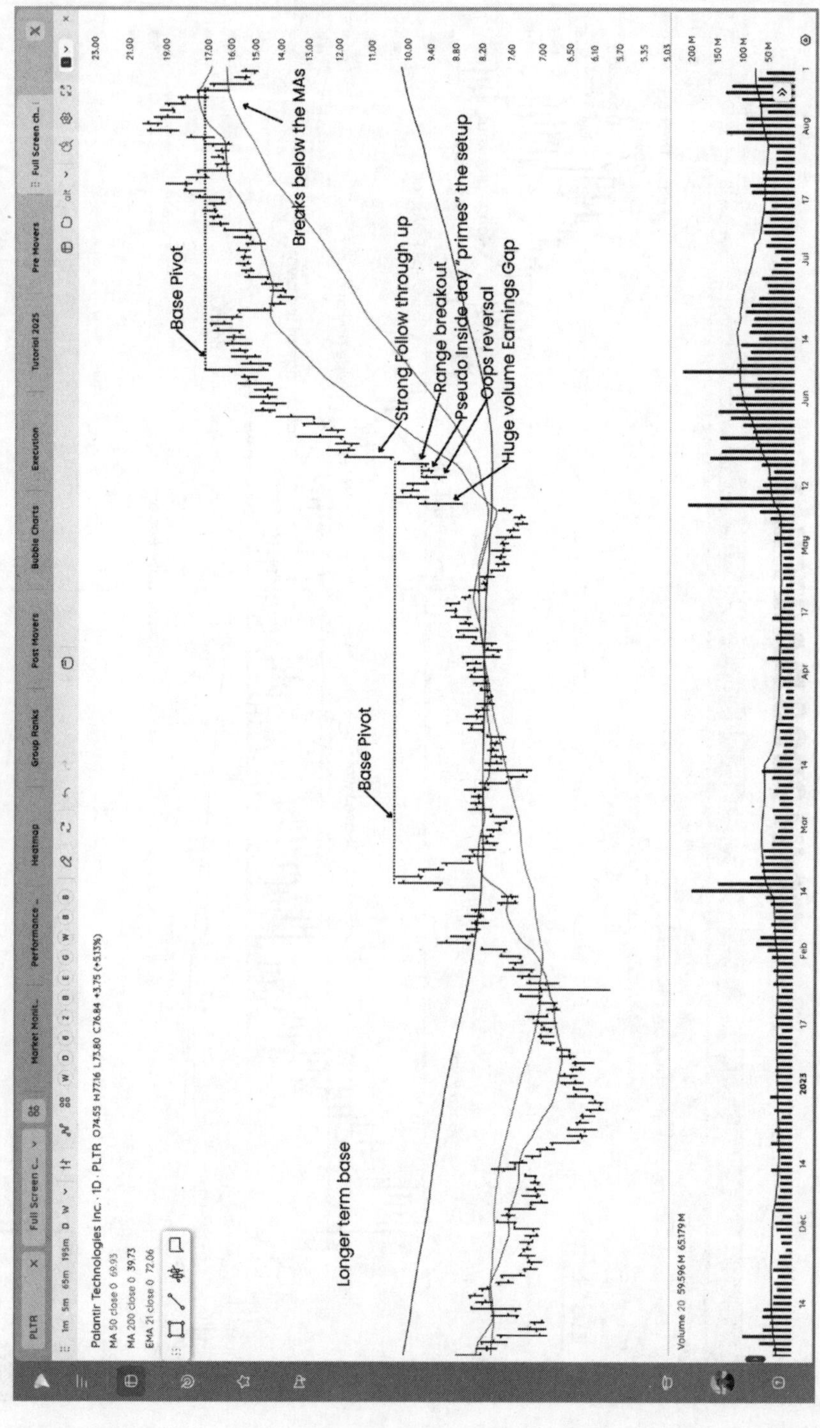

VRT 2023 DAILY 1/2

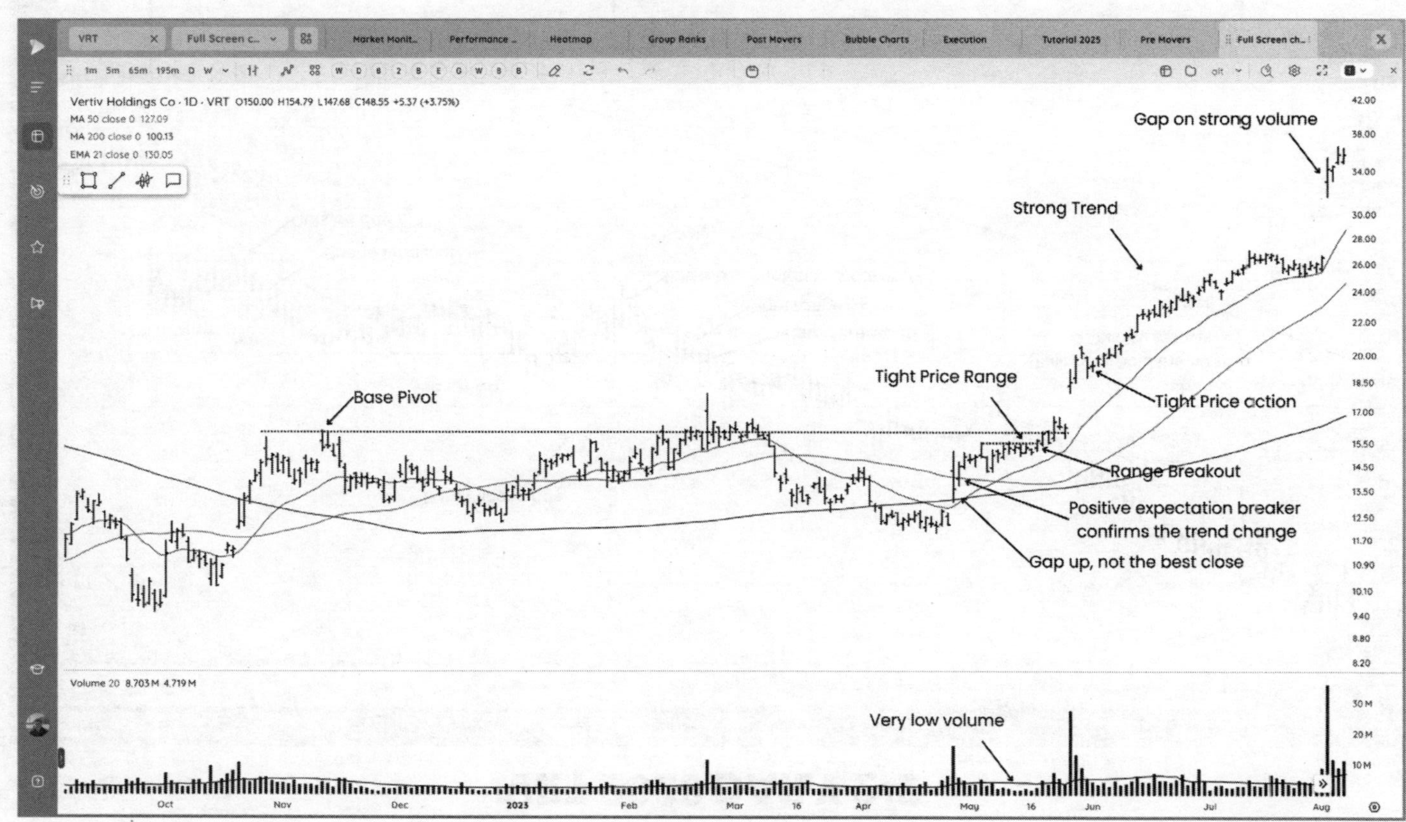

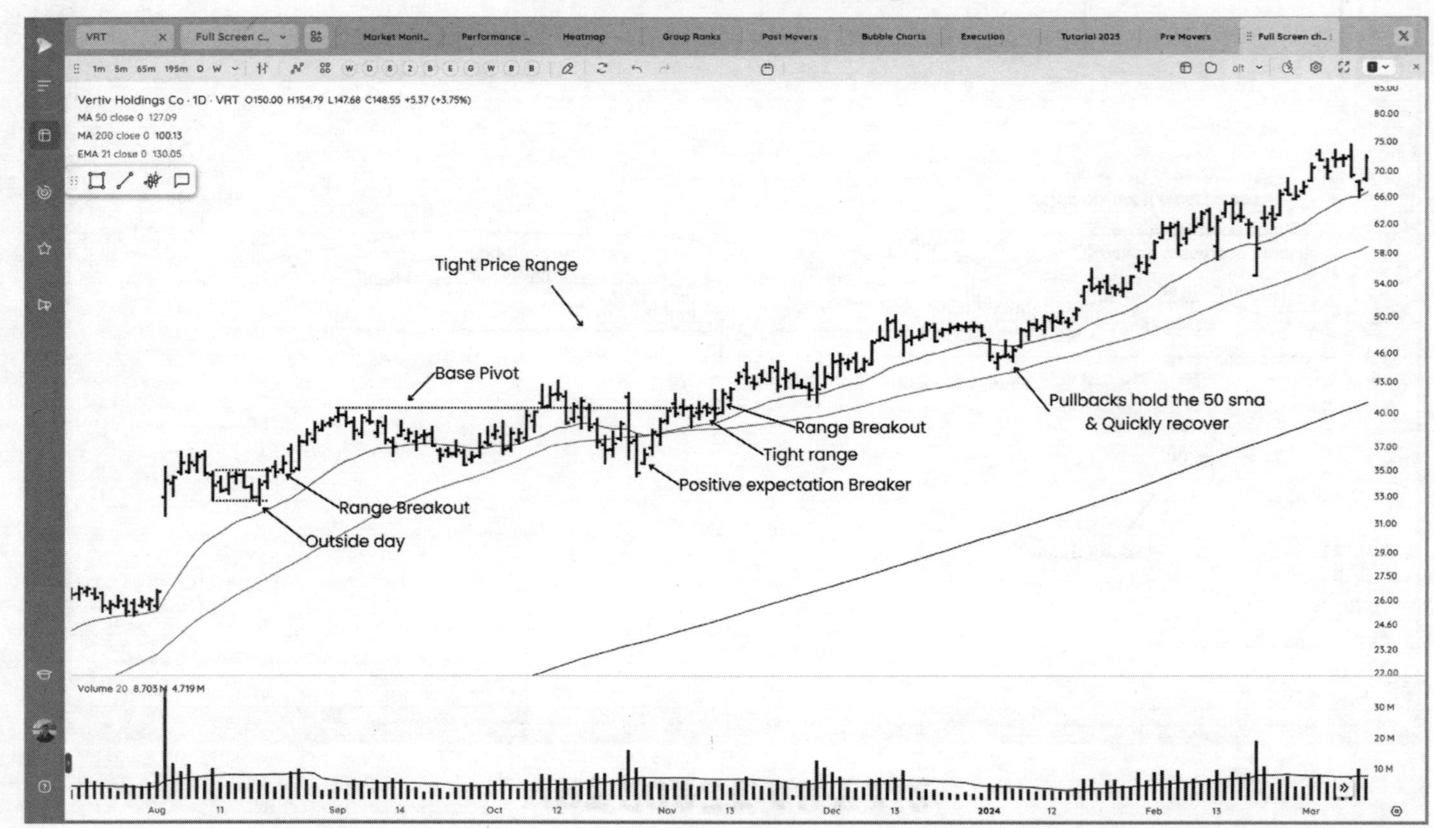
VRT 2023 DAILY 2/2
Vertiv Holdings Co · 1D · VRT O150.00 H154.79 L147.68 C148.55 +5.37 (+3.75%)
MA 50 close 0 127.09
MA 200 close 0 100.13
EMA 21 close 0 130.05
Tight Price Range
Base Pivot
Range Breakout
Outside day
Positive expectation Breaker
Tight range
Range Breakout
Pullbacks hold the 50 sma
& Quickly recover
Volume 20 8.703 M 4.719 M

VST 2023 DAILY

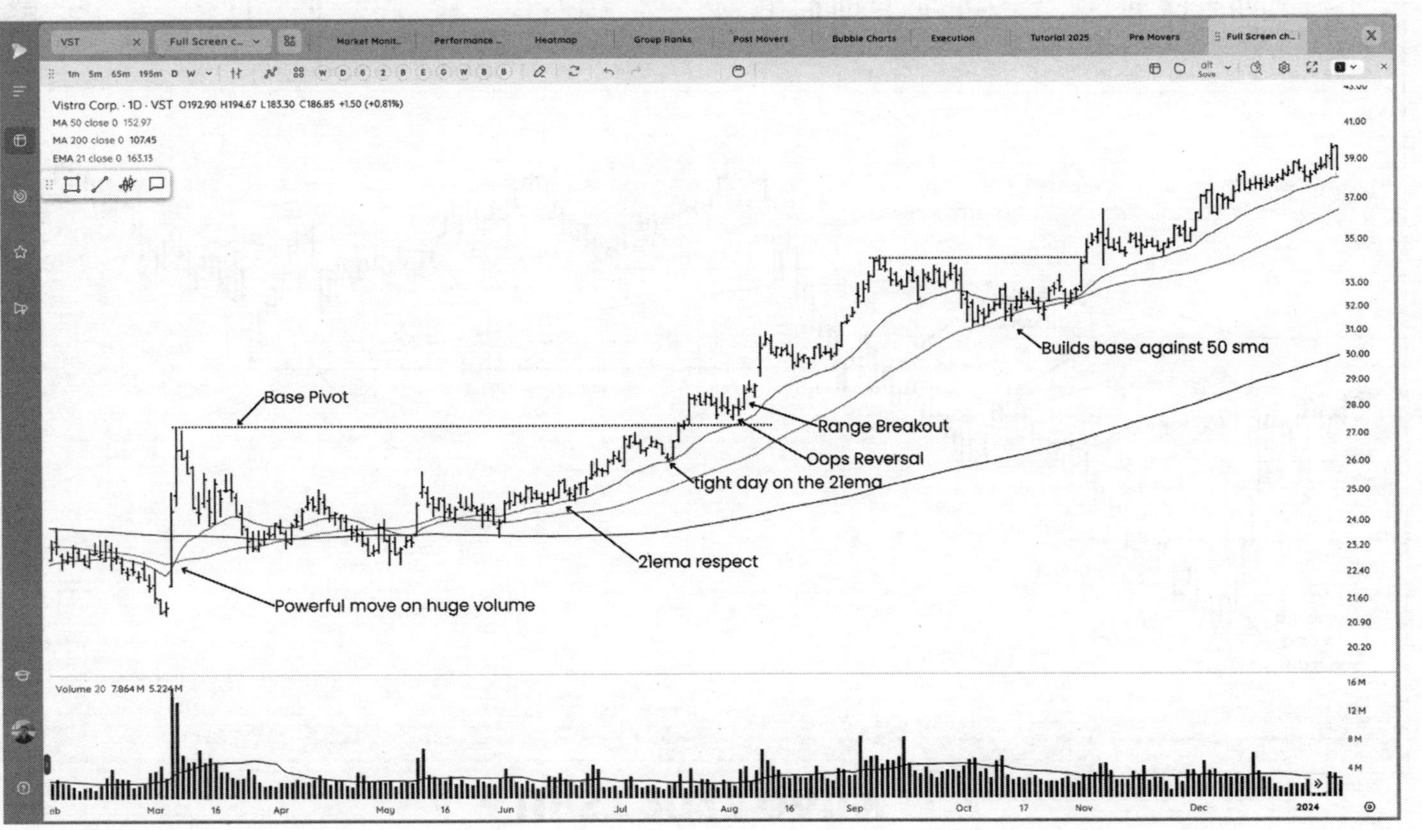

UPST 2023 DAILY

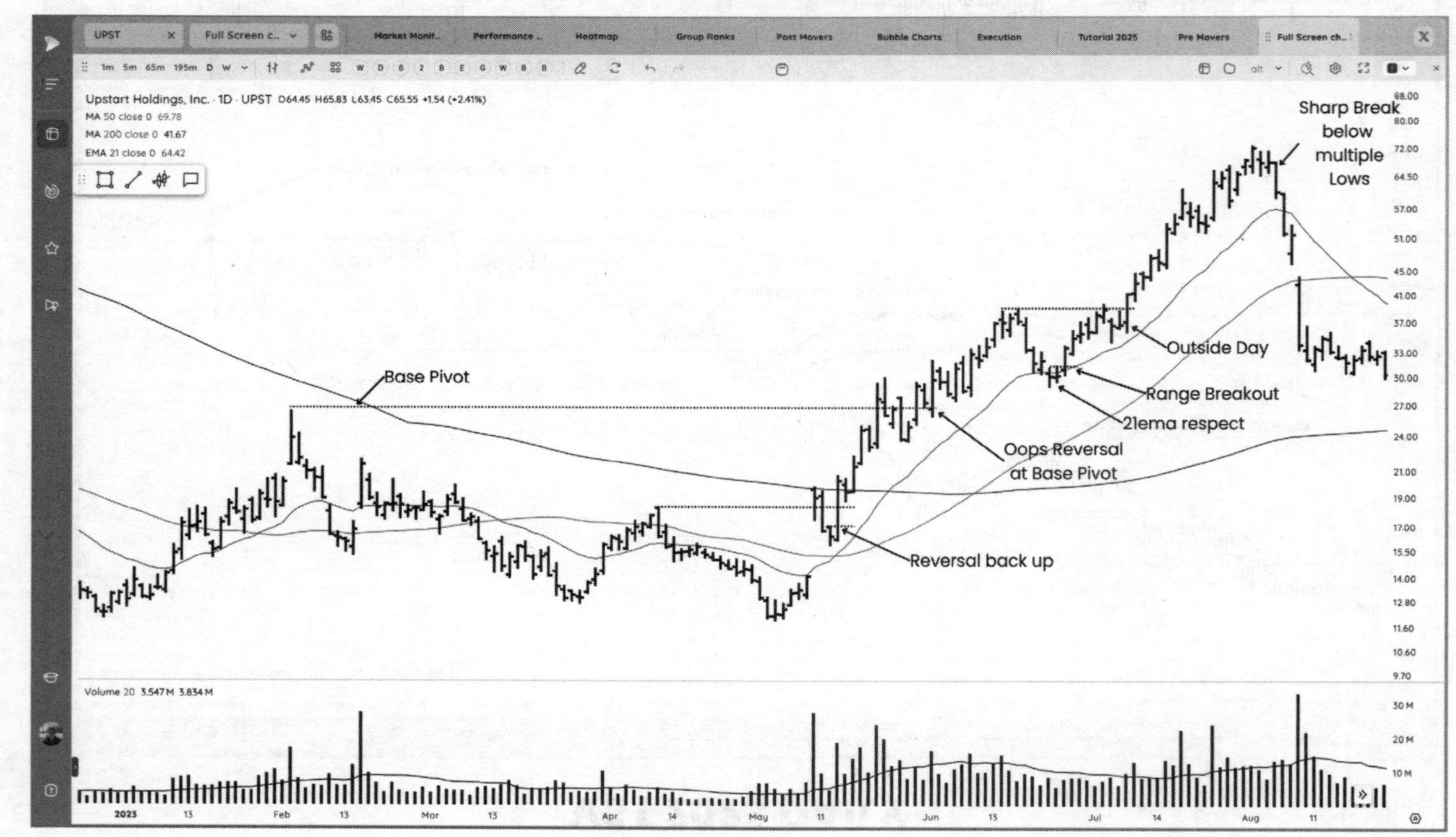

CRWD 2023 DAILY 1/2

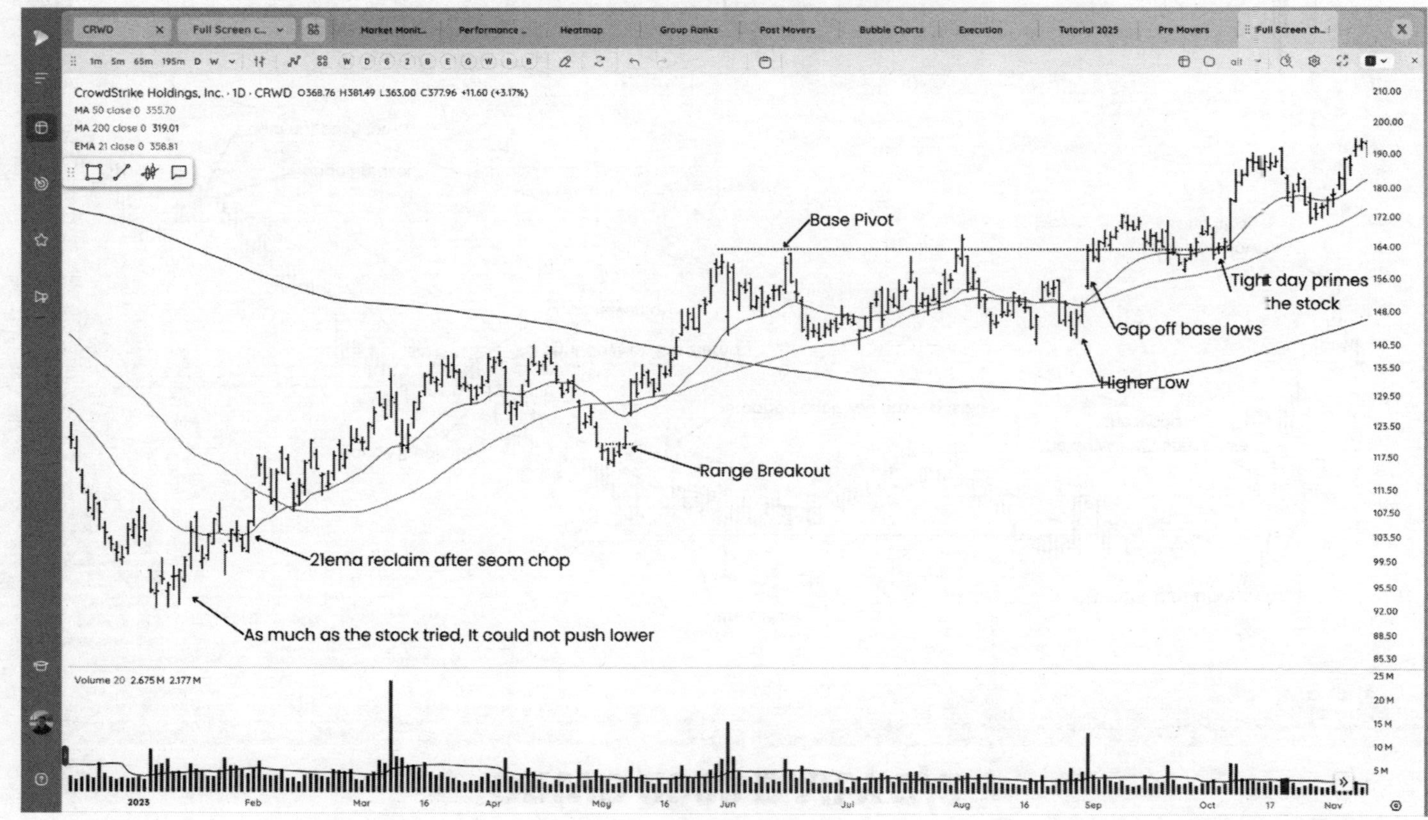

CRWD 2023 DAILY 2/2

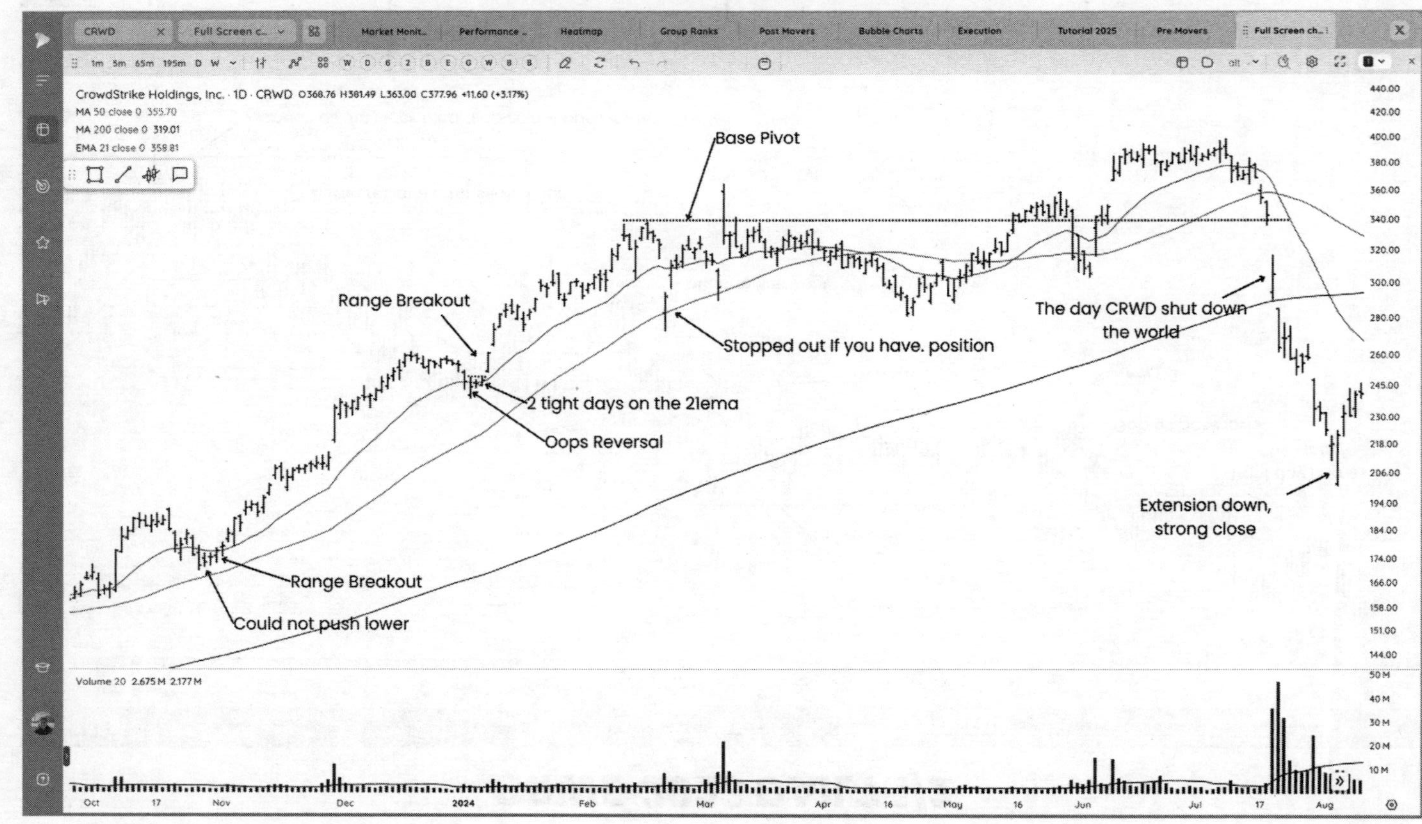

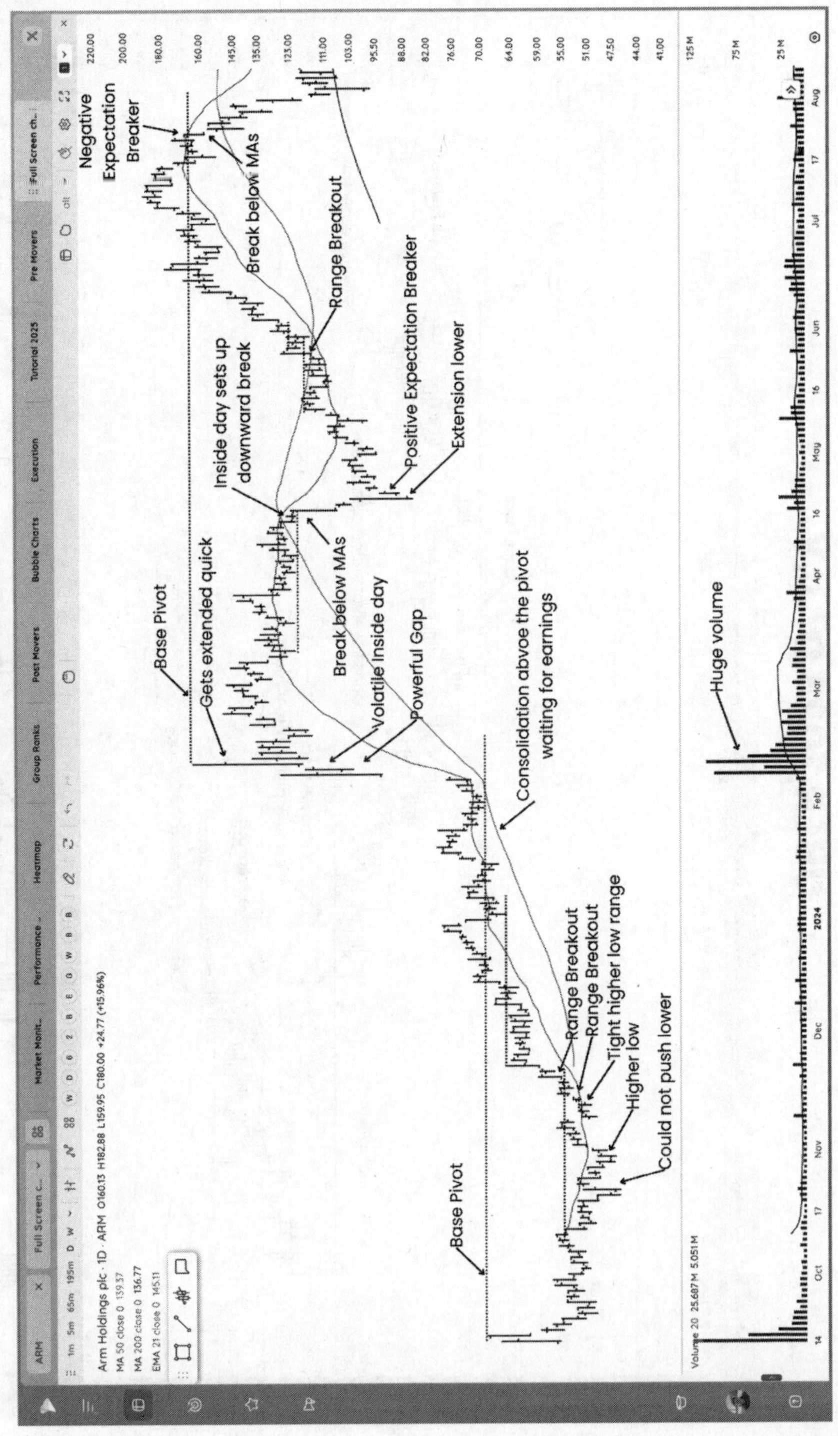
ARM 2023 DAILY
Arm Holdings plc · 1D · ARM O160.13 H182.88 L159.95 C180.00 +24.77 (+15.96%)
MA 50 close 0 139.37
MA 200 close 0 136.77
EMA 21 close 0 145.11
Base Pivot
Could not push lower
Higher low
Tight higher low range
Range Breakout
Range Breakout
Consolidation abvoe the pivot
waiting for earnings
Powerful Gap
Volatile Inside day
Break below MAs
Gets extended quick
Base Pivot
Inside day sets up
downward break
Positive Expectation Breaker
Extension lower
Range Breakout
Break below MAs
Negative
Expectation
Breaker
Huge volume
Volume 20 25.687 M 5.051 M

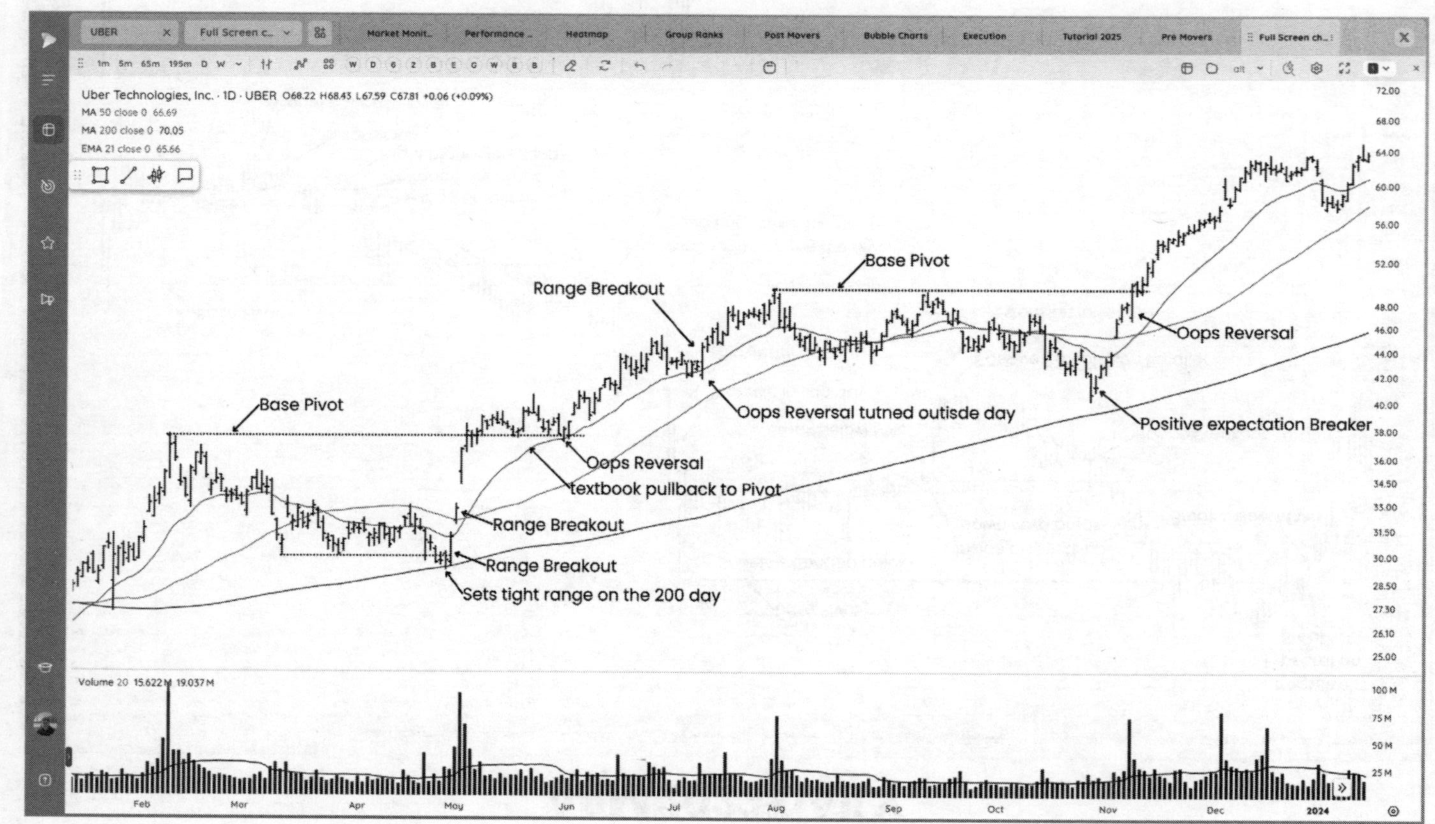
UBER 2023 DAILY
Uber Technologies, Inc. · 1D · UBER O68.22 H68.43 L67.59 C67.81 +0.06 (+0.09%)
MA 50 close 0 66.69
MA 200 close 0 70.05
EMA 21 close 0 65.66
Base Pivot
Range Breakout
Base Pivot
Oops Reversal
Oops Reversal tutned outisde day
Positive expectation Breaker
Oops Reversal
textbook pullback to Pivot
Range Breakout
Range Breakout
Sets tight range on the 200 day
Volume 20 15.622M 19.037M

META 2023 DAILY 1/2

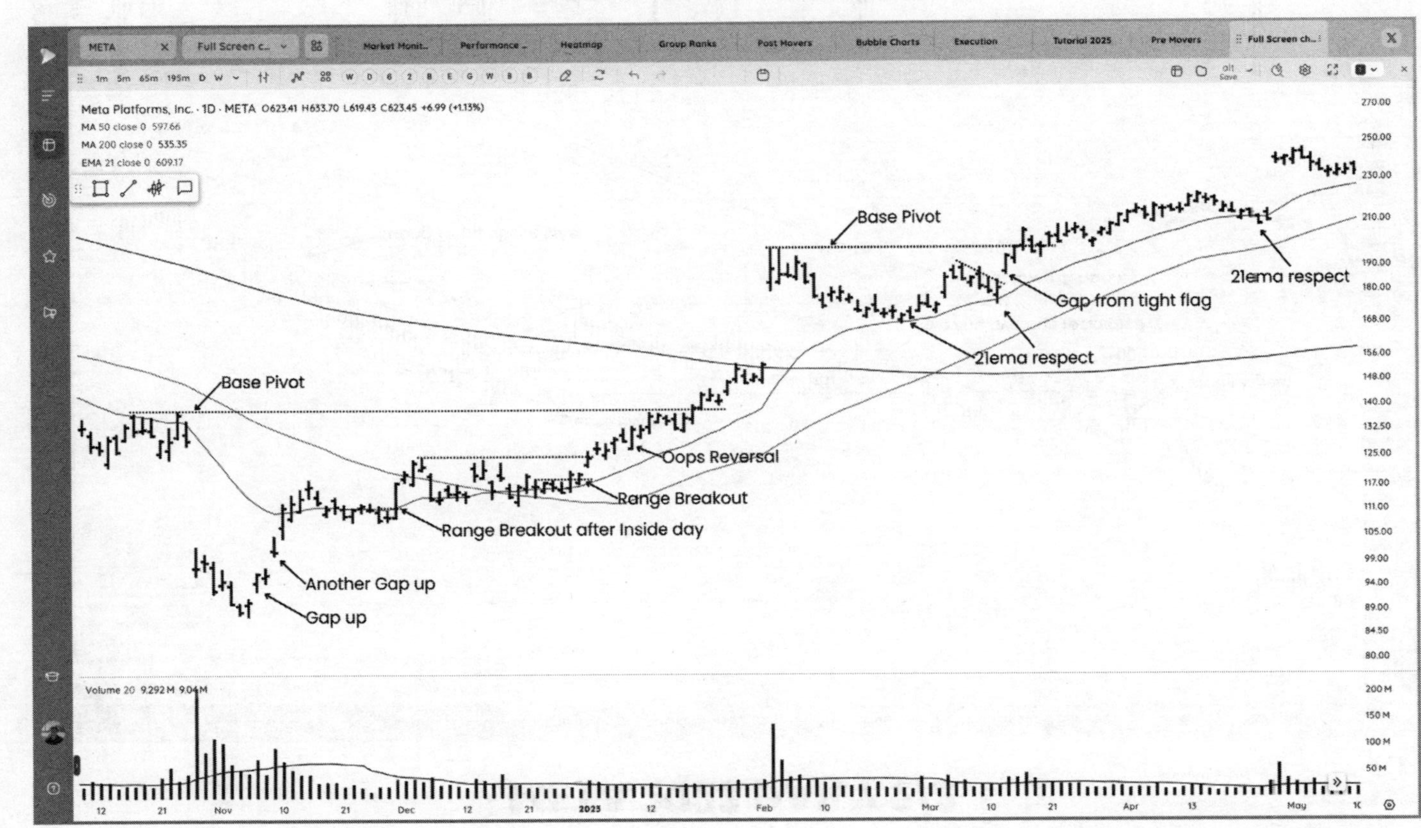

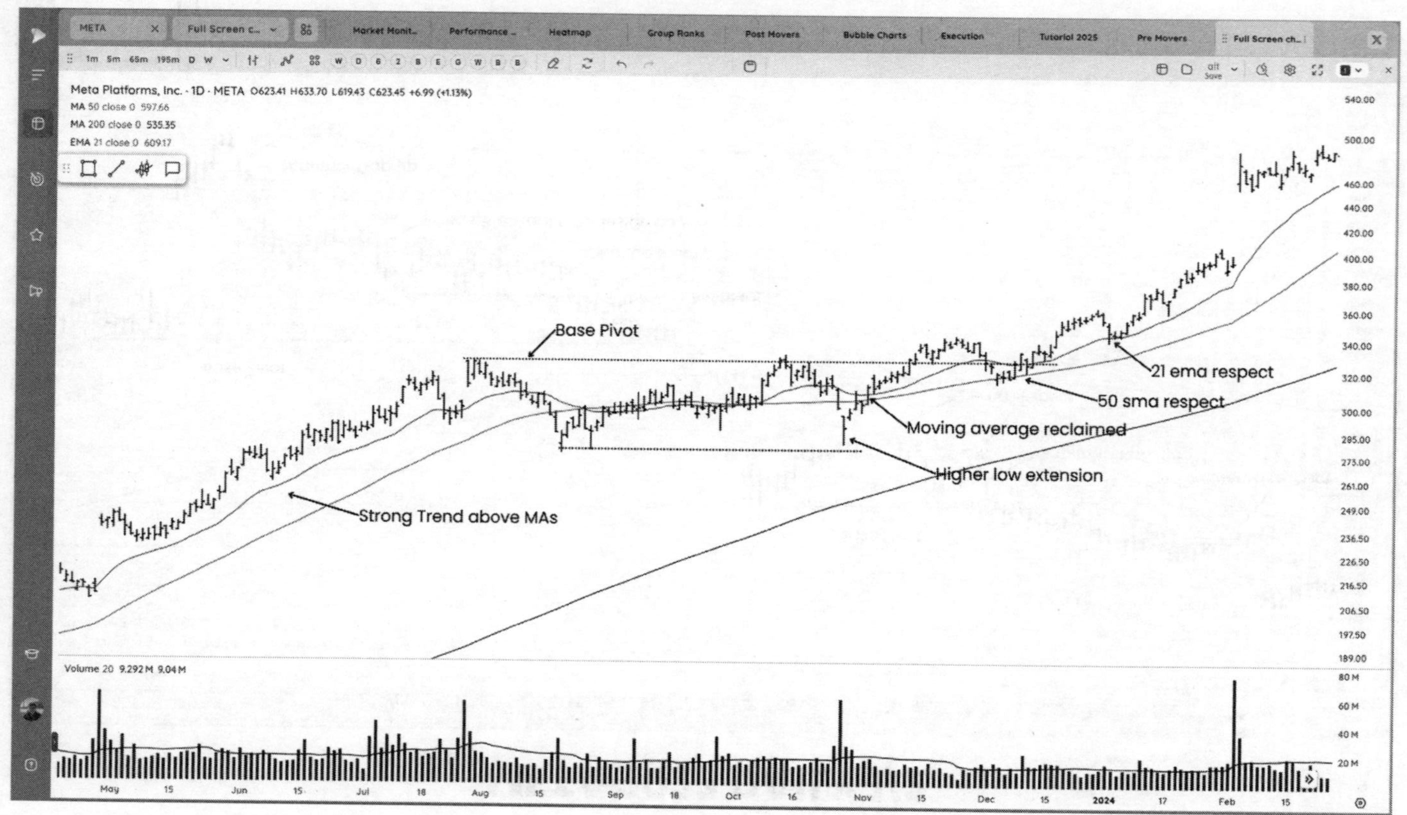
META 2023 DAILY 2/2
Meta Platforms, Inc. · 1D · META O623.41 H633.70 L619.43 C623.45 +6.99 (+1.13%)
MA 50 close 0 597.66
MA 200 close 0 535.35
EMA 21 close 0 609.17
Base Pivot
21 ema respect
50 sma respect
Moving average reclaimed
Higher low extension
Strong Trend above MAs
Volume 20 9.292 M 9.04 M

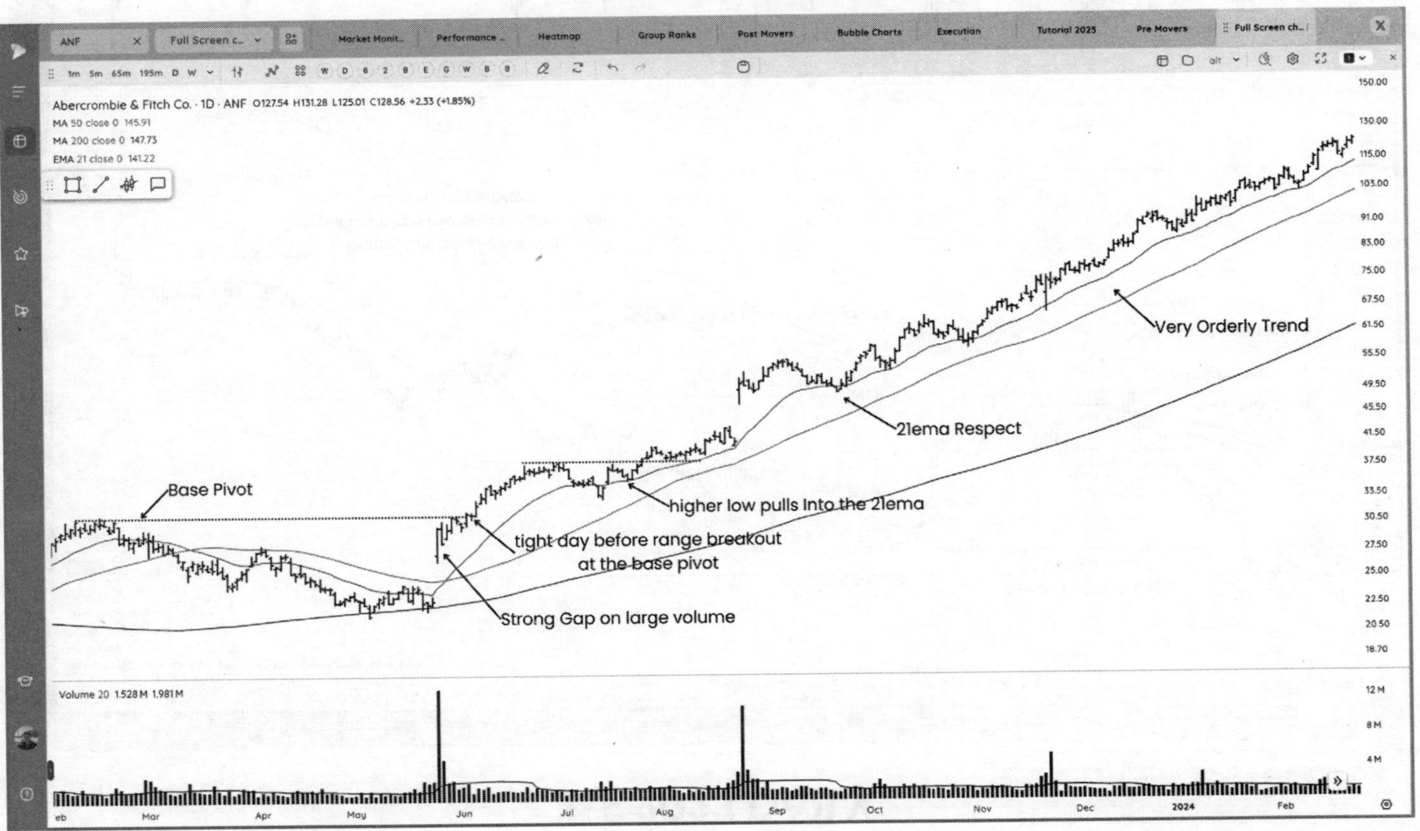
ANF 2023 DAILY
Abercrombie & Fitch Co. · 1D · ANF O127.54 H131.28 L125.01 C128.56 +2.33 (+1.85%)
MA 50 close 0 145.91
MA 200 close 0 147.73
EMA 21 close 0 141.22
Base Pivot
tight day before range breakout
at the base pivot
Strong Gap on large volume
higher low pulls into the 21ema
21ema Respect
Very Orderly Trend
Volume 20 1.528M 1.981M

ELF 2023 DAILY

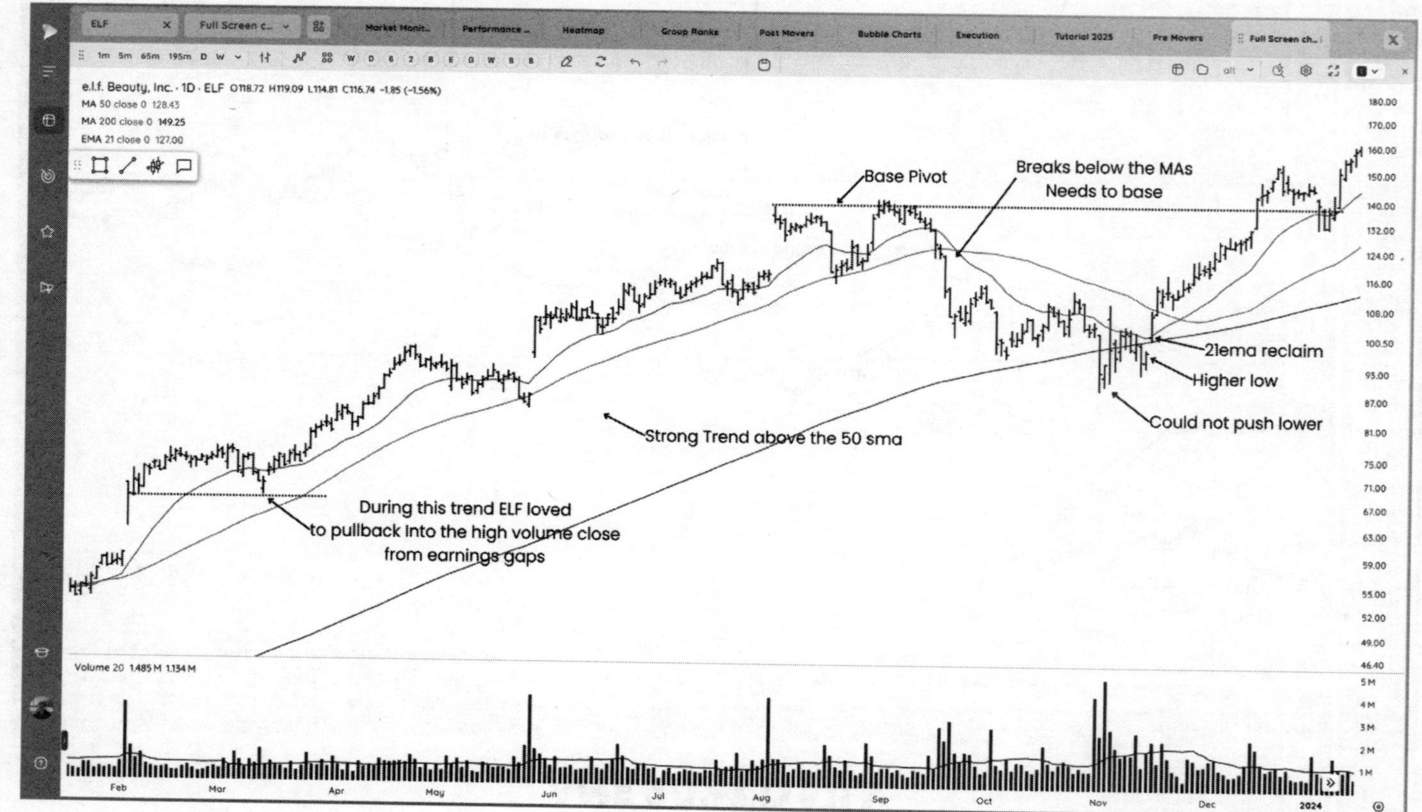

2024 MARKET LEADERS

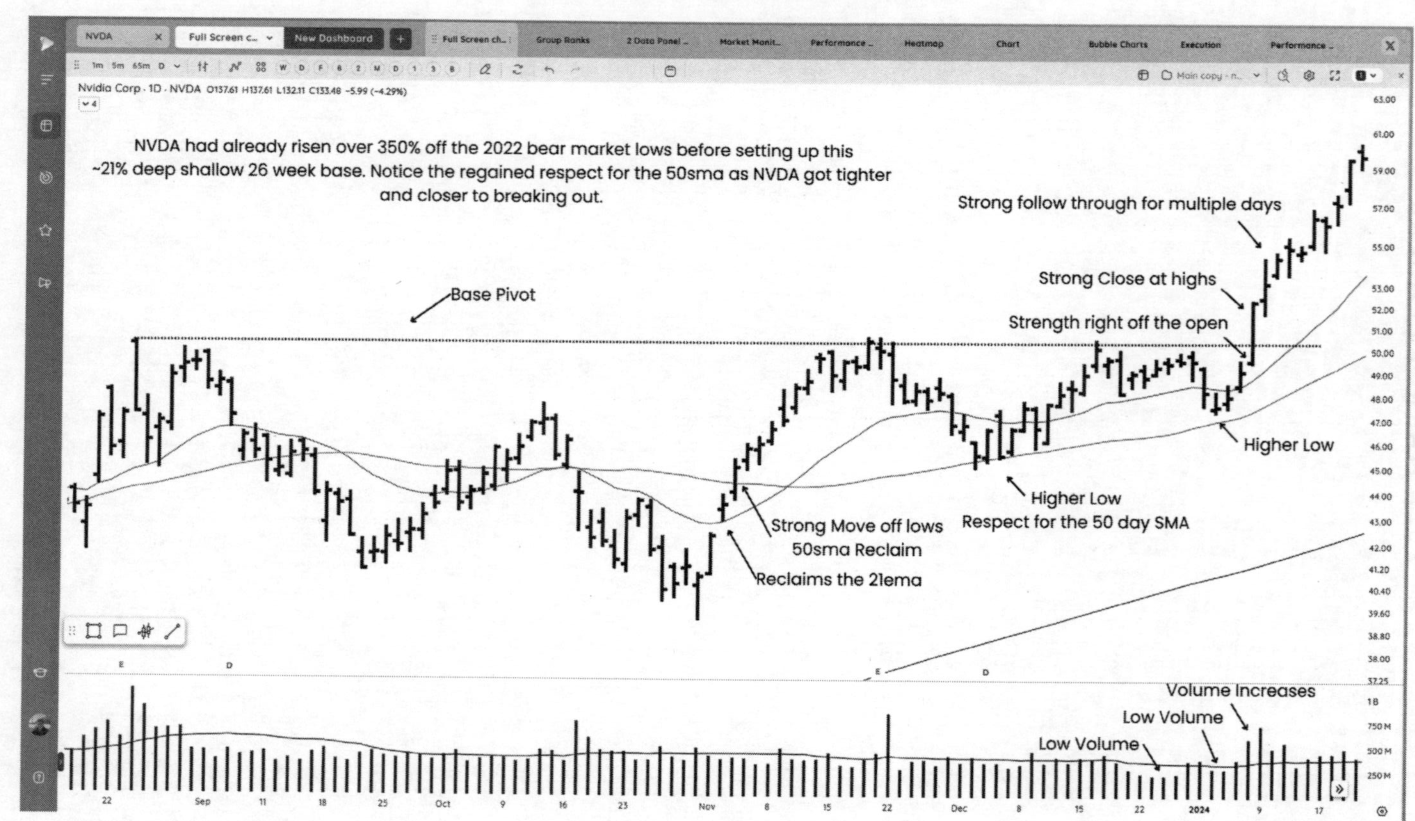
NVDA 2024 DAILY 1/3
Nvidia Corp · 1D · NVDA O137.61 H137.61 L132.11 C133.48 −5.99 (−4.29%)
NVDA had already risen over 350% off the 2022 bear market lows before setting up this
~21% deep shallow 26 week base. Notice the regained respect for the 50sma as NVDA got tighter
and closer to breaking out.
Base Pivot
Strong follow through for multiple days
Strong Close at highs
Strength right off the open
Higher Low
Higher Low
Respect for the 50 day SMA
Strong Move off lows
50sma Reclaim
Reclaims the 21ema
Volume Increases
Low Volume
Low Volume

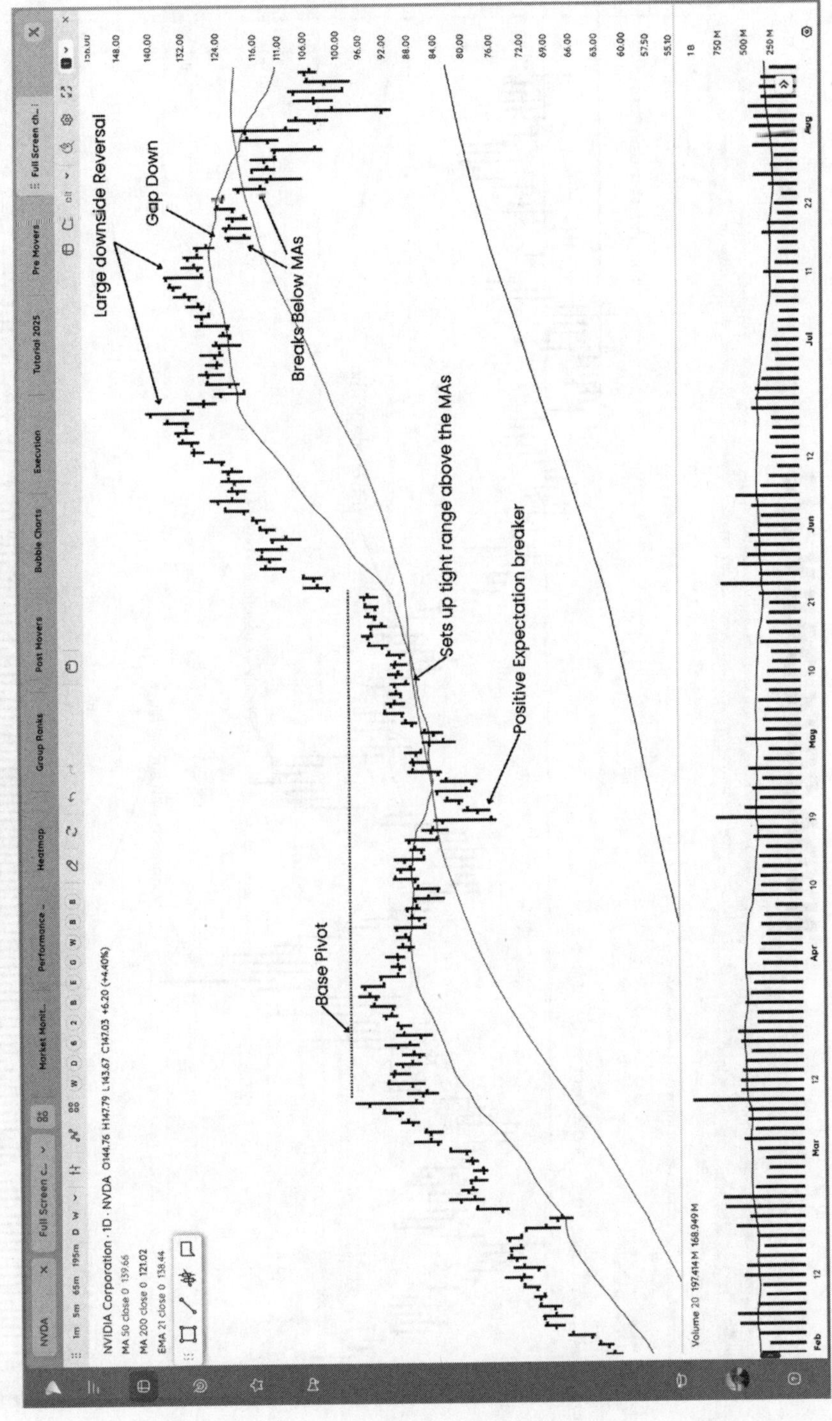
NVDA 2024 DAILY 2/3
NVIDIA Corporation · 1D · NVDA
MA 50 close 0 139.66
MA 200 close 0 121.02
EMA 21 close 0 138.44
Large downside Reversal
Gap Down
Breaks Below MAs
Sets up tight range above the MAs
Positive Expectation breaker
Base Pivot

NVDA 2024 DAILY 3/3

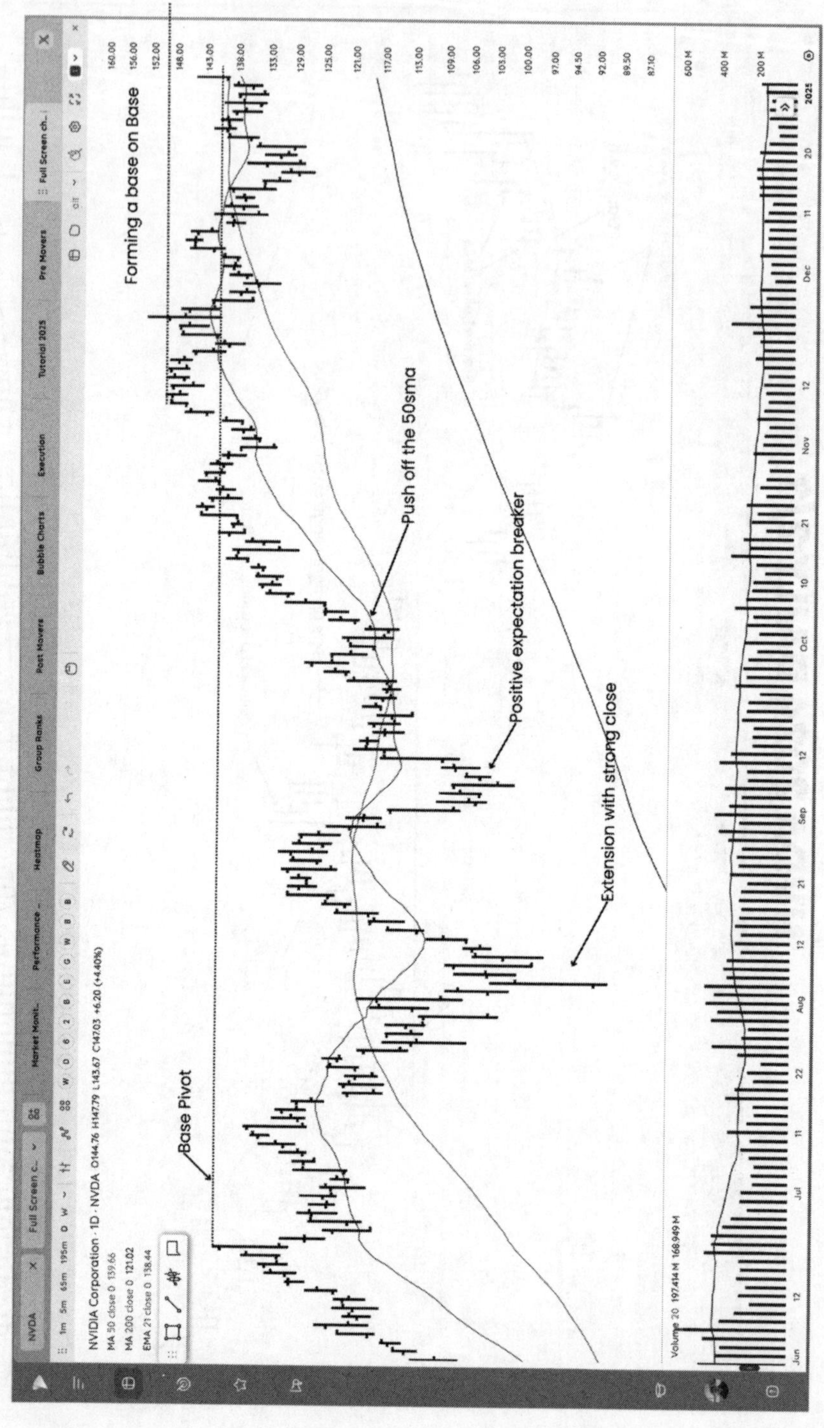

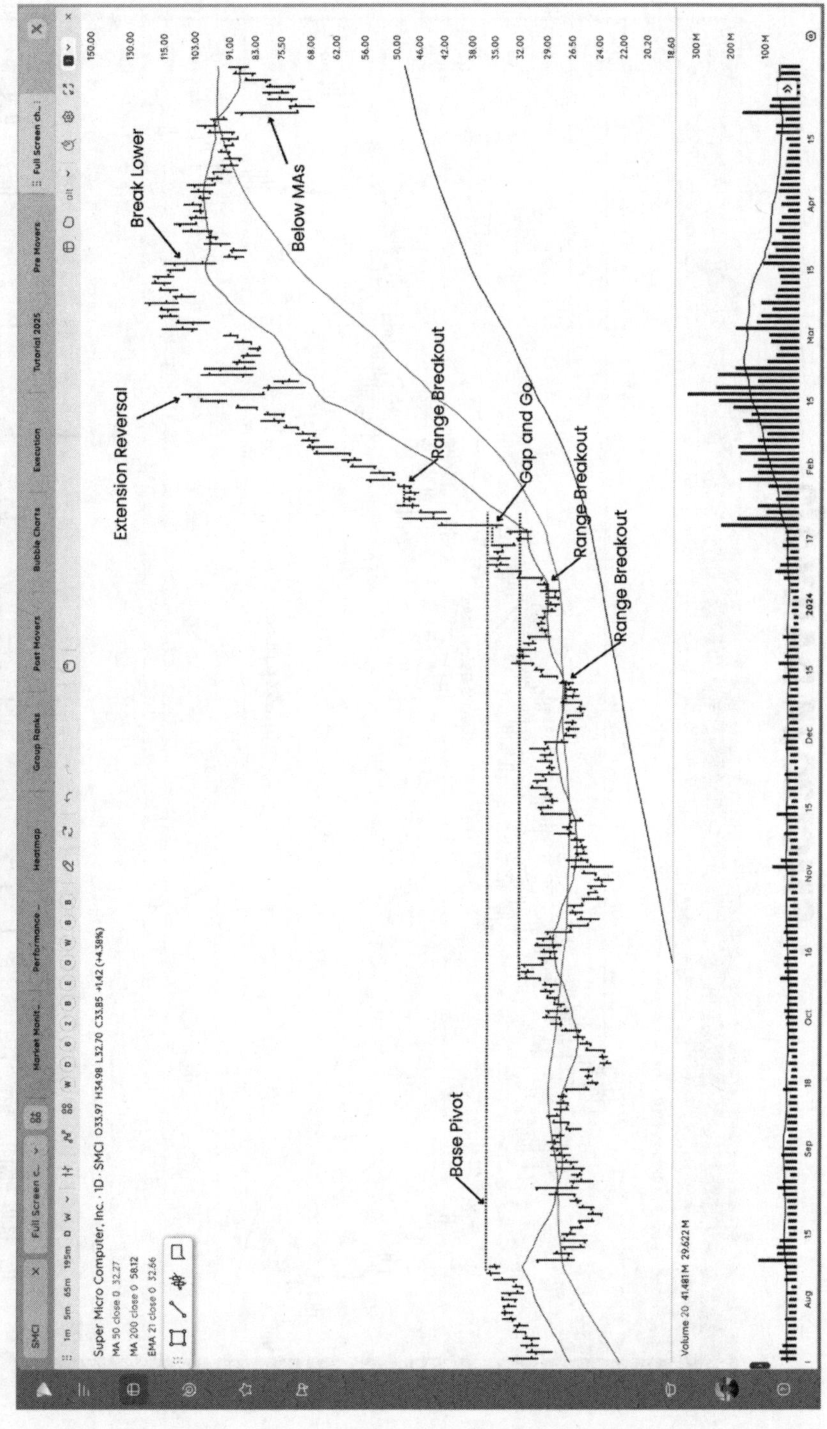
SMCI 2024 DAILY 1/2
Super Micro Computer, Inc. · 1D · SMCI O33.97 H34.98 L32.70 C33.85 +1.42 (+4.38%)
MA 50 close 0 32.27
MA 200 close 0 58.12
EMA 21 close 0 32.66
Extension Reversal
Break Lower
Below MAs
Range Breakout
Gap and Go
Range Breakout
Range Breakout
Base Pivot
Volume 20 41.481M 29.622M

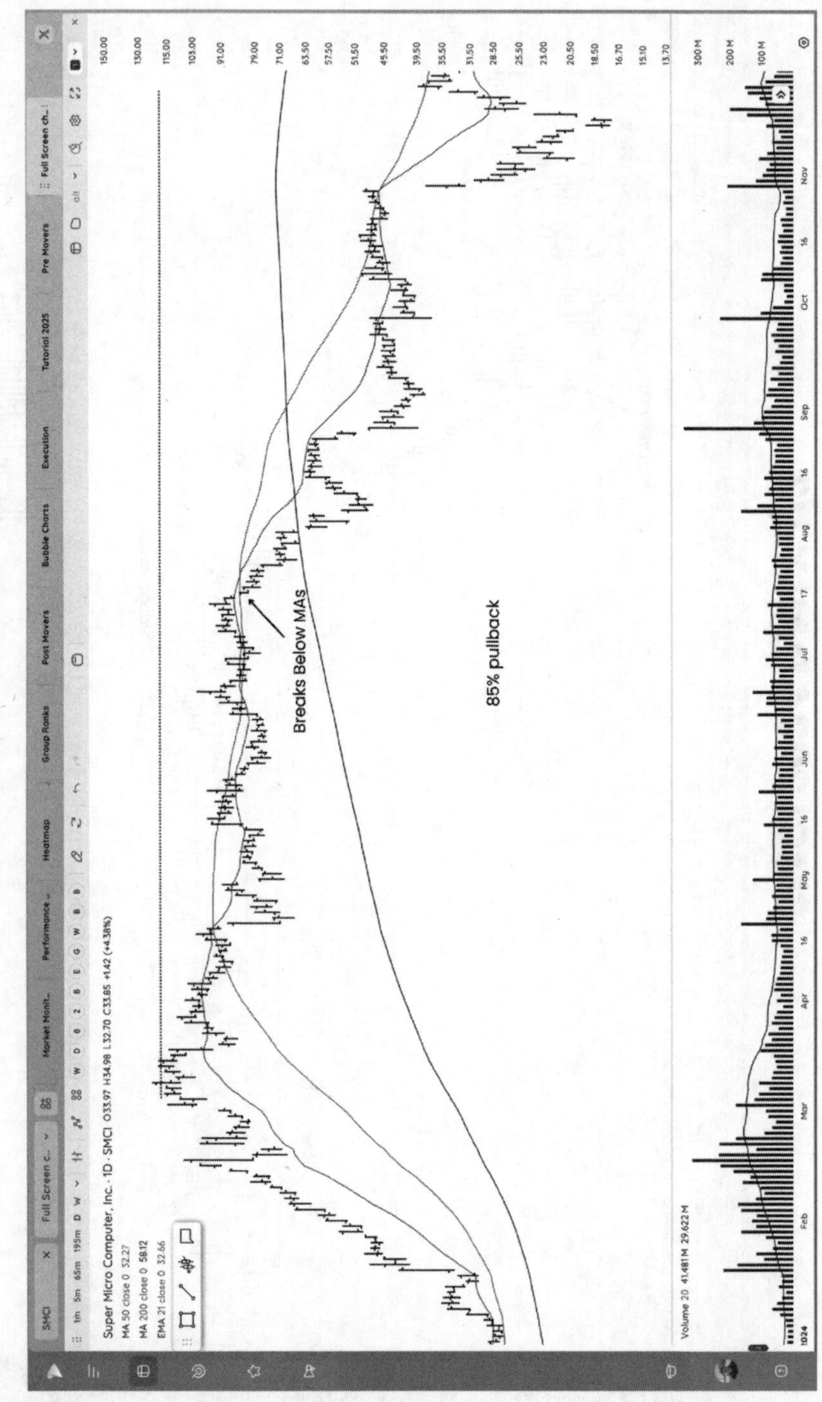
SMCI 2024 DAILY 2/2
Super Micro Computer, Inc. · 1D · SMCI O33.97 H34.98 L32.70 C33.85 +1.42 (+4.38%)
MA 50 close 0 52.27
MA 200 close 0 58.12
EMA 21 close 0 32.66
Breaks Below MAs
85% pullback
Volume 20 41.481M 29.622M

RDDT 2024 DAILY 1/2

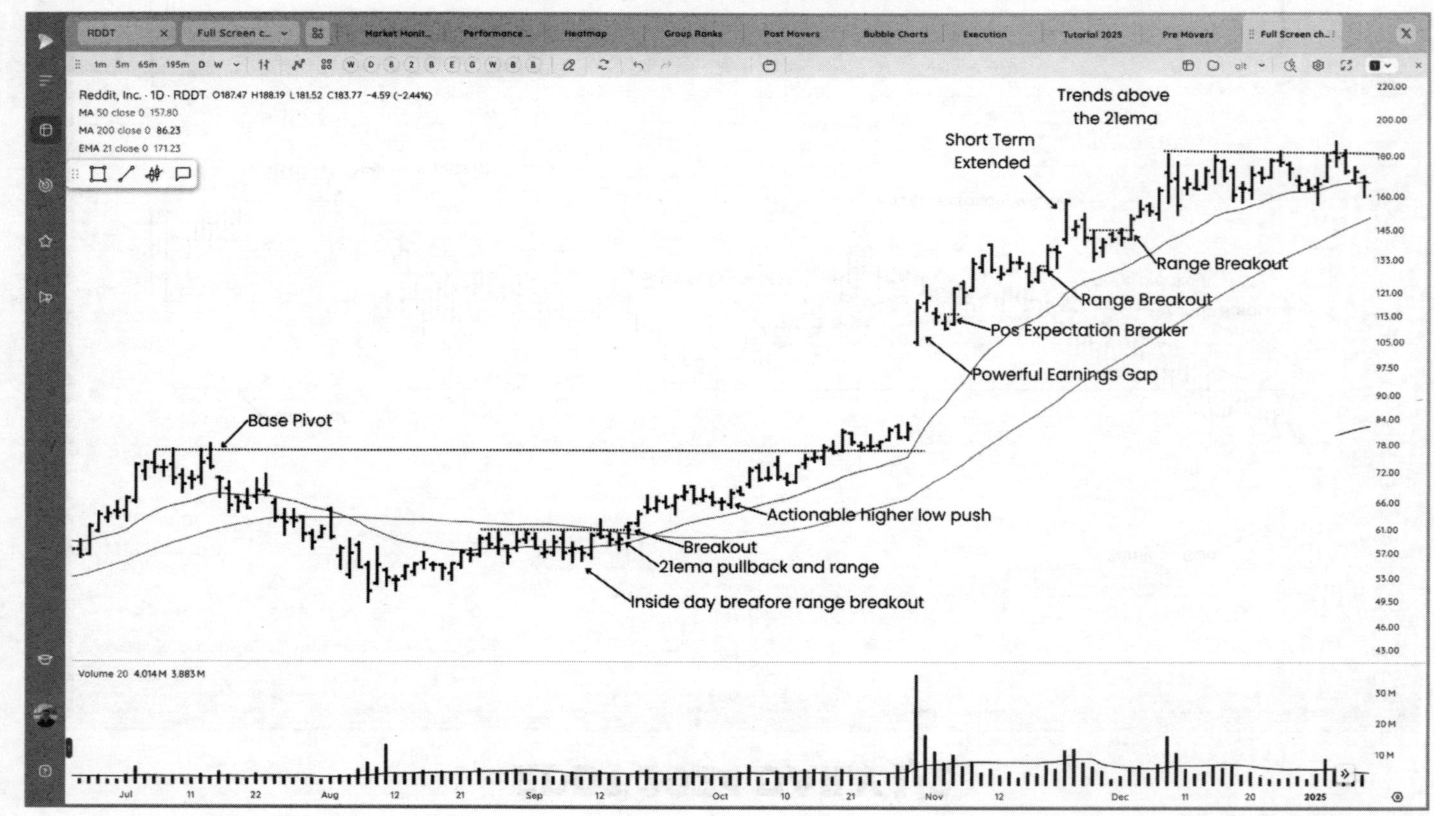
RDDT 2024 DAILY 2/2
Reddit, Inc. · 1D · RDDT O187.47 H188.19 L181.52 C183.77 −4.59 (−2.44%)
MA 50 close 0 157.80
MA 200 close 0 86.23
EMA 21 close 0 171.23
Base Pivot
Inside day breafore range breakout
21ema pullback and range
Breakout
Actionable higher low push
Powerful Earnings Gap
Pos Expectation Breaker
Range Breakout
Range Breakout
Short Term Extended
Trends above the 21ema
Volume 20 4.014 M 3.883 M

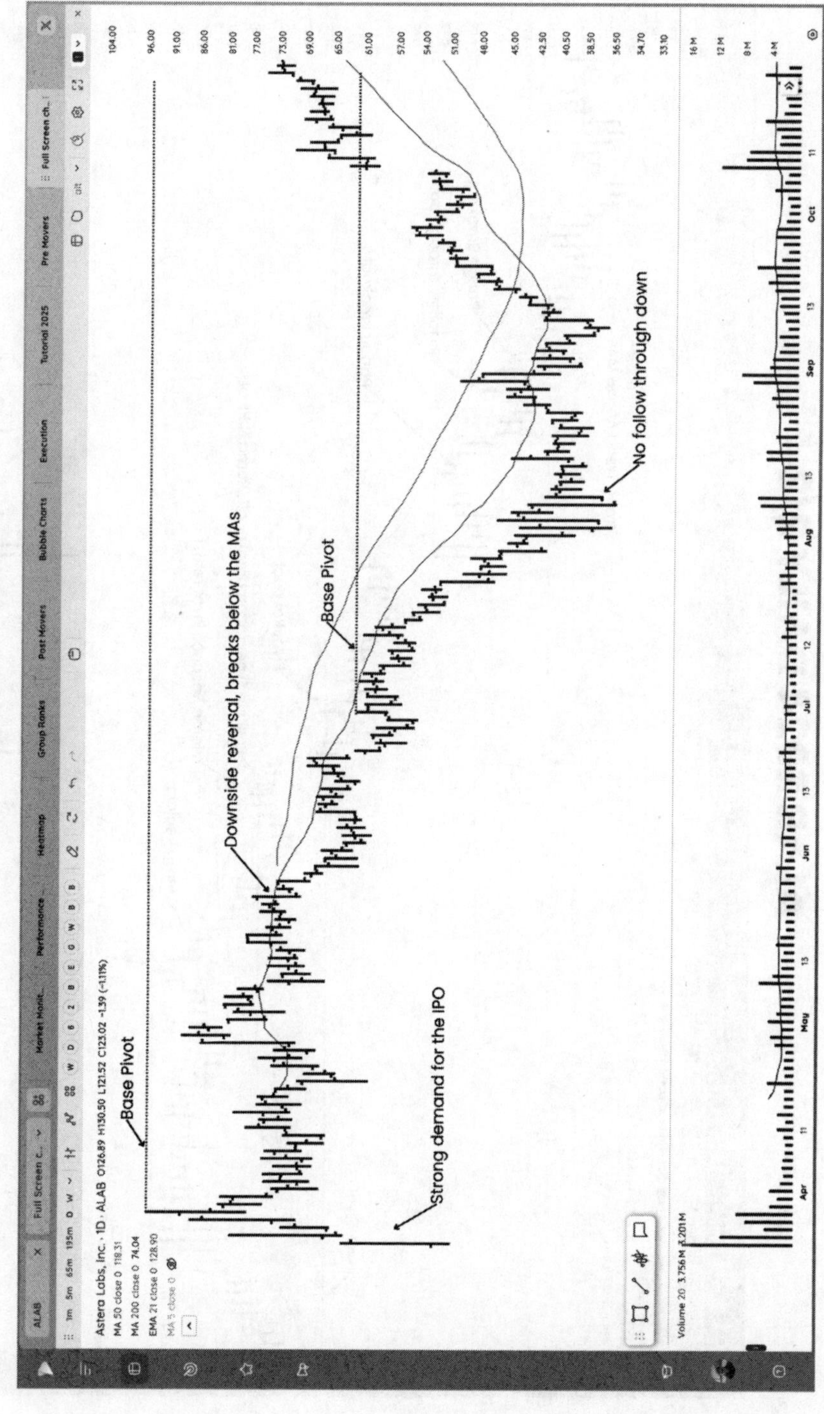
ALAB 2024 DAILY 1/2
Astera Labs, Inc. · 1D · ALAB O126.89 H130.50 L121.52 C123.02 −1.39 (−1.11%)
MA 50 close 0 118.31
MA 200 close 0 74.04
EMA 21 close 0 128.90
Base Pivot
Strong demand for the IPO
Downside reversal, breaks below the MAs
Base Pivot
No follow through down
Volume 20 3.756M 4.201M

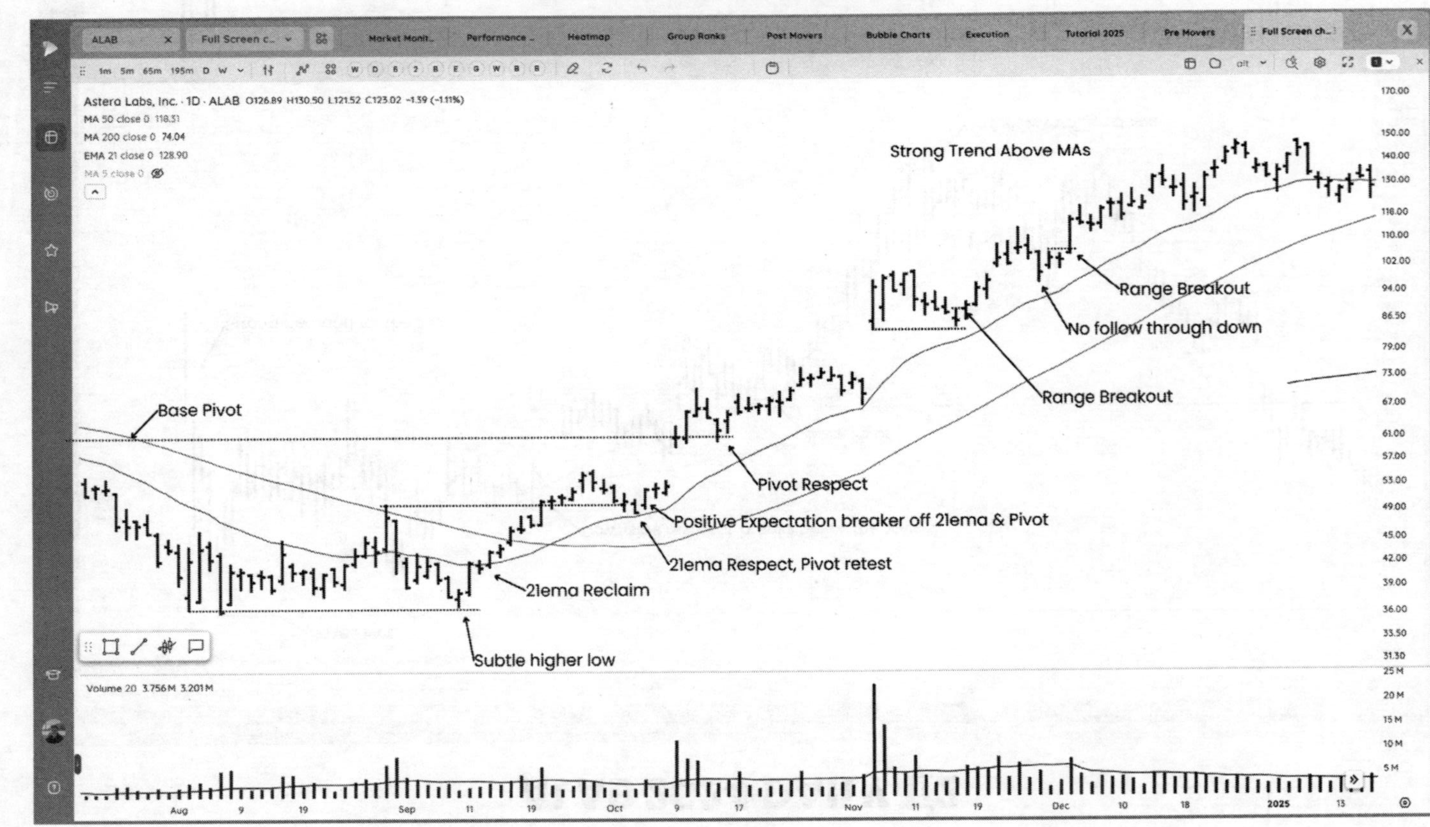
ALAB 2024 DAILY 2/2
Astera Labs, Inc. · 1D · ALAB O126.89 H130.50 L121.52 C123.02 −1.39 (−1.11%)
MA 50 close 0 118.31
MA 200 close 0 74.04
EMA 21 close 0 128.90
MA 5 close 0
Strong Trend Above MAs
Range Breakout
No follow through down
Range Breakout
Base Pivot
Pivot Respect
Positive Expectation breaker off 21ema & Pivot
21ema Respect, Pivot retest
21ema Reclaim
Subtle higher low
Volume 20 3.756M 3.201M

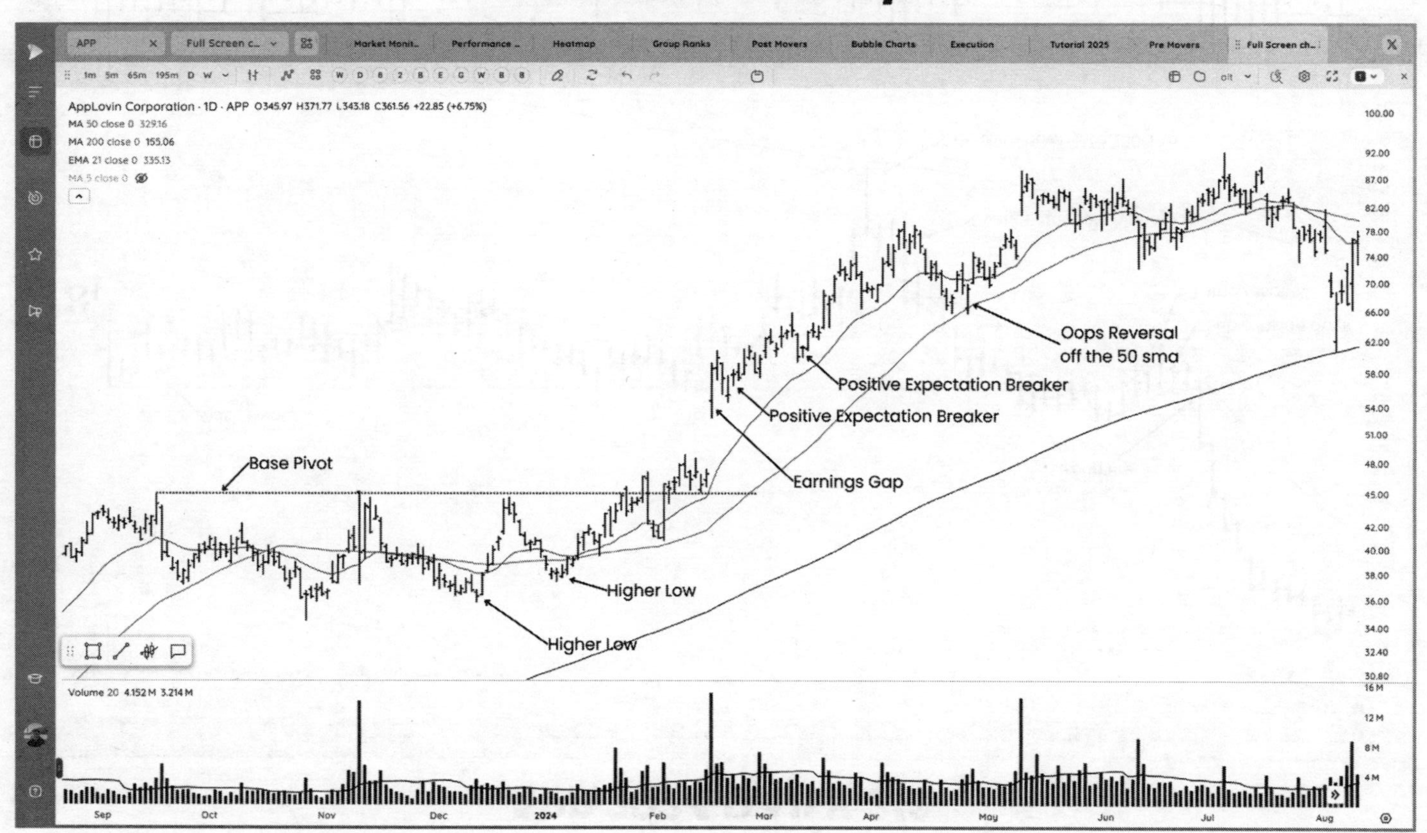
APP 2024 DAILY 1/3
AppLovin Corporation · 1D · APP O345.97 H371.77 L343.18 C361.56 +22.85 (+6.75%)
MA 50 close 0 329.16
MA 200 close 0 155.06
EMA 21 close 0 335.13
MA 5 close 0
Base Pivot
Higher Low
Higher Low
Earnings Gap
Positive Expectation Breaker
Positive Expectation Breaker
Oops Reversal
off the 50 sma
Volume 20 4.152 M 3.214 M
Sep
Oct
Nov
Dec
2024
Feb
Mar
Apr
May
Jun
Jul
Aug

APP 2024 DAILY 2/3
AppLovin Corporation · 1D · APP O345.97 H371.77 L343.18 C361.56 +22.85 (+6.75%)
MA 50 close 0 329.16
MA 200 close 0 155.06
EMA 21 close 0 335.13
Base Pivot
Strong Breakout
Double Inside days
50 sma respect
Oustide day sets higher low
Extension down into 200sma
Volume 20 4.152 M 3.214 M

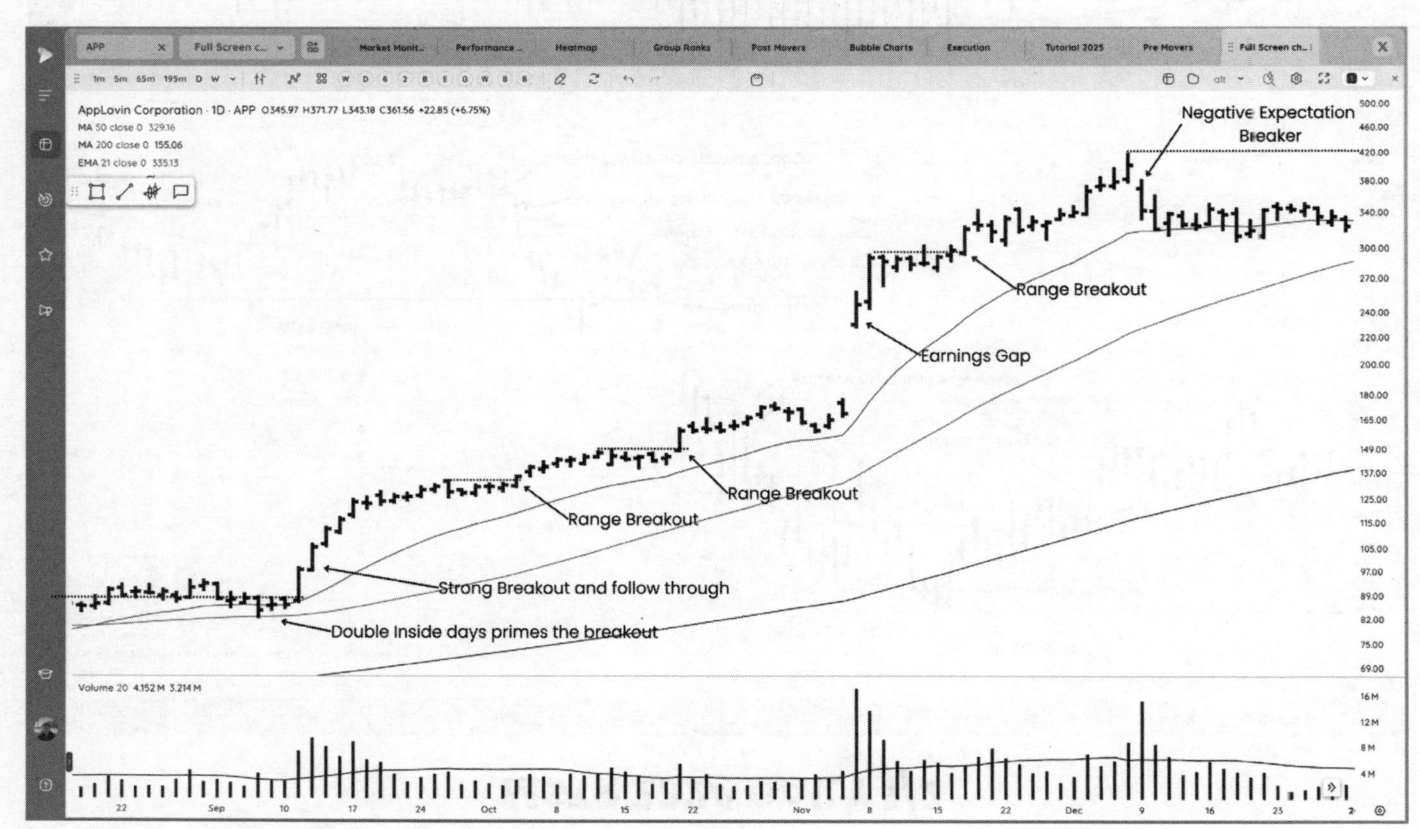
APP 2024 DAILY 3/3
AppLovin Corporation · 1D · APP O345.97 H371.77 L343.18 C361.56 +22.85 (+6.75%)
MA 50 close 0 329.16
MA 200 close 0 155.06
EMA 21 close 0 335.13
Negative Expectation Breaker
Range Breakout
Earnings Gap
Range Breakout
Range Breakout
Strong Breakout and follow through
Double Inside days primes the breakout
Volume 20 4.152 M 3.214 M

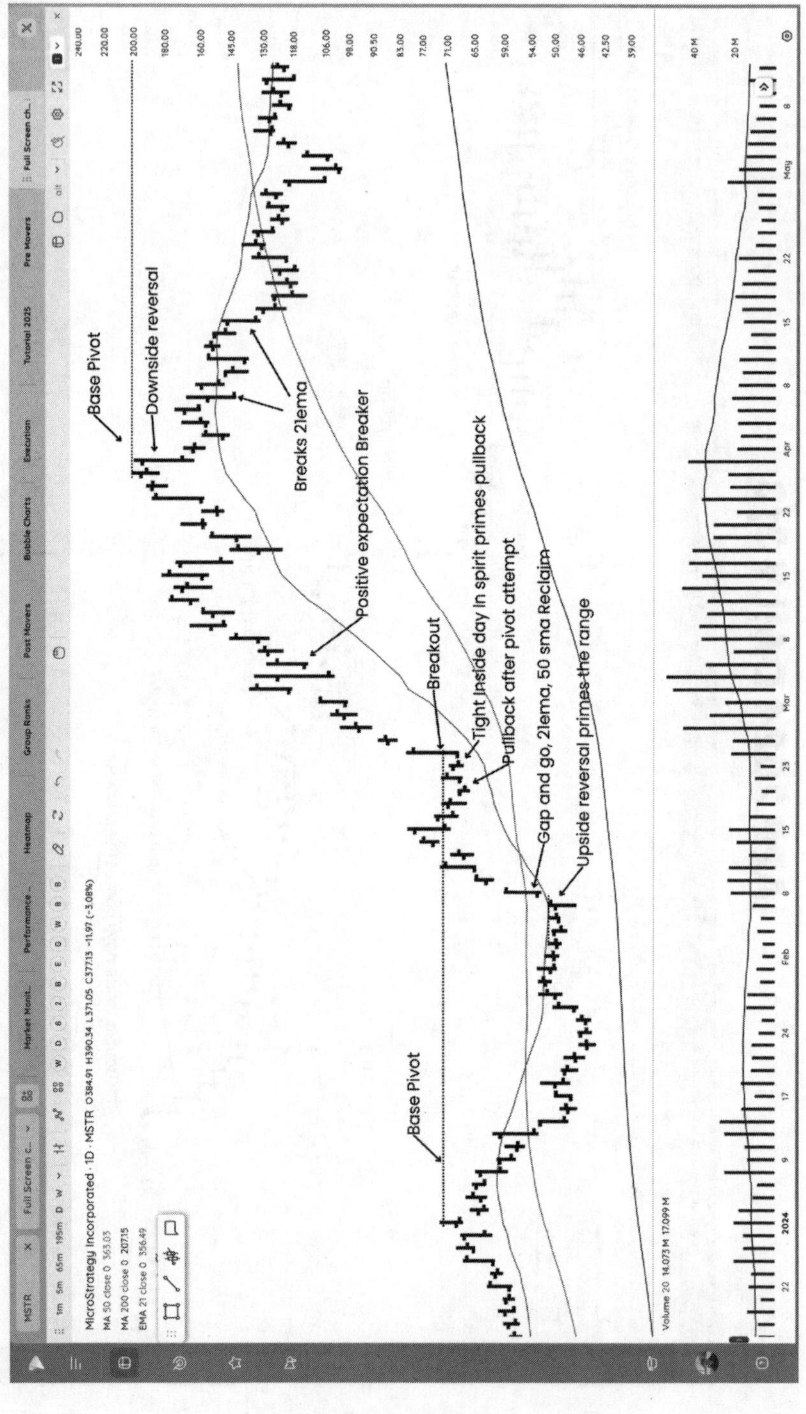
MSTR 2024 DAILY 1/2
Base Pivot
Downside reversal
Breaks 21ema
Positive expectation Breaker
Breakout
Tight inside day in spirit primes pullback
Pullback after pivot attempt
Gap and go, 21ema, 50 sma Reclaim
Upside reversal primes the range
Base Pivot

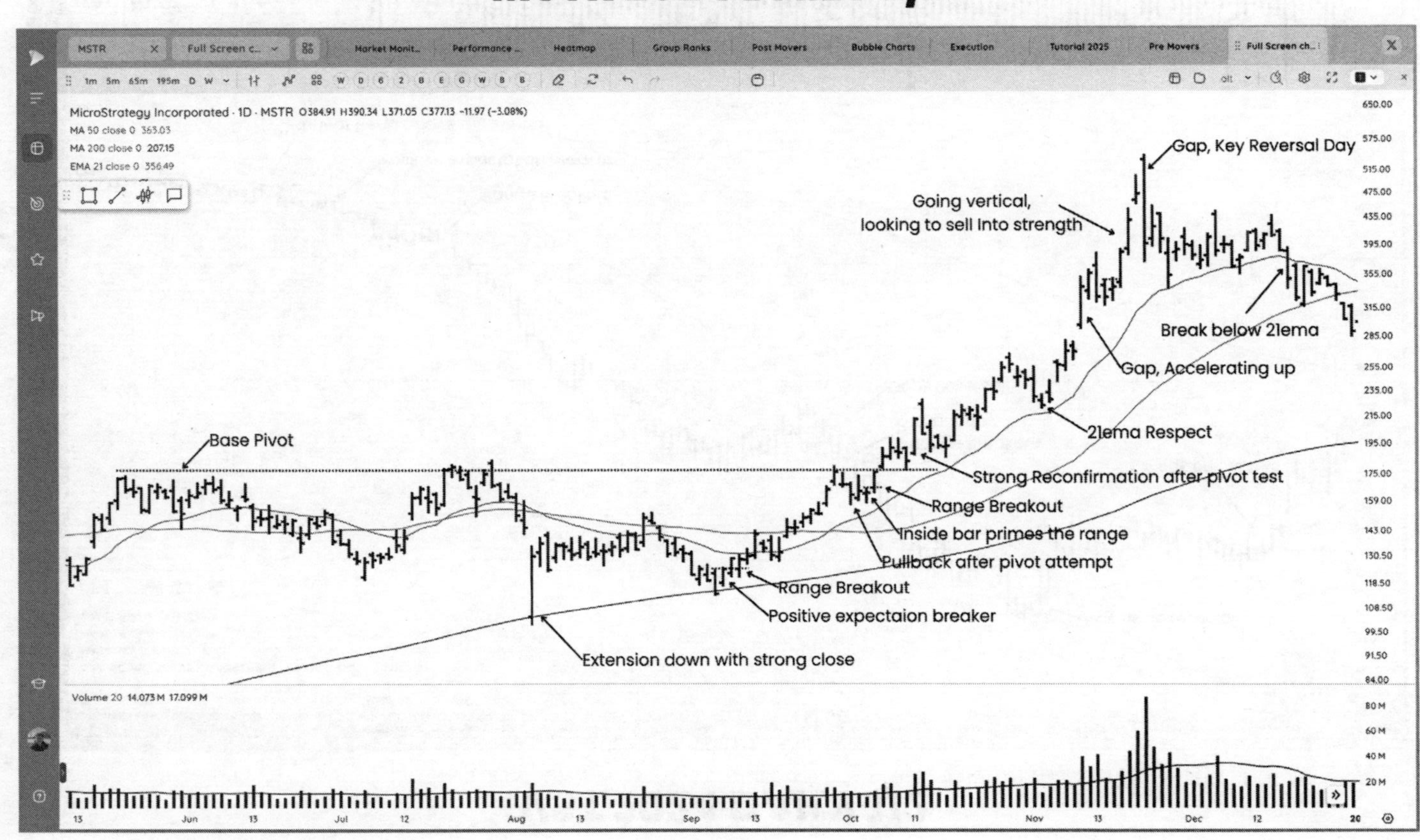
MSTR 2024 DAILY 2/2
MicroStrategy Incorporated · 1D · MSTR O384.91 H390.34 L371.05 C377.13 −11.97 (−3.08%)
MA 50 close 0 363.03
MA 200 close 0 207.15
EMA 21 close 0 356.49
Gap, Key Reversal Day
Going vertical,
looking to sell into strength
Break below 21ema
Gap, Accelerating up
21ema Respect
Base Pivot
Strong Reconfirmation after pivot test
Range Breakout
Inside bar primes the range
Pullback after pivot attempt
Range Breakout
Positive expectaion breaker
Extension down with strong close
Volume 20 14.073 M 17.099 M

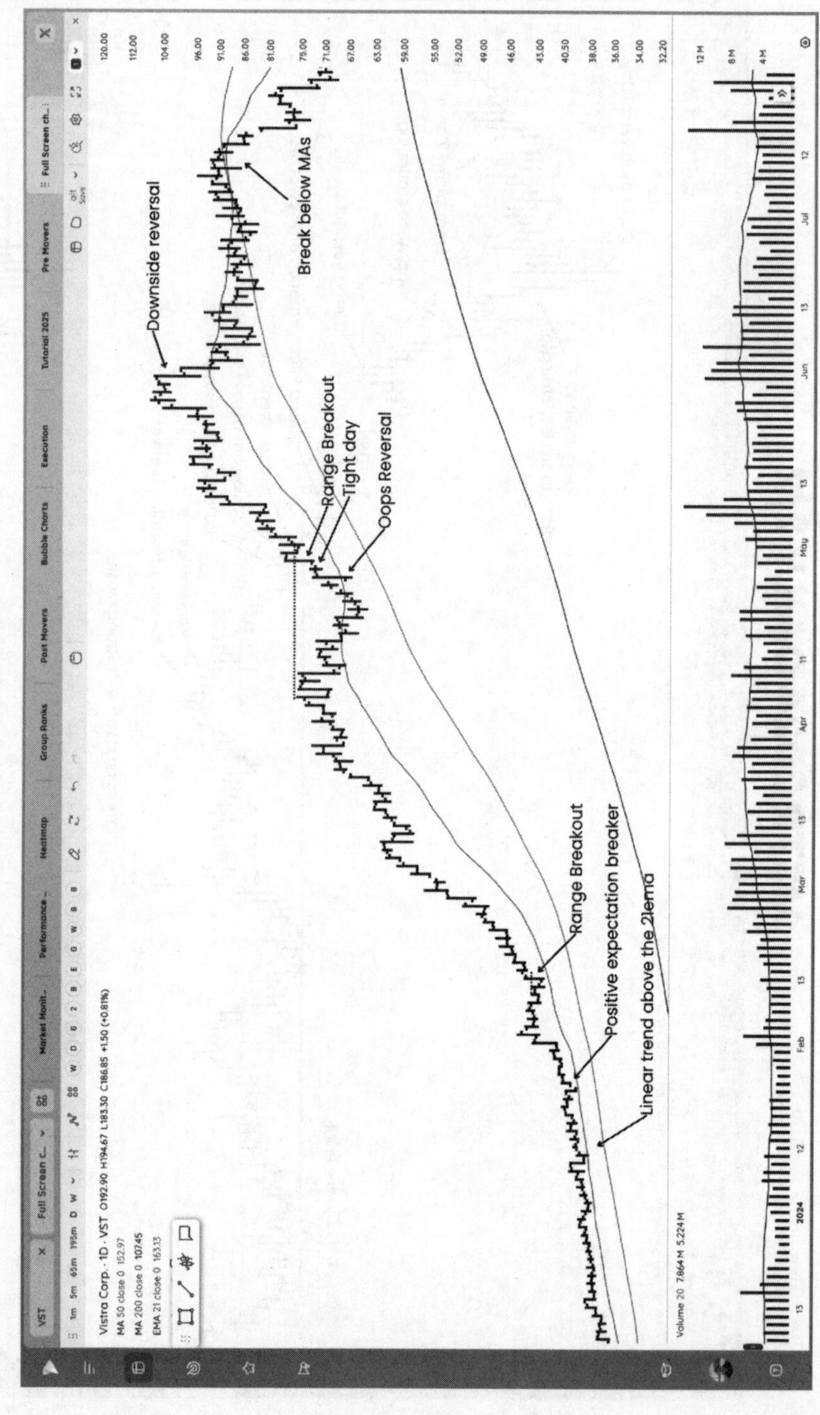
VST 2024 DAILY 1/2
Downside reversal
Break below MAs
Range Breakout
Tight day
Oops Reversal
Range Breakout
Positive expectation breaker
Linear trend above the 21ema

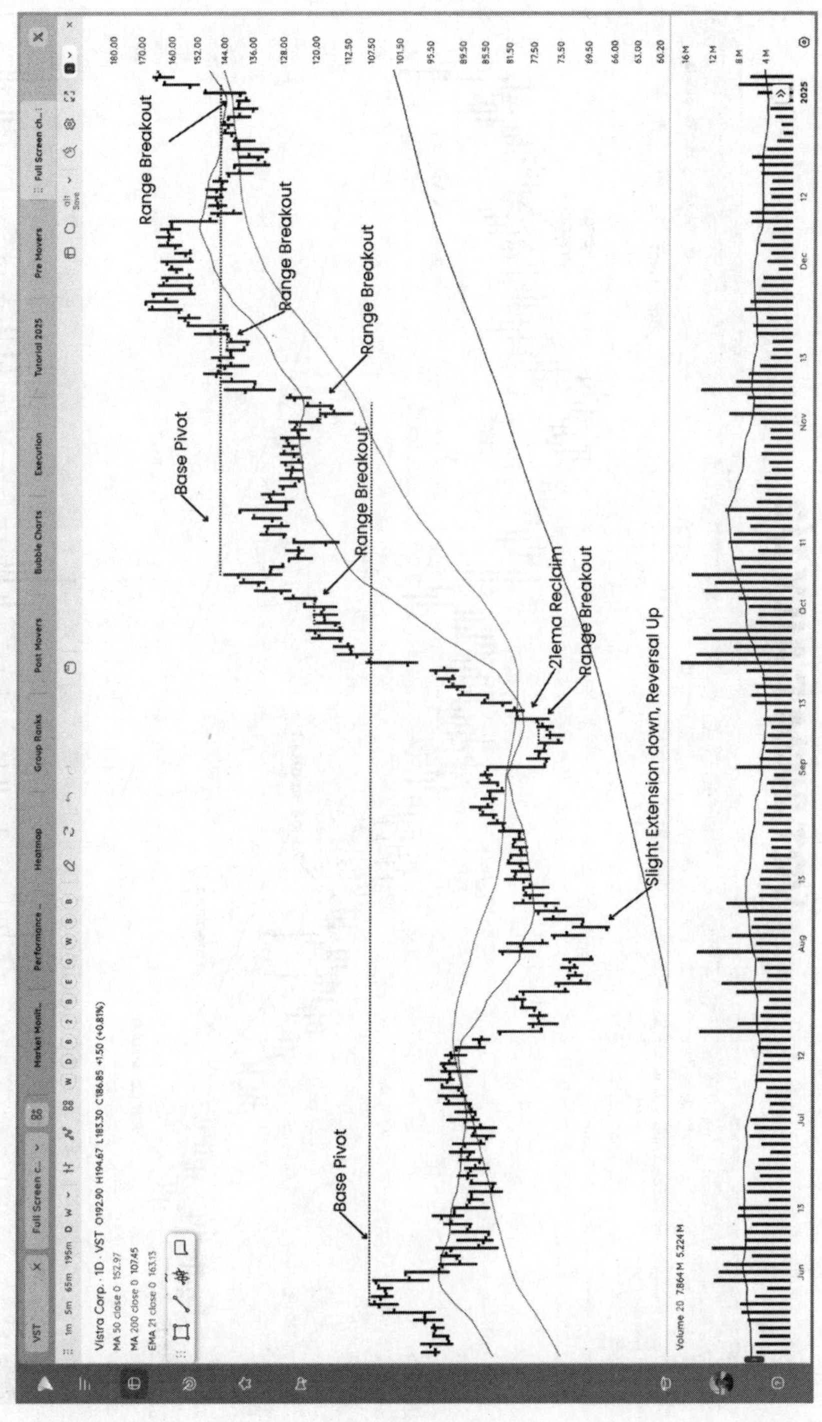
VST 2024 DAILY 2/2
Vistra Corp. · 1D · VST O192.90 H194.67 L183.30 C186.85 +1.50 (+0.81%)
MA 50 close 0 152.97
MA 200 close 0 107.45
EMA 21 close 0 163.13
Base Pivot
Base Pivot
Range Breakout
Range Breakout
Range Breakout
Range Breakout
Range Breakout
21ema Reclaim
Slight Extension down, Reversal Up
Volume 20 7.864 M 5.224 M

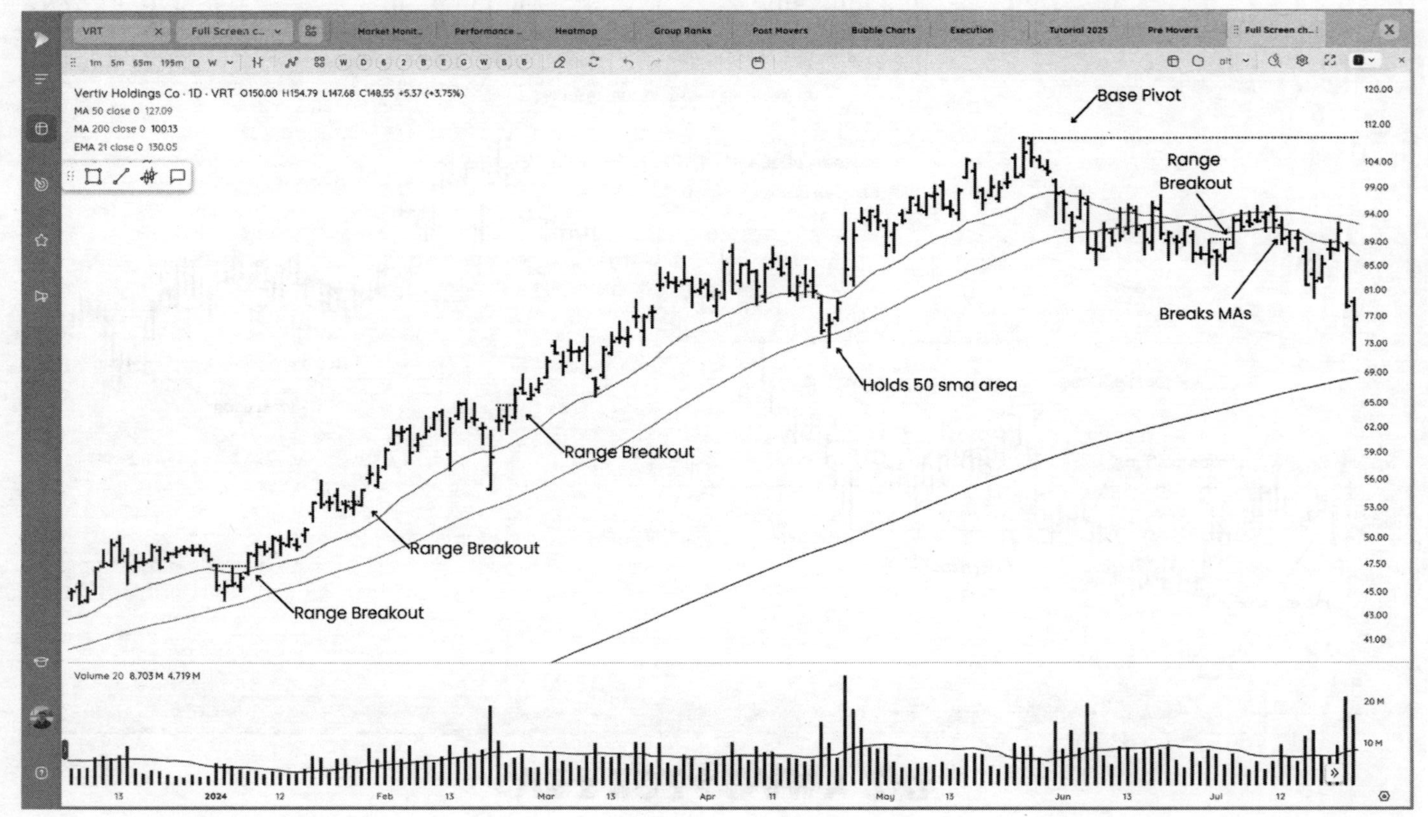
VRT 2024 DAILY 1/2
Vertiv Holdings Co · 1D · VRT O150.00 H154.79 L147.68 C148.55 +5.37 (+3.75%)
MA 50 close 0 127.09
MA 200 close 0 100.13
EMA 21 close 0 130.05
Base Pivot
Range Breakout
Breaks MAs
Holds 50 sma area
Range Breakout
Range Breakout
Range Breakout
Volume 20 8.703 M 4.719 M

VRT 2024 DAILY 2/2

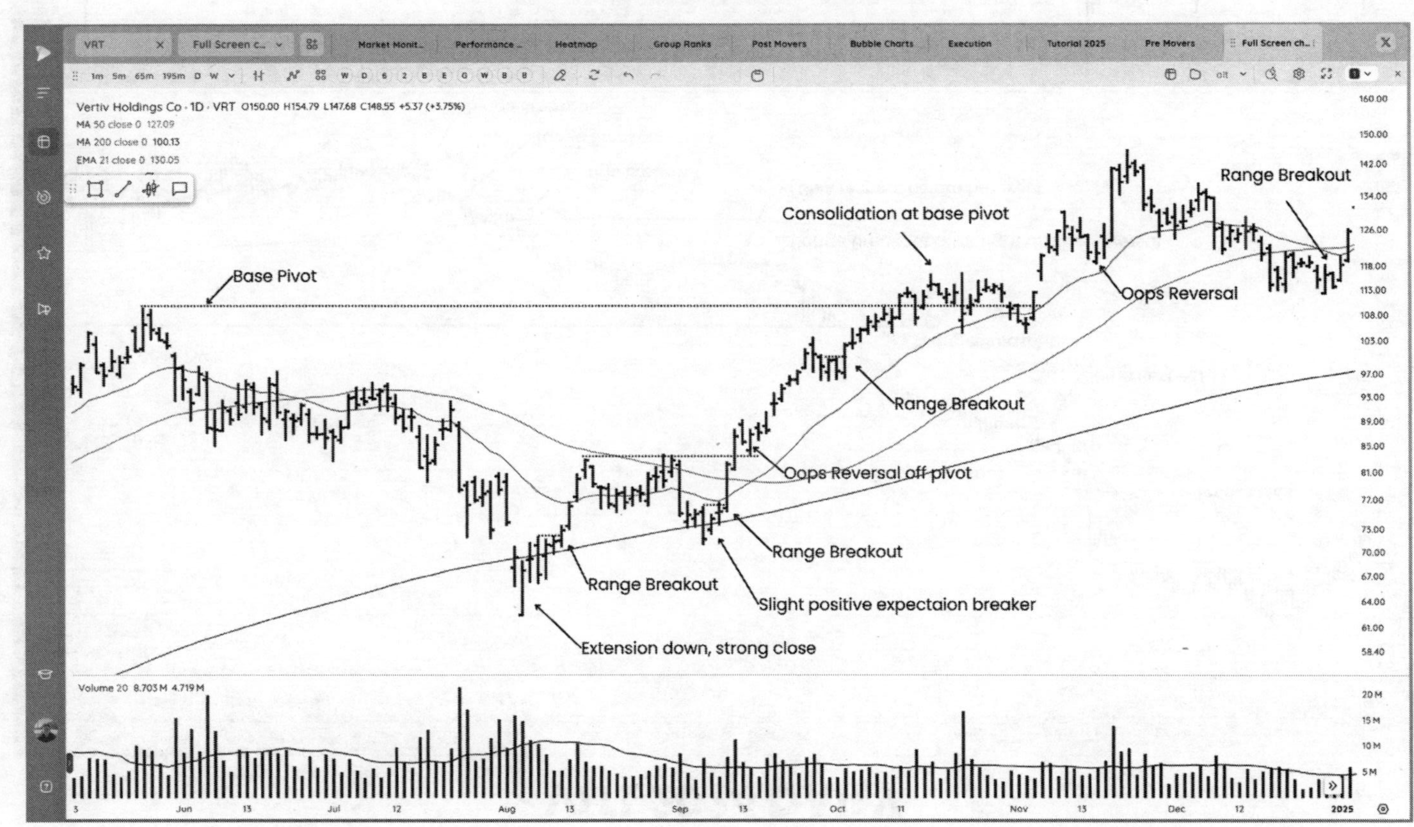

VITL 2024 DAILY

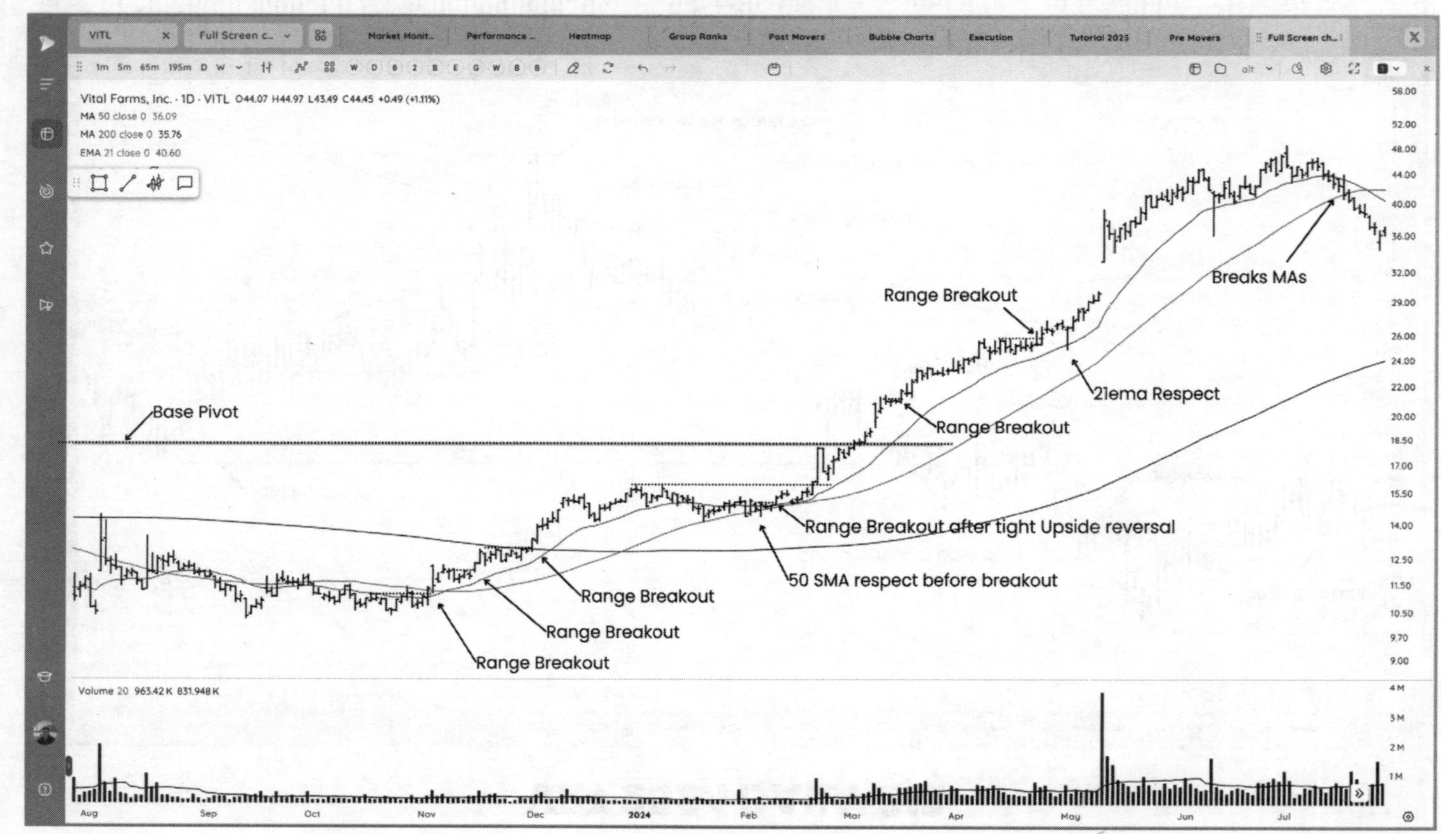

PLTR 2024 DAILY 1/2

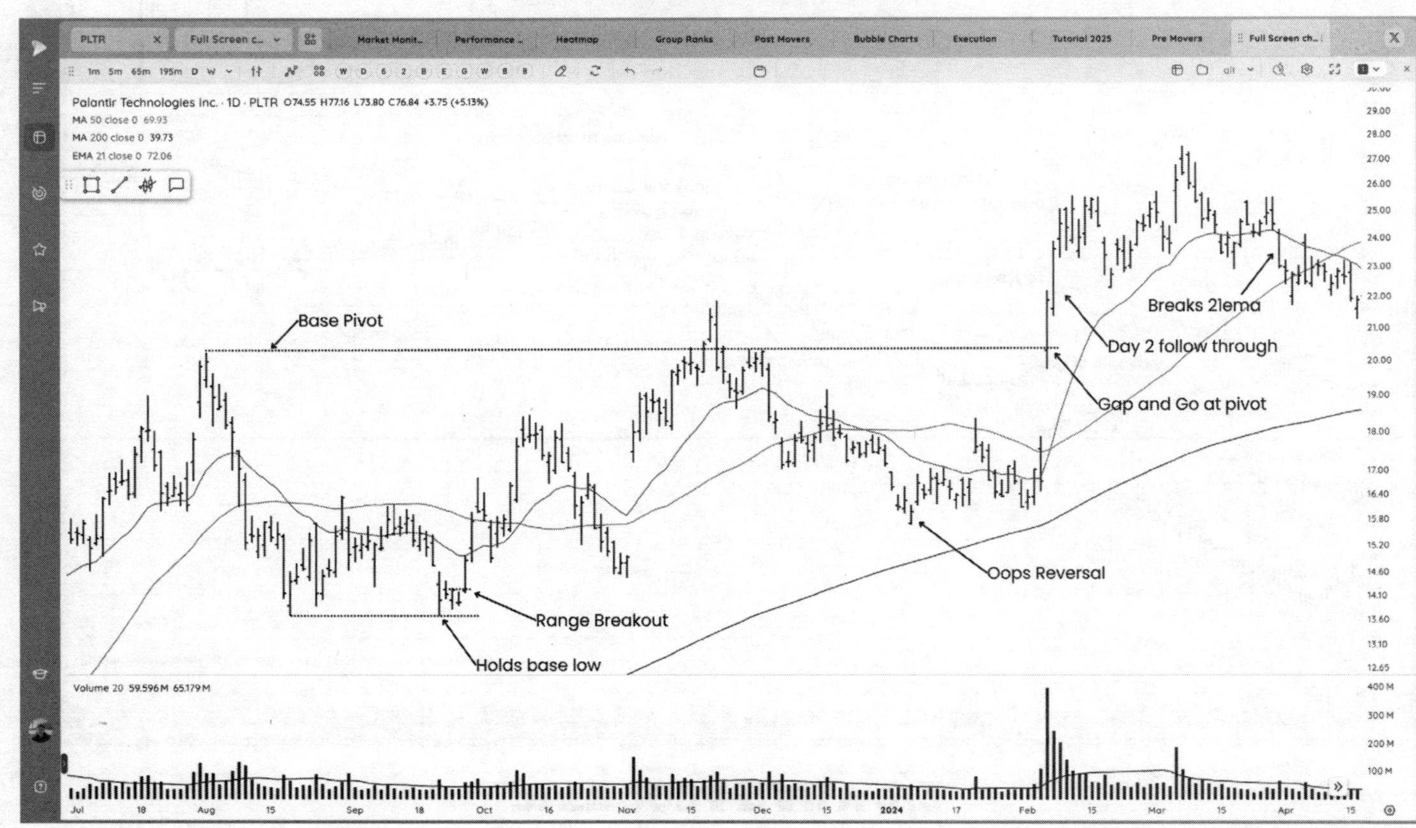

PLTR 2024 DAILY 2/2

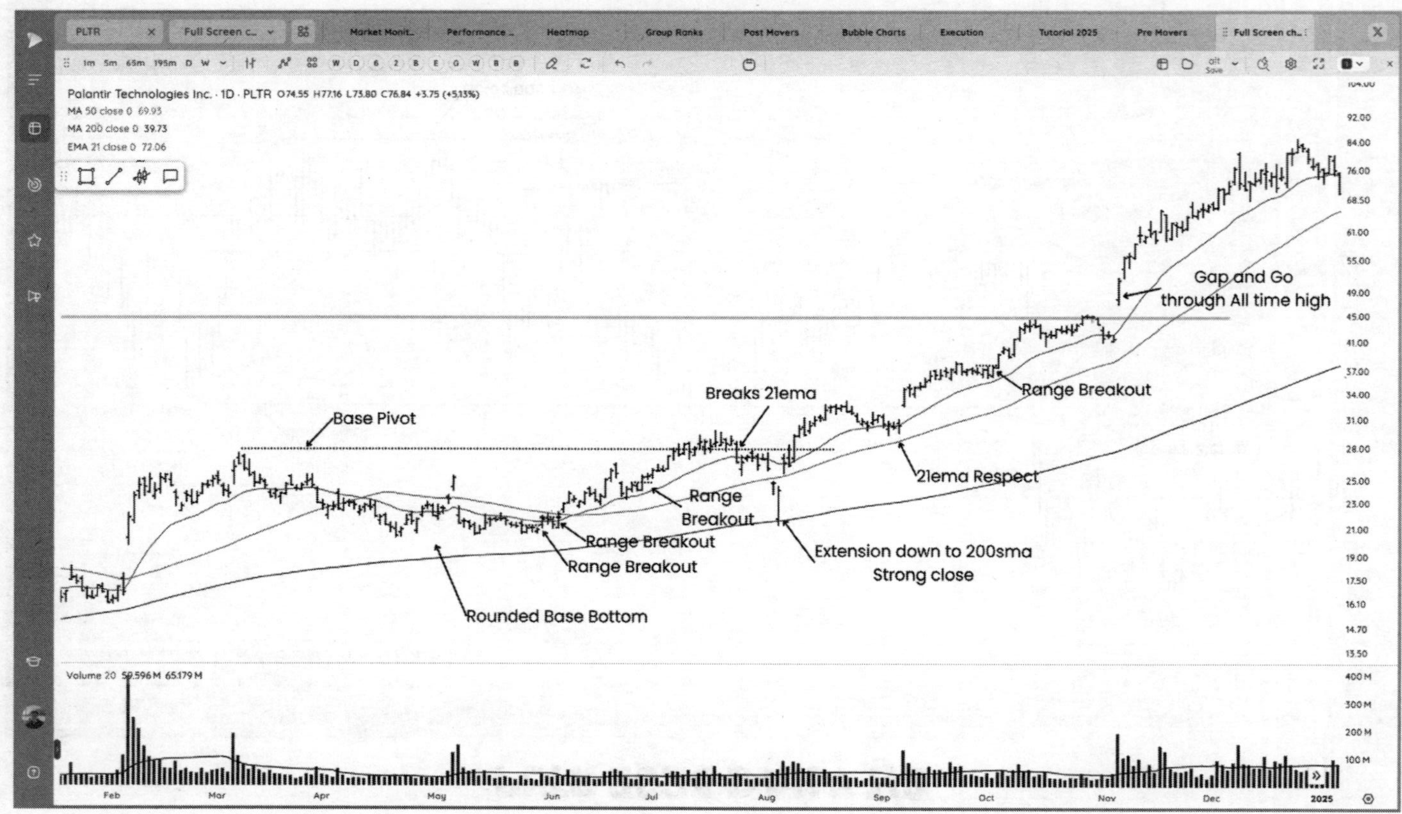

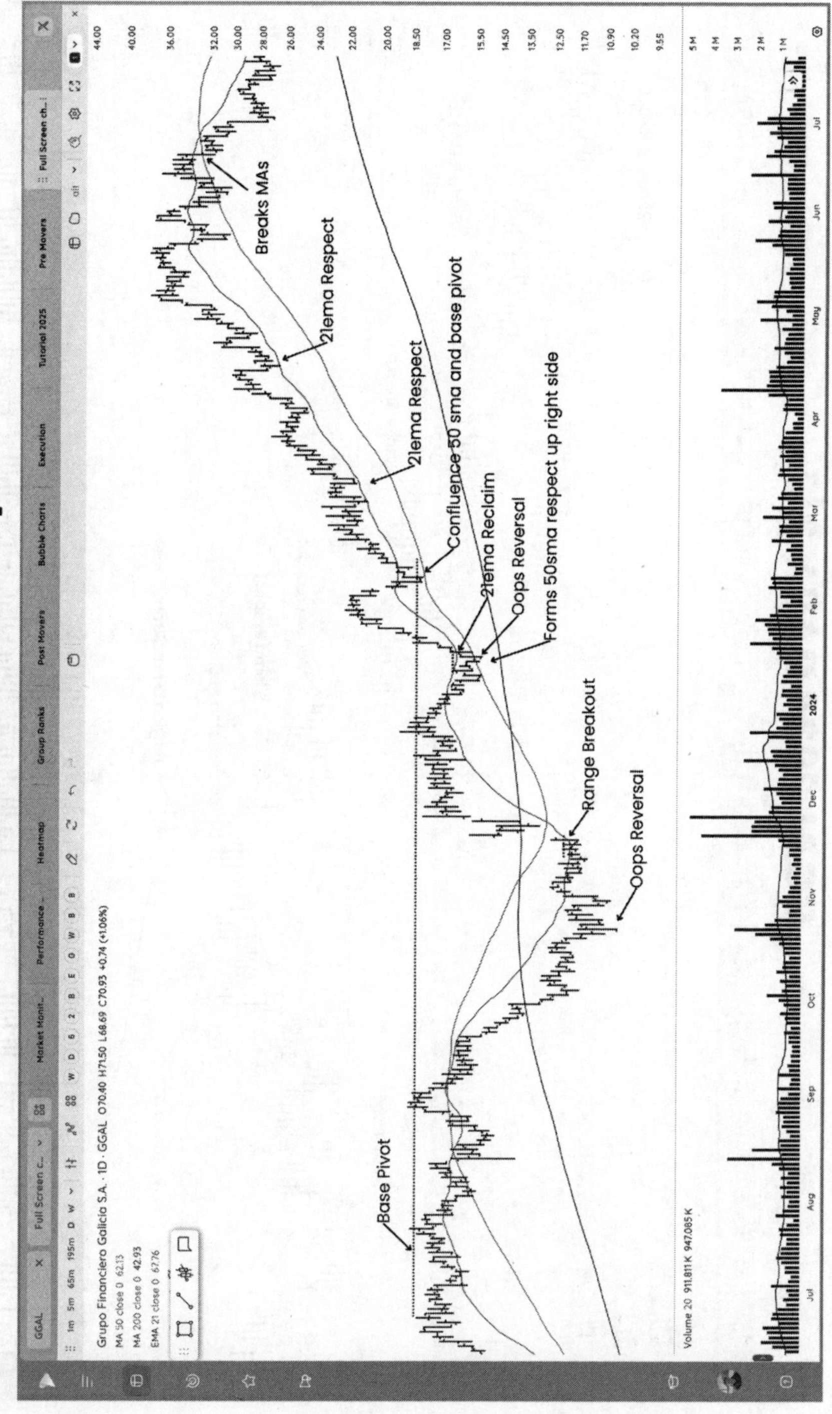
GGAL 2024 DAILY 1/2
Grupo Financiero Galicia S.A. · 1D · GGAL O70.40 H71.50 L68.69 C70.93 +0.74 (+1.06%)
MA 50 close 0 62.13
MA 200 close 0 42.93
EMA 21 close 0 67.76
Base Pivot
Oops Reversal
Range Breakout
Forms 50sma respect up right side
Oops Reversal
21ema Reclaim
Confluence 50 sma and base pivot
21ema Respect
21ema Respect
Breaks MAs
Volume 20 911.811K 947.085K

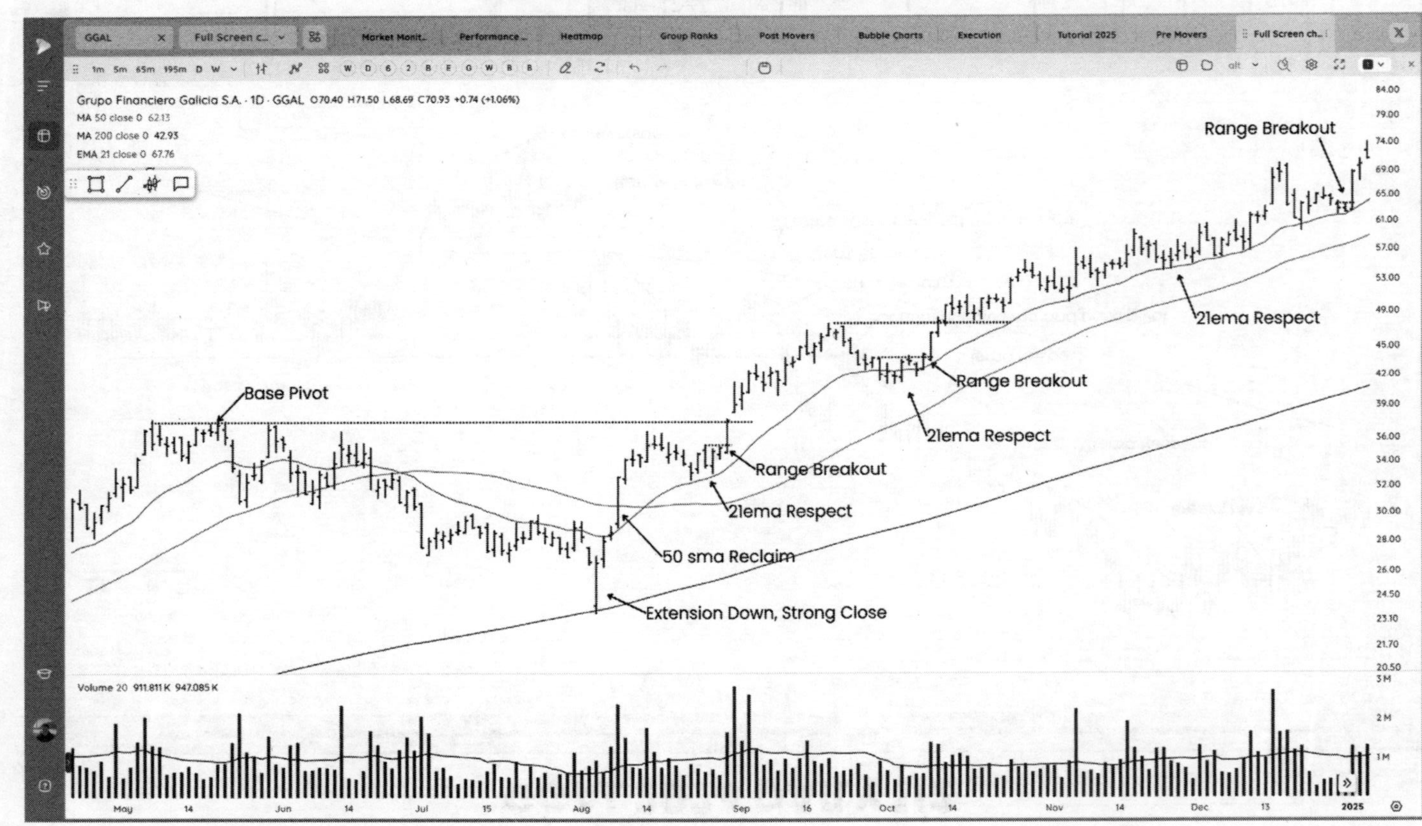
GGAL 2024 DAILY 2/2
Grupo Financiero Galicia S.A. · 1D · GGAL O70.40 H71.50 L68.69 C70.93 +0.74 (+1.06%)
MA 50 close 0 62.13
MA 200 close 0 42.93
EMA 21 close 0 67.76
Base Pivot
Extension Down, Strong Close
50 sma Reclaim
21ema Respect
Range Breakout
21ema Respect
Range Breakout
21ema Respect
Range Breakout
Volume 20 911.811 K 947.085 K

HOOD 2024 DAILY 1/2

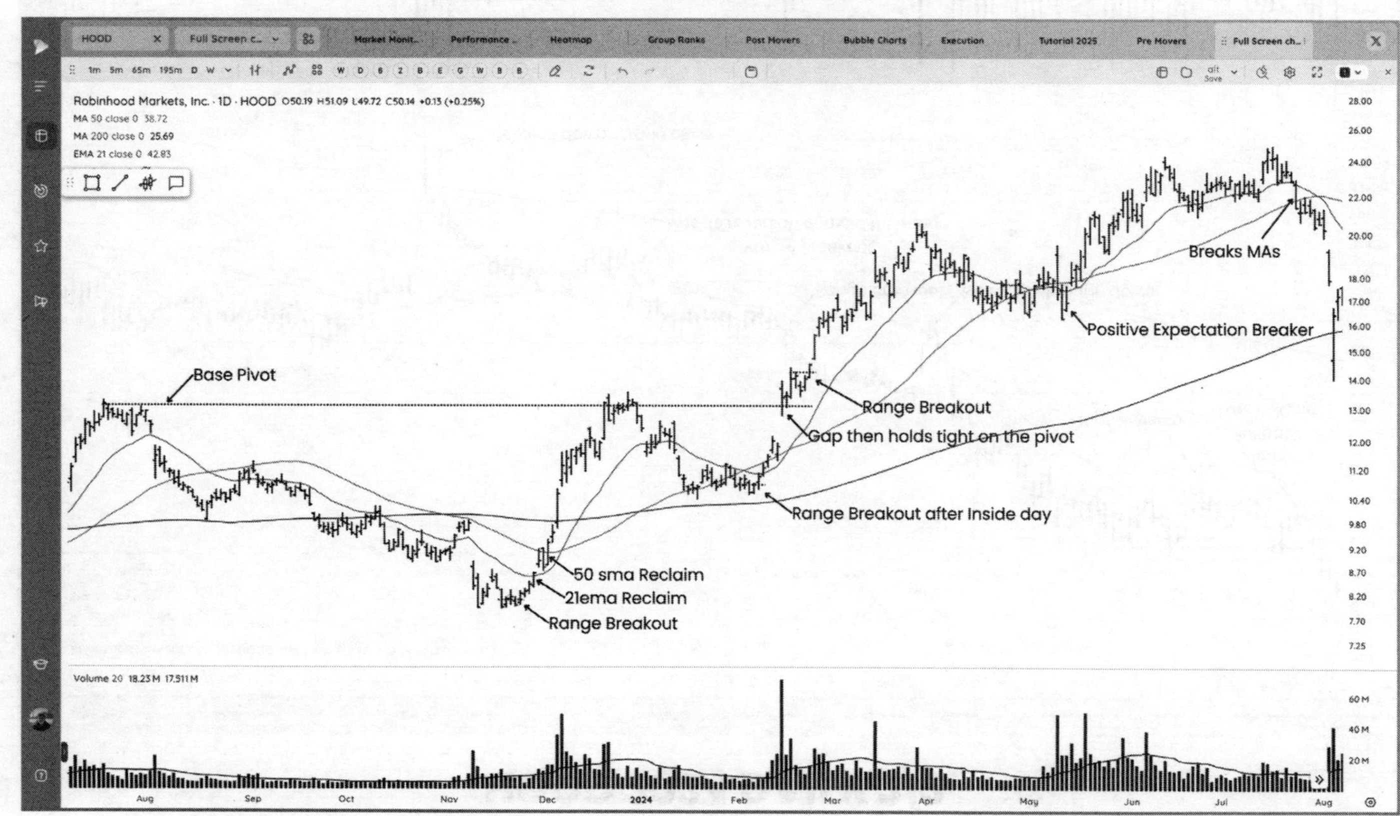

HOOD 2024 DAILY 2/2

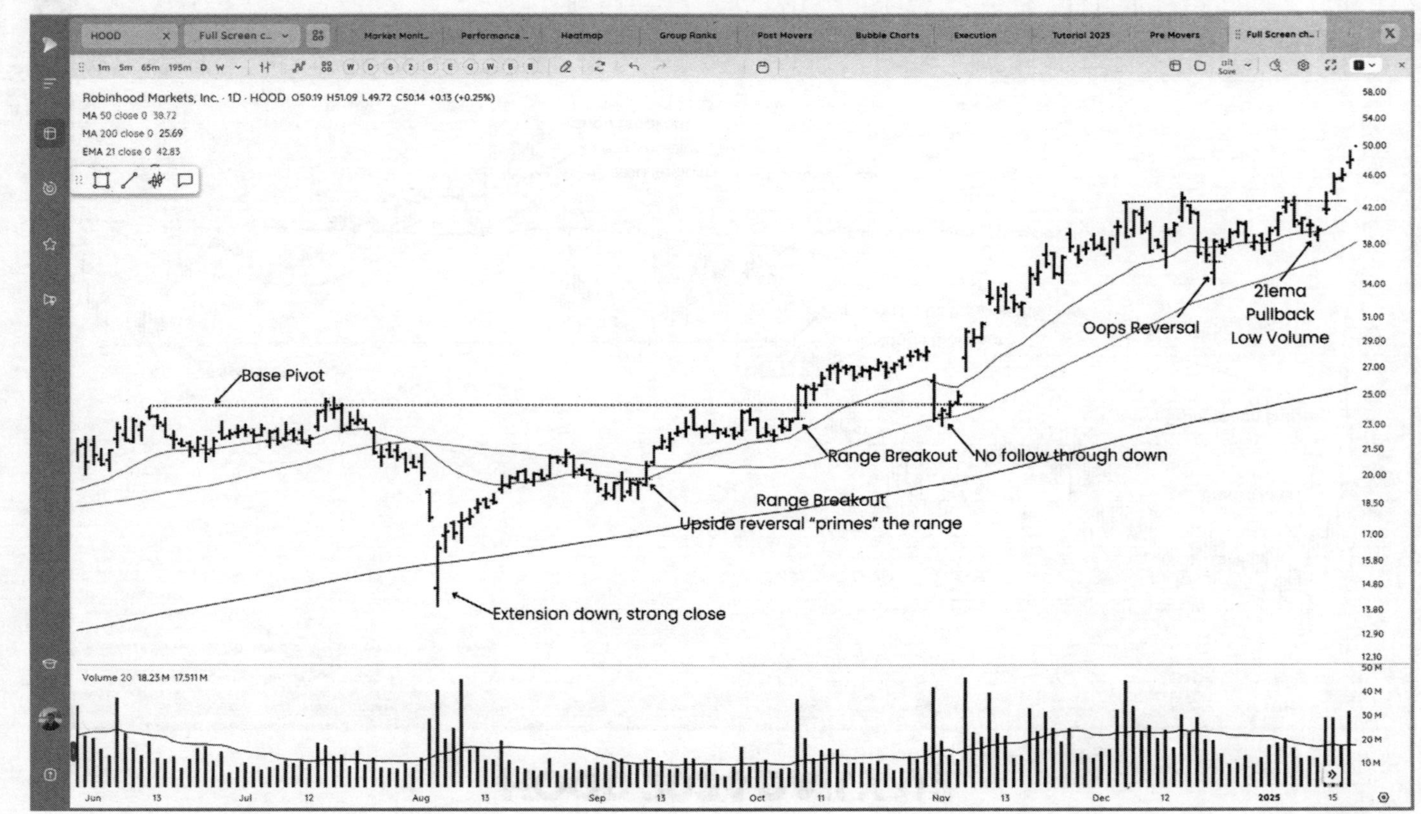

EAT 2024 DAILY 1/2

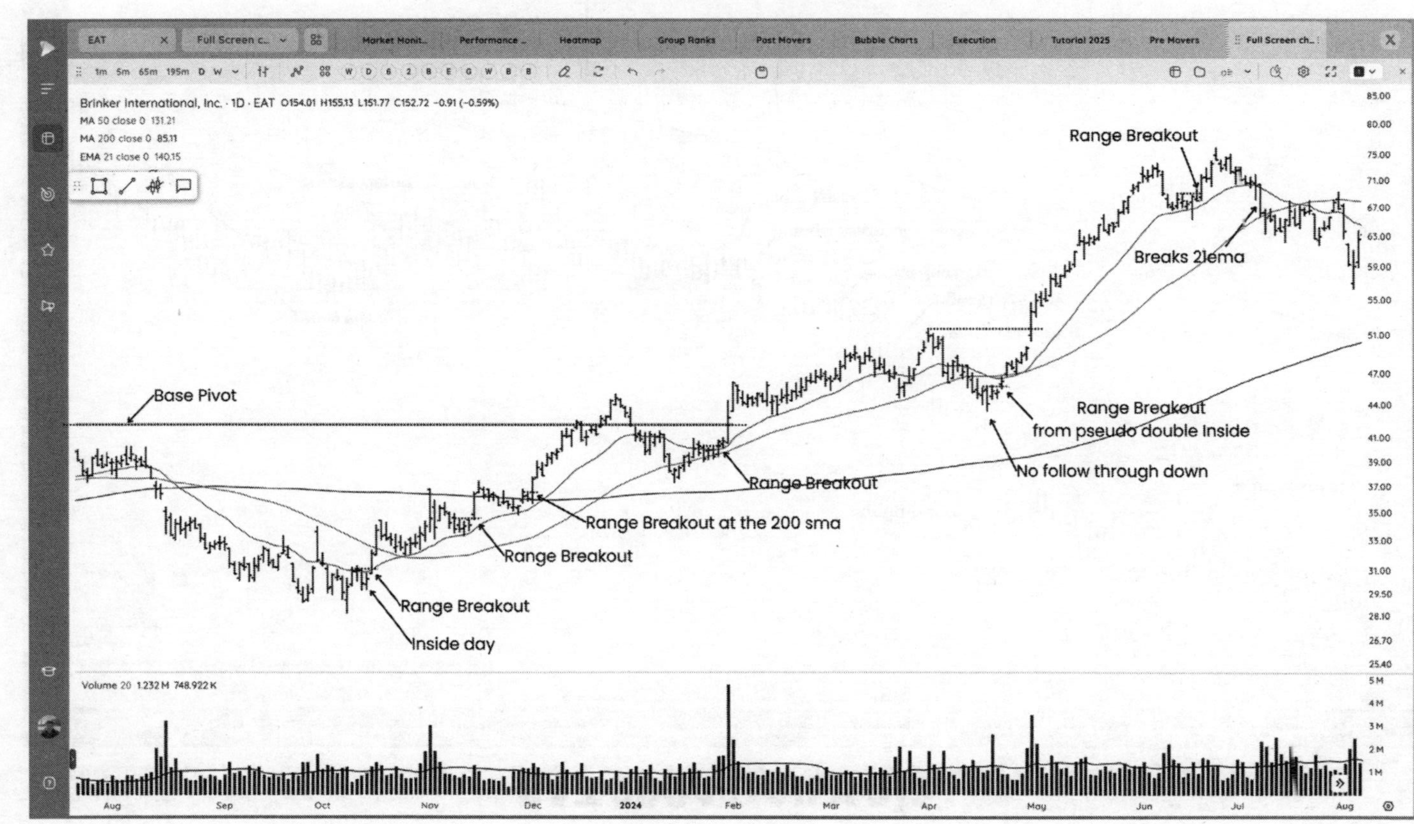

EAT 2024 DAILY 2/2

SOUN 2024 DAILY 1/2

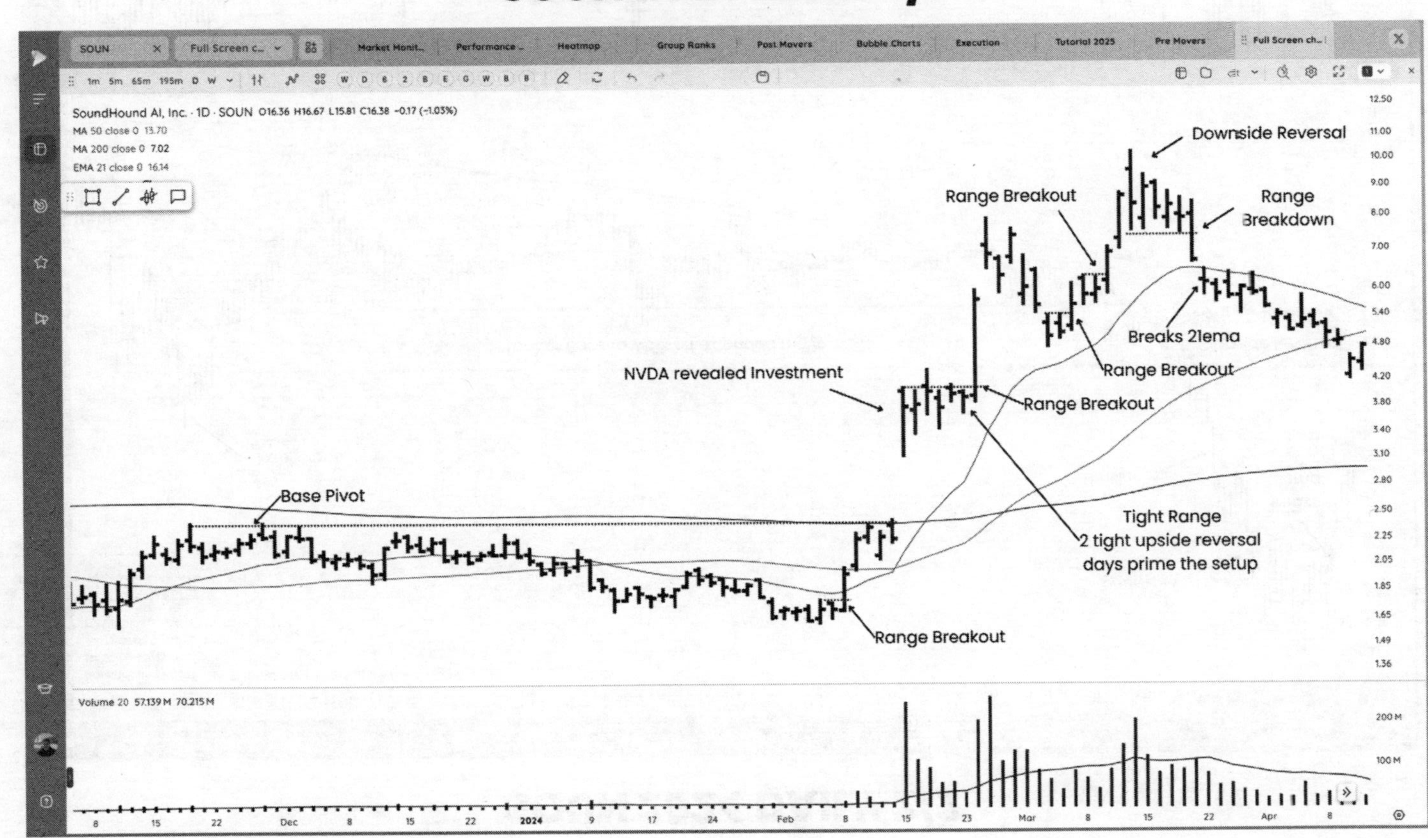

SOUN 2024 DAILY 2/2

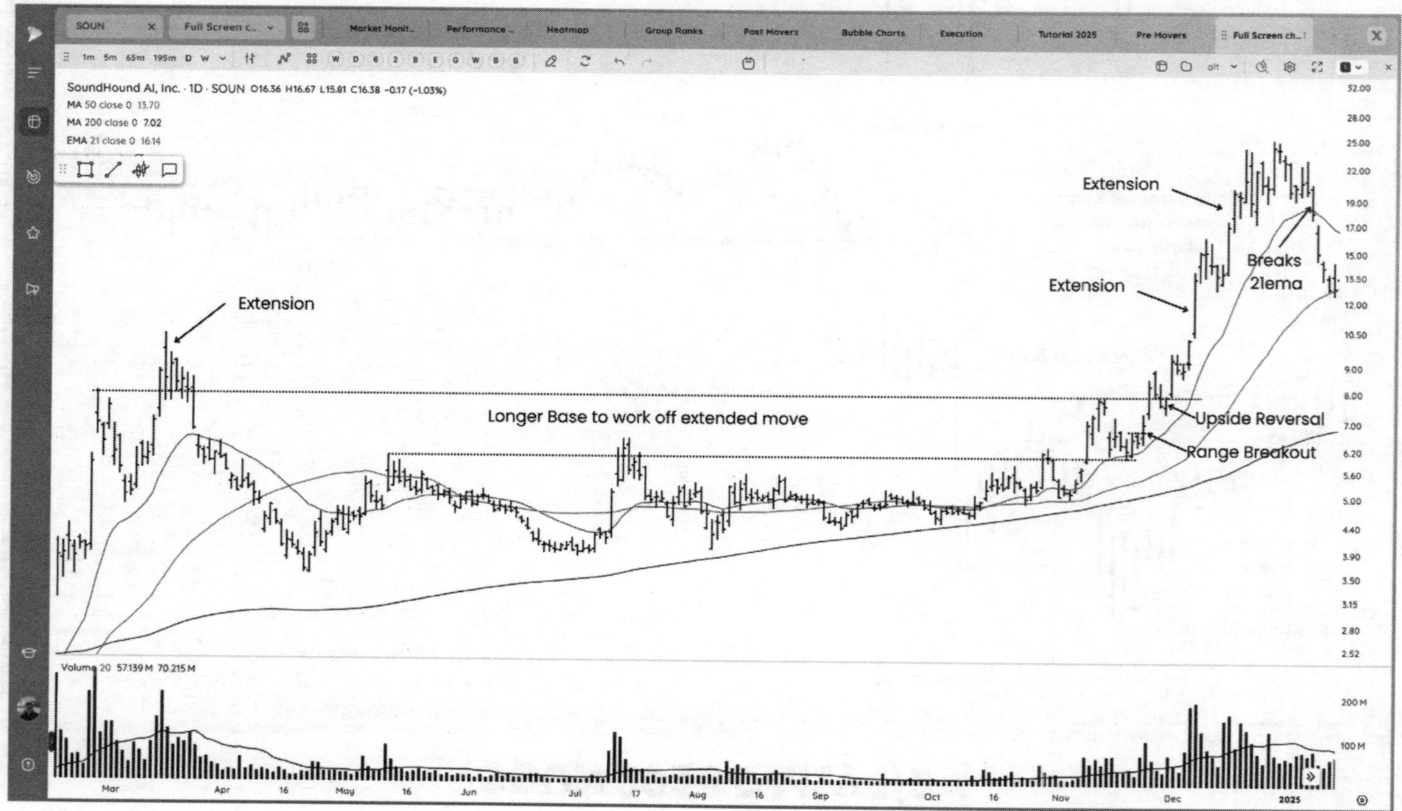

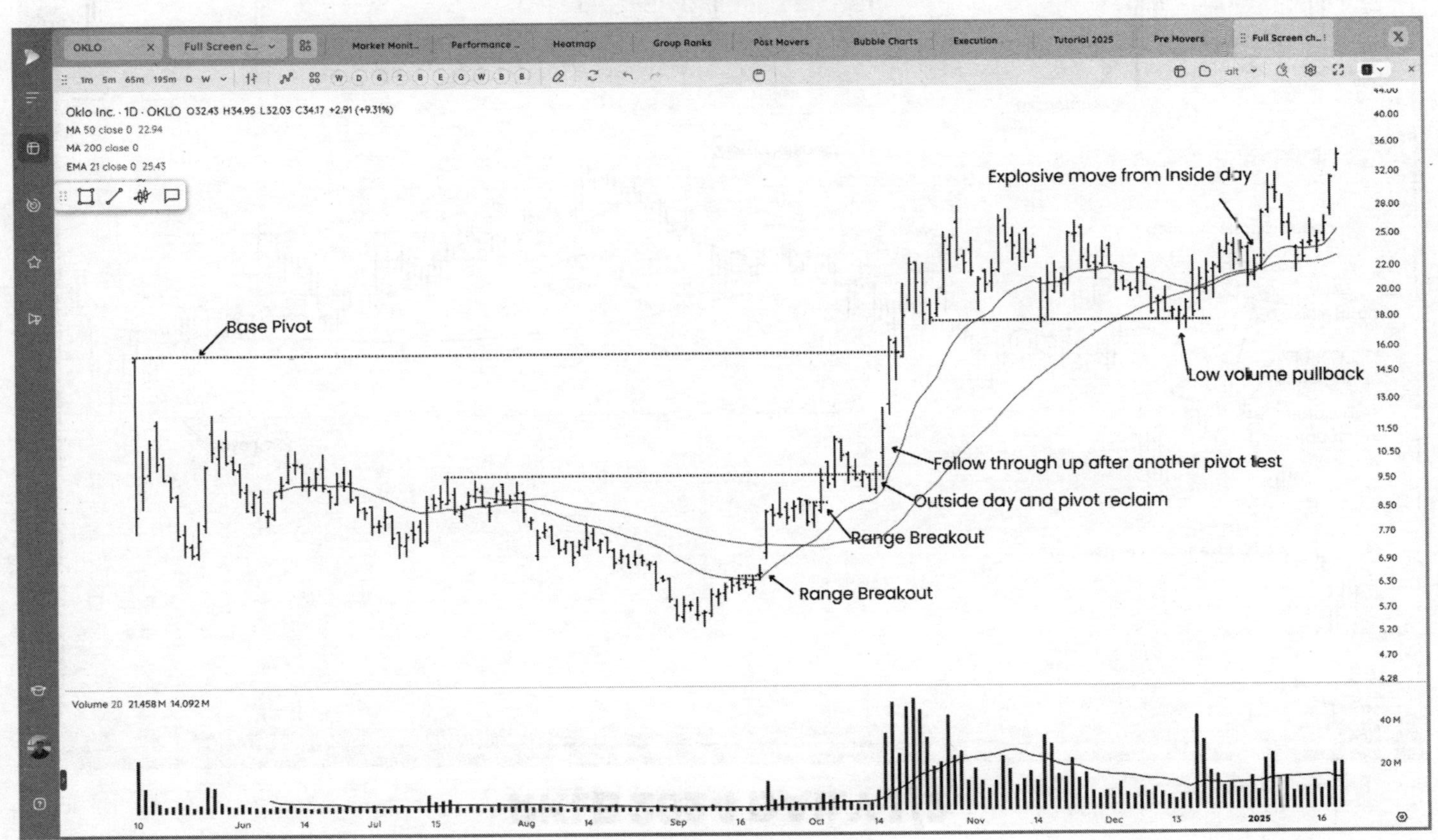
OKLO 2024 DAILY
Oklo Inc. · 1D · OKLO O32.43 H34.95 L32.03 C34.17 +2.91 (+9.31%)
MA 50 close 0 22.94
MA 200 close 0
EMA 21 close 0 25.43
Base Pivot
Explosive move from Inside day
Low volume pullback
Follow through up after another pivot test
Outside day and pivot reclaim
Range Breakout
Range Breakout
Volume 20 21.458M 14.092M

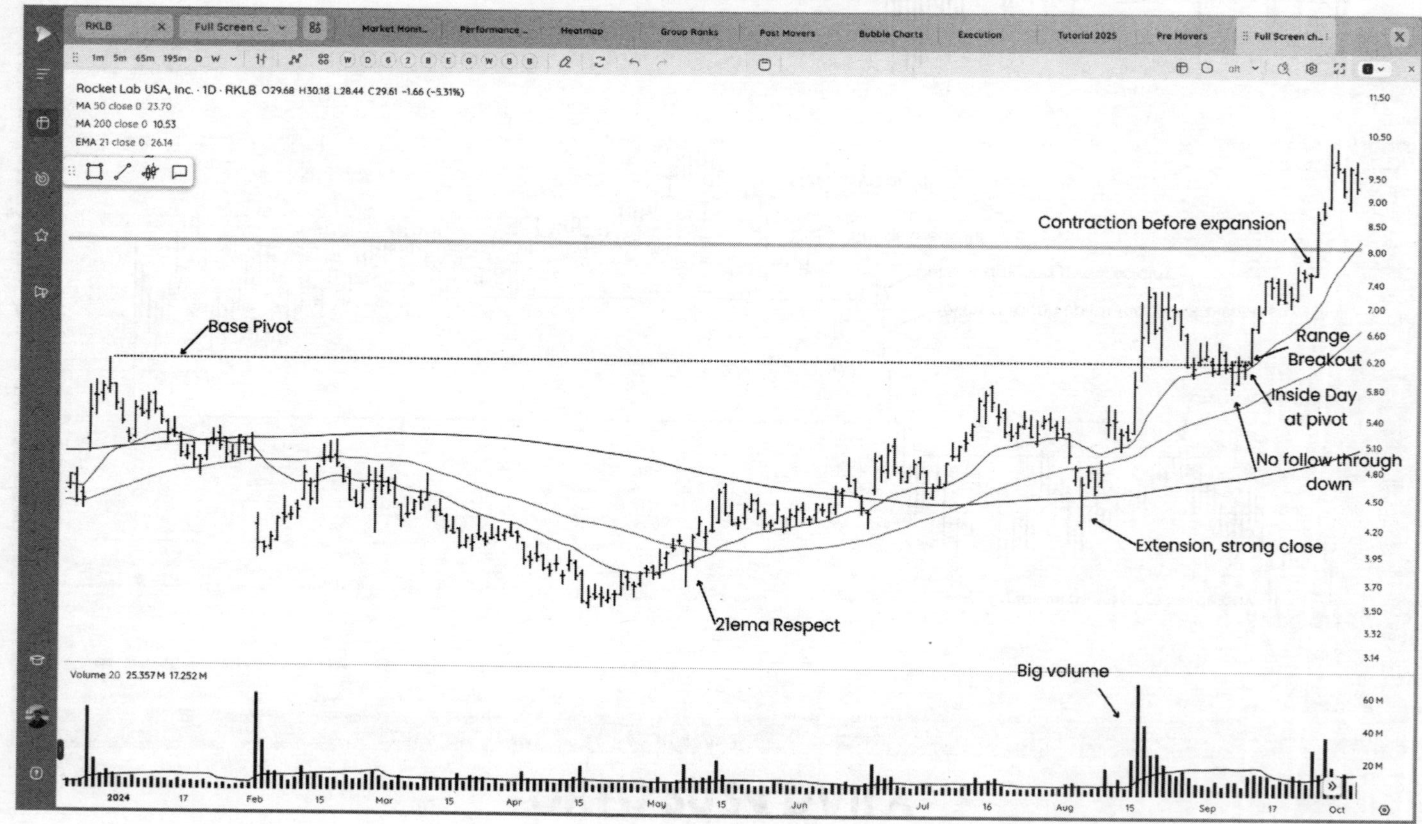
RKLB 2024 DAILY 1/2
Rocket Lab USA, Inc. · 1D · RKLB O29.68 H30.18 L28.44 C29.61 -1.66 (-5.31%)
MA 50 close 0 23.70
MA 200 close 0 10.53
EMA 21 close 0 26.14
Base Pivot
Contraction before expansion
Range
Breakout
Inside Day
at pivot
No follow through
down
Extension, strong close
21ema Respect
Big volume
Volume 20 25.357M 17.252M

RKLB 2024 DAILY 2/2

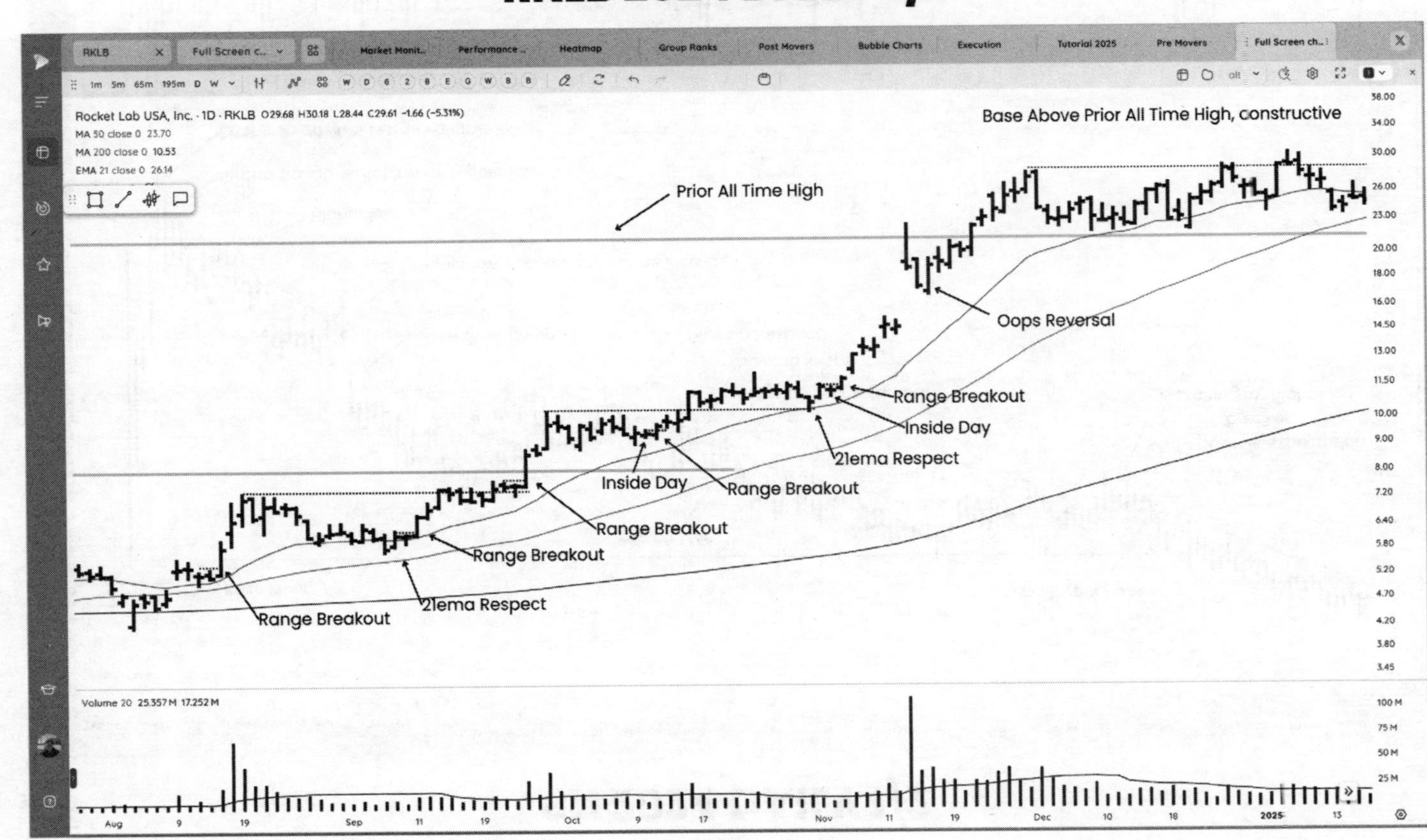

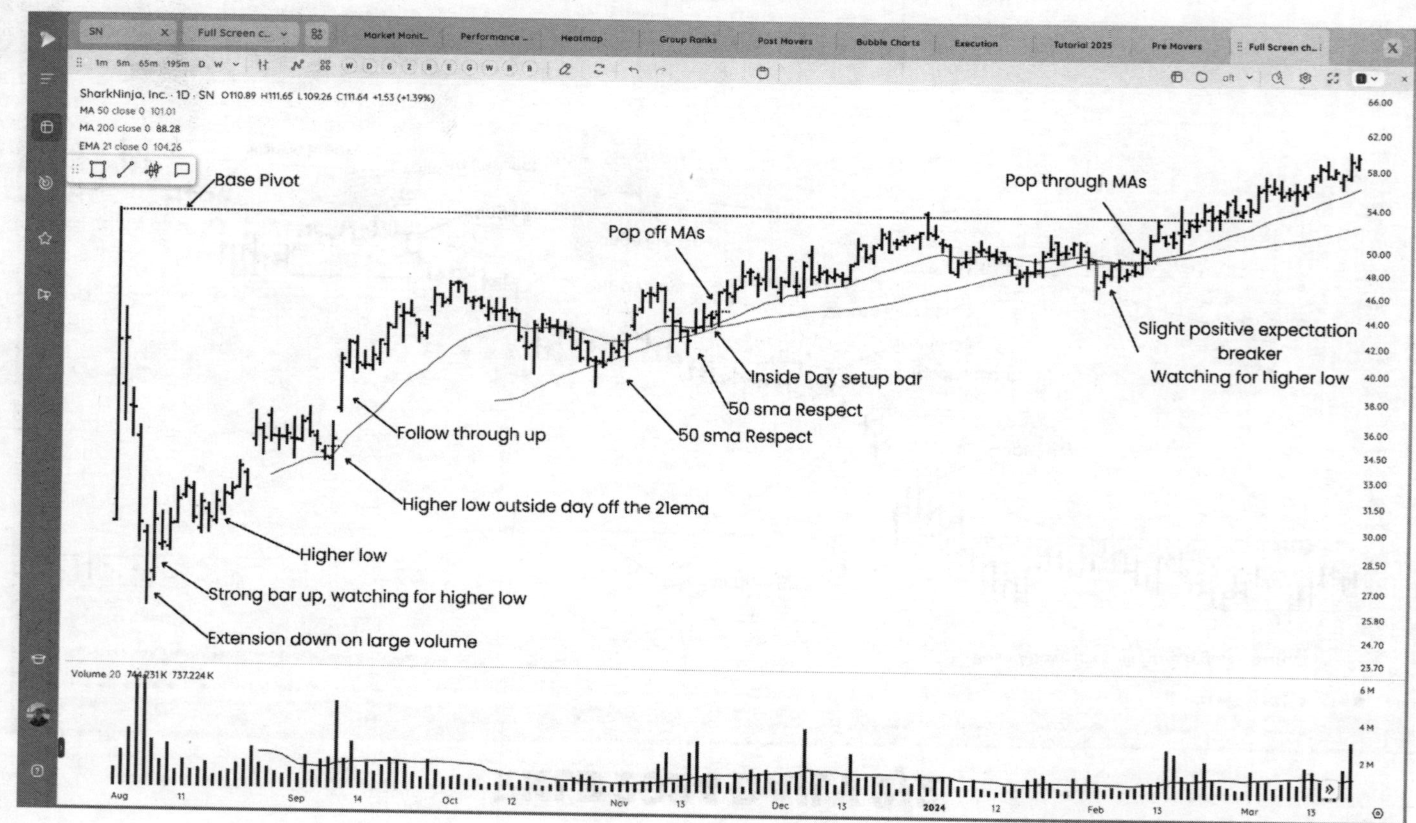
SN 2024 DAILY 1/2
SharkNinja, Inc. · 1D · SN
MA 50 close 0 101.01
MA 200 close 0 88.28
EMA 21 close 0 104.26
Base Pivot
Extension down on large volume
Strong bar up, watching for higher low
Higher low
Higher low outside day off the 21ema
Follow through up
50 sma Respect
50 sma Respect
Inside Day setup bar
Pop off MAs
Pop through MAs
Slight positive expectation
breaker
Watching for higher low

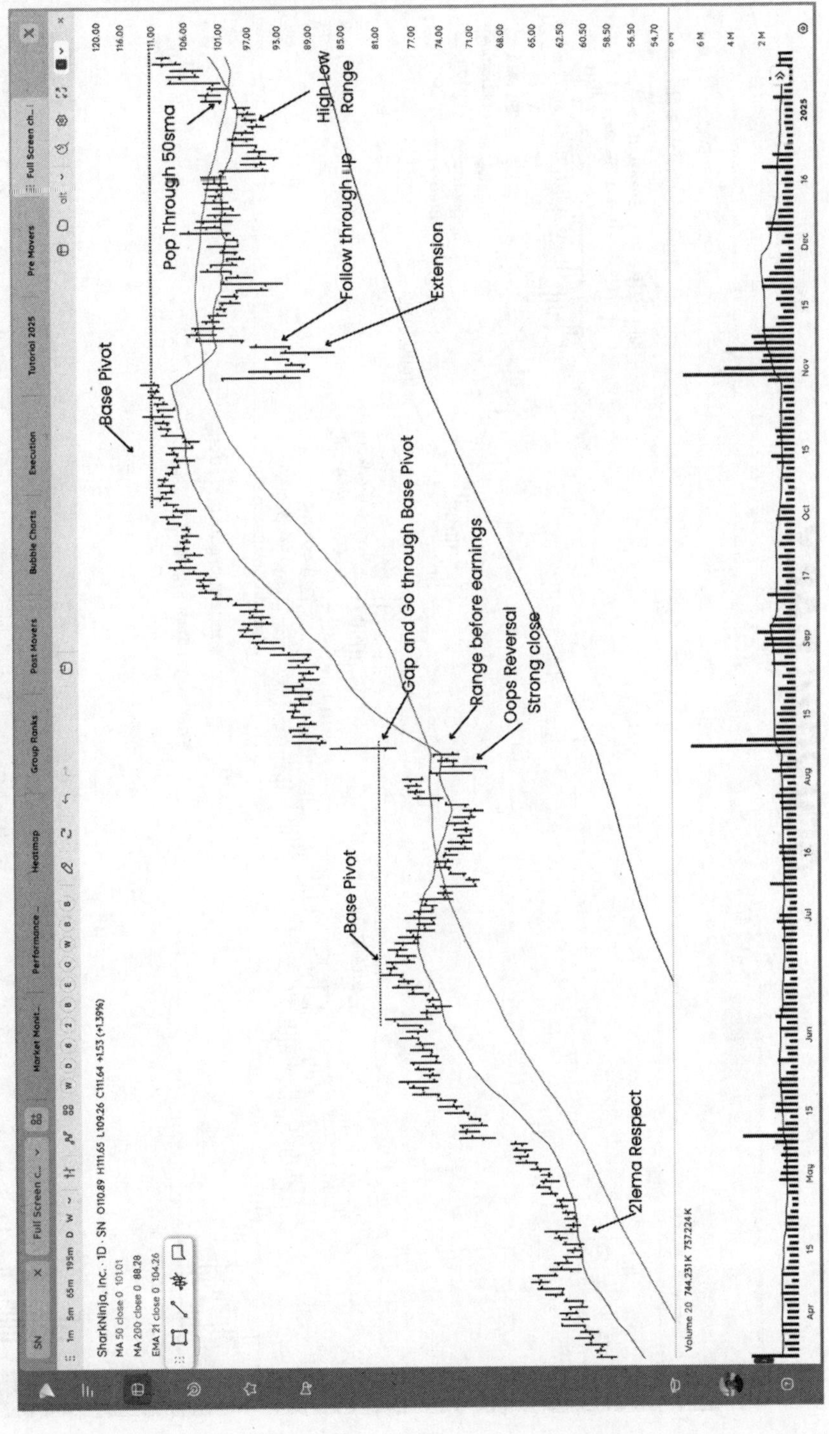
SN 2024 DAILY 2/2
SharkNinja, Inc. · 1D · SN O110.89 H111.65 L109.26 C111.64 +1.53 (+1.39%)
MA 50 close 0 101.01
MA 200 close 0 88.28
EMA 21 close 0 104.26
21ema Respect
Base Pivot
Gap and Go through Base Pivot
Range before earnings
Oops Reversal
Strong close
Base Pivot
Follow through up
Extension
Pop Through 50sma
High Low
Range
Volume 20 744.231K 737.224K

GEV 2024 DAILY

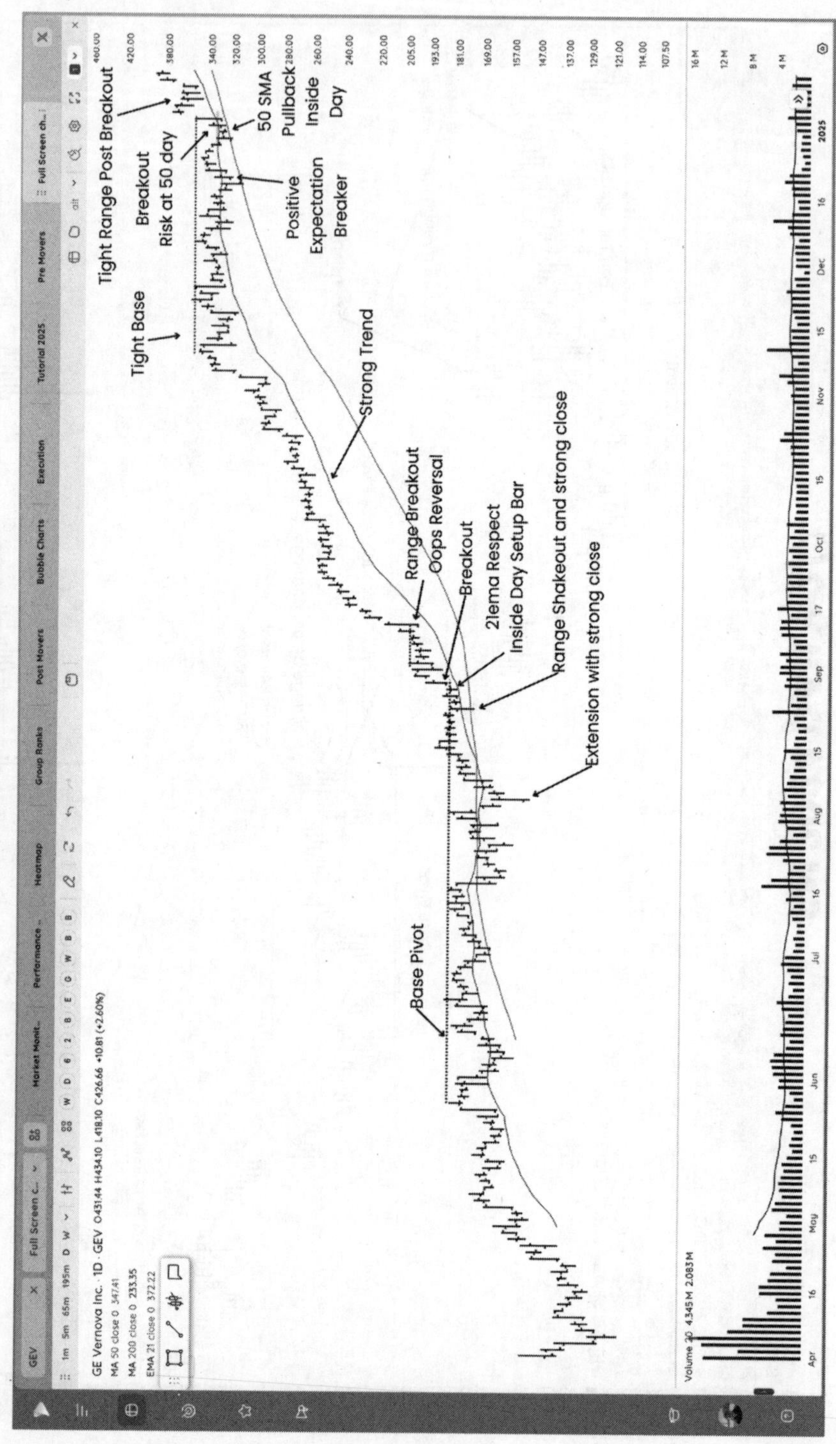

RBRK 2024 DAILY

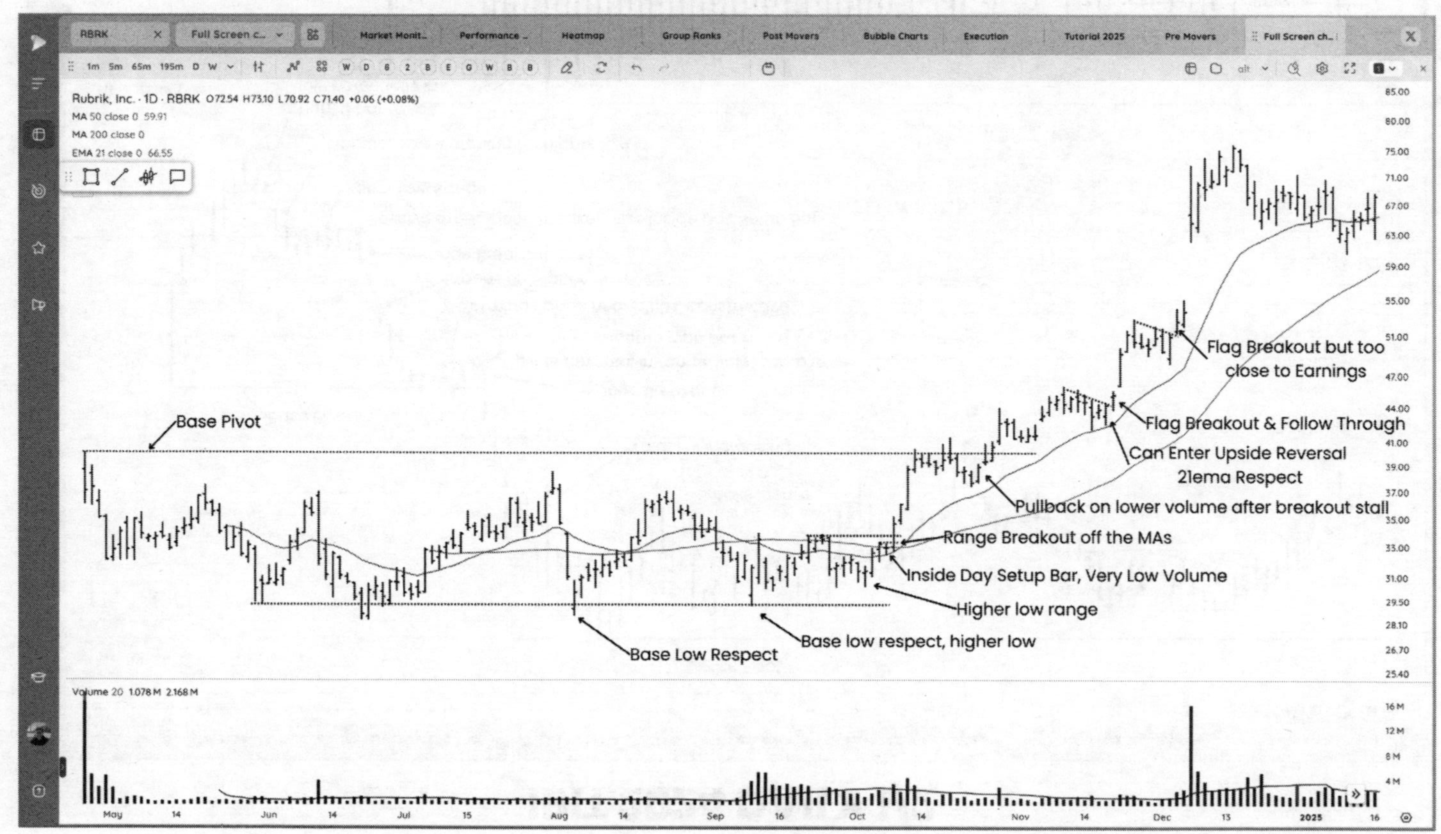

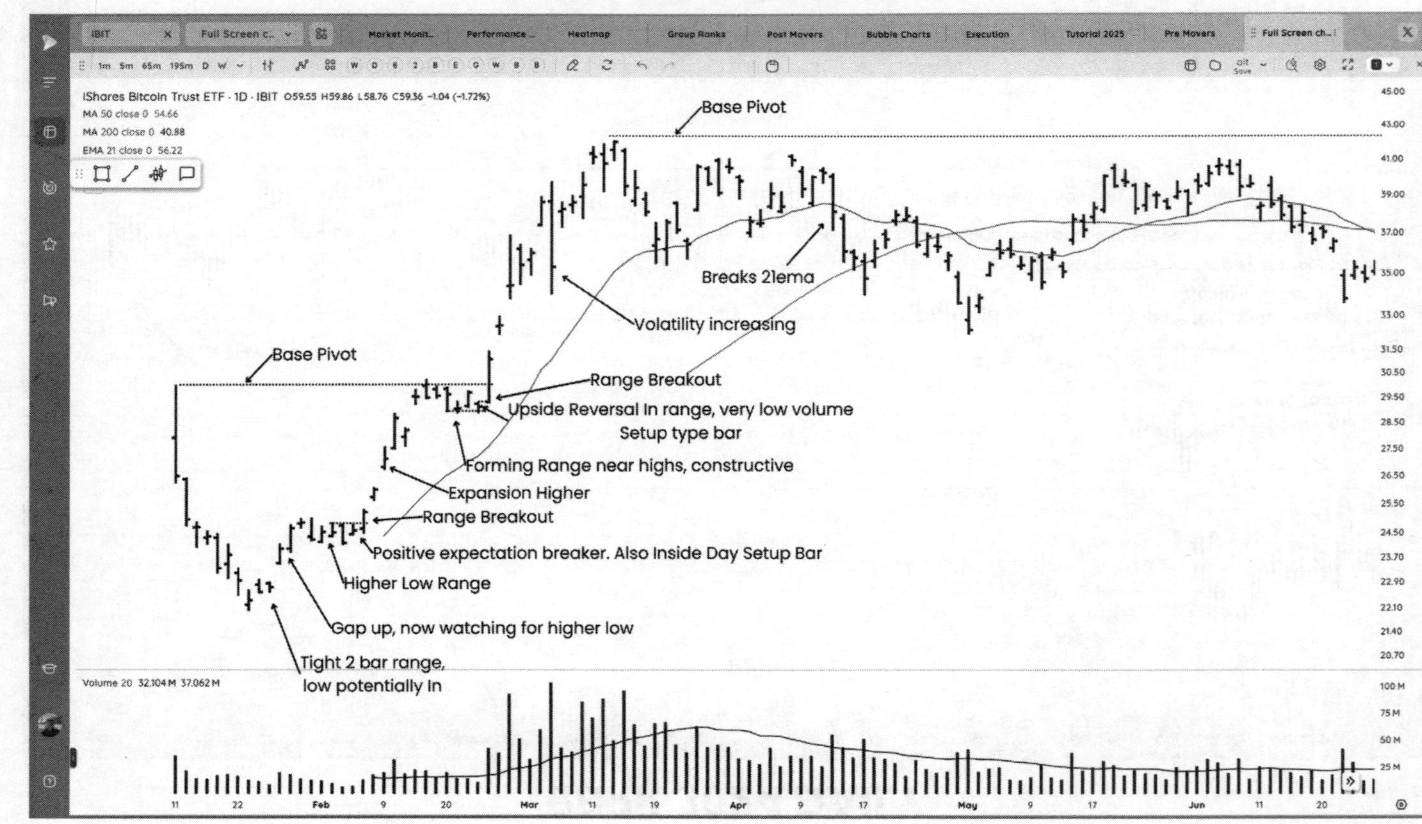
IBIT 2024 DAILY 1/2
iShares Bitcoin Trust ETF · 1D · IBIT O59.55 H59.86 L58.76 C59.36 −1.04 (−1.72%)
MA 50 close 0 54.66
MA 200 close 0 40.88
EMA 21 close 0 56.22
Base Pivot
Breaks 21ema
Volatility increasing
Base Pivot
Range Breakout
Upside Reversal in range, very low volume
Setup type bar
Forming Range near highs, constructive
Expansion Higher
Range Breakout
Positive expectation breaker. Also Inside Day Setup Bar
Higher Low Range
Gap up, now watching for higher low
Tight 2 bar range,
low potentially in
Volume 20 32.104M 37.062M

IBIT 2024 DAILY 2/2

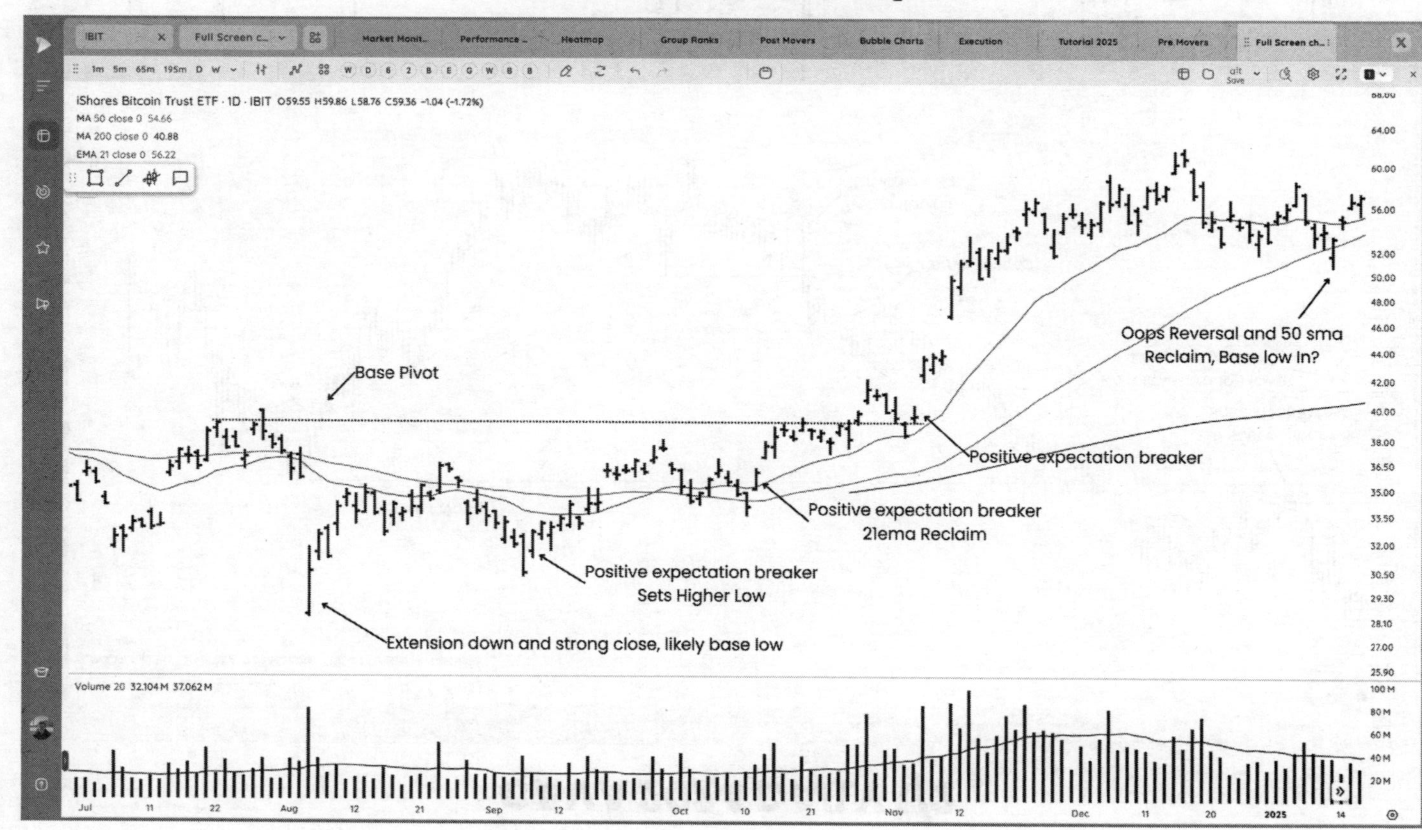

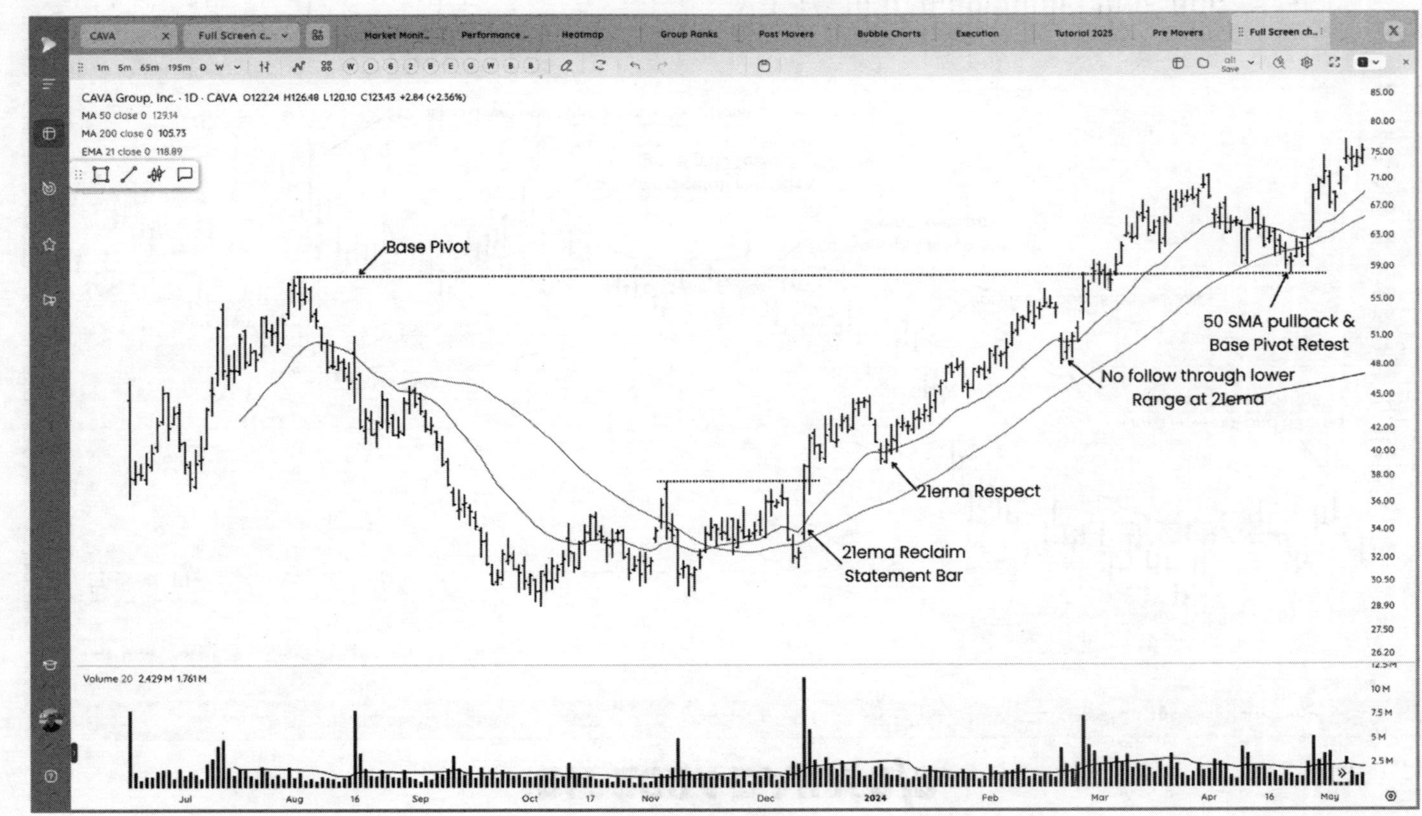
CAVA 2024 DAILY 1/2
CAVA Group, Inc. · 1D · CAVA O122.24 H126.48 L120.10 C123.43 +2.84 (+2.36%)
MA 50 close 0 129.14
MA 200 close 0 105.73
EMA 21 close 0 118.89
Base Pivot
50 SMA pullback &
Base Pivot Retest
No follow through lower
Range at 21ema
21ema Respect
21ema Reclaim
Statement Bar
Volume 20 2.429 M 1.761 M

CAVA 2024 DAILY 2/2

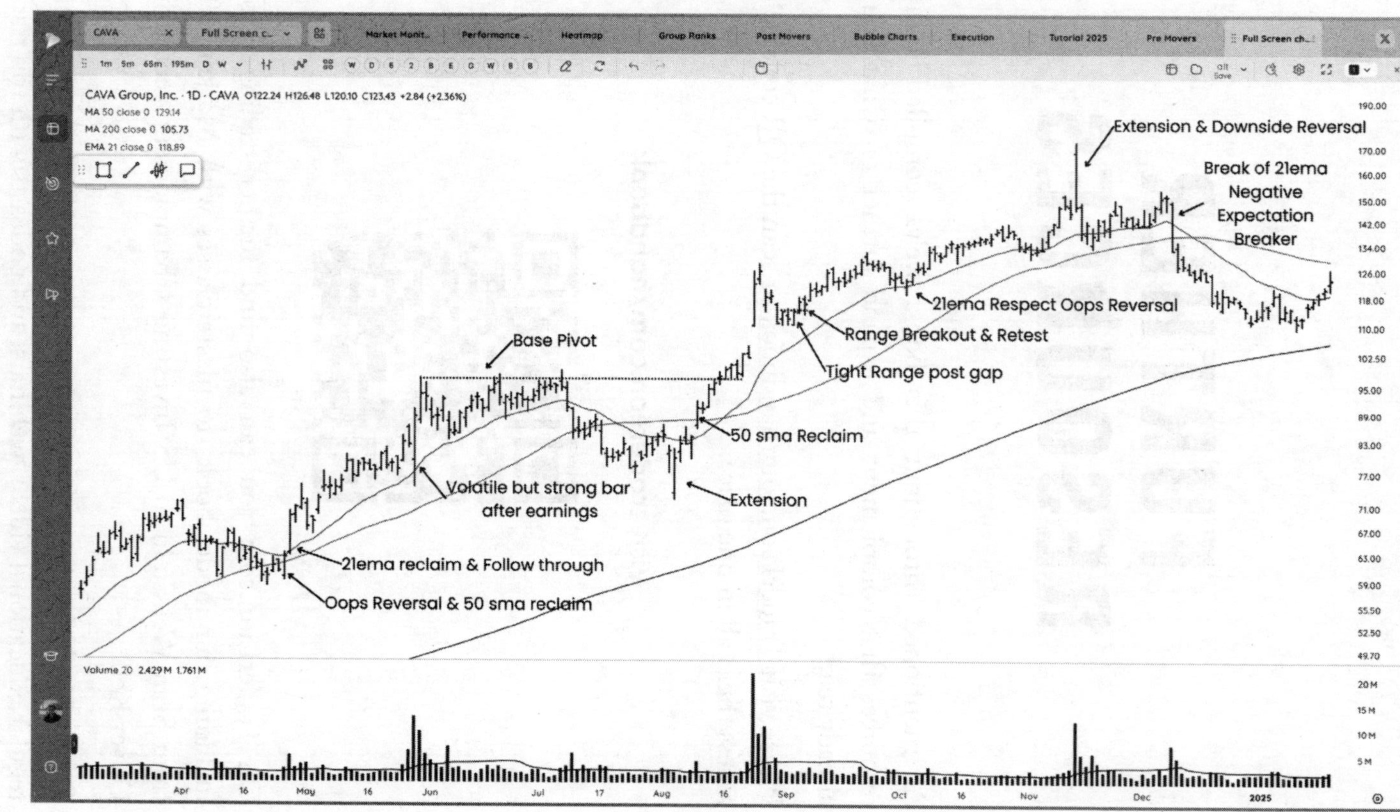

FURTHER RESOURCES

As mentioned throughout this book, we've compiled additional resources that complement and expand further on what you have already read.

Please visit TraderLion.com/handbook or scan the QR code below to access them all in one place.

Visit traderlion.com/handbook

On TraderLion.com you can also find further trading resources, including our model books to masterclasses with Market Wizards from Stan Weinstein to US Investing Championship record holder Oliver Kell.

On our YouTube channel www.youtube.com/@TraderLion we publish regular educational videos, webinars, and podcasts with top traders.

Finally, we highly recommend checking out Deepvue, the all in one chart analysis, screener, watchlist manager, and soon to be journaling software that we are developing to help traders find top ideas faster, and trade them more effectively.

Visit deepvue.com and use the code: **handbook** for a free monthly trial.

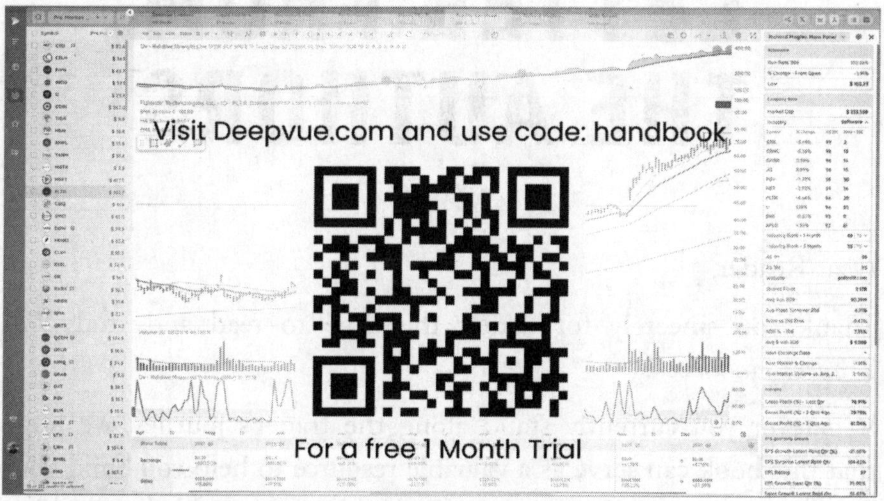

This offer is valid through December 31, 2025.

We hope these resources can help you accelerate your learning!

LETTER FROM THE AUTHORS

Dear Reader,

Thank you sincerely for taking the time to read and study *The Trader's Handbook*.

Wherever you currently stand along the trader's journey, we hope that this book can serve as a valuable resource to help you build your first trading system, improve your existing one, or add the finishing touches to your superperforming one.

As we stressed early on, take from this handbook the ideas that you find meaningful, test them and apply them for yourself, and then make them your own.

If you have found this handbook to be beneficial, please help us accomplish our goal of educating traders by leaving us a review where you purchased it, and by sharing this resource with other traders.

A great way to do this is by letting people know your thoughts about the handbook through X/Twitter. You can scan the QR code below to quickly share that you recommend the book.

Thank you very much in advance!

To close, we will leave you with this:

The markets present us with opportunities for action each day – be patient, deliberate, and systematic with how you participate. Above all else, continue your study of the markets, your trades, yourself, and search for ways to incrementally improve each day.

Wishing you success in your endeavours.

Richard Moglen, Ameet Rai, Ross Haber, and Nick Schmidt